W9-AEA-194

THE
HOMERIC HYMNS

THE HOMERIC HYMNS

EDITED BY

T. W. ALLEN
Fellow of Queen's College, Oxford

W. R. HALLIDAY
Principal of King's College, London

AND

E. E. SIKES
Fellow and President of St. John's College, Cambridge

Second edition

OXFORD
AT THE CLARENDON PRESS
1936

OXFORD
UNIVERSITY PRESS
AMEN HOUSE, E.C. 4
London Edinburgh Glasgow
New York Toronto Melbourne
Capetown Bombay Calcutta
Madras
HUMPHREY MILFORD
PUBLISHER TO THE
UNIVERSITY

PRINTED IN GREAT BRITAIN

PREFACE

THE first edition of this book was published by Macmillan & Co., Ltd., in the year 1904. Mr. E. E. Sikes of St. John's College, Cambridge, one of the two original editors, has long betaken himself to other provinces, and resisted entreaties to assist in a revision as long ago as 1911, the date of the last Oxford text. I therefore count myself fortunate to have induced Mr. W. R. Halliday, Principal of King's College, London, and lately Professor of Ancient History in the University of Liverpool, to take part in this edition. We present our acknowledgements to the Delegates of the Clarendon Press for accepting it, to Professor J. L. Myres (as we should have presented them to the late Lewis Farnell) for the recommendation he was pleased to give to it, and to the British Academy for a contribution towards the expenses of production.

The exigencies of publication made it desirable to utilize the plates of the edition of 1911. That apparatus criticus has received correction, but here and there the reader may find repetition. On the other hand the scale of the edition of 1911 only admitted of a minimum of conjectures being recorded; we have, therefore, to suit the convenience of the reader and as a warning to him, collected others in a pillory or limbo (p. 444); even here, however, we have found ourselves unable to give all of them a place. The edition of Eugen Abel (1895) leaves none out.

We hold the view, expressed in the preface to the text of 1911, that documents in a dead language, couched in a familiar dialect, require interpretation rather than alteration, and that interpretation consists in illustration, that is to say in the adducing of similar passages from other ancient authors or monuments. The difficulty of interpreting the Homeric Hymns lies in the circumstance that they are solitary survivors of a class. Much of their subject-matter is unique or nearly so. The nineteenth-century critics, whose scanty knowledge was directed towards assimilating the Hymns to the usage of Homer, and who were possessed by a belief that the Greeks and Latins spent their time in the falsification of their literature, and that mediaeval scribes were unable to read their own writing, altered the wording of the Hymns recklessly and to their ruin. We have done our best to collect illustrative material, with what success the reader may judge, and claim to have recovered the meaning of several passages.

Another result of the small scale of the edition of 1911 was that it was only possible to record the important variants of the MSS. In a book of the present size the reader may expect to find the less important variants also. We have therefore produced the more interesting of them under a separate heading (p. 93).

T. W. A.

November 1934.

CONTENTS

INDEXES:

ABBREVIATIONS BY WHICH MANUSCRIPTS ARE REFERRED TO

A = Parisinus 2763
At = Athous, Vatopedi 671
B = Parisinus 2765
Γ = Bruxellensis 11377–11380
C = Parisinus 2833
D = Ambrosianus B 98 sup.
E = Estensis iii E 11
G = Vaticanus Reginensis 91
H = Harleianus 1752
J = Estensis ii B 14
K = Laurentianus 31. 32
L_1 = Laurentianus 32. 45
L_2 = Laurentianus 70. 35
L_3 = Laurentianus 32. 4
L_4 = Laurentianus Aedil. 220
L_5 = Laurentianus 32. 7, editio princeps (marg.)
M = Leidensis 33 H (Mosquensis)
Mon. = Monacensis 333
N = Leidensis 74 C
O = Ambrosianus C 10 inf.
P = Vaticanus Palatinus 179
Π = Parisinus suppl. gr. 1095
Q = Ambrosianus S 31 sup.
R_1 = Riccardianus 53
R_2 = Riccardianus 52
R_3 = Riccardianus 3195 (nunc 3020)
S = Vaticanus 1880
T = Matritensis 24
V_1 = Venetus 456
V_2 = Venetus ix 37, editio princeps (marg.)
m = M man. 2
p = codd. A B C Γ G L_2 L_3 L_4 Mon. N O P Q R_1 R_2 V consensus
x = codd. E L Π T consensus
y = marginalia codd. E L Π T
z = codd. H J K consensus
𝔭 = Berlin papyrus 44 (*Berliner Klassikertexte* 1907, 7 sqq.)

INTRODUCTION

I.—THE MANUSCRIPTS

THE *Homeric Hymns* are contained, as far as is known, in the following thirty-one manuscripts. They are arranged according to the libraries in which they are found.[1]

LEIDEN,[2] UNIVERSITY LIBRARY.

M = xviii. 33 H (= 22); paper, 293 × 210 mm., 50 ff., s. xiii–xiv. Contains (ff. 1–30) *Iliad* Θ 435–N 134, (31–50) *Hom. Hymns* (i. 10–xviii. 4).

N = xviii. 74 C (= 28); vellum, 230 × 168 mm., 111 ff., s. xv. Contains Orpheus' *Argonautica* and *Hymns*, (53–104) *Hom. Hymns* (iii–xxxiii), Proclus' *Hymns*, Moschus' Ἔρως δραπέτης, Musaeus' *Hero and Leander*.

PARIS,[3] BIBLIOTHÈQUE NATIONALE.

A = grec 2763; paper, 220 × 146 mm., 244 ff., s. xv. Contains the Orphic *Argonautica* and *Hymns*, Proclus' and Callimachus' *Hymns*, (ff. 91–129) *Hom. Hymns* (iii–xxxiii), Moschus' Ἔρως δραπέτης, Musaeus' *Hero and Leander*, Hesiod's *Works and Days*, *Shield of Hercules*, *Theogony*, Theocritus. Smiley *l.c.* 1920. 112.

B = grec 2765; paper, 192 × 139 mm., ff. 58, s. xv. Contains Orpheus' and Proclus' *Hymns*, (ff. 23–58) *Hom. Hymns* (iii–xxxiii), Moschus' Ἔρως δραπέτης.

[1] The Callimachus MSS., which often coincide with those of the Homeric Hymns, are the subject of the detailed investigation of M. T. Smiley, *C. Q.* 1920 and 1921. We have taken some corrections from this source. See also P. Maas *Byzantinisch-Neugriechische Jahrbücher*, 1927, 205. The whole ground has recently been covered by P. S. Breuning, *De Hymnorum Homericorum memoria*, 1929.

[2] See Geel *Cat. librorum mstorum qui inde ab anno* 1741 *bibliothecae Lugduno-Batavae accesserunt*, 1852, p. 9.

[3] See H. Omont *Inventaire Sommaire des manuscrits grecs de la B.N.*, 1888, pp. 37, 47, 339.

C = grec 2833; vellum, 243 × 147 mm., ff. 214, s. xv. Contains Theocritus, (ff. 44–85) *Hom. Hymns* (iii–xxxiii), Moschus' Ἔρως δραπέτης, Musaeus' *Hero and Leander*, Hesiod, Dionysius' *Cosmography*, Theognis Phocylides.

Π = supplément grec 1095; paper, 335 × 228 mm., ff. 280, s. xv. Contains the *Iliad*, (ff. 225–45) *Hom. Hymns* (iii–xxxiii), Callimachus', Orpheus', Proclus' *Hymns*, the *Batrachomyomachia*. At the end is the inscription *Est Sancti Petri de Perusio*.[1] Smiley *l.c.* 1920. 106. A page in rotograph Breuning tab. 2.

MILAN, BIBLIOTECA AMBROSIANA.[2]

D = 120 B 98 sup.; vellum, 255 × 180 mm., ff. 227, s. xv. Contains Apollonius Rhodius' *Argonautica*, the *Batrachomyomachia*, Herodotus' *Life of Homer*, Maximus of Tyre's *Opuscula*, (ff. 178–209) *Hom. Hymns* (iii–xxxiii), Callimachus. Smiley 1921. 57.

O = 845 C 10 inf.; paper, 216 × 128 mm. ff. 143, s. xv.–xvi. Contains Plato's *Cratylus*, Orpheus' *Argonautica* and *Hymns*, Proclus' *Hymns*, (ff. 127–43) *Hom. Hymns* (iii–iv. 80). At the beginning this inscription: *codex non admodum ille quidem antiquus sed valde bonus. sternathiae in iapygia emptus 1606.*

Q = 734 S 31 sup.; paper, 230 × 158 mm., ff. 320, s. xv. Contains Orpheus' and Proclus' *Hymns*, (ff. 39–89) *Hom. Hymns* (iii–xxxiii), Moschus' Ἔρως δραπέτης, Callimachus, Pindar's *Olympian* and *Pythian Odes*. At the beginning these inscriptions: *liber iste est mei marci de passiris januensis* [in the margin *patavini* is added] *et amicorum*, and *J. V. Plli* (i.e. Pinelli). Smiley 1920. 112.

MODENA, BIBLIOTECA ESTENSE.[3]

E = iii. E 11 (= 164); paper, 292 × 203 mm., ff. 93, s. xv. Contains Orpheus' and Callimachus' *Hymns*, (ff. 50–84) *Hom. Hymns* (iii–xxxiii). At the end this inscription: γεώργϊος ὁ

[1] See Léopold Delisle *Catalogue des MSS. des fonds Libri et Barrois*, Paris, 1888, f. 125, and for other MSS. from this convent now in the Perugia library, *Centralblatt für Bibliothekswesen*, x. 470 f.

[2] See Martini e Bassi *Catalogus codicum graecorum bibliothecae ambrosianae*, 1906.

[3] See V. Puntoni *Indice dei codici greci della b. Estense di Modena*, 1896, pp. 487, 416.

οὐάλλα (corr. to βάλλας) πλακεντῖνος ἔγραψε; f. 12^v this: ἀλβέρτου πίου καρπαίων ἄρχοντος κτῆμα. Smiley 1920. 58. A reduced facsimile of the hand of this MS. (xxxiii. 10–end) is given in the *Miscellanea Fr. Ehrle* 1924 iv. 32.

J = ii. B 14 (= 51); paper, 216 × 152 mm., ff. 264, s. xv. Contains Aratus' *Phaenomena*, Tzetzes' περὶ ποιητῶν, (ff. 55–64) *Hom. Hymns* (viii–xviii, *h. Apoll.* 1–185 omitting 184), Hesiod's *Theogony* and *Shield of Hercules*, Lycophron's *Alexandra*, Pindar's *Pythian Odes*. At the beginning and the end a pair of inscriptions, of which the former is crossed out: γεωργίου τοῦ βάλλα ἐστι τὸ βιβλίον, and ἀλβέρτου τοῦ πίου καρπαίων ἄρχοντος κτῆμα.

Florence, Biblioteca Mediceo-Laurenziana.[1]

L_1 = plut. 32 cod. 45; vellum, 267 × 178 mm., ff. 170, s. xv. Contains Apollonius Rhodius' *Argonautica*, Orpheus' *Hymns*, (ff. 155–81) *Hom. Hymns* (iii–vii. 33).

L_2 = plut. 70 cod. 35; vellum, 252 × 178 mm., ff. 109, s. xv. Contains Herodotus' *Life of Homer*, Gorgias' *Encomium Helenae*, Orpheus' *Argonautica* and *Hymns*, Proclus' *Hymns*, (ff. 68–103) *Hom. Hymns* (iii–xxxiii), Moschus' Ἔρως δραπέτης, Musaeus' *Hero and Leander*. Written by Joannes Scutariota.

L_3 = plut. 32 cod. 4; paper, 407 × 229 mm., ff. 476, s. xv. Contains the *Iliad*, *Odyssey*, (ff. 450–76) *Hom. Hymns* (iii–xxxiii). Written by Joannes Rhosus.

K = plut. 31 cod. 32. Vellum, 269 × 185 mm., ff. 55. Contains Hesiod's *Shield of Hercules*, *Theogony* 1–577, (ff. 25–30) *Hom. Hymns* (viii–xviii, *h. Apoll.* 1–185, omitting 184), Aratus' *Phaenomena*.

L_4 = *Aedil.* 220; vellum, 256 × 175 mm., ff. 90, s. xv. Contains Orpheus' *Argonautica* and *Hymns*, Proclus' *Hymns*, *Hom. Hymns* (iii–xxxiii), Moschus' Ἔρως δραπέτης, Musaeus' *Hero and Leander*. Written by Scutariota.[2]

L_5 = plut. 32. 7, *editio princeps*, marginalia.

[1] See Bandini *Cat. codd. graec. bibl. Laur.* 1768, ii. 105, 126, 205.

[2] Rostagno *Indicis cod. graec. bibl. Laur. supplementum: Studi italiani di filologia classica* vi. 129 f.

Biblioteca Riccardiana.[1]

R_1 = 53 K II. 13; vellum, 223 × 143 mm., ff. 106, s. xv. Contains Orpheus' *Argonautica* and *Hymns*, Proclus' *Hymns*, (ff. 61–99) *Hom. Hymns* (iii–xxxiii), Moschus' Ἔρως δραπέτης, Musaeus' *Hero and Leander*. Written by Joannes Rhosus. At the beginning is written the name *Rinaldi*.

R_2 = 52 K II. 14; vellum, 214 × 144 mm., ff. 73, s. xv. Contains Orpheus' and Proclus' *Hymns*, (ff. 31–72) *Hom. Hymns* (iii–xxxiii), Moschus' Ἔρως δραπέτης. On f. 73[r] is found the signature ἐγράφη διὰ χειρὸς ἰωάννου τοῦ σκωταριώτου.

R_3 = 3195 (now 3020); paper, mm. 198 × 140, ff. 85, a. 1494, written by Bartolommeo Comparini. Contains the *Batrachomyomachia*, (ff. 6, 7) *Hom. Hymns* (ix, xii, xiii), and misc. Vitelli *op.c.* pp. 541–2.

Rome, Biblioteca Apostolica Vaticana.

S = *Vaticani greci* 1880; paper, 230 × 165 mm., ff. 266, s. xv. and xvi.; ff. 1–8 are s. xv., and contain *h. Apoll.* 1–357; the remainder are sixteenth-century notes. At the end is the inscription *Collectanea septem sophoclis tragediar. pertinent. interpretat. finiunt'. ult. Julij.* M.D.III. *mediol.*

G = *Regina* 91;[2] paper, 292 × 202, ff. 350, s. xvi. Contains the *Odyssey*, *Batrachomyomachia*, (ff. 306–350) *Hom. Hymns* (iii–xxxiii).

P = *Palatino* 179; vellum, 255 × 165 mm., ff. 140, s. xv. Contains Herodotus' *Life of Homer*, Gorgias' *Encomium Helenae*, Orpheus' *Argonautica* and *Hymns*, Proclus' *Hymns*, (ff. 86–129) *Hom. Hymns* (iii–xxxiii), Moschus' Ἔρως δραπέτης, Musaeus' *Hero and Leander*. At the beginning the inscription *Jannozii Manetti.*[3]

[1] G. Vitelli *Indice de' codici greci Riccardiani, Magliabecchiani e Marucelliani: Studi di fil. cl.* ii. 471 f.

[2] See *Codices mssti graeci Reginae Suecorum et Pii PP. II.* rec. et disp. Henricus Stevenson, senior, 1888, p. 66.

[3] *Codices mssti Palatini* rec. et disp. Henricus Stevenson, senior, 1885, p. 93.

VENICE, BIBLIOTECA DI S. MARCO.[1]

V_1 = 456; vellum, 341 × 252 mm., ff. 541, s. xv. Contains the *Iliad*, Quintus Smyrnaeus, the *Odyssey*, (ff. 509–38) *Hom. Hymns* (iii–xxxiii), Moschus' Ἔρως δραπέτης, *Batrachomyomachia.* At the beginning the inscription: κτῆμα βησσαρίωνος καρδινάλεως τοῦ τῶν τούσκλων. ἀριθμῶ α^ον^. *liber meus b. Car^l^· niceni numero* 1. *locus* 81, and a monogram of the letters A L F R.

V_2 = IX. 37, *editio princeps*, marginalia.

MUNICH, ROYAL LIBRARY.[2]

Mon. = 333; paper, 230 × 155 mm., ff. 110, s. xv. Contains Orpheus' *Argonautica* and *Hymns*, Proclus' *Hymns*, (ff. 72–90) *Hom. Hymns* (iii–iv. 192), Herodotus' *Life of Homer.*

BRUSSELS, BIBLIOTHÈQUE ROYALE.[3]

Γ = 74 (11377–11380); paper, 202 × 145 mm., ff. 94, s. xv. Contains Theognis, (ff. 27–63) *Hom. Hymns* (iii–xxxiii), Moschus' Ἔρως δραπέτης, Orpheus' and Proclus' *Hymns*. On f. 91 is found the signature:

ἀριστοβούλου οἶδε χειρὸς ἐκ διακόνου
ὕμνοι ὁμήρου λάβον, ἄξιοι ὕμνου πέρας.

MADRID, ROYAL LIBRARY.[4]

T = 4562 = 24; 280 × 180 mm., ff. 136, a. 1464. Contains Musaeus' *Hero and Leander*, Orpheus' *Argonautica* and *Hymns*, (ff. 56–83) *Hom. Hymns* (iii–xxxiii), Callimachus' *Hymns* and *Epigrams*. On f. 100^v^ κτῆμα κωνσταντίνου λασκάρεως ἐν μεδιολάνῳ ἐκγραφέν ᾱ ῡ ξ̄ δ̄. Smiley 1920. 57.

[1] See *Graeca D. Marci Bibliotheca cod. manu scriptorum*, 1740, p. 245.

[2] *Cat. cod. mstorum graecorum bibl. regiae Bavaricae*, auctore Ignatio Hardt, 1806, iii. 322 f.

[3] Cf. Henri Omont *Cat. des manuscrits grecs de la Bibliothèque Royale de Bruxelles*, 1885, no. 74, p. 25.

[4] See Iriarte *Regiae bibl. Matritensis codd. graeci*, 1769, p. 86.

LONDON, BRITISH MUSEUM.

H = Harley 1752; paper, 230 × 160 mm., ff. 191, s. xv. Contains (ff. 2–5) *Hom. Hymns* (viii–xviii, *h. Apoll.* 1–55), Orpheus' *Hymns* and *Argonautica*, Lycophron's *Alexandra*, Pindar's *Ol.*, *Pyth.* and *Nemean Odes.*[1]

ATHOS, VATOPEDI.[2]

At = 671; paper, 260 × 190 mm., ff. 247, s. xv. Contains Sophocles' *Ajax*, *Electra*, *Oed. Tyr.*, Euripides' *Hecuba*, *Orestes*, *Phoenissae*, (ff. 191–218) *Hom. Hymns* (iii, iv, v, vii), Callimachus. Constantinides *Classical Review* 1894, p.341, published the readings. Smiley 1921. 58.

SALAMANCA.

The University Library possesses a xv–xvith century paper MS. (i. 2. 13) which contains (vi. 2) hymn xxv. See Graux-Martin, *Notices sommaires des manuscrits grecs d'Espagne et de Portugal*, 1892, p. 179. This fragment has not been collated.

These MSS., with the exception of the Athous, L_4, the Matritensis, R_3, and the last, were collated for the edition of Alfred Goodwin, Oxford, 1893; the collation there used of the Brussels MS. (*Γ*) was due to Monsieur E. Ouverleaux, that of the Munich MS. to Herr S. Riezler. The hymn to Apollo in *Π* was collated, very accurately, by a Frenchman whose name we cannot recover. Since the publication of Goodwin's edition, the Madrid MS. has been partially collated by E. Bethe (*Hermes* 1893 552 ff.), and entirely by ourselves; the Athos MS. by Professor M. Constantinides; R_3, at our request and on the kind intervention of Professor Girolamo Vitelli, by Signor Alessandro Olivieri, and L_4 by Prof. Vitelli himself. M. Henri Omont has kindly

[1] There are a few marginal notes on the hymn to Hermes in the *editio princeps* in the British Museum add. MSS. 10627.

[2] See Sophronios Eustratiades and Arcadios *Catalogue of the Greek MSS. in the library of the Monastery of Vatopedi*, 1924.

answered a few questions about *Π*, and we have recollated it. We leave the account of the very gradual process by which this material was utilized by the earlier editors till p. lxxvii f.

G, as was noticed by Hollander, *Die handschriftliche Ueberlieferung der h. H.* p. 6, contains exactly the same matter as the second volume of the *editio princeps*, including the colophon; and, as the hand is fairly 1500 or later, may be taken to be a copy of the printed book, and therefore dismissed from consideration.

𝔭 = the Berlin papyrus 44, s. i B.C. (*Berliner Klassikertexte* 1907, 7 sqq.), which contains some lines of *Hymn* ii. See p. 110.

II.—THE RELATION OF THE MANUSCRIPTS TO EACH OTHER

The text of the *Hymns*, so far as it depends upon the MSS., may be said to be fairly settled; at least the account given *J.H.S.* 1895, xv. 138 f., which is followed here, has not been materially impugned. That account was based upon the treatise of Dr. H. Hollander, *Die handschriftliche Ueberlieferung der homerischen Hymnen*, Leipzig 1886, which established the main lines of the question.[1]

M

The celebrated book known as the Mosquensis evidently stands apart from the other MSS. on account of the frag-

[1] Other literature on the subject is: the same writer, 'Zur Ueberlieferung der hom. Hymnen', *Hermes*, 1891, pp. 170, 636; 'Ueber den Codex Estensis der hom. Hymnen', *Neue Jahrbücher für Philologie*, 1892, p. 544; 'Ueber die neu bekannt gewordenen Handschriften der hom. Hymnen', Osnabrück, 1895; A. Gemoll, *Homerische Blätter*, Striegau, 1895, p. 12 f.; E. Abel, preface to his edition, Prag 1886; Breuning l. c.

ment to Dionysus and the entire hymn to Demeter with which it opens; all other MSS. begin with the hymn to Apollo. This external singularity is confirmed by the character of its readings. Before we discuss these, it may be well to complete the description of the book itself.

It was found as early as 1777 by Christian Friedrich Matthaei, at that time Professor of Greek in Russia, in the library of the Synod at Moscow.[1] Matthaei acquired it together with other MSS., and sold it to the library at Leiden. It is a book of 50 leaves, written in two columns, with about 25 lines in a column; the hand is high and regular and is usually ascribed to the fourteenth century.[2] It has the ligatures which are common to the thirteenth and fourteenth centuries; in the height and uprightness of its strokes it resembles the Greek hand of Barberini 541 a. 1292 (Franchi-Lietzmann, pl. 38), Paris *grec* 1671 a. 1296 (Omont, Facsimilés datés, pl. LXVII, LXVIII), the Odyssey Harley 5674 (undated), and even Ven. 172 of a. 1175 (Wattenbach and von Velsen, pl. XV), though this is much larger and freer. On the other hand it shares the peculiarity of a single dot over iota with Ven. 292 of a. 1306 (W.V., pl. XX). We may therefore date it to the end of the thirteenth or the beginning of the fourteenth century. The sheets are arranged in quires of 5, or quinions, and the book runs at present:—

Quire 1. ff. 1–10; the signatures have perished, inc. Θ 435.

Quire 2. ff. 11–20; the signature ιαʹ at the beginning and the end.

[1] See v. Gebhardt, 'C. F. Matthäi und seine Sammlung griechischen Handschriften', *Centralblatt für Bibliothekswesen*, xv. 345 ff., 393 ff., 441 ff., 537 ff., esp. 442–62.

[2] The hand may be studied in the portion of the hymn to Demeter reproduced in Goodwin's edition, and in a page of the hymn to Hermes (57–107) prefixed to this book. It was collated with great care by Goodwin, and on two occasions by T. W. A.

Quire 3. ff. 21–30; the signature ιβ′ at either end: f. 30[v] expl. N 134.

Quire 4. ff. 31–39; no signature at the beginning; at the end ιδ′.

This quire consists of 9 leaves instead of 10; the last leaf, 39, is only half a sheet, and is glued to the back of the quire. The former half, therefore, of the first sheet has perished, carrying with it the signature: f. 31[r] inc. *καί οἱ ἀναστήσουσιν ἀγάλματα πόλλ' ἐνὶ νηοῖς* (*h. Dion.* 10).

Quire 5. ff. 40–49; at the beginning the signature ιε together with another numeral .s., which Maunde Thompson thought was part of another quire-numeration. The signature at the end has perished.

Quire 6. fol. 50; signature wanting. This is a single leaf glued at the back. The recto ceases with *h. Herm.* xviii. 4: the verso is blank.

On grounds both of palaeography and of contents the book is evidently fragmentary. The first quire must have been the tenth of the original book, and if the tenth began with Θ 435, it is natural to suppose that quires 1–9 contained the *Iliad* *A*–Θ 434. Heyne (*Iliad*, vol. I. xiii, xiv., vol. III. xc.) was informed by Matthaei (see v. Gebhardt *op.c.* p. 451 f.) that a book containing exactly this amount of Homer existed in the Imperial Library at Moscow (' Q 1 ' or ' Mosc. 1 ' among Iliad MSS.). Evidently the Hymn MS. once made one with this.[1]

Next, by the evidence of the signatures, one quire (ιγ′) has fallen out between f. 30 and f. 31, and one leaf, the

[1] The portion of the *Iliad* contained in M has been collated by Ludwich (*Index lect. Regimont.* 1891) and by ourselves. It is known for the Iliad as Le 2. Q 1 and Le 2 are closely related to another Iliad MS., U 11, with which they form the family *w*. On the catalogue of the library of the Imperial Russian Archives, see v. Gebhardt, *op. c.* pp. 393, 441.

first of ιδ′. What was contained on these eleven leaves it is impossible to divine. Somewhere within them the *Iliad* must have stopped and the *Hymns* have begun. The *Iliad* certainly was fragmentary, the *Hymns*, perhaps, fragmentary too. From the fact that f. 31 opens abruptly without a title we may assume that some more of the hymn to Dionysus stood in the gap, but how much cannot be guessed. The only certain conclusion that can be drawn is that the original of the Mosquensis must have been mutilated at this place. The succession of the signatures ιβ′, ιδ′ make this quite certain. The scribe of the Mosquensis must have lighted on a book once perhaps (like V), containing the Homeric corpus, but which had lost many quires. He copied the surviving fragment continuously.[2] Of the origin of M nothing is known beyond Matthaei's conjecture, printed by v. Gebhardt, p. 450, that it came from Athos.

The archetype was deficient at the end also, or we should not find the verso of that last leaf of M vacant. The original of M then was a MS. which contained the *Iliad*, perhaps the *Odyssey* also, and a complete hymn to Dionysus followed by the other hymns as we have them.

It was no doubt a minuscule MS. not necessarily much older than M. This is probable both on general grounds and because some of M's corruptions seemed to imply a minuscule origin: *Apoll.* 88 κωμή for βωμός, 367 δυσκλεέ' for δυσηλεγέ', 457 ἐκ μὴ τοῦ δέ for ἔκβητ' οὐδέ, *Dion.* vii. 17 δεσμὰ ἐθέλοντες for δεσμεύεθ' ἑλόντες. We may think of *Barocci* 50 s. x, which contains the Batrachomyomachia and Hero and Leander. Two omissions, *Apoll.* 22–73 and

¹ A mistaken attempt to compute the size of the Dionysus hymn was made by R. Thiele *Philologus* xxxiv. 193 f.; Bücheler's conclusions (preface to his edition, p. 2) are less improbable.

Aphr. 68–112, of nearly the same length, which have no obvious cause to explain them, have been supposed due to the loss of a single leaf in the archetype, which therefore contained 22-6 lines to the page. The class of argument is far from conclusive, but may stand for what it is worth.

The MS. is correctly written (its itacistic and other similar errors, without importance for the text, are collected by Dittmann, *Prolegomenon ad hymnum in Cererem homericum specimen* Halis Sax. 1882) and seldom corrected. Corrections of any weight in the first hand are *Dem.* 464 ερόεντα, *Apoll.* 391 ἴσως λείπει στίχος εἷς, *Herm.* 42 γρ. ὡς δοκεῖ μοι ἀγῶν' ἐξετό, 88, where γρ. " ην is superscribed, *Dem.* xiii. title.

A reader, perhaps coeval with the time of composition of the book, has affixed a sign consisting of a row of dots before several lines: *Dem.* 369, *Apoll.* 308 (ἤνεκ'), 384 (ποιήσατο), 460 (ἀδικότες), 502, *Herm.* 150, 260, 338 (τέρτομον), 411 (? ἀμβολάδην), 457 (? ἐπαίνει), 477, *Aphr.* 38, 113, 150, 188, *Dem.* xiii. 1 (this case seems to show the reviser was contemporary). Like similar marks in other MSS., these dots doubtless imply a perception or a suspicion of some error in the line as written, though it many cases the fault to which they point escapes us. (Plain references are given above in brackets.)

A hand later than M may be seen at work *Apoll.* 22, where he notices the lacuna λείπει στίχοι $\overline{\nu\alpha}$; 391, where he crosses out the note of m. 1; *Herm.* 518, κατὰ in place of μέγαν or κ́ μέγ′ (with τ′ and αν superscribed); 522, ἐκτεάτισται (τ superscribed); *Aphr.* x. 3; *Asclep.* xvi. 2. His principal field of activity, however, is on f. 35 (*Dem.* 387–478). At some unknown time between the fourteenth and sixteenth century, a V-shaped rent was made in the part of this leaf which contained the first column of the recto and the second column of the verso, and the greater part of 15 lines torn away. The loss is materially lightened by the circumstance that the original scribe repeated after 465 the vv. 449–53, and that these superfluous five lines are included in the lacuna on the verso. This gaping wound was repaired by this sixteenth-century scribe, who filled the space with a piece of thick paper, roughly cut to shape, the edge of which he pasted over the extremities of the original page. He then added the missing words by writing across the piece he had inserted.

The source from which he drew these supplements was evidently his own conjecture, for in the wide gap on the recto (388–395), he merely repeats the letters of the original which he has covered; the corresponding lines of the verso he does fill, but of these 463–5 are restored (rightly) after the model of 445–7, and 466–70 were a repetition of 449–53; the shorter lines it was not difficult for a moderate scholar to complete. We are therefore relieved from the necessity of supposing another MS. for the *hymn to Demeter* extant in the sixteenth century. The scribe's supplements are in most places correct: 399 his μοῖραν is a curious and unmetrical error for μέρος, 406 ἐρῶ for ἐρέω, 411 ἐνωροῦσ' for ἐνοροῦσ' are trivial, 466 δύο δὲ πὰρ σοὶ ἔσ- is a curious error, based evidently on 447; 474 it is hardly possible to decide if εἶπε was the original or not; the supplements of 473, 474, 475, which have perished in the original, are to be put to *m*'s credit, 476 admitted of easy restoration according to epic formula. The piece of paper inserted by *m* was removed during the librarianship of Pluygers; the state of the page generally may be studied in the facsimile in Goodwin's edition.

M distinguishes itself as to its contents by (*a*) some remarkable corruptions, (*b*) a number of peculiar readings.

(*a*) The corruptions may be classified as follows:

i. Permutation of letters:

Dem.	420	*ὠκύρθη*	= *ὠκυρόη* 𝔭, Hes. *Theog.* 360.
	423	*ταλαξαύρη*	= *γαλαξαύρη* ib. 353.
	476	*χρησμοσύνην*	= *δρησμοσύνην* Paus. ii. 14. 3.
Apoll.	119	*πρὸς*	= *πρὸ* cet.
	125	*ἐπώρξατο*	= *ἐπήρξατο* cet.
	156	*θ' οὗ*	= *ὅου* cet.
	213	*ἐλέλιψεν*	= *ἐνέλιπεν* cet.
	216	*πετρίην*	= *πιερίην* cet.
	234	*κεῖνον*	= *κεῖν'* cet.
	326	*ἔγωγ' ἐκθήσομαι*	= *ἐγὼ τεχνήσομαι* cet.
Herm.	55	*ἥντε*	= *ἠύτε* cet.
	79	*σάλδαλα*	= *σάνδαλα* cet.
	137	*οὐλοκαρηβα*	= *οὐλοκάρηνα* cet.
	138	*ηὔλησε*	= *ἤνυσε* cet.
	373	*ἀνάγκης*	= *ἀναγκαίης* cet.
	543	*μὴ*	= *μὲν* cet.
Aphr.	158	*δίνησι*	= *χλαίνησι* cet.
	159	*ἐκ τῶν*	= *ἄρκτων* cet.
Ares viii.	10	*πρὶν*	= *πρηὺ* cet.

to which must be added the definitely minuscular corruptions noticed above.[1]

ii. Omission or insertion of syllables or letters:

Dem.	122	*δὼς* (unmetrical).	
	228	*ἐπηλσίησι*	= *ἐπηλυσίη* (Ruhnken).
	267	*συναυξήσουσ'* (unmetrical).	
	419	*ῥόεια*	= *ῥοδεία* Hesiod *Theog.* 351.

[1] Some explanation of these graphical changes may be in place. *ὠκύρθη*, *ταλαξαύρη*, *χρησμοσύνην*, *θ' οὗ*, *πετρίην*, *δίνησι* and perhaps *ἔγωγ' ἐκθήσομαι* (Herod. ii. 42 *προεκθέσθαι προσχέσθαι*) seem to point to a confusion between uncials; *πρὸς* is a misinterpretation of *πρ̊*, *κεῖνον* of *κεῖν*'' (sc. *κεῖν'* out of *κειν*''). *ἥν τε* and *πρὶν* seem due to the similarity of *ηυ* written together to the ligature *ην*, *ἀνάγκης* is due to the omission of the symbol for *αι* ($\kappa = \kappa_{\varsigma}$), *ἐκ τῶν* comes from *ἄκτων*, *ρ* falling out.

Dem.	421	ἀκατάστη	= ἀκάστη Hes. *Theog.* 356.
	429	δρεπομένη (unmetrical).	
Apoll.	220	τῶ τ' οὐχάδε	= τό τοι οὐχ ἅδε cet.
	540	ἠέτ' ἐτήσιον	= ἠύτε τηύσιον cet.
Herm.	28	σκύλα	= σαῦλα cet.
	522	μήτ'	= μή ποτ' cet.
Aphr.	42	τέκε	= τέκετο cet.
	49	γελάσασα	= γελοιήσασα cet.
	66	κῆπον	= κύπρον cet.

iii. Misdivision :

Apoll.	272	προσάγοι ἐνηεῖ παιήονι	= προσάγοιεν ἰηπαιήονι cet.
	439	λιμένος δ' ἀμάθοισιν	= λιμέν'· ἧ δ' ἀμάθοισι cet.
Herm.	38	ζώουσι δὲ	= ζώουσ', ἣν δὲ cet.
	238	ὁλοσποδὸς	= ὕλης σποδὸς cet.
	308	ἐνέχων δὲ	= ἔνεχ' ὧδε cet.
	406	νεογνοίων	= νεογνὸς ἐὼν cet
	556	διδασκαλίαν	= διδάσκαλοι ἣν cet.

iv. Mistakes that do not fall under any particular head :

Dem.	13	κῶδις τ' ὀδμῇ (unmetrical)	
	28	πολυκλίστω (the same mistake *h. Apoll.* 347, where the other MSS. have πολυλλίστω).	
	51	φαινόλη (vox nihili)	
	362	θυσθύμαινε (vox nihili)	
	420	μηλοβόστη	= μηλόβοσις Hes. *Theog.* 354.
Apoll.	75	ἀίδης	= ἀδὴ οἳ cet.
	475	κεῖνοι	= ξεῖνοι cet.
	543	ὄμματα	= ἤματα cet.
Herm.	108	τύνη	= τέχνη cet.
	157	δύσαχ'	= ἦ τάχ' cet.
	338	τέρτομον	= κέρτομον cet.
	400	ὄχου	= ἦχ' οὗ cet.
	417	ἔθετ'	= ἔθελ' cet.
	493	θ' ἕξουσι	= τέξουσι cet.
	504	δραπέτην	= ἐτραπέτην cet.
	565	ἄνδρ' ἀδαῇ	= ἄνδρα δαείης cet.
	576	νομίζων	= -ν ὁμιλεῖ cet.

Aphr.	135	δοιώ τε κασιγνήτω	= σοῖς τε κασιγνήτοις cet.
	157	αὐτὴ	= ἄνακτι cet.

The number and character of these errors is remarkable; the majority of them are *voces nihili*, and clearly show that the text of the MS. has not undergone anything that can be called regular correction.

(*b*) Besides these obvious and unhealed blunders, M offers a considerable number of peculiar readings. An attempt was made, *J.H.S.* xv. 271 ff., to prove the superiority of these lections; it is unnecessary to repeat the argument in detail here. A list, however, of the more important of them is subjoined:

		M	cet.
Apoll.	82	ἔσται	ἐστίν
	99	φραδμοσύνης	φραδμοσύνη
	110	ἀπὸ	ἀπὲκ
	114	ἴθμαθ'	ἴσμαθ', ἴδμαθ', ἴσθμαθ'
	151	ἀθάνατος	ἀθανάτους
	192	ἀφραδέες	ἀμφαδέες
	198	ἀγαυή	ἀγητή
	200	ἐν δ'	ἔνθ'
	209	ὁππόταν ἱέμενος	ὅπποσ' ἀνωόμενος
	211	ἅμ' ἐρεχθεῖ	ἅμ' ἐρευθεῖ, ἀμαρύνθω
	216	πετρίην	πιερίης, πιερίη
	217	ἁγνιήνας	μαγνηΐδας
	224	τέμμισον	τευμησσὸν and τελμησσὸν
	249	πολλοὶ	ἐνθάδ'
	295	καλὰ	μακρὰ
	ib.	διηνεκὲς	διαμπερὲς
	308	ἥνεκ'	εὗτ'
	322	μητίσεαι	μήσεαι, ἔτι μήσεαι
	339	ἐστιν. ὅσον	ἦ πόσσον, ἦ παρόσον
	341	δὲ ἰδοῦσα	δ' ἐσιδοῦσα
	349	μῆνες	νύκτες
	350	ἐπιτελλομένου	περιτελλομένου

		M	cet.
Apoll.	352	θεοῖσι	βροτοῖσι
	402	οὔτις	ὅστις
	407	πρώτιστα	πρῶτα
	423	ἐύκτιτον	ἐϋκτίμενον
	447	ἔμβαλ' ἑκάστῳ	εἶλεν ἕκαστον
	459	ἐπὶ	ποτὶ
	501	εἰς ὅτε	εἰς ὅκε
	515	ἐρατὸν	. . . ατὸν, χρυσῆν, χαρίεν
	516	ῥήσσοντες	φρίσσοντες
Herm.	45	ἢ ὅτε	αἳ ὅτε, ἃς ὅτε
	59	ἐξονομάζων	ὀνομάζων
	65	ἆλτο	ὦρτο
	82	νεοθηλέαν ἀγκαλωρήν	νεοθηλέος ἄγκαλον ὕλης
	87	δέμων ἀνθοῦσαν	δόμων αἴθουσαν
	90	ἐπικάμπυλα ξύλα	ἐπικάμπυλος ὤμους
	91	πολὺ οἰνήσεις	πολὺ οἰμήσεις
	109	ἐνίαλλε	ἐπέλεψε
	110	ἄμπνυτο δὲ	ἀνὰ δ' ἄμπνυτο
	ib.	θυμὸς ἀυτμῇ.	θερμὸς ἀυτμή
	119	ἐκκρίνας	ἐγκλίνων
	120	πίονα	πίονι
	132	ἐπεπείθετο	οἱ ἐπείθετο
	148	ἰθύσας	ἰθύνας
	159	φεροντα	λαβόντα
	164	πολλὰ—ἄρμενα	παῦρα—αἴσυλα
	248	ἐμπλείους	ἐκπλείους
	259	μετ'	ἐν
	306	ἐέλμενος	ἐλιγμένος
	342	εὐθὺ πύλονδ'	εὐθυπόρονδ'
	352	πολὺν	μέγαν
	357	παλάμησεν	μάλ' ἄμησεν
	361	ἀλεγίζων	ἀλεγύνων, ἀλεείνων
	368	ἀγορεύσω	καταλέξω
	385	φωρὴν	φωνὴν
	401	ἐς	παρὰ
	402	ἐξήλαυνε	ἤλαυνε

		M	cet.
Herm.	403	ἀπάνευθεν	ἀπάτερθεν
	422	hab.	om.
	431	ἅπαντες	ἕκαστος
	440	γενετῆς	γενεῆς
	457, 458	hab.	om.
	471	δὲ	γε
	486	φεύγουσα	φθέγγουσα
	501	νέρθεν	καλὸν
	502	σμερδαλόεν	ἱμερόεν
	503	καί ῥα	ἔνθα
	ib.	βόας	βόες
	ib.	κατὰ	ποτὶ
	507	τὰ μὲν	τὸ μὲν
	515	ἅμα κλέψης	ἀνακλέψης
	544	φωνή τ' ἠδὲ πότησι	φωνῇ καὶ πτερύγεσσι
	552	σεμναὶ	μοῖραι
	560	θυίωσι	θυίσωσι, θύσωσι
Aphr.	8	γλαυκῶπιν	γλαυκώπιδ'
	18	πουλύχρυσα δὲ	καὶ γὰρ τῇ ἅδε
	67	ῥίμφα	θοῶς
	114	τρωὰς	τρωὸς
	118	χρυσηλακάτου	χρυσηλάτου
	132	μὲν	om.
	175	ἰοστεφάνου	ἐυστεφάνου
	205	τετιμένον	τετιμένος
	247	ἐν	μετ'
Artem. ix.	3	μέλητος	μελήτης, μιλήτης
Aphr. x.	3	θέει	φέρει
	4	μάκαιρα κυθήρης	θεὰ σαλαμῖνος
Dem. xiii.	2	περσεφόνειαν	φερσεφόνειαν
Mat. De. xiv.	6	θ'	δ'
Heracl. xv.	4	ῥα ἠμὲν	πρὶν μὲν
	5	πημαίνετ' ἀεθλεύων κραταιῶς	πομπῇσιν ὑπ' εὐρυσθῆος ἄνακτος
	6	ἔξοχα ἔργα	πολλὰ δ' ἀνέτλη

The conclusion arrived at (*op.c.* p. 300) was that out of some 150 peculiar readings in M, 6 appeared to be deliberate conjectures (*Apoll.* 198, 209, *Herm.* 306, 349, 361, 418), 34 to be semi-conscious corrections (*Apoll.* 125, 181, 284, 295, 350, 352, 367, 459, 496, 501, 505, *Herm.* 78, 82, 132, 141, 148, 208, 265, 287, 303, 383, 400, 401, 411, 431, 456, 568, 503, 524, 542, *Aphr.* 25, 135, 189, *Dion.* vii. 29), 80 to be substantive, and of these 34 independent though not necessarily preferable to their opposites (*Apoll.* 181, 308, 321, 326, 339, 436, 447, *Herm.* 45, 65, 90, 119, 159, 164, 200, 202, 259, 368, 403, 502, 503, 515, 518, 522, *Aphr.* 8, 18, 66, 67, 204, *Aphr.* x. 3, 4, 5, *Heracl.* xv. 4, 5, 6), 46 original (*Apoll.* 82, 99, 110, 114, 157, 192, 200, 272, 292, 293, 318, 322, 341, 349, 402, 407, 420, 423, 431, 516, *Herm.* 59, 82, 87, 91, 110, 138, 148, 246, 248, 339, 342, 385, 440, 453, 486, 501, 503, 516, 544, 560, *Aphr.* 114, 118, 125, 174, 229, *Artemis* ix. 3). The remainder (26) were graphic or phonetic corruptions.

These considerations, combined with the fact of the gross corruptions collected above, seem to put the claims of M to be considered the best MS. of the *Hymns* beyond doubt.[1] No stronger position can be held by a MS. than that it should combine a number of original readings with a number of palpable corruptions. The existence of the latter makes it all but impossible that the former are the work of revision or conjecture. The position given to M is of course merely relative; good readings and original readings are found in the other MSS. of the *Hymns*, but in less proportion.

[1] Ruhnken, naturally, believed in the excellence of M, but he has hardly been followed by any one except Hollander and now Breuning. The gradual discovery of E and L turned the tide in favour of that family, and current opinion down to Gemoll's edition looked upon M as a recension: some of the hottest denunciation of it came from Cobet *Mnemosyne* x. 310 f.

$x = \mathrm{E\,L_1}\,\varPi\,\mathrm{T}$

The relationship of E and L_1 has long been recognized; *Π* was added to them in Goodwin's edition. T's connexion, suspected by Hollander (*Hermes*, 1891, p. 170 f.), was made manifest by the collations of Bethe and ourselves. The four MSS. constitute a very close and well-defined family. The passages in which they all agree against the remainder are these:

		x	cet.
Apoll.	17	κύνθειον	κύνθιον, κύνιον
	35	αὐτοκανὴς	αὐτοκάνης
	46	σοι	om. plerique
	ib.	γαιέων	γαιάων
	59	full line	half line (plerique)
	65	γ' ἐροίμην	γενοίμην
	71	ἴδης	ἴδη
	73	ὤσει	ὤση
	74	κράτος	κρατὸς
	174	ἡμέτερον	ὑμέτερον
	216	πιερίης	πετρίην, πιερίη
	224	τευμησσὸν	τελμησσὸν, τέμμισον
	272	προάγοιεν (desunt ET)	προσάγοιεν
	284	ὑποκρέμαται (desunt ET)	ἐπικρέμαται
	322	μήσεαι	μητίσεαι, ἔτι μήσεαι
	339	ἢ πόσσον	ἢ παρόσον, ἐστιν ὅσον
	346	φραζάσκετο	φραζέσκετο
	538	hab.	om.
Herm.	36	τὸ om.	hab.
	45	αἳ ὅτε	ἂς ὅτε, ἢ ὅτε
	59	ὄνομα κλυτὸν	ὀνομακλυτὸν, ὀνομακλυτὴν
	72	ἀκειρασίους	ἀκηρασίους
	286	δραύλους	δ' ἀγραύλους
	303	οἰωνοῖσιν εὖ	οἰωνοῖσι σὺ

		x	cet.
Herm.	361	ἀλεγύνων	ἀλεείνων, ἀλεγίζων
	397	σπεύδοντο	σπεύδοντε
	398	δ' ἐπ'	ἐπ'
	560	θυίσωσι (deest Π)	θύσωσι, θυίωσιν
Aphr.	16	χρυσήλατον (deest Π)	χρυσηλάκατον
	20	πόλις (deest Π)	πόλεις, πόνος
	267	ἕστασ'	ἑστᾶσ'
vi.	12	κοσμίσθην	κοσμείσθην -ήσθην
vii.	39	κατεκριμνῶντο (deest L_1)	κατεκρημνῶντο
xiv.	2	ὑμνεῖ (deest L_1)	ὕμνει
	3	τρόμος	βρόμος
xix.	26	θαλέων	θαλέθων
	32	ψαφερότριχα	ψαφαρότριχα
xxvii.	13	μετὰ κασιγνήτοιο	μετὰ om.
xxviii.	10	ὀμβρίμης	ὀβρίμης
xxix.	3	ἔλαχε	ἔλαχες
xxx.	14	περεσανθέσιν	παρ' εὐανθέσιν
	16	καὶ	κε
xxxii.	6	χρυσέου	χρυσοῦ
	ib.	ἀκτῆρες.	ἀκτῖνες
	11	πλήθει	πλήθη
xxxiii.	11	με	μέγας

It has further been recognized that the pairs E and T, L_1 and *Π*, are more closely connected together; this results clearly from the following table. We call E T *a*, L_1 *Π* *b*.

		a	*b*
Apoll.	4	φαίδιμος	φαίδιμα
	38	νῆσος	νήσων
	ib.	λιπαροτάτη	λιπαρωτάτη
	44	πετρήεσσα	πετρήδε(σ)σα
	51	κε θέλεις	κε(θέ)λῃς
	59	π̊ερίτας (θ above π)	om.
	60	πεῖας (-αρ T)	πείαρ
	75	οἷ	οἱ

		a	*b*
Apoll.	78	ἄχη τεϊλάων	-α φήτει λάων
	86	τε om.	hab.
	88	σ' ἔξοχα	σέ γ' ἔξοχα
	96	om.	hab.
	102	ἐϋκτισμένης	ἐυκτιμένης
	128	ἀσπαίροντες	ἀσπαίροντα
	136	ση. in marg.	ση. om.
	162	βαμβαλιαστὺν	[βαμ] κρεμβαλιαστὺν
	171	ὑμέων	ἡμέων
	176	ἐπειδὴ	ἐπιδὴ
	180	μήλιτον	μίλητον
	217	μαγνιήνας	μαγνηΐδας, in marg. μαγνιήνας
	260	τελείεσσας	τελήεσσας
	261–89	om.	hab.
	325	ἦρ'	ἦρ'
	348	ἱεροῖς	ἱεροῖσι
	414	ἤθελον	ἔθελον
	423	ἐϋκτισμένον	ἐϋκτιμένον
	466	γάρ	δέ
	479	καλλοῖσι	λλοῖσι L_1 Π
	506–8	om.	hab.
	523	[ζάθεον] ἄδυτον ζάθεον E ἄδυτον ζάθεον T	αὐτοῦ δάπεδον, in marg. ἄδυτον ζάθεον
Herm.	45	ἀμαλδῦναι	ἀμαρυγαί, in marg. ἀμαλδῦναι
	81	συμμϊότων	συμμίσγ(τ L_1)ων
	86	αὐτοτροπήσας ὧς	αὐτοπρεπὴς ὧς, in marg. αὐτοτροπήσας
	100	μεγαμειδείοιο, the first ει corrected out of η	μεγαμηδείδ(ο)ιο
	168	ἄλιστοι	ἄπαστοι
	288	ἀντήσεις	ἀντήσης
	296	τλήμονα μετὰ	τλήμονα
	400	ἀντιβάλλετο E ἀντιτάλλετο T	ἀτιτάλλετο
Aphr.	10, 11	in one	in two.

		a	*b*
Aphr.	68	θεῶν, in marg. γρ. θηρῶν	θηρῶν
	97	om.	hab.
	113	ἡμετέρην	ὑμετέρην
	123	ἄκτιστον	ἄκτιτον
	156	μεταστρᾰφθεῖσα [ε above]	μεταστρεφθεῖσα
	174	βυρε	ηυρε
	186	ἔειπας	ἔειπες
	207	τρῶς E, τρὼς T	τρῶα
	214	ἶσα θεοῖσι	ἤματα πάντα, in marg. γρ. ἶσα θεοῖσι
	256	ἤδη	ἴδη
	262	σεληνοὶ	σιληνοὶ
	265	ἔφυγαν [σ above γ]	ἔφυσαν
Dion. vii.	3	νεῆνίη [α above η]	νεηνίη
	29	ἑκατέρω	ἑκαστέρω
			Here L_1 breaks off.
	37	φόβος	τάφος, in marg. φόβος Π
Ares viii.	9	εὐθαλέος	εὐθαρλέσεος Π
Pan xix.	7	κέλευθα	κάρηνα, in marg. γρ. κέλευθα Π
	48	ἱλάσομαι	λίσομαι [ἱλα above], in marg. ἵλαμαι, Π
Heph. xx.	8	om.	hab. Π
Apoll. xxi.	5	ἵλασμαι	ἵλαμαι Π
Dion. xxvi.	13	ὁράων	ὡράων Π
Ge xxx.	3	ἐπέρχεται	ἀπέρχεται Π
Diosc. xxxiii.	14	ἀνέμους, in marg. γρ. ἀέλλας	ἀέλλας Π

E and T are somewhat more nearly connected than L_1 and *Π*, but all four are remarkably close, and give a very clear representation of their archetype *x*. The readings of the original were elicited in detail *J.H.S.* xv. 164–74, and in most cases do not admit of doubt. One interesting point remains, and on it turns the decision of the respective value of *a* and *b*, and the assignment of a number of readings to another family. The reader will have noticed in the last table a certain number of marginal variants, sometimes introduced by γρ., and of variants superscribed. Their full list is as follows:

1. *Apoll.* 55. οὐδὲ τρύγην οἴσεις, οὔτ' ἆρ φυτὰ μυρία φύσεις.

οἰσεῖς πολλὸν E : οἰστεῖς[πολλὴν] T : οἰστεῖς[πολλῆν] L_1 : οἰστεῖς, in marg. πολλῆν Π.

2. ib. 59. δη[μ]ρὸν ἄναξ εἰ βόσκοις [θ]περίτας σ' ἔχωσιν, in marg. γρ. εἰ βοσκοισθε οἵ κε σ' ἔχωσιν E :

δηρὸν ἄναξ εἰ βόσκοις [θ]περίτας σ' ἔχωσιν T :
δη[μ]ρον ἄναξ εἰ βόσκοις σ' ἔχωσιν L_1 :
δηρὸν ἄναξ εἰ βόσκοις θεοί κέ σ' ἔχωσιν Π.

3. ib. 136–38 om. in text E T L_1 : hab. in marg. E L_1 T with the words σῃ. ἐν ἑτέρῳ κεῖνται καὶ οὗτοι οἱ στίχοι (E T) : ἐν ἑτέρῳ καὶ οὗτοι οἱ στίχοι κεῖνται (L_1 Π). Π has the verses in the text, evidently by error.

4. ib. 151. ἀνὴρ, in marg. αἰεί E T Π : ἀνὴρ αἰεὶ L_1.

5. ib. 162. βαμβαλιαστὺν E T : κρεμ[βαμ]βαλιαστὺν L_1 Π.

6. ib. 202. ἀμφὶ φαείνει[ηι] E : ἀμφιφαείνει[η] T : ἀμφι φαείνειη L_1 : ἀμφί φαείνει[η] Π.

7. ib. 211. ἢ ἅμ' ἐρευθεῖ in text E L_1 Π T : in marg. γρ. ἢ ἅμα φόρβαντι τριοπόῳ ἢ ἀμαρύνθῳ L_1 Π.

8. ib. 217. ἢ μαγνιήνας E T : ἢ μαγνηίδας L_1 Π : in marg. γρ. μαγνιήνας.

9. ib. 325[a] om. in text E L_1 Π T : add. in marg. with the words γρ. καὶ E T : γρ. καὶ οὕτως L_1 : γρ. Π.

10. ib. 523. ἄδυτον ζάθεον E T : αὐτοῦ δάπεδον, in marg. γρ'. ἄδυτον ζάθεον L_1 Π.

11. *Herm.* 45. ἀμαλδύναι E T : ἀμαρυγαί, in marg. γρ. ἀμαλδύ-[ναι L_1 Π.

12. ib. 86. αὐτοτροπήσας ὣς E T : αὐτοπρεπὴς ὣς, in marg. γρ. αὐτοτροπήσας (αὐτοτεοπήσας) L_1 Π.

13. ib. 168. ἄλιστοι E T : ἄπαστοι L_1 Π.

14. ib. 212. φοῖβος ἀπόλλων : in marg. γρ. μῦθον ἀκούσας E L_1 Π T.

15. ib. 224. ἔλπομαι εἶναι E T : ἤστην (-ιν Π) ὁμοῖα, in marg. γρ. ἔλπομαι εἶναι L_1 Π.

16. *Herm.* 241. δή ῥα νεόλλουτος προκαλεύμενος ἥδυμον ὕπνον: in marg. ἐν ἄλλω οὕτως· θῆρα νέον λοχάων προκαλεύμενος ἡδύ E L_1 Π (λοχεύων) (?T).

17. ib. 254. λίκνω E T: κλίνη L_1 Π, in marg. γρ. ἐν λίκνω.

τὸν
18. ib. 280. τὸν E(?T): ὡς L_1: τὸν ὡς Π.

19. ib. 288. ἀντήσεις ἀγέλησι βοῶν καὶ πώεσι μήλων: in marg. γρ΄. ἄντην βουκολίοισι καὶ εἰροπόκοις ὀίεσσιν E L_1 Π T (ἀντήσης in text L_1 Π).

20. ib. 322. δ' ἵκοντο κάρηνα E T: δὲ τέρθρον ἵκοντο, in marg. γρ΄. δ' ἵκοντο κάρηνα L_1 Π.

21. ib. 326. μετὰ χρυσόθρονον ἠῶ E T: ποτὶ πτύχας οὐλύμποιο, in marg. γρ΄. μετὰ χρυσόθρονον ἠῶ L_1 Π.

22. ib. 366. ἑρμῆς δ' ἄλλον μῦθον ἐν ἀθανάτοισιν ἔειπεν E T: ἑρμῆς δ' αὖθ' ἑτέρωθεν ἀμειβόμενος ἔπος ηὔδα L_1 Π, in marg. ἑρμῆς δ' ἄλλον μῦθον ἐν ἀθανάτοισιν ἔειπεν.

23. ib. 451. οἶμος, in marg. γρ. καὶ ὕμνος E L_1 Π T.

24. ib. 473. τῶν E T: καὶ L_1 Π, in marg. γρ. τῶν.

25. ib. 563. πειρῶνται δ' ἤπειτα πάρεξ ὁδὸν ἡγεμονεύειν: in marg. γρ. ψεύδονται δ' ἤπειτα δι' ἀλλήλων δονέουσαι E L_1 T (def. Π).

βη
26. *Aphr.* 99. βήσεα ET: πείσεα L_1 (def. Π).

27. ib. 205. τετιμένονος E L_1 Π T.

28. ib. 214. ἶσα θεοῖσι E T: ἤματα πάντα L_1 Π, in marg. γρ. ἶσα θεοῖσι.

τάχα
29. ib. 244. τάχα E T: κάτα L_1 Π.

30. *Dion.* vii. 37. φόβος E T: τάφος, in marg. φόβος Π (def. L_1).

31. *Ares* viii. 9. εὐθαλέος E T: εὐθαρλέσεος Π (def. L_1).

32. *Pan* xix. 7. κέλευθα E T: κάρηνα, in marg. γρ. κελευθα Π (def. L_1).

ἱλα
33. ib. 48. ἱλάσομαι E T: λίσομαι, in marg. ἵλαμαι Π (def. L_1).

In seven passages (3, 9, 14, 16, 19, 23, 25) it is explicitly said that there was a marginal variant in the joint archetype of the four MSS.; in three (1, 4, 27) the same is evident, the variant in one or other MS. having been absorbed into the text in such a way as to betray its origin; in one (7) the four MSS. agree in the text, but two of them (L_1 *Π*) mention a variant which does not appear in E T; in eighteen (5, 8, 10, 11, 12, 13, 15, 17, 20, 21, 22, 24, 26, 28, 29, 30, 31, 32) E T show in their text a reading which is marginal or superscribed in L_1 *Π*. The conclusion can only be that the scribe of *a*, the immediate archetype of E T, was careless compared to the scribe of *b*. He treated the marginalia of *x* differently in different passages, occasionally reproducing them as marginalia, occasionally simply ignoring them, but far more often copying them into his text. There can therefore be no doubt that *b* (= L *Π*) represents the original of the family more exactly than *a*, and the old question of the relative excellence of E and L_1 is answered in favour of L_1.[1]

We also acquire a number of important readings which, as they are neither *x* nor identical with M or *p*, we may regard as belonging to a different source, and call *y*.[2]

Apart from the *y* readings, the four MSS. represent *x* with great fidelity; this is particularly evident in a number of gaps which L_1 leaves in its words (*Apoll.* 7 λ ρεσσιν, 8 ανεκρ μασε, 12 τ π̔ γυια, 479 λλοῖσι, *Herm.* 5 μ ἆρ, *Aphr.* 6 ἔρ μέμηλεν, 133 ἀπ ρήτην): in the careful reproduction of *Apoll.* 59 in all four MSS., *Apoll.* 515 the mutilated word ατὸν or τόν, *Herm.* 42 the gap ὀρεσκώ λώνης in E L_1, only partially filled in *Π* (ὀρεσκώιο κολώνης), the similar gap *Herm.* 79 and the uncorrected blunder ὦτο (corrected indeed in T) *ib.* 65.

The archetype *x* was probably therefore damaged, and certainly minuscule; the typical corruption *Aphr.* 174 βυρε E T, ηυρε, L_1 *Π* for the κῦρε of M is sufficient evidence of

[1] Gemoll *Hom. Blätter* p. 12 f. and in the preface to his edition championed E against Hollander *op. c.* p. 16. See generally Breuning, pp. 8–20.

[2] Which Breuning, p. 54, n. 6 will not permit. But the expressions ἐν ἑτέρῳ, ἐν ἄλλῳ are current coin in the Byzantine period, and need not be referred to the ancient world.

that. (For a similar typical minuscule corruption cf. *Euthydemus* 298 D *βοϊδίων, κωβίων, ᾠιδίων*.)

The intrinsic character of the readings of *x* was examined *J.H.S.* xv. 269–71 with the conclusion that of twenty-eight peculiar readings two were conjectures (*Apoll.* 151, *Mat. Deor.* xiv. 3), nine semi-conscious alterations (*Apoll.* 71, 216, 284, 339, *Herm.* 86, 397, *Aphr.* 244, *Pan.* xix. 7, *Hest.* xxix. 3), and four correct and original (*Apoll.* 224, *Herm.* 232, 361, *Aphr.* 144). Its value consists in the fidelity of its copying, and the comparative absence of conjecture, for which the damaged state of the archetype afforded much opportunity.[1]

A number of other MSS. belong to the family *x*. First, At and D. The former was discovered at Athos by J. P. Mahaffy (*Athenaeum*, 1889, p. 631), and collated by Professor Constantinides, whose readings were published by

[1] The four MSS. have a certain number of readings peculiar to each, and which in the case of ET we may fairly call conjectures of their writers—Giorgio Valla (a native of Piacenza, 1430–99, cf. Heiberg, 'Beiträge zur Geschichte Georg Valla's und seine Bibliothek', *Beiheft zum Centralblatt f. Bibliothekswesen* xiv. 1896, and 'Nachfrägliches über G. V.', ib. xvi. 1898, p. 189 f., and for local Placentine literature Gabotto, *Nuovo Archivio Veneto*, 1891, p. 201 f.; for a reduced specimen of his hand, see *Miscellanea Fr. Ehrle* 1924, iv. 32), and the better-known Constantine Lascaris (Legrand, *Bibliothèque hellénique* i, p. lxxi f.). Peculiar to E are *Apoll.* 55 *οἰσεῖς* (for *οἰστεῖς*), 156 *ὅου* for *θ' οὗ*, 208 *μνηστῆρσιν*, *Herm.* 400 *ἀντιβάλλετο*; to T *Apoll.* 403 *ἀνασσείασκε*, *Herm.* 65 *ὦρτο* (for *ὦτο*), 286 *δ' ἀγραύλους*.

L_1 in addition to the gaps collected above has a few mistakes which seem to have arisen from misunderstanding symbols: *Apoll.* 17 *πρὸ* = *πρὸς*, 42 *μεερόπων* = *μερόπων*, 64 *δεξαίμ̈* (i.e. *δεξαίμιν*) = *δεξαίμων*, 178 *λυκ̈ι* = *λυκίην*, *μηον̈ι* = *μηονίην*, *Herm.* 565 *φρέντα* (i.e. *φρεν̄*) = *φρένα*, 570 *χθονὸν* = *χθὼν*.

Π's noticeable peculiarities are *Apoll.* 115 *μονοστόκος*, 136–8 in the text, evidently accidentally; 137 *οἴλατο* in marg., 479 *πολλοῖσι* (right), 510 *περὶ* marg. (right), *Herm.* 42 *κολώνης* (wrong), 79 *σάνδαλα αὐτίκ'* (gap in EL), 383 *ἐπιδέομαι*, *Herm.* 494–*Aphr.* 152 om., three leaves having been cut out (the stumps of them remain); Ares viii. 9 *εὐθαρλεσέος* (a curious conflation of *εὐθαρσέος* with *αλ* written above). Though the MS. contains many errors, it has been carefully revised, and a number of lines are marked with dots and crosses to indicate that they contain a suspicious spelling.

I. Bywater in the *Classical Review*, 1894, p. 341. Tracings made by Constantinides, and shown to us by Bywater, leave no doubt that At is a fifteenth-century MS., though the editors of the Vatopedi catalogue (p. xvi) put it in the fourteenth. Mr. Smiley should not have quoted Mahaffy and Wilamowitz, nor M. Breuning Gardthausen. Moreover, fourteenth-century bombycine MSS. even when smoothed do not 'resemble vellum', and Constantinides said *ἐπὶ χάρτου ἀρχαίου παρεμφεροῦς μεμβράνῃ* (*C. R.* 1894. 341). D, a Milan MS., has been longer known, and at one time was considered an important source. The two MSS. are closely connected; they have the following peculiarities in common.[1]

Apoll.	18	ὑπ' ἰνόποιο	Herm.	420	γέλασε
	41	in the place of 36		539	χρυσάραπι
	372–4	om.		540	βούλεται
	403	ἀνασείσασκε (with NV).		572	δ' om.
			Aphr.	13	σκύτινα
Herm.	54	κονάβισε		22	ἑστίῃ
	93	μηκέτι		46	μιγημέναι
	100	μεγαμηδείαο		174	ἦρε
	103	ἤλαυνον		214	ἀγήραος
	156	δέ σε	Asclep.	xvi. 3	φλεγύος (with KN)

The points in which At and D differ are few and clerical (*J.H.S.* xv. 149).

The pair At D belong to the *x* family, and the connexion is so obvious that a detailed proof need hardly be given (*J.H.S.* xv. 146). That within *x* they incline to the branch *b* appears from the following passages within the first 300 lines of the hymn to Apollo; (I quote D for At D, since the collation of At is not complete):

4	φαίδιμος *a*	φαίδιμα *b*D
20	τοι *a*	τε *b*D

[1] Breuning p. 29 gives them the collective letter *f*.

38	νῆσος *a*	νήσων *b*D
ib.	λιπαροτάτη *a*	λιπαρωτάτη *b*D
44	πετρήεσσα *a*D	πετρήδεσ(σ)α *b*
51	κε θέλεις *a*, κ' ἐθέλεις D	κε θέλῃς Π, κέλῃς L_1
60	πεῖας *a*	πείαρ *b*, πεῖαρ D
78	ἀκηδέα ἄχῃ τεϊλάων *a*	ἀκηδέα χήτει λαῶν *b*D
86	τε om. *a*D	hab. *b*
88	σ' ἔξοχα *a*	σέ γ' ἔξοχα *b*D
96	om. *a*	hab. *b*D
128	ἀσπαίροντες *a*	ἀσπαίροντα *b*D
162	βαμβαλιαστὺν *a*	κρεμβαλιαστὺν (βαμ above) *b*, κρεμβαλιαστὺν D
171	ἀφ' ὑμέων *a*	ἀφ' ἡμέων *b*D
176	ἐπειδὴ *a*	ἐπιδὴ *b*, ἐπὶ δὴ D
180	μήλιτον *a*	μίλητον *b*D
197	οὔτε λαχεῖα ET	οὔτε λάχεια *b*D
217	ἢ μαγνιήνας *a*	ἢ μαγνηΐδας *b*D
260	τελειέσσας *a*	τεληέσσας *b*D
261–89	om. *a*	hab. *b*D

In twenty variants, D agrees with *b* in seventeen, with *a* in three. The inference is plain. At D were derived from a member of the *x* family which did not, like *a*, absorb a certain number of the marginalia which were originally part of the archetype.

The pair, however, or D as representative of both, differ from *b* in a certain number of points, more curious than important, and which in most cases may fairly be called conjectures:

Apoll. 41 in AtD after 35; homoeoteleuton
72 ἀτιμήσω (η above ω)
83 ὄμωσεν
114 ἴδμαθ' (the same correction in Π, ἴσμαθ' with δ above σ)
130 ἀθανάτοισι
223 ἴξας
402 ἐπεφράσσατο

Apoll. 515 ἀγατὸν (an evident conjecture ; ατὸν *x*)
540 τηὖσιόν γ' ἔπος
Herm. 38 θάνης (as M)
47 marg. γρ. ταμῶν
70 θέων
99 σκοπιῇ AtD
100 μεγαμηδείαο AtD
103 ἤλαυνον AtD (102 ἤλασεν, 106 συνέλασσεν)
238 ἀμφικαλύπτει
261 ἔειπες
284 καθίσαι
289 καὶ ὕστατον, om. τε AtD
540 βούλεται AtD (a gloss; ξ 300 βούλετ', μήδετ': τ 326 βουλήν, μῆτιν)
Aphr. 13 σκύτινα AtD: conjecture
22 ἑστίη AtD (as M)
118 χρυσηλακάτου (as M)
174 ἧρε AtD (a conjecture, and a bad one, for the ηυρε of *b*; here AtD show clearly their closeness to *b*, since *a* has made βυρε of the original κῦρε)
203 ἥρπασε ὃν At, ἥρπασ' ἐὸν D
205 τετιμένος (τετιμένονος *x*)
214 ἀγήραος AtD
Ge xxx. 3 ὑπέρχεται
Helios xxxi. 4 ἀγακλειτὴν

These differences are evidently slight, and only rarely improvements. *ἀγατόν Apoll.* 515 is ingenious, but fortunately is shown by M and the quantity to be wrong; *σκύτινα Aphr.* 13 is also ingenious; *χρυσηλακάτου Aphr.* 118 and *ἀγακλειτήν Hel.* xxxi. 4 happen to be right. *ἑόν Aphr.* 203 is nearly correct.

H J K = *z*

Three other MSS. appear to be descended from D, or its archetype, and therefore form another ramification of *x*.

They are distinguished by their contents: *Hymns* viii–xvii, followed by *Apoll.* 1–186 (v. 185 is omitted, and of 186 only the words ἔνθεν δὲ πρὸς Ὄλυμπον are given; v. 184 comes after this half-line. In H even less than this remains, viz. *Apoll.* 1–55). No reason can be given for such curious contents, arranged in such an eccentric order; the archetype must have been a few quires of some book, out of order. M also fails suddenly in xviii, but this can hardly be more than a coincidence.

That the three MSS. belong to *x* appears from the following passages where H J K agree with *x* against M*p*:

Art. ix.	3	μελήτης HJK*x*	μιλήτης *p*, μέλητος M
Mat. de. xiv.	3	τρόμος HJK*x*	βρόμος M*p*
Apoll.	35	αὐτοκανὴς HJK*x*	αὐτοκάνης *p* (deest M)
	59	full line JK*x*	half line *p* (deest M)

and from these where H J K agree with *x* (and M, with which they can have no connexion) against *p*:

Ares viii.	9	εὐθαρσέος HJK*y*M	εὐθαλέος *px*
Mat. de. xiv.	3	τυμπάνων HJK*x*M	τυπάνων *p*
Apoll.	78	ἀκήδεα χήτει λαῶν JK (deest H)*x*M	ἕκαστά τε φῦλα νεπούδων *p*
	152	οἳ τότ' ἐπ' JK (deest H) M*x*	οἳ δή τότ' ἐπ- *p*
	162	κρεμβαλιαστὴν JK (deest H) M, βαμβαλιαστὺν *x*	κρεμβαλιασὺν *p*
	171	ἡμέων JK (deest H) *x*M	ὑμῶν *p*
	176	ἐπιδὴ JK (deest H), ἐπειδὴ *x*M	ἐπιδὴν *p*

That H J K are descended from D appears from these places:

Asclep. xvi.	3	φλεγύος AtDK, φλεγέος HJ	φλεγύου cet. (φλεγύος N)
Apoll.	41	after v. 35 AtDHJK	
	49	ἐβήσατο DK, βήσατο HJ	ἐβήσετο cet. (ἐβήσσατο L_1)

60 πεῖαρ DJK (deest H)	πείαρ L_1Π, πῖαρ *p*
72 ἀτιμήσω^{η} D, ἀτιμήση JK (in ras.), (deest H)	ἀτιμήσω *x*, ἀτιμήσας *p*
83 ὄμωσεν DK ὄμοσσεν$^{\text{γρ. ὅμωσεν}}$ J, (deest H)	ὄμοσ(σ)εν cet.
114 ἴδμαθ' DJK (deest H)	ἴσ^{δ}μαθ' *x*, ἴσθμαθ' *p*

The members differ among themselves; the peculiar readings are, in H:

Ares viii.	4 θέμιστα	θέμιστος cet.
Apoll.	46 οἱ	σοι cet. (. . οι T)

This is an excellent conjecture and usually printed.

In J:

Apoll.	57 ἀγινήσουσ'	ἀγινήσουσιν, ἀγίνουσιν cet.
	59 δὴ ῥὰ θεοί κε σ' ἔχωσι	δὴ ῥὰ om. cet.
	65 γενοίμην (and *p*S)	γ' ἐροίμην cet.
	70 αἰνῶς γε	γε om cet.
	74 ἄλλυδις	ἄλις cet.
	82 γρ. ἔσται (so M)	ἐστίν cet.
	86 πέλεται om. τε	πέλει cet.
	139 γ' ἀνθέει οὔρεος ἄνθεσιν ὕλη	τε ῥίον οὔρεος ἄνθεσιν ὕλης cet.
	151 ἄνδρας	ἀνὴρ *x*K, αἰεί cet.

Most of the peculiarities are evidently wild; *ἀγινήσουσ'*, *ἔσται*, and *γενοίμην* (if original) are good conjectures.

In K:

Dem. xiii.	1 δημήτηρ' K, etc.	δημήτρ' HJ
Apoll.	31 om. K cet.	κυδνὴ add. HJ
	39 κορύκου KD*x*, κωρύκου *p*	κουρίκου H, κουρύκου J
	51 κ' ἐθέλεις K, with DET*p*	κ' ἐθέλοις H, κεθέλοις J
	55 οἰσεῖς K cet., οἰστεῖς L_1Π	οἴσεις HJ
	158 ἂρ K cet.	ἂν HJ

H and J evidently are nearer to one another than to K. *οἴσεις*, though slight, is a good correction.

Traces of J's conjectures appear in K:

Apoll.	65 *γενοίμην* J	*γενοι* K m. 2
	151 *ἄνδρας* J	*ἄνδρας* K m. 2

All three MSS. differ from their immediate source, the original of AtD, in reading:

Apoll. 18 *ὑπ' οἰνώποιο* for *ὑπ' ἰνώποιο*
52 *ἐπὶ* for *ἐνὶ*

S

This MS. (Vat. 1880) was discovered by H. Rabe (whose collation was published by Arthur Ludwich *Neue Jahrbücher für Philologie*, 1892, pp. 239, 240); it was collated also by ourselves in 1893 and 1927. It consists of eight leaves (*Apoll.* 1–357), the first quire of a fifteenth-century MS. It agrees throughout with the *x* family, but in a small number of cases has the readings of *p* or HJK (the details are given *J.H.S.* xv. 152, 153). It is therefore, an emended member of the *x* stock. It has, however, a number of readings peculiar to itself, and in these its interest consists:

Apoll. 18 *ὑπ' ἰνώποιο*: this is correct. The nearest MS. reading is M's *ὑπὶ νώποιο*.

44 *ῥήναιά*: the rest accent *ῥηναία*.

53 *λήσ̆ει*. As the scribe has added a sigma, he may have thought his original *λήσει* a mistake, but it has suggested the undoubtedly right restoration: *λίσσει* cet.

54 *εὔβωλο σε ἔσεσθαι* (?).

57 *ἁγίνουσιν*: the rest *ἀγινήσουσιν* or *ἀγινήσουσ'*.

128 *ἔσχον*: the rest *ἴσχον*.

165 ἀλλ' ἄγεθ' ἱλήκοι as Thucydides : ἀλλάγε δὴ λητὼ vulg.
209 ὁππότ' ἀνωόμενος : ὅπποσ' ἀνωόμενος vulg.
216 πιερίην : πιερίης or πιερίη cet. (πετρίην M).
234 κείν' : κεῖν' cet.
297 υἱέες ἐργίνου : υἱέε σεργίνου cet.
325 ἤ' ἆρ : ἦρ', ἤρ' cet.

The readings on 53, 57, 165, 216, 297 are very remarkable, and that on 325, if *ἦά ῥ'* is intended, is a good conjecture. It is lamentable that more of this MS. has not been preserved.

Professor Hollander (*Über die neu bekannt gewordenen Handschriften der h. Hymnen*, 1895, pp. 10, 11) mentions a copy of the editio princeps of 1488 in the Laurentian Library at Florence (= L_5) on the margin of which are some readings entered in ink (he mentions the correction γενοίμην for γ' ἐροίμην, *Apoll.* 65), which agree with the readings of S. Hollander believes S (like G) to be a copy of the printed book. As was maintained *J.H.S.* xvii. 47, the converse seems more probable, viz. that the peculiar lections of S were copied by a reader into the margin of his edition. On the evidence of the hand, S may well have been written before 1488.

Editio Princeps

Homer was first printed at Florence in 1488 (E. Legrand, *Bibliographie hellénique* i. p. 939, *J.H.S.* xv. 156 f.). For the *Hymns*, at least, the edition is of importance, and fills the place exactly of a fifteenth-century MS. The editor, Demetrius Chalcondyles (Legrand *op.c.*, p. xciv f.), says of this portion of his work δεῖ μέντοι μὴ ἀγνοεῖν ὡς ἔν τε τῇ βατραχομυομαχίᾳ καὶ τοῖς ὕμνοις ἐνιαχοῦ διὰ τὴν τῶν ἀντιγράφων διαφθοράν, οὔτε ὁ τῶν ἐπῶν εἱρμὸς οὔτε μὴν τὸ τῆς διανοίας ὑγιὲς ἀπαρτίζεται. Demetrius followed on the whole a MS. of the *x* family (the passages are given *J.H.S.* xv. 155–7), but, as he implies in his preface, he corrected obvious errors; in many of his corrections he coincides with AtD (*ib.* 157); he may even have used D or a MS. like D to print from, and here and there various other MSS. (*ib.* p. 158); but many of his novelties are not found in any *x* or *p* MS., and therefore may fairly be set down to his own conjectures. These are:

Apoll.	63	μὲν	κεν cet.
	93	ῥείη	ῥέη cet.
	96	μεγάροισι	μεγάροις cet.
	220	ἅδε	-άδε cet.
	223	ἀπ'	ἐπ' cet.
	317	in marg. λείπει	
	318	ἔμβαλον	ἔμβαλεν cet.
	325	ἦν ἂρ	ἢ ῥ' ἐν and ἤ ῥ' ἐν cet.
	339	ἦ ὅσσον	ἦ πόσσον or παρόσον cet.
	361	καὶ ἔνθα om.	hab. cet.
	392	νῆα θοὴν	ἠμαθόην cet.
	407	οἳ τὰ πρῶτα	τὰ πρῶτα cet.
	411	ἶξον	ἴξον cet.
	414	ἤδ'	ἠδ' cet.
	419	παρὲκ	παρεκ cet.
	450	χαίτη	χαίτης cet.
	452	τίνες	πόθεν cet.
	502	ἔφαθ'	ἔφατ' cet.
Herm.	65	ἆλτο	ὦρτο cet. (except M)
	94	φὰς συνέσευε	φασὶν ἔσευε cet.
	175	φιλητεύων	δὲ φιλητεύων cet.
	214	φηλητὴν	φιλητὴν *x*, φηλωτὴν *p*
	236	χωόμενος	χωόμενον cet.
	292	φηλητέων	φιλητέων *x*, φηλιτέων *p*
	303	οἰωνοῖς· εὖ	οἰωνοῖσιν εὖ D*x*, οἰωνοῖσι σὺ *p*
	400	ἀτάλλετο	ἀτιτάλλετο cet.
	474	αὐτάγρετόν	αὖτ' ἄγρετόν cet.

Herm. 482	ἄρ'	ἂν cet.
491	αὖ	αὖτ' cet.
533	ἐρεείνης	ἐρεείνεις cet.
Aphr. 20	πτόλις	πόλις *x*, πόνος *p*
39	καταθνητῇσι	κατὰ θνητῇσι cet.
229	καὶ εὐγενέος	εὐγενέος cet.
Dion. vii. 13	λύγοι	λυδοὶ cet.
Pan xix. 31	κυλληνίον	κυλληνίου cet.
Pos. xxii. 3	αἰγάς	αἶγας cet.
Ge xxx. 15	παίζουσαι	παίζουσι cet.

Of these peculiarities the following are found in M, and as we cannot suppose Demetrius had access to any such source, the coincidence must be counted a confirmation: *Apoll.* 223 ἀπ', 318 ἔμβαλον, 392 νῆα θοήν, 502 ἔφαθ', *Herm.* 65 ἆλτο. The following are unique and also appear correct, and are no small tribute to Demetrius' ability: *Apoll.* 93 ῥείη, 96 μεγάροισι, 220 ἅδε, 317 marg. λείπει, 411 ἶξον, 419 παρέκ, 452 τίνες, *Herm.* 94 φὰς συνέσευε, 214 φηλητήν, 292 φηλητέων, 400 ἀτάλλετο, 474 αὐτάγρετόν, *Aphr.* 20 πτόλις, 39 καταθνητῇσι and other cases of καταθνητός, *Dion.* vii. 13 λύγοι, *Pos.* xxii. 3 αἰγάς, *Ge* xxx. 15 παίζουσαι.

p

The sixteen MSS. that remain constitute a large and also well-defined family, once, but without reason, considered inferior to the others, and even negligible. The passages in which these MSS. assert their relationship are:

		p	cet.
Apoll.	11	δὲ om. (as H)	hab.
	19	πάντων	πάντως and πάντοσσ'
	21	παντοτρόφον	πορτιτρόφον
	24	λίμναι	λιμένες
	28	λίγυπνόοις	λίγυπνοίοις

		p	cet.
Apoll.	29	θνητοῖς	θνητοῖσιν
	32	ἀγχίαλος	ἀγχίαλη
	42	πόλεις	πόλις
	46	σοι om.	hab.
	ib.	γαιάων	γαιέων
	54	εὔβουν	εὔβων
	59	δηρὸν ἄναξ εἰ βόσκοις	δηρὸν ἄναξ εἰ βόσκοις· θεοί κε σ' ἔχωσιν or the like
	65	πέρι τιμήεσσα	περιτιμήεσσα
	ib.	γενοίμην	γ' ἐροίμην
	72	ἀτιμήσας	ἀτιμήσω and ἀτιμήση
	ib.	ἐπείη	ἐπειὴ
	75	ἀδοίη	ἀδῄ οἱ and ἀδῆ οἱ
	78	ἕκαστά τε φῦλα νεπούδων	ἀκήδεα χήτει λαῶν
	129	δεσμά σ'	δέσματ' or δεσμάτ'
	143	τε (before νηοί)	τοι
	159	αὖθις	αὖτις
	162	κρεμβαλιασὺν	κρεμβαλιαστὺν (-ὴν)
	176	ἐπιδὴν	ἐπιδὴ, ἐπειδὴ
	178	ὑμνῶν	ὑμνέων
	184	ἔχον	ἔχων
	189	om.	hab.
	197	οὔτ' ἐλάχεια	οὔτε λάχεια or λαχεῖα
	211	om.	hab.
	215	ἀπόλλωνος	ἄπολλον
	216	πιερίη	πιερίης (πετρίην, πιερίην)
	224	τελμησσὸν	τευμησὸν, τέμμισον
	233	οἱ δὲ	οὐδὲ
	274	δέξαιο	δέξαι
	293	βωμῶ	νηῶ
	306	τυφάονα	τυφλὸν, τυφλόν τε
	322	ἔτι μήσεαι	μήσεαι, μητίσεαι
	326	καὶ νῦν τοιγὰρ	καὶ νῦν μὲν τοὶ γὰρ, καὶ νῦν μέντοι
	328	αἰσχύνασ'	αἰσχύνας

		p	cet.
Apoll.	339	ἢ παρόσον	ἢ πόσσον, or ἐστὶν. ὅσον
	344	om.	hab.
	351	ἐναλίγγιον	ἐναλίγκιον
	356	αἴσιον	αἴσιμον
	366	ἀδινήσουσι (pleriq.)	ἀγινήσουσι
	394	ἀγγελέουσι	ἀγέλλουσι, ἀγγέλουσι
	402	ἐπιφράσσαιτο	ἐπιφράσσατο, ἐπεφράσ(σ)ατο
	403	πάντοσ'	πάντοθ'
	416	om.	hab.
	460	σφας	σφεας
	515	χρυσῆν	χαρίεν (Athen.), ἐρατὸν (. . . ατὸν, ἄγατὸν)
	518	τε alterum om.	hab.
	538	om. (as M)	hab.
Herm.	10	δὴ om.	hab.
	20	γύων, or om.	γυίων
	45	ἃς ὅτε	αἳ ὅτε and ἣ ὅτε
	ib.	δυνηθῶσι	δινηθῶσι
	59	ὀνομακλυτὴν	ὀνομακλυτὸν and ὄνομα κλυτὸν
	127	χάρμα φέρων	χαρμοφέρων
	152	παρ' ἰγνύσι	περ' ἰγνύσι
	157	πλευροῖσι	πλευρῆσι
	159	φηλητεύσειν	φιλητεύσειν
	193	ἐβόσκετο om.	hab.
	209	εὐκραίροισιν	εὐκραιρῆσιν (-ησιν)
	214	φηλωτὴν	φιλητὴν or φιλοτὴν
	241	νήδυμον	ἥδυμον
	312	δέξαι	δέξο
	ib.	πὰρ	παρὰ
	313	ἐρέεινεν (as M*x*)	ἐρέεινον
	342	δΐα	δοιὰ
	356	κατέερξε	κατέρεξε
	361	ἀλεείνων	ἀλεγύνων, ἀλεγίζων
	386	κραταιῶ	κρατερῶ
	402	ἤλαυνε	ἐξήλαυνε

		p	cet.
Herm.	412	ἀγραύλοισι	ἀγραύλησι
	420	κονάβισσε	κονάβησε
	440	σὺ	σοί
	446	φηλητὰ	φιλητὰ
	449	νήδυμον	ἥδυμον
	478	ἑταῖρον	ἑταίρην
	481	φιλομειδέα	φιλοκυδέα
	ib.	χῶρον	κῶμον
	484	νόα	νόω
	495	πέρι ζαμενῶς	περιζαμενῶς
	502	κονάβισσε	κονάβησε
	530	ἀκήραον	ἀκήριον
	532–4	om.	hab.
	540	πιφάσκειν	πιφαύσκειν
	543	ἔλθοι	ἔλθη
	557	ἀλέγεινεν	ἀλέγυνεν
	560	θύσωσι	θυίσωσι, θυίωσιν
	ib.	ἐδωδυῖαι	ἐδηδυῖαι
Aphr.	20	πόνος	πόλις, πόλεις
	39, 50	θνητοῖσι	θνητῇσι
	71	πορδάλιες (nonnulli)	παρδάλιες
	82	τε καὶ (nonnulli)	καὶ
	136, 136^{a}	οὔ σφιν ἀεικελίη γυνὴ ἔσσομαι ἠὲ καὶ οὐκί	οὔ σφιν ἀεικελίη νυὸς ἔσσομαι ἀλλ' εἰκυῖα [εἴ τοι ἀεικελίη γυνὴ ἔσσομαι ἠὲ καὶ οὐκί]
	146	ἀγοράζεις	ἀγορεύεις
	152	προίοι (nonnulli)	προίη
	194	τοι om.	hab.
Art. ix.	3	μιλήτης	μελήτης, μέλητος
Ath. xi.	3	πόλεμοι	πτόλεμοι
Mat. de. xiv.	3	κροτάλη	κροτάλων
Ascl. xvi.	3	δωτίνω	δωτίω
Pan xix.	24	λυγγὸς	λυγκὸς
	26	θαλέθων	θαλέων
Ath. xxviii.	10	ὀβρίμης	ὀμβρίμης

	p	cet.
Hest. xxix.	3 ἔλαχες	ἔλαχε
Ge xxx.	14 παρ' εὐανθέσιν	περεσανθέσιν
Selene xxxii.	6 χρυσοῦ	χρυσέου
	ib. ἀκτῖνες	ἀκτῆρες
	11 πλήθη	πλήθει
Diosc. xxxiii.	14 ἀέλλαι	ἀέλλας

So many peculiarities reproduced with few corrections in sixteen MSS. are a considerable proof of fidelity. Within the family the divergences are not numerous or important. Those contained in the collations available to us are given *J.H.S.* xv. 177, 178;[1] the most important are the superscription νηῶ in NOPV$_1$ *Apoll.* 293, ἀγινήσουσι N and superscribed in L$_3$PR$_1$ *Apoll.* 366, the various reproductions of ἄπαστοι (λι superscribed) *Herm.* 168. The variants suggest a closer relationship between BΓO; Hollander *op.c.* p. 11 connects L$_2$PR$_{1,2}$. The ancestor of the whole family no doubt was minuscule (*J.H.S.* xv. 181); *Aphr.* 174 ἤυρε is proof of itself.

The impossible forms (*Apoll.* 28, 75, 162, 215, 351, 356, 366, *Herm.* 45, 342, 478, 484, 560) and omissions (*Apoll.* 11, 189, 211, 344, 416, *Herm.* 10, 193, 532–34, *Aphr.* 194) no doubt are against the credit of the archetype; but the inferiority is only comparative, and there is no reason to deny the quality of the family where it appears, or to call its good readings conjectures (a vindication of *p* against earlier disparagement was attempted, *J.H.S.* xv. 261–9; its good readings are twenty-three—*Apoll.* 32, 65, 71, 129, 227, 233, 272, 306, 403, *Herm.* 67, 209, 214, 292, 313, 412, 446, *Aphr.* 245, *Dion.* vii. 8, *Mat. de.* xiv. 3, *Pan* xix. 26, *Ath.* xxviii. 10, *Hest.* xxix. 3, *Selene* xxxii. 6).

[1] More are collected by Breuning pp. 26–8.

For clearness' sake the affinities of these MSS. are indicated by a tree :

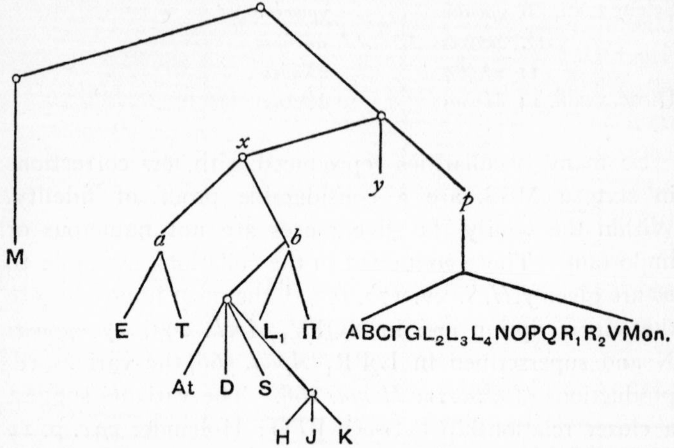

Too little has survived of R_3 to assign it to any particular family.

III. RELATION OF FAMILIES TO EACH OTHER

The merits of the three families M, *x*, and *p* may be expressed by the following table (*J.H.S.* xv. 304) :

	M	*x*	*p*
Conscious conjectures	6	2	11
Semi-conscious conjectures	34	9	17
Independent readings	35	0	1
Exclusively right readings	45	4	21
Clerical errors (about)	90	20	50

M is in all respects the most strongly characterized member ; its peculiarities are far more numerous than those of the other branches put together, while the quantity of uncorrected and half-corrected blunders are, as remarked above, a guarantee for the genuineness of the good readings. The other members offer a comparatively uniform vulgate, principally valuable as preserving the alternatives to M's independent lections and the originals of its blunders; among them *x* is remarkably faithful to its archetype; *p* has passed through the hands of peculiarly ignorant scribes, but a large proportion of genuine survivals remain in it. *y* being known only on the margin of *x* can hardly come under a numerical test; the characteristic of its variants is that they largely consist of whole lines.[1]

Whether further conclusions can be drawn as to the relationship between the families is doubtful. That *x* and *p* (and presumably *y*) hold together is obvious from their having lost the hymns to Dionysus and Demeter which were in the archetype of M and doubtless began the original collection: and this divergence is confirmed by the analysis of the agreements and differences between the families (*J.H.S.* xv. 261: *x* and *p* agree against M in eighty-five cases, M and *x* against *p* in forty-one, M and *p* against *x* in seven. *x* and *p* therefore seem about twice as near each other as M is to the nearest of them).

We have seen that the archetypes of all the families were minuscule, and possibly minuscule for several generations. That the families, at least M on one side and *xpy* on the other were apart for a long time would seem to result from the dissimilarity of their text; at one time however they were doubtless united in a single ancestor, of what period cannot be guessed. This assertion, in any

[1] e.g. *Apoll.* 136–8, *Herm.* 288, 366, 563, and phrases *Herm.* 241, 326. *y*'s readings at *Herm.* 45, 241, 288, 563 show it to be as severely corrupted as the other families. This is possibly due to long marginal transmission.

case natural, seems fortified by certain errors, which are held by all copies in common. They are the following:

Apoll. 59 δηρὸν ἄναξ εἰ βόσκοις κτλ. (M is wanting).
152 οἱ τότ' ἐπαντία σεῖο κτλ. (without construction).
165 ἀλλά γε λητὼ (without construction; Thucydides quotes ἀλλ' ἄγεθ' ἱλήκοι).
171 ἀφ' ἡμέων and sim. (meaningless).
209 ὅπποσ' ἀνωόμενος (vox nihili).
217 ἁγνιήνας, μαγνιήνας (voces nihili).
243 ἅμαρτον (id.)
255 ἡ δ' ἐσιδοῦσα (but ἡ δὲ ἰδοῦσα M v. 341).
297 υἱέε σεργίνου (vox nihili).
339 ἐστιν. ὅσον, ἢ πόσσον, ἢ παρόσον (senseless).
371 ἵμερον μένος (vox nihili).
392 ἠμαθόην (vox nihili: νῆα θοὴν M m. 2).
446 κρισσαγῶν (id.: κρισσαίων V_2, Casaubon).

Herm. 94 φασὶν ἔσευε (senseless).
242 ἄγρης· εἰνέτεόν τε (senseless).
431 πρέσβην (vox nihili).
457 ἐπαίνει (senseless).
473 παῖδ' ἀφνειὸν (unmetrical).

Aphr. 13 σάτινα (unmetrical).
252 στοναχήσεται (vox nihili).
254 ὀνότατον (clerical).

Dion. vii. 13 λυδοὶ (vox nihili).
43 μὴ δ' ἤδη or ἤδειν (voces nihili).

No other readings common to all the MSS. can be objectively proved corrupt. The corruptions are not of such a nature as to suggest any particular time or circumstances of origin (κρισσαγῶν *Apoll.* 446 is a common case of Romaic influence,[1] frequent in theological texts);

[1] e.g. Herod. vi. 126 ἐξήειρε -ήγειρε, 127 Παίου Πάγου, Athen. 508 F εὐάγων εὐαίων, Strabo 452 δηγονέως (= Δηιονέως), 469 αἰέστιν ἄγεστιν (= Vestam).

on the other hand, the most striking of them are simple disintegrations of letters natural to the transcription of a neglected author, and the original in most cases is not in doubt. It may be questioned whether the judgement usually passed on the tradition of these documents is not over severe.

The evidence of the MSS. ceases here. They carry us back to an undefined date, and perhaps, though certainty is impossible, not very far beyond the period of the introduction of the minuscule book-hand. It may be supposed that the archetype contained marginal variants, representing the abundant alternative readings of the classical period; and that the loss of the Dionysus and Demeter hymns in *xpy*, and of xviii. 5 to the end in M, was due to mechanical causes.[1]

We see further that the *Hymns* have come down to us in two connexions, either among the Homeric poems or in a selection of poets such as Callimachus, Orpheus, Proclus, portions of Hesiod, Pindar, Theocritus, and the poem ascribed to Musaeus. Of the twenty-eight MSS. of the *Hymns*, four (M, L_3, G, V) present them as part of the Homeric corpus; the remainder, except those in which the *Hymns* are quite alone, contain the selection more or less complete.

Between the *Homeric Hymns* and those of Callimachus, Orpheus, and Proclus there is a similarity of form, but they have not much in common with the other poems, and it is not easy to understand the reason for the collection. About its date and place there is no direct evidence, but the inclusion of Proclus (d. A.D. 485) brings it well down to the Byzantine period; with this the excerpting of

[1] Obvious parallels are Theognis book II, Theocritus *Idylls* 25 and 27, Lysias' 25th oration, and Juvenal *Sat.* xvi.

Pindar and Theocritus, a natural sign of decadence, agrees.[1] Signs of this association may be discerned here and there in the text of the *Hymns*: *Apoll.* 55 οἰσεῖς is due to the neighbourhood of Theocritus, and the lacuna in the line *Apoll.* 59 (in the family *p*) suggests similar omissions in Callimachus *Dem.* 15, 18.

The time at which the *Homeric Hymns* themselves were collected admits even less of being definitely fixed. The Orphic character of *h.* viii (denied by several critics, see the introduction to the hymn), should afford a *terminus a quo*, but the date of a given Orphic hymn cannot be fixed within several centuries.[2]

This account is unfortunately for the most part inferential; between the time of the Mosquensis (fourteenth century) and the last classical quotation we have no overt evidence to assist us. One testimony, however, of the fifteenth century there is, adduced first by O. Schneider *Callimachus*, i. p. vii. Giovanni Aurispa, in the celebrated letter to Ambrogio Traversari in which he enumerates his shipload of Greek MSS. conveyed to Italy from the Orient, specifies (*Ambrosii Traversarii Epistolae*, ed. Mehus, 1759, ii. col. 1027) 'Laudes Deorum Homeri, haud parvum opus.' It is hardly to be doubted that a copy of the *Hymns* is intended by this entry; what the nature and age

[1] Such a collection, made at the same period, seems to be described by Iulianus Aegyptius (s. vi. A.D.) in *Anth. Pal.* vii. 594 Μνῆμά τοι ὦ Θεόδωρε παναρτρεκὲς οὐκ ἐπὶ τύμβῳ | ἀλλ' ἐνὶ βιβλιακῶν μυριάσιν σελίδων, | αἷσιν ἐπεζώγρησας ἀπολλυμένων ἀπὸ λήθης | ἁρπάξας νοερῶν μόχθον ἀοιδοπόλων.

[2] Dieterich *de hymnis Orphicis*, 1891, p. 24 finds a *terminus ad quem* for the extant Orphica in the magical papyri which quote them, and which date from A.D. 100–150; the collection contains elements which may go back to 200 B.C., but cannot be earlier than Stoic allegorizing doctrine. There is no reason therefore on this account to bring down the date of the *Homeric Hymns* as a collection to the Christian era.

of the copy was, and whether it is one of those that survive, cannot be concluded.[1]

If we examine the nature of the variants which are given by the various families we find, graphical and phonetic corruptions and obvious blunders and glosses put aside, a considerable number of alternatives. Their number is increased by the quotations in ancient authors, the variants in which appear essentially of the same nature as the MS. divergences. We give here a list of these variants:

Dem.	476	καλὰ M	πᾶσιν Pausanias
Apoll.	136–38	βεβρίθει καθορῶσα διὸς λητοῦς τε γενέθλην γηθοσύνῃ ὅτι μιν θεὸς εἵλετο οἰκία θέσθαι νήσων ἠπείρου τε, φίλησε δὲ κηρόθι μᾶλλον *y*	
	139	ἤνθησ᾽ ὡς ὅτε τε ῥίον οὔρεος ἄνθεσιν ὕλης M*xp*	
	146	ἀλλά συ MSS.	ἀλλ᾽ ὅτε Thucydides
	149	οἱ δέ σε MSS.	ἔνθα σε Thuc.
	ib.	ὀρχηθμῷ MSS.	ὀρχηστυῖ Thuc.
	150	στήσωνται MSS.	καθέσωσι Thuc.
	162	κρεμβαλιαστὺν M*xp*	βαμβαλιαστὺν *y*
	168	ξεῖνος ταλαπείριος ἐλθών MSS. ταλαπείριος ἄλλος ἐπελθών Thuc.	
	249	πολλοὶ M	ἐνθάδ᾽ *xp*
	308	ἡνίκ᾽ ἄρα M	εὖτ᾽ ἄρα δὴ *xp*
	515	ἐρατὸν M*x*	χρυσῆν *p*, χαρίεν Athenaeus
	523	αὐτοῦ δάπεδον M*xp*	ἄδυτον ζάθεον *y*
Herm.	51	συμφώνους MSS.	θηλυτέρων Antig. Caryst.
	65	ἆλτο M	ὦρτο *xp*

[1] The idea started by Schneider *l.c.* and repeated by Wilamowitz-Möllendorf (*Callimachus* p. 6), Hollander *op.c.* p. 9, and Maas *op.c.* pp. 206, 207, that this MS. was the parent of the MSS. now existing, with the exception of M, may be dismissed. It is plain that the developed divergences between *x* and *p* and their various members could not be the fruit of a period beginning with the year 1423.

Herm.	82	νεοθηλέαν [ἀγκάλῳ ὤρην] M	νεοθηλέος ἄγκαλον ὕλης cet.
	90	ἐπικαμπύλα ξύλα M	ἐπικαμπύλος ὤμους *xp*
	159	φέροντα M	λαβόντα *xp*
	212	μῦθον ἀκούσας M*y*	φοῖβος ἀπόλλων *xp*
	224	ἔλπομαι εἶναι M*y*	ἔστιν ὁμοῖα *xp*
	288	ἀντήσεις ἀγέλῃσι βοῶν καὶ πώεσι μήλων M*xp*	ἄντην βουκολίοισι καὶ εἰροπόκοις ὀίεσσι *y*
	322	τέρθρον ἵκοντο M*x*	ἵκοντο κάρηνα *py*
	326	ποτὶ πτύχας οὐλύμποιο M*xp*	μετὰ χρυσόθρονον ἠῶ *y*
	352	πολὺν M	μέγαν *xp*
	366	δ' αὖθ' ἑτέρωθεν ἀμειβόμενος ἔπος ηὔδα M*xp*	δ' ἄλλον μῦθον ἐν ἀθανάτοισι ἔειπεν *y*
	368	ἀγορεύσω M	καταλέξω *xp*
	403	ἀπάνευθεν M	ἀπάτερθεν *xp*
	431	ἅπαντες M	ἕκαστος *xp*
	473	καὶ M*xp*	τῶν *y*
	502	σμερδαλέον M	ἱμερόεν *xp*
	503	καί ῥα M	ἔνθα *xp*
	518	κατὰ *m*	μέγαν M*xp*
	544	τ' ἠδὲ πότησι M	καὶ πτερύγεσσι *xp*
	552	σεμναὶ M	μοῖραι *xp*
	563	πειρῶνται δ' ἤπειτα παρὲξ ὁδὸν ἡγεμονεύειν M*xp*	ψεύδονται δ' ἤπειτα δι' ἀλλήλων δενέουσαι *y*
Aphr.	67	ῥίμφα M	θοῶς *xp*
	175	ἰοστεφάνου M	ἐυστεφάνου *xp*
	204–6	ἐπιοινοχοεύειν—τετιμένον—ἀφύσσειν M	ἐπιοινοχοεύοι—τετιμένος—ἀφύσσων *xp*
	214	ἶσα θεοῖσι M*y*	ἤματα πάντα *xp*
Aphr. vi.	18	ἰοστεφάνου M*x*	ἐυστεφάνου *p*
Ares viii.	9	εὐθαρσέος M	εὐθαλέος *xp*
Aphr. x	3	θέει M	φέρει *xp*
	4	μακαίρα κυθήρης M	θεὰ σαλαμῖνος *xp*
Heracl. xv.	5	πημαίνετ' ἀεθλεύων κραταιῶς M	πομπῇσιν ὑπ' εὐρυσθῆος ἄνακτος *xp*

	6 ἔξοχα ἔργα M	πολλὰ δ' ἀνέτλη *xp*
Pan. xix.	7 κάρηνα *x*	κέλευθα *py*
	48 λισομαι *xp*	ἵλαμαι *y*

Among these readings some may be preferable to others on different grounds, but none of them exhibit a definitely late origin, and none can certainly be explained as arising from its contrary by means of graphical corruption or interpretation. The members of each pair seem independent, and the age of the MS. variants seems guaranteed by the variants in the quotations, which are of the same nature, and go back to the fifth century B.C. They bear the same character as the variants in the Homeric text, which are abundantly testified to belong to the pre-Alexandrian age; and as the Homeric variants are usually supposed to have arisen in connexion with rhapsodizing or semi-oral transmission (and consist, therefore, mostly of epic reminiscences or equivalents), the same explanation may be offered of these. If this is the case, it is an additional argument for eclecticism in the constitution of the text; since, if the tradition of as early a period as the age of Thucydides exhibited alternatives, it is plainly a matter of chance which are found in what copy of the fifteenth century A.D.

There are a few passages in the *Hymns* where it has been thought that a pair of alternative lines or sequences of lines have found their way into the same text. There is no difficulty in believing such a process to have taken place, for contamination or conflation is a well-attested phenomenon; but where the guarantee of the overt difference between MSS. is wanting, the detection of such passages must rest upon considerations of grammar and sense; and the certainty of such a criterion in any particular case is materially diminished.[1] Lines which have been thought mutually incompatible, and, therefore, to be the result of two recensions fused together, are *Dion.* i. 13–15 and 16, *Apoll.* 136–8 and 139, *Aphr.* 97 and 98, 136 and 136ᵃ, 274–5 and 276–7, *Artemis* ix. 8 and 9, but no case except *Apoll.* 136–9 and *Aphr.* 136, 136ᵃ can be called certain. Cf. Nicander *Alex.* 556, 557.

IV. PROSODY

These MSS. were not collated by us with a view to recording their prosody and accentuation, though a certain number of these phenomena were noted by us and by our predecessors. These cases are not so numerous that any universal conclusion can be drawn, or in particular any argument *ex silentio*. Such phenomena, moreover, are incidental to Byzantine MSS. in general, and are found on a larger scale in the MSS. of the Iliad. A certain number have been collected by Reil, *Byzantinische Zeitschrift*, 1910, xix. 479 sq. Here, therefore, they have been withdrawn from the apparatus criticus except in a few special cases, and the more frequent instances are tabulated here.

I. ἂρ and ἄρ before a vowel. This, universal in MSS., arose from the example of ἄρ or ἂρ before a consonant. There was no doctrine of ἄρ an independent word, as there was of τάρ (La Roche, *H. T.* 359). The case of γάρ also assisted an unapocopated ἀρ.

(*a*) ἂρ. ii 20 M 181 M 208 M 228 M 432 M

[1] Hermann in his ed. p. xx f. is the principal exponent of this view. It is preferable to the other so-called critical method of excising and bracketing, and has a certain basis in fact; but its application is arbitrary and admits of very little check—as may be seen even from Hermann's remarks.

III 83 E 100 D E L_1 Π T 110 D E L_1 Π J 123 D E L_1 Π J 207 D 240 D L_1 243 D L_1 Π 292 codd. 307 D L_1 Π 379 D L_1 444 D L_1 Π 497 D L_1 Π 521 L_1 Π IV 39 D E L_1 47 M D L_1 Π 86 D E L_1 Π 154 D L_1 Π 278 D L_1 293 D L_1 Π 335 D L_1 Π 365 L_1 ib. D Π 409 D L_1 Π V 10 ἆρ vulg. 170 M D L_1 Π VII 37 D L_1 Π 51 D E Π XXXI 15 ἆρ codd.

(*b*) ἄρ. III 100 O 375 M D L_1 Π IV 278 M 293 M 409 E V 30 E 170 E VII 33 M E

(*c*) ἀρ'. III 83 L_1

II. δε quasi-enclitic. The influence of ὅδε ἥδε τόδε is manifest. Δε is included among enclitics by schol. Dion. Thrac. 466. 18 (an. Bekk. III. 1156). Cf. Vendryes p. 107, Chandler § 962.

(*a*) Demonstrative pronoun.

ὅδ' or ὅδε. II 80 M 300 M III 75 QT 362 M D L_1 Π IV 64 D E L_1 Π A B L_2 O 304 M D E Π 328 M D E L_1 496 M D L_1 510 D E L_1 V 166 M D L_1 Π 180 M D L_1 VII 44 D E Π 50 D E XXV 4 E XXVI 5 D E J 10 D E XXX 7 ET

ἥδ'. II 118 M 181 M 188 M 207 M 287 bis M 354 M 377 M III 190 L_1 Π 255 M (ἥδε O) 309 D L_1 O 341 D L_1 O Π 351 D O Π 354 M D L_1 Π 358 M IV 53 D L_1 O Π 419 D L_1 501 D L_1 E M V 72 D L_1 Q XXVII 9 D T (ἦδ' E) XXVIII 7 E XXXII 15 D E J

ἥδε. V 14 codd. (ἡδέ M)

τήνδ'. II 30 M 59 M 74 M 90 M 145 M 190 M 224 M 405 M 459 M IV 162 M D L_1 VI 5 D XXXIII 11 D

αἵδ'. III 102 D E L_1 Π 134 M D E L_1 J 445 L_1 O Π IV 560 M D E J L_1 XXVI 9 *x* D XXVII 18 E

τοίδ'. II 88 M

τώδ'. II 379 M τῶδε. V 283 codd. praeter M

τάδ'. II 456 M III 536 Π IV 123 M D L_1 342 L_1 Π 376 D E L_1 Π

τόδ'. IV 272 D L_1 Π 357 M D L_1 Π 459 codd. 577 L_1

τόνδ'. III 9 Π H IV 201 D L_1 Π 235 D L_1 260 M D L_1

281 D L_1 Π 333 D L_1 Π 354 M D L_1 434 D 463 M D L_1 V 76 O L_1 107 D 191 M 209 M D L_1 Π VII 13 D

οἶδ'. III 176 M D L_1 O Π 204 M D L_1 Π 404 O (*οἰδ'* Π) 502 Γ (*οἶδ'* M D C) V 73 *x* D Q 78 D L_1 Q 161 M D L_1 Π VI 15 M D L_1 Π VII 48 M D XXXIII 8 D E T 12 D E

τούς δ'. III 474 M D VII 8 DL_1

τάσ δ'. V 268 M D

ταί δ'. IV 197 M L_1 Π

ὅς δ'. II 481 M

(*b*) Other words:

τρισσάς δ'. V 7 L_1

ἁπαλοί δε. IV 273 L_1 Π

κρατί δ'. VI 7 L_1

ἐμήν δ'. VI 20 L_1

Ζεύς δε. IV 389 L_1 V 43 M L_1

ἐρατή δε. IV 421 L_1

βάν δε. II 185 M III 114 M L_1 Π 514 L_1 L_2

δηρόν δε. II 198 M

δός δ'. X 5 M XXVI 12 Π

εἰμί δ'. VII 56 M

τιμή δ'. II 263 M

ἱστόν δε. VII 40 M E Π

ἀμφί δε. IV 172 L_1

καλαί δε. VII 4 M L_1 Π

καλόν δε. IV 141 L_1 Π XXXI 13 B Π T

πολλός δε. IV 249 L_1

πολλαί δε. V 119 L_1

πολλά δε. IV 250 L_1 360 L_1 Π V 122 L_1

πολλήν δ'. V 123 L_1

αὐτός δ'. III 140 M IV 511 M

σύδ'. III 261 M IV 181 M 303 L_2 386 L_1 564 M_1 V 102 L_1 186 ML_1

σύδε. III 267 L_1 IV 181 E_1 467 M 477 D Π V 140 L_1 289 M L_1 Π

σοί δ'. V 127 L_1 M 196 L_1 Π

σοίδ'. v 276 M L_1

(*c*) δε of motion enclitic. This is universal in the Hymn-MSS. On the contrary doctrine which accented this δε see Apollonius *de adv.* 177. 21, Herodian ap. Ioann. Alex. 34. 4, Lehrs *qu. ep.* 40 sq. A few Iliad MS, and those mostly s. ix–x, have δέ.

Cf. e.g. II 126 Θορικόνδε M 253 πέδονδε M 484 οὔλυμπόνδε M III 23, 145 ἄλαδε codd. 28 χέρσονδε codd. 119 φόωσδε codd. 506 ἤπειρόνδε codd. IV 68 ὠκεανόνδε codd. 88 πεδίονδε codd. 186 ὀγχηστόνδ' codd. praeter D E (but ὀγχηστός is naturally oxytone) XXXI 16 ὠκεανόνδε codd.

3. Proclisis:

ταπρῶτα. II 86 M IV 428 MD V 185 M

διατριχὰ. II 86 M

καδ. II 285 M

τοπρὶν. II 451 M III 476 M D L_1 Π

τοπρῶτον. III 71 D 116 P S 493 M D IV 487 M V 179 M D Π τοπάρος XX 3 D E T

διαπροθύροιο. IV 271 D L_1 Π

κατακρατὸς. III 74 vulg. (κατὰ M L_1 Π)

προφόωσδε. III 119 E T J O

ἐπιδὴ. III 176 L_1 Π

παρδὲ. III 410 L_1 T συνδέ. XIX 19 T

ἀπεκ. III 110 L_1 Π ἀπἕκ O

παρεκ. III 419 codd. 547 M E L_1 V 36 (παρὲκ M)

ὑπεκ. III 428 vulg. (ὑπ' ἐκ Π T Γ)

διεκ. III 432 M D E L_1 Π T IV 158 M *x* B D Γ δι'ἐκ II 281 M 379 M

διαπρὸ. V 114 (exc. M D) ἐπειδὴ V 128 T 215 T VI 14 codd. XXVI 7 T III 355 κατακλυτὰ M (ὀνομακλυτὸς V 146 M)

ἀπογῆρας. V 224 E Π XIX 19 συνδέ E T IV 54 ὑποκαλὸν L_1

4. The contrary (i.e. separation):

πέρι τιμήεσσα. III 65 S περὶ *p*

κατὰ θνητοί (κτλ.). III 464 M D N 541 codd. praeter B V 3 M D N Q 39 E L_1 V_1 50 E T 52 E T 122 E L_1 T 192 codd. 200 M D E T N P 250 codd praeter Π 281 M D E N P T: *passim* in Homer.

κατὰ στυφέλω. IV 124 D ed. pr. M E T

κατ' οὐδαίῳ. IV 112 codd.

ὑπὸ βρύχιας. IV 116 E P T

διὰ πῦρ. IV 357 vulg. διαπῦρ M D L_1

αὖτ' ἄγρετον. IV 489 codd.

ἀμφὶ φαείνει. III 202 Π T

ἀπὸ ἐργμένη. V 47 T E

V 204 ἐπὶ οἰνοχοεύει T ἐπι L_1

κατ' ὄπισθε. IV 321 M

(*d*) Article unaccentuated:

II 153 ἥ μὲν . . . ἥ δὲ M 154 ἥ δὲ M

VII 19 ὅ δε D L_1

Article accentuated:

III 201 ὃ D O 397 οἳ L_1 495 ὃ L_1 Π T

5. Accentuation of words now usually unaccented:

(*a*) ῥα: ῥὰ II 145 M V 10 ῥά M 50 ῥὰ Q

This accentuation is universal in MSS.

(*b*) τις: III 226 πω τὶς Γ O

This usage also is universal. On the other hand τις with other enclitics is frequently not accented:

τι σε IV 407 D E L_1 ερ τι V 34 codd. praeter D L_1

(*c*) ἦδ': ἦδ' III 251 L_1 502 L_1 Π IV 246 L_1 Π 527 L_1 XXVII 9 E XXX 6 Π. This is the logical result of ἠδέ apocopated.

(*d*) εἰμί *sum.* I 18 ἐστὶ (for ἔστιν) M

II 148 φέρτεροι εἰσίν M 159 θεοείκελος ἐστί M 478 πως ἐστὶ (for ἔστι) M

III 64 ἐτήτυμον εἰμὶ *x* 176 ἐτήτυμον ἐστίν E L_1 S T, -ον ἔστιν P 82 πολυώνυμος ἐστὶν vulg. (-ός ἐστιν L_1)

IV 311 αἵτινες εἰσὶ M 339 λησίμβροτοι εἴσ' M, εἶσ' cet. 381 αἵτινες εἰσὶ M

V 31 τιμάοχος ἐστὶν codd.

VII 58 ἐστὶν M *x* D (for ἔστιν)

XIX 29 ἄγγελος ἐστὶν D E Π

(*e*) φημί:

IV 444 πώποτε φημὶ M 471 γε φασὶ M D E L_1 549 φῆμ' M E φημ' L_1

In these two cases ancient usage differed from ancient doctrine, and the enclitic rule is very seldom observed in MSS. Chandler § 937.

(*f*) μηδ':

μὴδ' II 323 M 362 M 467 M III 276 M D L_1 Π V 47 codd. 193 M D 290 μήδ' E μὴδ' M

This accentuation, contrary to modern usage, may be right.

(*g*) αἶ. III 56 OQ

(*h*) οὖ. IV 263 D M Π

(*i*) τοὶ γὰρ. II 406 M

6. Accent shifted:

(*a*) ἐνθάδε:

ἔνθαδ' III 58 Π 168 M IV 191 L_1

ἔνθαδε III 381 L_1 ἔνθαδέ (δὴ) III 381 Π

ἐνθάδ' III 385 D ἐνθάδε V 61 E

ἐνθὰδ' III 385 E Π

ἐνθαδ' III 58 L_1

(*b*) ὁπόταν. III 71 codd.

(*c*) ἤτοι. IV 365 D L_1 Π 368 D L_1 Π V 128 codd. praeter E 225 M Π N (δήτοι cet.) 230 codd. 237 δήτοι vulg. (δ' οὔτοι etc. cet.).

(*d*) ἐπειή. III 72 ἐπειή vulg. ἐπείη OPQ ἐπεὶ S 82 ἐπείη *p* ἐπειὴ J ἐπίη M L_1 Π ἐπιὴ T V 195 ἐπειὴ codd.

To these the Iliad MSS. add ἐπειῆ. Cf. La Roche *H.T.* 267

(*e*) μητιετα: μητιετά I 16 M V 202 M μητιέτα III 205 M IV 469 M Γ XXVIII 4 Π νεφεληγερετά II 78 M

The paroxytone is frequent, *H.T.* 309, 310.

(*f*) Aorist participle perispomenon:
θορῶν. III 233 Π
This curious usage is frequent in the Iliad MSS.

7. Retraction:
Omitted: III 52 ἐνὶ codd. 172 ἐνὶ D E L_1 Π T J 390 ἐνὶ D E L_1 Π VI 5 ἐνὶ E L_1 Π XV 2 ἐνὶ codd. V 77 ἀπὸ or ἀπο codd. 224 ἀπὸ ET 271 ἀπ' ὄζος codd. (ἄποζοι M) III 396 ὑπὸ M XV 5 ὑπ' codd. XIX 15 ὑπὸ and ὑπό codd. XXXII 4 ὑπο V_1 XXI 2 παρὰ codd. V 78 κατὰ T XXX 11 κατὰ codd.

Wrongly applied: III 329 ἄπο M D L_1 Π III 506 ἄνα M 491 ἔπι τ' Π III 336 ἔξ L_1

Accent on elided syllable retained: V 44 κεδὺ' L_1 III 234 κεῖνον M (= κεῖν') V 104 ἐμ' αὐτον L_1

With apocope: III 234 κεῖν' vulg. κείν' S IV 549 φήμ', φῆμ' M E, φημ' L_1

On anastrophe see Chandler §§ 908, 909, K.-R. I. 332. The rules, very artificial, were unknown to, or mistaken by, scribes.

8. Imperfect of αὐδᾶν:
V 91 ηὖδα L_1.
This usage occurs *passim* in Iliad MSS.

V. THE HOMERIC HYMNS IN ANTIQUITY

The history of these documents during the classical period may be recovered by two methods, the linguistic and the historical. The former is treated on pp. xcvi ff., the latter consists almost entirely in such evidence as is afforded by quotations.

The quotations of the *Homeric Hymns* are not abundant in antiquity.[1] We leave out allusions, clear or possible,

[1] A. Guttmann, *De Hymnorum Homericorum historia critica particulae quattuor*, 1869, p. 14 f.

and enumerate the actual citations, and first those of whose age there is no doubt.

FIFTH CENTURY B.C.

1. Thuc. iii. 104 δηλοῖ δὲ μάλιστα Ὅμηρος ὅτι τοιαῦτα ἦν [a festival at Delos] ἐν τοῖς ἔπεσι τοῖσδε, ἅ ἐστιν ἐκ προοιμίου Ἀπόλλωνος·

ἀλλ' ὅτε Δήλῳ Φοῖβε μάλιστά γε θυμὸν ἐτέρφθης,
ἔνθα τοι ἑλκεχίτωνες Ἰάονες ἠγερέθονται
σὺν σφοῖσιν τεκέεσσι γυναιξί τε σὴν ἐς ἀγυιάν·
ἔνθα σε πυγμαχίῃ τε καὶ ὀρχηστυῖ καὶ ἀοιδῇ
μνησάμενοι τέρπουσιν ὅταν καθέσωσιν ἀγῶνα.

ὅτι δὲ καὶ μουσικῆς ἀγὼν ἦν καὶ ἀγωνιούμενοι ἐφοίτων, ἐν τοῖσδε αὖ δηλοῖ, ἅ ἐστιν ἐκ τοῦ αὐτοῦ προοιμίου. τὸν γὰρ Δηλιακὸν χορὸν τῶν γυναικῶν ὑμνήσας ἐτελεύτα τοῦ ἐπαίνου ἐς τάδε τὰ ἔπη, ἐν οἷς καὶ ἑαυτοῦ ἐπεμνήσθη·

ἀλλ' ἄγεθ' ἱλήκοι μὲν Ἀπόλλων Ἀρτέμιδι ξύν,
χαίρετε δ' ὑμεῖς πᾶσαι· ἐμεῖο δὲ καὶ μετόπισθε
μνήσασθ' ὁππότε κέν τις ἐπιχθονίων ἀνθρώπων
ἐνθάδ' ἀνείρηται ταλαπείριος ἄλλος ἐπελθών·
ὦ κοῦραι τίς δ' ὔμμιν ἀνὴρ ἥδιστος ἀοιδῶν
ἐνθάδε πωλεῖται καὶ τέῳ τέρπεσθε μάλιστα ;
ὑμεῖς δ' εὖ μάλα πᾶσαι ὑποκρίνασθαι ἀφήμως,
τυφλὸς ἀνήρ, οἰκεῖ δὲ Χίῳ ἔνι παιπαλοέσσῃ.

= *Apoll.* 146–150, 165–172 with variants.

This citation, which was possibly intended as a reply to Herodotus' appeal to Olen's hymn (also with regard to Delos) iv. 35 (see further pp. lxxxiii ff.), evidently recognizes the *Hymn to Apollo* as Homeric. Thucydides calls it προοίμιον, the designation used by Pindar, who (*Nem.* ii. 1) alludes to a hymn to Zeus as *Διὸς* ἐκ προοιμίου.[1] Thucydides'

[1] Plutarch (*de mus.* 1133 c) uses the word of Terpander, Suidas of Arion (προοίμια εἰς ἔπη β'). Empedocles (Diog. Laert. viii. 2. 3) wrote a προοίμιον to Apollo. There seems no reason, however, with Welcker *Ep. Cycl.* i.

words have been used[1] to support the view that the document as we have it contains two hymns, one of which ended at this point; but the interpretation of the passage is that the words ἐτελεύτα τοῦ ἐπαίνου only mean 'he ended his compliment to the Delian women', after which he returned to his account of the God. (Cf. the introduction to the Hymn.) The variants (*J.H.S.* xv. 309, Gemoll *ad loc.*) seem independent, and not necessarily preferable one to the other. In a text which depends throughout on the MSS. we have not departed from them here. In one place the Thucydidean version seems to have preserved a reading which was common to the MSS. also, but has been corrupted in them; 165 ἀλλ' ἄγεθ' ἱλήκοι μὲν where the MSS. ἀλλ' ἄγε δὴ λητὼ μὲν gives no construction, and may easily be accounted for on graphical grounds (through λητοῖ); but in 171 Thucydides is farther from the truth (with ἀφήμως, εὐφήμως) than the MSS. (with ἀφ' ἡμέων, ἀφ' ὑμέων κ.τ.λ.).

328, to limit the word to the worship of Apollo. Cf. Plato's expressions *Laws* 722 D καὶ δή που κιθαρῳδικῆς ᾠδῆς λεγομένων νόμων καὶ πάσης μούσης προοίμια θαυμαστῶς ἐσπουδασμένα πρόκειται, Stesichorus fr. 46 μέτειμι δ' ἐφ' ἕτερον προοίμιον. From the account in Aristotle *Rhet.* iii. 14 (where the word is defined ἀρχὴ λόγου, ὅπερ ἐν ποιήσει πρόλογος καὶ ἐν αὐλήσει προαύλιον and applies to rhetoric, epos, tragedy, and comedy) it results that a prooemium has nothing to do with subject. See further p. xci. Analogous words are προαύλιον (above and Plato *Cratylus* 417 fin. ὥσπερ τοῦ τῆς Ἀθηναίας νόμου προαύλιον στομαυλῆσαι, Hesych. προαύλια· τὰ προαυλήματα· ὥσπερ προάμβουλα τὰ προκιθαρίσματα), and προνόμιον Steph. Byz. in Μίλητος (προνόμια αὐλῶν χίλια).

As a metaphor the word is common in literature from Pindar and Aeschylus onwards, especially in Plato (*Rep.* 531 D, 532 D, *Timaeus* 29 D, and often in the *Laws*), in the sense of 'introduction' to something. It is used of laws by Charondas in Stobaeus *Ecl.* iv. 2. 24, p. 154 Hense προστάσσει δὲ ὁ νόμος ἐπίστασθαι τὰ προοίμια τοὺς πολίτας ἅπαντας, καὶ ἐν ταῖς ἑορταῖς μετὰ τοὺς παιᾶνας λέγειν ᾧ ἂν προστάσσῃ ὁ ἑστιάτωρ ἵν' ἐμφυσιῶται ἑκάστῳ τὰ παραγγέλματα.

[1] First by Ruhnken *Ep. crit.* i. 7, 8; cf. Guttmann *op.c.* p. 16.

THIRD CENTURY B.C.

2. Antigonus of Carystus (born 295–290 B.C., Susemihl, *Geschichte d. gr. Lit. in der Alexandrinerzeit* i. p. 468) Ἱστοριῶν παραδόξων συναγωγή, c. vii (ed. Keller, 1877) ἴδιον δὲ καὶ τὸ περὶ τὰ ἔντερα τῶν προβάτων· τὰ μὲν γὰρ τῶν κριῶν ἐστιν ἄφωνα, τὰ δὲ τῶν θηλειῶν εὔφωνα, ὅθεν καὶ τὸν ποιητὴν ὑπολάβοι τις εἰρηκέναι, πολυπράγμονα πανταχοῦ καὶ περιττὸν ὄντα,

ἑπτὰ δὲ θηλυτέρων οἴων ἐτανύσσατο χορδάς.

= *Herm.* 51, with the variant θηλυτέρων for συμφώνους.

Antigonus, like every other scientist and antiquarian, seeks a support for his opinion in Homer. He quoted this verse because it contained the word θηλυτέρων, and the view[1] that he *conjectured* it is evidently preposterous. The translation of the phrase ὅθεν κ.τ.λ. will be 'and one may suppose this was the reason why Homer said'. Similar expressions in Antigonus are c. xxv ὅθεν δὴ καὶ ὁ ποιητὴς τὸ θρυλούμενον ἔγραψεν, c. xix ᾧ καὶ φαίνεται Φιλητᾶς προσέχειν, ἱκανῶς ὢν περίεργος. It might rather be questioned if συμφώνους, which is far the earliest instance of the word, were not an interpretation of θηλυτέρων, based upon the same belief which is stated in Antigonus. θηλύτερος in Homer is applied only to women or goddesses, except in the curious reading of the πολιτικαί Φ 454 νήσων θηλυτεράων for τηλεδαπάων.

FIRST CENTURY B.C.[2]

3. Diodorus Siculus i. 15. 7 (ed. Vogel 1888) μεμνῆσθαι δὲ τῆς Νύσης καὶ τὸν ποιητὴν [φασι] ἐν τοῖς ὕμνοις, ὅτι περὶ τὴν Αἴγυπτον γέγονεν, ἐν οἷς λέγει

ἔστι δέ τις Νύση, ὕπατον ὄρος, ἀνθέον ὕλῃ,
τηλοῦ Φοινίκης, σχεδὸν Αἰγύπτοιο ῥοάων.

= *h. Dion.* i. 8, 9.

[1] Held by Franke, Baumeister, Gemoll.

[2] Crates of Mallus, who belongs to the second century, quotes a line under the head of ἀρχαῖοι ὕμνοι, which may have come from the *Hymn to Dionysus*. See the notes to that Hymn.

4. Id. iii. 66. 3 μαρτυρεῖ δὲ τοῖς ὑφ' ἡμῶν λεγομένοις καὶ ὁ ποιητὴς ἐν τοῖς ὕμνοις . . .

οἱ μὲν γὰρ Δρακάνῳ σ' οἱ δ' Ἰκάρῳ ἠνεμοέσσῃ
φάσ', οἱ δ' ἐν Νάξῳ, δῖον γένος, εἰραφιῶτα,
οἱ δέ σ' ἐπ' Ἀλφειῷ ποταμῷ βαθυδινήεντι
κυσαμένην Σεμέλην τεκέειν Διὶ τερπικεραύνῳ,
ἄλλοι δ' ἐν Θήβῃσιν, ἄναξ, σε λέγουσι γενέσθαι,
ψευδόμενοι· σὲ δ' ἔτικτε πατὴρ ἀνδρῶν τε θεῶν τε
πολλὸν ἀπ' ἀνθρώπων, κρύπτων λευκώλενον Ἥρην.
ἔστι δέ τις Νύση, ὕπατον ὄρος, ἀνθέον ὕλῃ,
τηλοῦ Φοινίκης, σχεδὸν Αἰγύπτοιο ῥοάων.

= *h. Dion.* i. 1–9; verses 4 and 8, which are strictly dispensable, are only found in three MSS.

5. Id. iv. 2. 4 καὶ τὸν Ὅμηρον δὲ τούτοις μαρτυρῆσαι ἐν τοῖς ὕμνοις ἐν οἷς λέγει

ἔστι δέ κτλ. = *h. Dion.* i. 8, 9, as above.

The fact that two out of Diodorus' quotations are in the indirect narrative (in long paragraphs introduced by *φασί*), and are of the identical two lines which also are quoted by the scholiast on Apollonius Rhodius (below no. 14) in apparent connexion with the mythographer Herodorus, suggests that in both places Diodorus took the quotation from his sources. Of these he mentions by name only Dionysius (iii. 66 *Διονυσίῳ τῷ συνταξαμένῳ τὰς παλαιὰς μυθοποιίας· οὗτος γὰρ τά τε περὶ τὸν Διόνυσον καὶ τὰς Ἀμαζόνας ἔτι δὲ τοὺς Ἀργοναύτας καὶ τὰ κατὰ τὸν Ἰλιακὸν πόλεμον πραχθέντα καὶ πόλλ' ἕτερα συντέτακται, παρατιθεὶς τὰ ποιήματα τῶν ἀρχαίων, τῶν τε μυθολόγων καὶ τῶν ποιητῶν*), who is apparently the same as the Dionysius of Mitylene, whose *Ἀργόναυται* are as frequently utilized as those of Herodorus in the scholia on Apollonius (cf. Suidas *in v.*, Müller *FHG.* ii. 6 f., Susemihl *op.c.* ii. 45 f.). Without denying Diodorus the credit of possible original quotation, especially at iii. 66, it seems likely that the *Hymns* were excerpted and utilized by both Herodorus and Dionysius, antiquaries.

6. Philodemus περὶ εὐσεβείας (ed. Gomperz *Herkulanische Studien* ii. 1866), p. 42, tab. 91, vv. 12 ff.

κα[ὶ τ]ὴν Ἑ[κάτην]
ὀπαδ[ὸν Ἀρ]τέ[μιδος]
εἶναι Δήμη[τρος]
δὲ λάτριν Εὐρι[πίδης]
Ὅμηρος δ' ἐν [τοῖς]
[ὕμ]νοις πρόπ[ολον]
καὶ [ὀπ]άονα = *h. Dem.* 440.

There is perhaps another reference, p. 29, col. 57*a*

ἐν δὲ τοῖς . . .
. . ὅ]μηρος
]νθαιν (? αθαν[ατοις)
ονεα[ρ καὶ
τσκειν (? = τυκται)
κα]λλιμα[χος
ταραντι

cf. perhaps *Dem.* 269. In other parts of the work references seem made to ii. 2, iii. 305, v. 53, 218. See Philippson *Hermes* 1920. 248 sq.

7. The Berlin papyrus 44 (s. i. B. C.) quotes ii. 8–12, 17, 18, 33–6, 55, 56, 109, 248, 249, 256–62, 418–23. It shows that in this century part of the Homeric corpus was appropriated by the Orphics (see p. 110).

Second Century A.D.

8. Pausanias i. 38. 3 Ὁμήρῳ δὲ ἐς μὲν τὸ γένος ἐστὶν οὐδὲν αὐτοῦ πεποιημένον, ἐπονομάζει δὲ ἀγήνορα ἐν τοῖς ἔπεσι τὸν Εὔμολπον.
= *h. Dem.* 154.

9. Id. i. 38. 3 τὰ δὲ ἱερὰ τοῖν θεοῖν Εὔμολπος καὶ αἱ θυγατέρες δρῶσιν αἱ Κελεοῦ· καλοῦσι δὲ σφᾶς Πάμφως τε κατὰ ταὐτὰ καὶ Ὅμηρος Διογένειαν καὶ Παμμερόπην καὶ τρίτην Σαισάραν (in the MSS. there are variants on the last word, βαισάραν and σαιβάραν).

There is no line in our *Hymn to Demeter* containing the names of the three daughters of Celeus, but on the strength of this precise statement it has been supposed that they were mentioned after 108 or 477. See on v. 108.

10. Id. iv. 30. 3 πρῶτος δὲ ὧν οἶδα ἐποιήσατο ἐν τοῖς ἔπεσιν Ὅμηρος Τύχης μνήμην. ἐποιήσατο δὲ ἐν ὕμνῳ τῷ ἐς τὴν Δήμητρα, ἄλλας τε τῶν Ὠκεανοῦ θυγατέρας καταριθμούμενος, ὡς ὁμοῦ Κόρῃ τῇ Δήμητρος παίζοιεν, καὶ Τύχην ὡς Ὠκεανοῦ καὶ ταύτην παῖδα οὖσαν· καὶ οὕτως ἔχει τὰ ἔπη·

ἡμεῖς μὲν μάλα πᾶσαι ἀν' ἱμερτὸν λειμῶνα
Λευκίππη Φαινώ τε καὶ Ἠλέκτρη καὶ Ἰάνθη
Μηλόβοσίς τε Τύχη τε καὶ Ὠκυρόη καλυκῶπις.

= *h. Dem.* 417, 418, 420 : Paus. omits, intentionally or not, 419.

11. Id. x. 37. 4 Ὅμηρος μέντοι Κρῖσαν ἔν τε Ἰλιάδι ὁμοίως καὶ ὕμνῳ τῷ ἐς Ἀπόλλωνα ὀνόματι τῷ ἐξ ἀρχῆς καλεῖ τὴν πόλιν.

= *h. Apoll.* 269 &c.

Pausanias, who beside citing these lines, passes the judgement on the literary quality of the *Homeric Hymns* quoted in the next section (ix. 30. 12), and is our principal source for hymn-literature generally in antiquity, clearly recognizes these hymns as Homeric; his attitude is in marked contrast to that of his fellow-geographer Strabo. Considering this, it is remarkable that he uses only the *Hymn to Demeter* and *h. to Apollo*, and the latter only in one place; he ignores the *Hymn to Hermes* which he might have quoted (viii. 17 or ix. 26), and in treating *Τύχη* (10 above) neglects *h.* xi. 5. It is impossible to give an even plausible reason for this inconsistency: possibly the humorous character of the Hermes hymn detracted from its antiquarian authority; or Pausanias drew from Apollodorus and the other prose accounts of the story; or the Homeric hymn was overshadowed by Alcaeus (whom he quotes on the theft of Apollo's oxen, vii. 20).

12. Athenaeus 22 B οὕτως δ' ἦν εὔδοξον καὶ σοφὸν ἡ ὄρχησις ὥστε Πίνδαρος τὸν Ἀπόλλωνα ὀρχηστὴν καλεῖ—καὶ Ὅμηρος ἢ τῶν Ὁμηριδῶν τις ἐν τῷ εἰς Ἀπόλλωνα ὕμνῳ φησιν

Ἀπόλλων
φόρμιγγ' ἐν χείρεσσιν ἔχων χαρίεν κιθάριζε
καλὰ καὶ ὕψι βιβάς.

= *h. Apoll.* 514–16, with the variant χαρίεν for ἐρατὸν or χρυσῆν of the MSS.

This is the first quotation in which Homer is not positively given as the author. Athenaeus' quotation is repeated with his name by Eustathius *Od.* θ 383, f. 1602. 24.

13. Aristides *orat.* κατὰ τῶν ἐξορχουμένων 409 = ed. Dindorf ii. p. 559. τίς ἄριστος ἐπῶν ποιητής; Ὅμηρος. τίς δ' ὡς πλείστους ἀνθρώπων ἀρέσκει καὶ τῷ μάλιστα χαίρουσιν; ἢ τοῦτό γε καὶ αὐτὸς ὑπὲρ αὐτοῦ προείδετο· διαλεγόμενος γὰρ ταῖς Δηλιάσι καὶ καταλύων τὸ προοίμιον, εἴ τις ἔροιθ' ὑμᾶς φησὶν

ὦ κοῦραι τίς δ' ὔμμιν ἀνὴρ ἥδιστος ἀοιδῶν
ἐνθάδε πωλεῖται καὶ τέῳ τέρπεσθε μάλιστα;
ὑμεῖς δ' εὖ μάλα πᾶσαι ἀποκρίνασθαι ἀφ' ἡμῶν.
(*Apoll.* 169–71.)

The coincidence of the quotation with Thucydides iii. 104 is too marked for one to suppose Aristides to be making an original citation; the clause *διαλεγόμενος γὰρ ταῖς Δηλιάσι καὶ καταλύων τὸ προοίμιον* closely follows Thucydides' *τὸν γὰρ Δηλιακὸν χορὸν τῶν γυναικῶν ὑμνήσας ἐτελεύτα τοῦ ἐπαίνου*, and the rhetor, superficially excerpting from Thucydides, mistook the meaning of *ἐτελεύτα τοῦ ἐπαίνου*. This point is well made by Gemoll, p. 114[1] in

[1] Ruhnken's view (see *ante* p. lxvi) is maintained with needless subtlety by Guttmann *Hist. crit.* p. 16 f. It is certain that in Aristides' time there was but one hymn to Apollo; this appears from any fair interpretation of the manner in which Pausanias and Athenaeus cite it. (That Athenaeus cited the hymn as *ἐν τοῖς εἰς Ἀπόλλωνα ὕμνοις* is as much a legend as that the MS. titles of the hymns *ὁμήρου ὕμνοι*, &c., imply a plurality.) Aristides therefore can have derived his *καταλύων* only from an interpretation of the wording of Thucydides. Hence also Aristides quotes the hymn as Homeric, since Thucydides did.

his edition; see introd. to the *Hymn*, p. 186 f. Aristides, therefore, is not to be used as evidence to prove that two hymns to Apollo existed in his day. He is the last author, to whom a certain date can be assigned, that quotes the *Hymns*.

The following testimonies are less easy to date:

14. schol. Apoll. Rhod. ii. 1211 *περὶ δὲ τοῦ τὸν Τυφῶνα ἐν αὐτῇ κεῖσθαι καὶ Ἡρόδωρος ἱστορεῖ ἐν ᾧ καὶ τὴν Νύσαν ἱστορεῖ·*

> *ἔστι δέ τις Νύση ὕπατον κέρας ἀνθέον ὕλῃ*
> *τηλοῦ Φοινίκης σχεδὸν Αἰγύπτοιο ῥοάων.* = i. 8. 9.

This important testimony is unfortunately vague in its bearing. Herodorus, who is largely quoted in the scholia to Apollonius, sometimes as *ἐν τοῖς Ἀργοναύταις* or *Ἀργοναυτικοῖς*, is considered by C. F. Müller (*FHG*. iii. 27 f.) to be the same as the father of *Βρύσων* the sophist, and, therefore, of about 400 B.C. The scholion is incomplete and there is no indication of what is missing; the construc- of the second *ἱστορεῖ* seems to demand such an addition as *περὶ τὴν Αἴγυπτον γενέσθαι*, cl. Diodor. i. 15. There is nothing to show whether Herodorus' work on the Argonauts was in prose or verse (his other work, on Heracles, was in prose, as the quotation fr. 30, 39 shows); if Herodorus, like Ion of Chios in his own century, practised both prose and verse, the lines might well be a quotation from his poem, and the apparent variant *κέρας* (for *ὄρος*) would thus be explained, the more naturally that *κέρας*, according to the Lexica, is a late usage for a part of a mountain; in this case Herodorus would here have copied the hymn. On the other hand Herodorus' work may have been in prose (as we are explicitly told of the *Ἀργοναυτικά* of another source of the Apollonian scholia, Dionysius of Mitylene; see Suidas *in v.*, p. lxviii *supra*), in which case, as is usually supposed, the omission has taken place after the first *ἱστορεῖ*, and *καὶ Ὅμηρος* or *καὶ ὁ ποιητής* has fallen out. (But that Diodorus is nowhere quoted in these abundant scholia, it would be possible that the words were *καὶ ὁ Διόδωρος*, or again *Ἀπολλόδωρος*, as Guttmann *op.c.* p. 6 thought, where the identical ending *-ωρος* would explain the omission.)

If the quotation can be connected with Herodorus, a very ancient testimony—as good as that of Thucydides to the *Hymn to Apollo*—is gained to the Dionysus hymn, but the conclusion is far from certain. (Cf. Gemoll, p. 361, 2.)

15. Stephanus of Byzantium; Τευμησσός· ὄρος Βοιωτίας. Ὅμηρος ἐν τῷ εἰς Ἀπόλλωνα ὕμνῳ. ἄστυ, ὡς Δημοσθένης ἐν τρίτῳ Βιθυνιακῶν (fr. 3 *FHG* iv. 384)·

εἰς Μυκαλησσὸν ἰὼν καὶ Τευμησσὸν λεχεποίην.

ἐκλήθη δ' οὕτως ὡς Ἀντίμαχος πρώτῳ Θηβαΐδος (fr. 4).

= *h. Apoll.* 224.

According to the wording of the passage, the line seems to be quoted from the *Βιθυνιακά* of Demosthenes, which (as we see from the lines quoted by Stephanus *in vv.* *Ἀρτάκη*, *Ἡραία*) was a poem. Then Demosthenes would have appropriated the line of the hymn, and the case is somewhat parallel to that of Herodorus. Demosthenes' date is uncertain (Müller *FHG.* iv. 384–6), but Stephanus in *Χαλκεῖα* (= *fr.* 15) quotes Polybius as disagreeing with him, and Susemihl (*Gesch. d. gr. Lit. in d. Alex.* i. 404) accepts him as of the Alexandrine age. It must be remembered that Stephanus has been abbreviated.

16. schol. Genev. on Φ 319. Ἀπολλόδωρος δέ φησι περισσὸν τὸ σ̄ παρ' αὐτῷ εἶναι, ὡς παρ' Ὁμήρῳ τὴν φερέσβιον.[1]

[1] The reading seems correct, cf. schol. Π 163 ὡς ἐπὶ τῆς φερεσβίου, Strabo 66, &c. It is possible that Apollodorus is the authority at the base of this scholion and that on Ξ 114.

The word *φερέσβιος* does not occur in the *Iliad* or *Odyssey*, and the reference is presumably to the *Hymns*, in which it is frequent. On Apollodorus, who was a disciple of Aristarchus (and, therefore, of the second century B.C.), see La Roche *Hom. Textkritik*, pp. 73, 74, and Pauly-Wissowa s.v. If the note in these scholia is correct, it gives us the only instance of an Alexandrian noticing the *Hymns*.

17. schol. in Nicandri *Alexipharmaca* 130 ὅτι δὲ διὰ γλήχωνος ἔπιεν ἡ Δημήτηρ τὸν κυκεῶνα καὶ διὰ τὴν χλεύην τῆς Ἰάμβης ἐγέλασεν ἡ θεά, ἐν τοῖς εἰς Ὅμηρον ἀναφερομένοις ὕμνοις λέγεται.

= *Dem.* 192 ff.

The cautious ascription is noticeable, as in Athenaeus (no. 12).

18. schol. Pind. *Pyth.* iii. 14 ἐν δὲ τοῖς εἰς Ἡσίοδον ἀναφερομένοις ἔπεσι φέρεται ταῦτα περὶ τῆς Κορωνίδος . . . ἐν δὲ τοῖς Ὁμηρικοῖς ὕμνοις

ἰητῆρα νόσων Ἀσκληπιὸν ἄρχομ' ἀείδειν,
υἱὸν Ἀπόλλωνος, τὸν ἐγείνατο δῖα Κορωνὶς
Δωτίῳ ἐν πεδίῳ κούρη Φλεγύα βασιλῆος.

= xvi. 1–3, with the variant v. 3 Φλεγύα for Φλεγύου.

The age of any particular portion of the Pindaric scholia can probably not be fixed, but in general they go back to good sources, and quotations perhaps would not have been added later than Herodian's age. The point is of importance, as the quotation (which is unique) of the minor hymns tends to disprove a very late origin for xvi and its neighbours.[1] A classical grammarian of a good age would not have quoted Alexandrian literature as Homeric.

[1] *H.* xxv. 2–3 ἐκ γὰρ Μουσάων καὶ ἑκηβόλου Ἀπόλλωνος | ἄνδρες ἀοιδοὶ ἔασιν ἐπὶ χθονὶ καὶ κιθαρισταί are quoted by schol. Pind. *Pyth.* iv. 313, *Nem.* iii. 1, without an author's name. As they stand in Hesiod *Theog.* 94–7 it is probable the scholia quote them as from there.

19. *Certamen Homeri et Hesiodi* 315 (303 Rzach ed. 1913) ἐνδιατρίψας δὲ τῇ πόλει χρόνον τινὰ διέπλευσεν εἰς Δῆλον εἰς τὴν πανήγυριν. καὶ σταθεὶς ἐπὶ τὸν κεράτινον βωμὸν λέγει ὕμνον εἰς Ἀπόλλωνα οὗ ἡ ἀρχή

μνήσομαι οὐδὲ λάθωμαι Ἀπόλλωνος ἑκάτοιο. = *h. Apoll.* 1.

ῥηθέντος δὲ τοῦ ὕμνου οἱ μὲν Ἴωνες πολίτην αὐτὸν κοινὸν ἐποιήσαντο, Δήλιοι δὲ γράψαντες τὰ ἔπη εἰς λεύκωμα ἀνέθηκαν ἐν τῷ τῆς Ἀρτέμιδος ἱερῷ.

On the age of the *Certamen* and its connexion with Alcidamas see *Origins*, pp. 20 sqq. and references. It is probably impossible to assign a date to a particular portion, and the Delian inventories do not contain an entry of a hymn to Apollo as among the furniture of the temple of Artemis. There is no reason, however, to question so much of the story; a temple at Delos possessed Eudoxus' and Alcaeus' works, the latter in a θήκη τρίγωνος (Homolle, *Monuments grecs*, 1878, p. 49, Daremberg et Saglio, *Dict.*, p. 378, n. 181, cf. *BCH.* xxii. 268 f.), and a statue of Alcman (Plut. *de mus.* 1136 A), and the λευκώματα at Delos are mentioned in several inscriptions (*BCH.*, xiv. p. 399); for literature given the consecration of engraving in temples we have the Hesiod on lead at Helicon (Paus. ix. 31), Pindar's seventh *Olympian* in gold letters in the temple of Athena at Lindos (schol. Pind. *Ol.* vii. init. on the authority of Gorgon, a Rhodian antiquary, Susemihl *op.c.* ii. 329, *FHG.* iv. 410), his hymn at Thebes ἐν τριγώνῳ στήλῃ (Paus. ix. 6), the rite of the Megalai Theai on tin (ib. iv. 26. 8), the Τρωικὸς μῦθος at Carthaea (Ath. 456 F), a poem at Cos (Pliny, *N.H.* xx. 264), Nero's poem (Suet., *Ner.* 10), the discoveries of Archilochus on stone at Paros (*I.G.* xii. 445) and the *Delphian Hymns.* It is to be regretted that the Homeric hymn was not given a less perishable material than an *album.* (How ephemeral writing on a *λεύκωμα* was appears from the *Ἀθηναίων Πολιτεία*, c. 47, § 5, Plato *Laws*, 785 A.)

20. Tzetzes praef. in Lycophr. p. 3 Scheer = ii. 1.

These appear to be the quotations of the *Hymns*.[1] Allusions to them are the following:

21. Menander (in Walz *Rhet. graec.* ix. 320, Spengel *Rh. gr.* iii. 331 f.)[2] Περὶ ἐπιδεικτικῶν c. 17 (περὶ σμινθιακῶν): Ὅμηρος μὲν οὖν ὕμνους καὶ τῇ μεγάλῃ ποιήσει τοὺς πρὸς ἀξίαν ὕμνους εἴρηκε τοῦ θεοῦ [sc. Ἀπόλλωνος] καὶ παρέλιπε τοῖς μετ' αὐτὸν ὑπερβολὴν οὐδεμίαν.

22. Herodoti *vit. Hom.* c. 9 τήν τε ποίησιν αὐτοῖς ἐπεδείκνυντο, Ἀμφιάρεώ τε τὴν ἐξηλασίαν τὴν ἐς Θήβας, καὶ τοὺς ὕμνους τοὺς ἐς τοὺς θεοὺς πεποιημένους αὐτῷ, cf. *vita* v. 19–22.

23. schol. Pind. *Nem.* ii. init. Ὁμηρίδας ἔλεγον τὸ μὲν ἀρχαῖον τοὺς ἀπὸ τοῦ Ὁμήρου γένους, οἳ καὶ τὴν ποίησιν αὐτοῦ ἐκ διαδοχῆς ᾖδον· μετὰ δὲ ταῦτα καὶ οἱ ῥαψῳδοὶ οὐκέτι τὸ γένος εἰς Ὅμηρον ἀνάγοντες, ἐπιφανεῖς δὲ ἐγένοντο οἱ περὶ Κύναιθον, οὕς φασι πολλὰ τῶν ἐπῶν ποιήσαντας ἐμβαλεῖν εἰς τὴν Ὁμήρου ποίησιν. ἦν δὲ ὁ Κύναιθος Χῖος, ὃς καὶ τῶν ἐπιγραφομένων Ὁμήρου ποιημάτων τὸν εἰς Ἀπόλλωνα γραφόμενον ὕμνον λέγεται πεποιηκέναι. οὗτος οὖν ὁ Κύναιθος πρῶτος ἐν Συρακούσαις ἐραψῴδησε τὰ Ὁμήρου ἔπη κατὰ τὴν ἑξακοστὴν ἐννάτην Ὀλυμπιάδα, ὡς Ἱππόστρατός φησιν (the earlier part is in Eust. 6. 39).

Hippostratus was a Sicilian chronicler, cited frequently in the Pindaric scholia (*Pyth.* vi. 4, *Ol.* ii. 8 and 16), and in schol. *Theocr.* vi. 46, Phlegon *de mirac.*, 30 (cf. Müller *FHG.* iv. 432 f., Susemihl *op.c.* ii. 390), and the tradition

[1] θερμὸς ἀϋτμή cited by schol. Σ 222 is from Hesiod *Theog.* 696; on *EM.* 474. 30 see *h.* xxviii. 13.

[2] C. Bursian *Abh. d. 1. Cl. d. k. bayerischen Akad.* xvi. Bd. iii. Abth. 1882 considers that the treatises going under the name of Menander are the work of two writers; the former may be the Menander of Suidas who wrote commentaries on Aristides and Hermogenes, and have lived about A.D. 200; the other (to whose work the section περὶ σμινθιακῶν belongs) will have belonged to the end of the third or to the fourth century A.D.

of Cynaethus, of the greatest value seeing that it is the only account which professes to find a definite author of any hymn, comes to us as a piece of local history.

The date (ol. 69 = 504 B.C.) has long been recognized to be wrong, and must be so, since the hymn takes no account of the Pythia, the Pythian games, the chasm, the burning of the first temple at Delphi, or the temple of Apollo and the τροχοειδὴς λίμνη at Delos (see the introduction to the *Hymn*), and it is impossible to suppose that Homer was not recited at Syracuse till 504. The anecdote of Xenophanes and Hiero (Maxim. *ecl.* xli. 824 Migne) implies that Homer was well known in Sicily. In another fragment (no. 3) of Hippostratus the date has been altered. However, it seems idle to change ξθ′ into one numeral more than another.[1] The detailed character of the notice, and its coincidence with other sources which ascribe the hymn to the Homeridae, entitle it to respect, and Philodemus by citing Cynaethus together with Orpheus implies that he belonged to remote antiquity (*Herc. vol.* vi. 156, col. 7). Fick,[2] however, who resuscitated the story, was clearly wrong in supposing the hymn Sicilian. Cynaethus, like the other great rhapsodes, travelled round the Greek world[3] (another case is Arion, Herod. i. 24). The tradition evidently refers the hymn to Chios.

24. schol. Ar. *Birds* 574 Rav. ὅτι ψεύδεται παίζων. οὐ γὰρ ἐπὶ Ἴριδος ἀλλ' ἐπὶ Ἀθηνᾶς καὶ Ἥρας·

αἳ δὲ βάτην τρήρωσι πελειάσιν ἴθμαθ' ὁμοῖαι (E 778),

Ven. οἱ δὲ ἐν ἑτέροις ποιήμασιν Ὁμήρου φασιν τοῦτο γενέσθαι. εἰσὶ γὰρ αὐτοῦ καὶ ὕμνοι.

[1] Welcker *Ep. Cycl.* i. 228 wished to read τὴν ἕκτην ἢ τὴν ἐννάτην, but, as Gemoll justly observes, Syracuse was only founded ol. 11. 3 (= 733).

[2] *Odyssee* p. 278 f., *B.B.* ix. 201.

[3] As in fact the author of the *Hymn to Apollo* says of himself (174, 175).

25. Suidas *in v.* Ὅμηρος . . . . ἀναφέρεται δὲ ἐς αὐτὸν καὶ ἄλλα τινὰ ποιήματα . . . Κύκλος, Ὕμνοι, Κύπρια.[1]

We have next one or two resemblances in literature which suggest quotation. Aristophanes *Birds* 574 says:

αὐτίκα Νίκη πέτεται πτερύγοιν χρυσαῖν καὶ νὴ Δί' Ἔρως γε·
Ἶριν δέ γ' Ὅμηρος ἔφασκ' ἰκέλην εἶναι τρήρωνι πελείῃ.

But as the scholiast just quoted says, the comparison in Homer (*E* 778) is between Athena and Hera, not Iris, and a pigeon, and he implies that Aristophanes was by some taken to refer to *h. Apoll.* 114 βὰν δὲ ποσὶ τρήρωσι πελειάσιν ἴθμαθ' ὁμοῖαι (Iris and Eilithyia). This is possible, and the alteration Ἥρην for Ἶριν in the text of Aristophanes is uncalled for.

Further *Knights* 1016 ἴαχεν ἐξ ἀδύτοιο διὰ τριπόδων ἐριτίμων resembles *Apoll.* 443 ἐς δ' ἄδυτον κατέδυσε διὰ τριπόδων ἐριτίμων.[2] Aristophanes, perhaps, recognizes the Margites (*Birds* 909 and schol.) and *h.* xxxii 20 (*ib.* 913).

Lastly Heliodorus in Dion. Thrac. *art.* 94. 28 marg. καὶ ἄνα Λητοῦς υἱέ recalls *Apoll.* 545, and the commentary 566. 9 οὔτ' ἴδον οὔτ' ἤκουσα *Hermes* 263.

This is all the testimony, explicit and implicit, which can

[1] Homolle *BCH.* iv. 354 f. wishes to see in a Cnossian inscription of s. iii. B.C. found at Delos, in honour of a poet Dioscurides of Tarsus (συνταξάμενος ἐγκώμιον κατὰ τὸν ποιητὰν ὑπὲρ τῶ ἁμῶ ἔθνιος sc. Cnossus), an allusion to the *Hymn to Apollo* and the Cretan priests from Cnossus. This is possible, but can hardly be called certain. The allusion τ 178, 179 τῇσι δ' ἐνὶ Κνωσσὸς μεγάλη πόλις ἔνθα τε Μίνως | ἐννέωρος βασίλευε Διὸς μεγάλου ὀαριστής would fairly correspond to the vague expression κατὰ τὸν ποιητάν. Cf. Strabo's term 476 διαφερόντως δὲ τὴν Κνωσσὸν καὶ Ὅμηρος ὑ μ ν ε ῖ μεγάλην καλῶν καὶ βασίλειον τοῦ Μίνω and Paus. ix. 26. 3 ἐπῄνεσε of Homer's account of Onchestus.

[2] *Anth. Pal.* vii. 409. 5 (Antipater) εἰ δ' ὕμνων σκᾶπτρον Ὅμηρος ἔχει is intended of epos generally, as ὑμνοπόλων v. 10 and elsewhere.

be gathered from ancient literature. Compared to the vast mass of quotation from the *Iliad* and *Odyssey* it is slight, and the impression of neglect which we gather from it is supported by another class of evidence—the omission to quote the *Hymns* in contexts where they would naturally have been appealed to. This is most strikingly the case in the scholia to the *Iliad*. Thus *A* 176 the scholl. quote Hesiod *Theog*. 94–5 but not *h*. xxv. 2–3, where the same words occur; *B* 144 ὅτι Ζηνόδοτος γράφει φὴ κύματα. οὐδέποτε δὲ Ὅμηρος τὸ φή ἀντὶ τοῦ ὡς τέταχεν, Ξ 499 . . . ὅτι ὁ ποιητὴς οὐδέποτε οἶδε τὸ φή ἀντὶ τοῦ ὡς, οἱ δὲ μετ' αὐτόν, ὥσπερ Ἀντίμαχος καὶ οἱ περὶ Καλλίμαχον; this ignores *Herm*. 241, where φή ῥα for θή ῥα is almost certain. *I* 246 σημειοῦνταί τινες ὅτι τὴν ὅλην Πελοπόννησον οὐκ οἶδεν ὁ ποιητής, Ἡσίοδος δέ; but the author of the *Hymn to Apollo* has the word Peloponnesus 250 and 290. These passages might be increased, but they suffice to show that the learning of the Alexandrian school made no appeal to the *Hymns* on points where, if they were genuine, they would have affected Homeric usage; and therefore, however singular the absence of any reference to them in the whole body of extant scholia (except in the possible case of Apollodorus, above no. 16) may be, this silence is doubtless to be interpreted in the sense of the statement (*vita* v. 19 sqq.) that the Alexandrines considered the *Hymns* non-Homeric. Their real authors concealed their identity (using the εὐγνωμοσύνη which Olympiodorus, *in Cat*. ed. Berol. vol. xii, pars i, p. 137, assigns as one cause of the νοθεία of books) with more success than the authors of the Cycle, where there is at least one author assigned by tradition to each poem, and sometimes more than one. Cynaethus is the only fragment of tradition upon the *Hymns* that has come down to us.

The same conclusion may be drawn from the usage of writers who follow the Alexandrian view of Homer—Strabo and Apollonius the Sophist. Strabo, whose orthodoxy is more than scholastic, and contrasts strongly with the other geographers and antiquarians, ignores the *Hymns* in more than one important passage. Europe is unknown to Homer (Strabo, p. 531), but *Εὐρώπη* occurs *Apoll.* 251, 291; *ἄλφι* is un-Homeric (p. 560) and found only in Antimachus; he ignores *Dem.* 208; ***B*** 592 and *Λ* 711 are quoted for the town *Θρύον* (p. 349), *Apoll.* 423 is passed over. The consequence is that when in two places Strabo cites as after *ο* 294 a line which is not found in our *Odyssey* MSS., but which occurs (with a variant) *Apoll.* 425, we conclude not that Strabo is acknowledging the *Hymn* or even quoting it by a slip, but that his copy of the *Odyssey* contained this extra line. Of Apollonius it is enough to mention that his article *κνώδαλον* takes no account of *Herm.* 188, and that under *Φιλομηλείδης* he says *οὐ γὰρ Λητοίδην εἶπε τὸν Ἀπόλλωνα* (but cf. *h. Herm.* seven times). Among later authors Lydus *de mensibus* iii. 18 and Macrobius v. 168 (the latter an extensive quoter of Homer) state roundly that Homer has not the word *τύχη*, notwithstanding *Dem.* 420, *h.* xi. 5.

It results from all this evidence, positive and negative, that the *Homeric Hymns* were not included in the Homeric corpus by the grammarians of Alexandria or writers who took their tone from them; that they were considered Homeric and used as evidence of Homeric usage and history by historians and antiquarians from Thucydides downwards, in some cases with a qualification; and that by the public generally they were little read. This is especially shown by the proportions in which MSS. of the three Homeric works have survived. Of the *Iliad* there are over 200 MSS., of the *Odyssey* about 70, of the *Hymns* 30. Further, abundant papyri of the *Iliad* and *Odyssey* are now in existence, but the *Hymns* do not exist independently in one.

The neglect of these poems, so abundantly attested, seems to account for the many uncorrected corruptions which have propagated themselves in one or other of the families of MSS., especially in M; for the unsupplied loss of two hymns in all but one MS. and of nearly the whole of one in M; and for that absence of ancient commentaries which makes the interpretation of the longer hymns so difficult. The presence of full scholia on the hymns to Demeter, Apollo, and Hermes would have given the geographer and the folklorist wealth that it is difficult to imagine. There is a certain parallelism between the *Hymns* and another post-Homeric set of poems, the Epic Cycle. Our information about both is faulty and obscure. They date both from the sub-epic period, the eighth century and onwards (for the evidence see *Origins* 60 sq.). The real authors of both are not known for certain; but for all the poems of the Cycle there is one candidate, for some several; the *Hymns* are all anonymous save that to Apollo. No papyri quote either (except one which indirectly has a few lines from *h.* ii); the quotations are about equivalent and not abundant. On the evidence one might have supposed that both species perished during the classical period; but, in fact, while the Cycle lasted to the time of Proclus (s. v) (though even this is disputed), the *Hymns* came, as it were, to life, after a silence of 1,000 years, in a fourteenth-century MS., which is followed by a rather copious fifteenth-century tradition. We can only imagine the predecessors of these MSS. of the *Hymns*. The *Batrachomyomachia* and *Hero and Leander* exist, embedded in grammarians, in a tenth-century MS. (Barocci 50), and this may (or may not) be the appearance that the *Hymns* presented at that period. The neglect in the classical period of both sets of poems compared to Hesiod, of whom there is a steady crop of papyri, is remarkable. Traces of Byzantine study of the *Hymns* are slight, and consist in the marginalia of various MSS. These are

Ap. 39 or 40: Π τόπος ἐστὶ τοῦ ὀψικίου ὁ νῦν καλούμενος μαλάγινα περὶ οὗ φησὶ καὶ ὁ λυκόφρων [1464]

κλάρου μιμάλλων ἤτι φίκιον τέρας.

The note does not refer to *Αἰσαγέη* but to *Κλάρος* or *Μίμας*. The writer meant to connect *Μίμας*, *Μιμάλλωνες*, and *Μαλάγινα*. Identifications of ancient sites are frequent in Genesius, Symeon, Theophanes continuatus, Cinnamus, and other historians of the age of Constantine Porphyrogenitus, and in Constantine himself *de Them.* and *de admin. imperio*.

71: L_1Π τὸν ἥλιον φησὶ προυπάρχειν τοῦ ἀπόλλωνος.

147: L_1Π ὁ αὐτὸς ἐν τῇ ῡ ἰλιάδος [685] ἰαόνες ἑλκεσιχίτωνες.

172: L_1Π σή ὡς ἐντεῦθεν ἐμφαίνει ὅμηρος ἑαυτὸν Χῖον (Χίων L) εἶναι.

320: L_1Π ἐβάστασεν· εἰ δὲ μετὰ τοῦ η̄ [sc. κόμησεν] ἐπιμελείας ἠξίωσεν. ὁ αὐτὸς καὶ ἐν τῇ σ̄ τῆς ἰλιάδος [Σ 395]· ἤ μ' ἐσάωσ' ὅτε μ' ἄλγος ἀφίκ^α.

Herm. 36 L_1 Π C L_2 L_3 O R_1 R_2 σή τὸν ἡσίοδον [*OD.* 365] κλέψαντα (κεκλοφότα) τὸν στίχον.

336: L_1 Π ἤγουν (ἤτοι Π) φανερὸν κλέπτην.

Aphr. 244: L_1 Π τὸ ὅμοιον ὅμηρος πανταχοῦ ἐπὶ κακοῦ τιθέναι εἴωθεν.

The notes are nearly limited to L_1 *Π*, i.e. to their ancestor.

The Etymologica, which quote Hesiod and Apollonius of Rhodes, ignore the *Hymns*.

VI.—THE NATURE OF THE HOMERIC HYMNS.[1]

Ancient hymns fall into the classes of rhapsodic or hexameter, and melic. The greater part of what we know about the former comes from Pausanias. It may therefore be well first to collect the references to them in him, and then to add the few allusions in other authors.

Pausanias, who quotes a very large range of epic literature, uses five hymn-writers: Olen, Pamphos, Homer, Musaeus, and Orpheus, and, singular as it may seem to us, he does not give the preference either in age or in merit to Homer. Of Olen he quotes a hymn to Eilithyia (i. 18. 5, viii. 21. 3, ix. 27. 2), which was on the subject of the birth of Apollo and Artemis; as his other hymns, it was written for the Delians (viii. 21. 3), who used it in the worship of Eilithyia (i. 18. 5); one to Hera (ii. 13. 3); one to Achaia (v. 7. 8); this described her journey, as that of Eilithyia, from the Hyperboreans to Delos. He calls Olen a Lycian and regards him as the most ancient of the hymn-writers, older than Pamphos and Orpheus (ix. 27. 2); and quotes the Delphian poetess *Βοιώ* (x. 5. 4) as saying that Olen was the first to use oracles and to build the strain of hymns:

> Ὠλήν θ', ὃς γένετο πρῶτος Φοίβοιο προφάτας,
> πρῶτος δ' ἀρχαίων ἐπέων τεκτάνατ' ἀοιδάν.

Pausanias' statements are confirmed by the much older testimony of Herodotus iv. 35. After saying that Arge and Opis came to Delos from the Hyperboreans, bringing offerings to Eilithyia, he continues τὴν δὲ Ἄργην τε καὶ τὴν Ὦπιν ἅμα αὐτοῖσι τοῖσι θεοῖσι ἀπικέσθαι λέγουσι καί σφι τιμὰς ἄλλας δεδόσθαι πρὸς σφέων· καὶ γὰρ ἀγείρειν σφι

[1] Since the first edition of this book the admirable article *Hymnus* in P-W. by the late R. Wünsch has superseded previous literature. See also a short article in Hastings's *Encyclopedia of Religion and Ethics* 1914, vii. 40–42.

τὰς γυναῖκας ἐπονομαζούσας τὰ οὐνόματα ἐν τῷ ὕμνῳ τόν σφι Ὠλὴν ἀνὴρ Λύκιος ἐποίησε, παρὰ δὲ σφέων μαθόντας νησιώτας τε καὶ Ἴωνας ὑμνέειν Ὦπίν τε καὶ Ἄργην ὀνομάζοντάς τε καὶ ἀγείροντας. οὗτος δὲ ὁ Ὠλὴν καὶ τοὺς ἄλλους τοὺς παλαιοὺς ὕμνους ἐποίησε ἐκ Λυκίης ἐλθὼν τοὺς ἀειδομένους ἐν Δήλῳ. Olen appears therefore strictly associated with Delos, and to have written poems to contain the account of the divinities worshipped there.[1]

Pamphos is quoted for his hymn about Demeter (i. 38. 3, 39. 1, viii. 37. 9, ix. 31. 9), and it is not clear that he wrote anything else; for allusions quoted from him to Poseidon (Paus. vii. 21. 9), Artemis *Καλλίστη* (viii. 35. 8), the Graces (ix. 35. 4 *Πάμφως*[2] *μὲν δὴ πρῶτος ὧν ἴσμεν ᾖσεν ἐς Χάριτας*), Eros[3] (ix. 27. 2), and Zeus (Philostratus *Heroic.* 693=301) may have been contained in the account of Demeter. The statement in Philostratus, however, rather suggests a hymn to Zeus, and that Pamphos's verse was of a mystical and didactic character: *Παμφὼ σοφῶς μὲν ἐνθυμηθέντος ὅτι Ζεὺς εἴη τὸ ζῳογονοῦν καὶ δι' οὗ ἀνίσταται τὰ ἐκ τῆς γῆς πάντα, εὐηθέστερον δὲ χρησαμένου τῷ λόγῳ καὶ καταβεβλημένα ἔπη ἐς τὸν Δία ᾄσαντος· ἔστι γὰρ τὰ τοῦ Παμφὼ ἔπη*

> Ζεῦ κύδιστε μέγιστε θεῶν εἰλυμένε κόπρῳ
> μηλείῃ τε καὶ ἱππείῃ καὶ ἡμιονείῃ.

Pausanias regards him, as we have seen, as younger than

[1] We may add the allusion in Callimachus *h. Del.* 305

> οἱ μὲν ὑπαείδουσι νόμον Λυκίοιο γέροντος
> ὅν τοι ἀπὸ Ξάνθοιο θεοπρόπος ἤγαγεν Ὠλήν,

and the article in Suidas: Ὠλήν· Δυμαῖος ἢ Ὑπερβόρεος ἢ Λύκιος, ἐποποιός· μᾶλλον δὲ Λύκιος ἀπὸ Ξάνθου, ὡς δηλοῖ Καλλίμαχος καὶ ὁ Πολυίστωρ ἐν τοῖς περὶ Λυκίας.

[2] For the name cf. Παμφάη acc. Pindar *Nem.* x. 49.

[3] If there was no hymn, Plato's credit is saved when he says (*Sympos.* 177 B) that no poet had written hymns or paeans to Eros; but it is perhaps as probable that he ignored Pamphos.

Olen, older than Homer (viii. 37. 9) and Sappho (ix. 29. 7): his hymns were written 'for the Athenians' (vii. 21. 9, ix. 29. 7) and (ix. 27. 2) 'for the Lycomidae in their ritual', *ἵνα ἐπὶ τοῖς δρωμένοις Λυκομίδαι καὶ ταῦτα ᾄδωσιν.* They seem to have been executed by a choir of women who bore his name; Hesych. *Παμφίδες· γυναῖκες Ἀθήνησιν ἀπὸ Πάμφου τὸ γένος ἔχουσαι*, and they are perhaps the *Ἀττικοὶ ὕμνοι* of Pollux x. 162, where the word *σίφνις* is quoted as from the story of Demeter.

Orpheus (whose name Pausanias gives to the hymns with a qualification, i. 14. 3, 37. 4) wrote hymns (*τοὺς Ὀρφέως ὕμνους* ix. 30. 12), but except the story of Demeter (i. 14. 3) we do not hear of their subject.[1] They were part of the *τελετή* at Eleusis (i. 37. 4, x. 7. 2), the Lycomidae used them, as those of Pamphos (ix. 27. 2, 30. 12 *Λυκομίδαι δὲ ἴσασί τε καὶ ἐπᾴδουσι τοῖς δρωμένοις*), and an interesting distinction is drawn by Pausanias between their style and that of the *Homeric Hymns*: ix. 30. 12 *ὅστις δὲ περὶ ποιήσεως ἐπολυπραγμόνησεν ἤδη, τοὺς Ὀρφέως ὕμνους οἶδεν ὄντας ἕκαστόν τε αὐτῶν ἐπὶ βραχύτατον καὶ τὸ σύμπαν οὐκ ἐς ἀριθμὸν πολὺν πεποιημένους· Λυκομίδαι δὲ ἴσασί τε καὶ ἐπᾴδουσι τοῖς δρωμένοις. κόσμῳ μὲν δὴ τῶν ἐπῶν δευτερεῖα φέροιντο ἂν μετά γε Ὁμήρου τοὺς ὕμνους, τιμῆς δὲ ἐκ τοῦ θείου καὶ ἐς πλέον ἐκείνων ἥκουσι.* The same judgement is expressed by Menander *Περὶ ἐπιδεικτικῶν* c. 7; *παρέσχετο δὲ τὴν μὲν ἐν ποιήσει ἀρετὴν Ἡσίοδος, καὶ γνοίη τις ἂν μᾶλλον εἰ τοῖς Ὀρφέως παραθείη*, and is confirmed by the 'Orphica' which we possess; on which and their relation to the older Orphic hymns see Dieterich *de hymnis Orphicis*, 1891, and Kern in his edition.

[1] Diodorus (iii. 62) says the story of Dionysus was unfolded διὰ τῶν Ὀρφικῶν ποιημάτων. He quotes as from Orpheus lines about Demeter i. 12. 4, and about Dionysus i 11. 3 (*frr.* ed. Kern 302, 237, p. 300 no. 14).

With regard to Musaeus Pausanias is more trenchant; ἔστιν οὐδὲν Μουσαίου βεβαίως ὅτι μὴ μόνον ἐς Δήμητρα ὕμνος Λυκομίδαις (i. 22. 7; the same hymn, ὕμνος Μουσαίου Λυκομίδαις ποιηθεὶς ἐς Δήμητρα, iv. 1. 5, mentioned Phlyos, the hero of Phlya, the seat of the cult of the Lycomidae).[1] Otherwise the Εὐμολπία was ascribed to him (x. 5. 6). Pausanias seems to express doubt even of this hymn i. 14. 3) and states (x. 7. 2) that in character the Musaeus hymn closely resembled the Orphic. The verses that went under Musaeus' name he thinks were written by Onomacritus (i. 22. 7, an opinion he may have taken from Herodotus vii. 6). Kinkel *Epic. graec. fragg.* p. 218 gives other titles of Musaeus' supposed works.

From these notices we may draw conclusions as to the light in which the *Homeric Hymns* were regarded by a learned antiquarian such as Pausanias. The four other hymnographers are all connected with some place of worship, Olen with Delos, Pamphos, Orpheus, and Musaeus and especially the two latter, with Attica and Phlya, and the hymns are said to have been 'written for' them. The *Homeric Hymns* as a collection are not associated in this way with a particular locality, nor composed for the service of a particular temple, even if in later times the *Hymn to Apollo* hung on the walls of the temple of Artemis at Delos. The Orphic and Musaean poems were mystical, directly connected with τελεταί; they were also brief and without literary pretension. The *Homeric Hymns* were more literary and less devotional, and the ascription of them to Homer, of which Pausanias has no doubt, implies that in his mind they had the same origin as the rest of the

[1] On the worship conducted by the family or hereditary guild of the Λυκομίδαι at Phlya in Attica see Töpffer *Attische Genealogie* p. 208 f., Frazer on Paus. i. 31. 4, iv. 1. 5, 7, O. Kern *Hermes* xxv. 1 f.

epic corpus. When we go beyond Pausanias we find in earlier literature Plato (*Ion* 533 C, *Laws* 829 E) implying the existence in his day of hymns under the names of Orpheus and Thamyris. Both he and Aristophanes (*Frogs* 1032–3) mention Orpheus and Musaeus as religious teachers, and the latter implies that they were earlier than Homer. This opinion was usual in later times, e.g. in Aelian *VH.* xiv. 2, Ptol. Heph. in Phot. *Bibl.* 149 b 22; the Christians had the same faulty perspective of other authors: Lactantius *div. inst.* ii. 12. 4 *Empedocles . . . fortasse Trismegistum secutus* (so again *de ira Dei* ii. 11. 12); 15. 7 Asclepius was a disciple of Trismegistus. We may contrast the critical judgement of Herodotus ii. 53.

Hippias of Elis (ap. Clem. Alex. *strom.* vi. 267) quoted Orpheus, Musaeus, Homer, and Hesiod (and hence Theodoret ἑλλ. θερ. παθ. Migne lxxxiii. 841 gives a definite order: Orpheus first, then Linus, Musaeus, Thamyris, then Philammon contemporary with Troy, Homer and Hesiod long after Troy); the names of Orpheus and Musaeus are coupled by Euripides *Rhesus* 944; in Plato *Protagoras* 316 D they are among the sophists. Androtion (ap. Aelian *VH.* vii. 6) showed some critical faculty by doubting Orpheus' title to σοφία on the ground that the Thracians were unacquainted with letters. Plutarch *de musica* 1131 F sq., quoting Heraclides, who quoted the Sicyonian record, gives Amphion, Linus, Anthes, Pierus, Philammon.

In epic literature information about rhapsodic hymn-writing is not abundant. Demodocus' lay of Ares and Aphrodite (θ 266–366) bears a resemblance to one of the greater Homeric hymns, in so far as it is sung by a rhapsode, and is an episode in the history of divine beings, such as the Homeric *Hymn to Hermes* or *Aphrodite*. It wants, however, the formulae of invocation and farewell, and the addresses to the deity and reference to his qualities which are frequent in the real hymns. Still it may be conceded that it is a representation or adaptation, to suit his purposes, of a contemporary form of literature, by the author of *θ*. As a 'play within a play', it is naturally brief (100 lines), and an imperfect equivalent of its original. Historically the earliest mention of the recital of a hymn is in the autobiographical passage Hes. *OD.* 650 f. There Hesiod declares he had crossed the sea once in his life, from Aulis to Euboea,

> ἔνθα δ' ἐγὼν ἐπ' ἄεθλα δαΐφρονος Ἀμφιδάμαντος
> Χαλκίδα τ' εἰς ἐπέρησα· τὰ δὲ προπεφραδμένα πολλὰ
> ἄεθλ' ἔθεσαν παῖδες μεγαλήτορες· ἔνθα μέ φημι
> ὕμνῳ νικήσαντα φέρειν τρίποδ' ὠτώεντα.

The hymn was recited at games in honour of a departed prince, in competition, and was rewarded by a prize.[1] The subject was probably divine, to judge from the next quotation, Hes. *fr.* 265 (schol. Pind. *Nem.* ii. 1, derived perhaps from Nicocles, who may be the antiquarian *FHG.* iv. 464, Susemihl ii. 395), where the poet says:

> ἐν Δήλῳ τότε πρῶτον ἐγὼ καὶ Ὅμηρος ἀοιδοὶ
> μέλπομεν, ἐν νεαροῖς ὕμνοις ῥάψαντες ἀοιδήν,
> Φοῖβον Ἀπόλλωνα χρυσάορον, ὃν τέκε Λητώ.

We see clearly the Heliconian and Ionian schools meeting half-way between the Greek East and West; and an imaginative critic might fancy the Homerid singing about Delos, the Hesiodean about Pytho. The subjects in any case must have been the same. These passages, together

[1] Local tradition asserted that Amphidamas fell in the Lelantine war (Lesches in Plut. *Conv. Sept. Sap.* 153 F = c. 10, Proclus on *OD.* 650 = Plut. ed. Bernadakis vii. p. 82); this would fix the story to the somewhat vague date of that event. In any case it may well be historical as of a member of the Heliconian or Boeotian school at the period of its prosperity.

with *h. Ap.* 169 f., seem to show the 'Homeric' hymn in the light of a *πάρεργον* of the professional bard or rhapsode, and as delivered at an *ἀγών*, whether at a god's festival, or in honour of a prince.[1] One hymn, that to Apollo, is explicitly attributed to a rhapsode, Cynaethus of Chios (see ante, p. lxxvi, and Introd. to the hymn); and there is no more reason to doubt this ascription than that of the various Cyclic poems to Arctinus, Stasinus, Eugammon, &c. Similarity of language, style, and subject led to the other long hymns being regarded as Homeric, from whatever school they had actually sprung; and this is the view of our oldest authority Thucydides and his contemporary Herodorus (p. lxxii). As new forms of art appeared, the rhapsodic hymn lost its dignity and importance, and its place was taken by different forms of melos; the hexameter hymn continued to be written for private rites and mysteries, or, on a smaller scale in unworthy hands, for the public service of the cult-centres. A glorified specimen of the latter sort was inserted by Theocritus into his XVth Idyll, a hymn to Adonis, sung at the Adonia at Alexandria. The existence of short ritual hymns in the good classical period has been shown, from imitations in fifth-century literature, by Adami *Jahrb. f. class. Phil.* 1901, pp. 213–62, and a few notices remain of their writers, e.g. Plesirrous *ὁ Θεσσαλὸς ὑμνογράφος*, a contemporary of Herodotus, and Matris *ὁ Θηβαῖος ὑμνογράφος*, perhaps his contemporary (Ptol. Heph. in Phot. *Bibl.* 148 a 38 f.).

In the next age local antiquarian poets were frequent, especially at the different centres of worship.[2] Their com-

[1] A private contest is contemplated by Theognis 993.

[2] Julian *ep.* 89 = 302 clearly distinguishes between literary and ritual hymns: *ἐκμανθάνειν χρὴ τοὺς ὕμνους τῶν θεῶν, εἰσὶ δὲ οὗτοι πολλοὶ μὲν καὶ καλοί, πεποιημένοι παλαιοῖς καὶ νεοῖς· οὐ μὴν ἀλλ' ἐκείνους πειρατέον ἐπίστασθαι τοὺς ἐν τοῖς ἱεροῖς ᾀδομένους· οἱ πλεῖστοι γὰρ ὑπ' αὐτῶν τῶν θεῶν ἱκετευθέντων*

positions were usually choric. So we have Isyllus' poems on Asclepius (about B.C. 300 and of unusual literary merit, *C. I. Pel. et Ins.* 1902, i. [*IG.* iv] 950, Diehl *Anth. Lyr.* i. 28); Demoteles of Andros of the third century B.C. (*BCH.* iv. 346 *ποιητὴς ὢν πεπραγ[μά]τευται περί τε τὸ ἱερὸν καὶ τ[ὴν π]όλιν τὴν Δηλίων καὶ τοὺς μύθου[ς] τοὺς ἐπιχωρίους γέγραφεν*); Boeo the Delphian poetess (above, p. lxxxiii); the authors of the hymns lately found at Delphi—Aristonous of Corinth (Diehl i. 297); Cleochares of Athens (*BCH.* xviii. 71); Philodamus (Diehl i. 252)—and Dioscurides of Tarsus, who wrote an *ἐγκώμιον* on Cnossus (*BCH.* iv. 352, above, p. lxxviii. n. 1). In Arcadia the part that *ὕμνοι* played in education is shown by Polybius iv. 20: *σχεδὸν παρὰ μόνοις Ἀρκάσι πρῶτον μὲν οἱ παῖδες ἐκ νηπίων ᾄδειν ἐθίζονται κατὰ νόμους τοὺς ὕμνους καὶ παιᾶνας οἷς ἕκαστοι κατὰ τὰ πάτρια τοὺς ἐπιχωρίους ἥρωας καὶ θεοὺς ὑμνοῦσι· μετὰ δὲ ταῦτα τοὺς Φιλοξένου καὶ Τιμοθέου νόμους μανθάνοντες πολλῇ φιλοτιμίᾳ χορεύουσι κατ' ἐνιαυτὸν τοῖς Διονυσιακοῖς αὐληταῖς ἐν τοῖς θεάτροις.* (To Timotheus twenty-one hymns are ascribed, Suidas *s.v.*) Hymns may have been among the *πολλῶν καὶ πολλὰ ποιητῶν ποιήματα* sung at the Apaturia for the *ἆθλα ῥαψῳδίας* (*Timaeus* 21 B). At Stratonicea, under the Early Empire (*CIG.* 2715), a choir of thirty boys *ᾄσονται ὕμνον ὃν ἂν συντάξῃ Σώσανδρος ὁ γραμματικός*, in honour of Zeus and Hecate. Stobaeus *ecl.* i. 1 quotes Doric Hymns to Heracles, Pan, Asclepius, Hygea, Dioscuri, Curetes, Charites, Horae, Nymphs. A hymn to Hecate is quoted by Hippolytus *ref. haer.* iv. 35. 5.

Apart from temple-worship we are told that Melanippus of Cyme wrote an *ᾠδή* to Opis and Hecaerge (Paus. v. 7), the Erythraean sibyl Herophila a hymn to Apollo (Paus.

ἐδόθησαν, ὀλίγοι δέ τινες ἐποιήθησαν καὶ παρὰ ἀνθρώπων ὑπὸ πνεύματος ἐνθέου καὶ ψυχῆς ἀβάτου τοῖς κακοῖς ἐπὶ τῇ τῶν θεῶν τιμῇ συγκειμένων.

x. 12. 1), Eumelus of Corinth an ἆσμα προσόδιον (to Apollo) for a Messenian theoria going to Delos (Paus. iv. 4. 1, 33. 3: two lines preserved by Pausanias show that it was in Doric), Pronomus a προσόδιον ἐς Δῆλον τοῖς ἐπ' Εὐρίπῳ Χαλκιδεῦσιν (id. ix. 12. 6). In later times Socrates wrote a prooemium to Apollo in prison (*Phaedo* 60 D), Aratus a hymn to Pan (*Biographi graeci*, ed. Westermann p. 55), Euanthes, an epic poet, one to Glaucus (Athen. 296 C), a certain Niciades one to Persephone (*C. I. G.* no. 2338). The *Anthology* contains two curious hymns to Dionysus and Apollo (*Anth. Pal.* ix. 524, 525), in which each line consists of titles beginning with the same letter; *ib.* ix. 485 there is one to Thetis, ending with a prayer to Neoptolemus.

Next we collect the titles and classes of hymns given by ancient authors, and the extant evidence to support them. *Definition*: Didymus ἐν τῷ περὶ λυρικῶν ποιητῶν (Orion 155. 20, *EM.* 690. 34, 777. 1): ὕμνος . . . κεχώρισται ἐγκωμίων καὶ προσῳδιῶν καὶ ἐπαίνων οὐχ ὡς κἀκείνων μὴ ὄντων ὕμνων· γράφεται δὲ ὕμνος προσῳδίας, ὕμνος ἐγκωμίου, ὕμνος παιᾶνος, καὶ τὰ ὅμοια· διαστέλλεται ὡς εἴδη ἀπὸ γένους. ἀλλ' ἀντιδιαστέλλονται· προσόδια γὰρ Ἀθηναῖοι προσιόντες ναοῖς ἢ βωμοῖς πρὸς αὐλὸν ᾖδον, τὸν δὲ ὕμνον πρὸς κιθάραν: Proclus *Chrestomathia* ap. Phot. *Bibl.* ed. Bekk. 320 a 12 ἐκάλουν δὲ καθόλου πάντα τὰ εἰς τοὺς ὑπηρέτας (? ὑπερτέρους, Orion 155. 26 ὑπερέχοντας) γραφόμενα ὕμνους. διὸ καὶ τὸ προσόδιον καὶ τὰ ἄλλα τὰ προειρημένα φαίνονται ἀντιδιαστέλλοντες τῷ ὕμνῳ ὡς εἴδη πρὸς γένος . . . ὁ δὲ κύριος ὕμνος πρὸς κιθάραν ᾔδετο ἑστώτων: cf. also Zonaras 1767. 7, Acron in Horat. *Serm.* ii. 1 *eglogai haec nomina habent: si ad Iovem hymni: si ad Apollinem aut Dianam aut Latonam peanes; si ad Liberum aut Semelen dityrambi; si ad ceteros deos prosodia.* The distinction is maintained in literature: Plato

Laws 700 B καί τι ἦν εἶδος ᾠδῆς εὐχαὶ πρὸς θεούς, ὄνομα δὲ ὕμνοι ἐπεκαλοῦντο, as distinguished from θρῆνοι, παιᾶνες and διθύραμβοι, cf. 801 E ὕμνοι θεῶν καὶ ἐγκώμια κεκοινωνημένα εὐχαῖς and similar expressions in the *Ion* 534 C, Aristotle *poet.* 1448 b 27, Aelian *V.H.* ii. 39. Arrian *Anab.* iv. 11. 2 says ὕμνοι μὲν ἐς τοὺς θεοὺς ποιοῦνται, ἔπαινοι δὲ ἐς ἀνθρώπους; Menander in his Διαίρεσις τῶν ἐπιδεικτικῶν (*Rhet. gr.* ix. 127 sq. Walz) classifies hymns as κλητικοί, ἀποπεμπτικοί, φυσικοί, μυθικοί, γενεαλογικοί, πεπλασμένοι, εὐκτικοί, ἀπευκτικοί, and quotes Sappho, Alcaeus, and Bacchylides, but not Homer (though in another place he alludes to the hymn to Apollo, see p. lxxvi). In the *Medea* (190 sq.) a character says hymns were used at rejoicings (ἐπὶ μὲν θαλίαις ἐπί τ' εἰλαπίναις καὶ παρὰ δείπνοις . . . τερπνὰς ἀκοάς) and not to drive away grief: Ath. 627 F οἱ ἀρχαῖοι περιέλαβον ἔθεσι καὶ νόμοις τοὺς τῶν θεῶν ὕμνους ᾄδειν ἅπαντας ἐν ταῖς ἑστιάσεσιν, Anacreon, p. 63. 9 καλοῖς | ὑποπίνοντες ἐν ὕμνοις.

Hymnoedi used formulae of opening and closing: Aelius Dionysius ap. Eust. 239. 18, Hesych. in Νῦν δὲ θεοὶ κ.τ.λ., state that the most popular form of conclusion was νῦν (σὺν Suidas *in v.*, Zenobius 599) δὲ θεοὶ μάκαρες τῶν ἐσθλῶν ἄφθονοι ἔστε; nothing similar to this remains. Zenobius *l.c.* (in *Paroem. graec.* ed. Leutsch et Schneidewin, vol. 1) gives another, ἀλλὰ ἄναξ μάλα χαῖρε (Hesych. ἀλλ' ἄναξ· ἐξόδιον κιθαρῳδῶν τὸ καθαπάδον καὶ τὸ νῦν (?)), but as used by citharoedi. This approaches to the Homeric καὶ σὺ μὲν οὕτω χαῖρε.[1]

In general literature we find echoes or imitations of hymnal formulae frequently, from *I* 97 ἐν σοὶ μὲν λήξω

[1] Cf. more generally Aristides xiv. 228 κράτιστον οὖν ὥσπερ οἱ τῶν διθυράμβων τε καὶ παιάνων ποιηταὶ εὐχήν τινα προσθέντα οὕτω κατακλεῖσαι τὸν λόγον.

σέο δ' ἄρξομαι through Hesiod. *fr.* 192. 4, Bacchylides xvi. 130 Δάλιε . . . ὄπαζε θεόπομπον ἐσθλῶν τύχαν to Ion of Chios (χαῖρε δίδου δ' αἰῶνα i. 15), Theocritus (i. 130, ii. 14, xv. 142, xvii. 1, 135), Aratus 1, Philostr. *vit. Apoll. Tyan.* i. 37, epigr. ap. Plut. *vit. Aem. Paull.* 16 (σὺ δ' ἄναξ χαῖρε καὶ ἐσθλὰ δίδου), and even Nonnus (xix. 174, 192).

That ὕμνος, ὑμήν, ὑμέναιος are connected is remarked by P. Maas, *Philologus* 1907. 596, with whom we cordially agree (see also Boisacq *in v.*). The etymology of all three is non-Greek and Asiatic, as that of παιάν, κιθάρα, ἔλεγος, διθύραμβος and most musical terms.

When and how the Homeric hymns were recited has been much disputed, and without a certain result. The generic name for them is προοίμια (first in Pindar *Nem.* ii. below, then in Thuc. iii. 104 of the *Hymn to Apollo*; for other instances see p. lxv n. 1). It is natural to infer from this word that they were 'preludes', and Pindar *Nem.* ii. 1 distinctly states that the Homerids prefaced their rhapsodizing with a prooemium to Zeus; ὅθενπερ καὶ Ὁμηρίδαι | ῥαπτῶν ἐπέων τὰ πόλλ' ἀοιδοὶ | ἄρχονται Διὸς ἐκ προοιμίου; the scholiast *ad loc.* says that the rhapsodes as a rule began with a prooemium to Zeus, and sometimes with one to the Muses (so also schol. θ499 ἔθος γὰρ ἦν αὐτοῖς ἀπὸ θεοῦ προοιμιάζεσθαι). Many also of the lesser hymns contain clear allusions to festivals and recitations (*Aphr.* vi. 19 δὸς δ' ἐν ἀγῶνι | νίκην τῷδε φέρεσθαι, *Aphr.* x. 5 δὸς δ' ἱμερόεσσαν ἀοιδήν, *Dem.* xiii. 3 ἄρχε δ' ἀοιδῆς, *Hest.* xxiv. 5 χάριν δ' ἅμ' ὄπασσον ἀοιδῇ, *Mus.* xxv. 6 ἐμὴν τιμήσατ' ἀοιδήν, *Hel.* xxxi. 18 ἐκ σέο δ' ἀρξάμενος κλῄσω μερόπων γένος ἀνδρῶν | ἡμιθέων, *Sel.* xxxii. 18 σέο δ' ἀρχόμενος κλέα φωτῶν | ᾄσομαι ἡμιθέων, ὧν κλείουσ' ἔργματ' ἀοιδοί. See the notes on these passages). The minor hymns, both by these expressions and by their brevity, suggest that they were not used independently. Two of greater length, those to Pan and Dionysus, rather belong to a religious ceremony in honour of those gods, and either is longer than the Adonis hymn in Theocritus xv. The twenty-sixth hymn (also to Dionysus) explicitly talks of the recurrence of the festival 'next year'. These three hymns, therefore, seem to have no necessary connexion with recitations of Homer; and the same is even more the case with viii, xi, xii, xvii, xxii (see the introductions to these hymns). The usual view, therefore (expressed by Wolf *Prolegomena* p. cvi), that all the hymns were preludes to the recitation of *ῥαψῳδίαι*, cannot be maintained. This belief rested (besides on the passage of Pindar quoted above) on (i) the meaning of the word *προοίμιον*; this word, like many terms in music and the arts, may have shifted its significance, and, like 'prelude' in modern music, have been used of an independent composition which bore a technical resemblance to an actual prelude.[1] It is difficult to believe that the five greater hymns can have 'preluded' a rhapsody not necessarily longer than one of them. Wolf also relied (ii) on Plutarch *de mus.* 1133 C *τὰ γὰρ πρὸς τοὺς θεοὺς ὡς βούλονται ἀφοσιωσάμενοι ἐξέβαινον εὐθὺς ἐπί τε τὴν Ὁμήρου καὶ τῶν ἄλλων ποίησιν. δῆλον δὲ τοῦτ' ἐστὶ διὰ τῶν Τερπάνδρου προοιμίων.* The passage, however, refers not to rhapsodes at all, but to *νομοί* and their epic subjects, as a little before, 1132 B, Plutarch says: *οὐ λελυμένην δ' εἶναι τῶν προειρημένων τὴν τῶν ποιημάτων λέξιν καὶ μέτρον οὐκ ἔχουσαν, ἀλλὰ καθάπερ Στησιχόρου τε καὶ τῶν ἀρχαίων μελοποιῶν, οἳ ποιοῦντες ἔπη τούτοις μέλη περιετίθεσαν· καὶ γὰρ τὸν Τέρπανδρον, ἔφη, κιθαρῳδικῶν ποιητὴν ὄντα νόμων, κατὰ νόμον ἕκαστον τοῖς ἔπεσι τοῖς ἑαυτοῦ*

[1] e. g. Aristides li. 417 *μέτειμι δὲ ἐφ' ἕτερον προοίμιον κατὰ Στησίχορον*, i.e. a whole poem.

καὶ τοῖς Ὁμήρου μέλη περιτιθέντα ᾄδειν ἐν τοῖς ἀγῶσιν. That is, he says that the sequence of the nome was fixed; after a sufficient invocation, the poet proceeded to melic variations upon an epic theme. (So the Deliades in their paean, *h. Ap.* 158 ff.) The statement, therefore, that the *Homeric Hymns* were preludes to recitations of Homer must be corrected so as to apply only to certain of the minor hymns; and when Thucydides calls the Apollo hymn a prooemium, we must suppose him to be using a consecrated technical term like 'Prélude' or 'Ballade', which had lost its proper meaning. The presence of the formulae of opening and conclusion marks the *Hymns* as belonging to the same *genre*, and there is nothing incongruous in supposing Homerid rhapsodes at one time prefacing their recital of portions of Homer with invocatory verses of their own, and at another reciting, at ἀγῶνες and festivals, longer independent compositions in honour of the God of the place.[1]

[1] The story of Homer reciting the *Hymn to Apollo* upon the κερατών at Delos (p. lxxv) may, as Welcker *Ep. Cycl.* i. 328 remarks, contain an indication of the mode in which the *Hymns* were actually delivered. For the recitation of old poetry at local centres, cf. a Delphian inscription in Dittenberger *Sylloge* 663 ἐπειδὴ Κλεόδωρος καὶ Θρασύβουλος οἱ Θεοξενίδα Φενεᾶται παραγενόμενοί ποθ' ἁμὲ ἐπιδείξεις ἐποιήσαντο τῷ θεῷ διὰ τᾶς μουσικᾶς τέχνας ἐν αἷς καὶ εὐδοκίμουν προφερόμενοι ἀριθμοὺς τῶν ἀρχαίων ποιητῶν οἳ ἦσαν πρέποντες ποτί τε τὸν θεὸν καὶ τὴν πόλιν ἁμῶν κτλ. Such artists appear to resemble the poets described in the epitome of Ptolemy Heph. in Phot. *Bibl.* 148 a 38 f. ἔνθα περὶ τῶν κατὰ πόλεις τοὺς ὕμνους ποιησάντων. Mr. F. B. Jevons (*JHS.* vii. 291 f.) thought the minor hymns were invocations of a deity in whose honour a rhapsode was about to recite that portion of Homer in which the God was mentioned. That rhapsodies were performed in honour of gods we learn not only from the well-known instance of the Panathenaea but from Plato *Ion* 530 A, where Ion has come ἐξ Ἐπιδαύρου ἐκ τῶν Ἀσκληπιείων. (Socr.) Μῶν καὶ ῥαψῳδῶν ἀγῶνα τιθέασιν τῷ θεῷ οἱ Ἐπιδαύριοι; (Ion) Πάνυ γε, καὶ τῆς ἄλλης γε μουσικῆς: and from Clearchus of Soli ap. Athen. 275 B (= *FHG.* ii. 321, Welcker *Ep. Cycl.* p. 366; the text is uncertain) φαγήσια, οἱ δὲ φαγησιπόσια προσαγορεύουσι τὴν ἑορτήν· ἐξέλιπε δὲ αὕτη, καθάπερ ἡ τῶν

VII. LANGUAGE

The peculiarities of language in the several *Hymns* are enumerated in the introduction to each of them. It is necessary, however, to collect their more general linguistic features under one view, both to facilitate comparison, and to draw such conclusions as may be possible upon their age and place of origin.

The most obvious and important linguistic phenomenon in Greek Epos is the absence or presence of the Digamma.[1] Accordingly, before proceeding further, we give a conspectus of the passages in the *Hymns* where the effect of this letter is apparent or imperceptible. This list is based on that of H. Flach, 'Das nachhesiodische Digamma' in Bezzenberger's *Beiträge zur Kunde der indogermanischen Sprache*, 1878, vol. ii. p. 1–43.[2]

ῥαψῳδῶν ἦν ἦγον . . . καὶ τὴν τῶν Διονυσίων· ἐν ᾗ παριόντες ἕκαστοι (ἑκάστῳ Welcker) τῶν θεῶν οἷον τιμὴν ἐπετέλουν τὴν ῥαψῳδίαν. But the author does not state that the rhapsody was one in which the god appeared, and it would have been difficult to find a rhapsody to mention each of the gods in an honorific light. Further, the usual invocations of rhapsodes according to the schol. Pind. above were to Zeus and the Muses. The passage therefore has nothing to do with hymns. On Hesiod and hymns, see Friedländer *Hermes* 1914, 1.

[1] Albert Thumb 'zur Geschichte des griechischen Digamma' in *Indogermanische Forschungen*, 1898, ix. 294 ff. has superseded the older works (Knös *de digammo Homerico*, Upsala, 1873, Tudeer *de dialectorum graecarum digammo testimonia inscriptionum*, Helsingfors, 1879, R. Weiss *de digamm. in hym. Hom. quaest.* Budapest, 1889). Cf. also Solmsen *Untersuchungen zur griechischen Laut- und Verslehre*, 1901, p. 129 f., Meillet, *Mémoires de la soc. de la linguistique* xvi, Daniellson *Zur Lehre vom homerischen Digamma* I. G. F. 1909, 268, Kretschmer *Ἀντίδωρον*, p. 194. Convenient accounts are given by Monro *HG.* ed. 2, § 388 f., Kühner-Blass, 1892, i. 77 f., Brugmann *Griech. Gram.*[3] p. 37 ff.

[2] The corrections (other than the inclusion of ν ἐφ.) which it is necessary to make in Flach's list, though not many, are sufficient to alter his percentages materially. His data were somewhat vitiated by the emendations

Dionysus

This fragment (21 lines) is too short to yield results. Digamma is observed 10 *καί οἱ ἀναστήσουσι*, 14 *ἐπερρώσαντο ἄνακτος*; neglected 5 *Θήβῃσιν ἄναξ*.

Demeter

Observances of digamma:

26 Ἠέλιός τε ἄναξ, 37 τόφρα οἱ,[1] 51 δεκάτῃ οἱ, 52 ἤντετό οἱ Ἑκάτη (bis), 53 καί ῥά οἱ ἀγγελέουσα ἔπος (bis), 59 ἔφη Ἑκάτη, 65 ἢ ἔπει ἢ ἔργῳ (bis), 81 μεγάλα ἰαχοῦσαν, 93 πίονα ἔργα, 104 δώματα ἠχήεντα, 105 τὴν δὲ ἴδον, 112 ἱστάμεναι ἔπεα, 117 ἠμὲν ἔπει, 133 οὐδέ τι οἶδα, 164 δέ οἱ, 167 τίς σε ἰδοῦσα, 176 ἐπισχόμεναι ἑανῶν, 191 δέ οἱ, 195 δή οἱ, 199 οὔτε τι ἔργῳ, 205 ἢ δή οἱ and εὔαδεν, 207 θέμιτόν οἱ, 222 σε ἰδοῦσα, 235 δαίμονι ἶσος, 241 ἄντα ἐῴκει, 247 ὀλοφυρομένη ἔπεα, 275 καὶ εἶδος, 321 ἄφθιτα εἰδώς, 323 ἐμὸν ἔπος, 333 πρὶν ἴδοι, 336 παραιφάμενος ἐπέεσσιν, 338 ὄφρα ἑ, 342 τόν γε ἄνακτα, 349 ὄφρα ἑ, 357 μείδησεν δέ ἄναξ, 373 ἀμφὶ ἕ, 385 ἡ δὲ ἰδοῦσα, 419 Μελίτη Ἰάχη, 427 θαῦμα ἰδέσθαι, 440 ἐκ τοῦ οἱ, 445 νεῦσε δέ οἱ, 451 ἀλλὰ ἕκηλον, 488 δέ οἱ. = 47.

Neglects:

6 ἠδ' ἴα καλά, 10 πᾶσιν ἰδέσθαι, 17 ὄρουσεν ἄναξ, 37 τόφρα οἱ ἐλπίς, 66 θάλος εἴδεϊ, 75 Δήμητερ ἄνασσα, 117 καὶ ἔργῳ, 118 δ' ἐπέεσσιν, 139 σφίσιν ἐργάζωμαι, 140 ἀφήλικος ἔργα, 144 καί κ' ἔργα, 174 πόρτιες ἦαρος, 195 κέδν' εἰδυῖα,[2] 199 οὔτ' ἔπεϊ, 202 κέδν'

which Baumeister, whose text he used, had admitted. We have also removed from his lists the following forms, on what appear to be good philological grounds: ἑός &c. *passim*, ἤλπετο *Dem.* 35, ἐώθει *Herm.* 305, ἁλός *Ap.* 73. On the other hand, we have allowed ᾗσι *Ap.* 320, 375, ὅν *Ap.* 342, *Aphr.* 203, οἷς *Ap.* 348, ἱέμενοι *Ap.* 472 to stand, though the evidence is less certain in these cases.

[1] v. 46, which Flach gives as altered by Hermann (οὐδέ οἱ οἰωνῶν τις), yields no digamma in the MS. reading (οὔτ' οἰωνῶν τις).

[2] Cf. Flach p. 15 n. 14. Whatever view we take of the probability of an original ἰδυῖα (which nowhere occurs in the MSS. of the *Hymns*, while traces are left in those of the *Iliad*), it is surely plain that εἰδυῖα must take its place here among neglects. Whether the author used it depends on the age of the document, to establish which is the object of this calculation.

εἰδυῖα, 206 μελιηδέος οἴνου, 213 ἄπ' ἔολπα (ἀπὲολπα MS., which is the same as far as the digamma is concerned), 227 μιν ἔολπα, 246 δείσασ' ᾧ, 302 ἵμεν οἴκαδ' ἕκαστος (bis), 315 πολυήρατον εἶδος, 320 φωνήσασ' ἔπεα, 339 ὀφθαλμοῖσιν ἰδοῦσα (350, 409 id.), 347 καταφθιμένοισιν ἀνάσσων, 351 μήδεται ἔργον, 406 μῆτερ ἐρέω, 418 καὶ Ἰάνθη, 430 ἔκθορ' ἄναξ, 438 ἦλθ' Ἑκάτη, 440 ἔπλετ' ἄνασσα, 458 ἀσπασίως δ' ἴδον, 492 Δηοῖ ἄνασσα. = 35.

Apollo

Observances:

1 Ἀπόλλωνος ἑκάτοιο, 7 καί οἱ, 27 ἀμφιρύτῃ ἑκάτερθε, 45 ὠδίνουσα ἑκηβόλον, 46 εἴ τίς οἱ,[1] 50 ἀνειρομένη ἔπεα, 56 Ἀπόλλωνος ἑκαέργου, 63 ἑκάτοιο ἄνακτος, 66 Λητοῖ ἔπος, 74 κατὰ κρατὸς ἅλις αἰεί, 75 ἅδῃ οἱ, 90 γόνῳ ἑκάτοιο ἄνακτος (bis), 107 ὠκέα Ἶρις, 111 ἐκπροκαλεσσαμένη ἔπεα, 137 εἵλετο οἰκία, 139 ὅτε τε ῥίον, 140 ἀργυρότοξε ἄναξ, 157 Δηλιάδες ἑκατηβελέταο, 179 ὦ ἄνα, 184 ἄμβροτα εἵματ', 189 ἀμειβόμεναι ὀπί, 198 τε ἰδεῖν καὶ εἶδος (bis),[2] 229 ἔκιες ἑκατηβόλ', 237 οἱ δὲ ἄνακτι, 239 ἔκιες ἑκατηβόλ', 244 τοι ἅδε, 256 ἐχολώσατο εἶπέ τε, 257 Φοῖβε ἄναξ ἑκάεργε ἔπος (bis), 261 ἔκ τοι ἐρέω, 268 ἐσσὶ ἄναξ, 275 ὄφρα οἱ, 277 ἔκιες ἑκατηβόλ', 285 ἔνθα ἄναξ, 319 ἀλλά ἑ, 320 μετὰ ᾗσι, 341 ἡ δὲ ἰδοῦσα,[3] 342 τέρπετο ὅν, 348 τέρπετο οἷς, 350 περιτελλομένου ἔτεος, 357 γέ οἱ, 361 ἔνθα ἑλίσσετο, 372 δὲ ἄνακτα, 375 ἔγνω ᾗσιν, 382 ἐπὶ ῥίον, 391 ἐπὶ οἴνοπι, 400 δελφῖνι ἐοικώς, 413 Ἠελίοιο ἄνακτος, 420 πνοιῇ δὲ ἄναξ, 441 ἀστέρι εἰδόμενος, 449 ἀνέρι εἰδόμενος, 444 τὰ ἃ κῆλα, 467 ὄφρ' εὖ εἰδῶ, 471 οὔ τι ἑκόντες, 472 νόστου ἱέμενοι, 474 προσέφη ἑκάεργος, 477 καλὰ ἕκαστος, 486 ἐγὼ εἴπω, 488 ἠπείρου ἐρύσασθε, 490 ἐπὶ

[1] v. 46 εἴ τίς οἱ is the reading of the Harleian only, but appears a true correction of τίς σοι of the other MSS.

[2] v. 209 ἔκιες Ἀζαντίδα κούρην; there seems no ground for assuming a digamma before Ἀζαντίδα, besides that M reads ἀτλαντίδα, and the obscurity of the passage makes the word altogether doubtful.

[3] So M: the other MSS. ἡ δ' ἐσιδοῦσα. As an archaistic restoration is less probable than a linguistic degradation (well attested in the Homeric text), M may well have preserved the original. Cf. *Aphr.* 147.

ῥηγμῖνι, 505 id., 508 id., 516 δὲ ῥήσσοντες, 526 ὦ ἄν', 534 ῥηΐδιον ἔπος, 540 τηΰσιον ἔπος ἔσσεται ἠέ τι ἔργον (bis). = 69.

Neglects:

15 Ἀπόλλωνά τ' ἄνακτα, 22 σκοπιαί τοι ἅδον, 29 θνητοῖσιν ἀνάσσεις, 46 θέλοι οἰκία,[1] 71 πρῶτον ἴδῃ, 75 κεν ἅδῃ, 102 αἷ δ' Ἶριν, 106 ἔπειτ' ἐπέεσσιν, 153 κεν ἴδοιτο, 163 μιμεῖσθ' ἴσασιν and αὐτὸς ἕκαστος, 177 λήξω ἑκηβόλον, 181 μέγ' ἀνάσσεις, 255 ἐσιδοῦσα, 275 εἰποῦσ' Ἑκάτου, 276 μηδ' Ἑκάτοιο, 286 ἐπήρατον εἶπε, 301 κτεῖνεν ἄναξ, 312 κέδν' εἰδυῖαν, 355 πόλλ' ἔρδεσκε, 357 ἐφῆκεν ἄναξ, 382 ὦσεν ἄναξ, 385 ἔνθα δ' ἄνακτι, 393 τ' ἄνακτι, 395 κεν εἴπῃ, 415 ὀφθαλμοῖσιν ἰδέσθαι, 437 ἡγεμόνευε δ' ἄναξ, 440 ὄρουσεν ἄναξ, 447 ἔμβαλ' ἑκάστῳ,[2] 464 καταθνητοῖσιν ἔοικας, 506 νῆ' ἐρύσαντο, 514 σφιν ἄναξ, 534 ὔμμ' ἐρέω, 535 μάλ' ἕκαστος. = 34.

HERMES

Observances:

12 τε ἔργα, 16 κλυτὰ ἔργα, 26 ῥά οἱ, 61 κατὰ οἶκον, 80 θαύματα ἔργα, 92 τε ἰδών, 100 Μεγαμηδείδαο ἄνακτος, 117 δέ οἱ, 127 πίονα ἔργα, 164 αἴσυλα οἶδε, 177 τί οἱ, 234 ἠερόεν ἑκατηβόλος, 250 ἄργυφα εἵματα, 265 φωτὶ ἔοικα, 281 προσέφη ἑκάεργος, 313 τὰ ἕκαστα, 358 νυκτὶ ἐοικώς, 377 φωτὶ ἐοικώς,[3] 426 δέ οἱ, 439 τόδε εἰπέ, 440 θαυματὰ ἔργα, 454 ἐνδέξια ἔργα, 456 μήδεα οἶδας, 467 εὖ οἶδας, 516 ἐπαμοίβιμα ἔργα, 520 φίλα ἔρδοις, 550 τοι ἐρέω. = 27.

Neglects:

18 κλέψεν ἑκηβόλον, 46 ἅμ' ἔπος τε καὶ ἔργον (bis), 92 ἰδὼν μὴ ἰδών, 107 ἠδ' ἐρσήεντα, 120 δ' ἔργον, 129 προσέθηκεν ἑκάστῃ, 143 τίς οἱ, 154 θεὸς εἶπε, 179 ἔνθεν ἅλις, 180 χρυσὸν ἅλις, 182 ῥ' ἐπέεσσι, 192 κεράεσσιν ἑλικτάς, 199 ταῦτά μοι εἰπέ, 202 ὀφθαλμοῖσιν ἴδοιτο, 205

[1] v. 59 δηρὸν ἄναξ εἰ βόσκεις κτλ. is a *versus nihili*, and ἄναξ, which seems to yield a neglect, is especially inapplicable to Delos.

[2] This is the reading of M; the other lection εἷλεν ἕκαστον (*xp*) equally involves a neglect.

[3] Flach counted in v. 400 ἦχί ῥά οἱ, but this is only a conjecture and a bad one; ἦχοῦ δὴ is now established: in v. 224 he used the unwarranted conjecture λασιαύχενα for λασιαύχενος.

ἐστιν ἕκαστον, 215 ἤϊξεν ἄναξ, 218 εἰσενόησεν Ἑκηβόλος εἶπε (bis), 224 λασιαύχενος ἔλπομαι, 227 ἤϊξεν ἄναξ, 236 βουσὶν ἑκηβόλον, 239 Ἑκάεργον ἰδών, 241 προκαλεύμενος ἥδυμον, 266 ἐμὸν ἔργον, 285 κατ' οἶκον, 306 ἑελμένος εἶπε, 333 προσέειπεν ἄναξ, 343 δαίμονος ἔργα, 376 τ' οἶδε, 382 ὀπίζομαι οἶσθα, 389 ἐξεγέλασσεν ἰδών, 403 ἀπάτερθεν ἰδών, 417 ἐπρήϋνεν ἑκηβόλον, 421 ἤλυθ' ἰωή, 428 μοῖραν ἕκαστος, 431 γεγάασιν ἕκαστος, 449 καὶ ἥδυμον, 464 μ' Ἑκάεργε, 466 σήμερον εἰδήσεις, 472 θ' Ἑκάεργε,[1] 493 ἔνθεν ἅλις, 500 υἱὸς ἄναξ, 522 ὅσ' Ἑκηβόλος, 531 τε καὶ ἔργων, 535 τὸ γὰρ οἶδε, 559 κραίνουσιν ἕκαστα, 571 προβάτοισιν ἀνάσσων, 574 υἱὸν ἄναξ. = 49.

Aphrodite

Observances:

1 ἔννεπε ἔργα, 10 ἄρα οἱ πόλεμοι τε ἅδον καὶ ἔργον (ter), 11 ἀγλαὰ ἔργ', 15 ἀγλαὰ ἔργ' and θεῖσα ἑκάστῃ, 18 τῇ ἅδε, 21 κούρῃ ἅδεν, 30 μέσῳ οἴκῳ, 41 μέγα εἶδος, 43 μήδεα εἰδώς, 48 ἐπευξαμένη εἴπῃ, 53 δ' ἄρα οἱ, 56 ἔπειτα ἰδοῦσα, 59 δέ οἱ, 63 ῥά οἱ and ἀμβροσίῳ ἑανῷ, 82 καὶ εἶδος, 90 θαῦμα ἰδέσθαι, 92 χαῖρε ἄνασσ', 112 εὐτοιχήτοιο ἀνάσσει, 113 σάφα οἶδα, 116 εὖ οἶδα 139 τε ἅλις ἐσθῆτα (bis), 147 δὲ ἕκητι, 153 γύναι ἐικυῖα, 162 μέν οἱ, 164 λῦσε δέ οἱ and ἰδὲ εἵματα, 167 σάφα εἰδώς, 171 χροῒ ἕννυτο εἵματα (bis), 181 ὡς δὲ ἴδεν, 184 λισσόμενος ἔπεα, 185 θεὰ ἴδον, 205 θαῦμα ἰδεῖν, 207 οὐδέ τι ᾔδει, 208 ὅππῃ οἱ, 210 δέ οἱ, 212 δὲ ἕκαστα, 235 ἤδε δέ οἱ, 267 δέ ἑ, 277 ἐς πεμπτὸν ἔτος, 280 ποτὶ Ἴλιον. = 46.

Neglects:

6 δ' ἔργα, 9 γάρ οἱ and εὔαδεν ἔργα,[2] 21 ἅδεν ἔργ', 44 κέδν' εἰδυῖαν, 55 ἀθανάτοισιν ἐοικώς, 85 τε καὶ εἵματα,[3] 86 γὰρ ἕεστο, 91 εἶλεν ἔπος, 109 ἀθανάτῃσιν ἐΐσκεις, 122 ἤγαγεν ἔργα, 134 κέδν' εἰδυίῃ, 136 ἀλλ' ἐικυῖα,[4] 144 εἶλεν ἔπος, 151 εἴ κεν ἑκηβόλος, 157 ἔσκεν ἄνακτι,

[1] μαντείας θ' Ἑκάεργε the MSS. with unimportant variations (δ', τ', γ'): the particle was removed to suit an interpretation of the passage.

[2] By taking the conjecture οὐ γάρ οἱ ἅδε for the MS. reading οὐ γάρ οἱ εὔαδεν, Flach, naturally, avoids both neglects.

[3] τε καὶ εἶδος is a *v.l.* line 82.

[4] The other line of the apparent doublet avoids the neglect by the reading ἠὲ καὶ οὐκί.

163 θ' ἕλικας, 169 τε καὶ ἶφια, 176 ἀνέγειρεν ἔπος, 196 Τρώεσσιν ἀνάξει, 203 ἥρπασεν ὅν,[1] 232 τε καὶ εἵματα, 256 πρῶτον ἴδῃ, 278 πρῶτον ἴδῃς. = 24.

VII. Dionysus

Observances:

3 ἀνδρὶ ἐοικώς, 7 ἐπὶ οἴνοπα, 8 οἱ δὲ ἰδόντες, 16 αὐτίκα οἷς, 34 θαυματὰ ἔργα, 40 μέλας εἱλίσσετο, 42 οἱ δὲ ἰδόντες, 48 ὑπόδρα ἰδών, 52 ἐπεὶ ἴδον. = 9.

Neglects:

29 ἢ ἑκαστέρω, 30 ποτ' ἐρεῖ, 37 πάντας ἰδόντας, 54 πανόλβιον εἶπε. = 4.

XIX. Pan

Observances:

31 τέ οἱ, 48 χαῖρε ἄναξ. = 2.

Neglects:

14 δ' ἕσπερος, 17 τ' ἔαρος, 21 οὔρεος ἠχώ, 36 τερατωπὸν ἰδέσθαι, 37 πολύκροτον ἡδυγέλωτα. = 5.

Minor Hymns

Observances:

vi. Aphr.	6 ἄμβροτα εἵματα ἕσσαν (bis), 15 ἠσπάζοντο ἰδόντες, 16 ἠρήσαντο ἕκαστος, 17 καὶ οἴκαδ'.
xi. Ath.	2 πολεμήϊα ἔργα.
xv. Heracl.	9 χαῖρε ἄναξ.
xvi. Ascl.	5 χαῖρε ἄναξ.
xx. Heph.	2 ἀγλαὰ ἔργα.
xxi. Apoll.	5 χαῖρε ἄναξ.
xxiv. Hest.	1 ἥτε ἄνακτος Ἀπόλλωνος ἑκάτοιο (bis).
xxv. Mus.	5 γλυκερή οἱ.
xxix. Hest.	6 μελιηδέα οἶνον.
xxx. Ge	10 εὐθηνεῖ οἶκος.

[1] This reading appears to be implied by the chief MSS.; the variant ἥρπασ' ἑὸν would yield no neglect.

xxxi. Hel. 5 ἥ οἱ τέκε, 17 χαῖρε ἄναξ.
xxxii. Sel. 8 εἵματα ἑσσαμένη, 17 χαῖρε ἄνασσα.
xxxiii. Diosc. 16 οἱ δὲ ἰδόντες. = 20.

Neglects:

vi. 18 θαυμάζοντες ἰοστεφάνου,[1] 19 χαῖρ' ἑλικοβλέφαρε.
xii. 2 ὑπείροχον εἶδος.
xiv. 3 τυπάνων τ' ἰαχή, 5 τ' ἠχήεντα.
xv. 5 Εὐρυσθῆος ἄνακτος.
xxii. 3 θ' Ἑλικῶνα.
xxv. 2 καὶ ἑκηβόλου.
xxvi. 3 πατρὸς ἄνακτος, 5 πατρὸς ἕκητι.
xxvii. 20 τε καὶ ἔργμασιν.
xxix. 12 εἰδότες ἔργματα.
xxxi. 13 λάμπεται ἔσθος.
xxxii. 2 Διὸς ἵστορες, 3 γαῖαν ἑλίσσεται, 16 ἐκπρεπὲς εἶδος, 19 κλείουσ' ἔργματ'. = 17.

Tabulated the results are:

	Observances.	Neglects.
Demeter	47	35 = 1·342 : 1
Apoll.	69	34 = 2 : 1 approx.
Hermes	27	49 = 0·55 : 1
Aphrod.	46	24 = 1·9 : 1
Dion. vii	9	4 = 2·25 : 1
Pan xix	2	5 = 0·4 : 1
Minor Hymns	20	17 = 1·175 : 1[2]

These figures vary materially from those of Flach *op.c.* and of Fick ('Die ursprüngliche Sprache der h. H.' *B.B.* 1885, ix. 195 f.). The difference is mainly accounted for by the fact that we have not considered ν ἐφελκυστικόν before a once digammated word a certain sign of the

[1] Removed by *p*'s lection ἐυστεφάνου.

[2] For instances of mixed usage we may compare the Chest of Cypselus as reported by Pausanias; v. 18. 4 τάχ' ἄναξ, 19. 3 τυνδαρίδα ἑλέναν. Cf. also *IG.* xii. 148 -ντος hεκηβο[λωι, 442 τονδοικον.

original presence of the digamma in the document where it occurs. To believe this it would be necessary to prove that the *Hymns* started with an audible digamma, and that the scribes or reciters, as the digamma lost its force and they became aware of the hiatus, filled the gap with a ν. But the presence of an audible or living digamma in the later Homeric corpus is doubted on many sides. If it was at the beginning a fluctuating and semi-traditional sound, ν ἐφελκυστικόν may represent this original state of things, and be *prima facie* evidence that where it occurs F was not pronounced. As early as the sixth century we find ν ἐφ. on Ionic inscriptions before originally digammated vowels; Hoffmann, *Der ion. Dialekt* 30 ανεθηκεν hεκηβολωι, 32 ανεθηκεν εκηβολωι, 59 σοφιηισιν εκηβολ[ωι in prose ανδριασιν ερδεται, χρηιζωσιν εαδε in the rules of the Milesian guild, which, though late, may be a true copy (Wilamowitz, *Sitzungsb. d. preuss. Akad.* 1904, xix): before an aspirate *I.G. Sept.* 3225 εποιησεν *ho* ναξιος (Orchomenus). We have, therefore, not omitted consideration of ν ἐφ. in a calculation which aims at ascertaining the position of the digamma in these poems.

On the other hand, we have not ventured to follow Thumb (p. 328) in withdrawing the case of hiatus altogether from the computation. However independent of the digamma in historical times hiatus in instances such as δὲ ἔπος may have been, the digamma originally must have been the cause of it, and the gradual disappearance of hiatus has a chronological value.

These figures, once obtained, may be employed to determine the relation (1) of the *Hymns* to the *Iliad* and *Odyssey*; (2) of the hymns to one another.

1. The percentage of observances and neglects of the digamma in the *Iliad* and *Odyssey* has been worked out by

W. von Hartel in his 'Homerische Studien iii' (*Sitzungsberichte der k. Akademie der Wiss.*, Wien vol. 78, 1874; the separate edition has long been out of print). He gives 3,354 observances against 617 neglects, i.e. 5·43598 : 1. This total excludes ν ἐφελκ. (Hartel p. 61). If we count the cases of ν ἐφελκ. in the *Hymns* as observances, the ratios work out as

	Observances.	Neglects.
Dem.	53	29 = 1·82 : 1
Apoll.	81	22 = 4 : 1 approx.
Hermes	43	33 = 1·3 : 1
Aphr.	58	12 = 4·83 : 1
Dion. vii	9	4 = 2·25 : 1
Pan xix	2	5 = 0·4 : 1
Minor Hymns	20	17 = 1·175 : 1

Comparing Hartel's figures we see that the digamma has suffered weakening between the oldest of the hymns and the Homeric poems. This is natural and supported by external evidence, if we consider that, while the Homeric poems are most probably referred to the island of Chios at an early stage of its settlement and when the Aeolic part of its dialect was still alive (*Origins* 98 seq.), the *Hymn to Apollo* at least posits the Ionian colonization and the organized Delphic oracle. If, however, with Thumb p. 329, we limit the comparison to cases of elision only, some of the results in the *Hymns* are singularly even with Hartel's for the *Iliad* and *Odyssey*, viz.—

Apoll.	1 : 0·6
Aphr.	1 : 0·5
Homer	1 : 0·6

What the result on Hartel's figures of the introduction of ν ἐφ. would be can hardly be estimated, but it may be presumed the *Hymns* would still exhibit a larger number of neglected digammas.

How much later it may be inferred the *Hymns* are than Homer is another matter; there is no evidence to calculate the rate of digamma-decay, or to translate percentages of neglects into terms of chronology. Nor again is there agreement as to what ratio of observance is enough to constitute the digamma a 'living sound'; the older inquirers (Flach and Fick) assumed that in the *Hymns to Aphr.* and *Ap. Pyth.* it was alive, and in the Homeric poems; but it is now agreed on all hands that F belonged to Ionic as a dialect (Kretschmer *KZ.* 29, p. 390 f., Smyth *Ionic* § 386, Brugmann *Gr. Grammatik* ed. 3, p. 38), and it seems certain that it was alive in the *Iliad* and *Odyssey* when they were composed; but it is out of the question to refer any part of the *Hymns* to such a period. This consideration, and the low ratio of differences even in the best cases between observance and neglect make it very doubtful if F was a living sound in any of the hymns.

2. As regards the relation of the hymns to one another, digammas being admittedly indigenous to Ionic, and having disappeared almost entirely from both Ionic inscriptions and Iambic poets (see for the former Smyth or Hoffmann, or Thumb *op.c.*, p. 322 f., for the latter Hoffmann § 249 or Flach's statistics *op.c.*, p. 44 f.), and at a date varying from 800–700 B.C. in round numbers, it might be supposed *prima facie* that those hymns in which the digamma was best preserved were the oldest. Judged by this criterion the hymns fall into the following order of age:—*Apollo*, *Aphrodite*, *Demeter*, *Hermes*. The *Hymns to Dionysus* and *Pan* are excluded from the general calculation on account of their brevity; but as against *h. Pan*, *h. Dion.* appears remarkably the elder. The combined ratio of the minor

Hymns also does not strictly enter into the comparison; their total is very close to that of Demeter. The value, however, of the digamma as a criterion of age is gravely qualified by the extent to which any particular hymn depends upon Homer. It is obvious that lines borrowed from Homer containing observances or neglects of the digamma cannot be adduced as proof of the age of the hymn which borrows them. A later hymn, owing more to Homeric diction, may seem older than one whose writer was less bound by Homeric tradition. The *Homeric Hymns* differ considerably as to the degree of their dependence upon Homer; *h. Aphr.* is ὁμηρικώτατος in diction; twenty verses are taken from Homer with almost no alteration, and the poem abounds in hemistichs and formulae; out of 293 verses about 160 end in a Homeric formula (Windisch *De Hymn Hom. maj.* 1867, p. 47). The like statement applies to the latter part of the Apollo hymn; out of 368 verses thirty-eight are taken nearly unaltered from the *Iliad* or *Odyssey*, and nearly half contain formulae (Windisch, p. 11). It is plain, therefore, that the proportions of presence or absence of the digamma must not be pressed so as to establish a definite order between the greater hymns.[1] The figures appear when this allowance has been made to warrant these conclusions:

(1) *H. Hermes* is much later than the other three long hymns.

(2) *H. Ap.*, *h. Aphr.*, and *h. Dem.* are all old, but the percentages of observances and neglects do not differ so materially as to fix an order between them.

[1] This conclusion is denied, as against Windisch, Clemm, and others, by Flach *op.c.* p. 5 f., but, especially in view of the new theories held about the history of the digamma, its presence or absence cannot be held as more than one factor in determining the date of a document.

(3) The evidence of the digamma, as far as it goes, proves *h. Dion.* to be comparatively old (as against some theories mentioned in the Commentary.).

(4) *H. Pan* cannot belong to an early epic date.[1]

The digamma then at the time when the oldest hymn was written was dead in current pronunciation. If, therefore, as is currently held, the digamma ceased to be spoken in Asia after 850, and in Naxos and the Cyclades by 700, and perhaps somewhat later in Euboea, the oldest part of the *Hymns* cannot be put back beyond 800 at farthest. This limitation agrees with the external and historical evidence, which will be found in the Introductions to the different *Hymns*.

Besides the digamma there are few dialectal peculiarities in the *Hymns*. Their vocabulary, where it differs from Homer (see Fietkau, *De carm. Hesiod. atque hymnorum quatuor magnorum vocabulis non homericis*, Regimont. 1866), agrees with their general late-epic date. ἕκατι *h. Aphr.* 147 is perhaps a scribe's accident, due to Tragic associations. The same uncertainty attaches to μής *Herm.* 11, δελφοῦσα *h. Ap.* 244, etc., φύζαν *Herm.* 114, παῖδ' (πεδ') ἀφνειὸν *ib.* 473. The *Hymn to Hermes* is the only one which offers palpable peculiarities of language. Ἀθρόας 106, περ' ἰγνύσι 152 suggest peculiarities of the Hesiodic poems—e.g. λαγός (acc. pl.) *Scut.* 302, ἀποδρέπεν *OD.* 611, Φίκιον *Scut.* 33, Φῖκα *Theog.* 326, τροπᾶς *OD.* 564—which are recognized to be effects of the Boeotian dialect upon the Heliconian school (cf. e.g. Flach *op.c.* p. 5, n. 4). Φύζαν, which we have restored to the text *Herm.* 114, is obscure. The singularly low percentage of the digamma,

[1] No substantial results as to comparative dates can be drawn from the structure of the verse of the *Hymns*. The subject is treated exhaustively by La Roche *Wiener Studien* xx. 70–90, Eberhard *Metrische Beobachtungen zu d. h. H.* 1874 and 1887.

however, in the *Hymn to Hermes* would seem to contradict a theory of a Boeotian origin; and Fick's happy restoration of ἠχοῦ in v. 400 perhaps connects the hymn with Oropus or Eretria (*BB*. xxii. 272). For the Oropian inscription containing the form ηχοι see on *Herm*. 400. To these forms may be added θᾶττον 255; for in the same Oropian inscription we find ελαττον, which can hardly be an Atticism since the inscription contains non-Attic forms such as εντοθα = ἐνταῦθα, αφικνεμενων = ἀφικνουμένων, and especially the rhotacism δημοριων = δημοσίων. We should see in it an Euboean-Ionic dialect coloured by a few local peculiarities.[1] The Oropian syntax χαίρω σε ἐληλυθότα (Suid. and *EM*. *in v.*) resembles ἄλιον τὸν μῦθον ἀκούων 280. The hymn, therefore, seems attributable to the dialect of Oropus or Eretria. We hear of no school of rhapsodes at these places, but the neighbouring Chalcis could attract 'Hesiod' and 'Homer' to its games (Hes. *OD*. 650 f., quoted p. lxxxviii, *Certamen* 213 = 265 Rzach). A few writers of the early age are mentioned as of Chalcis; e.g. Tynnichus, the man of one paean (Plato *Ion*. 534 D ὃν πάντες ᾄδουσι), admired by Aeschylus for its antique simplicity (Porph. *de abst*. ii. 18; he was later than Alcman according to the story in Ptol. Heph. *Nov. Hist*. in Phot. *Bibl*. 151 a 9, cf. also Procopius *BG*. iv. 22); Hypodicus, who won the prize for the dithyramb at Athens in 508 (*Marmor Parium* § 61). Simonides an epic poet came from Carystus (Suid. *in v.*), Achaeus also and Euphorion were natives of Euboea or Chalcis, and in later days rhap-

[1] Rhotacism in Euboea is certainly un-Attic, and attracted Plato's notice (*Cratylus* 434 C), but it is not Boeotian either (Meister i. 151). Herodian, however, attributed it to 'Aeolians', and it is found in Thessaly (ib. 300) and is frequent in Elis, cf. Strabo 448 (where, however, it is final, while Eretrian rhotacism is usually medial, final however in an inscr. Ἐφ. Ἀρχ. 1902, 99).

sodes were a standing feature of the festivals at Oropus (*IG.* vii. 415–20) as well as those at Thespiae and Orchomenus. The neighbourhood of the serious Heliconian school may have induced an Euboean or Oropian to write a hymn in style somewhat of a parody upon Hesiod, which should contain the less dignified adventures of the God of gain.

The longer hymns then upon the evidence of their language appear to belong to the last stage of the epic period; the figures for the smaller hymns, though less cogent, since they assume the homogeneity of the poems, are a guarantee of their age on the whole, and compared with the ratios of the later epics [1] give them a place in the classical period; a conclusion agreeing with their style and the imitations in tragedy and comedy collected by Adami *l.c.*

These hymns, with a few exceptions, have no close analogies in later poetry: they do not resemble the *Batrachomyomachia* or the fourth-century parodies; they are simpler than the learned and artificial hymns of the Alexandrians; they are superior to the later official hymns found at Delphi; and, finally, they are far removed from the tone of the Orphic and Proclan hymns. The argument from style is strongly supported by the external evidence that a scholiast on Pindar quotes one hymn (xvi) as 'Homeric'.

But although the great majority of the minor hymns seem to belong to the end of the genuine epic period, a few are evidently later. The *Hymn to Pan* can hardly be older than the fifth century; the *Hymns to Helios* and *Selene* appear to be Alexandrine (see Comm. on xxxi); and the *Hymn to Ares*, anomalous in the collection, may date from any part of the period of Orphic influence (see *ante*, p. liv, n. 2).

[1] See Flach *BB.* ii. 44 f.

IX. BIBLIOGRAPHY

The editio princeps of 1488, its sources, and its contribution to the text of the author, have been described *ante*, p. xliii. The *Hymns* were printed with the rest of the Homeric corpus in the editions of Aldus (1504, &c.) and Giunta (1537). No new material was collected for these editions, and alterations in the text were merely clerical. The Aldine corrected *h. Ap.* 244 ἄδε, *h. Aphr.* 31 an accent. The *Hymns* were first translated by Georgius Dartona, in the Latin version of the *Odyssey* published by Andreas Divus at Venice in 1537.[1] Henri Estienne included the *Hymns* in his great edition of the *Poetae Graeci principes heroici carminis*, 1567, and on pp. xxvi, xxvii, printed the first notes on them. A certain number of quasi-clerical corrections are due to him (the best are *h. Ap.* 313 ποιήσατο for ἐποιήσατο, xix. 2 πίση for πίσση, xxv. 1 ἄρχωμαι for ἄρχομαι). A few bolder alterations which he makes are unacceptable, though πὰρ for ἄρα *h. Aphr.* 173 was for a time received and believed to be the reading of a Paris MS. One correction, however, is brilliant, and anticipates modern philology: λόον for λοῦον *h. Ap.* 120. The lawyer who goes by the name of Giphanius (van Giffen) may be quoted for his attempt to insert δ' after ὥσῃ *h. Ap.* 73; his edition of Homer came out at Strasbourg in 1572. The first scholar who seriously and with success applied his skill to the dark places of the *Hymns* was an avocat of Dijon, Bernard Martin (1574–1639), in his *Variarum lectionum libri quattuor Parisiis apud Petrum Chevalier*, 1605. This rare book (of which neither the Bodleian nor the British Museum possesses a copy) was reprinted 'cura Diederici van der Kemp,

[1] See Legrand *Bibliographie hellénique* iii. 367.

Trajecti ad Rhenum', in 1755. Particulars of Martin's life will be found in the preface, and in the local authorities quoted in the article upon him in the *Nouvelle Biographie générale*. He left his library to the Jesuits of Dijon, in whose house his portrait was to be seen in van der Kemp's time. His fame rests upon the brilliant emendations ὃς τότ' ἐπαντιάσει for οἳ τότ' ἐπαντία σεῖ(ο) *h. Ap.* 152, μνωόμενος for ἀνωόμενος *ib.* 209, ἐγρήσσων ἐτέον τε for ἄργης· εἰνέτεόν τε *h. Herm.* 242, φεύγουσα for φθέγγουσα (confirmed by M) *ib.* 486, στόμα χείσεται for στοναχήσεται *h. Aphr.* 252, Μέλητος for μελήτης *h.* ix. 3. His other conjectures, though less certain, are remarkable: *h. Ap.* 125 χερσὶ πορέξατο for χερσιν ἐπήρξατο, 165 a lacuna between this v. and 166, 209 ὥς ποτ' for ὅπποσ', *ib.* Ἀζανίδα or Ἀβαντίδα for Ἀζαντίδα, 371 ἱερὸν for ἵμερον, *h. Herm.* 86 φώς for ὥς, 87 κομέων for δέμων, 241 στῆ or βῆ or ὡς for δή, 410 λύοντο for φύοντο, 412 οἷα τι for ῥεῖά τε, 415 πύκν' for πῦρ (accepted till recently), 412 transposed after 415, 427 αἰνέοντ' or ὑμνέοντ' for κραίνων, 471 ὀμφάς for ὀμφῆς, 473 ἐγὼ παῖς σ' ὀξύνοον for ἔγωγε παῖδ' ἀφνειόν, 497 ἑκών for ἔχων, 498 ἐπέτειλεν for ἐπέτελλεν, 524 ἐπὶ ῥυθμῷ φιλότητος for ἐπ' ἀρθμῷ καὶ φιλότητι, *h. Aphr.* 254 ὀνομαστὸν for ὀνοτατὸν (accepted in every edition but Clarke's), xix. 6 αἰχμήενθ' for αὐχμήενθ', 12 αἰγιλόεντα for ἀργινόεντα, 14 ἔξαγεν or ἔκλασεν οἷας for ἔκλαγεν οἷον, 38 ἀναΐξασα[1] λίπεν for ἀναίξας λεῖπεν, xxii. 3 Ἑλίκην τε for Ἑλικῶνα (often accepted), xxix. alters the title to εἰς Ἑστίαν καὶ Ἑρμῆν, transposes v. 9 after v. 11 (usually accepted), 5 εἰλαπίναι θνητοῖς· σοὶ δὲ for εἰλ. θνητοῖσιν ἵν' οὐ, 12 νεοῖς for νόῳ. The courage implied in attacking so many of the worst passages, and the very considerable measure of success, with no suggestion from variants or commen-

[1] ἀναΐσπασα in the ed. of 1755 is presumably a misprint.

taries, give Martin's achievement a very high place. Some notes by Isaac Casaubon have been recovered from his copy of Stephanus in the Cambridge University Library.

The seventeenth century neglected the *Hymns*, and it is not till 1711 that we come to the edition of Joshua Barnes at Cambridge. It is unnecessary to characterize this remarkable book. With all its faults it held the field as a text till the time of Wolf (1807), and the next English edition (Samuel Clarke 1740) was almost a reprint. Barnes's chief merit is probably his collection of Homeric parallels, which have since played so great a part in the study of these documents. His best conjectures are his divination of φή in δή *Hermes* 241 (repeated by Hermann and confirmed by *y*'s θῆ), μεγάλου **Κοίοιο** for μεγάλοιο **Κρόνοιο** *h. Ap.* 62, τεθυωμένα for τεθυώδεα *ib.* 184, and particularly ὕλη for ὕλην *ib.* 228. His extraordinary Latin renderings, however, exposed him to the just ridicule of Jacques Philippe D'Orville (1696–1751) the well-known collector, dilettante, and scholar. A selection of D'Orville's comments and conjectures upon the *Hymns* was published in the *Journal of Philology* xxv. 250 f.; some of his conjectures anticipate later scholars (*h. Ap.* 142 ἂν for αὖ, *h. Herm.* 497 ἔχειν for ἔχων, xix. 18 ἐπιπροιεῖσα for ἐπιπροχέουσα) and one of them is confirmed by M (*h. Ap.* 211, *tutius etiam legatur* ἅμ' ἐρεχθεῖ, for ἐρευθεῖ). He alludes to the *Hymns* also in his *Critica Vannus* 1737. Another object of D'Orville's lash was Michael Maittaire, known as an early dialectologist, who published the *Hymn to Apollo* as part of his *Miscellanea Graecorum aliquot Scriptorum Carmina cum Versione Latina et Notis*, London, 1722. He first wished to take βεβλήαται *h. Ap.* 20 as a singular. Samuel Clarke's edition (1740) was, as we said above, almost a re-issue of Barnes's, as Ernesti's

(1759–60) was of Clarke's. *ὀνοταστόν* for *ὀνόταττον h. Aphr.* 254 is its most conspicuous novelty. In the learned *Verisimilium libri duo* of Joannes Pierson, Lugd. Bat. 1752, there are a few good things. *ἀβλαύτοις* (*incredibile dictu*) was for many years read after his conjecture for *ἀβλαβέως h. Herm.* 83; *ἄγρης* is certain for *ἄκρης* xix. 15.

Down to this period ever since 1488 no single manuscript of the *Hymns* had been collated. During the three centuries scholars accomplished what they did without the suggestion of variants. It is singular that D'Orville, an industrious collector in other provinces, who travelled in Italy, visited Milan and Florence, and catalogued the Biblioteca Estense, where E was lying, should have copied down no various readings. The modern and scientific study of the *Hymns* begins with the Dutch professor David Ruhnken, who, in his *Epistola critica* to Valckenaer (1749), published the readings of two 'MSS. Regii' (the actual Paris MSS. grec 2763 = A, and 2833 = C). This book was the work of Ruhnken's youth, and it produced no immediate follower. When, however, thirty years afterwards the Moscow MS. fell into his hands, Ruhnken republished his *Epistola critica* together with a text of the new poem (1782 and 1808). This discovery fairly launched the *Hymns*; there followed in succession the works of Mitscherlich (*Hymn to Demeter* alone, 1787, with, at the end, the emendations of Nicolas Ignarra), Ilgen (1796), A. Matthiae (*Animadversiones* 1800, edition 1805), Hermann (1806), Voss (*Demeter* only, 1826), Franke (1828). Wolf's text (1807) and Bothe's text with notes (1835) are occasionally quoted. It is unnecessary to analyse these commentaries in detail. Ilgen accumulated parallels, Matthiae contributed new ideas and acute emendations (nearly all of which have at last been removed from the text),

Hermann principally grammar and a theory of the formation of the text. Franke's small book summed up this period with judgement and impartiality. In the other books a certain opposition is noticeable; Matthiae harked back to Ruhnken, while Hermann championed Ilgen.

Still with all the advance in criticism and the collection of illustrations achieved by these publications, the collation of MSS. had only increased by one Paris MS. (no. 2765 = B), examined together with Ruhnken's pair by Coray (Matthiae *Animadver.* p. ix–xi). The next and last period of investigation should have been introduced by Schneidewin (from whom we actually have some work on the *Hymns to Apollo* and *Hermes*; *v.* Baumeister p. 92). His incomplete edition was taken up by Baumeister in the well-known book (1860) which for so long was the principal authority for these documents. At this time the critical material before the world was the textus receptus, M, and ABC. Baumeister re-introduced the family from which Demetrius, unknown to mankind, had originally drawn. Schneidewin had obtained from Keil collations of D and L_1, and information of the existence of P, G, and Q (*ed.* pp. 93, 94). The discovery of L_1 turned attention to the x family, and between 1860 and 1886, the date of Abel's and Gemoll's editions, there had been collated by various hands the MSS. D, E, G, L_2, P, R_1, R_2, N, V (Abel *praef.* p. xiii, Gemoll p. vi, Hollander *op. citando*, pp. 3, 4). The x family, perhaps as the newest, dethroned M from the position it had held since its discovery, and the question was only whether E or L_1 were the better representative of x. The claims of M were re-introduced and temperately weighed by H. Hollander in his treatise *Die handschriftliche Ueberlieferung der hom. Hymnen* Leipzig 1886, which definitely settled the relation of the

MSS. All these MSS., with the addition of O, *Π*, *Γ*, S, L_3, H, J, K, and Mon., were collated for the edition of Alfred Goodwin, Oxford 1893. Since that date there have been added T, At, R_3, L_4, and the marginalia of two copies of the editio princeps (L_5 and V_2).

Subsequent literature is noticed in the commentary. It is sufficient to mention the text of E. Abel, Prag 1886, the text and commentary of Albert Gemoll, Leipzig 1886, the separate editions of the *Hymn to Demeter* by Bücheler 1869 and V. Puntoni 1896, and of that *to Hermes* by Arthur Ludwich 1890, the same scholar's *Homerische Hymnenbau* 1908 (with texts of Apollo, Hermes, Aphrodite, Pan, Ge, Helios, Selene, Dioscuri), the text and translation by H. G. Evelyn-White 1914, and the translations of the *Hymns* by J. Edgar, 1891, and Andrew Lang, 1899, the latter with a discussion on many points in connexion with the folklore of the poems. The hymns have been published at Oxford in *Homeri opera ed. D. B. Monro, Oxonii* 1896, and in *Homeri opera* vol. v, 1911.

ΟΜΗΡΟΥ ΥΜΝΟΙ

I. *Fragmenta Hymni in Bacchum*

Versus 1-9 citantur a Diodoro III, 66. 3 ; 8, 9 tantum ib. I, 15. 7, IV, 2. 4, schol. Apoll. Rhod. II, 1211, Eudoc. 932, p. 406.

οἱ μὲν γὰρ Δρακάνῳ σ', οἱ δ' Ἰκάρῳ ἠνεμοέσσῃ
φάσ', οἱ δ' ἐν Νάξῳ, δῖον γένος εἰραφιῶτα,
οἱ δέ σ' ἐπ' Ἀλφειῷ ποταμῷ βαθυδινήεντι
κυσαμένην Σεμέλην τεκέειν Διὶ τερπικεραύνῳ,
ἄλλοι δ' ἐν Θήβῃσιν ἄναξ σε λέγουσι γενέσθαι
ψευδόμενοι· σὲ δ' ἔτικτε πατὴρ ἀνδρῶν τε θεῶν τε
πολλὸν ἀπ' ἀνθρώπων κρύπτων λευκώλενον Ἥρην.
ἔστι δέ τις Νύσῃ ὕπατον ὄρος ἀνθέον ὕλῃ
τηλοῦ Φοινίκης σχεδὸν Αἰγύπτοιο ῥοάων

hic incipit fol. xxxi codicis M

καί οἱ ἀναστήσουσιν ἀγάλματα πόλλ' ἐνὶ νηοῖς.
ὣς δὲ τάμεν τρία, σοὶ πάντως τριετηρίσιν αἰεὶ
ἄνθρωποι ῥέξουσι τεληέσσας ἑκατόμβας.
ἦ καὶ κυανέῃσιν ἐπ' ὀφρύσι νεῦσε Κρονίων·
ἀμβρόσιαι δ' ἄρα χαῖται ἐπερρώσαντο ἄνακτος
κρατὸς ἀπ' ἀθανάτοιο, μέγαν δ' ἐλέλιξεν Ὄλυμπον.
ὣς εἰπὼν ἐκέλευσε καρήατι μητίετα Ζεύς.
ἵληθ' εἰραφιῶτα γυναιμανές· οἱ δέ σ' ἀοιδοὶ
ᾄδομεν ἀρχόμενοι λήγοντές τ', οὐδέ πῃ ἔστι

8 κέρας pro ὄρος scholiasta Apollonii sed cf. Ap. Rh. iv. 282 ἀνθέον (ἔνθεον MSS.) ὕλᾳ Alcman 58. 1   10 οἱ] sc. Semelae   11 ὣς δέ, τὰ μὲν τρίασοι πάντως M   τάμεν (*secuit*) nos   16 ἐπένευσε Ruhnken, sed cf. Ψ 642 Ω 326

σεῖ' ἐπιληθόμενῳ ἱερῆς μεμνῆσθαι ἀοιδῆς.
καὶ σὺ μὲν οὕτω χαῖρε Διώνυσ' εἰραφιῶτα,
σὺν μητρὶ Σεμέλῃ ἥν περ καλέουσι Θυώνην.

II. Εἰς Δημήτραν

Δήμητρ' ἠΰκομον σεμνὴν θεὰν ἄρχομ' ἀείδειν,
αὐτὴν ἠδὲ θύγατρα τανύσφυρον ἣν Ἀϊδωνεὺς
ἥρπαξεν, δῶκεν δὲ βαρύκτυπος εὐρυόπα Ζεύς,
νόσφιν Δήμητρος χρυσαόρου ἀγλαοκάρπου
παίζουσαν κούρῃσι σὺν Ὠκεανοῦ βαθυκόλποις,
ἄνθεά τ' αἰνυμένην ῥόδα καὶ κρόκον ἠδ' ἴα καλὰ
λειμῶν' ἂμ μαλακὸν καὶ ἀγαλλίδας ἠδ' ὑάκινθον
νάρκισσόν θ', ὃν φῦσε δόλον καλυκώπιδι κούρῃ
Γαῖα Διὸς βουλῇσι χαριζομένη πολυδέκτῃ
θαυμαστὸν γανόωντα, σέβας τότε πᾶσιν ἰδέσθαι
ἀθανάτοις τε θεοῖς ἠδὲ θνητοῖς ἀνθρώποις·
τοῦ καὶ ἀπὸ ῥίζης ἑκατὸν κάρα ἐξεπεφύκει,
κῶζ' ἥδιστ' ὀδμή, πᾶς δ' οὐρανὸς εὐρὺς ὕπερθε
γαῖά τε πᾶσ' ἐγέλασσε καὶ ἁλμυρὸν οἶδμα θαλάσσης.
ἡ δ' ἄρα θαμβήσασ' ὠρέξατο χερσὶν ἅμ' ἄμφω
καλὸν ἄθυρμα λαβεῖν· χάνε δὲ χθὼν εὐρυάγυια
Νύσιον ἂμ πεδίον τῇ ὄρουσεν ἄναξ πολυδέγμων
ἵπποις ἀθανάτοισι Κρόνου πολυώνυμος υἱός.
ἁρπάξας δ' ἀέκουσαν ἐπὶ χρυσέοισιν ὄχοισιν

19 *ἐπιλαθόμενοι* M, *ἐπιληθόμενον* Ruhnken cl. vii. 59. vel ex hoc vel ex alio hymno versum
αὐτῇσι σταφυλῇσι μελαίνῃσιν κομόωντες
sumpsit Crates *ἐν δευτέρῳ Ἀττικῆς διαλέκτου* ap. Athen. 653 B (p. 65 Wachsmuth): quidni et fr. homericum xxiv. p. 150 *βαρύβρομα θωύσσοντες* hinc venerit? 21 *ἣν καλέουσι* M corr. m. p.

II. *codex*: M. Tit. *τοῦ αὐτοῦ ὕμνοι εἰς τὴν δήμητραν* litteris rubris M 1 *δημήτηρ'* M corr. Ruhnken (cf. 315) 2 *και τανυσφορον ειπει[ν]* Philodem. Voll. Herc. vi. col. vii. 157 Gomperz *Szgb. Ak. Wien.* 1890. 29 7 *λειμῶνα μαλακὸν* M corr. Hermann (*ἂν* Ruhnken) 8 *ἔφυσε* Ilgen cl. 428 *καλυκώπιδι*—12 *ἀπὸ ῥί* = 𝔓 c. 4. 12–16 10 *τότε* M: *ὅτε* 𝔓: *τό γε* Goodwin 13 *κῶδις τ' ὀδμῇ* M corr. Tyrrell 17, 18 = 𝔓 c. 5. 1–3 18 *ἀθανάτα[ισι* 𝔓

ἦγ' ὀλοφυρομένην· ἰάχησε δ' ἄρ' ὄρθια φωνῇ
κεκλομένη πατέρα Κρονίδην ὕπατον καὶ ἄριστον.
οὐδέ τις ἀθανάτων οὐδὲ θνητῶν ἀνθρώπων
ἤκουσεν φωνῆς, οὐδ' ἀγλαόκαρποι ἐλαῖαι,
εἰ μὴ Περσαίου θυγάτηρ ἀταλὰ φρονέουσα
ἄϊεν ἐξ ἄντρου Ἑκάτη λιπαροκρήδεμνος,
Ἠέλιός τε ἄναξ Ὑπερίονος ἀγλαὸς υἱός,
κούρης κεκλομένης πατέρα Κρονίδην· ὁ δὲ νόσφιν
ἧστο θεῶν ἀπάνευθε πολυλλίστῳ ἐνὶ νηῷ
δέγμενος ἱερὰ καλὰ παρὰ θνητῶν ἀνθρώπων.
τὴν δ' ἀεκαζομένην ἦγεν Διὸς ἐννεσίῃσι
πατροκασίγνητος πολυσημάντωρ πολυδέγμων
ἵπποις ἀθανάτοισι Κρόνου πολυώνυμος υἱός.
ὄφρα μὲν οὖν γαῖάν τε καὶ οὐρανὸν ἀστερόεντα
λεῦσσε θεὰ καὶ πόντον ἀγάρροον ἰχθυόεντα
αὐγάς τ' ἠελίου, ἔτι δ' ἤλπετο μητέρα κεδνὴν
ὄψεσθαι καὶ φῦλα θεῶν αἰειγενετάων,
τόφρα οἱ ἐλπὶς ἔθελγε μέγαν νόον ἀχνυμένης περ·
ἤχησαν δ' ὀρέων κορυφαὶ καὶ βένθεα πόντου
φωνῇ ὑπ' ἀθανάτῃ, τῆς δ' ἔκλυε πότνια μήτηρ.
ὀξὺ δέ μιν κραδίην ἄχος ἔλλαβεν, ἀμφὶ δὲ χαίταις
ἀμβροσίαις κρήδεμνα δαΐζετο χερσὶ φίλῃσι,
κυάνεον δὲ κάλυμμα κατ' ἀμφοτέρων βάλετ' ὤμων,
σεύατο δ' ὥς τ' οἰωνὸς ἐπὶ τραφερήν τε καὶ ὑγρὴν
μαιομένη· τῇ δ' οὔ τις ἐτήτυμα μυθήσασθαι
ἤθελεν οὔτε θεῶν οὔτε θνητῶν ἀνθρώπων,
οὔτ' οἰωνῶν τις τῇ ἐτήτυμος ἄγγελος ἦλθεν.
ἐννῆμαρ μὲν ἔπειτα κατὰ χθόνα πότνια Δηὼ
στρωφᾶτ' αἰθομένας δαΐδας μετὰ χερσὶν ἔχουσα,
οὐδέ ποτ' ἀμβροσίης καὶ νέκταρος ἡδυπότοιο

28 πολυκλίστω M corr. Ruhnken cl. h. Ap. 347 ε 445 33–36 = 𝔭 c. 5. 3–6. 35 ἔτι ἤλπετο 𝔭 37 lacunam post h. v. statuit Hermann, sed cf. 127, 315, 445, h. Herm. 110, T 80 et de re Galen. vi. 106, x. 275 K. 49 ἢ δεπότοιο M corr. Ruhnken cl. ο 507

πάσσατ᾽ ἀκηχεμένη, οὐδὲ χρόα βάλλετο λουτροῖς.
ἀλλ᾽ ὅτε δὴ δεκάτη οἱ ἐπήλυθε φαινολὶς Ἠὼς
ἤντετό οἱ Ἑκάτη σέλας ἐν χείρεσσιν ἔχουσα,
καί ῥά οἱ ἀγγελέουσα ἔπος φάτο φώνησέν τε·
πότνια Δημήτηρ ὡρηφόρε ἀγλαόδωρε
τίς θεῶν οὐρανίων ἠὲ θνητῶν ἀνθρώπων
ἥρπασε Περσεφόνην καὶ σὸν φίλον ἤκαχε θυμόν;
φωνῆς γὰρ ἤκουσ᾽, ἀτὰρ οὐκ ἴδον ὀφθαλμοῖσιν
ὅς τις ἔην· σοὶ δ᾽ ὦκα λέγω νημερτέα πάντα.
ὣς ἄρ᾽ ἔφη Ἑκάτη· τὴν δ᾽ οὐκ ἠμείβετο μύθῳ
Ῥείης ἠϋκόμου θυγάτηρ, ἀλλ᾽ ὦκα σὺν αὐτῇ
ἤϊξ᾽ αἰθομένας δαΐδας μετὰ χερσὶν ἔχουσα.
Ἠέλιον δ᾽ ἵκοντο θεῶν σκοπὸν ἠδὲ καὶ ἀνδρῶν,
στὰν δ᾽ ἵππων προπάροιθε καὶ εἴρετο δῖα θεάων·
Ἠέλι᾽ αἴδεσσαί με θεὰν σύ περ, εἴ ποτε δή σευ
ἢ ἔπει ἢ ἔργῳ κραδίην καὶ θυμὸν ἴηνα.
κούρην τὴν ἔτεκον γλυκερὸν θάλος εἴδεϊ κυδρὴν
τῆς ἁδινὴν ὄπ᾽ ἄκουσα δι᾽ αἰθέρος ἀτρυγέτοιο
ὥς τε βιαζομένης, ἀτὰρ οὐκ ἴδον ὀφθαλμοῖσιν.
ἀλλὰ σὺ γὰρ δὴ πᾶσαν ἐπὶ χθόνα καὶ κατὰ πόντον
αἰθέρος ἐκ δίης καταδέρκεαι ἀκτίνεσσι,
νημερτέως μοι ἔνισπε φίλον τέκος εἴ που ὄπωπας
ὅς τις νόσφιν ἐμεῖο λαβὼν ἀέκουσαν ἀνάγκῃ
οἴχεται ἠὲ θεῶν ἢ καὶ θνητῶν ἀνθρώπων.
Ὣς φάτο, τὴν δ᾽ Ὑπεριονίδης ἠμείβετο μύθῳ·
Ῥείης ἠϋκόμου θυγάτηρ Δήμητερ ἄνασσα
εἰδήσεις· δὴ γὰρ μέγα ἅζομαι ἠδ᾽ ἐλεαίρω
ἀχνυμένην περὶ παιδὶ τανυσφύρῳ· οὐδέ τις ἄλλος
αἴτιος ἀθανάτων εἰ μὴ νεφεληγερέτα Ζεύς,

50 πᾶσατ᾽ M corr. Ruhnken 51 φαινόλη M corr. Ruhnken cl. Sapph. 95 55, 56 = 𝔭 c. 7. 3–5 55 θεὸς οὐράνιος 𝔭 56 ἥπα]φε θυμόν 𝔭 64 θέας ὕπερ M corr. Ludwich cl. 116 70 καταδέρκεται M 71 ὄπωπεν M corr. Ruhnken 72 ἐμοῖο M corr. Ruhnken 76 μέγα σ᾽ Ruhnken, sed cf. Hes. Theog. 532, Theogn. 280

ὅς μιν ἔδωκ' Ἀΐδῃ θαλερὴν κεκλῆσθαι ἄκοιτιν
αὐτοκασιγνήτῳ· ὁ δ' ὑπὸ ζόφον ἠερόεντα
ἁρπάξας ἵπποισιν ἄγεν μεγάλα ἰάχουσαν.
ἀλλὰ θεὰ κατάπαυε μέγαν γόον· οὐδέ τι σὲ χρὴ
μὰψ αὔτως ἄπλητον ἔχειν χόλον· οὔ τοι ἀεικὴς
γαμβρὸς ἐν ἀθανάτοις πολυσημάντωρ Ἀϊδωνεὺς
αὐτοκασίγνητος καὶ ὁμόσπορος· ἀμφὶ δὲ τιμὴν
ἔλλαχεν ὡς τὰ πρῶτα διάτριχα δασμὸς ἐτύχθη·
τοῖς μεταναιετάει τῶν ἔλλαχε κοίρανος εἶναι.
  Ὣς εἰπὼν ἵπποισιν ἐκέκλετο, τοὶ δ' ὑπ' ὀμοκλῆς
ῥίμφ' ἔφερον θοὸν ἅρμα τανύπτεροι ὥς τ' οἰωνοί·
τὴν δ' ἄχος αἰνότερον καὶ κύντερον ἵκετο θυμόν.
χωσαμένη δ' ἤπειτα κελαινεφέϊ Κρονίωνι
νοσφισθεῖσα θεῶν ἀγορὴν καὶ μακρὸν Ὄλυμπον
ᾤχετ' ἐπ' ἀνθρώπων πόλιας καὶ πίονα ἔργα
εἶδος ἀμαλδύνουσα πολὺν χρόνον· οὐδέ τις ἀνδρῶν
εἰσορόων γίγνωσκε βαθυζώνων τε γυναικῶν
πρίν γ' ὅτε δὴ Κελεοῖο δαΐφρονος ἵκετο δῶμα,
ὃς τότ' Ἐλευσῖνος θυοέσσης κοίρανος ἦεν.
ἕζετο δ' ἐγγὺς ὁδοῖο φίλον τετιημένη ἦτορ
Παρθενίῳ φρέατι ὅθεν ὑδρεύοντο πολῖται
ἐν σκιῇ, αὐτὰρ ὕπερθε πεφύκει θάμνος ἐλαίης,
γρηῒ παλαιγενέϊ ἐναλίγκιος, ἥ τε τόκοιο
εἴργηται δώρων τε φιλοστεφάνου Ἀφροδίτης,
οἷαί τε τροφοί εἰσι θεμιστοπόλων βασιλήων
παίδων καὶ ταμίαι κατὰ δώματα ἠχήεντα.
τὴν δὲ ἴδον Κελεοῖο Ἐλευσινίδαο θύγατρες
ἐρχόμεναι μεθ' ὕδωρ εὐήρυτον ὄφρα φέροιεν
κάλπισι χαλκείῃσι φίλα πρὸς δώματα πατρός,
τέσσαρες ὥς τε θεαὶ κουρήϊον ἄνθος ἔχουσαι,

83 cf. Paus. ii. 28. 4 *γαμβρὸν οὐ μεμπτόν*, Aph. 136   87 *μ*[illegible] *ναίεται* M corr. Voss   98 *τετιημένος* M corr. Ruhnken   99 [illegible] *θείῳ φρέατι* Wolf: *φρειάτι Παρθενίῳ* Porson: *πὰρ φρέατ' Ἀνθείῳ* T[illegible]
107 *φίλου* Matthiae et 180

Καλλιδίκη καὶ Κλεισιδίκη Δημώ τ' ἐρόεσσα
Καλλιθόη θ', ἣ τῶν προγενεστάτη ἦεν ἁπασῶν·
οὐδ' ἔγνων· χαλεποὶ δὲ θεοὶ θνητοῖσιν ὁρᾶσθαι.
ἀγχοῦ δ' ἱστάμεναι ἔπεα πτερόεντα προσηύδων·
Τίς πόθεν ἐσσὶ γρηῢ παλαιγενέων ἀνθρώπων;
τίπτε δὲ νόσφι πόληος ἀπέστιχες οὐδὲ δόμοισι
πιλνᾷς; ἔνθα γυναῖκες ἀνὰ μέγαρα σκιόεντα
τηλίκαι ὡς σύ περ ὧδε καὶ ὁπλότεραι γεγάασιν,
αἵ κέ σε φίλωνται ἠμὲν ἔπει ἠδὲ καὶ ἔργῳ.
Ὣς ἔφαθ', ἣ δ' ἐπέεσσιν ἀμείβετο πότνα θεάων·
τέκνα φίλ' αἵ τινές ἐστε γυναικῶν θηλυτεράων
χαίρετ', ἐγὼ δ' ὑμῖν μυθήσομαι· οὔ τοι ἀεικὲς
ὑμῖν εἰρομένῃσιν ἀληθέα μυθήσασθαι.
†Δὼς ἐμοί γ' ὄνομ' ἐστί· τὸ γὰρ θέτο πότνια μήτηρ·
νῦν αὖτε Κρήτηθεν ἐπ' εὐρέα νῶτα θαλάσσης
ἤλυθον οὐκ ἐθέλουσα, βίῃ δ' ἀέκουσαν ἀνάγκῃ
ἄνδρες ληϊστῆρες ἀπήγαγον. οἱ μὲν ἔπειτα
νηῒ θοῇ Θορικὸν δὲ κατέσχεθον, ἔνθα γυναῖκες
ἠπείρου ἐπέβησαν ἀολλέες ἠδὲ καὶ αὐτοὶ
δεῖπνον ἐπηρτύνοντο παρὰ πρυμνήσια νηός·
ἀλλ' ἐμοὶ οὐ δόρποιο μελίφρονος ἤρατο θυμός,
λάθρῃ δ' ὁρμηθεῖσα δι' ἠπείροιο μελαίνης
φεῦγον ὑπερφιάλους σημάντορας, ὄφρα κε μή με
ἀπριάτην περάσαντες ἐμῆς ἀπονάιατο τιμῆς.
οὕτω δεῦρ' ἱκόμην ἀλαλημένη, οὐδέ τι οἶδα
ἥ τις δὴ γαῖ' ἐστὶ καὶ οἵ τινες ἐγγεγάασιν.

109 cf. 𝔓 c. 4. 2, 3 *καλλιόπης δὲ καὶ κλ[ει]σι[δί]κης καὶ Δαμ[ω]ν[άσ]σης* 109, 110 Paus. i. 38. 3 *τὰ δὲ ἱερὰ τοῖν θεοῖν Εὔμολπος καὶ αἱ θυγατέρες δρῶσιν αἱ Κελεοῦ· καλοῦσι δὲ σφᾶς Πάμφως τε κατὰ ταὐτὰ καὶ Ὅμηρος Διογένειαν καὶ Παμμερόπην καὶ τρίτην Σαισάραν* 112 δ' add. Ruhnken 115 *πιλνᾶς* M : *πίλνασαι* Voss : *πιλνᾷ* Hermann 117 *φίλονται* M corr. Voss 118 *ἔφαν* Voss 119 *φίλα· τίνες* M corr. Fontein 120 *οὔτι* M 121 *εἰρομένοισιν* M 122 *Δωσὼ* Passow : *Δωρὶς* Ruhnken : *Δμωὶς* Mitscherlich : *Δωὶς* Hermann, Bechtel : *Δωὰς* Hermann : *Δηὼ* Fontein : *Δὼς μὲν* Brunck 132 *ἀπονοίατο* M corr. Ruhnken 134 *ἐκγεγάασιν* M corr. Ruhnken

ἀλλ' ὑμῖν μὲν πάντες Ὀλύμπια δώματ' ἔχοντες
δοῖεν κουριδίους ἄνδρας καὶ τέκνα τεκέσθαι
ὡς ἐθέλουσι τοκῆες· ἐμὲ δ' αὖτ' οἰκτείρατε κοῦραι

προφρονέως φίλα τέκνα τέων πρὸς δώμαθ' ἵκωμαι
ἀνέρος ἠδὲ γυναικός, ἵνα σφίσιν ἐργάζωμαι
πρόφρων οἷα γυναικὸς ἀφήλικος ἔργα τέτυκται·
καί κεν παῖδα νεογνὸν ἐν ἀγκοίνῃσιν ἔχουσα
καλὰ τιθηνοίμην καὶ δώματα τηρήσαιμι
καί κε λέχος στορέσαιμι μυχῷ θαλάμων εὐπήκτων
δεσπόσυνον καί κ' ἔργα διαθρήσαιμι γυναικός.
Φῆ ῥα θεά· τὴν δ' αὐτίκ' ἀμείβετο παρθένος ἀδμὴς
Καλλιδίκη Κελεοῖο θυγατρῶν εἶδος ἀρίστη·
Μαῖα θεῶν μὲν δῶρα καὶ ἀχνύμενοί περ ἀνάγκῃ
τέτλαμεν ἄνθρωποι· δὴ γὰρ πολὺ φέρτεροί εἰσιν.
ταῦτα δέ τοι σαφέως ὑποθήσομαι ἠδ' ὀνομήνω
ἀνέρας οἷσιν ἔπεστι μέγα κράτος ἐνθάδε τιμῆς,
δήμου τε προὔχουσιν, ἰδὲ κρήδεμνα πόληος
εἰρύαται βουλῇσι καὶ ἰθείῃσι δίκῃσιν.
ἠμὲν Τριπτολέμου πυκιμήδεος ἠδὲ Διόκλου
ἠδὲ Πολυξείνου καὶ ἀμύμονος Εὐμόλποιο
καὶ Δολίχου καὶ πατρὸς ἀγήνορος ἡμετέροιο
τῶν πάντων ἄλοχοι κατὰ δώματα πορσαίνουσι·
τάων οὐκ ἄν τίς σε κατὰ πρώτιστον ὀπωπὴν
εἶδος ἀτιμήσασα δόμων ἀπονοσφίσσειεν,
ἀλλά σε δέξονται· δὴ γὰρ θεοείκελός ἐσσι.
εἰ δὲ θέλεις, ἐπίμεινον, ἵνα πρὸς δώματα πατρὸς
ἔλθωμεν καὶ μητρὶ βαθυζώνῳ Μετανείρῃ

137 *ἔμ' αὖτ'* Fontein : *ἐμὲ δ' οἰκτείρατε* Ilgen : *ἐμοὶ δ' αὖτ' εἴπατε* Cobet. lacunam statuimus cuius sententia fuerit *τοῦτο δέ μοι σαφέως ὑποθήκατε ὄφρα πύθωμαι* cl. 149 138 *τέως* pro *τέων* Ruhnken 141 *ἔχουσα* ex *ἔχουσιν* M m. p. 144 *διαθήσαιμι γυναικὸς* M corr. Bothe : *διδασκήσαιμι γυναῖκας* Voss : *διασκήσαιμι* Sikes : *διαθλήσαιμι* Ignarra : *διαντλήσαιμι* Mitscherlich 153 *ἡ μὲν . . . ἡ δὲ* 154 *ἡ δὲ* M corr. Matthiae 154 Pausanias i. 38. 2 *Ὁμήρῳ δὲ ἐς μὲν τὸ γένος ἐστὶν οὐδὲν αὐτοῦ πεποιημένον, ἐπονομάζει δὲ ἀγήνορα ἐν τοῖς ἔπεσι τὸν Εὔμολπον,* unde *ἀγήνορος* hic *ἀμύμονος* 155 Ruhnken

εἴπωμεν τάδε πάντα διαμπερές, αἴ κέ σ' ἀνώγῃ
ἡμέτερον δ' ἰέναι μηδ' ἄλλων δώματ' ἐρευνᾶν.
τηλύγετος δέ οἱ υἱὸς ἐνὶ μεγάρῳ εὐπήκτῳ
ὀψίγονος τρέφεται, πολυεύχετος ἀσπάσιός τε.
εἰ τόν γ' ἐκθρέψαιο καὶ ἥβης μέτρον ἵκοιτο
ῥεῖά κέ τίς σε ἰδοῦσα γυναικῶν θηλυτεράων
ζηλώσαι· τόσα κέν τοι ἀπὸ θρεπτήρια δοίη.
  Ὣς ἔφαθ'· ἡ δ' ἐπένευσε καρήατι, ταὶ δὲ φαεινὰ
πλησάμεναι ὕδατος φέρον ἄγγεα κυδιάουσαι.
ῥίμφα δὲ πατρὸς ἵκοντο μέγαν δόμον, ὦκα δὲ μητρὶ
ἔννεπον ὡς εἶδόν τε καὶ ἔκλυον. ἡ δὲ μάλ' ὦκα
ἐλθούσας ἐκέλευε καλεῖν ἐπ' ἀπείρονι μισθῷ.
αἱ δ' ὥς τ' ἢ ἔλαφοι ἢ πόρτιες ἤαρος ὥρῃ
ἅλλοντ' ἂν λειμῶνα κορεσσάμεναι φρένα φορβῇ,
ὣς αἱ ἐπισχόμεναι ἑανῶν πτύχας ἱμεροέντων
ἤϊξαν κοίλην κατ' ἀμαξιτόν, ἀμφὶ δὲ χαῖται
ὤμοις ἀΐσσοντο κροκηΐῳ ἄνθει ὁμοῖαι.
τέτμον δ' ἐγγὺς ὁδοῦ κυδρὴν θεὰν ἔνθα πάρος περ
κάλλιπον· αὐτὰρ ἔπειτα φίλα πρὸς δώματα πατρὸς
ἡγεῦνθ', ἡ δ' ἄρ' ὄπισθε φίλον τετιημένη ἦτορ
στεῖχε κατὰ κρῆθεν κεκαλυμμένη, ἀμφὶ δὲ πέπλος
κυάνεος ῥαδινοῖσι θεᾶς ἐλελίζετο ποσσίν.
αἶψα δὲ δώμαθ' ἵκοντο διοτρεφέος Κελεοῖο,
βὰν δὲ δι' αἰθούσης ἔνθα σφίσι πότνια μήτηρ
ἧστο παρὰ σταθμὸν τέγεος πύκα ποιητοῖο
παῖδ' ὑπὸ κόλπῳ ἔχουσα νέον θάλος· αἱ δὲ παρ' αὐτὴν
ἔδραμον, ἡ δ' ἄρ' ἐπ' οὐδὸν ἔβη ποσὶ καί ῥα μελάθρου
κῦρε κάρη, πλῆσεν δὲ θύρας σέλαος θείοιο.
τὴν δ' αἰδώς τε σέβας τε ἰδὲ χλωρὸν δέος εἷλεν·
εἶξε δέ οἱ κλισμοῖο καὶ ἑδριάασθαι ἄνωγεν.

174 αἴδ' ὥς τοι M corr. Brunck εἴαρος Ruhnken; cf. 401 180 φίλου Matthiae ut 107 182 κατ' ἄκρηθεν M corr. Ruhnken 183 θεῆς M corr. Ruhnken

ἀλλ' οὐ Δημήτηρ ὡρηφόρος ἀγλαόδωρος
ἤθελεν ἑδριάασθαι ἐπὶ κλισμοῖο φαεινοῦ,
ἀλλ' ἀκέουσα ἔμιμνε κατ' ὄμματα καλὰ βαλοῦσα,
πρίν γ' ὅτε δή οἱ ἔθηκεν Ἰάμβη κέδν' εἰδυῖα
πηκτὸν ἕδος, καθύπερθε δ' ἐπ' ἀργύφεον βάλε κῶας.
ἔνθα καθεζομένη προκατέσχετο χερσὶ καλύπτρην·
δηρὸν δ' ἄφθογγος τετιημένη ἧστ' ἐπὶ δίφρου,
οὐδέ τιν' οὔτ' ἔπεϊ προσπτύσσετο οὔτε τι ἔργῳ,
ἀλλ' ἀγέλαστος ἄπαστος ἐδητύος ἠδὲ ποτῆτος
ἧστο πόθῳ μινύθουσα βαθυζώνοιο θυγατρός,
πρίν γ' ὅτε δὴ χλεύῃς μιν Ἰάμβη κέδν' εἰδυῖα
πολλὰ παρασκώπτουσ' ἐτρέψατο πότνιαν ἁγνὴν
μειδῆσαι γελάσαι τε καὶ ἵλαον σχεῖν θυμόν·
ἣ δή οἱ καὶ ἔπειτα μεθύστερον εὔαδεν ὀργαῖς.
τῇ δὲ δέπας Μετάνειρα δίδου μελιηδέος οἴνου
πλήσασ', ἣ δ' ἀνένευσ'· οὐ γὰρ θεμιτόν οἱ ἔφασκε
πίνειν οἶνον ἐρυθρόν, ἄνωγε δ' ἄρ' ἄλφι καὶ ὕδωρ
δοῦναι μίξασαν πιέμεν γλήχωνι τερείνῃ.
ἣ δὲ κυκεῶ τεύξασα θεᾷ πόρεν ὡς ἐκέλευε·
δεξαμένη δ' ὁσίης ἕνεκεν πολυπότνια Δηὼ

τῇσι δὲ μύθων ἦρχεν ἐΰζωνος Μετάνειρα·
Χαῖρε γύναι, ἐπεὶ οὔ σε κακῶν ἄπ' ἔολπα τοκήων
ἔμμεναι ἀλλ' ἀγαθῶν· ἐπί τοι πρέπει ὄμμασιν αἰδὼς
καὶ χάρις, ὡς εἴ πέρ τε θεμιστοπόλων βασιλήων.
ἀλλὰ θεῶν μὲν δῶρα καὶ ἀχνύμενοί περ ἀνάγκῃ
τέτλαμεν ἄνθρωποι· ἐπὶ γὰρ ζυγὸς αὐχένι κεῖται.
νῦν δ' ἐπεὶ ἵκεο δεῦρο, παρέσσεται ὅσσα τ' ἐμοί περ.
παῖδα δέ μοι τρέφε τόνδε, τὸν ὀψίγονον καὶ ἄελπτον

192 *ὡραφόρος* M corr. Ruhnken 196 *κῶα* M corr. Ruhnken 202 *χλεύης* M corr. Ruhnken 203 *παρασκώπτουσα τρέψατο* M corr. Voss 205 *ἤδη* M, *ἔβαδεν* M corr. Ruhnken 207 *οἱ*] *τοι* M corr. Matthiae 211 lacunam statuimus cuius sententia fuerit *ἔκπιεν, ἡ δὲ λαβοῦσα δέπας θέτο ἔνθ' ἀνάειρε* pro *ἕνεκεν* *ἔλαχεν* Schaefer: *ἐπέβη* Voss *πίε πότνια* Franke

ὤπασαν ἀθάνατοι, πολυάρητος δέ μοί ἐστιν.
εἰ τόν γε θρέψαιο καὶ ἥβης μέτρον ἵκοιτο
ἦ ῥά κέ τίς σε ἰδοῦσα γυναικῶν θηλυτεράων
ζηλώσαι· τόσα κέν τοι ἀπὸ θρεπτήρια δοίην.
Τὴν δ' αὖτε προσέειπεν ἐϋστέφανος Δημήτηρ·
καὶ σὺ γύναι μάλα χαῖρε, θεοὶ δέ τοι ἐσθλὰ πόροιεν.
παῖδα δέ τοι πρόφρων ὑποδέξομαι ὥς με κελεύεις·
θρέψω, κοὔ μιν ἔολπα κακοφραδίῃσι τιθήνης
οὔτ' ἄρ' ἐπηλυσίη δηλήσεται οὔθ' ὑποτάμνον·
οἶδα γὰρ ἀντίτομον μέγα φέρτερον ὑλοτόμοιο,
οἶδα δ' ἐπηλυσίης πολυπήμονος ἐσθλὸν ἐρυσμόν.
Ὣς ἄρα φωνήσασα θυώδεϊ δέξατο κόλπῳ
χερσίν τ' ἀθανάτοισι· γεγήθει δὲ φρένα μήτηρ.
ὣς ἡ μὲν Κελεοῖο δαΐφρονος ἀγλαὸν υἱὸν
Δημοφόωνθ', ὃν ἔτικτεν ἐΰζωνος Μετάνειρα,
ἔτρεφεν ἐν μεγάροις· ὁ δ' ἀέξετο δαίμονι ἶσος
οὔτ' οὖν σῖτον ἔδων, οὐ θησάμενος ⟨γάλα μητρὸς⟩
Δημήτηρ
χρίεσκ' ἀμβροσίῃ ὡς εἰ θεοῦ ἐκγεγαῶτα,
ἡδὺ καταπνείουσα καὶ ἐν κόλποισιν ἔχουσα·
νύκτας δὲ κρύπτεσκε πυρὸς μένει ἠΰτε δαλὸν
λάθρα φίλων γονέων· τοῖς δὲ μέγα θαῦμ' ἐτέτυκτο
ὡς προθαλὴς τελέθεσκε, θεοῖσι δὲ ἄντα ἐῴκει.
καί κέν μιν ποίησεν ἀγήρων τ' ἀθάνατόν τε
εἰ μὴ ἄρ' ἀφραδίῃσιν ἐΰζωνος Μετάνειρα
νύκτ' ἐπιτηρήσασα θυώδεος ἐκ θαλάμοιο
σκέψατο· κώκυσεν δὲ καὶ ἄμφω πλήξατο μηρὼ
δείσασ' ᾧ περὶ παιδὶ καὶ ἀάσθη μέγα θυμῷ,

220 *πολυήρατος* M corr. Ruhnken 228 *ἐπηλσίησι δηλήσεται οὔθ' ὑποταμνὸν* M : *ἐπηλυσίη* Ruhnken, cl. Herm. 37 pro *ὑποταμνὸν ὑποταμνῶν* Ignarra : *οὔτε τομαῖον* Voss : *ὑπόθαμνον* et *ὀρόδαμνος* commendat Buecheler. subcidens vermis est 229 *ὑλοτόμοιο*] *οὐλοτόμοιο* Voss. et silvicida vermis 236 *θησάμενος δημήτηρ* M. lacunam a Mitscherlichio statutam explevit Hermann, cf. Herm. 267 237 *ἀλλά μιν ἠματίη μὲν ἐυστέφανος Δημήτηρ* Stoll 240 *λάθρα ἑῶν* Spitzner

καί ῥ' ὀλοφυρομένη ἔπεα πτερόεντα προσηύδα·
Τέκνον Δημοφόων ξείνη σε πυρὶ ἔνι πολλῷ
κρύπτει, ἐμοὶ δὲ γόον καὶ κήδεα λυγρὰ τίθησιν.
Ὣς φάτ' ὀδυρομένη· τῆς δ' ἄϊε δῖα θεάων.
τῇ δὲ χολωσαμένη καλλιστέφανος Δημήτηρ
παῖδα φίλον, τὸν ἄελπτον ἐνὶ μεγάροισιν ἔτικτε,
χείρεσσ' ἀθανάτῃσιν ἀπὸ ἕο θῆκε πέδον δὲ
ἐξανελοῦσα πυρὸς θυμῷ κοτέσασα μάλ' αἰνῶς,
καί ῥ' ἄμυδις προσέειπεν ἐΰζωνον Μετάνειραν·
Νήϊδες ἄνθρωποι καὶ ἀφράδμονες οὔτ' ἀγαθοῖο
αἶσαν ἐπερχομένου προγνώμεναι οὔτε κακοῖο·
καὶ σὺ γὰρ ἀφραδίῃσι τεῇς μήκιστον ἀάσθης.
ἴστω γὰρ θεῶν ὅρκος ἀμείλικτον Στυγὸς ὕδωρ
ἀθάνατόν κέν τοι καὶ ἀγήραον ἤματα πάντα
παῖδα φίλον ποίησα καὶ ἄφθιτον ὤπασα τιμήν·
νῦν δ' οὐκ ἔσθ' ὥς κεν θάνατον καὶ κῆρας ἀλύξαι.
τιμὴ δ' ἄφθιτος αἰὲν ἐπέσσεται οὕνεκα γούνων
ἡμετέρων ἐπέβη καὶ ἐν ἀγκοίνῃσιν ἴαυσεν.
ὥρῃσιν δ' ἄρα τῷ γε περιπλομένων ἐνιαυτῶν
παῖδες Ἐλευσινίων πόλεμον καὶ φύλοπιν αἰνὴν
αἰὲν ἐν ἀλλήλοισι συνάξουσ' ἤματα πάντα.
εἰμὶ δὲ Δημήτηρ τιμάοχος, ἥ τε μέγιστον
ἀθανάτοις θνητοῖσί τ' ὄνεαρ καὶ χάρμα τέτυκται.
ἀλλ' ἄγε μοι νηόν τε μέγαν καὶ βωμὸν ὑπ' αὐτῷ

248, 249 = 𝔭 c. 6. 12–14   248 πυρῇ ἔνι πο]λλῆ 𝔭 nescio an recte; cf. 287 η 13 ι 251 Herod. ii. 39   253 ἄπω M corr. Matthiae   256-262 = 𝔭 c. 6 15–20 qui ita se habent:

ἄφρονε[s] ἄνθ[ρω]ποι δυστλήμονες [οὔτε κακοῖο
ἐπ]ερ[χομένου πρ]ογνώμονες οὔτ' ἀ[γ]α[θοῖο
γ]ὰρ ἀβραδί[ῃs]μος πολὺ πείρατι νυκτὸς
τη εκ.α ἥρπασεν ἀ̣γ̣ήρ
νῦν δ' οὐ]κ ἔσθ' ὥς [κεν θά]νατον [. . . .

cf. et Orphica fr. 76 Abel.   257 προγνώμενοι M corr. Matthiae: -ες 𝔭   258 νήκεστον Voss cl. Hes. Opp. 283   259-261 om. 𝔭   261 ποιήσασα M corr. Ruhnken   263 ἄφθιτον M corr. Ruhnken   267 συναυξήσουσ' M corr. Ignarra   268 𝔭 c. 7. 2, 3 εἰμὶ δὲ Δη[μ]ήτηρ ὡρηφόρ[ος ἀγλαό]δωρος, cf. 54   269 ἀθανάτοις θνητοῖσιν ὔνειαρ M: θνητοῖσί τ' Ruhnken: ὄνεαρ Ilgen

τευχόντων πᾶς δῆμος ὑπαὶ πόλιν αἰπύ τε τεῖχος
Καλλιχόρου καθύπερθεν ἐπὶ προὔχοντι κολωνῷ·
ὄργια δ' αὐτὴ ἐγὼν ὑποθήσομαι ὡς ἂν ἔπειτα
εὐαγέως ἕρδοντες ἐμὸν νόον ἱλάσκοισθε.
Ὣς εἰποῦσα θεὰ μέγεθος καὶ εἶδος ἄμειψε
γῆρας ἀπωσαμένη, περί τ' ἀμφί τε κάλλος ἄητο·
ὀδμὴ δ' ἱμερόεσσα θυηέντων ἀπὸ πέπλων
σκίδνατο, τῆλε δὲ φέγγος ἀπὸ χροὸς ἀθανάτοιο
λάμπε θεᾶς, ξανθαὶ δὲ κόμαι κατενήνοθεν ὤμους,
αὐγῆς δ' ἐπλήσθη πυκινὸς δόμος ἀστεροπῆς ὥς.
βῆ δὲ διὲκ μεγάρων, τῆς δ' αὐτίκα γούνατ' ἔλυντο,
δηρὸν δ' ἄφθογγος γένετο χρόνον, οὐδέ τι παιδὸς
μνήσατο τηλυγέτοιο ἀπὸ δαπέδου ἀνελέσθαι.
τοῦ δὲ κασίγνηται φωνὴν ἐσάκουσαν ἐλεεινήν,
κὰδ δ' ἄρ' ἀπ' εὐστρώτων λεχέων θόρον· ἡ μὲν ἔπειτα
παῖδ' ἀνὰ χερσὶν ἑλοῦσα ἑῷ ἐγκάτθετο κόλπῳ,
ἡ δ' ἄρα πῦρ ἀνέκαι', ἡ δ' ἔσσυτο πόσσ' ἁπαλοῖσι
μητέρ' ἀναστήσουσα θυώδεος ἐκ θαλάμοιο.
ἀγρόμεναι δέ μιν ἀμφὶς ἐλούεον ἀσπαίροντα
ἀμφαγαπαζόμεναι· τοῦ δ' οὐ μειλίσσετο θυμός·
χειρότεραι γὰρ δή μιν ἔχον τροφοὶ ἠδὲ τιθῆναι.
Αἳ μὲν παννύχιαι κυδρὴν θεὸν ἱλάσκοντο
δείματι παλλόμεναι· ἅμα δ' ἠοῖ φαινομένηφιν
εὐρυβίῃ Κελεῷ νημερτέα μυθήσαντο,
ὡς ἐπέτελλε θεὰ καλλιστέφανος Δημήτηρ.
αὐτὰρ ὅ γ' εἰς ἀγορὴν καλέσας πολυπείρονα λαὸν
ἤνωγ' ἠϋκόμῳ Δημήτερι πίονα νηὸν
ποιῆσαι καὶ βωμὸν ἐπὶ προὔχοντι κολωνῷ.
οἱ δὲ μάλ' αἶψ' ἐπίθοντο καὶ ἔκλυον αὐδήσαντος,
τεῦχον δ' ὡς ἐπέτελλ'· ὁ δ' ἀέξετο δαίμονος αἴσῃ.
αὐτὰρ ἐπεὶ τέλεσαν καὶ ἐρώησαν καμάτοιο

274 *νηὸν* M corr. Ruhnken 279 *θεῆς* M corr. Hermann 280 *αὐτῆς* M corr. Ruhnken 287 *πυρὰν ἔκαι'* M corr. Ruhnken, v. 248 299 *αἶψα πίθοντο* M ante corr. 301 *ἐτέλεσσαν* M corr. Valckenaer

βάν ῥ' ἴμεν οἶκαδ' ἕκαστος· ἀτὰρ ξανθὴ Δημήτηρ
ἔνθα καθεζομένη μακάρων ἀπὸ νόσφιν ἁπάντων
μίμνε πόθῳ μινύθουσα βαθυζώνοιο θυγατρός.
αἰνότατον δ' ἐνιαυτὸν ἐπὶ χθόνα πουλυβότειραν
ποίησ' ἀνθρώποις καὶ κύντατον, οὐδέ τι γαῖα
σπέρμ' ἀνίει· κρύπτεν γὰρ ἐϋστέφανος Δημήτηρ.
πολλὰ δὲ καμπύλ' ἄροτρα μάτην βόες ἕλκον ἀρούραις,
πολλὸν δὲ κρῖ λευκὸν ἐτώσιον ἔμπεσε γαίῃ.
καί νύ κε πάμπαν ὄλεσσε γένος μερόπων ἀνθρώπων
λιμοῦ ὑπ' ἀργαλέης, γεράων τ' ἐρικυδέα τιμὴν
καὶ θυσιῶν ἤμερσεν Ὀλύμπια δώματ' ἔχοντας,
εἰ μὴ Ζεὺς ἐνόησεν ἑῷ τ' ἐφράσσατο θυμῷ.
Ἶριν δὲ πρῶτον χρυσόπτερον ὦρσε καλέσσαι
Δήμητρ' ἠΰκομον πολυήρατον εἶδος ἔχουσαν.
ὣς ἔφαθ'· ἡ δὲ Ζηνὶ κελαινεφέϊ Κρονίωνι
πείθετο καὶ μεσσηγὺ διέδραμεν ὦκα πόδεσσιν.
ἵκετο δὲ πτολίεθρον Ἐλευσῖνος θυοέσσης,
εὗρεν δ' ἐν νηῷ Δημήτερα κυανόπεπλον,
καί μιν φωνήσασ' ἔπεα πτερόεντα προσηύδα·
Δήμητερ καλέει σε πατὴρ Ζεὺς ἄφθιτα εἰδὼς
ἐλθέμεναι μετὰ φῦλα θεῶν αἰειγενετάων.
ἀλλ' ἴθι, μηδ' ἀτέλεστον ἐμὸν ἔπος ἐκ Διὸς ἔστω.
Ὣς φάτο λισσομένη· τῆς δ' οὐκ ἐπεπείθετο θυμός.
αὖτις ἔπειτα πατὴρ μάκαρας θεοὺς αἰὲν ἐόντας
πάντας ἐπιπροΐαλλεν· ἀμοιβηδὶς δὲ κιόντες
κίκλησκον καὶ πολλὰ δίδον περικαλλέα δῶρα,
τιμάς θ' ἅς κ' †ἐθέλοιτο† μετ' ἀθανάτοισιν ἑλέσθαι·
ἀλλ' οὔ τις πεῖσαι δύνατο φρένας οὐδὲ νόημα
θυμῷ χωομένης, στερεῶς δ' ἠναίνετο μύθους.

302 *βὰν δ'* M corr. Wyttenbach 304 *θυγατρός* ex *γυναικός* corr. M 308 *εἷλκον* M 314 *ἥρην* M corr. Ruhnken, contra *ἥρην* pro *Ἶριν* Bentleius ad Ar. Av. 575 317 *τὸ μεσηγὺ* Ilgen cl. Ap. 108 325 *πατὴρ* add. Valckenaer, cf. 345 328 *κεν ἕλοιτο μετ' ἀθανάτοισι θεοῖσι* Hermann cl. 444 : *κε βόλοιτο* nos cl. Λ 319 329 *ἠδὲ* Brunck mutatione facili (E 484 O 409 P 42 Ω 750 al.) sed vix necessaria

οὐ μὲν γάρ ποτ' ἔφασκε θυώδεος Οὐλύμποιο
πρίν γ' ἐπιβήσεσθαι, οὐ πρὶν γῆς καρπὸν ἀνήσειν,
πρὶν ἴδοι ὀφθαλμοῖσιν ἑὴν εὐώπιδα κούρην.
Αὐτὰρ ἐπεὶ τό γ' ἄκουσε βαρύκτυπος εὐρύοπα Ζεὺς
εἰς Ἔρεβος πέμψε χρυσόρραπιν Ἀργειφόντην,
ὄφρ' Ἀΐδην μαλακοῖσι παραιφάμενος ἐπέεσσιν
ἁγνὴν Περσεφόνειαν ἀπὸ ζόφου ἠερόεντος
ἐς φάος ἐξαγάγοι μετὰ δαίμονας, ὄφρα ἑ μήτηρ
ὀφθαλμοῖσιν ἰδοῦσα μεταλήξειε χόλοιο.
Ἑρμῆς δ' οὐκ ἀπίθησεν, ἄφαρ δ' ὑπὸ κεύθεα γαίης
ἐσσυμένως κατόρουσε λιπὼν ἕδος Οὐλύμποιο.
τέτμε δὲ τόν γε ἄνακτα δόμων ἔντοσθεν ἐόντα
ἥμενον ἐν λεχέεσσι σὺν αἰδοίῃ παρακοίτι
πόλλ' ἀεκαζομένῃ μητρὸς πόθῳ· ἡ δ' ἀποτηλοῦ
ἔργοις θεῶν μακάρων ⏑⏑– μητίσετο βουλῇ.
ἀγχοῦ δ' ἱστάμενος προσέφη κρατὺς Ἀργειφόντης·
Ἅιδη κυανοχαῖτα καταφθιμένοισιν ἀνάσσων
Ζεύς σε πατὴρ ἤνωγεν ἀγαυὴν Περσεφόνειαν
ἐξαγαγεῖν Ἐρέβευσφι μετὰ σφέας, ὄφρα ἑ μήτηρ
ὀφθαλμοῖσιν ἰδοῦσα χόλου καὶ μήνιος αἰνῆς
ἀθανάτοις παύσειεν· ἐπεὶ μέγα μήδεται ἔργον
φθῖσαι φῦλ' ἀμενηνὰ χαμαιγενέων ἀνθρώπων
σπέρμ' ὑπὸ γῆς κρύπτουσα, καταφθινύθουσα δὲ τιμὰς
ἀθανάτων. ἡ δ' αἰνὸν ἔχει χόλον, οὐδὲ θεοῖσι
μίσγεται, ἀλλ' ἀπάνευθε θυώδεος ἔνδοθι νηοῦ
ἧσται, Ἐλευσῖνος κραναὸν πτολίεθρον ἔχουσα.

332 ἐπιβήσεσθ' M corr. Voss 344 ἠδ' ἐπ' ἀτλήτων M : ἀποτηλοῦ satis probabiliter Ilgen, cf. ἀπάνευθε 355 : ἔτ' ἄπλητον idem : ἀτελέστων Ruhnken : ἔτ' ἄληκτον Voss : ἐπ' ἀλιτρῶν seu ἀπατηλῶν Mitscherlich : ἐπ' ἀλάστοις Hermann : ἐπὶ ἔργοις | ἀτλήτοισι C. Burney in marg. ed. Ruhnkenianae 345 ἔργοις θεῶν] ὀργισθεῖσα Ignarra : excidisse videtur anapaestus cl. 325, ex. gr. θάνατον (O 349), τι κακὸν (Ap. 325 a). ἔργοις ἀθανάτων μακάρων μηνίετο βουλήν Ruhnken : ἔργοισιν μακάρων ὀλοὴν Hermann : δεινὴν μηνίετο βουλὴν Voss 348 σε] με Wyttenbach 351 λήξειεν C. Burney, Hermann cl. 410

Ὣς φάτο· μείδησεν δὲ ἄναξ ἐνέρων Ἀϊδωνεὺς
ὀφρύσιν, οὐδ' ἀπίθησε Διὸς βασιλῆος ἐφετμῆς.
ἐσσυμένως δ' ἐκέλευσε δαΐφρονι Περσεφονείῃ·
ἔρχεο Περσεφόνη παρὰ μητέρα κυανόπεπλον
ἤπιον ἐν στήθεσσι μένος καὶ θυμὸν ἔχουσα,
μηδέ τι δυσθύμαινε λίην περιώσιον ἄλλων.
οὔ τοι ἐν ἀθανάτοισιν ἀεικὴς ἔσσομ' ἀκοίτης
αὐτοκασίγνητος πατρὸς Διός· ἔνθα δ' ἐοῦσα
δεσπόσσεις πάντων ὁπόσα ζώει τε καὶ ἕρπει,
τιμὰς δὲ σχήσησθα μετ' ἀθανάτοισι μεγίστας,
τῶν δ' ἀδικησάντων τίσις ἔσσεται ἤματα πάντα
οἵ κεν μὴ θυσίαισι τεὸν μένος ἱλάσκωνται
εὐαγέως ἔρδοντες ἐναίσιμα δῶρα τελοῦντες.
Ὣς φάτο· γήθησεν δὲ περίφρων Περσεφόνεια,
καρπαλίμως δ' ἀνόρουσ' ὑπὸ χάρματος· αὐτὰρ ὅ γ' αὐτὸς
ῥοιῆς κόκκον ἔδωκε φαγεῖν μελιηδέα λάθρῃ
ἀμφὶ ἓ νωμήσας, ἵνα μὴ μένοι ἤματα πάντα
αὖθι παρ' αἰδοίῃ Δημήτερι κυανοπέπλῳ.
ἵππους δὲ προπάροιθεν ὑπὸ χρυσέοισιν ὄχεσφιν
ἔντυεν ἀθανάτους πολυσημάντωρ Ἀϊδωνεύς.
ἣ δ' ὀχέων ἐπέβη, παρὰ δὲ κρατὺς Ἀργειφόντης
ἡνία καὶ μάστιγα λαβὼν μετὰ χερσὶ φίλῃσι
σεῦε διὲκ μεγάρων· τὼ δ' οὐκ ἄκοντε πετέσθην.
ῥίμφα δὲ μακρὰ κέλευθα διήνυσαν, οὐδὲ θάλασσα
οὔθ' ὕδωρ ποταμῶν οὔτ' ἄγκεα ποιήεντα
ἵππων ἀθανάτων οὔτ' ἄκριες ἔσχεθον ὁρμήν,
ἀλλ' ὑπὲρ αὐτάων βαθὺν ἠέρα τέμνον ἰόντες.
στῆσε δ' ἄγων ὅθι μίμνεν ἐϋστέφανος Δημήτηρ
νηοῖο προπάροιθε θυώδεος· ἣ δὲ ἰδοῦσα

357 ἀνέρων M corr. Ruhnken: eadem tria verba I. G. Sic. Ital. 1842 362 θυσθύμαινε M corr. Ruhnken 363 ἄκοιτις M corr. Ruhnken 364 ἰοῦσα M corr. Ruhnken 366 σχήσεισθα Boissonade alii 368 ἱλάσκονται M corr. Valckenaer 373 ἀμφί ἑ Ruhnken alii: ἀμφὶς Santen

ἤϊξ' ἠΰτε μαινὰς ὄρος κάτα δάσκιον ὕλῃς.
Περσεφόνη δ' ἑτέρ[ωθεν ἐπεὶ ἴδεν ὄμματα καλὰ]
μητρὸς ἑῆς κατ' [ἄρ' ἥ γ' ὄχεα προλιποῦσα καὶ ἵππους]
ἆλτο θέει[ν, δειρῇ δέ οἱ ἔμπεσεν ἀμφιχυθεῖσα·]
τῇ δὲ [φίλην ἔτι παῖδα ἑῆς μετὰ χερσὶν ἐχούσῃ]
α[ἶψα δόλον θυμός τιν' ὀΐσατο, τρέσσε δ' ἄρ' αἰνῶς]
πα[υ]ομ[ένη φιλότητος, ἄφαρ δ' ἐρεείνετο μύθῳ·]
Τέκνον μή ῥά τί μοι σ[ύ γε πάσσαο νέρθεν ἐοῦσα]
βρώμης; ἐξαύδα, [μὴ κεῦθ', ἵνα εἴδομεν ἄμφω·]
ὣς μὲν γάρ κ' ἀνιοῦσα π[αρὰ στυγεροῦ 'Αΐδαο]
καὶ παρ' ἐμοὶ καὶ πατρὶ κελ[αινεφέϊ Κρονίωνι]
ναιετάοις πάντεσσι τετιμ[ένη ἀθανάτοι]σιν.
εἰ δέ, πτᾶσα πάλιν ⟨σύ γ'⟩ ἰοῦσ' ὑπ[ὸ κεύθεσι γαίης]
οἰκήσεις ὡρέων τρίτατον μέρ[ος εἰς ἐνιαυτόν,]
τὰς δὲ δύω παρ' ἐμοί τε καὶ [ἄλλοις ἀθανά]τοισιν.
ὁππότε δ' ἄνθεσι γαῖ' εὐώδε[σιν] ἠαρινο[ῖσι]
παντοδαποῖς θάλλει, τότ' ἀπὸ ζόφου ἠερόεντος
αὖτις ἄνει μέγα θαῦμα θεοῖς θνητοῖς τ' ἀνθρώποις.

καὶ τίνι σ' ἐξαπάτησε δόλῳ κρατερ[ὸς Πολυδ]έγμων;
Τὴν δ' αὖ Περσεφόνη περικαλλὴς ἀντίον ηὔδα·
τοιγὰρ ἐγώ σοι μῆτερ ἐρέω νημερτέα πάντα·
εὖτέ μοι 'Ερμῆς ἦ[λθ]' ἐριούνιος ἄγγελος ὠκὺς
πὰρ πατέρος Κρονίδαο καὶ ἄλλων οὐρανιώνων

386 *ὕλης* M: cf. Anacreon 51, Anacreontea 32. 7, Moschus iii. 89 Hecataeus 172 *οὔρεα δασέα ὕλῃσι*, C. R. 1906. 290: *ὕλῃ* Ruhnken 387 lacunam quae versus 387–405, 462–478 hausit explevit scriba s. xvi (*m*): quae dedimus supplementa Alfredi Goodwin ingenio plerumque debentur 392 *παομένη* leg. E. Maunde Thompson 394 *βρώμῃς* M corr. Voss *μὴ κεῦθ'* Ilgen *ἵνα εἴδομεν ἄμφω* Hermann 395 *κε νέουσα* M corr. Ruhnken 396 suppl. *m* 397 *ναιετάεις* M (ss. *οι*) *τετιμημένη* *m* corr. Ruhnken 398 *εἰ δὲ πτᾶσα πάλιν ἰοῦσ' ὑπ* M reposuimus C. R. 1901. 97 *ὑπὸ κεύθεσι γαίης* *m* 399 *ὀρέων* M corr. Ilgen *μοῖραν εἰς ἐνιαυτὸν* *m* sed *μέρ* M 400 suppl. *m* 401 suppl. *m* 403 *ἀνεῖ* M corr. Wyttenbach lacunam statuit Ruhnken: *εἰπὲ δὲ πῶς σ' ἥρπαξεν ὑπὸ ζόφον ἠερόεντα* suppl. Goodwin 404 *καί τιν' ἐξαπάτησε* M corr. Ruhnken 407 suppl. Mitscherlich

ἐλθεῖν ἐξ Ἐρέβευς, ἵνα μ' ὀφθαλμοῖσιν ἰδοῦσα
λήξαις ἀθανάτοισι χόλου καὶ μήνιος αἰνῆς,
αὐτὰρ ἐγὼν ἀνόρουσ' ὑπὸ χάρματος, αὐτὰρ ὁ λάθρῃ
ἔμβαλέ μοι ῥοιῆς κόκκον, μελιηδέ' ἐδωδήν,
ἄκουσαν δὲ βίῃ με προσηνάγκασσε πάσασθαι.
ὡς δέ μ' ἀναρπάξας Κρονίδεω πυκινὴν διὰ μῆτιν
ᾤχετο πατρὸς ἐμοῖο φέρων ὑπὸ κεύθεα γαίης
ἐξερέω καὶ πάντα διίξομαι ὡς ἐρεείνεις.
ἡμεῖς μὲν μάλα πᾶσαι ἀν' ἱμερτὸν λειμῶνα,
Λευκίππη Φαινώ τε καὶ Ἠλέκτρη καὶ Ἰάνθη
καὶ Μελίτη Ἰάχη τε Ῥόδειά τε Καλλιρόη τε
Μηλόβοσίς τε Τύχη τε καὶ Ὠκυρόη καλυκῶπις
Χρυσηΐς τ' Ἰάνειρά τ' Ἀκάστη τ' Ἀδμήτη τε
καὶ Ῥοδόπη Πλουτώ τε καὶ ἱμερόεσσα Καλυψὼ
καὶ Στὺξ Οὐρανίη τε Γαλαξαύρη τ' ἐρατεινὴ
Παλλάς τ' ἐγρεμάχη καὶ Ἄρτεμις ἰοχέαιρα
παίζομεν ἠδ' ἄνθεα δρέπομεν χείρεσσ' ἐρόεντα,
μίγδα κρόκον τ' ἀγανὸν καὶ ἀγαλλίδας ἠδ' ὑάκινθον
καὶ ῥοδέας κάλυκας καὶ λείρια, θαῦμα ἰδέσθαι,
νάρκισσόν θ' ὃν ἔφυσ' ὥς περ κρόκον εὐρεῖα χθών.
αὐτὰρ ἐγὼ δρεπόμην περὶ χάρματι, γαῖα δ' ἔνερθε

411 αὐτίκ' Ilgen : εἶθαρ Ruhnken 418–423 = 𝔭 c. 2. 7–13. Paus. iv. 30. 4 πρῶτος δὲ ὧν οἶδα ἐποιήσατο ἐν τοῖς ἔπεσιν Ὅμηρος Τύχης μνήμην. ἐποιήσατο δὲ ἐν τῷ ὕμνῳ τῷ ἐς τὴν Δήμητρα, ἄλλας τε τῶν Ὠκεανοῦ θυγατέρας καταριθμούμενος, ὡς ὁμοῦ Κόρῃ τῇ Δήμητρος παίζοιεν, καὶ Τύχην ὡς Ὠκεανοῦ καὶ ταύτην παῖδα οὖσαν. καὶ οὕτως ἔχει τὰ ἔπη·

ἡμεῖς μὲν μάλα πᾶσαι ἀν' ἱμερτὸν λειμῶνα
Λευκίππη Φαινώ τε καὶ Ἠλέκτρη καὶ Ἰάνθη
Μηλόβοσίς τε Τύχη τε καὶ Ὠκυρόη καλυκῶπις.

Oceanides recenset et Hesiodus Theog. 349 sqq. 418 φανερη 𝔭 Ἰάνθη τ' Ἠλέκτρη τε Hes. Theog. 349 419 om. 𝔭 Paus. Ἱππώ τε Κλυμένη τε Ῥόδειά τε Καλλιρόη τε Hes. 351 ῥόεια M 420 ita 𝔭 Paus. Μηλόβοσίς τε Θόη τε καὶ εὐειδὴς Πολυδώρη Hes. 354 μηλοβόστη τε corr. ex μηλοβοείη seu μηλοβότη τε M ὠκύρθη M 421 ita 𝔭 ἀκατάστη M 422 hab. 𝔭 423 ita 𝔭 cf. Hes. 353, 361 ταλαξαύρη M 426 κροκοέντα γανὸν M corr. Voss 427 ῥόδα ἐς M corr. Heyne 428 cf. 178, Ap. Rhod. iii. 855, Diosc. iv. 161 (158), Hipponax 41 ἔστι δ' οἷά περ κρόκος 429 δρεπομένη M corr. Ruhnken

χώρησεν, τῇ δ' ἔκθορ' ἄναξ κρατερὸς πολυδέγμων.
βῆ δὲ φέρων ὑπὸ γαῖαν ἐν ἅρμασι χρυσείοισι
πόλλ' ἀεκαζομένην, ἐβόησα δ' ἄρ' ὄρθια φωνῇ.
ταῦτά τοι ἀχνυμένη περ ἀληθέα πάντ' ἀγορεύω.
Ὣς τότε μὲν πρόπαν ἦμαρ ὁμόφρονα θυμὸν ἔχουσαι
πολλὰ μάλ' ἀλλήλων κραδίην καὶ θυμὸν ἴαινον
ἀμφαγαπαζόμεναι, ἀχέων δ' ἀπεπαύετο θυμός.
γηθοσύνας δὲ δέχοντο παρ' ἀλλήλων ἔδιδ[όν τε.]
τῇσιν δ' ἐγγύθεν ἦλθ' Ἑκάτη λιπαροκρήδεμνος,
πολλὰ δ' ἄρ' ἀμφαγάπησε κόρην Δημήτερος ἁγνῆς·
ἐκ τοῦ οἱ πρόπολος καὶ ὀπάων ἔπλετ' ἄνασσα.
ταῖς δὲ μετάγγελον ἧκε βαρύκτυπος εὐρύοπα Ζεὺς
Ῥείην ἠΰκομον ἣν μητέρα κυανόπεπλον
ἀξέμεναι μετὰ φῦλα θεῶν, ὑπέδεκτο δὲ τιμὰς
δωσέμεν, ἅς κεν ἕλοιτο μετ' ἀθανάτοισι θεοῖσι·
νεῦσε δέ οἱ κούρην ἔτεος περιτελλομένοιο
τὴν τριτάτην μὲν μοῖραν ὑπὸ ζόφον ἠερόεντα,
τὰς δὲ δύω παρὰ μητρὶ καὶ ἄλλοις ἀθανάτοισιν.
ὣς ἔφατ'· οὐδ' ἀπίθησε θεὰ Διὸς ἀγγελιάων.
ἐσσυμένως δ' ἤϊξε κατ' Οὐλύμποιο καρήνων,
εἰς δ' ἄρα Ῥάριον ἷξε, φερέσβιον οὖθαρ ἀρούρης
τὸ πρίν, ἀτὰρ τότε γ' οὔ τι φερέσβιον, ἀλλὰ ἕκηλον
ἑστήκει πανάφυλλον· ἔκευθε δ' ἄρα κρῖ λευκὸν
μήδεσι Δήμητρος καλλισφύρου· αὐτὰρ ἔπειτα
μέλλεν ἄφαρ ταναοῖσι κομήσειν ἀσταχύεσσιν
ἦρος ἀεξομένοιο, πέδῳ δ' ἄρα πίονες ὄγμοι
βρισέμεν ἀσταχύων, τὰ δ' ἐν ἐλλεδανοῖσι δεδέσθαι.
ἔνθ' ἐπέβη πρώτιστον ἀπ' αἰθέρος ἀτρυγέτοιο·
ἀσπασίως δ' ἴδον ἀλλήλας, κεχάρηντο δὲ θυμῷ.
τὴν δ' ὧδε προσέειπε Ῥέη λιπαροκρήδεμνος·

437 *γηθόσυναι* M corr. Ruhnken *ἐδίδ* M : *ἐδίδοντο* *m* corr. Ruhnken 440 *πρόπολον καὶ ὀπάονα* cit. Philodemus de piet. 40. 5 (*Ὅμηρος ἐν τοῖς ὕμνοις*) 441 *μετ'* M 442 *Δημήτερα* Fontein, cf. Herod. iv. 53. 6 450 *ῥίον* M corr. Ruhnken 452 *εἱστήκει* M corr. Hermann

Δεῦρο τέκος, καλέει σε βαρύκτυπος εὐρύοπα Ζεὺς
ἐλθέμεναι μετὰ φῦλα θεῶν, ὑπέδεκτο δὲ τιμὰς
[δωσέμεν, ἅς κ' ἐθέλῃσθα] μετ' ἀθανάτοισι θεοῖσι.
[νεῦσε δέ σοι κούρην ἔτεος π]εριτελλομένοιο
[τὴν τριτάτην μὲν μοῖραν ὑπὸ ζόφον ἠ]ερόεντα,
[τὰς δὲ δύω παρὰ σοί τε καὶ ἄλλοις] ἀθανάτοισιν.
[ὣς ἄρ' ἔφη τελέ]εσθαι· ἑῷ δ' ἐπένευσε κάρητι.
[ἀλλ' ἴθι τέκνον] ἐμὸν καὶ πείθεο, μηδέ τι λίην
ἀ[ζηχὲς μεν]έαινε κελαινεφέϊ Κρονίωνι·
α[ἶψα δὲ κα]ρπὸν ἄεξε φερέσβιον ἀνθρώποισιν.
  Ὣ[ς ἔφατ', οὐ]δ' ἀπίθησεν ἐϋστέφανος Δημήτηρ,
αἶψα δὲ καρπὸν ἀνῆκεν ἀρουράων ἐριβώλων.
πᾶσα δὲ φύλλοισίν τε καὶ ἄνθεσιν εὐρεῖα χθὼν
ἔβρισ'· ἡ δὲ κιοῦσα θεμιστοπόλοις βασιλεῦσι
δ[εῖξε,] Τριπτολέμῳ τε Διοκλεῖ τε πληξίππῳ,
Εὐμόλπου τε βίῃ Κελεῷ θ' ἡγήτορι λαῶν,
δρησμοσύνην θ' ἱερῶν καὶ ἐπέφραδεν ὄργια πᾶσι,
Τριπτολέμῳ τε Πολυξείνῳ τ', ἐπὶ τοῖς δὲ Διοκλεῖ,
σεμνά, τά τ' οὔ πως ἔστι παρεξ[ίμ]εν [οὔτε πυθέσθαι,]
οὔτ' ἀχέειν· μέγα γάρ τι θεῶν σέβας ἰσχάνει αὐδήν.
ὄλβιος ὃς τάδ' ὄπωπεν ἐπιχθονίων ἀνθρώπων·
ὃς δ' ἀτελὴς ἱερῶν, ὅς τ' ἄμμορος, οὔ ποθ' ὁμοίων
αἶσαν ἔχει φθίμενός περ ὑπὸ ζόφῳ εὐρώεντι.
  Αὐτὰρ ἐπεὶ δὴ πάνθ' ὑπεθήκατο δῖα θεάων,
βάν ῥ' ἴμεν Οὔλυμπον δὲ θεῶν μεθ' ὁμήγυριν ἄλλων.
ἔνθα δὲ ναιετάουσι παραὶ Διὶ τερπικεραύνῳ

462 et seqq. suppl. *m* 464 ερόεντα (ss. ι̃) M (et olim ζόφον ss. ω?) cf. 482 465 expl. Ruhnken: post h.v. versus 449–453 repetivit M expunxit *m* 466 expl. Goodwin: δύο δὲ πὰρ σοὶ ἔσ *m* 467 suppl. *m* 468 suppl. *m* 469 suppl. *m* 470 suppl. *m* 474–6 cit. Paus. ii. 14. 3 474 δ^ M: δεῖξεν Paus.: εἶπε *m* 476 χρησμοσύνην M: δρησμοσύνην Paus. ὄργια καλὰ M: πᾶσι Paus. 478 παρεξ ΄ . ˘ . (ss. εν) M: παρεξίμεν Matthiae: παρεξέμεν Ruhnken οὔτε olim M ut vid. πυθέσθαι add. *m* 479 σ . . . σ M ut vid.: σέβας Cobet: ἄχος *m*: ἄγος Valckenaer 484 θέων M corr. Ruhnken

σεμναί τ' αἰδοῖαί τε· μέγ' ὄλβιος ὅν τιν' ἐκεῖναι
προφρονέως φίλωνται ἐπιχθονίων ἀνθρώπων·
αἶψα δέ οἱ πέμπουσιν ἐφέστιον ἐς μέγα δῶμα
Πλοῦτον, ὃς ἀνθρώποις ἄφενος θνητοῖσι δίδωσιν.
'Αλλ' ἄγ' 'Ελευσῖνος θυοέσσης δῆμον ἔχουσαι
καὶ Πάρον ἀμφιρύτην ῎Αντρωνά τε πετρήεντα,
πότνια ἀγλαόδωρ' ὡρηφόρε Δηοῖ ἄνασσα
αὐτὴ καὶ κούρη περικαλλὴς Περσεφόνεια
πρόφρονες ἀντ' ᾠδῆς βίοτον θυμήρε' ὀπάζειν.
αὐτὰρ ἐγὼ καὶ σεῖο καὶ ἄλλης μνήσομ' ἀοιδῆς.

III. Εἰς 'Απόλλωνα

Μνήσομαι οὐδὲ λάθωμαι 'Απόλλωνος ἑκάτοιο,
ὅν τε θεοὶ κατὰ δῶμα Διὸς τρομέουσιν ἰόντα·
καί ῥά τ' ἀναΐσσουσιν ἐπὶ σχεδὸν ἐρχομένοιο
πάντες ἀφ' ἑδράων, ὅτε φαίδιμα τόξα τιταίνει.
Λητὼ δ' οἴη μίμνε παραὶ Διὶ τερπικεραύνῳ,
ἥ ῥα βιόν τ' ἐχάλασσε καὶ ἐκλήϊσε φαρέτρην,
καί οἱ ἀπ' ἰφθίμων ὤμων χείρεσσιν ἑλοῦσα
τόξον ἀνεκρέμασε πρὸς κίονα πατρὸς ἑοῖο
πασσάλου ἐκ χρυσέου· τὸν δ' εἰς θρόνον εἷσεν ἄγουσα.
τῷ δ' ἄρα νέκταρ ἔδωκε πατὴρ δέπαϊ χρυσείῳ
δεικνύμενος φίλον υἱόν, ἔπειτα δὲ δαίμονες ἄλλοι
ἔνθα καθίζουσιν· χαίρει δέ τε πότνια Λητώ,
οὕνεκα τοξοφόρον καὶ καρτερὸν υἱὸν ἔτικτεν.

488 *μέγαν δόμον* M corr. Ruhnken 490 *ἀλλὰ θελευσῖνος* M corr. Ruhnken 494 *ὄπαζε* M corr. Voss

III. *Codices*: M *p x y z* (usque ad 185) S (usque ad 357). Τιτvlvs: *τοῦ αὐτοῦ ὁμήρου ὕμνοι εἰς ἀπόλλωνα* M: *ὁμήρου ὕμνος εἰς ἀπόλλωνα* D L[1]: *ὁμήρου ὕμνοι εἰς ἀπόλλωνα* E Π S T ed. pr. (*α*[os] add. E T): *ὕμνοι ὁμήρου· εἰς τὸν* (om. Mon.) *ἀπόλλωνα p* (*ὕμνος εἰς* V): *εἰς ἀπόλλωνα* J: *ἐς ἀπόλλω* H om. K 1 cit. Certamen Hom. et Hes. 316 *σταθεὶς ἐπὶ τὸν κεράτινον βωμὸν λέγει ὕμνον εἰς 'Απόλλωνα οὗ ἡ ἀρχὴ* [v. 1], Tzetzes praef. in Lycophr. f. 3 Scheer 3 *τ'* Hermann: *γ'* codd. *ἐπὶ x z* D V[1] Peppmueller: *ἐπισχεδὸν* M *p* 5 *παρὰ* ed. pr. 9 *ἧσεν* M 11 *δὲ* om. *p* H S

χαῖρε μάκαιρ' ὦ Λητοῖ, ἐπεὶ τέκες ἀγλαὰ τέκνα
Ἀπόλλωνά τ' ἄνακτα καὶ Ἄρτεμιν ἰοχέαιραν,
τὴν μὲν ἐν Ὀρτυγίῃ, τὸν δὲ κραναῇ ἐνὶ Δήλῳ,
κεκλιμένη πρὸς μακρὸν ὄρος καὶ Κύνθιον ὄχθον,
ἀγχοτάτω φοίνικος ὑπ' Ἰνωποῖο ῥεέθροις.
  Πῶς τάρ σ' ὑμνήσω πάντως εὔυμνον ἐόντα;
πάντῃ γάρ τοι, Φοῖβε, νομὸς βεβλήαται ᾠδῆς,
ἠμὲν ἀν' ἤπειρον πορτιτρόφον ἠδ' ἀνὰ νήσους.
πᾶσαι δὲ σκοπιαί τοι ἅδον καὶ πρώονες ἄκροι
ὑψηλῶν ὀρέων ποταμοί θ' ἅλα δὲ προρέοντες,
ἀκταί τ' εἰς ἅλα κεκλιμέναι λιμένες τε θαλάσσης.
ἦ ὥς σε πρῶτον Λητὼ τέκε χάρμα βροτοῖσι,
κλινθεῖσα πρὸς Κύνθου ὄρος κραναῇ ἐνὶ νήσῳ
Δήλῳ ἐν ἀμφιρύτῃ; ἑκάτερθε δὲ κῦμα κελαινὸν
ἐξῄει χέρσον δὲ λιγυπνοίοις ἀνέμοισιν·
ἔνθεν ἀπορνύμενος πᾶσι θνητοῖσιν ἀνάσσεις.
ὅσσους Κρήτη τ' ἐντὸς ἔχει καὶ δῆμος Ἀθηνῶν
νῆσός τ' Αἰγίνη ναυσικλειτή τ' Εὔβοια
Αἰγαί τ' Εἰρεσίαι τε καὶ ἀγχιάλη Πεπάρηθος
Θρηΐκιός τ' Ἀθόως καὶ Πηλίου ἄκρα κάρηνα
Θρηϊκίη τε Σάμος Ἴδης τ' ὄρεα σκιόεντα
Σκῦρος καὶ Φώκαια καὶ Αὐτοκάνης ὄρος αἰπὺ

14 μάκαιρα λητοῖ M 18 ἐπ' Reiz οἰνώποιο *z*: ἰνώποιο sim. cet. (ποταμοῦ ss. T), -οῖο Schneidewin 19 γάρ codd. πάντοσσ' M: πάντων A B C O Q 20 νόμος codd.: νόμοι Matthiae: νομοὶ Barnes 21 παντοτρόφον *p*, πρὸς ss. T 23–73 om. M: λείπουσι στίχοι να̅ *m* 24 λίμναι *p*, cf. Herod. iv. 195 25 ἦ ὡς A ed. pr.: ἠώς cet. 26 κύνθου Holstein cl. 141: κύνθος codd.: κύνθος· καὶ θηλυκῶς καὶ οὐδετέρως Steph. Byz. 28 ἐξείει *x*: ἔξεισι T mg. λιγυπνόοις *p* 30 τ' add. Hermann Ἀθηνέων Hermann 31 αἴγινα codd. (αἰγίνα J Π O Q) em. Barnes, cf. Herod. iii. 59 ναυσικλείτη codd. corr. Barnes εὔβοια κυδνὴ H J: Steph. Byz. Κύδνα· πόλις Μακεδονίας. Θεαγένης ἐν Μακεδονικοῖς ⟨F. H. G. iv. 509 fr. 5⟩· ἣ κατὰ παραφθορὰν Πύδνα λέγεται. legit pro Αἰγαί ut videtur quidam. Κύδνα et oppidum Lycium, Ptol. Geogr. v. 3 (Πύδναι Stadiasm. 248) 32 Πειρεσίαι Ruhnken ἀγχίαλος *p*: ἀγχιάλην Π 33 ἄθως codd. corr. Barnes 35 αὐτοκανὴς *x z* AtDS: ΑΥΤΟΚΑΝΑ nummi sequitur in *z* AtD v. 41

Ἴμβρος τ' εὐκτιμένη καὶ Λῆμνος ἀμιχθαλόεσσα
Λέσβος τ' ἠγαθέη Μάκαρος ἕδος Αἰολίωνος
καὶ Χίος, ἣ νήσων λιπαρωτάτη εἰν ἁλὶ κεῖται,
παιπαλόεις τε Μίμας καὶ Κωρύκου ἄκρα κάρηνα
καὶ Κλάρος αἰγλήεσσα καὶ Αἰσαγέης ὄρος αἰπὺ
καὶ Σάμος ὑδρηλὴ Μυκάλης τ' αἰπεινὰ κάρηνα
Μίλητός τε Κόως τε, πόλις Μερόπων ἀνθρώπων,
καὶ Κνίδος αἰπεινὴ καὶ Κάρπαθος ἠνεμόεσσα
Νάξος τ' ἠδὲ Πάρος Ῥήναιά τε πετρήεσσα,
τόσσον ἔπ' ὠδίνουσα Ἑκηβόλον ἵκετο Λητώ,
εἴ τίς οἱ γαιέων υἱεῖ θέλοι οἰκία θέσθαι.
αἱ δὲ μάλ' ἐτρόμεον καὶ ἐδείδισαν, οὐδέ τις ἔτλη
Φοῖβον δέξασθαι καὶ πιοτέρη περ ἐοῦσα
πρίν γ' ὅτε δή ῥ' ἐπὶ Δήλου ἐβήσετο πότνια Λητώ,
καί μιν ἀνειρομένη ἔπεα πτερόεντα προσηύδα·
Δῆλ' εἰ γάρ κ' ἐθέλοις ἕδος ἔμμεναι υἷος ἐμοῖο
Φοίβου Ἀπόλλωνος, θέσθαι τ' ἔνι πίονα νηόν·
ἄλλος δ' οὔ τις σεῖό ποθ' ἅψεται, οὐδέ σε λήσει,
οὐδ' εὔβων σέ γ' ἔσεσθαι ὀΐομαι οὔτ' εὔμηλον,
οὐδὲ τρύγην οἴσεις, οὔτ' ἂρ φυτὰ μυρία φύσεις.

38 νῆσος E T 39 κορύκου x D K : κουρύκου J : κουρίκου H 40 ἀσαγέης Mon. τόπος ἐστὶ τοῦ ὀψικίου ὁ νῦν καλούμενος μαλάγινα περὶ οὗ φησὶ καὶ ὁ λυκόφρων ⟨1464, 5⟩ κλάρου μιμάλλων ἥτι φίκιον τέρας Π marg. dici quidem oppidum Malaginam seu Melam in themate Obsequii monuit J. G. C. Anderson : quid vero ita sibi scholiasta voluerit nescimus. cf. et Αἰσαγέη, Αἰγαγέη Nic. Ther. 218, Αἰγανέη Anth. Pal. vii. 390, Ἀγχαλέη Hipponact. 99 42 πόλεις p 44 ῥήναιά S : ῥηναία cet. cum Steph. Byz. : Ῥήνεια Lobeck πετρήδεσ(σ)α L[1] Π v. om. Mon. 45 ἐπωδίνουσα codd. corr. Barnes 46 οἱ H L[5] T corr. : σοι cet. praeter p : εἴ τις γαιάων p (σοὶ add. A m. rec.) θέλοι L[5] Mon. S : θέλει cet. 48 προτέρη Q 49 ἐβήσατο D K L[1] (σσ) : βήσατο H J 51 κ' ἐθέλοις H S : κεθέλοις J : κεθέλης L[1] (κέλης) Π : -εις cet. ἐμοῖο A H L[1] Π R[1] S : ἐμεῖο cet. cf. 314 52 ἐπὶ J : ἐνὶ cet. corr. Hermann 53 ἄλλως J L[5] S Bothe λήσει Agar C. R. x. 388 : λήσει (ss. σ) S : λίσσει cet. cf. λ 102 υ 85, Theogn. 20, Anth. Pal. vii. 513. 3, Herod. iii. 2, Batr. 93 54 ὀυδ' Γ O Π Q S εὔβουν p : εὔβωλο S γ' add. Hermann, cf. 88 (σ' ἐσέσεσθαι L[1]) 55 οἴσεις H J (οἰστεῖς L[1] Π : οἰσεῖς cet.) : πολλὴν y

αἰ δέ κ' Ἀπόλλωνος ἑκαέργου νηὸν ἔχησθα,
ἄνθρωποί τοι πάντες ἀγινήσουσ' ἑκατόμβας
ἐνθάδ' ἀγειρόμενοι, κνίση δέ τοι ἄσπετος αἰεὶ
δημοῦ ἀναΐξει, βοσκήσεις θ' οἵ κέ σ' ἔχωσι
χειρὸς ἀπ' ἀλλοτρίης, ἐπεὶ οὔ τοι πῖαρ ὑπ' οὖδας.
Ὣς φάτο· χαῖρε δὲ Δῆλος, ἀμειβομένη δὲ προσηύδα·
Λητοῖ κυδίστη θύγατερ μεγάλου Κοίοιο,
ἀσπασίη κεν ἐγώ γε γονὴν ἑκάτοιο ἄνακτος
δεξαίμην· αἰνῶς γὰρ ἐτήτυμόν εἰμι δυσηχὴς
ἀνδράσιν, ὧδε δέ κεν περιτιμήεσσα γενοίμην.
ἀλλὰ τόδε τρομέω Λητοῖ ἔπος, οὐδέ σε κεύσω·
λίην γάρ τινά φασιν ἀτάσθαλον Ἀπόλλωνα
ἔσσεσθαι, μέγα δὲ πρυτανευσέμεν ἀθανάτοισι
καὶ θνητοῖσι βροτοῖσιν ἐπὶ ζείδωρον ἄρουραν.
τῷ ῥ' αἰνῶς δείδοικα κατὰ φρένα καὶ κατὰ θυμὸν
μὴ ὁπότ' ἂν τὸ πρῶτον ἴδῃ φάος ἠελίοιο
νῆσον ἀτιμήσας, ἐπεὶ ἦ κραναήπεδός εἰμι,
ποσσὶ καταστρέψας ὤσῃ ἁλὸς ἐν πελάγεσσιν.
ἔνθ' ἐμὲ μὲν μέγα κῦμα κατὰ κρατὸς ἅλις αἰεὶ
κλύσσει, ὁ δ' ἄλλην γαῖαν ἀφίξεται ἥ κεν ἅδῃ οἱ
τεύξασθαι νηόν τε καὶ ἄλσεα δενδρήεντα·
πουλύποδες δ' ἐν ἐμοὶ θαλάμας φῶκαί τε μέλαιναι

57 ita J : ἀγινήσουσιν vulg.: ἀγινησοῦσα V[2] : ἀγίνουσιν S ed. pr. 59 δημοῦ Cobet, reliqua Stoll : δηρὸν (ss. μ) ἄναξ εἰ βόσκοις περί (ss. θ) τας s ἔχωσιν E T (om. μ hic) : δηρον (ss. μ) ἄναξ εἰ βόσκοις σ' ἔχωσιν L[1] : δηρὸν ἄναξ εἰ βόσκοις θεοί κε σ' ἔχωσιν D K (-εις) Π : γρ. εἰ βόσκοισθε οἵ κε σ' ἔχωσιν margo E : δηρὸν ἄνακτ' εἰ βόσκεις· δὴ ῥὰ θεοί κε σ' ἔχωσι J : δηρὸν ἄνακτ' εἰ βόσκοις θεοί κε σ' ἔχωσι S, ἄνακτ' et L[5] : δηρὸν ἄναξ εἰ βόσκοις (ss. ει) θύτας οἵκε σ' ἔχωσι ἄνακτ' Γ m. 2 : θύτάς θ' οἳ κέ σ' ἔχωσι, et δήμον. δηρὸν ἄνακτ' εἰ βόσκοις V[2] : δηρὸν . . . βόσκοις *p* 60 πῖαρ] πεῖαρ O J K T : πείαρ L[1] Π : πεῖας E 62 μεγάλοιο κρόνοιο codd. corr. Barnes 63 κεν] μὲν ed. pr. S 65 γ' ἐροίμην *x* D K 71 ἴδης *x* D K : ὅτι (om. L[1] Π) τὸν ἥλιον φασὶν (φησὶ O) προυπάρχειν τοῦ ἀπόλλωνος L[1] O Π marg. 72 ita *p* : ἀτιμήσω *x* D K uv. : ἀτιμήσῃ J S D ss. K T corr. (ex -ω uv.) 73 ὤσει *x* At D J S tuetur Marx *Rh. Mus.* 1907. 620 74 ἄλλυδις J : ἄλλυδις ἄλλο Stephanus 75 ἁδῆ οἱ sim. *x* : ἀδοίη *p* : ἀΐδης M N 76 ἄλγεα Π

οἰκία ποιήσονται ἀκηδέα χήτεϊ λαῶν·
ἀλλ' εἴ μοι τλαίης γε θεὰ μέγαν ὅρκον ὀμόσσαι,
ἐνθάδε μιν πρῶτον τεύξειν περικαλλέα νηὸν
ἔμμεναι ἀνθρώπων χρηστήριον, αὐτὰρ ἔπειτα

πάντας ἐπ' ἀνθρώπους, ἐπεὶ ἦ πολυώνυμος ἔσται.
Ὣς ἄρ' ἔφη· Λητὼ δὲ θεῶν μέγαν ὅρκον ὄμοσσεν·
ἴστω νῦν τάδε γαῖα καὶ οὐρανὸς εὐρὺς ὕπερθεν
καὶ τὸ κατειβόμενον Στυγὸς ὕδωρ, ὅς τε μέγιστος
ὅρκος δεινότατός τε πέλει μακάρεσσι θεοῖσιν·
ἦ μὴν Φοίβου τῇδε θυώδης ἔσσεται αἰεὶ
βωμὸς καὶ τέμενος, τίσει δέ σέ γ' ἔξοχα πάντων.
Αὐτὰρ ἐπεί ῥ' ὄμοσέν τε τελεύτησέν τε τὸν ὅρκον,
Δῆλος μὲν μάλα χαῖρε γόνῳ ἑκάτοιο ἄνακτος,
Λητὼ δ' ἐννῆμάρ τε καὶ ἐννέα νύκτας ἀέλπτοις
ὠδίνεσσι πέπαρτο. θεαὶ δ' ἔσαν ἔνδοθι πᾶσαι
ὅσσαι ἄρισται ἔσαν, Διώνη τε Ῥείη τε
Ἰχναίη τε Θέμις καὶ ἀγάστονος Ἀμφιτρίτη,
ἄλλαι τ' ἀθάναται, νόσφιν λευκωλένου Ἥρης·
ἧστο γὰρ ἐν μεγάροισι Διὸς νεφεληγερέταο.
μούνη δ' οὐκ ἐπέπυστο μογοστόκος Εἰλείθυια·
ἧστο γὰρ ἄκρῳ Ὀλύμπῳ ὑπὸ χρυσέοισι νέφεσσιν
Ἥρης φραδμοσύνῃς λευκωλένου, ἥ μιν ἔρυκε
ζηλοσύνῃ ὅ τ' ἄρ' υἱὸν ἀμύμονά τε κρατερόν τε
Λητὼ τέξεσθαι καλλιπλόκαμος τότ' ἔμελλεν.
Αἳ δ' Ἶριν προὔπεμψαν ἐϋκτιμένης ἀπὸ νήσου
ἀξέμεν Εἰλείθυιαν, ὑποσχόμεναι μέγαν ὅρμον
χρυσείοισι λίνοισιν ἐερμένον ἐννεάπηχυν·

78 ἄχη τεϊλάων E T: ἕκαστά τε φῦλα νεπούδων *p* 81 lac. stat. Hermann: ex gr. τευξάσθω νηούς τε καὶ ἄλσεα δενδρήεντα 82 ἔσται M, γρ. J: ἐστὶν cet. 83 ὄμοσεν *x*: ὄμωσεν D K, γρ. J 86 τε om. E T D J πέλεται J 87 μη L[1] Π: ἦ μή Π marg. αἰὲν codd. corr. Barnes 88 σ' ἔξοχα *x*: σε ἔξοχα J S (γ' add. m. pr.) 93 ἔσαν] ἔασι Wolf: ἔσαν δὲ Tucker ῥέη codd. corr. ed. pr. 96 v. om. M E T μεγάροις codd. corr. ed. pr. 99 φραδμοσύνης M: -η cet. corr. Baumeister 104 ἐεργμένον codd. corr. Barnes, cf. A 486 E 89 σ 296

νόσφιν δ' ἤνωγον καλέειν λευκωλένου Ἥρης
μή μιν ἔπειτ' ἐπέεσσιν ἀποστρέψειεν ἰοῦσαν.
αὐτὰρ ἐπεὶ τό γ' ἄκουσε ποδήνεμος ὠκέα Ἶρις
βῆ ῥα θέειν, ταχέως δὲ διήνυσε πᾶν τὸ μεσηγύ.
αὐτὰρ ἐπεί ῥ' ἵκανε θεῶν ἕδος αἰπὺν Ὄλυμπον
αὐτίκ' ἄρ' Εἰλείθυιαν ἀπὸ μεγάροιο θύραζε
ἐκπροκαλεσσαμένη ἔπεα πτερόεντα προσηύδα
πάντα μάλ' ὡς ἐπέτελλον Ὀλύμπια δώματ' ἔχουσαι.
τῇ δ' ἄρα θυμὸν ἔπειθεν ἐνὶ στήθεσσι φίλοισι,
βὰν δὲ ποσὶ τρήρωσι πελειάσιν ἴθμαθ' ὁμοῖαι.
εὖτ' ἐπὶ Δήλου ἔβαινε μογοστόκος Εἰλείθυια,
τὴν τότε δὴ τόκος εἷλε, μενοίνησεν δὲ τεκέσθαι.
ἀμφὶ δὲ φοίνικι βάλε πήχεε, γοῦνα δ' ἔρεισε
λειμῶνι μαλακῷ, μείδησε δὲ γαῖ' ὑπένερθεν·
ἐκ δ' ἔθορε πρὸ φόως δέ, θεαὶ δ' ὀλόλυξαν ἅπασαι.
ἔνθα σὲ ἤϊε Φοῖβε θεαὶ λόον ὕδατι καλῷ
ἁγνῶς καὶ καθαρῶς, σπάρξαν δ' ἐν φάρεϊ λευκῷ
λεπτῷ νηγατέῳ· περὶ δὲ χρύσεον στρόφον ἧκαν.
οὐδ' ἄρ' Ἀπόλλωνα χρυσάορα θήσατο μήτηρ,
ἀλλὰ Θέμις νέκταρ τε καὶ ἀμβροσίην ἐρατεινὴν
ἀθανάτῃσιν χερσὶν ἐπήρξατο· χαῖρε δὲ Λητὼ
οὕνεκα τοξοφόρον καὶ καρτερὸν υἱὸν ἔτικτεν.

Αὐτὰρ ἐπεὶ δὴ Φοῖβε κατέβρως ἄμβροτον εἶδαρ,
οὔ σέ γ' ἔπειτ' ἴσχον χρύσεοι στρόφοι ἀσπαίροντα,
οὐδ' ἔτι δεσμά σ' ἔρυκε, λύοντο δὲ πείρατα πάντα.
αὐτίκα δ' ἀθανάτῃσι μετηύδα Φοῖβος Ἀπόλλων·

110 ἀπὸ M: ἀπὲκ (ἀπ' ἐκ) cet. 112 ἔχοντες E T 114 Ar. Aves 575 Ἶριν δέ γ' Ὅμηρος ἔφασκ' ἰκέλην εἶναι τρήρωνι πελείῃ. schol. ad loc. ὅτι ψεύδεται παίζων· οὐ γὰρ ἐπὶ Ἴριδος ἀλλ' ἐπὶ Ἀθηνᾶς καὶ Ἥρας ⟨E 778⟩

αἱ δὲ βάτην τρήρωσι πελειάσιν ἴθμαθ' ὁμοῖαι.

οἱ δὲ ἐν ἑτέροις ποιήμασιν ὁμήρου φασὶ τοῦτο φέρεσθαι. εἰσὶ γὰρ αὐτοῦ καὶ ὕμνοι. ἴθμαθ' M: ἴσμαθ' *x*, cf. Marx l. c.: ἴσθμαθ' *p* S commendat Jacobsohn *Hermes* 1910. 201: ἴδμαθ' *z* D, Π ss. eaedem varietates E 778 115 μονοστόκος L[1] Π: μογοστόλος E 116 μενήνυσε M 119 ἐν L[1] Π 120 λοῦον codd. corr. Steph. 122 στροφὸν codd. corr. Stephanus, item 128 125 ἀθανάτοισι K V[1] ἐπώρξατο M 128 ἔσχον S ἀσπαίροντες E T 129 δεσμά σ' *p*: δεσμά τ' seu δέσμα τ' cet. 130 ἀθανάτοισι D J E ed. pr.

εἴη μοι κίθαρίς τε φίλη καὶ καμπύλα τόξα,
χρήσω δ' ἀνθρώποισι Διὸς νημερτέα βουλήν.
Ὣς εἰπὼν ἐβίβασκεν ἀπὸ χθονὸς εὐρυοδείης
Φοῖβος ἀκερσεκόμης ἑκατηβόλος· αἱ δ' ἄρα πᾶσαι
θάμβεον ἀθάναται, χρυσῷ δ' ἄρα Δῆλος ἅπασα
Ↄ βεβρίθει καθορῶσα Διὸς Λητοῦς τε γενέθλην,
Ↄ γηθοσύνῃ ὅτι μιν θεὸς εἵλετο οἰκία θέσθαι
Ↄ νήσων ἠπείρου τε, φίλησε δὲ κηρόθι μᾶλλον.
• ἤνθησ' ὡς ὅτε τε ῥίον οὔρεος ἄνθεσιν ὕλης.
Αὐτὸς δ' ἀργυρότοξε ἄναξ ἑκατηβόλ' Ἄπολλον,
ἄλλοτε μέν τ' ἐπὶ Κύνθου ἐβήσαο παιπαλόεντος,
ἄλλοτε δ' ἂν νήσους τε καὶ ἀνέρας ἠλάσκαζες.
πολλοί τοι νηοί τε καὶ ἄλσεα δενδρήεντα,
πᾶσαι δὲ σκοπιαί τε φίλαι καὶ πρώονες ἄκροι
ὑψηλῶν ὀρέων, ποταμοί θ' ἅλα δὲ προρέοντες·
ἀλλὰ σὺ Δήλῳ Φοῖβε μάλιστ' ἐπιτέρπεαι ἦτορ,
ἔνθα τοι ἑλκεχίτωνες Ἰάονες ἠγερέθονται
αὐτοῖς σὺν παίδεσσι καὶ αἰδοίῃς ἀλόχοισιν.
οἱ δέ σε πυγμαχίῃ τε καὶ ὀρχηθμῷ καὶ ἀοιδῇ
μνησάμενοι τέρπουσιν ὅταν στήσωνται ἀγῶνα.
φαίη κ' ἀθανάτους καὶ ἀγήρως ἔμμεναι αἰεὶ
ὃς τότ' ἐπαντιάσει' ὅτ' Ἰάονες ἀθρόοι εἶεν·

132 δ'] τ' *x* M P S 133 ἐπὶ Matthiae, sed cf. E 13 τ 389 χ 72, I. G. Ins. Aeg. iii. 449 136–138 om. codd. praeter *y*: (scilicet exstant in marg. E L^1 T praefixis in E T Ↄ Ↄ et ἐν ἑτέρῳ κεῖνται καὶ οὗτοι οἱ στίχοι, in textu Π signis Ↄ ante vv. 136, 137 isdemque verbis καὶ οὗτοι οἱ στίχοι κεῖνται praefixis: in marg. O m. 2, in textu S ed. pr.:) 136–138 et 139 alius esse recensionis signis indicavimus 137 οἴλατο Π marg. (voluitne ἵλατο?) 139 ὡς ὅτε γ' ἀνθέει οὔρεος ἄνθεσιν ὕλη J similia D'Orville *J. Ph.* xxv. 251 142 ἂν D'Orville: αὖ codd., cf. B 198 144 ἄκραι J 145 ὑψηλῶντ' ὀρέων ποταμοὶ ἅλ. M 146–150 Thuc. iii. 104 δηλοῖ δὲ μάλιστα Ὅμηρος ὅτι τοιαῦτα ἦν ἐν τοῖς ἔπεσι τοῖσδε, ἅ ἐστιν ἐκ προοιμίου Ἀπόλλωνος 146 ἀλλ' ὅτε Thuc. ἐπετέρπεο M μάλιστά γε θυμὸν ἐτέρφθης Thuc. 147 ὁ αὐτὸς ἐν τῇ ν̄ Ἰλιάδος [685] ἰαόνες ἑλκεσιχίτωνες L^1 Π: cf. Asii Samii fr. 13 Kink. 148 σὺν σφοῖσιν τεκέεσσι γυναιξί τε σὴν ἐς ἀγυιάν Thuc. 149 ἔνθα σε Thuc. ὀρχηστυῖ Thuc. 150 καθέσωσιν Thuc. 151 ἀθάνατος M, Bernardus Martin αἰεὶ] ἀνὴρ *x* (ἀνὴρ αἰεὶ L^1) At D K: ἄνδρας J K m 2 152 οἳ τότ' ἐπ' ἀντιᾶσι τ' ἰάονες M: οἳ τότ' ἐπάντια σεῖο τ' ἰάονες *x z* At D S: οἳ δὴ τότ' ἐπαντία σεῖο *p* corr. Martin, cf. Herod. i. 124

πάντων γάρ κεν ἴδοιτο χάριν, τέρψαιτο δὲ θυμὸν
ἄνδρας τ' εἰσορόων καλλιζώνους τε γυναῖκας
νῆάς τ' ὠκείας ἠδ' αὐτῶν κτήματα πολλά.
πρὸς δὲ τόδε μέγα θαῦμα, ὅου κλέος οὔποτ' ὀλεῖται,
κοῦραι Δηλιάδες Ἑκατηβελέταο θεράπναι·
αἵ τ' ἐπεὶ ἂρ πρῶτον μὲν Ἀπόλλων' ὑμνήσωσιν,
αὖτις δ' αὖ Λητώ τε καὶ Ἄρτεμιν ἰοχέαιραν,
μνησάμεναι ἀνδρῶν τε παλαιῶν ἠδὲ γυναικῶν
ὕμνον ἀείδουσιν, θέλγουσι δὲ φῦλ' ἀνθρώπων.
πάντων δ' ἀνθρώπων φωνὰς καὶ κρεμβαλιαστὺν
μιμεῖσθ' ἴσασιν· φαίη δέ κεν αὐτὸς ἕκαστος
φθέγγεσθ'· οὕτω σφιν καλὴ συνάρηρεν ἀοιδή.
ἀλλ' ἄγεθ' ἱλήκοι μὲν Ἀπόλλων Ἀρτέμιδι ξύν,
χαίρετε δ' ὑμεῖς πᾶσαι· ἐμεῖο δὲ καὶ μετόπισθε
μνήσασθ', ὁππότε κέν τις ἐπιχθονίων ἀνθρώπων
ἐνθάδ' ἀνείρηται ξεῖνος ταλαπείριος ἐλθών·
ὦ κοῦραι, τίς δ' ὔμμιν ἀνὴρ ἥδιστος ἀοιδῶν
ἐνθάδε πωλεῖται, καὶ τέῳ τέρπεσθε μάλιστα;
ὑμεῖς δ' εὖ μάλα πᾶσαι ὑποκρίνασθ' ἀμφ' ἡμέων·
τυφλὸς ἀνήρ, οἰκεῖ δὲ Χίῳ ἔνι παιπαλοέσσῃ,

156 τόδ' αὖ J ὅου B E : θ' οὗ M : ὃ οὗ sim. cet. cf. Herm. 400 157 δηλιάδες δ' codd. praeter M 158 ἂρ] ἂν z 159 αὖθις p 162 βαμβαλιαστὺν E T : κρεμβαλιαστὺν (ss. βαμ) L¹ Π : κρεμβαλιαστὺν D L³ Q S ed. pr. : -στὴν M J K Mon. -σὺν p (plerique) 163 μιμεῖσθαι codd. corr. Barnes 164 ἀοιδῇ L¹ 165 Thuc. l. c. ὅτι δὲ καὶ μουσικῆς ἀγὼν ἦν καὶ ἀγωνιούμενοι ἐφοίτων ἐν τοῖσδε αὖ δηλοῖ, ἅ ἐστιν ἐκ τοῦ αὐτοῦ προοιμίου· τὸν γὰρ Δηλιακὸν χορὸν τῶν γυναικῶν ὑμνήσας ἐτελεύτα τοῦ ἐπαίνου ἐς τάδε τὰ ἔπη, ἐν οἷς καὶ ἑαυτοῦ ἐπεμνήσθη [165–172]. Aristides xxxiv. 35 διαλεγόμενος γὰρ ταῖς Δηλιάσι καὶ καταλύων τὸ προοίμιον εἴ τις ἔροιθ' ὑμᾶς φησὶν [169–172] cf. xxviii. 19 ἀλλά γε λητὼ μὲν καὶ ἀπόλλων M : ἀλλ' ἄγε δὴ λητὼ μὲν ἀπόλλων cet. praeter S : ἀλλ' ἄγεθ' ἱλήκοι μὲν ἀπόλλων L⁵ S Thucydidis codd. vetustiores : reposuit Normann 166 ἐμεῖο D K L² N R² V¹ : ἐμοῖο cet. 168 ταλαπείριος ἄλλος ἐπελθών Thuc. 171 ὑποκρίνασθε codd. (-θαι S : ὑποκρίνεσθ' M : ἀπ- Aristid.) ἀφ' ἡμέων M D L¹ Π At D z : ἀφ' ἡμῶν Aristides : ἀφ' ὑμέων E T S : ἀφ' ὑμῶν p : ἀφήμως Thuc. codices antiquiores εὐφήμως recentiores : correxit F. Marx *Rh. Mus.* 1907. 620. poeta ap. Suidam in v. Κοκκύαι. ἀ⟨μ⟩φ' ὑμέων κοκύῃσι καθημένη ἀρχαίῃσι 172 σῆ ἐντεῦθεν ἔστιν εἰδέναι τὸν ὅμηρον χῖον εἶναι T marg. : σῆ ὡς ἐντεῦθεν φαίνει (ἐμφ. L¹) ὅμηρος ἑαυτὸν χῖον εἶναι L¹ Π marg.

τοῦ πᾶσαι μετόπισθεν ἀριστεύουσιν ἀοιδαί.
ἡμεῖς δ' ὑμέτερον κλέος οἴσομεν ὅσσον ἐπ' αἶαν
ἀνθρώπων στρεφόμεσθα πόλεις εὖ ναιεταώσας·
οἱ δ' ἐπὶ δὴ πείσονται, ἐπεὶ καὶ ἐτήτυμόν ἐστιν.
αὐτὰρ ἐγὼν οὐ λήξω ἑκηβόλον Ἀπόλλωνα
ὑμνέων ἀργυρότοξον ὃν ἠΰκομος τέκε Λητώ.
ὦ ἄνα, καὶ Λυκίην καὶ Μῃονίην ἐρατεινὴν
καὶ Μίλητον ἔχεις ἔναλον πόλιν ἱμερόεσσαν,
αὐτὸς δ' αὖ Δήλοιο περικλύστου μέγ' ἀνάσσεις.
εἶσι δὲ φορμίζων Λητοῦς ἐρικυδέος υἱὸς
φόρμιγγι γλαφυρῇ πρὸς Πυθὼ πετρήεσσαν,
ἄμβροτα εἵματ' ἔχων τεθυωμένα· τοῖο δὲ φόρμιγξ
χρυσέου ὑπὸ πλήκτρου καναχὴν ἔχει ἱμερόεσσαν.
ἔνθεν δὲ πρὸς Ὄλυμπον ἀπὸ χθονὸς ὥς τε νόημα
εἶσι Διὸς πρὸς δῶμα θεῶν μεθ' ὁμήγυριν ἄλλων·
αὐτίκα δ' ἀθανάτοισι μέλει κίθαρις καὶ ἀοιδή.
Μοῦσαι μέν θ' ἅμα πᾶσαι ἀμειβόμεναι ὀπὶ καλῇ
ὑμνεῦσίν ῥα θεῶν δῶρ' ἄμβροτα ἠδ' ἀνθρώπων
τλημοσύνας, ὅσ' ἔχοντες ὑπ' ἀθανάτοισι θεοῖσι
ζώουσ' ἀφραδέες καὶ ἀμήχανοι, οὐδὲ δύνανται
εὑρέμεναι θανάτοιό τ' ἄκος καὶ γήραος ἄλκαρ·
αὐτὰρ ἐϋπλόκαμοι Χάριτες καὶ ἐΰφρονες Ὧραι
Ἁρμονίη θ' Ἥβη τε Διὸς θυγάτηρ τ' Ἀφροδίτη
ὀρχεῦντ' ἀλλήλων ἐπὶ καρπῷ χεῖρας ἔχουσαι·
τῇσι μὲν οὔτ' αἰσχρὴ μεταμέλπεται οὔτ' ἐλάχεια,
ἀλλὰ μάλα μεγάλη τε ἰδεῖν καὶ εἶδος ἀγητὴ
Ἄρτεμις ἰοχέαιρα ὁμότροφος Ἀπόλλωνι.
ἐν δ' αὖ τῇσιν Ἄρης καὶ ἐΰσκοπος Ἀργειφόντης

174 ἡμέτερον *x* At D 176 ἐπειδὴ M E T S: ἐπιδὴν *p* 178 ὑμνῶν *p* 181 δ' αὖ] γὰρ M περικλύστου] ita M: περικλύστης cet.: περικλύστης (ss. οιο) Γ (sc. om. μέγ') 184 ἔχον *p* L[1] Π τεθυώδεα codd.: θυώδεα (ss. τε) Γ: εὐωδέα Pierson: corr. Barnes pro hoc versu ἔνθεν δὲ πρὸς ὄλυμπον (186) *z* quae hic desinit 189 om. *p* 192 ἀμφαδέες libri praeter M Γ marg., cf. Nonn. v. 349 197 οὔτε λάχεια omnes praeter *p* (-εῖα M E T) 198 ἀγητὴ] ἀγαυὴ M 200 ἔνθ' codd. praeter M αὐτῇσιν M

παίζουσ᾽· αὐτὰρ ὁ Φοῖβος Ἀπόλλων ἐγκιθαρίζει
καλὰ καὶ ὕψι βιβάς, αἴγλη δέ μιν ἀμφιφαείνει
μαρμαρυγαί τε ποδῶν καὶ ἐϋκλώστοιο χιτῶνος.
οἱ δ᾽ ἐπιτέρπονται θυμὸν μέγαν εἰσορόωντες
Λητώ τε χρυσοπλόκαμος καὶ μητίετα Ζεὺς
υἷα φίλον παίζοντα μετ᾽ ἀθανάτοισι θεοῖσι.
πῶς τ᾽ ἄρ σ᾽ ὑμνήσω πάντως εὔυμνον ἐόντα;
ἠέ σ᾽ ἐνὶ μνηστῇσιν ἀείδω καὶ φιλότητι
ὅππως μνωόμενος ἔκιες Ἀζαντίδα κούρην
Ἴσχυ᾽ ἅμ᾽ ἀντιθέῳ Ἐλατιονίδῃ εὐίππῳ;
ἢ ἅμα Φόρβαντι Τριοπέῳ γένος, ἢ ἅμ᾽ Ἐρευθεῖ;
ἢ ἅμα Λευκίππῳ καὶ Λευκίπποιο δάμαρτι
πεζός, ὁ δ᾽ ἵπποισιν; οὐ μὴν Τρίοπός γ᾽ ἐνέλειπεν.
ἢ ὡς τὸ πρῶτον χρηστήριον ἀνθρώποισι
ζητεύων κατὰ γαῖαν ἔβης ἑκατηβόλ᾽ Ἄπολλον;
Πιερίην μὲν πρῶτον ἀπ᾽ Οὐλύμποιο κατῆλθες·
Λέκτον τ᾽ ἠμαθόεντα παρέστιχες ἠδ᾽ Αἰνιῆνας
καὶ διὰ Περραιβούς· τάχα δ᾽ εἰς Ἰαωλκὸν ἵκανες,
Κηναίου τ᾽ ἐπέβης ναυσικλείτης Εὐβοίης·
στῆς δ᾽ ἐπὶ Ληλάντῳ πεδίῳ, τό τοι οὐχ ἅδε θυμῷ
τεύξασθαι νηόν τε καὶ ἄλσεα δενδρήεντα.

202 *ἀμφιφαείνῃ* L^3 N Q R^2 V,[1] *η* ss. *x* L^2, *γρ.* marg. Γ R^1: *-ειῆ* O: *-ειη* L^1: *-ει* (ss. *η*) Π T, (ss. *ηι*) E   203 *μαρμαρυγὰς* O ut Bothe   204 *μέγα* M   207 *πάντοσ᾽* M   208 *μνηστῇρσιν* E   209 *ὁππόταν ἱέμενος* M: *ὁππότ᾽ ἀνωόμενος* S: *ὅπποσ᾽ ἀνωόμενος* cet. corr. Martin: *ὁππόσα μαιόμενος κίες εἰς* Ludwich   *ἀτλαντίδα* M: *Ἀζανίδα* Martin   210 *ἐλατιονίδῃ* E B ed. pr.: *ἐλατινιονίδῃ* cet. (*ἐλατινονίδῃ* M)   211 v. om. *p* At   *τριοπέῳ* correximus: *τριόπῳ* (*τριοπῷ* M) *γένος x* M: *τριοπόῳ* om. *γένος* marg. L^1 Π   *ἅμ᾽ ἐρεχθεῖ* M D'Orville: *ἀμαρύνθῳ* marg. L^1 Π: *Ἐρύμανθος* Ptol. Heph. 146 b 41   213 *ἐνέλειπεν* A Q S: *ἐνέλιπεν* vulg.: *ἐλέλιψεν* M   214 *ὡς*] *καὶ* E L^1 T   215 *ἀπόλλωνος p* (= *ἀπόλλων* ss. *ο*)   216 *πιερίην* S: *πετρίην* M, cf. Herod. viii. 44: *πιερίης x* D ed. pr.: *πιερίη p*   217 *Λέκτον*] *Λύγκον* Hermann: *Λάκμον* Baumeister   *ἠμαθόεντα*] *Ἠμαθίην τε* Matthiae   *Αἰνιῆνας*] *ἠδ᾽ ἁγνιήνας* M: *ἢ μαγνιήνας y*, *γρ.* V^2: *μαγνηΐδας* (ss. *ν*) Γ: *ἢ μαγνηίδας x p*: *μαγνηΐας* At: *Ἐνιῆνας* Matthiae. mirus gentium ordo   218 *ἰωλκὸν* codd. (*ἰολκὸν* M) corr. Barnes   219 *κυναίου* A B: *κϋναί* Γ   220 *τῶτ᾽* M   *οὐχάδε* codd. (*ἅδε* Π), corr. ed. pr.   221 *τεύξεσθαι* L^1 Π

ἔνθεν δ' Εὔριπον διαβὰς ἑκατηβόλ' Ἄπολλον
βῆς ἀν' ὄρος ζάθεον χλωρόν· τάχα δ' ἶξες ἀπ' αὐτοῦ
ἐς Μυκαλησσὸν ἰὼν καὶ Τευμησσὸν λεχεποίην.
Θήβης δ' εἰσαφίκανες ἕδος καταειμένον ὕλῃ·
οὐ γάρ πώ τις ἔναιε βροτῶν ἱερῇ ἐνὶ Θήβῃ,
οὐδ' ἄρα πω τότε γ' ἦσαν ἀταρπιτοὶ οὐδὲ κέλευθοι
Θήβης ἂμ πεδίον πυρηφόρον, ἀλλ' ἔχεν ὕλη.
ἔνθεν δὲ προτέρω ἔκιες ἑκατηβόλ' Ἄπολλον,
Ὀγχηστὸν δ' ἶξες Ποσιδήϊον ἀγλαὸν ἄλσος·
ἔνθα νεοδμὴς πῶλος ἀναπνέει ἀχθόμενός περ
ἕλκων ἅρματα καλά, χαμαὶ δ' ἐλατὴρ ἀγαθός περ
ἐκ δίφροιο θορὼν ὁδὸν ἔρχεται· οἱ δὲ τέως μὲν
κείν' ὄχεα κροτέουσιν ἀνακτορίην ἀφιέντες.
εἰ δέ κεν ἅρματ' ἀγῇσιν ἐν ἄλσεϊ δενδρήεντι,
ἵππους μὲν κομέουσι, τὰ δὲ κλίναντες ἐῶσιν·
ὣς γὰρ τὰ πρώτισθ' ὁσίη γένεθ'· οἱ δὲ ἄνακτι
εὔχονται, δίφρον δὲ θεοῦ τότε μοῖρα φυλάσσει.
ἔνθεν δὲ προτέρω ἔκιες ἑκατηβόλ' Ἄπολλον·
Κηφισὸν δ' ἄρ' ἔπειτα κιχήσαο καλλιρέεθρον,
ὅς τε Λιλαίηθεν προχέει καλλίρροον ὕδωρ·
τὸν διαβὰς Ἑκάεργε καὶ Ὠκαλέην πολύπυργον
ἔνθεν ἄρ' εἰς Ἁλίαρτον ἀφίκεο ποιήεντα.
βῆς δ' ἐπὶ Τελφούσης· τόθι τοι ἅδε χῶρος ἀπήμων
τεύξασθαι νηόν τε καὶ ἄλσεα δενδρήεντα.

223 ἶξες *x p*: ἴξας D S ed. pr.: εἶξας M ἀπ' M ed. pr. ἐπ' cet. 224 μυκάλισσον M τέμμισον M: τελμησσὸν *p*: Τευμησσός, ὄρος Βοιωτίας. Ὅμηρος ἐν τῷ εἰς Ἀπόλλωνα ὕμνῳ citato h. v. Steph. Byz. 227 πω τότε *p* D: πώποτε cet. 228 ἀμπεδίον codd. corr. Ilgen ὕλην codd. corr. Barnes 230 ὄγχηστον hic codd. τὰ εἰς σ̄τ̄ο̄ς̄ τῷ η̄ παραληγόμενα κύρια ὀξύνεται, Ὀγχηστὸς ἄλσος [B 506] Herodian. i. 223. 29 Lentz; cf. Herm. 88, 186, 190 231 ἀναπνείει codd. praeter M N S 232 om. (ex homoeotel.) M B O 233 οὐδὲ L¹ Π 234 κείν' vulg.: κεῖνον M (sc. κεῖν'): κεῖν' S κρατεόυσιν M ἀφιέν (ss. τ) M 235 ἄγησιν codd. corr. Ilgen, Cobet 241 προχέει] προίει Hesiod. fr. 37 243 ἁλἴαρτον Γ m. 2 '*leg.* ἁλιαρ' Casaubon: ἅμαρτον, ἅμαρτον cet. 244 δελφούσης (ss. τ) Γ: δελφούσης cet. οἱ codd. praeter M E

στῆς δὲ μάλ' ἄγχ' αὐτῆς καί μιν πρὸς μῦθον ἔειπες·
  Τελφοῦσ' ἐνθάδε δὴ φρονέω περικαλλέα νηὸν
ἀνθρώπων τεῦξαι χρηστήριον, οἵ τέ μοι αἰεὶ
ἐνθάδ' ἀγινήσουσι τεληέσσας ἑκατόμβας,
ἠμὲν ὅσοι Πελοπόννησον πίειραν ἔχουσιν
ἠδ' ὅσοι Εὐρώπην τε καὶ ἀμφιρύτους κάτα νήσους,
χρησόμενοι· τοῖσιν δέ τ' ἐγὼ νημερτέα βουλὴν
πᾶσι θεμιστεύοιμι χρέων ἐνὶ πίονι νηῷ.
  Ὣς εἰπὼν διέθηκε θεμείλια Φοῖβος Ἀπόλλων
εὐρέα καὶ μάλα μακρὰ διηνεκές· ἣ δὲ ἰδοῦσα
Τελφοῦσα κραδίην ἐχολώσατο εἶπέ τε μῦθον·
  Φοῖβε ἄναξ ἑκάεργε ἔπος τί τοι ἐν φρεσὶ θήσω,
ἐνθάδ' ἐπεὶ φρονέεις τεῦξαι περικαλλέα νηὸν
ἔμμεναι ἀνθρώποις χρηστήριον, οἳ δέ τοι αἰεὶ
ἐνθάδ' ἀγινήσουσι τεληέσσας ἑκατόμβας·
ἀλλ' ἔκ τοι ἐρέω, σὺ δ' ἐνὶ φρεσὶ βάλλεο σῇσι·
πημανέει σ' αἰεὶ κτύπος ἵππων ὠκειάων
ἀρδόμενοί τ' οὐρῆες ἐμῶν ἱερῶν ἀπὸ πηγέων·
ἔνθα τις ἀνθρώπων βουλήσεται εἰσοράασθαι
ἅρματά τ' εὐποίητα καὶ ὠκυπόδων κτύπον ἵππων
ἢ νηόν τε μέγαν καὶ κτήματα πόλλ' ἐνεόντα.
ἀλλ' εἰ δή τι πίθοιο, σὺ δὲ κρείσσων καὶ ἀρείων
ἐσσὶ ἄναξ ἐμέθεν, σεῦ δὲ σθένος ἐστὶ μέγιστον·
ἐν Κρίσῃ ποίησαι ὑπὸ πτυχὶ Παρνησοῖο.
ἔνθ' οὔθ' ἅρματα καλὰ δονήσεται, οὔτε τοι ἵππων
ὠκυπόδων κτύπος ἔσται ἐΰδμητον περὶ βωμόν.
ἀλλά τοι ὣς προσάγοιεν Ἰηπαιήονι δῶρα

247 δελφοῦσ' (256 δελφοῦσα) praeter M codd. 249 ἐνθάδ'] πολλοὶ M 251 ἀμφιρύτας codd. praeter M 252 τ'] κ' Ilgen, cf. 292 253 θεμιστεύσοιμι B Γ, cf. 293 ἐν M 255 ἣ δὲ ἰδοῦσα Hermann cl. 341 : δ' ἐσιδοῦσα codd. 259 ἀνθρώποισι codd. praeter *p* 260 τελειέσσας E T *p* (praeter P R[1]) 261–289 om. E T 263 πηγῶν M 269 κρίση M : -ει V[1] : κρίσση cet. ποιῆσαι M παρνησοῖο M : -ασ(σ)οῖο cet. 272 τοι M : καὶ cet. προάγοιεν *x* D S ed. pr. : προσάγοιεν cet. (προσάγοι ἐνηεῖ παιήονι M)

ἀνθρώπων κλυτὰ φῦλα, σὺ δὲ φρένας ἀμφιγεγηθὼς
δέξαι' ἱερὰ καλὰ περικτιόνων ἀνθρώπων.
  Ὣς εἰποῦσ' Ἑκάτου πέπιθε φρένας, ὄφρα οἱ αὐτῇ
Τελφούσῃ κλέος εἴη ἐπὶ χθονὶ μηδ' Ἑκάτοιο.
ἔνθεν δὲ προτέρω ἔκιες ἑκατηβόλ' Ἄπολλον,
ἷξες δ' ἐς Φλεγύων ἀνδρῶν πόλιν ὑβριστάων,
οἳ Διὸς οὐκ ἀλέγοντες ἐπὶ χθονὶ ναιετάασκον
ἐν καλῇ βήσσῃ Κηφισίδος ἐγγύθι λίμνης.
ἔνθεν καρπαλίμως προσέβης πρὸς δειράδα θύων,
ἵκεο δ' ἐς Κρίσην ὑπὸ Παρνησὸν νιφόεντα
κνημὸν πρὸς ζέφυρον τετραμμένον, αὐτὰρ ὕπερθεν
πέτρη ἐπικρέμαται, κοίλη δ' ὑποδέδρομε βῆσσα
τρηχεῖ'· ἔνθα ἄναξ τεκμήρατο Φοῖβος Ἀπόλλων
νηὸν ποιήσασθαι ἐπήρατον εἶπέ τε μῦθον·
  ἐνθάδε δὴ φρονέω τεύξειν περικαλλέα νηὸν
ἔμμεναι ἀνθρώποις χρηστήριον οἵ τέ μοι αἰεὶ
ἐνθάδ' ἀγινήσουσι τεληέσσας ἑκατόμβας,
ἠμὲν ὅσοι Πελοπόννησον πίειραν ἔχουσιν,
ἠδ' ὅσοι Εὐρώπην τε καὶ ἀμφιρύτους κατὰ νήσους,
χρησόμενοι· τοῖσιν δ' ἄρ' ἐγὼ νημερτέα βουλὴν
πᾶσι θεμιστεύοιμι χρέων ἐνὶ πίονι νηῷ.
  Ὣς εἰπὼν διέθηκε θεμείλια Φοῖβος Ἀπόλλων
εὐρέα καὶ μάλα μακρὰ διηνεκές· αὐτὰρ ἐπ' αὐτοῖς
λάϊνον οὐδὸν ἔθηκε Τροφώνιος ἠδ' Ἀγαμήδης
υἱέες Ἐργίνου, φίλοι ἀθανάτοισι θεοῖσιν·
ἀμφὶ δὲ νηὸν ἔνασσαν ἀθέσφατα φῦλ' ἀνθρώπων
κτιστοῖσιν λάεσσιν ἀοίδιμον ἔμμεναι αἰεί.

274 δέξαι M *x* D S : δέξαιο *p* corr. Ilgen   276 τελφούσῃ M L[1] ss. : δελφούσῃ cet.   hινα κλεος ειη I. G. Ins. Aeg. 737   279 ναιετάεσκον M   282 ἶκες S   κρίσσην praeter M libri   283 κνῆμον D L[1] Π   284 πέτρος M   ὑποκρέμαται *x* At D S ed. pr.   290–293 bina signa (⩽) praefixa habet T   291 ἠδ'] οἵδ' *x* N ed. pr.   ἀμφιρύτας ed. pr.   292 τοῖσιν] τῇσιν *x* D ed. pr.   ἄρ' M : ἂν cet.   293–320 om. B   293 θεμιστεύσοιμι praeter M omnes, cf. 253   νηῷ] βωμῷ *p* (νηῷ νιῷ ss. N O P V[1])   295 μακρὰ] καλὰ M   διηνεκὲς M : διαμπερὲς cet., cf. 255   297 υἱέε σεργίνου vulg. : υ. σεργῖνος Π corr. S V[2] ed. pr.   299 ξεστοῖσιν Ernesti : ῥυτοῖσιν, τυκτοῖσιν alii

ἀγχοῦ δὲ κρήνη καλλίρροος ἔνθα δράκαιναν
κτεῖνεν ἄναξ Διὸς υἱὸς ἀπὸ κρατεροῖο βιοῖο
ζατρεφέα μεγάλην τέρας ἄγριον, ἣ κακὰ πολλὰ
ἀνθρώπους ἔρδεσκεν ἐπὶ χθονί, πολλὰ μὲν αὐτοὺς
πολλὰ δὲ μῆλα ταναύποδ᾽ ἐπεὶ πέλε πῆμα δαφοινόν.
καί ποτε δεξαμένη χρυσοθρόνου ἔτρεφεν Ἥρης
δεινόν τ᾽ ἀργαλέον τε Τυφάονα πῆμα βροτοῖσιν,
ὅν ποτ᾽ ἄρ᾽ Ἥρη ἔτικτε χολωσαμένη Διὶ πατρὶ
ἡνίκ᾽ ἄρα Κρονίδης ἐρικυδέα γείνατ᾽ Ἀθήνην
ἐν κορυφῇ· ἡ δ᾽ αἶψα χολώσατο πότνια Ἥρη
ἠδὲ καὶ ἀγρομένοισι μετ᾽ ἀθανάτοισιν ἔειπε·
κέκλυτέ μευ πάντες τε θεοὶ πᾶσαί τε θέαιναι,
ὡς ἔμ᾽ ἀτιμάζειν ἄρχει νεφεληγερέτα Ζεὺς
πρῶτος, ἐπεί μ᾽ ἄλοχον ποιήσατο κέδν᾽ εἰδυῖαν·
καὶ νῦν νόσφιν ἐμεῖο τέκε γλαυκῶπιν Ἀθήνην,
ἣ πᾶσιν μακάρεσσι μεταπρέπει ἀθανάτοισιν·
αὐτὰρ ὅ γ᾽ ἠπεδανὸς γέγονεν μετὰ πᾶσι θεοῖσι
παῖς ἐμὸς Ἥφαιστος ῥικνὸς πόδας ὃν τέκον αὐτὴ

ῥίψ᾽ ἀνὰ χερσὶν ἑλοῦσα καὶ ἔμβαλον εὐρέϊ πόντῳ·
ἀλλά ἑ Νηρῆος θυγάτηρ Θέτις ἀργυρόπεζα
δέξατο καὶ μετὰ ᾗσι κασιγνήτῃσι κόμισσεν·
ὡς ὄφελ᾽ ἄλλο θεοῖσι χαρίσσασθαι μακάρεσσι.
σχέτλιε ποικιλομῆτα τί νῦν μητίσεαι ἄλλο;

304 *ταναύποδ᾽* *x* S ed. pr.: *τανύποδ᾽* cet., cf. Herm. 232, ι 464 306 *τυφάονα* *p* S ed. pr., cf. 352: *τυφλὸν* *x* At D: *τυφλὸν τε* M 308 *ἥνεκ᾽ ἄρα* M praefixis punctis: *εὖτ᾽ ἄρα δὴ* cet. 309 *κορυφῆς*, s m. 2, Γ: *ἄλλως ἐκ κορυφῆς* V², idem Barnes 310 *ἠδὲ* M D N 311 *θεαὶ* pro *θεοὶ* A Γ L² O P 313 *ἐποιήσατο* codd. corr. Steph. 314 *ἐμοῖο* M Γ 317 *λείπει* marg. ed. pr., lacunam stat. Matthiae *αὐτὴ* ex *αὐτὸς* uv. T 318 *ῥίψ᾽ ἀνὰ* (ss. *δε*) Γ: *ῥίψα δὲ χερσὶν* V² *ἐλοῦσα* (ss. *ὼν*) T *ἔμβαλον* M ed. pr. Γ ss.: *ἔμβαλεν* cet. 320 *κόμισεν* codd. corr. Steph.: *ἐβάστασεν· εἰ δὲ μετὰ τοῦ η̄ ἐπιμελείας ἠξίωσεν· ὁ αὐτὸς καὶ ἐν τῇ σ̄ ἰλιάδος* [395]· *ἥ μ᾽ ἐσάωσ᾽ ὅτε μ᾽ ἄλγος ἀφίκ* (ss. *α*) marg. L¹ Π 321 *χαρίσασθαι* M: *χαρίζεσθαι* cet., cf. 430 322 *σχέτλια* M *μητίσεαι* M: *μήσεαι* *x* D: *ἔτι μήσεαι* *p*

πῶς ἔτλης οἶος τεκέειν γλαυκῶπιδ' Ἀθήνην;
οὐκ ἂν ἐγὼ τεκόμην; καὶ σὴ κεκλημένη ἔμπης
ἦα ῥ' ἐν ἀθανάτοισιν οἳ οὐρανὸν εὐρὺν ἔχουσι.
φράζεο νῦν μή τοί τι κακὸν μητίσομ' ὀπίσσω·
καὶ νῦν μέν τοι ἐγὼ τεχνήσομαι ὥς κε γένηται
παῖς ἐμὸς ὅς κε θεοῖσι μεταπρέποι ἀθανάτοισιν,
οὔτε σὸν αἰσχύνασ' ἱερὸν λέχος οὔτ' ἐμὸν αὐτῆς,
οὐδέ τοι εἰς εὐνὴν πωλήσομαι, ἀλλ' ἀπὸ σεῖο
τηλόθεν οὖσα θεοῖσι μετέσσομαι ἀθανάτοισιν.
Ὣς εἰποῦσ' ἀπονόσφι θεῶν κίε χωομένη περ.
αὐτίκ' ἔπειτ' ἠρᾶτο βοῶπις πότνια Ἥρη,
χειρὶ καταπρηνεῖ δ' ἔλασε χθόνα καὶ φάτο μῦθον·
κέκλυτε νῦν μοι γαῖα καὶ οὐρανὸς εὐρὺς ὕπερθεν,
Τιτῆνές τε θεοὶ τοὶ ὑπὸ χθονὶ ναιετάοντες
Τάρταρον ἀμφὶ μέγαν, τῶν ἐξ ἄνδρες τε θεοί τε·
αὐτοὶ νῦν μευ πάντες ἀκούσατε καὶ δότε παῖδα
νόσφι Διός, μηδέν τι βίην ἐπιδευέα κείνου·
ἀλλ' ὅ γε φέρτερος ἔστω ὅσον Κρόνου εὐρύοπα Ζεύς.
Ὣς ἄρα φωνήσασ' ἵμασε χθόνα χειρὶ παχείῃ·
κινήθη δ' ἄρα γαῖα φερέσβιος, ἡ δὲ ἰδοῦσα
τέρπετο ὃν κατὰ θυμόν, ὀΐετο γὰρ τελέεσθαι.
ἐκ τούτου δὴ ἔπειτα τελεσφόρον εἰς ἐνιαυτὸν
οὔτε ποτ' εἰς εὐνὴν Διὸς ἤλυθε μητιόεντος,
οὔτε ποτ' εἰς θῶκον πολυδαίδαλον ὡς τὸ πάρος περ
αὐτῷ ἐφεζομένη πυκινὰς φραζέσκετο βουλάς·

325 ἦ ρ' ἐν M D L¹ Π : ἦ ρ' ἐν E T : ἦ ρ' ἐν *p* : ἦ' ἂρ S : ἦν Γ m. 2 ed. pr. corr. Matthiae 325ª om. codd. praeter *y* (γρ. Π : γρ. καὶ E T : γρ. καὶ οὕτως L¹) : μήτι τοι marg. L¹ Π T : τοί om. marg. E 326 ita M, καὶ νῦν τοίγαρ *p* ed. pr. (γάρ τοι Γ) : καὶ νῦν μὲν τοὶ γὰρ *x* At D ἐγὼ τεχνήσομαι] ἔγωγ' ἐκθήσομαι M 328 αἰσχύνας codd. praeter *p* 331 περ] κῆρ Barnes 335 lacunam hic statuit Peppmueller 336 ἔξ L¹ 338 μὴ δ' ἀντιβίην M 339 ἐστιν. ὅσον M : ἦ ὅσσον ed. pr. : ἦ πόσσον *x* D (πόσον subscr. *s*T): ἦ παρόσον *p* : ἔστω correximus : εἴη Hermann 341 schol. Genev. Φ 319 Ἀπολλόδωρος δέ φησι περισσὸν τὸ σ̄ παρ' αὐτῷ εἶναι, ὡς παρ' Ὁμήρῳ τὴν φερέσβιον ἡ δ' ἐσιδοῦσα praeter M codd. 342 ᾤετο M 344 om. *p* E (ex homoearch.) 346 φραζάσκετο *x* D

ἀλλ' ἥ γ' ἐν νηοῖσι πολυλλίστοισι μένουσα
τέρπετο οἷς ἱεροῖσι βοῶπις πότνια Ἥρη.
ἀλλ' ὅτε δὴ μῆνές τε καὶ ἡμέραι ἐξετελεῦντο
ἂψ περιτελλομένου ἔτεος καὶ ἐπήλυθον ὧραι,
ἡ δ' ἔτεκ' οὔτε θεοῖς ἐναλίγκιον οὔτε βροτοῖσι
δεινόν τ' ἀργαλέον τε Τυφάονα πῆμα βροτοῖσιν.
αὐτίκα τόνδε λαβοῦσα βοῶπις πότνια Ἥρη
δῶκεν ἔπειτα φέρουσα κακῷ κακόν, ἡ δ' ὑπέδεκτο·
ὃς κακὰ πόλλ' ἔρδεσκε κατὰ κλυτὰ φῦλ' ἀνθρώπων.
ὃς τῇ γ' ἀντιάσειε, φέρεσκέ μιν αἴσιμον ἦμαρ
πρίν γέ οἱ ἰὸν ἐφῆκεν ἄναξ ἑκάεργος Ἀπόλλων
καρτερόν· ἡ δ' ὀδύνῃσιν ἐρεχθομένη χαλεπῇσι
κεῖτο μέγ' ἀσθμαίνουσα κυλινδομένη κατὰ χῶρον.
θεσπεσίη δ' ἐνοπὴ γένετ' ἄσπετος, ἡ δὲ καθ' ὕλην
πυκνὰ μάλ' ἔνθα καὶ ἔνθα ἑλίσσετο, λεῖπε δὲ θυμὸν
φοινὸν ἀποπνείουσ', ὁ δ' ἐπηύξατο Φοῖβος Ἀπόλλων·
ἐνταυθοῖ νῦν πύθευ ἐπὶ χθονὶ βωτιανείρῃ,
οὐδὲ σύ γε ζωοῖσι κακὸν δήλημα βροτοῖσιν
ἔσσεαι, οἳ γαίης πολυφόρβου καρπὸν ἔδοντες
ἐνθάδ' ἀγινήσουσι τεληέσσας ἑκατόμβας,
οὐδέ τί τοι θάνατόν γε δυσηλεγέ' οὔτε Τυφωεὺς
ἀρκέσει οὔτε Χίμαιρα δυσώνυμος, ἀλλὰ σέ γ' αὐτοῦ
πύσει γαῖα μέλαινα καὶ ἠλέκτωρ Ὑπερίων.
Ὣς φάτ' ἐπευχόμενος, τὴν δὲ σκότος ὄσσε κάλυψε.
τὴν δ' αὐτοῦ κατέπυσ' ἱερὸν μένος Ἠελίοιο·
ἐξ οὗ νῦν Πυθὼ κικλήσκεται, οἱ δὲ ἄνακτα
Πύθειον καλέουσιν ἐπώνυμον οὕνεκα κεῖθι
αὐτοῦ πῦσε πέλωρ μένος ὀξέος Ἠελίοιο.

347 πολυκλίστοισι M : πολυαλίστοισι At, cf. Dem. 28 349 μῆνες M : νύκτες cet. 350 ἐπιτελλομένου M 351 ἐναλίγγιον p 352 τυφῶνα πῆμα θεοῖσιν M 356 τώγ' M αἴσιον p 357 hic finitur S 358 χαλεπῇσι p M corr. : -οῖσι cet. 363 πουλυβοτείρῃ At 364 δήλομα L[1] 366 ἀδινήσουσι p (praeter N et L[3] P R[1] ss.) 367 δυσκλεέ' M τυφωνεύς M 370 ὄσσ' ἐκάλυψε M 371 ἵμερον codd. corr. Casaubon '*leg.* ἱερ.', Martin 373 πύθιον codd. corr. Barnes 374 αὐτοῦς O πέλας M

Καὶ τότ᾽ ἄρ᾽ ἔγνω ᾗσιν ἐνὶ φρεσὶ Φοῖβος Ἀπόλλων
οὕνεκά μιν κρήνη καλλίρροος ἐξαπάφησε·
βῆ δ᾽ ἐπὶ Τελφούσῃ κοχολωμένος, αἶψα δ᾽ ἵκανε·
στῆ δὲ μάλ᾽ ἄγχ᾽ αὐτῆς καί μιν πρὸς μῦθον ἔειπε·
Τελφοῦσ᾽, οὐκ ἄρ᾽ ἔμελλες ἐμὸν νόον ἐξαπαφοῦσα
χῶρον ἔχουσ᾽ ἐρατὸν προρέειν καλλίρροον ὕδωρ.
ἐνθάδε δὴ καὶ ἐμὸν κλέος ἔσσεται, οὐδὲ σὸν οἴης.
Ἦ καὶ ἐπὶ ῥίον ὦσεν ἄναξ ἑκάεργος Ἀπόλλων
πέτρῃσι προχυτῇσιν, ἀπέκρυψεν δὲ ῥέεθρα,
καὶ βωμὸν ποιήσατ᾽ ἐν ἄλσεϊ δενδρήεντι
ἄγχι μάλα κρήνης καλλιρρόου· ἔνθα δ᾽ ἄνακτι
πάντες ἐπίκλησιν Τελφουσίῳ εὐχετόωνται
οὕνεκα Τελφούσης ἱερῆς ᾔσχυνε ῥέεθρα.
Καὶ τότε δὴ κατὰ θυμὸν ἐφράζετο Φοῖβος Ἀπόλλων
οὕς τινας ἀνθρώπους ὀργιόνας εἰσαγάγοιτο
οἳ θεραπεύσονται Πυθοῖ ἔνι πετρηέσσῃ·
ταῦτ᾽ ἄρα ὁρμαίνων ἐνόησ᾽ ἐπὶ οἴνοπι πόντῳ
νῆα θοήν· ἐν δ᾽ ἄνδρες ἔσαν πολέες τε καὶ ἐσθλοί,
Κρῆτες ἀπὸ Κνωσοῦ Μινωΐου, οἵ ῥά τ᾽ ἄνακτι
ἱερά τε ῥέζουσι καὶ ἀγγέλλουσι θέμιστας
Φοίβου Ἀπόλλωνος χρυσαόρου, ὅττι κεν εἴπῃ
χρείων ἐκ δάφνης γυάλων ὕπο Παρνησοῖο.
οἱ μὲν ἐπὶ πρῆξιν καὶ χρήματα νηῒ μελαίνῃ
ἐς Πύλον ἠμαθόεντα Πυλοιγενέας τ᾽ ἀνθρώπους
ἔπλεον· αὐτὰρ ὁ τοῖσι συνήνετο Φοῖβος Ἀπόλλων·
ἐν πόντῳ δ᾽ ἐπόρουσε δέμας δελφῖνι ἐοικὼς
νηῒ θοῇ, καὶ κεῖτο πέλωρ μέγα τε δεινόν τε·
τῶν δ᾽ ὅς τις κατὰ θυμὸν ἐπιφράσσαιτο νοῆσαι

377 κεχολωμένοι L¹ : -ον E 382 ἧσεν E T 386 τελφούσιον (ss. ω) Γ 389 ὀργίοτας E T (-οτ- corr. fort. ex -ων-): ὀργίονας cet. 391 ἴσως λείπει στίχος εἷς M marg. ταῦτ᾽ ἄρ᾽ ἄμ᾽ Ludwich 392 ἠμαθόην codd. corr. M T man. rec. (νημ̣̈αθόην, ν praefixo) Γ marg. ed. pr. ἔνθ᾽ M 393 κνώσσου p E M : κνωσσοῦ cet. corr. Baumeister 394 ῥέζουσι E T : ῥέξ- cet. ἀγγελέουσι p γρ. V² 398 πυληγενέας codd. corr. Fick, cf. B 54 402 οὔτις M, Γ marg. ἐπιφράσσαιτο p : ἐπιφράσσατο seu ἐπεφράσ(σ)ατο cet.

πάντοσ' ἀνασσείασκε, τίνασσε δὲ νήϊα δοῦρα.
οἱ δ' ἀκέων ἐνὶ νηῒ καθήατο δειμαίνοντες,
οὐδ' οἵ γ' ὅπλ' ἔλυον κοίλην ἀνὰ νῆα μέλαιναν,
οὐδ' ἔλυον λαῖφος νηὸς κυανοπρώροιο·
ἀλλ' ὡς τὰ πρώτιστα κατεστήσαντο βοεῦσιν
ὣς ἔπλεον· κραιπνὸς δὲ νότος κατόπισθεν ἔγειρε
νῆα θοήν· πρῶτον δὲ παρημείβοντο Μάλειαν,
πὰρ δὲ Λακωνίδα γαῖαν ἁλιστέφανον πτολίεθρον
ἷξον καὶ χῶρον τερψιμβρότου Ἠελίοιο
Ταίναρον, ἔνθα τε μῆλα βαθύτριχα βόσκεται αἰεὶ
Ἠελίοιο ἄνακτος, ἔχει δ' ἐπιτερπέα χῶρον.
οἱ μὲν ἄρ' ἔνθ' ἔθελον νῆα σχεῖν ἠδ' ἀποβάντες
φράσσασθαι μέγα θαῦμα καὶ ὀφθαλμοῖσιν ἰδέσθαι
εἰ μενέει νηὸς γλαφυρῆς δαπέδοισι πέλωρον,
ἦ εἰς οἶδμ' ἅλιον πολυΐχθυον ἀμφὶς ὀρούσει·
ἀλλ' οὐ πηδαλίοισιν ἐπείθετο νηῦς εὐεργής,
ἀλλὰ παρὲκ Πελοπόννησον πίειραν ἔχουσα
ἤϊ' ὁδόν, πνοιῇ δὲ ἄναξ ἑκάεργος Ἀπόλλων
ῥηϊδίως ἴθυν'· ἡ δὲ πρήσσουσα κέλευθον
Ἀρήνην ἵκανε καὶ Ἀργυφέην ἐρατεινὴν
καὶ Θρύον Ἀλφειοῖο πόρον καὶ ἐΰκτιτον Αἶπυ
καὶ Πύλον ἠμαθόεντα Πυλοιγενέας τ' ἀνθρώπους·
βῆ δὲ παρὰ Κρουνοὺς καὶ Χαλκίδα καὶ παρὰ Δύμην
ἠδὲ παρ' Ἤλιδα δῖαν ὅθι κρατέουσιν Ἐπειοί·

403 πάντοσ' *p*: πάντοθ' cet. ἀνασσείασκε M T: ἀνασ(σ)είσασκε cet. δουρός M 404 καθείατο codd. 406 ita M: οὐδὲ λύον cet. 407 πρώτιστα M: πρῶτα cet.: οἳ τὰ πρῶτα ed. pr. 408 ἔπειγε Ruhnken, sed cf. Herod. vii. 49 Ap. Rhod. i. 666, 1159, iii. 295 Anth. Pal. vi. 21. 12 Quintus Smyrnaeus ix. 271 410 Ἕλος τ' ἔφαλον pro ἁλιστέφανον Matthiae 416 om. *p* 417 ἀμφὶς] αὖθις Pierson 420 ἤϊ' M: ἦεν cet. πνοιὴν M 423 ἐΰκτιτον M Γ marg.: ἐυκτίμενον, ἐυκτίσμενον cet., cf. B 592 Quint. Smyrn. xii. 91 αἶπυ M O T marg.: αἰπὺ L[1] T: αἰπύ cet. 424 πυληγενέας codd.: πολυγενέας ed. pr. cf. 398. idem fere iter narrat Stesich. fr. 44 425 *o* 295 βὰν δὲ παρὰ κρουνοὺς καὶ χαλκίδα καλλιρέεθρον in codd. Odysseae omissum cit. Strabo 350, 447 (et hic quidem πετρήεσσαν e B 640 fort. petitum) 426 = *o* 298

εὖτε Φερὰς ἐπέβαλλεν ἀγαλλομένη Διὸς οὔρῳ
καί σφιν ὑπὲκ νεφέων Ἰθάκης τ' ὄρος αἰπὺ πέφαντο,
Δουλίχιόν τε Σάμη τε καὶ ὑλήεσσα Ζάκυνθος.
ἀλλ' ὅτε δὴ Πελοπόννησον παρενίσατο πᾶσαν,
καὶ δὴ ἐπὶ Κρίσης κατεφαίνετο κόλπος ἀπείρων
ὅς τε διὲκ Πελοπόννησον πίειραν ἐέργει,
ἦλθ' ἄνεμος ζέφυρος μέγας αἴθριος ἐκ Διὸς αἴσης
λάβρος ἐπαιγίζων ἐξ αἰθέρος, ὄφρα τάχιστα
νηῦς ἀνύσειε θέουσα θαλάσσης ἁλμυρὸν ὕδωρ.
ἄψορροι δὴ ἔπειτα πρὸς ἠῶ τ' ἠέλιόν τε
ἔπλεον, ἡγεμόνευε δ' ἄναξ Διὸς υἱὸς Ἀπόλλων·
ἶξον δ' ἐς Κρίσην εὐδείελον ἀμπελόεσσαν
ἐς λιμέν', ἡ δ' ἀμάθοισιν ἐχρίμψατο ποντοπόρος νηῦς.
ἔνθ' ἐκ νηὸς ὄρουσεν ἄναξ ἑκάεργος Ἀπόλλων
ἀστέρι εἰδόμενος μέσῳ ἤματι· τοῦ δ' ἀπὸ πολλαὶ
σπινθαρίδες πωτῶντο, σέλας δ' εἰς οὐρανὸν ἶκεν·
ἐς δ' ἄδυτον κατέδυσε διὰ τριπόδων ἐριτίμων.
ἔνθ' ἄρ' ὅ γε φλόγα δαῖε πιφαυσκόμενος τὰ ἃ κῆλα,
πᾶσαν δὲ Κρίσην κάτεχεν σέλας· αἱ δ' ὀλόλυξαν
Κρισαίων ἄλοχοι καλλίζωνοί τε θύγατρες
Φοίβου ὑπὸ ῥιπῆς· μέγα γὰρ δέος ἔμβαλ' ἑκάστῳ.
ἔνθεν δ' αὖτ' ἐπὶ νῆα νόημ' ὣς ἆλτο πέτεσθαι
ἀνέρι εἰδόμενος αἰζηῷ τε κρατερῷ τε
πρωθήβῃ, χαίτῃς εἰλυμένος εὐρέας ὤμους·

427 φέρας M : φερᾶς L^1 ἡ δὲ φερὰς ἐπέβαλλεν ἐπειγομένη Διὸς οὔρῳ ο 297 (ἀγαλλομένη cit. Strabo 350): ubi φεαῖς (seu φεὰς) leg. Aristarchus, cf. et Rhian. ap. Steph. Byz. in Ἀρτεμίτα 428 πέφανται M : πέφαντο corr. ex πέφανται Mon.: πέφαντο cet. 429 = α 246 ι 24 π 123 430 παρενίσατο M : παρενίσσετο cet. 431 ἐπὶ M R^1: ἐπεὶ cet. κρίσης M : κρίσσης cet. 436 ἄψορρον M, cf. Ω 330 Hes. Theog. 659 438 κρίσσην praeter M codd., item 445 439 ἐς λιμένος δ' ἀμάθοισιν M : ἐλλιμέν' E 441 ἤματι μέσω (ss. β, α) E T 442 πώτοντο M ἧκεν codd. corr. Barnes 443 κατέδυσσε *x* ed. pr. ἴαχεν ἐξ ἀδύτοιο διὰ τριπόδων ἐριτίμων Ar. Eq. 1016 444 ἐν δ' codd. corr. Hermann φλόγ' ἔδαιε praeter *x* M codd. πιφασκόμενος Γ V^1 E L^1: ἐπιφ. Π 445 κρίσιν M : κρίσσην cet. 446 κρισ(σ)αγῶν vulg.: κρισσαίων V^2 Casaubon : -σ- Hermann 447 εἶλεν ἕκαστον *x p* 450 χαίτη Γ corr., ed. pr.

καί σφεας φωνήσας ἔπεα πτερόεντα προσηύδα·
ὦ ξεῖνοι τίνες ἐστέ; πόθεν πλεῖθ' ὑγρὰ κέλευθα;
ἤ τι κατὰ πρῆξιν, ἦ μαψιδίως ἀλάλησθε
οἷά τε ληϊστῆρες ὑπεὶρ ἅλα, τοί τ' ἀλόωνται
ψυχὰς παρθέμενοι κακὸν ἀλλοδαποῖσι φέροντες;
τίφθ' οὕτως ἧσθον τετιηότες, οὐδ' ἐπὶ γαῖαν
ἔκβητ', οὐδὲ καθ' ὅπλα μελαίνης νηὸς ἔθεσθε;
αὕτη μέν γε δίκη πέλει ἀνδρῶν ἀλφηστάων
ὁππόταν ἐκ πόντοιο ποτὶ χθονὶ νηῒ μελαίνῃ
ἔλθωσιν καμάτῳ ἀδηκότες, αὐτίκα δέ σφεας
σίτοιο γλυκεροῖο περὶ φρένας ἵμερος αἱρεῖ.
Ὣς φάτο καί σφιν θάρσος ἐνὶ στήθεσσιν ἔθηκε.
τὸν καὶ ἀμειβόμενος Κρητῶν ἀγὸς ἀντίον ηὔδα·
ξεῖν', ἐπεὶ οὐ μὲν γάρ τι καταθνητοῖσιν ἔοικας,
οὐ δέμας οὐδὲ φυήν, ἀλλ' ἀθανάτοισι θεοῖσιν,
οὖλέ τε καὶ μέγα χαῖρε, θεοὶ δέ τοι ὄλβια δοῖεν.
καί μοι τοῦτ' ἀγόρευσον ἐτήτυμον ὄφρ' εὖ εἰδῶ·
τίς δῆμος; τίς γαῖα; τίνες βροτοὶ ἐγγεγάασιν;
ἄλλῃ γὰρ φρονέοντες ἐπεπλέομεν μέγα λαῖτμα
εἰς Πύλον ἐκ Κρήτης, ἔνθεν γένος εὐχόμεθ' εἶναι·
νῦν δ' ὧδε ξὺν νηῒ κατήλθομεν οὔ τι ἑκόντες
νόστου ἱέμενοι ἄλλην ὁδὸν ἄλλα κέλευθα·
ἀλλά τις ἀθανάτων δεῦρ' ἤγαγεν οὐκ ἐθέλοντας.
Τοὺς δ' ἀπαμειβόμενος προσέφη ἑκάεργος Ἀπόλλων·
ξεῖνοι, τοὶ Κνωσὸν πολυδένδρεον ἀμφινέμεσθε
τὸ πρίν, ἀτὰρ νῦν οὐκ ἔθ' ὑπότροποι αὖθις ἔσεσθε
ἔς τε πόλιν ἐρατὴν καὶ δώματα καλὰ ἕκαστος
ἔς τε φίλας ἀλόχους, ἀλλ' ἐνθάδε πίονα νηὸν
ἕξετ' ἐμὸν πολλοῖσι τετιμένον ἀνθρώποισιν·
εἰμὶ δ' ἐγὼ Διὸς υἱός, Ἀπόλλων δ' εὔχομαι εἶναι,
ὑμέας δ' ἤγαγον ἐνθάδ' ὑπὲρ μέγα λαῖτμα θαλάσσης

452 *πόθεν ἐστὲ* codd., *τίνες* Γ ss., ed. pr., cf. Dem. 411, Merc. 453   459 *ἐπὶ* M   460 *σφας* *p*   466 *γάρ τοι* E T   468 *ἐκγεγάασιν* libri, corr. Ilgen   475 *κνωσσὸν* libri   479 *ἐμὸν*   *λλοῖσι* L[1] Π: *καλλοῖσι* E T

οὔ τι κακὰ φρονέων, ἀλλ' ἐνθάδε πίονα νηὸν
ἕξετ' ἐμὸν πᾶσιν μάλα τίμιον ἀνθρώποισι,
βουλάς τ' ἀθανάτων εἰδήσετε, τῶν ἰότητι
αἰεὶ τιμήσεσθε διαμπερὲς ἤματα πάντα.
ἀλλ' ἄγεθ' ὡς ἂν ἐγὼ εἴπω πείθεσθε τάχιστα·
ἱστία μὲν πρῶτον κάθετον λύσαντε βοείας,
νῆα δ' ἔπειτα θοὴν ἀν' ἐπ' ἠπείρου ἐρύσασθε,
ἐκ δὲ κτήμαθ' ἕλεσθε καὶ ἔντεα νηὸς ἐΐσης,
καὶ βωμὸν ποιήσατ' ἐπὶ ῥηγμῖνι θαλάσσης,
πῦρ ἐπικαίοντες ἐπί τ' ἄλφιτα λευκὰ θύοντες·
εὔχεσθαι δὴ ἔπειτα παριστάμενοι περὶ βωμόν.
ὡς μὲν ἐγὼ τὸ πρῶτον ἐν ἠεροειδέϊ πόντῳ
εἰδόμενος δελφῖνι θοῆς ἐπὶ νηὸς ὄρουσα,
ὣς ἐμοὶ εὔχεσθαι δελφινίῳ· αὐτὰρ ὁ βωμὸς
αὐτὸς δέλφειος καὶ ἐπόψιος ἔσσεται αἰεί.
δειπνῆσαί τ' ἄρ' ἔπειτα θοῇ παρὰ νηῒ μελαίνῃ,
καὶ σπεῖσαι μακάρεσσι θεοῖς οἳ Ὄλυμπον ἔχουσιν.
αὐτὰρ ἐπὴν σίτοιο μελίφρονος ἐξ ἔρον ἧσθε,
ἔρχεσθαί θ' ἅμ' ἐμοὶ καὶ ἰηπαιήον' ἀείδειν
εἰς ὅ κε χῶρον ἵκησθον ἵν' ἕξετε πίονα νηόν.
Ὣς ἔφαθ'· οἱ δ' ἄρα τοῦ μάλα μὲν κλύον ἠδ' ἐπίθοντο.
ἱστία μὲν πρῶτον κάθεσαν, λῦσαν δὲ βοείας,
ἱστὸν δ' ἱστοδόκῃ πέλασαν προτόνοισιν ὑφέντες,
ἐκ δὲ καὶ αὐτοὶ βαῖνον ἐπὶ ῥηγμῖνι θαλάσσης,
ἐκ δ' ἁλὸς ἤπειρον δὲ θοὴν ἀνὰ νῆ' ἐρύσαντο
ὑψοῦ ἐπὶ ψαμάθοις, παρὰ δ' ἕρματα μακρὰ τάνυσσαν,
καὶ βωμὸν ποίησαν ἐπὶ ῥηγμῖνι θαλάσσης·
πῦρ δ' ἐπικαίοντες ἐπί τ' ἄλφιτα λευκὰ θύοντες
εὔχονθ' ὡς ἐκέλευε παριστάμενοι περὶ βωμόν.
δόρπον ἔπειθ' εἵλοντο θοῇ παρὰ νηῒ μελαίνῃ,

488 θοὴν ἐπὶ ἠπείρου codd. (ἐπ' ἠπ- M T) corr. Agar cl. 506 491 ἐπικαίοντές γ' M Γ O 496 δελφίνιος M : δέλφιος A D O P Q 501 εἰς ὅτε M 505 βῆσαν M 507 περὶ δ' ἕργματα M 510 περὶ Π marg. Ernesti : παρὰ cet., cf. 492

καὶ σπεῖσαν μακάρεσσι θεοῖς οἳ Ὄλυμπον ἔχουσιν.
αὐτὰρ ἐπεὶ πόσιος καὶ ἐδητύος ἐξ ἔρον ἕντο
βάν ῥ' ἴμεν· ἦρχε δ' ἄρα σφιν ἄναξ Διὸς υἱὸς Ἀπόλλων
φόρμιγγ' ἐν χείρεσσιν ἔχων ἐρατὸν κιθαρίζων
καλὰ καὶ ὕψι βιβάς· οἱ δὲ ῥήσσοντες ἕποντο
Κρῆτες πρὸς Πυθὼ καὶ ἰηπαιήον' ἄειδον,
οἷοί τε Κρητῶν παιήονες οἷσί τε Μοῦσα
ἐν στήθεσσιν ἔθηκε θεὰ μελίγηρυν ἀοιδήν.
ἄκμητοι δὲ λόφον προσέβαν ποσίν, αἶψα δ' ἵκοντο
Παρνησὸν καὶ χῶρον ἐπήρατον ἔνθ' ἄρ' ἔμελλεν
οἰκήσειν πολλοῖσι τετιμένος ἀνθρώποισι·
δεῖξε δ' ἄγων ἄδυτον ζάθεον καὶ πίονα νηόν.
τῶν δ' ὠρίνετο θυμὸς ἐνὶ στήθεσσι φίλοισι·
τὸν καὶ ἀνειρόμενος Κρητῶν ἀγὸς ἀντίον ηὔδα·
ὦ ἄν' ἐπεὶ δὴ τῆλε φίλων καὶ πατρίδος αἴης
ἤγαγες· οὕτω που τῷ σῷ φίλον ἔπλετο θυμῷ·
πῶς καὶ νῦν βιόμεσθα; τό σε φράζεσθαι ἄνωγμεν.
οὔτε τρυγηφόρος ἥδε γ' ἐπήρατος οὔτ' εὐλείμων,
ὥς τ' ἀπό τ' εὖ ζώειν καὶ ἅμ' ἀνθρώποισιν ὀπηδεῖν.
Τοὺς δ' ἐπιμειδήσας προσέφη Διὸς υἱὸς Ἀπόλλων·
νήπιοι ἄνθρωποι δυστλήμονες οἳ μελεδῶνας
βούλεσθ' ἀργαλέους τε πόνους καὶ στείνεα θυμῷ·
ῥηΐδιον ἔπος ὔμμ' ἐρέω καὶ ἐπὶ φρεσὶ θήσω.
δεξιτερῇ μάλ' ἕκαστος ἔχων ἐν χειρὶ μάχαιραν
σφάζειν αἰεὶ μῆλα· τὰ δ' ἄφθονα πάντα παρέσται,
ὅσσα ἐμοί κ' ἀγάγωσι περικλυτὰ φῦλ' ἀνθρώπων·
νηὸν δὲ προφύλαχθε, δέδεχθε δὲ φῦλ' ἀνθρώπων

515 ἐρατὸν M, Barnes: ἔχων ατὸν E T: ἔχω ατὸν L[1] Π: ἀγατὸν D ed. pr.: χρυσῆν *p*: χαρίεν Athen. 22 C (Ὅμηρος ἢ τῶν Ὁμηριδῶν τις ἐν τῷ εἰς Ἀπόλλωνα ὕμνῳ φησὶν [514 Ἀπόλλων—516 βιβάς]) 516 ῥήσσοντες M Γ: φρίσσοντες cet. 522 τετιμημένος M At Γ 523 ἄδυτον ζάθεον *y* γρ. V[2]: αὐτοῦ δάπεδον cet. 525 τῶν *x* ed. pr.: τὸν cet. (cum V[2]) 530 τ' εὖ] τίνας uv. T ss. 532 μελεδώνας L[1] Π 534 ῥηιδίως M 536 μᾶλα *p* (μάλα B Γ) 537 ὅσσα] αἰὲν M ὅσσ' ἅμ' ἐμοί κ' Ludwich 538 om. *p* M (ex homoeotel.) νηὸν δὲ Ilgen: τε codd.

ἐνθάδ' ἀγειρομένων καὶ ἐμὴν ἰθύν τε μάλιστα

ἠέ τι τηΰσιον ἔπος ἔσσεται ἠέ τι ἔργον,
ὕβρις θ', ἣ θέμις ἐστὶ καταθνητῶν ἀνθρώπων,
ἄλλοι ἔπειθ' ὑμῖν σημάντορες ἄνδρες ἔσονται,
τῶν ὑπ' ἀναγκαίῃ δεδμήσεσθ' ἤματα πάντα.
εἴρηταί τοι πάντα, σὺ δὲ φρεσὶ σῇσι φύλαξαι.
Καὶ σὺ μὲν οὕτω χαῖρε Διὸς καὶ Λητοῦς υἱέ·
αὐτὰρ ἐγὼ καὶ σεῖο καὶ ἄλλης μνήσομ' ἀοιδῆς.

IV. Εἰς Ἑρμῆν

Ἑρμῆν ὕμνει Μοῦσα Διὸς καὶ Μαιάδος υἱόν,
Κυλλήνης μεδέοντα καὶ Ἀρκαδίης πολυμήλου,
ἄγγελον ἀθανάτων ἐριούνιον, ὃν τέκε Μαῖα
νύμφη ἐϋπλόκαμος Διὸς ἐν φιλότητι μιγεῖσα
αἰδοίη· μακάρων δὲ θεῶν ἠλεύαθ' ὅμιλον
ἄντρον ἔσω ναίουσα παλίσκιον, ἔνθα Κρονίων
νύμφῃ ἐϋπλοκάμῳ μισγέσκετο νυκτὸς ἀμολγῷ,
ὄφρα κατὰ γλυκὺς ὕπνος ἔχοι λευκώλενον Ἥρην,
λήθων ἀθανάτους τε θεοὺς θνητούς τ' ἀνθρώπους.
ἀλλ' ὅτε δὴ μεγάλοιο Διὸς νόος ἐξετελεῖτο,
τῇ δ' ἤδη δέκατος μεὶς οὐρανῷ ἐστήρικτο,
εἴς τε φόως ἄγαγεν, ἀρίσημά τε ἔργα τέτυκτο·
καὶ τότ' ἐγείνατο παῖδα πολύτροπον, αἱμυλομήτην,
ληϊστῆρ', ἐλατῆρα βοῶν, ἡγήτορ' ὀνείρων,

539 ἰθύντε T τὰ μάλιστα D'Orville: καὶ ἐμὴν ἴθυντε θέμιστα Baumeister (Hes. Opp. 9 δίκῃ δ' ἴθυνε θέμιστας), lacunam nos. 540 ἠέ τ' ἐτήσιον M: μάταιον ss. T γ' ἔπος D ed. pr. 543 δεδμήσασθ' M ὄμματα M 544 δ' ἐνὶ M

IV. *codices* M *x y p* (Mon. usque ad 192 O usque ad 80) Titvlvs. τοῦ αὐτοῦ ὕμνοι εἰς ἑρμῆν M: ὕμνος δεύτερος εἰς ἑρμῆν E T: εἰς ἑρμῆν D L[1] Π ed. pr.: εἰς τὸν ἑρμῆν *p* 1 ὑμνεῖ *x* At D ed. pr. 5 ἠλαύνετ' At 10 δὴ om. *p* 11 μὴς (ss. εἰς) M: μεῖς D ed. pr., cf. T 117 13 τότε γείνατο *x* M

νυκτὸς ὀπωπητῆρα, πυληδόκον, ὃς τάχ' ἔμελλεν
ἀμφανέειν κλυτὰ ἔργα μετ' ἀθανάτοισι θεοῖσιν.
ἠῷος γεγονὼς μέσῳ ἤματι ἐγκιθάριζεν,
ἑσπέριος βοῦς κλέψεν ἑκηβόλου Ἀπόλλωνος,
τετράδι τῇ προτέρῃ τῇ μιν τέκε πότνια Μαῖα.
ὃς καὶ ἐπεὶ δὴ μητρὸς ἀπ' ἀθανάτων θόρε γυίων
οὐκέτι δηρὸν ἔκειτο μένων ἱερῷ ἐνὶ λίκνῳ,
ἀλλ' ὅ γ' ἀναΐξας ζήτει βόας Ἀπόλλωνος
οὐδὸν ὑπερβαίνων ὑψηρεφέος ἄντροιο.
ἔνθα χέλυν εὑρὼν ἐκτήσατο μυρίον ὄλβον·
Ἑρμῆς τοι πρώτιστα χέλυν τεκτήνατ' ἀοιδόν,
ἥ ῥά οἱ ἀντεβόλησεν ἐπ' αὐλείῃσι θύρῃσι
βοσκομένη προπάροιθε δόμων ἐριθηλέα ποίην,
σαῦλα ποσὶν βαίνουσα· Διὸς δ' ἐριούνιος υἱὸς
ἀθρήσας ἐγέλασσε καὶ αὐτίκα μῦθον ἔειπε·
σύμβολον ἤδη μοι μέγ' ὀνήσιμον, οὐκ ὀνοτάζω.
χαῖρε φυὴν ἐρόεσσα χοροιτύπε δαιτὸς ἑταίρη,
ἀσπασίη προφανεῖσα· πόθεν τόδε καλὸν ἄθυρμα
αἰόλον ὄστρακον ἕσσο χέλυς ὄρεσι ζώουσα;
ἀλλ' οἴσω σ' εἰς δῶμα λαβών· ὄφελός τί μοι ἔσσῃ,
οὐδ' ἀποτιμήσω· σὺ δέ με πρώτιστον ὀνήσεις.
οἴκοι βέλτερον εἶναι, ἐπεὶ βλαβερὸν τὸ θύρηφιν·
ἦ γὰρ ἐπηλυσίης πολυπήμονος ἔσσεαι ἔχμα
ζώουσ'· ἢν δὲ θάνῃς τότε κεν μάλα καλὸν ἀείδοις.
Ὣς ἄρ' ἔφη· καὶ χερσὶν ἅμ' ἀμφοτέρῃσιν ἀείρας
ἂψ εἴσω κίε δῶμα φέρων ἐρατεινὸν ἄθυρμα.
ἔνθ' ἀναπηλήσας γλυφάνῳ πολιοῖο σιδήρου

15 ὀπωπ[ητῆρα Kaibel Ep. Gr. 1032. 1 = I. G. Sic. Ital. 2557 21 ἱερῶς E T 33 ἕσσο Matthiae, Tyrrell: ἐσσὶ codd. 36 βέλτιον B Γ: σῆ τὸν ἡσίοδον κλέψαντα (κεκλοφότα p) τὸν στίχον [Opp. 365] L[1] Π C L[2] L[3] O R[1] R[2]: cf. Cercidas fr. 3 (P. L. G. ii. 514), carm. pop. 21 ib. iii. 662: σῆ· περὶ ἀποδημήσεως Π τὸ om. x D 37 ἐπηλύσιος B Γ R[1] ἔχμα Ruhnken: αἰχμὰ codd. (αἶχμα M: αἰγχμὰ L[1]) 38 θάνῃς M D ed. pr.: θάνοις cet. κεν Hermann: ἂν codd. ἀείδεις (ss. οις) E T 41 ἀναπειρήνας Stephanus: ἀναπηδήσας Barnes: ἀναπιλήσας perperam Hermann: ἀναπειλήσας Agar

αἰῶν' ἐξετόρησεν ὀρεσκῴοιο χελώνης.
ὡς δ' ὁπότ' ὠκὺ νόημα διὰ στέρνοιο περήσῃ
ἀνέρος ὅν τε θαμιναὶ ἐπιστρωφῶσι μέριμναι,
ἢ ὅτε δινηθῶσιν ἀπ' ὀφθαλμῶν ἀμαρυγαί,
ὣς ἅμ' ἔπος τε καὶ ἔργον ἐμήδετο κύδιμος Ἑρμῆς.
πῆξε δ' ἄρ' ἐν μέτροισι ταμὼν δόνακας καλάμοιο
πειρήνας διὰ νῶτα διὰ ῥινοῖο χελώνης.
ἀμφὶ δὲ δέρμα τάνυσσε βοὸς πραπίδεσσιν ἑῇσι,
καὶ πήχεις ἐνέθηκ', ἐπὶ δὲ ζυγὸν ἤραρεν ἀμφοῖν,
ἑπτὰ δὲ συμφώνους ὀΐων ἐτανύσσατο χορδάς.
αὐτὰρ ἐπεὶ δὴ τεῦξε φέρων ἐρατεινὸν ἄθυρμα
πλήκτρῳ ἐπειρήτιζε κατὰ μέλος, ἡ δ' ὑπὸ χειρὸς
σμερδαλέον κονάβησε· θεὸς δ' ὑπὸ καλὸν ἄειδεν
ἐξ αὐτοσχεδίης πειρώμενος, ἠΰτε κοῦροι
ἡβηταὶ θαλίῃσι παραιβόλα κερτομέουσιν,
ἀμφὶ Δία Κρονίδην καὶ Μαιάδα καλλιπέδιλον
†ὃν πάρος ὠρίζεσκον† ἑταιρείῃ φιλότητι,
ἥν τ' αὐτοῦ γενεὴν ὀνομακλυτὸν ἐξονομάζων·
ἀμφιπόλους τε γέραιρε καὶ ἀγλαὰ δώματα νύμφης,
καὶ τρίποδας κατὰ οἶκον ἐπηετανούς τε λέβητας.
καὶ τὰ μὲν οὖν ἤειδε, τὰ δὲ φρεσὶν ἄλλα μενοίνα.
καὶ τὴν μὲν κατέθηκε φέρων ἱερῷ ἐνὶ λίκνῳ
φόρμιγγα γλαφυρήν· ὁ δ' ἄρα κρειῶν ἐρατίζων

42 αἰὼν M, marg. γρ. ὡς δοκεῖ μοι ἀγῶν' ἐξετό ὀρεσκώ λώνης E L[1]: ὀρεσκώιο κολώνης Π: ὀρεσκώηι λώνης T uv. ante corr. 43 περήσῃ B Franke: περήσει cet. 44 θαμιναὶ codd., Ruhnken: cf. Choerobosc. An. Ox. ii. 180, Matro 79, Nicand. Ther. 239, Call. Aet. 36 (Ox. Pap. vii. 1011), Xen. Anab. iv. 1. 16 (v. l.): θαμειαὶ Barnes 45 ἢ ὅτε M V[2], marg. Γ: αἳ ὅτε x: ἃς ὅτε p δυνηθῶσιν p At ἀμαλδύναι y 46 ἐμήσατο E 47 ταμὼν] λαβὼν D 48 τετρήνας Matthiae, cf. vv. ll. Herod. ii. 11 pro διὰ ῥινοῖο coni. κραταιρίνοιο Barnes (cl. Herod. i. 47): διατρήτοιο Ludwich 51 συμφώνους] θηλυτέρων Antigonus Carystius c. 7: voce συμφωνούσας utitur Ion Chius 3. 2 53 μέρος codd. 54 κονάβησε M: -ισ(σ)ε cet. 55 ἧντε κόραοι M 56 παραίβολα M 58 ὃν codd. (ὃν πάρος Nonnus ii. 269): ὡς Γ corr., V[2]: οἳ Clarke ἠρίζεσκον Γ: ἐρίζεσκον (ss. ἠ) V[2]: ὡρίζ. M καὶ ἑταιρείῃ M 59 ὀνομακλυτὴν p ὀνομάζων praeter M codd.

ἆλτο κατὰ σκοπιὴν εὐώδεος ἐκ μεγάροιο,
ὁρμαίνων δόλον αἰπὺν ἐνὶ φρεσὶν οἷά τε φῶτες
φηληταὶ διέπουσι μελαίνης νυκτὸς ἐν ὥρῃ.
Ἠέλιος μὲν ἔδυνε κατὰ χθονὸς ὠκεανὸν δὲ
αὐτοῖσίν θ' ἵπποισι καὶ ἅρμασιν, αὐτὰρ ἄρ' Ἑρμῆς
Πιερίης ἀφίκανε θεῶν ὄρεα σκιόεντα,
ἔνθα θεῶν μακάρων βόες ἄμβροτοι αὖλιν ἔχεσκον
βοσκόμεναι λειμῶνας ἀκηρασίους ἐρατεινούς.
τῶν τότε Μαιάδος υἱὸς ἐΰσκοπος Ἀργειφόντης
πεντήκοντ' ἀγέλης ἀπετάμνετο βοῦς ἐριμύκους.
πλανοδίας δ' ἤλαυνε διὰ ψαμαθώδεα χῶρον
ἴχνι' ἀποστρέψας· δολίης δ' οὐ λήθετο τέχνης
ἀντία ποιήσας ὁπλάς, τὰς πρόσθεν ὄπισθεν,
τὰς δ' ὄπιθεν πρόσθεν, κατὰ δ' ἔμπαλιν αὐτὸς ἔβαινε.
σάνδαλα δ' αὐτίκα ῥιψὶν ἐπὶ ψαμάθοις ἁλίῃσιν
ἄφραστ' ἠδ' ἀνόητα διέπλεκε, θαυματὰ ἔργα,
συμμίσγων μυρίκας καὶ μυρσινοειδέας ὄζους.
τῶν τότε συνδήσας νεοθηλέαν ἀγκάλῳ ὥρην
ἀβλαβέως ὑπὸ ποσσὶν ἐδήσατο σάνδαλα κοῦφα
αὐτοῖσιν πετάλοισι, τὰ κύδιμος Ἀργειφόντης
ἔσπασε Πιερίηθεν ὁδοιπορίην ἀλεείνων,
οἷά τ' ἐπειγόμενος δολιχὴν ὁδόν, αὐτοτροπήσας.

65 ἆλτο M : ὦρτο *p* V^2 : ὦτο *x*, cf. Υ 62 67 φιληταὶ M D, cf. 159, 175 69 αὐτὰρ ὅγ' Barnes 70 Πηρείη (B 766) non Πιερίη in fabula pristina videtur stetisse : cf. Antonini Lib. 23 (αἱ δὲ ἐνέμοντο ἵναπερ ἦσαν αἱ Ἀδμήτου βόες) θεῶν (sc. θεῖα, cf. 551 ω 67 Υ 53) codd. praeter D ed. pr. 72 ἀκειρασίους *x* D ed. pr. 74 ἀγέλας M 76 ἴχνη codd. corr. Hermann cl. 218 al. 78 πρώτας M 79 αὐτίκ' om. *x* (σάνδαλα ἔριψεν E : σάνδαλα κ' ἔριψεν L^1 : σάνδαλα αὐτίκ' ἔριψεν Π : δ' αὐτί- in spatio vacuo suppl. T) ἔριψεν codd. em. Postgate 81 συμμϊότων E T : συμμίστων L^1 82 νεοθηλέος ἄγκαλον (ἀγκαλὸν *x* At Γ ed. pr.) ὕλης vulg. : νεοθηλέαν ἀγκαλωρήν M 83 ἀβλαδέως Headlam *J. Ph.* 1910. 2 85 ἀλεείνων] ἀλεγύνων Windisch cl. 361 86 αὐτοτροπήσας M V^2 *py* (-τραπήσας Mon. V^1 : αὐτοτροπήσας ὣς E T, γρ. αὐτοτροπήσας Π marg.) : αὐτοπρεπὴς ὣς L^1 Π D ed. pr. : φὼς pro ὣς Martin

τὸν δὲ γέρων ἐνόησε δέμων ἀνθοῦσαν ἀλωὴν
ἱέμενον πεδίον δὲ δι' Ὀγχηστὸν λεχεποίην·
τὸν πρότερος προσέφη Μαίης ἐρικυδέος υἱός·
ὦ γέρον ὅς τε φυτὰ σκάπτεις ἐπικαμπύλος ὤμους,
ἦ πολυοινήσεις εὖτ' ἂν τάδε πάντα φέρῃσι

καί τε ἰδὼν μὴ ἰδὼν εἶναι καὶ κωφὸς ἀκούσας,
καὶ σιγᾶν, ὅτε μή τι καταβλάπτῃ τὸ σὸν αὐτοῦ.
Τόσσον φὰς συνέσευε βοῶν ἴφθιμα κάρηνα.
πολλὰ δ' ὄρη σκιόεντα καὶ αὐλῶνας κελαδεινοὺς
καὶ πεδί' ἀνθεμόεντα διήλασε κύδιμος Ἑρμῆς.
ὀρφναίη δ' ἐπίκουρος ἐπαύετο δαιμονίη νὺξ
ἡ πλείων, τάχα δ' ὄρθρος ἐγίγνετο δημιοεργός·
ἡ δὲ νέον σκοπιὴν προσεβήσατο δῖα Σελήνη
Πάλλαντος θυγάτηρ Μεγαμηδείδαο ἄνακτος,
τῆμος ἐπ' Ἀλφειὸν ποταμὸν Διὸς ἄλκιμος υἱὸς
Φοίβου Ἀπόλλωνος βοῦς ἤλασεν εὐρυμετώπους.
ἀδμῆτες δ' ἵκανον ἐς αὔλιον ὑψιμέλαθρον
καὶ ληνοὺς προπάροιθεν ἀριπρεπέος λειμῶνος.
ἔνθ' ἐπεὶ εὖ βοτάνης ἐπεφόρβει βοῦς ἐριμύκους
καὶ τὰς μὲν συνέλασσεν ἐς αὔλιον ἀθρόας οὔσας
λωτὸν ἐρεπτομένας ἠδ' ἑρσήεντα κύπειρον,
σὺν δ' ἐφόρει ξύλα πολλά, πυρὸς δ' ἐπεμαίετο τέχνην.
δάφνης ἀγλαὸν ὄζον ἑλὼν ἐπέλεψε σιδήρῳ

ἄρμενον ἐν παλάμῃ, ἄμπνυτο δὲ θερμὸς ἀϋτμή·

87 δέμων ἀνθοῦσαν M : δόμων αἴθουσαν cet. 88 ὀγχηστῶν λεχεποίων M ante corr. 90 ἐπικαμπύλα ξύλα M 91 πολυοινήσεις Ilgen: πολὺ οἰν. M : πολὺ οἰμ- (οἰμ-)ήσεις cet., cf. χρηστοινεῖν Strabo 637: lacunam stat. Groddeck quam verbis εἴκε πίθῃ μάλα περ μεμνημένος ἐν φρεσὶ σῇσι E. White explevit 93 σῖγαν E L[1] 94 φασὶν ἔσευε codd. (ἔσκευε L[1]) corr. ed. pr. 99 σκοπιῇ At D ed. pr. 103 ἤλαυνον At D 108 τέχνην] τύνη M : τέχνῃ Ilgen 109 ἐπέλεψε *x p* cet.: ἐνίαλλε M, unde λείαινε Postgate, cf. Quintus xii. 136, Plat. Tim. 65 E lacunam hic statuit Kuhn *Herabkunft des Feuers* 36 110 ἀνὰ δ' ἄμπνυτο praeter M codd. θυμὸς αὐτμῇ M

Ἑρμῆς τοι πρώτιστα πυρήϊα πῦρ τ' ἀνέδωκε.
πολλὰ δὲ κάγκανα κᾶλα κατουδαίῳ ἐνὶ βόθρῳ
οὖλα λαβὼν ἐπέθηκεν ἐπηετανά· λάμπετο δὲ φλὸξ
τηλόσε φῦζαν ἱεῖσα πυρὸς μέγα δαιομένοιο.
ὄφρα δὲ πῦρ ἀνέκαιε βίη κλυτοῦ Ἡφαίστοιο,
τόφρα δ' ὑποβρύχιας ἕλικας βοῦς ἕλκε θύραζε
δοιὰς ἄγχι πυρός, δύναμις δέ οἱ ἔπλετο πολλή·
ἀμφοτέρας δ' ἐπὶ νῶτα χαμαὶ βάλε φυσιοώσας·
ἐγκλίνων δ' ἐκύλινδε δι' αἰῶνας τετορήσας,
ἔργῳ δ' ἔργον ὄπαζε ταμὼν κρέα πίονα δημῷ·
ὤπτα δ' ἀμφ' ὀβελοῖσι πεπαρμένα δουρατέοισι,
σάρκας ὁμοῦ καὶ νῶτα γεράσμια καὶ μέλαν αἷμα
ἐργμένον ἐν χολάδεσσι, τὰ δ' αὐτοῦ κεῖτ' ἐπὶ χώρης.
ῥινοὺς δ' ἐξετάνυσσε καταστυφέλῳ ἐνὶ πέτρῃ,
ὡς ἔτι νῦν τὰ μέτασσα πολυχρόνιοι πεφύασι
δηρὸν δὴ μετὰ ταῦτα καὶ ἄκριτον. αὐτὰρ ἔπειτα
Ἑρμῆς χαρμόφρων εἰρύσατο πίονα ἔργα
λείῳ ἐπὶ πλαταμῶνι καὶ ἔσχισε δώδεκα μοίρας
κληροπαλεῖς· τέλεον δὲ γέρας προσέθηκεν ἑκάστῃ.
ἔνθ' ὁσίης κρεάων ἠράσσατο κύδιμος Ἑρμῆς·
ὀδμὴ γάρ μιν ἔτειρε καὶ ἀθάνατόν περ ἐόντα
ἡδεῖ'· ἀλλ' οὐδ' ὥς οἱ ἐπείθετο θυμὸς ἀγήνωρ
καί τε μάλ' ἱμείροντι περῆν' ἱερῆς κατὰ δειρῆς.
ἀλλὰ τὰ μὲν κατέθηκεν ἐς αὔλιον ὑψιμέλαθρον,

111 *πύρια* (ss. *ή*) *x* praeter Π   112 *κᾶλα p* : *καλὰ, κάλα* cet.   114 *φύσαν* E: *φύζαν* cet.: *φῦσαν* D'Orville, Hemsterhuys   116 *ὑποβρύχους* Ludwich   *εἶλκε* codd.   119 *ἐγκλίνων*] *ἐκκρίνας* M   *αἰῶνος p* T corr. : *αἰῶνας* cet.   120 *πίονι* praeter M codd., cf. Ψ 750 al.   124 *κατὰ* M D ed. pr.   *στυφελῇ* M   125 *τὰ μέτασσα* M, O. Müller *Hyperbor. Röm. Stud.* 310 (An. Ox. i. 280 *παρὰ τὴν μετὰ μέτασσα*) : *τὰ μετ'* (*τάμετ'* E L[1]) *ἄσσα* (*ἄσσα*) cet. : *τὰ μέταζε* Baumeister   127 *χαρμοφέρων* M *x* : *χάρμα φέρων p*, corr. Stephanus : *χαρμόφρων· ὁ Ἑρμῆς* Hesych.   132 *ἐπεπείθετο* M om. *οἱ*   133 *περῆν* M : *πέρην' x* At D ed. pr. : *πέρην p* : *περᾶν* Barnes : *περῆν'* Clarke : *πιεῖν* Ludwich : *παρεῖν'* Tucker, cf. xxx. 8

δημὸν καὶ κρέα πολλά, μετήορα δ' αἶψ' ἀνάειρε,
σῆμα νέης φωρῆς· ἐπὶ δὲ ξύλα κάγκαν' ἀείρας
οὐλόποδ' οὐλοκάρηνα πυρὸς κατεδάμνατ' ἀϋτμῇ.
αὐτὰρ ἐπεί τοι πάντα κατὰ χρέος ἤνυσε δαίμων
σάνδαλα μὲν προέηκεν ἐς Ἀλφειὸν βαθυδίνην,
ἀνθρακιὴν δ' ἐμάρανε, κόνιν δ' ἀμάθυνε μέλαιναν
παννύχιος· καλὸν δὲ φόως κατέλαμπε Σελήνης.
Κυλλήνης δ' αἶψ' αὖτις ἀφίκετο δῖα κάρηνα
ὄρθριος, οὐδέ τίς οἱ δολιχῆς ὁδοῦ ἀντεβόλησεν
οὔτε θεῶν μακάρων οὔτε θνητῶν ἀνθρώπων,
οὐδὲ κύνες λελάκοντο· Διὸς δ' ἐριούνιος Ἑρμῆς
δοχμωθεὶς μεγάροιο διὰ κλήϊθρον ἔδυνεν
αὔρῃ ὀπωρινῇ ἐναλίγκιος ἠΰτ' ὀμίχλη.
ἰθύσας δ' ἄντρου ἐξίκετο πίονα νηὸν
ἦκα ποσὶ προβιβῶν· οὐ γὰρ κτύπεν ὥς περ ἐπ' οὔδει.
ἐσσυμένως δ' ἄρα λίκνον ἐπῴχετο κύδιμος Ἑρμῆς·
σπάργανον ἀμφ' ὤμοις εἰλυμένος ἠΰτε τέκνον
νήπιον ἐν παλάμῃσι περ' ἰγνύσι λαῖφος ἀθύρων
κεῖτο, χέλυν ἐρατὴν ἐπ' ἀριστερὰ χειρὸς ἐέργων.
μητέρα δ' οὐκ ἄρ' ἔληθε θεὰν θεός, εἶπέ τε μῦθον·
　τίπτε σὺ ποικιλομῆτα πόθεν τόδε νυκτὸς ἐν ὥρῃ
ἔρχῃ ἀναιδείην ἐπιειμένε; νῦν σε μάλ' οἴω
ἢ τάχ' ἀμήχανα δεσμὰ περὶ πλευρῇσιν ἔχοντα
Λητοΐδου ὑπὸ χερσὶ διὲκ προθύροιο περήσειν,
ἢ σὲ φέροντα μεταξὺ κατ' ἄγκεα φηλητεύσειν.
ἔρρε πάλιν· μεγάλην σε πατὴρ ἐφύτευσε μέριμναν
θνητοῖς ἀνθρώποισι καὶ ἀθανάτοισι θεοῖσι.
　Τὴν δ' Ἑρμῆς μύθοισιν ἀμείβετο κερδαλέοισι·

136 v. om. M : *φωνῆς* codd. corr. Hermann cl. 385　138 *τοι* A ed. om. cet.　*ἐπειδὴ* M　141 *παννύχιον* M　*ἐπέλαμπε* codd. praeter M　148 *ἰθύνας* praeter M codices　151 *ἠλυμένος* M　152 *περιγνύσι* M O : *περ' ἰγ.* *x* ed. pr. : *παρ' ἰγ.* *p*　155 *τάδε* codd. corr. Wolf, cf. *α* 409　157 *ἢ τάχ'*] *δύσαχ'* M : *δὴ τάχ'* Bywater　*πλευροῖσι* *p*　159 *φέροντα* M : *λαβόντα* cet. : *λαθόντα* Matthiae : fort. *βαλόντα*, cf. 256　*φηλητεύσειν* *p* : *φιλ-* cet., cf. 67　161 *θνητῶν* (ss. *οῖς*) E T

μῆτερ ἐμὴ τί με ταῦτα †τιτύσκεαι† ἠΰτε τέκνον
νήπιον, ὃς μάλα παῦρα μετὰ φρεσὶν αἴσυλα οἶδε,
ταρβαλέον καὶ μητρὸς ὑπαιδείδοικεν ἐνιπάς;
αὐτὰρ ἐγὼ τέχνης ἐπιβήσομαι ἥ τις ἀρίστη
βουκολέων ἐμὲ καὶ σὲ διαμπερές· οὐδὲ θεοῖσι
νῶϊ μετ' ἀθανάτοισιν ἀδώρητοι καὶ ἄλιστοι
αὐτοῦ τῇδε μένοντες ἀνεξόμεθ', ὡς σὺ κελεύεις.
βέλτερον ἤματα πάντα μετ' ἀθανάτοις ὀαρίζειν
πλούσιον ἀφνειὸν πολυλήϊον ἢ κατὰ δῶμα
ἄντρῳ ἐν ἠερόεντι θαασσέμεν· ἀμφὶ δὲ τιμῆς
κἀγὼ τῆς ὁσίης ἐπιβήσομαι ἧς περ Ἀπόλλων.
εἰ δέ κε μὴ δώῃσι πατὴρ ἐμός, ἦ τοι ἔγωγε
πειρήσω, δύναμαι, φηλητέων ὄρχαμος εἶναι.
εἰ δέ μ' ἐρευνήσει Λητοῦς ἐρικυδέος υἱός,
ἄλλο τί οἱ καὶ μεῖζον ὀΐομαι ἀντιβολήσειν.
εἶμι γὰρ εἰς Πυθῶνα μέγαν δόμον ἀντιτορήσων·
ἔνθεν ἅλις τρίποδας περικαλλέας ἠδὲ λέβητας
πορθήσω καὶ χρυσόν, ἅλις τ' αἴθωνα σίδηρον
καὶ πολλὴν ἐσθῆτα· σὺ δ' ὄψεαι αἴ κ' ἐθέλῃσθα.
  Ὣς οἱ μέν ῥ' ἐπέεσσι πρὸς ἀλλήλους ἀγόρευον
υἱός τ' αἰγιόχοιο Διὸς καὶ πότνια Μαῖα.
ἠὼς δ' ἠριγένεια φόως θνητοῖσι φέρουσα
ὤρνυτ' ἀπ' Ὠκεανοῖο βαθυρρόου· αὐτὰρ Ἀπόλλων
Ὀγχηστὸν δ' ἀφίκανε κιὼν πολυήρατον ἄλσος
ἁγνὸν ἐρισφαράγου Γαιηόχου· ἔνθα γέροντα
κνώδαλον εὗρε νέμοντα παρὲξ ὁδοῦ ἕρκος ἀλωῆς.

163 δεδίσκεαι Pierson cl. Υ 201   164 πολλὰ ἐνὶ . . . ἄρμενα M   165 ταρβαλέων L[1]   167 βουκολέων Ludwich (βουκολέειν Gemoll): βουλεύων codd., cf. Ξ 445   168 ἄλιστοι y (sc. E T in textu, L[1] Π ss.): ἄπαστοι (ss. λι) L[2] Mon. N P R[1]: ἄπλιστοι A C L[3] Q: ἄπ στοι B: ἄπαστοι M At Γ D V[1] ed. pr.   169 ἀεξόμεθ' M   171 πολυλήϊλον E T   173 ἧπερ E   175 δύναμαι δὲ φιλητεύων (φιλητέον M) codd. corr. ed. pr., Steph., Bothe   183 μήτηρ pro μαῖα M   186 ὄγχηστόνδ' Π: ὀγχηστὸν δ' D E: ὀγχηστόνδ' cet., v. h. Apoll. 230   188 κνώδαλον] κάνδαλον Ilgen: ἰκμάδα Groddeck: τρόχμαλον seu νωχαλὸν Hermann: κλῶνας ὄγ' Schneidewin: καμπύλον Stoll: νώδαλον Ridgeway: κώδαλον Rossbach   νέμοντα] ἐλῶντα Ilgen: λέγοντα Schneidewin: ἀμῶντα Tyrrell: δέμοντα Barnes, Fick

τὸν πρότερος προσέφη Λητοῦς ἐρικυδέος υἱός·
Ὦ γέρον Ὀγχηστοῖο βατοδρόπε ποιήεντος
βοῦς ἀπὸ Πιερίης διζήμενος ἐνθάδ' ἱκάνω
πάσας θηλείας, πάσας κεράεσσιν ἑλικτάς,
ἐξ ἀγέλης· ὁ δὲ ταῦρος ἐβόσκετο μοῦνος ἀπ' ἄλλων
κυάνεος, χαροποὶ δὲ κύνες κατόπισθεν ἕποντο
τέσσαρες ἠΰτε φῶτες ὁμόφρονες· οἱ μὲν ἔλειφθεν
οἵ τε κύνες ὅ τε ταῦρος, ὃ δὴ περὶ θαῦμα τέτυκται·
ταὶ δ' ἔβαν ἠελίοιο νέον καταδυομένοιο
ἐκ μαλακοῦ λειμῶνος ἀπὸ γλυκεροῖο νομοῖο.
ταῦτά μοι εἰπὲ γεραιὲ παλαιγενὲς εἴ που ὄπωπας
ἀνέρα ταῖσδ' ἐπὶ βουσὶ διαπρήσσοντα κέλευθον.
Τὸν δ' ὁ γέρων μύθοισιν ἀμειβόμενος προσέειπεν·
ὦ φίλος ἀργαλέον μὲν ὅσ' ὀφθαλμοῖσιν ἴδοιτο
πάντα λέγειν· πολλοὶ γὰρ ὁδὸν πρήσσουσιν ὁδῖται,
τῶν οἱ μὲν κακὰ πολλὰ μεμαότες, οἱ δὲ μάλ' ἐσθλὰ
φοιτῶσιν· χαλεπὸν δὲ δαήμεναί ἐστιν ἕκαστον.
αὐτὰρ ἐγὼ πρόπαν ἦμαρ ἐς ἠέλιον καταδύντα
ἔσκαπτον περὶ γουνὸν ἀλωῆς οἰνοπέδοιο·
παῖδα δ' ἔδοξα φέριστε, σαφὲς δ' οὐκ οἶδα, νοῆσαι,
ὅς τις ὁ παῖς ἅμα βουσὶν ἐϋκραίρῃσιν ὀπήδει
νήπιος, εἶχε δὲ ῥάβδον, ἐπιστροφάδην δ' ἐβάδιζεν,
ἐξοπίσω δ' ἀνέεργε, κάρη δ' ἔχεν ἀντίον αὐτῷ.
Φῆ ῥ' ὁ γέρων· ὁ δὲ θᾶττον ὁδὸν κίε μῦθον ἀκούσας.
οἰωνὸν δ' ἐνόει τανυσίπτερον, αὐτίκα δ' ἔγνω
φηλητὴν γεγαῶτα Διὸς παῖδα Κρονίωνος.
ἐσσυμένως δ' ἤϊξεν ἄναξ Διὸς υἱὸς Ἀπόλλων
ἐς Πύλον ἠγαθέην διζήμενος εἰλίποδας βοῦς,
πορφυρέῃ νεφέλῃ κεκαλυμμένος εὐρέας ὤμους·

193 ἐβόσκετο om. *p* 200 κέλευθα M 202 ἴδοιμι M : ἴδοιο Ernesti 203 ὁδῖται (ss. σ, sc. ὁδισταί) E 205 πρήσσουσιν M 208 νοήσας M 209 εὐκραίροισιν *p* 211 ἔχον Hermann 212 φῆ δ' L^2 θᾶσσον codd., cf. 255 μῦθον ἀκούσας M *y* A B C Γ : φοῖβος ἀπόλλων cet. 214 φηλητὴν ed. pr. : φηλωτὴν *p* : φιλοτὴν E T : φιλητὴν cet. 217 πορφυρέην L^1 : πορφυρη (ss. εί) E

ἴχνιά τ' εἰσενόησεν Ἑκηβόλος εἶπέ τε μῦθον·
"Ὢ πόποι ἦ μέγα θαῦμα τόδ' ὀφθαλμοῖσιν ὁρῶμαι·
ἴχνια μὲν τάδε γ' ἐστὶ βοῶν ὀρθοκραιράων,
ἀλλὰ πάλιν τέτραπται ἐς ἀσφοδελὸν λειμῶνα·
βήματα δ' οὔτ' ἀνδρὸς τάδε γίγνεται οὔτε γυναικὸς
οὔτε λύκων πολιῶν οὔτ' ἄρκτων οὔτε λεόντων·
οὔτε τι κενταύρου λασιαύχενος ἔλπομαι εἶναι
ὅς τις τοῖα πέλωρα βιβᾷ ποσὶ καρπαλίμοισιν·
αἰνὰ μὲν ἔνθεν ὁδοῖο, τὰ δ' αἰνότερ' ἔνθεν ὁδοῖο."
Ὣς εἰπὼν ἤϊξεν ἄναξ Διὸς υἱὸς Ἀπόλλων,
Κυλλήνης δ' ἀφίκανεν ὄρος καταείμενον ὕλῃ
πέτρης εἰς κευθμῶνα βαθύσκιον, ἔνθα τε νύμφη
ἀμβροσίη ἐλόχευσε Διὸς παῖδα Κρονίωνος.
ὀδμὴ δ' ἱμερόεσσα δι' οὔρεος ἠγαθέοιο
κίδνατο, πολλὰ δὲ μῆλα ταναύποδα βόσκετο ποίην.
ἔνθα τότε σπεύδων κατεβήσατο λάϊνον οὐδὸν
ἄντρον ἐς ἠερόεν ἑκατηβόλος αὐτὸς Ἀπόλλων.
Τὸν δ' ὡς οὖν ἐνόησε Διὸς καὶ Μαιάδος υἱὸς
χωόμενον περὶ βουσὶν ἑκηβόλον Ἀπόλλωνα,
σπάργαν' ἔσω κατέδυνε θυήεντ'· ἠΰτε πολλὴν
πρέμνων ἀνθρακιὴν ὕλης σποδὸς ἀμφικαλύπτει,
ὣς Ἑρμῆς Ἑκάεργον ἰδὼν ἀνεείλε' ἓ αὐτόν.
ἐν δ' ὀλίγῳ συνέλασσε κάρη χεῖράς τε πόδας τε
φή ῥα νεόλλουτος προκαλεύμενος ἥδυμον ὕπνον,
ἐγρήσσων ἐτεόν γε· χέλυν δ' ὑπὸ μασχάλῃ εἶχε.
γνῶ δ' οὐδ' ἠγνοίησε Διὸς καὶ Λητοῦς υἱὸς

218, 219 om. M 224 ἔλπομαι εἶναι M *y*: ἔστιν ὁμοῖα cet. (ἥστιν Π: ἥστην L[1]): cf. Batr. 170 b (ἦσαν ὁμοῖοι) 230 κρονίωνα M 232 ταναύποδα *x*: τανύποδα cet., cf. Apoll. 304 238 ὁλοσποδὸς M: ὕλης σποδὸς cet. i. q. τῇ ξυλίνῃ σποδῷ Strab. 269, cf. ἄνθρακα δρυός Galen. xiv. 521 K, μηρίων σποδόν Herod. iv. 35 ἀμφικαλύπτοι codd. praeter D ed. pr. 239 ἀλέεινεν (-ον E Π) codd. em. Postgate (ἀνέειλεν Lohsee): ἀλέαινεν Ilgen 241 δή ῥα νεόλλουτος M *x p*: θῆρα νέον λοχάων (-εύων Π mg.) *y*: φή Barnes νήδυμον *p* προκαλούμενος M 242 ἄγρης (ἄγρην B: ἄγρην (ss. *s*) εἰνεόν γε Γ) εἰνέτεόν τε codd.: ἐγρήσσων invenit Martin, cetera Hermann δ' om. codd. add. Hermann

νύμφην τ' οὐρείην περικαλλέα καὶ φίλον υἱόν,
παῖδ' ὀλίγον δολίῃς εἰλυμένον ἐντροπίῃσι.
παπτήνας δ' ἀνὰ πάντα μυχὸν μεγάλοιο δόμοιο
τρεῖς ἀδύτους ἀνέῳγε λαβὼν κληῖδα φαεινὴν
νέκταρος ἐμπλείους ἠδ' ἀμβροσίης ἐρατεινῆς·
πολλὸς δὲ χρυσός τε καὶ ἄργυρος ἔνδον ἔκειτο,
πολλὰ δὲ φοινικόεντα καὶ ἄργυφα εἵματα νύμφης,
οἷα θεῶν μακάρων ἱεροὶ δόμοι ἐντὸς ἔχουσιν.
ἔνθ' ἐπεὶ ἐξερέεινε μυχοὺς μεγάλοιο δόμοιο
Λητοΐδης μύθοισι προσηύδα κύδιμον Ἑρμῆν·
Ὦ παῖ ὃς ἐν λίκνῳ κατάκειαι, μήνυέ μοι βοῦς
θᾶττον· ἐπεὶ τάχα νῶϊ διοισόμεθ' οὐ κατὰ κόσμον.
ῥίψω γάρ σε βαλὼν ἐς Τάρταρον ἠερόεντα,
εἰς ζόφον αἰνόμορον καὶ ἀμήχανον· οὐδέ σε μήτηρ
ἐς φάος οὐδὲ πατὴρ ἀναλύσεται, ἀλλ' ὑπὸ γαίῃ
ἐρρήσεις ὀλίγοισι μετ' ἀνδράσιν ἡγεμονεύων.
Τὸν δ' Ἑρμῆς μύθοισιν ἀμείβετο κερδαλέοισι·
Λητοΐδη τίνα τοῦτον ἀπηνέα μῦθον ἔειπας
καὶ βοῦς ἀγραύλους διζήμενος ἐνθάδ' ἱκάνεις;
οὐκ ἴδον, οὐ πυθόμην, οὐκ ἄλλου μῦθον ἄκουσα·
οὐκ ἂν μηνύσαιμ', οὐκ ἂν μήνυτρον ἀροίμην·
οὐδὲ βοῶν ἐλατῆρι κραταιῷ φωτὶ ἔοικα,
οὐδ' ἐμὸν ἔργον τοῦτο, πάρος δέ μοι ἄλλα μέμηλεν·
ὕπνος ἐμοί γε μέμηλε καὶ ἡμετέρης γάλα μητρός,
σπάργανά τ' ἀμφ' ὤμοισιν ἔχειν καὶ θερμὰ λοετρά.
μή τις τοῦτο πύθοιτο πόθεν τόδε νεῖκος ἐτύχθη·
καί κεν δὴ μέγα θαῦμα μετ' ἀθανάτοισι γένοιτο
παῖδα νέον γεγαῶτα διὰ προθύροιο περῆσαι
βουσὶ μετ' ἀγραύλοισι· τὸ δ' ἀπρεπέως ἀγορεύεις.

246 ἀνὰ M : ἄρα cet. 248 ἐμπλείους M : ἐκπλείους cet. 254 λίκνῳ] κλίνῃ *x* At D κατάκηαι *p* praeter N 256 λαβὼν Ilgen 259 ὀλίγοισι *parvulis* : κἀμὲ τὸν ἐν σμικροῖς ὀλίγον θεόν Anth. Pal. ix. 334 : ὀμφακίας νεκροὺς *infantes* Lucian Catapl. 5 μετ' M : ἐν cet. 265 οὔτε codd. corr. Baumeister : οὔτι Hermann 269 πόθου pro πόθεν T 272 ἀγραύλησι M

χθὲς γενόμην, ἁπαλοὶ δὲ πόδες, τρηχεῖα δ' ὑπὸ χθών.
εἰ δὲ θέλεις πατρὸς κεφαλὴν μέγαν ὅρκον ὀμοῦμαι·
μὴ μὲν ἐγὼ μήτ' αὐτὸς ὑπίσχομαι αἴτιος εἶναι,
μήτε τιν' ἄλλον ὄπωπα βοῶν κλοπὸν ὑμετεράων,
αἵ τινες αἱ βόες εἰσί· τὸ δὲ κλέος οἶον ἀκούω.
Ὣς ἄρ' ἔφη καὶ πυκνὸν ἀπὸ βλεφάρων ἀμαρύσσων
ὀφρύσι ῥιπτάζεσκεν ὁρώμενος ἔνθα καὶ ἔνθα,
μάκρ' ἀποσυρίζων, ἅλιον τὸν μῦθον ἀκούων.
τὸν δ' ἁπαλὸν γελάσας προσέφη ἑκάεργος Ἀπόλλων·
Ὦ πέπον ἠπεροπευτὰ δολοφραδὲς ἦ σε μάλ' οἴω
πολλάκις ἀντιτοροῦντα δόμους εὖ ναιετάοντας
ἔννυχον οὔ χ' ἕνα μοῦνον ἐπ' οὔδεϊ φῶτα καθίσσαι
σκευάζοντα κατ' οἶκον ἄτερ ψόφου, οἷ' ἀγορεύεις.
πολλοὺς δ' ἀγραύλους ἀκαχήσεις μηλοβοτῆρας
οὔρεος ἐν βήσσῃς, ὁπόταν κρειῶν ἐρατίζων
ἀντῇς βουκολίοισι καὶ εἰροπόκοις ὀΐεσσιν.
ἀλλ' ἄγε, μὴ πύματόν τε καὶ ὕστατον ὕπνον ἰαύσῃς,
ἐκ λίκνου κατάβαινε μελαίνης νυκτὸς ἑταῖρε.
τοῦτο γὰρ οὖν καὶ ἔπειτα μετ' ἀθανάτοις γέρας ἕξεις·
ἀρχὸς φηλητέων κεκλήσεαι ἤματα πάντα.
Ὣς ἄρ' ἔφη καὶ παῖδα λαβὼν φέρε Φοῖβος Ἀπόλλων.
σὺν δ' ἄρα φρασσάμενος τότε δὴ κρατὺς Ἀργειφόντης
οἰωνὸν προέηκεν ἀειρόμενος μετὰ χερσί,
τλήμονα γαστρὸς ἔριθον ἀτάσθαλον ἀγγελιώτην.
ἐσσυμένως δὲ μετ' αὐτὸν ἐπέπταρε, τοῖο δ' Ἀπόλλων
ἔκλυεν, ἐκ χειρῶν δὲ χαμαὶ βάλε κύδιμον Ἑρμῆν.

273 δ' ὀσποχθὼν L[1] 279 ῥιπάζεσκεν M 280 τὸν y At D : ὡς M ed. pr. : ὡς τὸν p 284 οὐχ (οὐδ' M) codd. em. Tucker 286 δραύλους x D (δραύλους ss. δ' ἀγραύλους T) 287 κρειῶν] μήλων M 288 ἄντην βουκολίοισι καὶ εἰροπόκοις οἴεσσιν y corr. Gemoll : ἀντήσῃς (-εις) ἀγέλῃσι βοῶν καὶ πώεσι μήλων cet. 289 ἰαύσεις M : ἰαύῃς Π 290 νυκτὸς δὲ φίλῃ καὶ ἑταίρῃ carmen ap. Origen. in haeret. 72 (P. L. G. iii. 682) 292 αὖχος M : ἀργὸς E φηλητέων ed. pr. : φηλι////τέων corr. ex φιλητέων P : φηλιτέων p praeter B R^2 : φιλητέων cet. 296 τλήμονα μετὰ E T, cf. xxvii. 13

ἕζετο δὲ προπάροιθε καὶ ἐσσύμενός περ ὁδοῖο
Ἑρμῆν κερτομέων, καί μιν πρὸς μῦθον ἔειπε·
Θάρσει σπαργανιῶτα Διὸς καὶ Μαιάδος υἱέ·
εὑρήσω καὶ ἔπειτα βοῶν ἴφθιμα κάρηνα
τούτοις οἰωνοῖσι· σὺ δ' αὖθ' ὁδὸν ἡγεμονεύσεις.
Ὣς φάθ'· ὁ δ' αὖτ' ἀνόρουσε θοῶς Κυλλήνιος Ἑρμῆς
σπουδῇ ἰών· ἄμφω δὲ παρ' οὔατα χερσὶν ἐώθει,
σπάργανον ἀμφ' ὤμοισιν ἐελμένος, εἶπε δὲ μῦθον·
Πῇ με φέρεις Ἑκάεργε θεῶν ζαμενέστατε πάντων;
ἦ με βοῶν ἕνεχ' ὧδε χολούμενος ὀρσολοπεύεις;
ὢ πόποι εἴθ' ἀπόλοιτο βοῶν γένος· οὐ γὰρ ἐγώ γε
ὑμετέρας ἔκλεψα βόας, οὐδ' ἄλλον ὄπωπα,
αἵ τινές εἰσι βόες· τὸ δὲ δὴ κλέος οἶον ἀκούω.
δὸς δὲ δίκην καὶ δέξο παρὰ Ζηνὶ Κρονίωνι.
Αὐτὰρ ἐπεὶ τὰ ἕκαστα διαρρήδην ἐρέεινον
Ἑρμῆς τ' οἰοπόλος καὶ Λητοῦς ἀγλαὸς υἱὸς
ἀμφὶς θυμὸν ἔχοντες· ὁ μὲν νημερτέα φωνὴν

οὐκ ἀδίκως ἐπὶ βουσὶν ἐλάζυτο κύδιμον Ἑρμῆν,
αὐτὰρ ὁ τέχνῃσίν τε καὶ αἱμυλίοισι λόγοισιν
ἤθελεν ἐξαπατᾶν Κυλλήνιος Ἀργυρότοξον·
αὐτὰρ ἐπεὶ πολύμητις ἐὼν πολυμήχανον εὗρεν
ἐσσυμένως δὴ ἔπειτα διὰ ψαμάθοιο βάδιζε
πρόσθεν, ἀτὰρ κατόπισθε Διὸς καὶ Λητοῦς υἱός.
αἶψα δὲ τέρθρον ἵκοντο θυώδεος Οὐλύμποιο
ἐς πατέρα Κρονίωνα Διὸς περικαλλέα τέκνα·
κεῖθι γὰρ ἀμφοτέροισι δίκης κατέκειτο τάλαντα.

303 *αὐτοῖς* M *οἰωνοῖς εὖ* ed. pr. : *οἰωνοῖσιν εὖ* *x* D : *σὺ* M *p* (*εὖ* Γ marg.) 305 commate interpunximus 306 *σπάργανον*, D'Orville *ἐέλμενος* M : *ἐλιγμένος* (*ἑλ-*) cet. : *ἐελμένον* Baumeister : *ἐλελιγμένον* Gemoll 308 *ἐνέχωνδὲ* M *ὀρσοπολεύεις* *p* : *ὀρσολοπεύεις. ἀλλαχῶς ὀρσοπολεύεις* V[2] 312 *δέξαι πὰρ* *p* 313 *ἔπειτα* M *ἐρέεινεν* *x p* M ed. pr. 315 *φωνὴν* codd. : *φῶρα* Windisch, cf. 136, 385 lacuna fortasse statuenda servato *φωνήν* 322 ita M L[1] Π : *δ' ἵκοντο κάρηνα* *p y* ed. pr.

†εὐμιλίη† δ' ἔχ' Ὄλυμπον ἀγάννιφον, ἀθάνατοι δὲ
ἄφθιτοι ἠγερέθοντο μετὰ χρυσόθρονον ἠῶ.
ἔστησαν δ' Ἑρμῆς τε καὶ ἀργυρότοξος Ἀπόλλων
πρόσθε Διὸς γούνων· ὁ δ' ἀνείρετο φαίδιμον υἱὸν
Ζεὺς ὑψιβρεμέτης καί μιν πρὸς μῦθον ἔειπε·
Φοῖβε πόθεν ταύτην μενοεικέα ληΐδ' ἐλαύνεις
παῖδα νέον γεγαῶτα φυὴν κήρυκος ἔχοντα;
σπουδαῖον τόδε χρῆμα θεῶν μεθ' ὁμήγυριν ἦλθε.
Τὸν δ' αὖτε προσέειπεν ἄναξ ἑκάεργος Ἀπόλλων·
ὦ πάτερ ἦ τάχα μῦθον ἀκούσεαι οὐκ ἀλαπαδνὸν
κερτομέων ὡς οἶος ἐγὼ φιλολήϊός εἰμι.
παῖδά τιν' εὗρον τόνδε διαπρύσιον κεραϊστὴν
Κυλλήνης ἐν ὄρεσσι πολὺν διὰ χῶρον ἀνύσσας
κέρτομον, οἷον ἐγώ γε θεῶν οὐκ ἄλλον ὄπωπα
οὐδ' ἀνδρῶν, ὁπόσοι λησίμβροτοί εἰσ' ἐπὶ γαῖαν.
κλέψας δ' ἐκ λειμῶνος ἐμὰς βοῦς ᾤχετ' ἐλαύνων
ἑσπέριος παρὰ θῖνα πολυφλοίσβοιο θαλάσσης
εὐθὺ Πύλον δ' ἐλάων· τὰ δ' ἄρ' ἴχνια δοιὰ πέλωρα
οἷά τ' ἀγάσσασθαι καὶ ἀγαυοῦ δαίμονος ἔργα.
τῇσιν μὲν γὰρ βουσὶν ἐς ἀσφοδελὸν λειμῶνα
ἀντία βήματ' ἔχουσα κόνις ἀνέφαινε μέλαινα·
αὐτὸς δ' οὗτος †ὅδ' ἐκτὸς† ἀμήχανος, οὔτ' ἄρα ποσσὶν
οὔτ' ἄρα χερσὶν ἔβαινε διὰ ψαμαθώδεα χῶρον·
ἀλλ' ἄλλην τινὰ μῆτιν ἔχων διέτριβε κέλευθα
τοῖα πέλωρ' ὡς εἴ τις ἀραιῇσι δρυσὶ βαίνοι.
ὄφρα μὲν οὖν ἐδίωκε διὰ ψαμαθώδεα χῶρον,

325 *εὐμιλίη* M : *εὐμυλίη* cet. : *εὐμελίη, εὐνομίη, στωμυλίη* D'Orville : *αἱμυλίη* Heyne : *εὐμελίη, ἐμμελίη* Hermann : *εὐελίη* Franke : *ἀδμωλὴ* Bergk : *εὐδίη* Baumeister : *αἰθρίη* Schmitt : *εὐκηλίη* Sikes : *εὐμολίη* Ludwich an *οὐμιλίη* sc. *ὁμιλίη*? 326 ita *y* : *ποτὶ πτύχας οὐλύμποιο* cet. 336 *ἤγουν* (*ἢ* Π ss. *τ*) *φανερὸν κλέπτην* marg. L[1] Π 339 *γαῖαν* M : *γαίη x p* 342 *εὐθύπυλονδ'* M : *εὐθυπόρονδ'* cet. *δῖα p* : *δοιὰ* cet. 343 *ἀγάσ(σ)εσθαι* codd. praeter M 344 *τοῖσι* M 349 *βαίνων* M

ῥεῖα μάλ᾽ ἴχνια πάντα διέπρεπεν ἐν κονίῃσιν·
αὐτὰρ ἐπεὶ ψαμάθοιο μέγαν στίβον ἐξεπέρησεν,
ἄφραστος γένετ᾽ ὦκα βοῶν στίβος ἠδὲ καὶ αὐτοῦ
χῶρον ἀνὰ κρατερόν· τὸν δ᾽ ἐφράσατο βροτὸς ἀνὴρ
εἰς Πύλον εὐθὺς ἐλῶντα βοῶν γένος εὐρυμετώπων.
αὐτὰρ ἐπεὶ δὴ τὰς μὲν ἐν ἡσυχίῃ κατέερξε
καὶ διαπυρπαλάμησεν ὁδοῦ τὸ μὲν ἔνθα τὸ δ᾽ ἔνθα,
ἐν λίκνῳ κατέκειτο μελαίνῃ νυκτὶ ἐοικὼς
ἄντρῳ ἐν ἠερόεντι κατὰ ζόφον, οὐδέ κεν αὐτὸν
αἰετὸς ὀξὺ λάων ἐσκέψατο· πολλὰ δὲ χερσὶν
αὐγὰς ὠμόργαζε δολοφροσύνην ἀλεγύνων.
αὐτὸς δ᾽ αὐτίκα μῦθον ἀπηλεγέως ἀγόρευεν·
οὐκ ἴδον, οὐ πυθόμην, οὐκ ἄλλου μῦθον ἄκουσα,
οὐδέ κε μηνύσαιμ᾽, οὐδ᾽ ἂν μήνυτρον ἀροίμην.
  Ἦ τοι ἄρ᾽ ὣς εἰπὼν κατ᾽ ἄρ᾽ ἕζετο Φοῖβος Ἀπόλλων·
Ἑρμῆς δ᾽ ἄλλον μῦθον ἐν ἀθανάτοισιν ἔειπε,
δείξατο δ᾽ εἰς Κρονίωνα θεῶν σημάντορα πάντων·
  Ζεῦ πάτερ ἦ τοι ἐγώ σοι ἀληθείην ἀγορεύσω·
νημερτής τε γάρ εἰμι καὶ οὐκ οἶδα ψεύδεσθαι.
ἦλθεν ἐς ἡμετέρου διζήμενος εἰλίποδας βοῦς
σήμερον ἠελίοιο νέον ἐπιτελλομένοιο,
οὐδὲ θεῶν μακάρων ἄγε μάρτυρας οὐδὲ κατόπτας.
μηνύειν δ᾽ ἐκέλευεν ἀναγκαίης ὑπὸ πολλῆς,
πολλὰ δέ μ᾽ ἠπείλησε βαλεῖν ἐς Τάρταρον εὐρύν,
οὕνεχ᾽ ὁ μὲν τέρεν ἄνθος ἔχει φιλοκυδέος ἥβης,
αὐτὰρ ἐγὼ χθιζὸς γενόμην· τὰ δέ τ᾽ οἶδε καὶ αὐτός·
οὔ τι βοῶν ἐλατῆρι κραταιῷ φωτὶ ἐοικώς.

352 *μέγαν*] *πολὺν* M   356 *κατέερξε* *p*: *κατέρεξε* cet.   357 *διαπῦρ* M D L[1]: *παλάμησεν* M: *διὰ πῦρ μάλ᾽ ἄμησεν* cet. corr. Ilgen, cf. Stolz *Wiener Studien* 1903. 251   360 *λάων* (ss. *βλέπων*) E L[1]   361 *ὠ(ώ)μάρταζε* codd. (*ὠμόρταζε* T) em. Ilgen cl. *σ* 199   *ἀλεγύνων* *x* O: *ἀλεγίζων* M: *ἀλεείνων* *p*, cf. 557   362 *ἀπολεγέως* E L[1] Π   366 ita *y*: *ἑρμῆς δ᾽ αὖθ᾽ ἑτέρωθεν ἀμειβόμενος ἔπος ηὔδα* cet.   368 *ἀγορεύσω* M: *καταλέξω* cet., cf. K 384 al.   370 *ἡμέτερον* Barnes, cf. *β* 55, *η* 301, *ρ* 534   371 *νέον γ᾽* *p* (praeter A Q): *γ᾽* add. D m. p.

πείθεο, καὶ γὰρ ἐμεῖο πατὴρ φίλος εὔχεαι εἶναι,
ὡς οὐκ οἴκαδ' ἔλασσα βόας, ὣς ὄλβιος εἴην,
οὐδ' ὑπὲρ οὐδὸν ἔβην· τὸ δέ τ' ἀτρεκέως ἀγορεύω.
Ἠέλιον δὲ μάλ' αἰδέομαι καὶ δαίμονας ἄλλους,
καὶ σὲ φιλῶ καὶ τοῦτον ὀπίζομαι· οἶσθα καὶ αὐτὸς
ὡς οὐκ αἴτιός εἰμι· μέγαν δ' †ἐπιδαίομαι ὅρκον·
οὐ μὰ τάδ' ἀθανάτων εὐκόσμητα προθύραια.
καί ποτ' ἐγὼ τούτῳ τίσω ποτὶ νηλέα φωρὴν
καὶ κρατερῷ περ ἐόντι· σὺ δ' ὁπλοτέροισιν ἄρηγε.
  Ὣς φάτ' ἐπιλλίζων Κυλλήνιος Ἀργειφόντης,
καὶ τὸ σπάργανον εἶχεν ἐπ' ὠλένῃ οὐδ' ἀπέβαλλε.
Ζεὺς δὲ μέγ' ἐξεγέλασσεν ἰδὼν κακομηδέα παῖδα
εὖ καὶ ἐπισταμένως ἀρνεύμενον ἀμφὶ βόεσσιν.
ἀμφοτέρους δ' ἐκέλευσεν ὁμόφρονα θυμὸν ἔχοντας
ζητεύειν, Ἑρμῆν δὲ διάκτορον ἡγεμονεύειν,
καὶ δεῖξαι τὸν χῶρον ἐπ' ἀβλαβίῃσι νόοιο
ὅππῃ δὴ αὖτ' ἀπέκρυψε βοῶν ἴφθιμα κάρηνα.
νεῦσεν δὲ Κρονίδης, ἐπεπείθετο δ' ἀγλαὸς Ἑρμῆς·
ῥηϊδίως γὰρ ἔπειθε Διὸς νόος αἰγιόχοιο.
τὼ δ' ἄμφω σπεύδοντε Διὸς περικαλλέα τέκνα
ἐς Πύλον ἠμαθόεντα ἐπ' Ἀλφειοῦ πόρον ἷξον·
ἀγροὺς δ' ἐξίκοντο καὶ αὔλιον ὑψιμέλαθρον
ἠχοῦ δὴ τὰ χρήματ' ἀτάλλετο νυκτὸς ἐν ὥρῃ.
ἔνθ' Ἑρμῆς μὲν ἔπειτα κιὼν παρὰ λάϊνον ἄντρον
εἰς φῶς ἐξήλαυνε βοῶν ἴφθιμα κάρηνα·
Λητοΐδης δ' ἀπάτερθεν ἰδὼν ἐνόησε βοείας

381 δὲ om. codd. praeter M 382 ita M: *καί σε* cet. 383 *ἐπιδεύομαι* M: *ἐπιδαίομαι* cet. (*δαι* in ras. L²: *ἐπιδεόμαι* Π): *ἐπιδώσομαι* Barnes: *ἐπιμαίομαι* Herwerden: an *μέγαν δ' ἄρ' ἐπαιδέομ' ὅρκον*? olim *μέγαν δ' ἔπι ὅρκον ὀμοῦμαι* proposuimus 385 *ποτὶ* M: *ποτὲ* cet., cf. *ρ* 191 *φωρὴν* M: *φωνὴν* cet. 386 *κραταιῷ* *p*, cf. 265 394 *ἴφιμα* L¹ T 397 *σπεύδοντο* *x* At D ed. pr. Γ ss. 398 *δ' ἐπ'* *x* At D ed. pr. 400 corr. Fick coll. *ηχοι* I. G. vii. 235. 16: *ὄχου δὲ τὰ χρήματα τιτάλλετο* M: *ἦχ' οὐ, ἦχ' οὗ, ἦχ' οὐ* sim. cet. *ἀτιτάλλετο* vulg.: *ἀντιβάλλετο* E: *ἀντιτάλλετο* T, em. ed. pr. 401 *ἐς* pro *παρὰ* M 402 *ἤλαυνε* *p* 403 *ἀπάνευθεν* M, cf. E 445

πέτρῃ ἐπ' ἠλιβάτῳ, τάχα δ' ἤρετο κύδιμον Ἑρμῆν·
Πῶς ἐδύνω δολομῆτα δύω βόε δειροτομῆσαι,
ὧδε νεογνὸς ἐὼν καὶ νήπιος; αὐτὸς ἐγώ γε
θαυμαίνω κατόπισθε τὸ σὸν κράτος· οὐδὲ τί σε χρὴ
μακρὸν ἀέξεσθαι Κυλλήνιε Μαιάδος υἱέ.
Ὣς ἄρ' ἔφη, καὶ χερσὶ περίστρεφε καρτερὰ δεσμὰ

ἄγνου· ταὶ δ' ὑπὸ ποσσὶ κατὰ χθονὸς αἶψα φύοντο
αὐτόθεν ἐμβολάδην ἐστραμμέναι ἀλλήλῃσι
ῥεῖά τε καὶ πάσῃσιν ἐπ' ἀγραύλοισι βόεσσιν
Ἑρμέω βουλῇσι κλεψίφρονος· αὐτὰρ Ἀπόλλων
θαύμασεν ἀθρήσας. τότε δὴ κρατὺς Ἀργειφόντης
χῶρον ὑποβλήδην ἐσκέψατο πῦρ ἀμαρύσσων

ἐγκρύψαι μεμαώς· Λητοῦς δ' ἐρικυδέος υἱὸν
ῥεῖα μάλ' ἐπρήϋνεν ἑκηβόλον, ὡς ἔθελ' αὐτός,
καὶ κρατερόν περ ἐόντα· λαβὼν δ' ἐπ' ἀριστερὰ χειρὸς
πλήκτρῳ ἐπειρήτιζε κατὰ μέλος· ἡ δ' ὑπὸ χειρὸς
σμερδαλέον κονάβησε, γέλασσε δὲ Φοῖβος Ἀπόλλων
γηθήσας, ἐρατὴ δὲ διὰ φρένας ἤλυθ' ἰωὴ
θεσπεσίης ἐνοπῆς, καί μιν γλυκὺς ἵμερος ᾕρει
θυμῷ ἀκουάζοντα· λύρῃ δ' ἐρατὸν κιθαρίζων
στῆ ῥ' ὅ γε θαρσήσας ἐπ' ἀριστερὰ Μαιάδος υἱὸς
Φοίβου Ἀπόλλωνος, τάχα δὲ λιγέως κιθαρίζων
γηρύετ' ἀμβολάδην, ἐρατὴ δέ οἱ ἕσπετο φωνή,
κραίνων ἀθανάτους τε θεοὺς καὶ γαῖαν ἐρεμνὴν
ὡς τὰ πρῶτα γένοντο καὶ ὡς λάχε μοῖραν ἕκαστος.

404 *γαίῃ κατ'* M *εἴρετο* M 406 *νεογνοίων* M 408 *ἀέξασθαι* M 409 lacunam hic et 415 stat. Baumeister 410 *ἀγνοῦ* L[1] T (ex *ἁγ.*): *ἅγνου, ἁγνοῦ* cet.: *ἄγνους* Ludwich *φέροντο* V[2] 411 *ἀμβολάδην* M 412 *ἀγραύλῃσι* M *x* 414 *ὅτε* V[2] 417 *ἐπράυνεν* E T (*-εν* ex *-αν*) 418 *χειρὸς*] *λύρην* M 420 *κονάβισσε* *p* 422 v. om. praeter M omnes 425 *λλιγέως* *x* 426 *ἕπετο* T 427 *κραίνων*] *κλείων* Hermann: *αἰνῶν* Steph.: *οὐρανὸν* Tucker *κραίνειν· τιμᾶν. κραίνουσι· πληροῦσι, παρέχουσι, τιμῶσι.* Hesych., cf. *τ* 567, Emped. 111. 2 Diels

Μνημοσύνην μὲν πρῶτα θεῶν ἐγέραιρεν ἀοιδῇ
μητέρα Μουσάων, ἡ γὰρ λάχε Μαιάδος υἱόν·
τοὺς δὲ κατὰ πρέσβιν τε καὶ ὡς γεγάασιν ἕκαστος
ἀθανάτους ἐγέραιρε θεοὺς Διὸς ἀγλαὸς υἱὸς
πάντ' ἐνέπων κατὰ κόσμον, ἐπωλένιον κιθαρίζων.
τὸν δ' ἔρος ἐν στήθεσσιν ἀμήχανος αἴνυτο θυμόν,
καί μιν φωνήσας ἔπεα πτερόεντα προσηύδα·
Βουφόνε μηχανιῶτα πονεύμενε δαιτὸς ἑταῖρε
πεντήκοντα βοῶν ἀντάξια ταῦτα μέμηλας.
ἡσυχίως καὶ ἔπειτα διακρινέεσθαι ὀΐω.
νῦν δ' ἄγε μοι τόδε εἰπὲ πολύτροπε Μαιάδος υἱὲ
ἦ σοί γ' ἐκ γενετῆς τάδ' ἅμ' ἕσπετο θαυματὰ ἔργα
ἦέ τις ἀθανάτων ἠὲ θνητῶν ἀνθρώπων
δῶρον ἀγαυὸν ἔδωκε καὶ ἔφρασε θέσπιν ἀοιδήν;
θαυμασίην γὰρ τήνδε νεήφατον ὄσσαν ἀκούω,
ἣν οὔ πώ ποτέ φημι δαήμεναι οὔτε τιν' ἀνδρῶν,
οὔτε τιν' ἀθανάτων οἳ Ὀλύμπια δώματ' ἔχουσι,
νόσφι σέθεν φηλῆτα Διὸς καὶ Μαιάδος υἱέ.
τίς τέχνη, τίς μοῦσα ἀμηχανέων μελεδώνων,
τίς τρίβος; ἀτρεκέως γὰρ ἅμα τρία πάντα πάρεστιν
εὐφροσύνην καὶ ἔρωτα καὶ ἥδυμον ὕπνον ἑλέσθαι.
καὶ γὰρ ἐγὼ Μούσῃσιν Ὀλυμπιάδεσσιν ὀπηδός,
τῇσι χοροί τε μέλουσι καὶ ἀγλαὸς οἶμος ἀοιδῆς
καὶ μολπὴ τεθαλυῖα καὶ ἱμερόεις βρόμος αὐλῶν·
ἀλλ' οὔ πώ τί μοι ὧδε μετὰ φρεσὶν ἄλλο μέλησεν
οἷα νέων θαλίῃς ἐνδέξια ἔργα πέλονται·
θαυμάζω Διὸς υἱὲ τάδ' ὡς ἐρατὸν κιθαρίζεις.
νῦν δ' ἐπεὶ οὖν ὀλίγος περ ἐὼν κλυτὰ μήδεα οἶδας,

431 πρέσβην codd. em. Matthiae, cf. 515 ἅπαντες M 438 διακρίνεσθαι M D 440 σοί γ'] σὺ p γενεῆς praeter M libri 443 super νεήφατον nonnihil scriptum habet T (ην? ειν?) 446 φηλητὰ p At: φιλητὰ cet. acc. corr. Barnes 448 τρὶς Γ 449 νήδυμον p 451 ὕμνος M y: οἶμος cet. 453 ἄλλο M: ὧδε cet., cf. Apoll. 452 456 οἶσθα M

ἶζε πέπον καὶ μῦθον ἐπαίνει πρεσβυτέροισι.
νῦν γάρ τοι κλέος ἔσται ἐν ἀθανάτοισι θεοῖσι
σοί τ' αὐτῷ καὶ μητρί· τὸ δ' ἀτρεκέως ἀγορεύσω·
ναὶ μὰ τόδε κρανέϊνον ἀκόντιον ἦ μὲν ἐγώ σε
κυδρὸν ἐν ἀθανάτοισι καὶ ὄλβιον †ἡγεμονεύσω,
δώσω τ' ἀγλαὰ δῶρα καὶ ἐς τέλος οὐκ ἀπατήσω.

Τὸν δ' Ἑρμῆς μύθοισιν ἀμείβετο κερδαλέοισιν·
εἰρωτᾷς μ' Ἑκάεργε περιφραδές· αὐτὰρ ἐγώ σοι
τέχνης ἡμετέρης ἐπιβήμεναι οὔ τι μεγαίρω.
σήμερον εἰδήσεις· ἐθέλω δέ τοι ἤπιος εἶναι
βουλῇ καὶ μύθοισι, σὺ δὲ φρεσὶ πάντ' εὖ οἶδας.
πρῶτος γὰρ Διὸς υἱὲ μετ' ἀθανάτοισι θαάσσεις
ἠΰς τε κρατερός τε· φιλεῖ δέ σε μητίετα Ζεὺς
ἐκ πάσης ὁσίης, ἔπορεν δέ τοι ἀγλαὰ δῶρα·
καὶ τιμὰς σὲ δέ φασι δαήμεναι ἐκ Διὸς ὀμφῆς
μαντείας θ' Ἑκάεργε Διὸς πάρα, θέσφατα πάντα·
τῶν νῦν αὐτὸς ἔγωγε †παῖδ' ἀφνειὸν† δεδάηκα.
σοὶ δ' αὐτάγρετόν ἐστι δαήμεναι ὅττι μενοινᾷς.
ἀλλ' ἐπεὶ οὖν τοι θυμὸς ἐπιθύει κιθαρίζειν,
μέλπεο καὶ κιθάριζε καὶ ἀγλαΐας ἀλέγυνε
δέγμενος ἐξ ἐμέθεν· σὺ δέ μοι φίλε κῦδος ὄπαζε.
εὐμόλπει μετὰ χερσὶν ἔχων λιγύφωνον ἑταίρην
καλὰ καὶ εὖ κατὰ κόσμον ἐπιστάμενος ἀγορεύειν.
εὔκηλος μὲν ἔπειτα φέρειν εἰς δαῖτα θάλειαν
καὶ χορὸν ἱμερόεντα καὶ ἐς φιλοκυδέα κῶμον,

457, 458 om. praeter M omnes 457 θυμὸν cod. em. Ruhnken, cf. σ 167 (v. l.) Σ 313 sec. Epaphroditum. Δ 412 τέττα σιωπῇ ἧσο, ἐμῷ δ' ἐπιπείθεο μύθῳ 460 ita Ilgen : κρανάϊνον A At Γ : κρανάϊον cet. (αϊ in ras V^1), cf. Herod. vii. 92 ἔγωγε E L^1 T 461 ἡγεμόν' εἴσω Tyrrell 468 θοάσσεις M 471 σέ γέ *px* ita interpunximus : καὶ τιμάς· σὲ δέ φασι δ. ἐκ Δ. ὀμ. μαντείας θ' ἑκάεργε· Διὸς παρὰ θέσφατα πάντα codd. 472 μαντείας θ' M A Q Π corr. δ' V^1 : τ' cet. πάρα Steph. : παρὰ, παρα codd. 473 τῶν *y* V^2 : καὶ cet. ἔγωγε παῖδ' ἀφνειὸν codd. : ἐγώ σε Hermann, cf. 460 : πεδ' ἀφνειῶν Tyrrell 474 αὖτ' ἄγρετόν codd. em. ed. pr. 478 γλυκύφωνον E T ἑταῖρον *p* 479 ἐπισταμένως codd. em. Barnes 481 φιλομειδέα *p* χῶρον *p*

εὐφροσύνην νυκτός τε καὶ ἤματος. ὅς τις ἂν αὐτὴν
τέχνῃ καὶ σοφίῃ δεδαημένος ἐξερεείνῃ
φθεγγομένη παντοῖα νόῳ χαρίεντα διδάσκει
ῥεῖα συνηθείῃσιν ἀθυρομένη μαλακῇσιν,
ἐργασίην φεύγουσα δυήπαθον· ὃς δέ κεν αὐτὴν
νῆϊς ἐὼν τὸ πρῶτον ἐπιζαφελῶς ἐρεείνῃ,
μὰψ αὔτως κεν ἔπειτα μετήορά τε θρυλίζοι.
σοὶ δ' αὐτάγρετόν ἐστι δαήμεναι ὅττι μενοινᾷς.
καί τοι ἐγὼ δώσω ταύτην Διὸς ἀγλαὲ κοῦρε·
ἡμεῖς δ' αὖτ' ὄρεός τε καὶ ἱπποβότου πεδίοιο
βουσὶ νομοὺς Ἑκάεργε νομεύσομεν ἀγραύλοισιν.
ἔνθεν ἅλις τέξουσι βόες ταύροισι μιγεῖσαι
μίγδην θηλείας τε καὶ ἄρσενας· οὐδέ τί σε χρὴ
κερδαλέον περ ἐόντα περιζαμενῶς κεχολῶσθαι.
Ὣς εἰπὼν ὤρεξ', ὁ δ' ἐδέξατο Φοῖβος Ἀπόλλων,
Ἑρμῇ δ' ἐγγυάλιξεν ἔχων μάστιγα φαεινήν,
βουκολίας τ' ἐπέτελλεν· ἔδεκτο δὲ Μαιάδος υἱὸς
γηθήσας· κίθαριν δὲ λαβὼν ἐπ' ἀριστερὰ χειρὸς
Λητοῦς ἀγλαὸς υἱὸς ἄναξ ἑκάεργος Ἀπόλλων
πλήκτρῳ ἐπειρήτιζε κατὰ μέλος, ἡ δ' ὑπὸ νέρθεν
σμερδαλέον κονάβησε, θεὸς δ' ὑπὸ καλὸν ἄεισεν.
Ἔνθα βόες μὲν ἔπειτα ποτὶ ζάθεον λειμῶνα
ἐτραπέτην· αὐτοὶ δὲ Διὸς περικαλλέα τέκνα
ἄψορροι πρὸς Ὄλυμπον ἀγάννιφον ἐρρώσαντο
τερπόμενοι φόρμιγγι, χάρη δ' ἄρα μητίετα Ζεύς,

482 ὅστις ἂν καὶ M : ὅστις ἄρ' ed. pr. 483 ἐξερεείνει (ss. η) T 484 νόα p 486 ita M : φθέγγουσα x p 487 ἰὼν M ἐρέεινε praeter M omnes (ἐρέεινε T) 488 θρυαλίζοι codd. em. Ruhnken, Schneidewin 489 αὖτ' ἄγρετόν codd. corr. ed. Aldina 491 αὖ ed. pr. 493 θ' ἕξουσι M 494–Ven. 152 evulsi e Π 497 ἔχειν D'Orville : ἑκὼν Martin : fort. ἑλών 499 om. M 501 ὑπὸ νέρθεν M : ὑπὸ καλὸν cet. 502 σμερδαλέον M : ἱμερόεν cet. κονάβισσε p καλὸν M : μέλος cet. (-λλ- E L^1 T) 503 ἔνθα] καί ῥα M βόας M ποτὶ] κατὰ M 504 δραπέτην M

ἄμφω δ' ἐς φιλότητα συνήγαγε. καὶ τὰ μὲν Ἑρμῆς
Λητοΐδην ἐφίλησε διαμπερὲς ὡς ἔτι καὶ νῦν,
σήματ' ἐπεὶ κίθαριν μὲν Ἑκηβόλῳ ἐγγυάλιξεν
ἱμερτήν, δεδαὼς ὁ δ' ἐπωλένιον κιθάριζεν·
αὐτὸς δ' αὖθ' ἑτέρης σοφίης ἐκμάσσατο τέχνην·
συρίγγων ἐνοπὴν ποιήσατο τηλόθ' ἀκουστήν.
καὶ τότε Λητοΐδης Ἑρμῆν πρὸς μῦθον ἔειπε·

Δείδια Μαιάδος υἱὲ διάκτορε ποικιλομῆτα
μή μοι ἀνακλέψῃς κίθαριν καὶ καμπύλα τόξα·
τιμὴν γὰρ πὰρ Ζηνὸς ἔχεις ἐπαμοίβιμα ἔργα
θήσειν ἀνθρώποισι κατὰ χθόνα πουλυβότειραν.
ἀλλ' εἴ μοι τλαίης γε θεῶν μέγαν ὅρκον ὀμόσσαι,
ἢ κεφαλῇ νεύσας ἢ ἐπὶ Στυγὸς ὄβριμον ὕδωρ,
πάντ' ἂν ἐμῷ θυμῷ κεχαρισμένα καὶ φίλα ἔρδοις.

Καὶ τότε Μαιάδος υἱὸς ὑποσχόμενος κατένευσε
μή ποτ' ἀποκλέψειν ὅσ' Ἑκηβόλος ἐκτεάτισται,
μηδέ ποτ' ἐμπελάσειν πυκινῷ δόμῳ· αὐτὰρ Ἀπόλλων
Λητοΐδης κατένευσεν ἐπ' ἀρθμῷ καὶ φιλότητι
μή τινα φίλτερον ἄλλον ἐν ἀθανάτοισιν ἔσεσθαι,
μήτε θεὸν μήτ' ἄνδρα Διὸς γόνον· ἐκ δὲ τέλειον

σύμβολον ἀθανάτων ποιήσομαι ἠδ' ἅμα πάντων
πιστὸν ἐμῷ θυμῷ καὶ τίμιον· αὐτὰρ ἔπειτα
ὄλβου καὶ πλούτου δώσω περικαλλέα ῥάβδον
χρυσείην τριπέτηλον, ἀκήριον ἥ σε φυλάξει
πάντας ἐπικραίνουσα θεμοὺς ἐπέων τε καὶ ἔργων
τῶν ἀγαθῶν ὅσα φημὶ δαήμεναι ἐκ Διὸς ὀμφῆς.

507 καὶ τὰ μὲν M : καὶ τὸ μὲν cet. interpunxit Tucker 509 σήματ' M : σῆματ' cet. 510 om. M : interpunxit Ludwich ὑπωλένιον codd. corr. Ilgen, cf. 433 515 ἅμα κλέψῃς M, cf. γ 276 κιθάρην praeter E M omnes 516 ἐπ' ἀμοίβημα M corr. Ludwich : ἐπαμοίβια cet. 518 μέγαν] κατὰ m in rasura : fuerat uv. κ' (ss. τ) μεγ' (ss. αν) 522 μήτ' pro μή ποτ' M ἐκτετάτισται E T, M ss. 524 ἀριθμῷ M cf. Ap. Rhod. ii. 755 526 lacunam statuimus 530 ἀκήραον p L[1] (-αον ss. ϊ) 531 θεοὺς codd. : θεμοὺς Ludwich : οἴμους Hermann : (πᾶν τοι) τέλος Bothe : ἄθλους Sikes

μαντείην δὲ φέριστε διοτρεφὲς ἣν ἐρεείνεις
οὔτε σε θέσφατόν ἐστι δαήμεναι οὔτε τιν' ἄλλον
ἀθανάτων· τὸ γὰρ οἶδε Διὸς νόος· αὐτὰρ ἐγώ γε
πιστωθεὶς κατένευσα καὶ ὤμοσα καρτερὸν ὅρκον
μή τινα νόσφιν ἐμεῖο θεῶν αἰειγενετάων
ἄλλον γ' εἴσεσθαι Ζηνὸς πυκινόφρονα βουλήν.
καὶ σὺ κασίγνητε χρυσόρραπι μή με κέλευε
θέσφατα πιφαύσκειν ὅσα μήδεται εὐρύοπα Ζεύς.
ἀνθρώπων δ' ἄλλον δηλήσομαι, ἄλλον ὀνήσω,
πολλὰ περιτροπέων ἀμεγάρτων φῦλ' ἀνθρώπων.
καὶ μὲν ἐμῆς ὀμφῆς ἀπονήσεται ὅς τις ἂν ἔλθῃ
φωνῇ τ' ἠδὲ ποτῇσι τεληέντων οἰωνῶν·
οὗτος ἐμῆς ὀμφῆς ἀπονήσεται οὐδ' ἀπατήσω.
ὃς δέ κε μαψιλόγοισι πιθήσας οἰωνοῖσι
μαντείην ἐθέλῃσι παρὲκ νόον ἐξερεείνειν
ἡμετέρην, νοέειν δὲ θεῶν πλέον αἰὲν ἐόντων,
φήμ' ἁλίην ὁδὸν εἶσιν, ἐγὼ δέ κε δῶρα δεχοίμην.
ἄλλο δέ τοι ἐρέω Μαίης ἐρικυδέος υἱὲ
καὶ Διὸς αἰγιόχοιο, θεῶν ἐριούνιε δαῖμον·
σεμναὶ γάρ τινες εἰσὶ κασίγνηται γεγαυῖαι
παρθένοι ὠκείῃσιν ἀγαλλόμεναι πτερύγεσσι
τρεῖς· κατὰ δὲ κρατὸς πεπαλαγμέναι ἄλφιτα λευκὰ
οἰκία ναιετάουσιν ὑπὸ πτυχὶ Παρνησοῖο
μαντείης ἀπάνευθε διδάσκαλοι ἣν ἐπὶ βουσὶ
παῖς ἔτ' ἐὼν μελέτησα· πατὴρ δ' ἐμὸς οὐκ ἀλέγιζεν.
ἐντεῦθεν δὴ ἔπειτα ποτώμεναι ἄλλοτε ἄλλῃ
κηρία βόσκονται καί τε κραίνουσιν ἕκαστα.
αἱ δ' ὅτε μὲν θυίωσιν ἐδηδυῖαι μέλι χλωρὸν

533 διαμπερὲς pro διοτρεφὲς M 534 ἄλλων M 535 om. E T 538 θυμὸν T ante corr. 539 χρυσάραπι At D 540 πιφάσκειν *p* βούλεται At D 542 περιτραπῶν M 543 καὶ μὴν At : καὶ μὴ M 544 φωνή τ' ἠδὲ πότησι M : φωνῇ καὶ πτερύγεσσι cet. 547 ἐθελήσει *x* M At D 550 υἱὸς M 552 σεμναὶ M : μοῖραι cet. : Θριαὶ Hermann 556 διδασκαλίαν ἐπὶ M 557 ita Hermann cl. 361, Quintus ii. 428 : ἀλέγυνεν *x* M D At : ἀλέγεινεν *p* 558 ἄλλοτ' ἐπ' ἄλλῃ libri corr. Schneidewin 560 θυίωσιν M : θυίσωσιν *x* D : θύσωσι *p* ἐδωδυῖαι *p*

προφρονέως ἐθέλουσιν ἀληθείην ἀγορεύειν·
ἢν δ' ἀπονοσφισθῶσι θεῶν ἠδεῖαν ἐδωδὴν
ψεύδονται δὴ ἔπειτα δι' ἀλλήλων δονέουσαι.
τάς τοι ἔπειτα δίδωμι, σὺ δ' ἀτρεκέως ἐρεείνων
σὴν αὐτοῦ φρένα τέρπε, καὶ εἰ βροτὸν ἄνδρα δαείης
πολλάκι σῆς ὀμφῆς ἐπακούσεται αἴ κε τύχῃσι.
ταῦτ' ἔχε Μαιάδος υἱὲ καὶ ἀγραύλους ἕλικας βοῦς,
ἵππους τ' ἀμφιπόλευε καὶ ἡμιόνους ταλαεργοὺς

καὶ χαροποῖσι λέουσι καὶ ἀργιόδουσι σύεσσι
καὶ κυσὶ καὶ μήλοισιν, ὅσα τρέφει εὐρεῖα χθών,
πᾶσι δ' ἐπὶ προβάτοισιν ἀνάσσειν κύδιμον Ἑρμῆν,
οἶον δ' εἰς Ἀΐδην τετελεσμένον ἄγγελον εἶναι,
ὅς τ' ἄδοτός περ ἐὼν δώσει γέρας οὐκ ἐλάχιστον.
Οὕτω Μαιάδος υἱὸν ἄναξ ἐφίλησεν Ἀπόλλων
παντοίῃ φιλότητι, χάριν δ' ἐπέθηκε Κρονίων.
πᾶσι δ' ὅ γε θνητοῖσι καὶ ἀθανάτοισιν ὁμιλεῖ·
παῦρα μὲν οὖν ὀνίνησι, τὸ δ' ἄκριτον ἠπεροπεύει
νύκτα δι' ὀρφναίην φῦλα θνητῶν ἀνθρώπων.
Καὶ σὺ μὲν οὕτω χαῖρε Διὸς καὶ Μαιάδος υἱέ·
αὐτὰρ ἐγὼ καὶ σεῖο καὶ ἄλλης μνήσομ' ἀοιδῆς.

V. Εἰς Ἀφροδίτην

Μοῦσά μοι ἔννεπε ἔργα πολυχρύσου Ἀφροδίτης
Κύπριδος, ἥ τε θεοῖσιν ἐπὶ γλυκὺν ἵμερον ὦρσε
καί τ' ἐδαμάσσατο φῦλα καταθνητῶν ἀνθρώπων,
οἰωνούς τε διιπετέας καὶ θηρία πάντα,

561 ἐθέλωσι *x* 563 ita *y* (δενέουσαι) V² (δὲ νέουσαι), corr. Baumeister: πειρῶνται δ' ἤπειτα παρὲξ ὁδὸν ἡγεμονεύειν cet. 565 ἣν At E ἄνδρ' ἀδαῆ in extremo versu M 568 lacunam stat. Wolf 568 post 571 transp. E 570 χθονὸν L¹ 572 δ' om. At D 576 ἀθανάτοισι νομίζων M

V. *codices* M *x* (praeter Π) *p* (praeter Mon. O) Titulus: τοῦ αὐτοῦ ὁμήρου ὕμνοι εἰς ἀφροδίτην M ὕμνος εἰς ἀφροδίτην *p* At εἰς ἀφροδίτην D E L¹ ed. pr.: εἰς ἀφροδίτην γ (ss. ος) T 4 διιπετέα M

ἠμὲν ὅσ' ἤπειρος πολλὰ τρέφει ἠδ' ὅσα πόντος·
πᾶσιν δ' ἔργα μέμηλεν ἐϋστεφάνου Κυθερείης.
τρισσὰς δ' οὐ δύναται πεπιθεῖν φρένας οὐδ' ἀπατῆσαι·
κούρην τ' αἰγιόχοιο Διὸς γλαυκῶπιν Ἀθήνην·
οὐ γάρ οἱ εὔαδεν ἔργα πολυχρύσου Ἀφροδίτης,
ἀλλ' ἄρα οἱ πόλεμοί τε ἅδον καὶ ἔργον Ἄρηος,
ὑσμῖναί τε μάχαι τε καὶ ἀγλαὰ ἔργ' ἀλεγύνειν.
πρώτη τέκτονας ἄνδρας ἐπιχθονίους ἐδίδαξε
ποιῆσαι σατίνας καὶ ἅρματα ποικίλα χαλκῷ·
ἡ δέ τε παρθενικὰς ἁπαλόχροας ἐν μεγάροισιν
ἀγλαὰ ἔργ' ἐδίδαξεν ἐπὶ φρεσὶ θεῖσα ἑκάστῃ.
οὐδέ ποτ' Ἀρτέμιδα χρυσηλάκατον κελαδεινὴν
δάμναται ἐν φιλότητι φιλομμειδὴς Ἀφροδίτη·
καὶ γὰρ τῇ ἅδε τόξα καὶ οὔρεσι θῆρας ἐναίρειν,
φόρμιγγές τε χοροί τε διαπρύσιοί τ' ὀλολυγαὶ
ἄλσεά τε σκιόεντα δικαίων τε πτόλις ἀνδρῶν.
οὐδὲ μὲν αἰδοίῃ κούρῃ ἅδεν ἔργ' Ἀφροδίτης
Ἱστίῃ, ἣν πρώτην τέκετο Κρόνος ἀγκυλομήτης,
αὖτις δ' ὁπλοτάτην, βουλῇ Διὸς αἰγιόχοιο,
πότνιαν, ἣν ἐμνῶντο Ποσειδάων καὶ Ἀπόλλων·
ἡ δὲ μάλ' οὐκ ἔθελεν ἀλλὰ στερεῶς ἀπέειπεν,
ὤμοσε δὲ μέγαν ὅρκον, ὃ δὴ τετελεσμένος ἐστίν,
ἁψαμένη κεφαλῆς πατρὸς Διὸς αἰγιόχοιο
παρθένος ἔσσεσθαι πάντ' ἤματα, δῖα θεάων.
τῇ δὲ πατὴρ Ζεὺς δῶκε καλὸν γέρας ἀντὶ γάμοιο,
καί τε μέσῳ οἴκῳ κατ' ἄρ' ἕζετο πῖαρ ἑλοῦσα.
πᾶσιν δ' ἐν νηοῖσι θεῶν τιμάοχός ἐστι
καὶ παρὰ πᾶσι βροτοῖσι θεῶν πρέσβειρα τέτυκται.
τάων οὐ δύναται πεπιθεῖν φρένας οὐδ' ἀπατῆσαι·

8 ita M: *γλαυκώπιδ'* cet. 10 *ἅδον* Q, ex *ἅδον* M: *ἅδεν* At Γ: *ἅδεν* cet. 11 om. E 13 *σάτινα* vulg.: *σκύτινα* At D: *σάκεα* V² marg. Γ corr. Barnes 16 *χρυσήλατον* *x* D, cf. 118 17 *φιλομειδὴς* *x* M D ed. pr., cf. 49, 56 18 *καὶ γὰρ τῇ ἅδε*] *πουλύχρυσα δὲ* M 20 *πτόλις* Γ marg. ed. pr.: *πόλις* *x* At D: *πόλεις* M: *πόνος* *p* 22 *ἑστίη* M At D 25 *στερρῶς* M 30 *πεῖαρ* M

τῶν δ' ἄλλων οὔ πέρ τι πεφυγμένον ἔστ' Ἀφροδίτην
οὔτε θεῶν μακάρων οὔτε θνητῶν ἀνθρώπων.
καί τε παρὲκ Ζηνὸς νόον ἤγαγε τερπικεραύνου,
ὅς τε μέγιστός τ' ἐστί, μεγίστης τ' ἔμμορε τιμῆς·
καί τε τοῦ εὖτε θέλοι πυκινὰς φρένας ἐξαπαφοῦσα
ῥηϊδίως συνέμιξε καταθνητῇσι γυναιξὶν
Ἥρης ἐκλελαθοῦσα κασιγνήτης ἀλόχου τε,
ἣ μέγα εἶδος ἀρίστη ἐν ἀθανάτῃσι θεῇσι,
κυδίστην δ' ἄρα μιν τέκετο Κρόνος ἀγκυλομήτης
μήτηρ τε Ῥείη· Ζεὺς δ' ἄφθιτα μήδεα εἰδὼς
αἰδοίην ἄλοχον ποιήσατο κέδν' εἰδυῖαν.
Τῇ δὲ καὶ αὐτῇ Ζεὺς γλυκὺν ἵμερον ἔμβαλε θυμῷ
ἀνδρὶ καταθνητῷ μιχθήμεναι, ὄφρα τάχιστα
μηδ' αὐτὴ βροτέης εὐνῆς ἀποεργμένη εἴη
καί ποτ' ἐπευξαμένη εἴπῃ μετὰ πᾶσι θεοῖσιν
ἡδὺ γελοιήσασα φιλομμειδὴς Ἀφροδίτη
ὥς ῥα θεοὺς συνέμιξε καταθνητῇσι γυναιξὶ
καί τε καταθνητοὺς υἱεῖς τέκον ἀθανάτοισιν,
ὥς τε θεὰς ἀνέμιξε καταθνητοῖς ἀνθρώποις.
Ἀγχίσεω δ' ἄρα οἱ γλυκὺν ἵμερον ἔμβαλε θυμῷ,
ὃς τότ' ἐν ἀκροπόλοις ὄρεσιν πολυπιδάκου Ἴδης
βουκολέεσκεν βοῦς δέμας ἀθανάτοισιν ἐοικώς.
τὸν δὴ ἔπειτα ἰδοῦσα φιλομμειδὴς Ἀφροδίτη
ἠράσατ', ἐκπάγλως δὲ κατὰ φρένας ἵμερος εἷλεν.
ἐς Κύπρον δ' ἐλθοῦσα θυώδεα νηὸν ἔδυνεν
ἐς Πάφον· ἔνθα δέ οἱ τέμενος βωμός τε θυώδης·
ἔνθ' ἥ γ' εἰσελθοῦσα θύρας ἐπέθηκε φαεινάς.
ἔνθα δέ μιν Χάριτες λοῦσαν καὶ χρῖσαν ἐλαίῳ
ἀμβρότῳ, οἷα θεοὺς ἐπενήνοθεν αἰὲν ἐόντας,

38 ἐθέλῃ M 39 κατὰ codd. (et 46, 50, 51, 52) θνητοῖσι *p* 46 μιγημέναι At D 47 ἀπὸ T 49 γελάσασα M φιλομειδὴς libri et 56 (ubi -μ- ss. μ T), 65 50 σύμμιξε M θνητοῖσι *p* 51 τέκεν praeter M libri 52 συνέμιξε Schäfer 57 ἐκπάγλης L[1]

ἀμβροσίῳ ἑδανῷ, τό ῥά οἱ τεθυωμένον ἦεν.
ἑσσαμένη δ' εὖ πάντα περὶ χροῒ εἵματα καλὰ
χρυσῷ κοσμηθεῖσα φιλομμειδὴς Ἀφροδίτη
σεύατ' ἐπὶ Τροίης προλιποῦσ' εὐώδεα Κύπρον
ὕψι μετὰ νέφεσιν ῥίμφα πρήσσουσα κέλευθον.
Ἴδην δ' ἵκανεν πολυπίδακα, μητέρα θηρῶν,
βῆ δ' ἰθὺς σταθμοῖο δι' οὔρεος· οἱ δὲ μετ' αὐτὴν
σαίνοντες πολιοί τε λύκοι χαροποί τε λέοντες
ἄρκτοι παρδάλιές τε θοαὶ προκάδων ἀκόρητοι
ἤϊσαν· ἡ δ' ὁρόωσα μετὰ φρεσὶ τέρπετο θυμὸν
καὶ τοῖς ἐν στήθεσσι βάλ' ἵμερον, οἱ δ' ἅμα πάντες
σύνδυο κοιμήσαντο κατὰ σκιόεντας ἐναύλους.
αὐτὴ δ' ἐς κλισίας εὐποιήτους ἀφίκανε·
τὸν δ' εὗρε σταθμοῖσι λελειμμένον οἶον ἀπ' ἄλλων
Ἀγχίσην ἥρωα θεῶν ἄπο κάλλος ἔχοντα.
οἱ δ' ἅμα βουσὶν ἕποντο νομοὺς κάτα ποιήεντας
πάντες, ὁ δὲ σταθμοῖσι λελειμμένος οἶος ἀπ' ἄλλων
πωλεῖτ' ἔνθα καὶ ἔνθα διαπρύσιον κιθαρίζων.
στῆ δ' αὐτοῦ προπάροιθε Διὸς θυγάτηρ Ἀφροδίτη
παρθένῳ ἀδμήτῃ μέγεθος καὶ εἶδος ὁμοίη,
μή μιν ταρβήσειεν ἐν ὀφθαλμοῖσι νοήσας.
Ἀγχίσης δ' ὁρόων ἐφράζετο θαύμαινέν τε
εἶδός τε μέγεθος καὶ εἵματα σιγαλόεντα.
πέπλον μὲν γὰρ ἕεστο φαεινότερον πυρὸς αὐγῆς,
εἶχε δ' ἐπιγναμπτὰς ἕλικας κάλυκάς τε φαεινάς,
ὅρμοι δ' ἀμφ' ἁπαλῇ δειρῇ περικαλλέες ἦσαν
καλοὶ χρύσειοι παμποίκιλοι· ὡς δὲ σελήνη
στήθεσιν ἀμφ' ἁπαλοῖσιν ἐλάμπετο, θαῦμα ἰδέσθαι.
Ἀγχίσην δ' ἔρος εἷλεν, ἔπος δέ μιν ἀντίον ηὔδα·

63 ἑανῷ, ἐανῷ codd. em. Clarke cl. Ξ 172 66 τροίης M : τροίην cet. κῆπον M 67 νέφεσι ῥίμφα M : νεφέεσσι θοῶς cet. 68–112 om. M 68 θεῶν, mg. γρ. θηρῶν E T 71 πορδάλιες B Γ L^2 L^3 N R^1 R^2, cf. N 103 P 20 Φ 573 δ 457 72 ἤεσ(σ)αν codd. em. Ilgen 82 τε καὶ A B C Γ L^3 Q R^1 84 θάμβαινέν p, cf. Pind. Ol. iii. 83 85 τε καὶ codd. 87 ἐπὶ Q : ἔπι Barnes

Χαῖρε ἄνασσ', ἥ τις μακάρων τάδε δώμαθ' ἱκάνεις,
Ἄρτεμις ἢ Λητὼ ἠὲ χρυσέη Ἀφροδίτη
ἢ Θέμις ἠϋγενὴς ἠὲ γλαυκῶπις Ἀθήνη
ἤ πού τις Χαρίτων δεῦρ' ἤλυθες, αἵ τε θεοῖσι
πᾶσιν ἑταιρίζουσι καὶ ἀθάνατοι καλέονται,
ἤ τις νυμφάων αἵ τ' ἄλσεα καλὰ νέμονται,
ἢ νυμφῶν αἳ καλὸν ὄρος τόδε ναιετάουσι
καὶ πηγὰς ποταμῶν καὶ πίσεα ποιήεντα.
σοὶ δ' ἐγὼ ἐν σκοπιῇ, περιφαινομένῳ ἐνὶ χώρῳ,
βωμὸν ποιήσω, ῥέξω δέ τοι ἱερὰ καλὰ
ὥρῃσιν πάσῃσι· σὺ δ' εὔφρονα θυμὸν ἔχουσα
δός με μετὰ Τρώεσσιν ἀριπρεπέ' ἔμμεναι ἄνδρα,
ποίει δ' εἰσοπίσω θαλερὸν γόνον, αὐτὰρ ἔμ' αὐτὸν
δηρὸν ἐῢ ζώειν καὶ ὁρᾶν φάος ἠελίοιο
ὄλβιον ἐν λαοῖς καὶ γήραος οὐδὸν ἱκέσθαι.
Τὸν δ' ἠμείβετ' ἔπειτα Διὸς θυγάτηρ Ἀφροδίτη·
Ἀγχίση, κύδιστε χαμαιγενέων ἀνθρώπων,
οὔ τίς τοι θεός εἰμι· τί μ' ἀθανάτῃσιν ἐΐσκεις ;
ἀλλὰ καταθνητή γε, γυνὴ δέ με γείνατο μήτηρ.
Ὀτρεὺς δ' ἐστὶ πατὴρ ὄνομα κλυτός, εἴ που ἀκούεις,
ὃς πάσης Φρυγίης εὐτειχήτοιο ἀνάσσει.
γλῶσσαν δ' ὑμετέρην καὶ ἡμετέρην σάφα οἶδα·
Τρῳὰς γὰρ μεγάρῳ με τροφὸς τρέφεν, ἡ δὲ διὰ πρὸ
σμικρὴν παῖδ' ἀτίταλλε φίλης παρὰ μητρὸς ἑλοῦσα.
ὣς δή τοι γλῶσσάν γε καὶ ὑμετέρην εὖ οἶδα.
νῦν δέ μ' ἀνήρπαξε χρυσόρραπις Ἀργειφόντης
ἐκ χοροῦ Ἀρτέμιδος χρυσηλακάτου κελαδεινῆς.
πολλαὶ δὲ νύμφαι καὶ παρθένοι ἀλφεσίβοιαι
παίζομεν, ἀμφὶ δ' ὅμιλος ἀπείριτος ἐστεφάνωτο·

93 *χρυσῇ* libri em. Barnes 97 om. E T 99 *πείσεα* (ss. *βη*) L[1] corr. Clarke Ruhnken: *βήσεα* cet. 105 *ἐΰζώειν* libri praeter T 110 *γε* Gemoll: *τε* libri 113 *ὑμετέρην καὶ ὑμετέρην* E T (priorem corr. T) 114 *τρῳὰς* M: *τρωὸς* cet. *διὰ* M D: *δια* cet. 116 *γε* Hermann: *τε* libri 117 *ἀνήρπαζε* E T 118 *χρυσηλάτου* libri praeter M D ed. pr.

ἔνθεν μ' ἥρπαξε χρυσόρραπις Ἀργειφόντης,
πολλὰ δ' ἔπ' ἤγαγεν ἔργα καταθνητῶν ἀνθρώπων,
πολλὴν δ' ἄκληρόν τε καὶ ἄκτιτον, ἣν διὰ θῆρες
ὠμοφάγοι φοιτῶσι κατὰ σκιόεντας ἐναύλους,
οὐδὲ ποσὶ ψαύσειν ἐδόκουν φυσιζόου αἴης·
Ἀγχίσεω δέ με φάσκε παραὶ λέχεσιν καλέεσθαι
κουριδίην ἄλοχον, σοὶ δ' ἀγλαὰ τέκνα τεκεῖσθαι.
αὐτὰρ ἐπεὶ δὴ δεῖξε καὶ ἔφρασεν ἦ τοι ὅ γ' αὖτις
ἀθανάτων μετὰ φῦλ' ἀπέβη κρατὺς Ἀργειφόντης·
αὐτὰρ ἐγώ σ' ἱκόμην, κρατερὴ δέ μοι ἔπλετ' ἀνάγκη.
ἀλλά σε πρὸς Ζηνὸς γουνάζομαι ἠδὲ τοκήων
ἐσθλῶν· οὐ μὲν γάρ κε κακοὶ τοιόνδε τέκοιεν·
ἀδμήτην μ' ἀγαγὼν καὶ ἀπειρήτην φιλότητος
πατρί τε σῷ δεῖξον καὶ μητέρι κεδνὰ ἰδυίῃ
σοῖς τε κασιγνήτοις οἵ τοι ὁμόθεν γεγάασιν·
οὔ σφιν ἀεικελίη νυὸς ἔσσομαι, ἀλλ' εἰκυῖα.
πέμψαι δ' ἄγγελον ὦκα μετὰ Φρύγας αἰολοπώλους
εἰπεῖν πατρί τ' ἐμῷ καὶ μητέρι κηδομένῃ περ·
οἱ δέ κέ τοι χρυσόν τε ἅλις ἐσθῆτά θ' ὑφαντὴν
πέμψουσιν, σὺ δὲ πολλὰ καὶ ἀγλαὰ δέχθαι ἄποινα.
ταῦτα δὲ ποιήσας δαίνυ γάμον ἱμερόεντα
τίμιον ἀνθρώποισι καὶ ἀθανάτοισι θεοῖσιν.
Ὣς εἰποῦσα θεὰ γλυκὺν ἵμερον ἔμβαλε θυμῷ.
Ἀγχίσην δ' ἔρος εἷλεν, ἔπος τ' ἔφατ' ἔκ τ' ὀνόμαζεν·
Εἰ μὲν θνητή τ' ἐσσί, γυνὴ δέ σε γείνατο μήτηρ,
Ὀτρεὺς δ' ἐστὶ πατὴρ ὄνομα κλυτός, ὡς ἀγορεύεις,
ἀθανάτου δὲ ἕκητι διακτόρου ἐνθάδ' ἱκάνεις

122 *ἐπήγαγεν* codd. em. Barnes 123 *ἄκτιστον* E T (*ἄκτιστον* ss. *τ* T) 125 *ψαύειν* praeter M libri *φυσιζώου* codd. em. Steph. 127 *τεκέσθαι* Buttmann: *τελεῖσθαι* Tucker 132 *μὲν* om. praeter M T omnes *κε* M: *τοι* V[1] ed. pr.: *τε* cet., cf. δ 64 135 *δοιώ τε κασιγνήτω* M post 136 add. *εἴ τοι ἀεικελίη γυνὴ ἔσσομαι ἠὲ καὶ οὐκί* M *x* At D, cf. Dem. 83, 84 pro 136, 136a *οὔ σφιν ἀεικελίη γυνὴ ἔσσομαι ἠὲ καὶ οὐκὶ* *p* 139 *οὐδέ τε* A Q: *οἱ δέ τε* cet. praeter M *τοι* add. Matthiae *χρυσόν κεν* praeter M libri 144 *ἔρως* *p* M 146 *ἀγοράζεις* *p* (*ἀγορεύεις* N, marg. *ἀγοράζεις*) 147 *ἀθανάτοιο δ' ἕκητι* libri praeter M (*ἕκατι* M N)

Ἑρμέω, ἐμὴ δ' ἄλοχος κεκλήσεαι ἤματα πάντα·
οὔ τις ἔπειτα θεῶν οὔτε θνητῶν ἀνθρώπων
ἐνθάδε με σχήσει πρὶν σῇ φιλότητι μιγῆναι
αὐτίκα νῦν· οὐδ' εἴ κεν ἑκηβόλος αὐτὸς Ἀπόλλων
τόξου ἀπ' ἀργυρέου προϊῇ βέλεα στονόεντα.
βουλοίμην κεν ἔπειτα, γύναι εἰκυῖα θεῇσι,
σῆς εὐνῆς ἐπιβὰς δῦναι δόμον Ἄϊδος εἴσω.
  Ὣς εἰπὼν λάβε χεῖρα· φιλομμειδὴς δ' Ἀφροδίτη
ἕρπε μεταστρεφθεῖσα κατ' ὄμματα καλὰ βαλοῦσα
ἐς λέχος εὔστρωτον, ὅθι περ πάρος ἔσκεν ἄνακτι
χλαίνῃσιν μαλακῇς ἐστρωμένον· αὐτὰρ ὕπερθεν
ἄρκτων δέρματ' ἔκειτο βαρυφθόγγων τε λεόντων,
τοὺς αὐτὸς κατέπεφνεν ἐν οὔρεσιν ὑψηλοῖσιν.
οἱ δ' ἐπεὶ οὖν λεχέων εὐποιήτων ἐπέβησαν,
κόσμον μέν οἱ πρῶτον ἀπὸ χροὸς εἷλε φαεινόν,
πόρπας τε γναμπτάς θ' ἕλικας κάλυκάς τε καὶ ὅρμους.
λῦσε δέ οἱ ζώνην ἰδὲ εἵματα σιγαλόεντα
ἔκδυε καὶ κατέθηκεν ἐπὶ θρόνου ἀργυροήλου
Ἀγχίσης· ὁ δ' ἔπειτα θεῶν ἰότητι καὶ αἴσῃ
ἀθανάτῃ παρέλεκτο θεᾷ βροτός, οὐ σάφα εἰδώς.
  Ἦμος δ' ἂψ εἰς αὖλιν ἀποκλίνουσι νομῆες
βοῦς τε καὶ ἴφια μῆλα νομῶν ἐξ ἀνθεμοέντων,
τῆμος ἄρ' Ἀγχίσῃ μὲν ἐπὶ γλυκὺν ὕπνον ἔχευε
νήδυμον, αὐτὴ δὲ χροῒ ἕννυτο εἵματα καλά.
ἑσσαμένη δ' εὖ πάντα περὶ χροῒ δῖα θεάων
ἔστη ἄρα κλισίῃ, εὐποιήτοιο μελάθρου
κῦρε κάρη, κάλλος δὲ παρειάων ἀπέλαμπεν
ἄμβροτον, οἷόν τ' ἐστὶν ἐϋστεφάνου Κυθερείης.

152 *προΐοι* Γ L[3] N Q R[1] V[1]: *προοίοι* L[2] R[2]: *προΐῃ* cet. 155 ita A B L[2] N ss.: *φιλομει-* cet. 156 *μεταστραφθεῖσα* (ss. ε) E T 157 *λέχον* M *ἔσκεν αὐτὴ* M 158 *δίνησι* pro *χλαίνῃσιν* M 159 *ἄρκτων*] *ἐκ τῶν* M 164 *ἠδ'* M 173 *ἄρα*] *πὰρ* Stephanus *κεὐποιήτοιο* Sikes: *εὐποιήτου δὲ* Ruhnken 174 *κῦρε* M, cf. Dem. 189: *βυρε* E T: *ἤυρε* L[1] Π *p*: *ἦρε* At D: *ἦρε* ed. pr. 175 *ἰοστεφάνου* M, cf. vi. 18

ἐξ ὕπνου τ' ἀνέγειρεν, ἔπος τ' ἔφατ' ἔκ τ' ὀνόμαζεν·
Ὄρσεο Δαρδανίδη· τί νυ νήγρετον ὕπνον ἰαύεις;
καὶ φράσαι εἴ τοι ὁμοίη ἐγὼν ἰνδάλλομαι εἶναι
οἵην δή με τὸ πρῶτον ἐν ὀφθαλμοῖσι νόησας;
Ὣς φάθ'· ὁ δ' ἐξ ὕπνοιο μάλ' ἐμμαπέως ὑπάκουσεν.
ὡς δὲ ἴδεν δειρήν τε καὶ ὄμματα κάλ' Ἀφροδίτης
τάρβησέν τε καὶ ὄσσε παρακλιδὸν ἔτραπεν ἄλλῃ.
ἂψ δ' αὖτις χλαίνῃ τε καλύψατο καλὰ πρόσωπα,
καί μιν λισσόμενος ἔπεα πτερόεντα προσηύδα·
Αὐτίκα σ' ὡς τὰ πρῶτα θεὰ ἴδον ὀφθαλμοῖσιν
ἔγνων ὡς θεὸς ἦσθα· σὺ δ' οὐ νημερτὲς ἔειπες.
ἀλλά σε πρὸς Ζηνὸς γουνάζομαι αἰγιόχοιο
μή με ζῶντ' ἀμενηνὸν ἐν ἀνθρώποισιν ἐάσῃς
ναίειν, ἀλλ' ἐλέαιρ'· ἐπεὶ οὐ βιοθάλμιος ἀνὴρ
γίγνεται ὅς τε θεαῖς εὐνάζεται ἀθανάτῃσι.
Τὸν δ' ἠμείβετ' ἔπειτα Διὸς θυγάτηρ Ἀφροδίτη·
Ἀγχίση, κύδιστε καταθνητῶν ἀνθρώπων,
θάρσει, μηδέ τι σῇσι μετὰ φρεσὶ δείδιθι λίην·
οὐ γάρ τοί τι δέος παθέειν κακὸν ἐξ ἐμέθεν γε
οὐδ' ἄλλων μακάρων, ἐπεὶ ἦ φίλος ἐσσὶ θεοῖσι.
σοὶ δ' ἔσται φίλος υἱὸς ὃς ἐν Τρώεσσιν ἀνάξει
καὶ παῖδες παίδεσσι διαμπερὲς ἐκγεγάονται·
τῷ δὲ καὶ Αἰνείας ὄνομ' ἔσσεται οὕνεκά μ' αἰνὸν
ἔσχεν ἄχος ἕνεκα βροτοῦ ἀνέρος ἔμπεσον εὐνῇ·
ἀγχίθεοι δὲ μάλιστα καταθνητῶν ἀνθρώπων
αἰεὶ ἀφ' ὑμετέρης γενεῆς εἶδός τε φυήν τε.
ἦ τοι μὲν ξανθὸν Γανυμήδεα μητίετα Ζεὺς
ἥρπασεν ὃν διὰ κάλλος ἵν' ἀθανάτοισι μετείη
καί τε Διὸς κατὰ δῶμα θεοῖς ἐπιοινοχοεύοι,

178 τοι] τι *x* ed. pr. ἀγὼν M 179 με om. La Roche, τὸ Hermann 181 δ' εἶδε M 186 ἔειπας (ss. ε) E T 189 βιοφθάλμιος M N P, cf. Pind. Ol. vii. 20 190 ἀθανάτοισι Γ N 194 τι τοι M : τοι om. *p* 197 ἐκγεγάοντες Baumeister 198 καὶ om. D L[1] 200 ἀγχίθεοι Barnes, separatim codd. 202 ἤτοι codd. praeter E 203 ita At Γ, Hermann : ἥρπασ' ἐνὸν *x* M (αἰνὸν M) : ἑὸν *p* D 204 ἐπιοινοχοεύειν M : ἐπὶ οινοχοεύει E (ss. οι) T (ἐπ' Π)

θαῦμα ἰδεῖν, πάντεσσι τετιμένος ἀθανάτοισι,
χρυσέου ἐκ κρητῆρος ἀφύσσων νέκταρ ἐρυθρόν.
Τρῶα δὲ πένθος ἄλαστον ἔχε φρένας, οὐδέ τι ᾔδει
ὅππῃ οἱ φίλον υἱὸν ἀνήρπασε θέσπις ἄελλα·
τὸν δὴ ἔπειτα γόασκε διαμπερὲς ἤματα πάντα.
καί μιν Ζεὺς ἐλέησε, δίδου δέ οἱ υἷος ἄποινα
ἵππους ἀρσίποδας, τοί τ' ἀθανάτους φορέουσι.
τούς οἱ δῶρον ἔδωκεν ἔχειν· εἶπεν δὲ ἕκαστα
Ζηνὸς ἐφημοσύνῃσι διάκτορος Ἀργειφόντης,
ὡς ἔοι ἀθάνατος καὶ ἀγήρως ἶσα θεοῖσιν.
αὐτὰρ ἐπεὶ δὴ Ζηνὸς ὅ γ' ἔκλυεν ἀγγελιάων
οὐκέτ' ἔπειτα γόασκε, γεγήθει δὲ φρένας ἔνδον,
γηθόσυνος δ' ἵπποισιν ἀελλοπόδεσσιν ὀχεῖτο.
ὣς δ' αὖ Τιθωνὸν χρυσόθρονος ἥρπασεν Ἠὼς
ὑμετέρης γενεῆς ἐπιείκελον ἀθανάτοισι.
βῆ δ' ἴμεν αἰτήσουσα κελαινεφέα Κρονίωνα
ἀθάνατόν τ' εἶναι καὶ ζώειν ἤματα πάντα·
τῇ δὲ Ζεὺς ἐπένευσε καὶ ἐκρήηνεν ἐέλδωρ.
νηπίη, οὐδ' ἐνόησε μετὰ φρεσὶ πότνια Ἠὼς
ἥβην αἰτῆσαι, ξῦσαί τ' ἄπο γῆρας ὀλοιόν.
τὸν δ' ἤ τοι εἵως μὲν ἔχεν πολυήρατος ἥβη,
Ἠοῖ τερπόμενος χρυσοθρόνῳ ἠριγενείῃ
ναῖε παρ' Ὠκεανοῖο ῥοῇς ἐπὶ πείρασι γαίης·
αὐτὰρ ἐπεὶ πρῶται πολιαὶ κατέχυντο ἔθειραι
καλῆς ἐκ κεφαλῆς εὐηγενέος τε γενείου,
τοῦ δ' ἤ τοι εὐνῆς μὲν ἀπείχετο πότνια Ἠώς,
αὐτὸν δ' αὖτ' ἀτίταλλεν ἐνὶ μεγάροισιν ἔχουσα
σίτῳ τ' ἀμβροσίῃ τε καὶ εἵματα καλὰ διδοῦσα.
ἀλλ' ὅτε δὴ πάμπαν στυγερὸν κατὰ γῆρας ἔπειγεν

205 *τετιμένον* M : *τετιμένονος* *x* (sc. *-ον* ss. *ος*) 206 *κρατῆρος* praeter M omnes *ἀφύσσειν* M 207 *τρῶς* E T, mg. Π 208 *ὅποι* M 212 *δὲ* Wolf : *τε* libri 214 *ἀγήραος* At D, cf. Θ 539 *ἶσα θεοῖσι* M *y* : *ἤματα πάντα* cet. 218 *χρυσόθρονον* *p* 224 *ἄπο* E T : *ἀπὸ* cet. 225 *δ' ἤτοι* M N Π : *δήτοι* cet. 229 *εὐγενέος* codd. praeter M : *καὶ εὐγενέος* ed. pr. 230 *δή τοι* codd. em. Hermann

οὐδέ τι κινῆσαι μελέων δύνατ' οὐδ' ἀναεῖραι,
ἥδε δέ οἱ κατὰ θυμὸν ἀρίστη φαίνετο βουλή·
ἐν θαλάμῳ κατέθηκε, θύρας δ' ἐπέθηκε φαεινάς.
τοῦ δ' ἦ τοι φωνὴ ῥεῖ ἄσπετος, οὐδέ τι κῖκυς
ἔσθ' οἵη πάρος ἔσκεν ἐνὶ γναμπτοῖσι μέλεσσιν.
οὐκ ἂν ἐγώ γε σὲ τοῖον ἐν ἀθανάτοισιν ἑλοίμην
ἀθάνατόν τ' εἶναι καὶ ζώειν ἤματα πάντα.
ἀλλ' εἰ μὲν τοιοῦτος ἐὼν εἶδός τε δέμας τε
ζώοις, ἡμέτερός τε πόσις κεκλημένος εἴης,
οὐκ ἂν ἔπειτά μ' ἄχος πυκινὰς φρένας ἀμφικαλύπτοι.
νῦν δέ σε μὲν τάχα γῆρας ὁμοίιον ἀμφικαλύψει
νηλειές, τό τ' ἔπειτα παρίσταται ἀνθρώποισιν,
οὐλόμενον καματηρόν, ὅ τε στυγέουσι θεοί περ.
αὐτὰρ ἐμοὶ μέγ' ὄνειδος ἐν ἀθανάτοισι θεοῖσιν
ἔσσεται ἤματα πάντα διαμπερὲς εἵνεκα σεῖο,
οἳ πρὶν ἐμοὺς ὀάρους καὶ μήτιας, αἷς ποτε πάντας
ἀθανάτους συνέμιξα καταθνητῇσι γυναιξί,
τάρβεσκον· πάντας γὰρ ἐμὸν δάμνασκε νόημα.
νῦν δὲ δὴ οὐκέτι μοι στόμα χείσεται ἐξονομῆναι
τοῦτο μετ' ἀθανάτοισιν, ἐπεὶ μάλα πολλὸν ἀάσθην
σχέτλιον οὐκ ὀνοταστόν, ἀπεπλάγχθην δὲ νόοιο,
παῖδα δ' ὑπὸ ζώνῃ ἐθέμην βροτῷ εὐνηθεῖσα.
τὸν μὲν ἐπὴν δὴ πρῶτον ἴδῃ φάος ἠελίοιο,
νύμφαι μιν θρέψουσιν ὀρεσκῷοι βαθύκολποι,
αἳ τόδε ναιετάουσιν ὄρος μέγα τε ζάθεόν τε·
αἵ ῥ' οὔτε θνητοῖς οὔτ' ἀθανάτοισιν ἕπονται·
δηρὸν μὲν ζώουσι καὶ ἄμβροτον εἶδαρ ἔδουσι,
καί τε μετ' ἀθανάτοισι καλὸν χορὸν ἐρρώσαντο.

237 δ' ἦτοι] δ' οὔτοι Α Γ L[2] N P V[1]: δ' οὔτϊ B: δήτι D: δήτοι cet. κίκυς libri corr. Abel 244 καταγῆρας (ss. τάχα) L[1] Π marg. τὸ ὁμοίιον (ὅμοιον L[1]) ὅμηρος πανταχοῦ ἐπὶ κακοῦ τιθέναι εἴωθεν L[1] Π 245 νηλειεὺς E T (ε¦s): νηλεὲς Π τ' p: γ' x M At D: σ' Π 247 ἐν M ed. pr.: μετ' cet. 252 στοναχήσεται codd. em. Martin 254 ὀνότατον codd. corr. Clarke: ὀνομαστὸν Martin 255 ζώνην M 256 ἐπεὶ M ἴδῃ] ἤδη E T

τῇσι δὲ Σειληνοί τε καὶ εὔσκοπος Ἀργειφόντης
μίσγοντ᾽ ἐν φιλότητι μυχῷ σπείων ἐροέντων.
τῇσι δ᾽ ἅμ᾽ ἢ ἐλάται ἠὲ δρύες ὑψικάρηνοι
γεινομένῃσιν ἔφυσαν ἐπὶ χθονὶ βωτιανείρῃ
καλαὶ τηλεθάουσαι ἐν οὔρεσιν ὑψηλοῖσιν.
ἑστᾶσ᾽ ἠλίβατοι, τεμένη δέ ἑ κικλήσκουσιν
ἀθανάτων· τὰς δ᾽ οὔ τι βροτοὶ κείρουσι σιδήρῳ.
ἀλλ᾽ ὅτε κεν δὴ μοῖρα παρεστήκῃ θανάτοιο
ἀζάνεται μὲν πρῶτον ἐπὶ χθονὶ δένδρεα καλά,
φλοιὸς δ᾽ ἀμφιπεριφθινύθει, πίπτουσι δ᾽ ἄπ᾽ ὄζοι,
τῶν δέ χ᾽ ὁμοῦ ψυχὴ λείποι φάος ἠελίοιο.
αἱ μὲν ἐμὸν θρέψουσι παρὰ σφίσιν υἱὸν ἔχουσαι.
τὸν μὲν ἐπὴν δὴ πρῶτον ἕλῃ πολυήρατος ἥβη
ἄξουσίν σοι δεῦρο θεαί, δείξουσί τε παῖδα·
σοὶ δ᾽ ἐγώ, ὄφρα κε ταῦτα μετὰ φρεσὶ πάντα διέλθω,
ἐς πέμπτον ἔτος αὖτις ἐλεύσομαι υἱὸν ἄγουσα.
τὸν μὲν ἐπὴν δὴ πρῶτον ἴδῃς θάλος ὀφθαλμοῖσι,
γηθήσεις ὁρόων· μάλα γὰρ θεοείκελος ἔσται·
ἄξεις δ᾽ αὐτίκα νιν ποτὶ Ἴλιον ἠνεμόεσσαν.
ἢν δέ τις εἴρηταί σε καταθνητῶν ἀνθρώπων
ἥ τις σοὶ φίλον υἱὸν ὑπὸ ζώνῃ θέτο μήτηρ,
τῷ δὲ σὺ μυθεῖσθαι μεμνημένος ὥς σε κελεύω·
φασίν τοι νύμφης καλυκώπιδος ἔκγονον εἶναι
αἳ τόδε ναιετάουσιν ὄρος καταειμένον ὕλῃ.
εἰ δέ κεν ἐξείπῃς καὶ ἐπεύξεαι ἄφρονι θυμῷ
ἐν φιλότητι μιγῆναι ἐϋστεφάνῳ Κυθερείῃ,
Ζεύς σε χολωσάμενος βαλέει ψολόεντι κεραυνῷ.

262 σιληνοὶ M L[1] Π D ed. pr.: σεληνοὶ E T: σειληνοὶ *p* 263 μυχῶν E T (ν T): χυμῷ L[1] 265 ἔφυγαν (ss. σ) E T 266 ἐν οὔρεσι δ᾽ L 267 ἕστασ᾽ *x* M ed. pr. 268 οὔτοι *p* D 269 παρεστήκοι *p*: -ει cet. corr. Stephanus 271 ἀπ᾽ ὄζοι codd. (ἄποζοι M) corr. Steph. 272 δέ θ᾽ Hermann ψυχῇ E T (-ῆ) λείπει codd. 275 ἄξουσί τοι M 276 κε add. Barnes 279 γηθήσαις *p* 280 ἄξαις *p* νιν codd. (νῦν M): μιν Hermann 281 εἰρήσεταί T σε om. L[1] 284 φάσθαι Matthiae ἔγγονον codd. em. Barnes 288 σε] τε B Γ

εἴρηταί τοι πάντα· σὺ δὲ φρεσὶ σῇσι νοήσας
ἴσχεο μηδ' ὀνόμαινε, θεῶν δ' ἐποπίζεο μῆνιν.
῝Ως εἰποῦσ' ἤϊξε πρὸς οὐρανὸν ἠνεμόεντα.
Χαῖρε θεὰ Κύπροιο ἐϋκτιμένης μεδέουσα·
σεῦ δ' ἐγὼ ἀρξάμενος μεταβήσομαι ἄλλον ἐς ὕμνον.

VI. Εἰς Ἀφροδίτην

Αἰδοίην χρυσοστέφανον καλὴν Ἀφροδίτην
ᾄσομαι, ἣ πάσης Κύπρου κρήδεμνα λέλογχεν
εἰναλίης, ὅθι μιν Ζεφύρου μένος ὑγρὸν ἀέντος
ἤνεικεν κατὰ κῦμα πολυφλοίσβοιο θαλάσσης
ἀφρῷ ἔνι μαλακῷ· τὴν δὲ χρυσάμπυκες Ὧραι
δέξαντ' ἀσπασίως, περὶ δ' ἄμβροτα εἵματα ἕσσαν,
κρατὶ δ' ἐπ' ἀθανάτῳ στεφάνην εὔτυκτον ἔθηκαν
καλὴν χρυσείην, ἐν δὲ τρητοῖσι λοβοῖσιν
ἄνθεμ' ὀρειχάλκου χρυσοῖό τε τιμήεντος,
δειρῇ δ' ἀμφ' ἁπαλῇ καὶ στήθεσιν ἀργυφέοισιν
ὅρμοισι χρυσέοισιν ἐκόσμεον οἷσί περ αὐταὶ
Ὧραι κοσμείσθην χρυσάμπυκες ὁππότ' ἴοιεν
ἐς χορὸν ἱμερόεντα θεῶν καὶ δώματα πατρός.
αὐτὰρ ἐπεὶ δὴ πάντα περὶ χροῒ κόσμον ἔθηκαν
ἦγον ἐς ἀθανάτους· οἱ δ' ἠσπάζοντο ἰδόντες
χερσί τ' ἐδεξιόωντο καὶ ἠρήσαντο ἕκαστος
εἶναι κουριδίην ἄλοχον καὶ οἴκαδ' ἄγεσθαι,
εἶδος θαυμάζοντες ἰοστεφάνου Κυθερείης.
Χαῖρ' ἑλικοβλέφαρε γλυκυμείλιχε, δὸς δ' ἐν ἀγῶνι
νίκην τῷδε φέρεσθαι, ἐμὴν δ' ἔντυνον ἀοιδήν.
αὐτὰρ ἐγὼ καὶ σεῖο καὶ ἄλλης μνήσομ' ἀοιδῆς.

290 *ὀνόμηνε* codd. em. Hermann 292 *εὐκτισμένης* E T
VI. *codices*: M *x p* praeter Mon. O TITVLVS: *τοῦ αὐτοῦ εἰς τὴν αὐτὴν ἀφροδίτην* M : *εἰς τὴν αὐτὴν* vulg. : *εἰς ἀφροδίτην* E N : *ἔτι εἰς ἀφροδίτην* V[1] : in B Γ continuatur hymnus cum priore. 7 *εὐτικτον* *x* At D ed. pr. 9 *ἔνθεμ'* *p* 12 *κοσμίσθην* *x* D ed. pr. : *κοσμήσθην* M *ὁππότϊ ἦεν* M 15 *ἰδέσθαι* M 16 *τε δεξιόωντο* *x* 18 *ἐϋστεφάνου* *p* (*ἰο* P ss.), cf. Aphr. 175 19 *δός δ' ἀγγῶον* L[1]

VII. Εἰς Διόνυσον

Ἀμφὶ Διώνυσον Σεμέλης ἐρικυδέος υἱὸν
μνήσομαι, ὡς ἐφάνη παρὰ θῖν' ἁλὸς ἀτρυγέτοιο
ἀκτῇ ἐπὶ προβλῆτι νεηνίῃ ἀνδρὶ ἐοικὼς
πρωθήβῃ· καλαὶ δὲ περισσείοντο ἔθειραι
κυάνεαι, φᾶρος δὲ περὶ στιβαροῖς ἔχεν ὤμοις
πορφύρεον· τάχα δ' ἄνδρες ἐϋσσέλμου ἀπὸ νηὸς
ληϊσταὶ προγένοντο θοῶς ἐπὶ οἴνοπα πόντον
Τυρσηνοί· τοὺς δ' ἦγε κακὸς μόρος· οἱ δὲ ἰδόντες
νεῦσαν ἐς ἀλλήλους, τάχα δ' ἔκθορον, αἶψα δ' ἑλόντες
εἷσαν ἐπὶ σφετέρης νηὸς κεχαρημένοι ἦτορ.
υἱὸν γάρ μιν ἔφαντο διοτρεφέων βασιλήων
εἶναι, καὶ δεσμοῖς ἔθελον δεῖν ἀργαλέοισι.
τὸν δ' οὐκ ἴσχανε δεσμά, λύγοι δ' ἀπὸ τηλόσ' ἔπιπτον
χειρῶν ἠδὲ ποδῶν· ὁ δὲ μειδιάων ἐκάθητο
ὄμμασι κυανέοισι, κυβερνήτης δὲ νοήσας
αὐτίκα οἷς ἑτάροισιν ἐκέκλετο φώνησέν τε·
Δαιμόνιοι τίνα τόνδε θεὸν δεσμεύεθ' ἑλόντες
καρτερόν; οὐδὲ φέρειν δύναταί μιν νηῦς εὐεργής.
ἢ γὰρ Ζεὺς ὅδε γ' ἐστὶν ἢ ἀργυρότοξος Ἀπόλλων
ἠὲ Ποσειδάων· ἐπεὶ οὐ θνητοῖσι βροτοῖσιν
εἴκελος, ἀλλὰ θεοῖς οἳ Ὀλύμπια δώματ' ἔχουσιν.
ἀλλ' ἄγετ' αὐτὸν ἀφῶμεν ἐπ' ἠπείροιο μελαίνης
αὐτίκα, μηδ' ἐπὶ χεῖρας ἰάλλετε μή τι χολωθεὶς
ὄρσῃ ἀργαλέους τ' ἀνέμους καὶ λαίλαπα πολλήν.
Ὣς φάτο· τὸν δ' ἀρχὸς στυγερῷ ἠνίπαπε μύθῳ·
δαιμόνι' οὖρον ὅρα, ἅμα δ' ἱστίον ἕλκεο νηὸς

VII. *codices*: M *x* (L[1] usque ad v. 34) *p* praeter Mon. O Titulus: *τοῦ αὐτοῦ εἰς διόνυσον* M : *εἰς τὸν διόνυσον p* : *διόνυσος ἢ λησταί x* D ed. pr. 3 *νεανίη* ET 5 *φάρος* codd. em. Steph. 8 *ἤγαγε* codd. praeter *p* 9 om. L[1] 13 *λυδοὶ* libri praeter M (*ληδοὶ*), corr. ed. pr. 17 *θεῶν δεσμὰ ἐθέλοντες* M 21 *ἴκελος* codd. em. Steph.

σύμπανθ' ὅπλα λαβών· ὅδε δ' αὖτ' ἄνδρεσσι μελήσει.
ἔλπομαι ἢ Αἴγυπτον ἀφίξεται ἢ ὅ γε Κύπρον
ἢ ἐς Ὑπερβορέους ἢ ἑκαστέρω· ἐς δὲ τελευτὴν
ἔκ ποτ' ἐρεῖ αὑτοῦ τε φίλους καὶ κτήματα πάντα
οὕς τε κασιγνήτους, ἐπεὶ ἡμῖν ἔμβαλε δαίμων.
Ὣς εἰπὼν ἱστόν τε καὶ ἱστίον ἕλκετο νηός.
ἔμπνευσεν δ' ἄνεμος μέσον ἱστίον, ἀμφὶ δ' ἄρ' ὅπλα
καττάνυσαν· τάχα δέ σφιν ἐφαίνετο θαυματὰ ἔργα.
οἶνος μὲν πρώτιστα θοὴν ἀνὰ νῆα μέλαιναν
ἡδύποτος κελάρυζ' εὐώδης, ὤρνυτο δ' ὀδμὴ
ἀμβροσίη· ναύτας δὲ τάφος λάβε πάντας ἰδόντας.
αὐτίκα δ' ἀκρότατον παρὰ ἱστίον ἐξετανύσθη
ἄμπελος ἔνθα καὶ ἔνθα, κατεκρημνῶντο δὲ πολλοὶ
βότρυες· ἀμφ' ἱστὸν δὲ μέλας εἱλίσσετο κισσὸς
ἄνθεσι τηλεθάων, χαρίεις δ' ἐπὶ καρπὸς ὀρώρει·
πάντες δὲ σκαλμοὶ στεφάνους ἔχον· οἱ δὲ ἰδόντες
νῆ' ἤδη τότ' ἔπειτα κυβερνήτην ἐκέλευον
γῇ πελάαν· ὁ δ' ἄρα σφι λέων γένετ' ἔνδοθι νηὸς
δεινὸς ἐπ' ἀκροτάτης, μέγα δ' ἔβραχεν, ἐν δ' ἄρα μέσσῃ
ἄρκτον ἐποίησεν λασιαύχενα σήματα φαίνων·
ἂν δ' ἔστη μεμαυῖα, λέων δ' ἐπὶ σέλματος ἄκρου
δεινὸν ὑπόδρα ἰδών· οἱ δ' εἰς πρύμνην ἐφόβηθεν,
ἀμφὶ κυβερνήτην δὲ σαόφρονα θυμὸν ἔχοντα
ἔσταν ἄρ' ἐκπληγέντες· ὁ δ' ἐξαπίνης ἐπορούσας
ἀρχὸν ἕλ', οἱ δὲ θύραζε κακὸν μόρον ἐξαλύοντες
πάντες ὁμῶς πήδησαν ἐπεὶ ἴδον εἰς ἅλα δῖαν,
δελφῖνες δ' ἐγένοντο· κυβερνήτην δ' ἐλεήσας
ἔσχεθε καί μιν ἔθηκε πανόλβιον εἶπέ τε μῦθον·

29 ὁ ἐκαστέρω M (sc. ὅγ', cf. υ 245 ἤ δέ ε g): ἑκατέρω E T τελευτὴν (ss. ε) M: ἐς δὲ τελευτὴν Theognis 755 34 in voce σφιν finitur L[1] 36 κελάρυξ' M E ὄρνυτο Γ N V[1] 37 φόβος y (E) M: ἤγουν φόβος marg. P 39 κατεκριμνῶντο x D ed. pr. 43 ita Hermann cl. Apoll. 392, Herod. v. 85: μὴ δ' ἤδη M: μὴ δή δειν p Π T At: μὴ δείδειν Γ: μὴ δέ δειν E: Μηδείδην Barnes

Θάρσει † δῖ' ἑκάτωρ τῷ ἐμῷ κεχαρισμένε θυμῷ·
εἰμὶ δ' ἐγὼ Διόνυσος ἐρίβρομος ὃν τέκε μήτηρ
Καδμηῒς Σεμέλη Διὸς ἐν φιλότητι μιγεῖσα.
Χαῖρε τέκος Σεμέλης εὐώπιδος· οὐδέ πῃ ἔστι
σεῖό γε ληθόμενον γλυκερὴν κοσμῆσαι ἀοιδήν.

VIII. Εἰς Ἄρεα

Ἄρες ὑπερμενέτα, βρισάρματε, χρυσεοπήληξ,
ὀβριμόθυμε, φέρασπι, πολισσόε, χαλκοκορυστά,
καρτερόχειρ, ἀμόγητε, δορυσθενές, ἕρκος Ὀλύμπου,
Νίκης εὐπολέμοιο πάτερ, συναρωγὲ Θέμιστος,
ἀντιβίοισι τύραννε, δικαιοτάτων ἀγὲ φωτῶν,
ἠνορέης σκηπτοῦχε, πυραυγέα κύκλον ἑλίσσων
αἰθέρος ἑπταπόροις ἐνὶ τείρεσιν ἔνθα σε πῶλοι
ζαφλεγέες τριτάτης ὑπὲρ ἄντυγος αἰὲν ἔχουσι·
κλῦθι βροτῶν ἐπίκουρε, δοτὴρ εὐθαλέος ἥβης,
πρηῢ καταστίλβων σέλας ὑψόθεν ἐς βιότητα
ἡμετέρην καὶ κάρτος ἀρήϊον, ὥς κε δυναίμην
σεύασθαι κακότητα πικρὴν ἀπ' ἐμοῖο καρήνου,
καὶ ψυχῆς ἀπατηλὸν ὑπογνάμψαι φρεσὶν ὁρμὴν
θυμοῦ τ' αὖ μένος ὀξὺ κατισχέμεν ὅς μ' ἐρέθῃσι
φυλόπιδος κρυερῆς ἐπιβαινέμεν· ἀλλὰ σὺ θάρσος
δὸς μάκαρ, εἰρήνης τε μένειν ἐν ἀπήμοσι θεσμοῖς
δυσμενέων προφυγόντα μόθον κῆράς τε βιαίους.

55 *δῖ' ἑκάτωρ* M: *δῖε κάτωρ* cet. alibi Acoetes audit, cf. et Κα(σ)τρεύς Apollod. ii. 23   *τῶ 'μῶ* x M D: *τὼμῶ* p corr. Ilgen

VIII. *codices* M x praeter L[1] p praeter Mon. O z At D   Titvlvs: *τοῦ αὐτοῦ εἰς ἄρεα* M: *εἰς ἀρέα* x D J K: *εἰς τὸν ἀρέα* L[3] R[1] V[1]: *εἰς τὸν ἄρην* cet. (*ὁμήρου ὕμνοι εἰς θεούς εἰς ἄρην* H)   2 *ὀμβριμόθυμε* x D H ed. pr.   3 *δορισθενὲς* M   4 *θέμιστα* H   7 *ἑπταπύροις* M   9 *εὐθαλέος* p E T: *εὐθαρλέσεος* Π (sc. *εὐθαλεος* ss. *ρσ*): *εὐθαρσέος* M: *εὐθηλ-* Gemoll   10 *πρηῢ*] *πρὶν* M   11 *ὥς τε* V[1]   12 *σεύασθαι* M: *-εσθαι* cet.   *ἐμοῖο* B: *ἐμεῖο* cet.   13 *ὑπογνάμψαι* M: *-άψαι* cet.

IX. Εἰς Ἄρτεμιν

Ἄρτεμιν ὕμνει Μοῦσα κασιγνήτην Ἑκάτοιο,
παρθένον ἰοχέαιραν, ὁμότροφον Ἀπόλλωνος,
ἥ θ' ἵππους ἄρσασα βαθυσχοίνοιο Μέλητος
ῥίμφα διὰ Σμύρνης παγχρύσεον ἅρμα διώκει
ἐς Κλάρον ἀμπελόεσσαν, ὅθ' ἀργυρότοξος Ἀπόλλων
ἧσται μιμνάζων ἑκατηβόλον ἰοχέαιραν.
Καὶ σὺ μὲν οὕτω χαῖρε θεαί θ' ἅμα πᾶσαι ἀοιδῇ·
αὐτὰρ ἐγώ σε πρῶτα καὶ ἐκ σέθεν ἄρχομ' ἀείδειν,
σεῦ δ' ἐγὼ ἀρξάμενος μεταβήσομαι ἄλλον ἐς ὕμνον.

X. Εἰς Ἀφροδίτην

Κυπρογενῆ Κυθέρειαν ἀείσομαι ἥ τε βροτοῖσι
μείλιχα δῶρα δίδωσιν, ἐφ' ἱμερτῷ δὲ προσώπῳ
αἰεὶ μειδιάει καὶ ἐφ' ἱμερτὸν θέει ἄνθος.
Χαῖρε θεὰ Σαλαμῖνος ἐϋκτιμένης μεδέουσα
εἰναλίης τε Κύπρου· δὸς δ' ἱμερόεσσαν ἀοιδήν.
αὐτὰρ ἐγὼ καὶ σεῖο καὶ ἄλλης μνήσομ' ἀοιδῆς.

XI. Εἰς Ἀθηνᾶν

Παλλάδ' Ἀθηναίην ἐρυσίπτολιν ἄρχομ' ἀείδειν
δεινήν, ᾗ σὺν Ἄρηϊ μέλει πολεμήϊα ἔργα
περθόμεναί τε πόληες ἀϋτή τε πτόλεμοί τε,
καί τ' ἐρρύσατο λαὸν ἰόντα τε νισόμενόν τε.
Χαῖρε θεά, δὸς δ' ἄμμι τύχην εὐδαιμονίην τε.

IX. *codices*: qui ad h. viii et R[3] Τɪᴛᴠʟᴠs: *εἰς ἄρτεμιν x z* M D: *εἰς τὴν ἄρτεμιν p* 1 *ὑμνεῖ* E T At D H ed. pr. 3 ita M (*-νοῖο*) *μελήτης x z* At D L[3]: *μιλήτης p* praeter L[3] 7 *θ'* M: *δ'* cet. 8 *σέ τε* M: *σέθ'* E T

X. post h. xi invenitur in M. *codices*: qui ad h. viii Τɪᴛᴠʟᴠs: *εἰς ἀφροδίτην x z* M D ed. pr.: *εἰς τὴν ἀφροδίτην p* praeter L[3] 1 *υπρογενῆ* D V[1]: *οὐπρογενῆ* B: *ευπρογενῆ* E K T 3 *ἐφιμερτὸν x* J *θέει* M, cf. ζ 45 υ 357: *φέρει* cet. 4 *χαῖρε μάκαιρα κυθήρης εὐκτιμένης μεδέουσα* M 5 *εἰναλίης τε κύπρου* M: *καὶ πάσης κύπρου* cet.

XI. *codices*: qui ad h. viii Τɪᴛᴠʟᴠs: *εἰς τὴν ἀθηνᾶν p*: *εἰς ἀθηνᾶν* cet. 3 *πόλιες* praeter M N P codd. *αὐτοί* M V[1] *πόλεμοι p*

XII. Εἰς Ἥραν

Ἥρην ἀείδω χρυσόθρονον ἣν τέκε Ῥείη,
ἀθανάτην βασίλειαν ὑπείροχον εἶδος ἔχουσαν
Ζηνὸς ἐριγδούποιο κασιγνήτην ἄλοχόν τε
κυδρήν, ἣν πάντες μάκαρες κατὰ μακρὸν Ὄλυμπον
ἁζόμενοι τίουσιν ὁμῶς Διὶ τερπικεραύνῳ.

XIII. Εἰς Δημήτραν

Δήμητρ' ἠΰκομον σεμνὴν θεὰν ἄρχομ' ἀείδειν,
αὐτὴν καὶ κούρην, περικαλλέα Περσεφόνειαν.
Χαῖρε θεὰ καὶ τήνδε σάου πόλιν, ἄρχε δ' ἀοιδῆς.

XIV. Εἰς Μητέρα Θεῶν

Μητέρα μοι πάντων τε θεῶν πάντων τ' ἀνθρώπων
ὕμνει Μοῦσα λίγεια Διὸς θυγάτηρ μεγάλοιο,
ᾗ κροτάλων τυπάνων τ' ἰαχὴ σύν τε βρόμος αὐλῶν
εὔαδεν, ἠδὲ λύκων κλαγγὴ χαροπῶν τε λεόντων,
οὔρεά τ' ἠχήεντα καὶ ὑλήεντες ἔναυλοι.
Καὶ σὺ μὲν οὕτω χαῖρε θεαί θ' ἅμα πᾶσαι ἀοιδῇ.

XII. *codices*: qui ad h. viii et R³ Titulus: *εἰς τὴν ἥραν p* : *εἰς ἥραν* cet. (*ἥρην* K) 1 *ἥραν* M R³ 4 *κυδνὴν* J (= *κεδνὴν* ss. *υ*)

XIII. *codices*: qui ad h. viii et R³ Titulus: *εἰς μητ' . . ρα θεῶν* (ss. *δή ραν*) M : *εἰς δήμητραν x* D H K ed. pr. : *εἰς δήμητρα* J : *εἰς τὴν δήμητραν καὶ περσεφόνην p* : (*περσεφόην* L² : *περσεφόνειαν* P) 1 *Μημήτηρ'* M : *δημήτηρ'* E K : *δημήτηρ'* (ss. *δη*) T : *δημήτρ'* H J : *δημήτερ' p* D corr. ed. pr. *θεὰν* M : *θεὸν* cet. 2 *φερσεφόνειαν x p* D, cf. Dem. 493 3 *χαῖρε . . . πόλιν* = Call. Dem. 134 *σάω* Barnes, cf. *ρ* 595 Call. Epigr. 35 Alcman 45 *Μῶσ' ἄγε . . . ἄρχ' ἐρατῶν ἐπέων* Pind. Nem. iii. 10

XIV. *codices*: M, qui ad h. viii Titulus: *εἰς μητέρα θεῶν* M D Π ed. pr. : *εἰς μητέρα τῶν θεῶν* E T : *εἰς τὴν ῥέαν p* : *εἰς ῥέαν* H J, om. K 2 *ὑμνεῖ x* At D H 3 *κροτάλη p* *τυπάνων p* praeter Γ R² : *τυμπάνων* cet. (*τυπάνων* ss. *μ* L²) : *τυπάνα* E marg., cf. Ap. Rhod. i. 1139 Anth. Pal. vi. 165. 5 *βρόμος p* M V², cf. h. Merc. 452 : *τρόμος* cet. 6 *θ'* M : *δ'* cet. *ἀοιδῆς* E T

XV. Εἰς Ἡρακλέα λεοντόθυμον

Ἡρακλέα Διὸς υἱὸν ἀείσομαι, ὃν μέγ' ἄριστον
γείνατ' ἐπιχθονίων Θήβῃς ἔνι καλλιχόροισιν
Ἀλκμήνη μιχθεῖσα κελαινεφέϊ Κρονίωνι·
ὃς πρὶν μὲν κατὰ γαῖαν ἀθέσφατον ἠδὲ θάλασσαν
πλαζόμενος πομπῇσιν ὕπ' Εὐρυσθῆος ἄνακτος
πολλὰ μὲν αὐτὸς ἔρεξεν ἀτάσθαλα, πολλὰ δ' ἀνέτλη·
νῦν δ' ἤδη κατὰ καλὸν ἕδος νιφόεντος Ὀλύμπου
ναίει τερπόμενος καὶ ἔχει καλλίσφυρον Ἥβην
Χαῖρε ἄναξ Διὸς υἱέ· δίδου δ' ἀρετήν τε καὶ ὄλβον.

XVI. Εἰς Ἀσκληπιόν

Ἰητῆρα νόσων Ἀσκληπιὸν ἄρχομ' ἀείδειν
υἱὸν Ἀπόλλωνος τὸν ἐγείνατο δῖα Κορωνὶς
Δωτίῳ ἐν πεδίῳ κούρη Φλεγύου βασιλῆος,
χάρμα μέγ' ἀνθρώποισι, κακῶν θελκτῆρ' ὀδυνάων.
Καὶ σὺ μὲν οὕτω χαῖρε ἄναξ· λίτομαι δέ σ' ἀοιδῇ.

XVII. Εἰς Διοσκούρους

Κάστορα καὶ Πολυδεύκε' ἀείσεο Μοῦσα λίγεια,
Τυνδαρίδας οἳ Ζηνὸς Ὀλυμπίου ἐξεγένοντο·
τοὺς ὑπὸ Ταϋγέτου κορυφῇς τέκε πότνια Λήδη

XV. *codices*: qui ad h. viii Titvlvs: *εἰς ἡρακλέα λεοντόθυμον* *x* M D ed. pr.: *εἰς τὸν ἡρακλέα* *p*: *εἰς ἡρακλέα* H: *εἰς ἡρακλῆ* J, om. K 4 *ὃς ῥὰ ἠμὲν* M 5 *πλαζόμενος πημαίνετ'* (ss. *η*) *ἀεθλεύων κραταιῶς* M: *ἀεθλεύων δὲ κρ.* Ilgen 6 *ἔξοχα ἔργα* M: *πολλὰ δ' ἀνέτλη* cet.

XVI. *codices*: qui ad h. viii Titvlvs: *εἰς τὸν ἀσκληπιὸν* *p* M: *εἰς ἀσκληπιὸν* cet. om. K 1-3 cit. schol. Pind. Pyth. iii. 14 (*ἐν τοῖς Ὁμηρικοῖς ὕμνοις*) 2 *κορωνίς* om. M add. m. 2 3 *δωτίνω* *p* *φλεγύος* At D K N: *φλεγέος* H J: *φλεγύα* scholiasta Pindari 4 *κακὸν* H J *θελγηθρον ανε[ιῶν]* I. G. xiv. 2557

XVII. *codices*: qui ad h. viii Titvlvs: *εἰς τοὺς διοσκούρους* M: *εἰς διοσκούρους* *x* D ed. pr.: *εἰς κάστορα καὶ πολυδεύκη* H J *p* (sed haec quidem *πολυδεύκην*), om. K 1 *ἀείδεο* Steph. 3 *λήδα* V[1]

λάθρῃ ὑποδμηθεῖσα κελαινεφέϊ Κρονίωνι.
Χαίρετε Τυνδαρίδαι, ταχέων ἐπιβήτορες ἵππων.

XVIII. Εἰς Ἑρμῆν

Ἑρμῆν ἀείδω Κυλλήνιον Ἀργειφόντην
Κυλλήνης μεδέοντα καὶ Ἀρκαδίης πολυμήλου,
ἄγγελον ἀθανάτων ἐριούνιον ὃν τέκε Μαῖα
Ἄτλαντος θυγάτηρ Διὸς ἐν φιλότητι μιγεῖσα
αἰδοίη· μακάρων δὲ θεῶν ἀλέεινεν ὅμιλον
ἄντρῳ ναιετάουσα παλισκίῳ ἔνθα Κρονίων
νύμφῃ ἐϋπλοκάμῳ μισγέσκετο νυκτὸς ἀμολγῷ,
εὖτε κατὰ γλυκὺς ὕπνος ἔχοι λευκώλενον Ἥρην·
λάνθανε δ' ἀθανάτους τε θεοὺς θνητούς τ' ἀνθρώπους.
Καὶ σὺ μὲν οὕτω χαῖρε Διὸς καὶ Μαιάδος υἱέ·
σεῦ δ' ἐγὼ ἀρξάμενος μεταβήσομαι ἄλλον ἐς ὕμνον.
χαῖρ' Ἑρμῆ χαριδῶτα διάκτορε, δῶτορ ἐάων.

XIX. Εἰς Πᾶνα

Ἀμφί μοι Ἑρμείαο φίλον γόνον ἔννεπε Μοῦσα,
αἰγιπόδην δικέρωτα φιλόκροτον ὅς τ' ἀνὰ πίση
δενδρήεντ' ἄμυδις φοιτᾷ χοροήθεσι νύμφαις
αἵ τε κατ' αἰγίλιπος πέτρης στείβουσι κάρηνα
Πᾶν' ἀνακεκλόμεναι νόμιον θεὸν ἀγλαέθειρον
αὐχμήενθ', ὃς πάντα λόφον νιφόεντα λέλογχε
καὶ κορυφὰς ὀρέων καὶ πετρήεντα κέλευθα.
φοιτᾷ δ' ἔνθα καὶ ἔνθα διὰ ῥωπήϊα πυκνά,
ἄλλοτε μὲν ῥείθροισιν ἐφελκόμενος μαλακοῖσιν,

5 ἐπιβήτορες] ἐπ' ἀμήτων M

XVIII. *codices*: qui ad h. viii Tɪᴛᴠʟᴠs: εἰς τὸν ἑρμῆν *p*: εἰς ἑρμῆν cet. om. K 2 πολυμήλου (ss. ης) M 4 in hoc versu expl. M 6 πολυσκίω J 8 ἔχει *p* H (οι ss.) 12 ἑάων Π P N corr. V[1]

XIX. *codices*: *x* praeter L[1] *p* praeter Mon. O Tɪᴛᴠʟᴠs: εἰς τὸν πᾶνα *p*: εἰς πᾶνα cet. 2 αἰγοπόδην codd. em. Hermann πίσση libri corr. Steph. 4 στείβουσαι E T 7 κάρηνα D Π ed. pr.: κέλευθα cet.

ἄλλοτε δ' αὖ πέτρῃσιν ἐν ἠλιβάτοισι διοιχνεῖ,
ἀκροτάτην κορυφὴν μηλοσκόπον εἰσαναβαίνων.
πολλάκι δ' ἀργινόεντα διέδραμεν οὔρεα μακρά,
πολλάκι δ' ἐν κνημοῖσι διήλασε θῆρας ἐναίρων
ὀξέα δερκόμενος· τότε δ' ἕσπερος ἔκλαγεν οἶον
ἄγρης ἐξανιών, δονάκων ὕπο μοῦσαν ἀθύρων
νήδυμον· οὐκ ἂν τόν γε παραδράμοι ἐν μελέεσσιν
ὄρνις ἥ τ' ἔαρος πολυανθέος ἐν πετάλοισι
θρῆνον ἐπιπροχέουσ' ἀχέει μελίγηρυν ἀοιδήν.
σὺν δέ σφιν τότε νύμφαι ὀρεστιάδες λιγύμολποι
φοιτῶσαι πυκνὰ ποσσὶν ἐπὶ κρήνῃ μελανύδρῳ
μέλπονται, κορυφὴν δὲ περιστένει οὔρεος ἠχώ·
δαίμων δ' ἔνθα καὶ ἔνθα χορῶν τοτὲ δ' ἐς μέσον ἕρπων
πυκνὰ ποσὶν διέπει, λαῖφος δ' ἐπὶ νῶτα δαφοινὸν
λυγκὸς ἔχει λιγυρῇσιν ἀγαλλόμενος φρένα μολπαῖς
ἐν μαλακῷ λειμῶνι τόθι κρόκος ἠδ' ὑάκινθος
εὐώδης θαλέθων καταμίσγεται ἄκριτα ποίῃ.
ὑμνεῦσιν δὲ θεοὺς μάκαρας καὶ μακρὸν Ὄλυμπον·
οἷόν θ' Ἑρμείην ἐριούνιον ἔξοχον ἄλλων
ἔννεπον ὡς ὅ γ' ἅπασι θεοῖς θοὸς ἄγγελός ἐστι
καί ῥ' ὅ γ' ἐς Ἀρκαδίην πολυπίδακα, μητέρα μήλων,
ἐξίκετ', ἔνθα τέ οἱ τέμενος Κυλληνίου ἐστίν.
ἔνθ' ὅ γε καὶ θεὸς ὢν ψαφαρότριχα μῆλ' ἐνόμευεν
ἀνδρὶ πάρα θνητῷ· θάλε γὰρ πόθος ὑγρὸς ἐπελθὼν
νύμφῃ ἐϋπλοκάμῳ Δρύοπος φιλότητι μιγῆναι·

11 *μηλόσκοπον* codd. em. Gemoll 12 *αἰγινόεντα* codd. em. Barnes 14 *τοτὲ* V[1] *οἶον* libri corr. Peppmüller (sc. *μόνον*, cf. Hes. Theog. 26, Aesch. Ag. 136, C. I. A. iii, p. i. 171 B v. 22 *ου μα[ν το]υδε χαριν σε τελεσφορε αιδομεν οιον*) 15 *ἄκρης* codd. (*ἄκρη* V[1]) em. Pierson 18 *ἐπιπροχέουσα χέει* codd. em. Ilgen: *ἰαχεῖ* Ruhnken 20 *πύκα* Barnes 22 *τότε ἐς* codd. δ' add. Buttmann 24 *λυγγὸς p* 26 *θαλέθων p*: *θαλέων* cet. cf. Ap. Rh. ii. 843 *ποίην* libri corr. Hermann 29 *θεοῖς θεὸς* V[1] 31 *τε* Hermann: *δέ* codd. *κυλληνίον* ed. pr. 32 *ψαφερότριχα x* At D: *ψαφορότριχα* A Q 33 *θάλε* libri: *λάθε* Ruhnken

ἐκ δ' ἐτέλεσσε γάμον θαλερόν, τέκε δ' ἐν μεγάροισιν
Ἑρμείῃ φίλον υἱὸν ἄφαρ τερατωπὸν ἰδέσθαι,
αἰγιπόδην δικέρωτα πολύκροτον ἡδυγέλωτα·
φεῦγε δ' ἀναΐξασα, λίπεν δ' ἄρα παῖδα τιθήνη·
δεῖσε γὰρ ὡς ἴδεν ὄψιν ἀμείλιχον ἠϋγένειον.
τὸν δ' αἶψ' Ἑρμείας ἐριούνιος εἰς χέρα θῆκε
δεξάμενος, χαῖρεν δὲ νόῳ περιώσια δαίμων.
ῥίμφα δ' ἐς ἀθανάτων ἕδρας κίε παῖδα καλύψας
δέρμασιν ἐν πυκινοῖσιν ὀρεσκῴοιο λαγωοῦ·
πὰρ δὲ Ζηνὶ καθῖζε καὶ ἄλλοις ἀθανάτοισιν,
δεῖξε δὲ κοῦρον ἑόν· πάντες δ' ἄρα θυμὸν ἔτερφθεν
ἀθάνατοι, περίαλλα δ' ὁ Βάκχειος Διόνυσος·
Πᾶνα δέ μιν καλέεσκον ὅτι φρένα πᾶσιν ἔτερψε.
Καὶ σὺ μὲν οὕτω χαῖρε ἄναξ, ἵλαμαι δέ σ' ἀοιδῇ·
αὐτὰρ ἐγὼ καὶ σεῖο καὶ ἄλλης μνήσομ' ἀοιδῆς.

XX. Εἰς Ἥφαιστον

Ἥφαιστον κλυτόμητιν ἀείδεο Μοῦσα λίγεια,
ὃς μετ' Ἀθηναίης γλαυκώπιδος ἀγλαὰ ἔργα
ἀνθρώπους ἐδίδαξεν ἐπὶ χθονός, οἳ τὸ πάρος περ
ἄντροις ναιετάασκον ἐν οὔρεσιν ἠΰτε θῆρες.
νῦν δὲ δι' Ἥφαιστον κλυτοτέχνην ἔργα δαέντες
ῥηϊδίως αἰῶνα τελεσφόρον εἰς ἐνιαυτὸν
εὔκηλοι διάγουσιν ἐνὶ σφετέροισι δόμοισιν.
Ἀλλ' ἵληθ' Ἥφαιστε· δίδου δ' ἀρετήν τε καὶ ὄλβον.

38 *ἀναίξας λεῖπεν* libri corr. Martin 44 *κάθιζε* T V[1] 45 *ἔτερφθον* libri : *-ον* ss. *ε* Γ 48 *ἵλαμαι* Π marg. : *λίσομαι* (ss. *ἵλα*) Π : *ἱλάσομαι* E T : *λίσσομαι* D : *λίσομαι* cet.

XX. *codices*: qui h. xix et hymnos xxi–xxxiii continent Titvlvs : *εἰς τὸν ἥφαιστον p* : *εἰς ἥφαιστον* cet. 4 *ναιετάεσκον* B Γ 8 om. E T

XXI. Εἰς Ἀπόλλωνα

Φοῖβε σὲ μὲν καὶ κύκνος ὑπὸ πτερύγων λίγ' ἀείδει
ὄχθῃ ἐπιθρῴσκων ποταμὸν πάρα δινήεντα
Πηνειόν· σὲ δ' ἀοιδὸς ἔχων φόρμιγγα λίγειαν
ἡδυεπὴς πρῶτόν τε καὶ ὕστατον αἰὲν ἀείδει.
Καὶ σὺ μὲν οὕτω χαῖρε ἄναξ, ἵλαμαι δέ σ' ἀοιδῇ.

XXII. Εἰς Ποσειδῶνα

Ἀμφὶ Ποσειδάωνα θεὸν μέγαν ἄρχομ' ἀείδειν
γαίης κινητῆρα καὶ ἀτρυγέτοιο θαλάσσης
πόντιον, ὅς θ' Ἑλικῶνα καὶ εὐρείας ἔχει Αἰγάς.
διχθά τοι Ἐννοσίγαιε θεοὶ τιμὴν ἐδάσαντο
ἵππων τε δμητῆρ' ἔμεναι σωτῆρά τε νηῶν.
Χαῖρε Ποσείδαον γαιήοχε κυανοχαῖτα,
καὶ μάκαρ εὐμενὲς ἦτορ ἔχων πλώουσιν ἄρηγε.

XXIII. Εἰς Δία

Ζῆνα θεῶν τὸν ἄριστον ἀείσομαι ἠδὲ μέγιστον
εὐρύοπα κρείοντα τελεσφόρον, ὅς τε Θέμιστι
ἐγκλιδὸν ἑζομένῃ πυκινοὺς ὀάρους ὀαρίζει.
Ἵληθ' εὐρύοπα Κρονίδη κύδιστε μέγιστε.

XXIV. Εἰς Ἑστίαν

Ἑστίη, ἥ τε ἄνακτος Ἀπόλλωνος ἑκάτοιο
Πυθοῖ ἐν ἠγαθέῃ ἱερὸν δόμον ἀμφιπολεύεις,
αἰεὶ σῶν πλοκάμων ἀπολείβεται ὑγρὸν ἔλαιον·

XXI. Titvlvs: *εἰς τὸν ἀπόλλωνα p* : *εἰς ἀπόλλωνα* cet. 1 *Φοῖφε* (ss. *β*) T 5 *ἵλασμαι* E T

XXII. Titvlvs: *εἰς τὸν ποσειδῶνα p* : *εἰς ποσειδῶνα* cet. 1 *θεῶν p* 3 cf. vit. Herod. 236 *αἶγας* libri corr. ed. pr.

XXIII. Titvlvs: *εἰς τὸν δία p* : *εἰς δία* ed. pr. : *εἰς ὕπατον κρονίδην x* : *εἰς ὕπατον κρονίδην ἢ δία* D 2 *θέμιτι* libri corr. Barnes, cf. O 87 π 403

XXIV. Titvlvs: *εἰς τὴν ἑστίαν p* : *εἰς ἑστίαν* cet. 3 *καὶ ἐεὶ* Tucker

ἔρχεο τόνδ' ἀνὰ οἶκον, ἐπέρχεο θυμὸν ἔχουσα
σὺν Διὶ μητιόεντι· χάριν δ' ἅμ' ὄπασσον ἀοιδῇ.

XXV. Εἰς Μούσας καὶ Ἀπόλλωνα

Μουσάων ἄρχωμαι Ἀπόλλωνός τε Διός τε·
ἐκ γὰρ Μουσάων καὶ ἑκηβόλου Ἀπόλλωνος
ἄνδρες ἀοιδοὶ ἔασιν ἐπὶ χθονὶ καὶ κιθαρισταί,
ἐκ δὲ Διὸς βασιλῆες· ὁ δ' ὄλβιος ὅν τινα Μοῦσαι
φίλωνται· γλυκερή οἱ ἀπὸ στόματος ῥέει αὐδή.
Χαίρετε τέκνα Διὸς καὶ ἐμὴν τιμήσατ' ἀοιδήν·
αὐτὰρ ἐγὼν ὑμέων τε καὶ ἄλλης μνήσομ' ἀοιδῆς.

XXVI. Εἰς Διόνυσον

Κισσοκόμην Διόνυσον ἐρίβρομον ἄρχομ' ἀείδειν
Ζηνὸς καὶ Σεμέλης ἐρικυδέος ἀγλαὸν υἱόν,
ὃν τρέφον ἠΰκομοι νύμφαι παρὰ πατρὸς ἄνακτος
δεξάμεναι κόλποισι καὶ ἐνδυκέως ἀτίταλλον
Νύσης ἐν γυάλοις· ὁ δ' ἀέξετο πατρὸς ἕκητι
ἄντρῳ ἐν εὐώδει μεταρίθμιος ἀθανάτοισιν.
αὐτὰρ ἐπεὶ δὴ τόνδε θεαὶ πολύυμνον ἔθρεψαν,
δὴ τότε φοιτίζεσκε καθ' ὑλήεντας ἐναύλους
κισσῷ καὶ δάφνῃ πεπυκασμένος· αἱ δ' ἅμ' ἕποντο
νύμφαι, ὁ δ' ἐξηγεῖτο· βρόμος δ' ἔχεν ἄσπετον ὕλην.
Καὶ σὺ μὲν οὕτω χαῖρε πολυστάφυλ' ὦ Διόνυσε·
δὸς δ' ἡμᾶς χαίροντας ἐς ὥρας αὖτις ἱκέσθαι,
ἐκ δ' αὖθ' ὡράων εἰς τοὺς πολλοὺς ἐνιαυτούς.

4 ἔν' ἔρχεο Tucker cl. O 710. cf. et Ap. Rh. iv. 1030 5 om. E add. marg.

XXV. Titvlvs: εἰς μούσας ἀπόλλωνα καὶ δία *p*: εἰς μούσας καὶ ἀπόλλωνα cet. 1 ἄρχομαι libri em. Stephanus 2–5 = Hes. Theog. 94–7 2 ἐκ γάρ τοι Μουσέων schol. Pind. Pyth. iv. 313, Nem. iii. 1 3 χθόνα Hes. Theog. 95 5 φιλεῦνται codd. Hes. Theog. 97 plures

XXVI. Titvlvs: εἰς τὸν διόνυσον *p*: εἰς διόνυσον cet., om. T, add. aliquis 13 ὀράων E T

XXVII. Εἰς Ἄρτεμιν

Ἄρτεμιν ἀείδω χρυσηλάκατον κελαδεινὴν
παρθένον αἰδοίην ἐλαφηβόλον ἰοχέαιραν
αὐτοκασιγνήτην χρυσαόρου Ἀπόλλωνος,
ἣ κατ' ὄρη σκιόεντα καὶ ἄκριας ἠνεμοέσσας
ἄγρῃ τερπομένη παγχρύσεα τόξα τιταίνει
πέμπουσα στονόεντα βέλη· τρομέει δὲ κάρηνα
ὑψηλῶν ὀρέων, ἰαχεῖ δ' ἔπι δάσκιος ὕλη
δεινὸν ὑπὸ κλαγγῆς θηρῶν, φρίσσει δέ τε γαῖα
πόντος τ' ἰχθυόεις· ἡ δ' ἄλκιμον ἦτορ ἔχουσα
πάντῃ ἐπιστρέφεται θηρῶν ὀλέκουσα γενέθλην.
αὐτὰρ ἐπὴν τερφθῇ θηροσκόπος ἰοχέαιρα
εὐφρήνῃ δὲ νόον χαλάσασ' εὐκαμπέα τόξα,
ἔρχεται ἐς μέγα δῶμα κασιγνήτοιο φίλοιο
Φοίβου Ἀπόλλωνος Δελφῶν ἐς πίονα δῆμον
Μουσῶν καὶ Χαρίτων καλὸν χορὸν ἀρτυνέουσα.
ἔνθα κατακρεμάσασα παλίντονα τόξα καὶ ἰοὺς
ἡγεῖται χαρίεντα περὶ χροῒ κόσμον ἔχουσα,
ἐξάρχουσα χορούς· αἱ δ' ἀμβροσίην ὄπ' ἰεῖσαι
ὑμνεῦσιν Λητὼ καλλίσφυρον ὡς τέκε παῖδας
ἀθανάτων βουλῇ τε καὶ ἔργμασιν ἔξοχ' ἀρίστους,
Χαίρετε τέκνα Διὸς καὶ Λητοῦς ἠϋκόμοιο·
αὐτὰρ ἐγὼν ὑμέων καὶ ἄλλης μνήσομ' ἀοιδῆς.

XXVIII. Εἰς Ἀθηνᾶν

Παλλάδ' Ἀθηναίην κυδρὴν θεὸν ἄρχομ' ἀείδειν
γλαυκῶπιν πολύμητιν ἀμείλιχον ἦτορ ἔχουσαν
παρθένον αἰδοίην ἐρυσίπτολιν ἀλκήεσσαν
Τριτογενῆ, τὴν αὐτὸς ἐγείνατο μητίετα Ζεὺς

XXVII. Titvlvs: *εἰς τὴν ἄρτεμιν p*: *εἰς ἄρτεμιν* cet. om. T 7 *ἐπιδάσκιος* libri corr. Hermann 8 *δεινῆς* Π 13 *μετὰ κασιγνήτοιο x* D, cf. Herm. 296 18 *ἀμβροσίων* Π 22 *τε καὶ* Barnes

XXVIII. Titvlvs: *εἰς τὴν ἀθηνᾶν p*: *εἰς ἀθηνᾶν* cet.

σεμνῆς ἐκ κεφαλῆς, πολεμήϊα τεύχε' ἔχουσαν
χρύσεα παμφανόωντα· σέβας δ' ἔχε πάντας ὁρῶντας
ἀθανάτους· ἡ δὲ πρόσθεν Διὸς αἰγιόχοιο
ἐσσυμένως ὤρουσεν ἀπ' ἀθανάτοιο καρήνου
σείσασ' ὀξὺν ἄκοντα· μέγας δ' ἐλελίζετ' Ὄλυμπος
δεινὸν ὑπὸ βρίμης γλαυκώπιδος, ἀμφὶ δὲ γαῖα
σμερδαλέον ἰάχησεν, ἐκινήθη δ' ἄρα πόντος
κύμασι πορφυρέοισι κυκώμενος, ἔσχετο δ' ἅλμη
ἐξαπίνης· στῆσεν δ' Ὑπερίονος ἀγλαὸς υἱὸς
ἵππους ὠκύποδας δηρὸν χρόνον εἰσότε κούρη
εἵλετ' ἀπ' ἀθανάτων ὤμων θεοείκελα τεύχη
Παλλὰς Ἀθηναίη· γήθησε δὲ μητίετα Ζεύς.
Καὶ σὺ μὲν οὕτω χαῖρε Διὸς τέκος αἰγιόχοιο·
αὐτὰρ ἐγὼ καὶ σεῖο καὶ ἄλλης μνήσομ' ἀοιδῆς.

XXIX. Εἰς Ἑστίαν

Ἑστίη ἣ πάντων ἐν δώμασιν ὑψηλοῖσιν
ἀθανάτων τε θεῶν χαμαὶ ἐρχομένων τ' ἀνθρώπων
ἕδρην ἀΐδιον ἔλαχες πρεσβηΐδα τιμὴν
καλὸν ἔχουσα γέρας καὶ τιμήν· οὐ γὰρ ἄτερ σοῦ
εἰλαπίναι θνητοῖσιν ἵν' οὐ πρώτῃ πυμάτῃ τε
Ἑστίῃ ἀρχόμενος σπένδει μελιηδέα οἶνον·
καὶ σύ μοι Ἀργειφόντα Διὸς καὶ Μαιάδος υἱὲ
ἄγγελε τῶν μακάρων χρυσόρραπι δῶτορ ἐάων,
ναίετε δώματα καλά, φίλα φρεσὶν ἀλλήλοισιν

ἵλαος ὢν ἐπάρηγε σὺν αἰδοίῃ τε φίλῃ τε
Ἑστίῃ· ἀμφότεροι γὰρ ἐπιχθονίων ἀνθρώπων
εἰδότες ἔργματα καλὰ νόῳ θ' ἕσπεσθε καὶ ἥβῃ.

10 ὑπ' ὀμβρίμης *x* D ed. pr.: ὑπ' ὀβρίμης cet. corr. Ruhnken 12 δ' N ed. pr.: θ' codd. 14 δειρὸν E T V[1] εἰς ὅ κε ed. pr., cf. ω 134
XXIX. Titvlvs: εἰς τὴν ἑστίαν *p*: εἰς ἑστίαν cet. 3 ἔλαχες *p*: ἔλαχε cet. 6 ἑστίη D Q: ἱστίη cet. 8 ἑάων codd. em. Steph. 9 lacunam statuimus: v. 9 post 11 transp. Martin, White 11 ἑστίη D: ἱστίη cet. 12 θ' ex τ' A, ss. Π: τ' cet.

Χαῖρε Κρόνου θύγατερ, σύ τε καὶ χρυσόρραπις Ἑρμῆς.
αὐτὰρ ἐγὼν ὑμέων τε καὶ ἄλλης μνήσομ' ἀοιδῆς.

XXX. Εἰς Γῆν μητέρα πάντων

Γαῖαν παμμήτειραν ἀείσομαι ἠϋθέμεθλον
πρεσβίστην, ἣ φέρβει ἐπὶ χθονὶ πάνθ' ὁπόσ' ἐστίν·
ἠμὲν ὅσα χθόνα δῖαν ἐπέρχεται ἠδ' ὅσα πόντον
ἠδ' ὅσα πωτῶνται, τάδε φέρβεται ἐκ σέθεν ὄλβου.
ἐκ σέο δ' εὔπαιδές τε καὶ εὔκαρποι τελέθουσι
πότνια, σεῦ δ' ἔχεται δοῦναι βίον ἠδ' ἀφελέσθαι
θνητοῖς ἀνθρώποισιν· ὃ δ' ὄλβιος ὅν κε σὺ θυμῷ
πρόφρων τιμήσῃς· τῷ τ' ἄφθονα πάντα πάρεστι.
βρίθει μέν σφιν ἄρουρα φερέσβιος, ἠδὲ κατ' ἀγροὺς
κτήνεσιν εὐθηνεῖ, οἶκος δ' ἐμπίπλαται ἐσθλῶν·
αὐτοὶ δ' εὐνομίῃσι πόλιν κάτα καλλιγύναικα
κοιρανέουσ', ὄλβος δὲ πολὺς καὶ πλοῦτος ὀπηδεῖ·
παῖδες δ' εὐφροσύνῃ νεοθηλέϊ κυδιόωσι,
παρθενικαί τε χοροῖς φερεσανθέσιν εὔφρονι θυμῷ
παίζουσαι σκαίρουσι κατ' ἄνθεα μαλθακὰ ποίης,
οὕς κε σὺ τιμήσῃς σεμνὴ θεὰ ἄφθονε δαῖμον.
Χαῖρε θεῶν μήτηρ, ἄλοχ' Οὐρανοῦ ἀστερόεντος,
πρόφρων δ' ἀντ' ᾠδῆς βίοτον θυμήρε' ὄπαζε·
αὐτὰρ ἐγὼ καὶ σεῖο καὶ ἄλλης μνήσομ' ἀοιδῆς.

XXXI. Εἰς Ἥλιον

Ἥλιον ὑμνεῖν αὖτε Διὸς τέκος ἄρχεο Μοῦσα
Καλλιόπη φαέθοντα, τὸν Εὐρυφάεσσα βοῶπις

XXX. Titulus: εἰς γῆν μητέρα πάντων *x* D ed. pr.: εἰς τὴν γῆν *p* (imaginem terrae add. A P Q, solis L[2]) 3 ὑπέρχεται D ed. pr.: ἀπέρχεται Π 8 τιμήσεις libri em. Franke περ (πέρ) ἐστι *x* D L[2] N P: πέρεστι B: πάρεστι cet. 13 ἢ πάντες marg. E 14 περεσανθέσιν *x* D ed. pr.: παρ' εὐανθέσιν *p* V[2] corr. Ernesti 15 παίζουσι χαίρουσι libri (παίζουσαι Γ ss. ed. pr.) corr. Ruhnken μαλακὰ codd. em. Stephanus 16 κε] καὶ *x* D τιμήσεις codd. em. Franke
XXXI. Titulus: εἰς τὸν ἥλιον *p*: εἰς ἥλιον cet. solis imaginem add. A P Q R[1] R[2]

γείνατο Γαίης παιδὶ καὶ Οὐρανοῦ ἀστερόεντος·
γῆμε γὰρ Εὐρυφάεσσαν ἀγακλειτὴν Ὑπερίων
αὐτοκασιγνήτην, ἥ οἱ τέκε κάλλιμα τέκνα
Ἠῶ τε ῥοδόπηχυν ἐϋπλόκαμόν τε Σελήνην
Ἠέλιόν τ' ἀκάμαντ' ἐπιείκελον ἀθανάτοισιν,
ὃς φαίνει θνητοῖσι καὶ ἀθανάτοισι θεοῖσιν
ἵπποις ἐμβεβαώς· σμερδνὸν δ' ὅ γε δέρκεται ὄσσοις
χρυσῆς ἐκ κόρυθος, λαμπραὶ δ' ἀκτῖνες ἀπ' αὐτοῦ
αἰγλῆεν στίλβουσι, παρὰ κροτάφων τε παρειαὶ
λαμπραὶ ἀπὸ κρατὸς χαρίεν κατέχουσι πρόσωπον
τηλαυγές· καλὸν δὲ περὶ χροῒ λάμπεται ἔσθος
λεπτουργὲς πνοιῇ ἀνέμων, ὑπὸ δ' ἄρσενες ἵπποι

ἔνθ' ἄρ' ὅ γε στήσας χρυσόζυγον ἅρμα καὶ ἵππους
θεσπέσιος πέμπῃσι δι' οὐρανοῦ ὠκεανὸν δέ.
Χαῖρε ἄναξ, πρόφρων δὲ βίον θυμήρε' ὄπαζε·
ἐκ σέο δ' ἀρξάμενος κλῄσω μερόπων γένος ἀνδρῶν
ἡμιθέων ὧν ἔργα θεοὶ θνητοῖσιν ἔδειξαν.

XXXII. Εἰς Σελήνην

Μήνην ἀείδειν τανυσίπτερον ἔσπετε Μοῦσαι
ἡδυεπεῖς κοῦραι Κρονίδεω Διὸς ἵστορες ᾠδῆς·
ἧς ἄπο αἴγλη γαῖαν ἑλίσσεται οὐρανόδεικτος
κρατὸς ἀπ' ἀθανάτοιο, πολὺς δ' ὑπὸ κόσμος ὄρωρεν
αἴγλης λαμπούσης· στίλβει δέ τ' ἀλάμπετος ἀὴρ
χρυσέου ἀπὸ στεφάνου, ἀκτῖνες δ' ἐνδιάονται,
εὖτ' ἂν ἀπ' Ὠκεανοῖο λοεσσαμένη χρόα καλὸν
εἵματα ἑσσαμένη τηλαυγέα δῖα Σελήνη

4 ἀγακλυτὴν praeter D libri, cf. Π 463 al. 5 οἵη B Γ 10 χρυσέης Barnes 11 C. I. A. II. i. 703. vv. 10, 11 κρανιδιον . . . παρειας ουκ εχον, sim. 676, 701; χαλκοπαρῄου M 183 al. 14 lacunam stat. Hermann

XXXII. Titvlvs: εἰς τὴν σελήνην p E T: εἰς σελήνην cet. lunae imaginem habent A Q R[1] R[2], lunae phasium P 1 σελήνην Γ ἀείδει R[1]: εὐειδῆ Bothe: ἀϊδίην Sikes ἕσπεται E: ἕσπετε cet. corr. Baumeister 4 κόσμον D E Π 5 δ' ἀλάμπετος libri corr. Barnes 6 χρυσοῦ p ἀκτῆρες x At D ed. pr.: ἀκτῖνες p ἐνδαίονται Roscher 8 ἥματα Γ N V[1] (ἧμ-)

ζευξαμένη πώλους ἐριαύχενας αἰγλήεντας
ἐσσυμένως προτέρωσ᾽ ἐλάσῃ καλλίτριχας ἵππους
ἑσπερίη διχόμηνος· ὅ τε πλήθει μέγας ὄγμος,
λαμπρόταταί τ᾽ αὐγαὶ τότ᾽ ἀεξομένης τελέθουσιν
οὐρανόθεν· τέκμωρ δὲ βροτοῖς καὶ σῆμα τέτυκται.
τῇ ῥά ποτε Κρονίδης ἐμίγη φιλότητι καὶ εὐνῇ·
ἡ δ᾽ ὑποκυσαμένη Πανδείην γείνατο κούρην
ἐκπρεπὲς εἶδος ἔχουσαν ἐν ἀθανάτοισι θεοῖσι.
Χαῖρε ἄνασσα θεὰ λευκώλενε δῖα Σελήνη
πρόφρον ἐϋπλόκαμος· σέο δ᾽ ἀρχόμενος κλέα φωτῶν
ᾄσομαι ἡμιθέων ὧν κλείουσ᾽ ἔργματ᾽ ἀοιδοὶ
Μουσάων θεράποντες ἀπὸ στομάτων ἐροέντων.

XXXIII. Εἰς Διοσκούρους

Ἀμφὶ Διὸς κούρους ἑλικώπιδες ἔσπετε Μοῦσαι
Τυνδαρίδας Λήδης καλλισφύρου ἀγλαὰ τέκνα,
Κάστορά θ᾽ ἱππόδαμον καὶ ἀμώμητον Πολυδεύκεα,
τοὺς ὑπὸ Ταϋγέτου κορυφῇ ὄρεος μεγάλοιο
μιχθεῖσ᾽ ἐν φιλότητι κελαινεφέϊ Κρονίωνι
σωτῆρας τέκε παῖδας ἐπιχθονίων ἀνθρώπων
ὠκυπόρων τε νεῶν, ὅτε τε σπέρχωσιν ἄελλαι
χειμέριαι κατὰ πόντον ἀμείλιχον· οἱ δ᾽ ἀπὸ νηῶν
εὐχόμενοι καλέουσι Διὸς κούρους μεγάλοιο
ἄρνεσσιν λευκοῖσιν ἐπ᾽ ἀκρωτήρια βάντες
πρύμνης· τὴν δ᾽ ἄνεμός τε μέγας καὶ κῦμα θαλάσσης
θῆκαν ὑποβρυχίην, οἱ δ᾽ ἐξαπίνης ἐφάνησαν
ξουθῇσι πτερύγεσσι δι᾽ αἰθέρος ἀΐξαντες,
αὐτίκα δ᾽ ἀργαλέων ἀνέμων κατέπαυσαν ἀέλλας,
κύματα δ᾽ ἐστόρεσαν λευκῆς ἁλὸς ἐν πελάγεσσι,

11 πλήθη *p* praeter B C V¹ 12 τελέθωσιν libri corr. Baumeister 17 λευκώλενος T (corr. in ε) : λευκώλενες E

XXXIII. Titulus : εἰς διοσκούρους *x* D ed. pr. : εἰς κάστορα καὶ πολυδεύκην *p* 1 ἕσπετε D N T V¹ ed. pr. 9 διϝος κωροιν μεγαλοιο I. G. III. i. 649 (s. vi a. C. n.) 11 ἄνεμός τε καὶ (ss. με) E : με καὶ Π T 14 ἀέλλας C Π : ἀνέμους, marg. γρ. ἀέλλας E T : ἀέλλαι cet.

ναύταις σήματα καλὰ πόνου σφίσιν· οἱ δὲ ἰδόντες
γήθησαν, παύσαντο δ' ὀϊζυροῖο πόνοιο.
Χαίρετε Τυνδαρίδαι ταχέων ἐπιβήτορες ἵππων·
αὐτὰρ ἐγὼν ὑμέων καὶ ἄλλης μνήσομ' ἀοιδῆς.

Εἰς Ξένους

Αἰδεῖσθε ξενίων κεχρημένον ἠδὲ δόμοιο
οἳ πόλιν αἰπεινὴν νύμφης ἐρατώπιδος Ἥρης
ναίετε, Σαιδήνης πόδα νείατον ὑψικόμοιο,
ἀμβρόσιον πίνοντες ὕδωρ ξανθοῦ ποταμοῖο
Ἕρμου καλὰ ῥέοντος ὃν ἀθάνατος τέκετο Ζεύς.

16 σφίσιν] κρίσιν Baumeister: λύσιν Abel: σβέσιν nos: πόνου ἀπονόσφισιν Bury om. ναύταις   ad calcem δευρὶ πέλας λάχε τῶν ἐς δαίμονας ὕμνων ὁμήρου *p* praeter V[1]

Poemation εἰς ξένους habent C D E Π T ed. pr.: exstat et in vita Herodotea c. ix   2 ita codd., κύμην ἐριώπιδα κούρην Herod.   3 ναίετ' ἐς ᾅδην ἧς πόδα codd.: σαρδήνης Herod.: Σαιδηνή, ὄρος Κύμης Steph. Byz.   4 θείου Herod.   5 ἕβρου codd.: ἕρμου Herod.: Ἑρμοῦ πεδίον, τόπος πλησίον Κύμης, Ἔφορος ὀκτωκαιδεκάτῃ ⟨fr. 131⟩ Steph. Byz.   δινήεντος Herod.   τέλος τῶν ὕμνων ὁμήρου E T: τέλος τῶν ὁμήρου ὕμνων Π

CODICUM VARIETAS LEVIOR

I 11 τριετήρισιν M 16 μητιετὰ M 20 διόνυσ' M

II 12 ῥρίζης M 20 ὀρθία M 26 τ' ἄναξ M 47 χθόνια M 54 ὡριφόρε M 57 εἶδον M, id. 68 78 νεφεληγερετά M 95 γίνωσκε M 101 παλαιγενέη M 113 γρηῦ M 114 πόλιος M 134 γᾶι, εα m. rec. M 147 ἠχνύμενοί M 155 δολιχοῦ M 162 ἀνώγει M 173 καλέειν M 189 κύρε M 208 ἀμφὶ M 213 ἀπέολπα M 215 ὡσεί M 234 δημοφόονθ' M 242 ἀγή-ρον M 272 προύχοντι M 281 δἰὲκ M, id. 379 285 καδ M 297 δημήτορι et ναὸν M 309 γαῖα M 315 δημήτηρ' M corr. Ruhnken 323 μὴδ' M 331 ποτε φάσκε M 343 παρα-κοίτῇ M 346 κρατερὸς M corr. Ruhnken 348 ἄνωγεν M 362 μὴ δέ τι M 369 post τελοῦντες . . . . . M 384 ἀγῶν' M 389 ἅλτο M 432 ἂρ M 456 βρυσέμεν M 451 τοπρὶν M 458 εἶδον corr. m. p. M 487 φιλῶνται M corr. Voss

III 7 λ ρεσσιν L_1 12 τπ̄ τνϊα L_1 16 ὀρτιγύη M 17 κύνιον M κύνθειον L_1 Π 22 ἅδον Γ ἅδον M ἆδον cet. ἄκραι M 35 σκύρος codd. 65 πέρι S περὶ *p* 72 ἐπειὴ T 87 ἥ μιν M 88 κωμὸς M 102 ἴριν codd. 107 ἶρις M ἴρις cet. 127 ἄβρο-τον M 128 στροφοὶ codd. 129 οὐδέτι M T 139 ῥρίον L_1 Π T 142 ἰλάσκαζες M 143 δενδρόεντα L_1 Π 146 σε in ras. J 169 ὔμμιν M E D N O P S ὑμῖν Aristid. 172 ἐνὶ J L_1 205 μητιέτα M 210 ἰσχύ' M 225 δ' εἰσ' ἀφίκανες M 226 πως L_1 230 ἶξες S ed. pr. ἶξες M ἵξες cet. 235 δενδρόεντι Π (sim. 245) 244 ἆδε M *x* ἅδε *p* S corr. Aldina prima 270 οὐτέ τι M 276 μὴ δ' L_1 278 ἶξες P S ἵξες seu ἴξες cet. 303 ἔρδεσκεν M D E L_1 ἕρδ. cet. 348 et 353 βοῶπες L_1 355 κατακλυτὰ M 368 οὐδὲ M T 375 βοῖβος M 379 ἐξαπάφουσα L_1 396 ὑπὸ M 411 ἶξον M ἵξον cet. corr. ed. pr. τερψιβρότου M 417 πολυίχθιον M ἀμφισορούσει M T 419 παρεκ L_1 428 ὑπὲὲκ T ὑπεκ L_1 432 διεκ L_1 T 438 ἵξον M ἴξον cet. corr. ed. pr. 447 ῥρiπῆς *x* 453 πρᾶξιν

M 457 ἐκ μὴ τοῦ δὲ M 458 αὐτὴ M 460 ἀδικότες M 464 κατὰ M 475 κεῖνοι pro ξεῖνοι M 487 λύσατε M 489 εἴσσης x Γ N 490 ῥῥηγμῖνι x 506 ἄνα M 508 ῥῥηγμῖνι L_1 ῥῥ- Π 517 πυθῶ M ἴη παιήον' M ἰη. παιήον' L_1 519 μελίγυρυν M 540 ἢ ἔτι Π 541 κατὰ M L_1 T

IV 12 ἄγαγ' M 15 πολύδοκον M 17 ἐνκιθαρίζειν E 18 ἔκλεψεν M 20 καὶ om. M γύων A B Γ L_3 O Q R_1 om. L_2 P R_2 22 ζητεῖ M 26 αὐλίησι codd. corr. Steph. 45 ἀμαλδύναι in text T 48 πειρῆνας *p* 50 πήχυς M δὲ om. M B Γ N 59 ὄνομα κλυτὸν x D 79 ἀλίοισιν Γ 80 θαυμαστὰ B Γ N V 86 γρ. αὐτοτεοπήσας L_1 93 μηκέτι At D 98 ἐγένετο M 100 μέγα M μεγαμηδείδοιο L_1 μέγα μηδείδιο Π μεγαμηδείαο At D μεγαμειδείοιο priore ει ex η correcto E T 122 γ' ἐράσμια M 123 ἔργμενον M 132 ᾔδει seu ἤδει codd. em. Ruhnken 137 οὐλοκάρηβα M 138 ηὔλησε M 143 ὄρθρια E 148 ἄντρον M_1 149 προβιβῶν M x D 150 ἐσσυμένης L_1 Π 158 διεκ E T 190 βατόδροπε M 196 τέτυκτον Π 218, 219 om. M 232 πόαν M 236 χωόμενος ed. pr. 245 εἰλύμενον E 247 κληίδα M D Π 261 ἔειπες D ed. pr. 263 πιθόμην E D 265 κατερῶ M 289 ἀλλάγε and πήματόν M D 294 κρατὸς M κρατοὺς L_1 321 κάτ' ὄπισθε M 338 τέρτομον praefixis punctis M 339 εἴσ' L_1 355 ἑλῶντα x A D V_1 (-οντα) 356 ἡσυχία M 363 ἄλλον E 367 πάντα 373 ἀνάγκης M 375 φιλοκύδεος M 384 οὔ M D L_1 Π πρόθυρα M 398 ἴξον codd. em. ed. pr. 413 ἑρμείω M 417 ἔθετ' M 429 ἀοιδὸν M 431 καὶ κατὰ (for κατὰ) M 444 πώποτε φημὶ M 451 χορὸς om. τε M 453 μέλησιν M 454 θαλιῆσ' M 461 κύδεα M 469 μητιέτα M 513 ἑρμῇ ex ἑρμῆς M 514 ποικολομήτα E 517 πολυβ- M x At D 519 ὄμβριμον E L_1 D 537 ἐμοῖο M 549 φῆμ' M φημ' L_1 547 παρεις E L_1 566 αἶ x 576 ὁμίλει x D

V 7 πεπίθειν M 8 γ' pro τ' M 10 ἀλλὰ ῥά M 18 τοι pro τῇ Q 21 ἄδεν x D N 34 περ τι codd. praeter D L_1 36 τι M παρ' ἐκ M παρεκ E L_1 Q T 42 τέκε M 44 κεδν'

E κεδν' L_1 47 βροτέας M ἀποειρομένη M 52 ὡς δὲ M 56 φιλομειδὴς codd. praeter T corr. 58 ἐκ κύπρον L_1 61 χρίσαν M D E χρίσσαν L_1 N 65 φιλομειδὴς E T 67 πρήσασα Γ 74 σὺν δύο L_1 76 οἶος Q T 77 ἀπὸ Q ἀπο cet. corr. Steph. 78 κατὰ T 79 οἶος E T Q 86 ἔστο ed. pr. 104 ἐμ' αὐτὸν L_1 117 μ' om. M 120 ἐστεφάνωντο E 122 κατὰ E L_1 128 ἤτοι codd. praeter E 141 δαῖνυ M δαίννυ D L_1 145 τέ pro δέ M σ' ἐγείνατο M 146 ὀνομακλυτὸς M 170 ἔχευαν Π 173 εὖ ποιητοῖο M 179 οἶκοι δήμε M νοήσας M 183 τ' ἐκαλύψατο M 190 γίνεται M 192 κατὰ E 200 κατὰ E T 201 ἀμφ' M 202 μητιετὰ M 210 υἱὸς E 215 ἐπειδὴ T 219 ἡμετέρης Π 222 ἐπίνευσε M ἐκρήηνεν T 239 ἔγωγέ σε T 241 τοῖος M 250 κατὰ M E T θνητοῖσι M 281 κατὰ E T 283 τῶδε codd. praeter M

VI 2 αἴσομαι M D 4 ἤνυκε M 5 ἐνὶ E L_1 Π 14 ἐπειδὴ T 17 ἀγέσθαι M

VII 6 ἐυσέλμου M *x* D N 13 ἀποτηλὸς ἔπιπτον M ἀποτηλόσ' E L_1 T V_1 19 ἢ pr. L_1 23 μήτ' ἐπὶ M

VIII 1 ἄρες M E Π T 2 πολίσσοε M 5 ἄγε E 10 βιοτῆτα M 13 ἀπατηλὴν M

IX 4 παγχρύσιον D X 4 εὔκτισμένης E T

XI 4 ἐρύσατο M Γ νισσομ- codd. praeter M

XV 2 ἐνὶ T 5 ὑπ' E T J 6 ἔρεζεν Π

XIX 46 ὀμβάγχειος E

XX 3 τοπάρος D E T

XXI 2 παρὰ E V_1

XXII 6 ποσειδάων Γ N

XXVI 5 νύσσης codd. em. Barnes ἔξετο Π 7 ἐπειδὴ T

XXVII 14 εἰς *x* D N

XXVIII 4 *μητιέτα* Π

XXIX 4 *σου* E T   12 *ἔπεσθε* T

XXX 6 *ποτνία* E   11 *κατὰ* E T V_1

XXXI 11 *κροτάφην* Π   12 *χάριεν* Γ   15 om. E   17 *θυμήρη* V_1

XXXII 6 *ἄπὸ* T

COMMENTARY

I

Hymn to Dionysus

The loss of one quire and a leaf in M, and probably more in its archetype (p. xv), has deprived us of all but the last twelve verses of this hymn. The lines quoted by Diodorus, first connected with the hymn by Ruhnken, came apparently from the beginning; there is no reason to doubt, with Baumeister, the connexion of the two fragments. Another line is perhaps preserved by Athenaeus 653 B Κράτης ἐν δευτέρῳ Ἀττικῆς διαλέκτου ἐν τοῖς ὕμνοις τοῖς ἀρχαίοις φάσκων ἀντὶ τοῦ βότρυος τὴν σταφυλὴν κεῖσθαι διὰ τούτου

αὐτῇσι σταφυλῇσιν μελαίνῃσιν κομόωντες

(p. 65 Wachsmuth). The fairy story of the vine which flowered, fruited, and ripened in a single day (Soph. *fr.* 255 Pearson)—perhaps connected with an annual spring festival of the miraculous creation of wine (*CR.* xlii. 19, Bonner *AJA.* 1929. 1)—may have occurred in the hymn and included this line. Another fragment perhaps is preserved by Suidas in Θωύσσοντες, viz. Ὅμηρος· βαρύβρομα θωύσσοντες (Homer ed. 1911 v. 151).

On the source of the quotation in the Σ to *Ap. Rh.* ii. 1211, see p. lxxii.

Date. From its position in M it is probable that this was a long hymn, on the scale of those to Dem., Apoll., Hermes, and Aphr. Otherwise it would have been placed among the short preludes. Diodorus attributed it to Homer (iv. 2 καὶ τὸν Ὅμηρον δὲ τούτοις μαρτυρῆσαι ἐν τοῖς ὕμνοις). The other hymn to Dionysus in the collection (vii) is in a different style, and comparisons of the two hymns are useless. It is probable that the seventh hymn is later, and that its composer borrowed the concluding formula οὐδέ πῃ ἔστι from 18, 19. There is nothing either mythological or linguistic in the fragments of this hymn which suggests a late period.

Subject of the Hymn. For the legends and cult of Dionysus in general see P.-R. 659 f., Roscher i. 1029 f., P.-W. v. 1010 f., Farnell v. 85 f., Nilsson *GF.* 258 f., Rose *Handbook* 149 f. For the various forms of the name, and supposed meanings attributed to it, see P.-W. v. 1010 f., P.-R. 660, 664, Roscher iv. 665 f. To these interpretations, ancient and modern, no value can be attached (see below).

Our fragment deals with two topics, the birthplace of the God and the origin of the *trieteris.* As regards the first there exists everywhere an intelligible tendency for old-established cults of a God or saint to lay claim to be the original scene of revelation or birth, or to possess the tomb of the object of their worship, and a rivalry of claim is particularly likely to occur in the case of a God whose cult like that of Dionysus entered Greece from abroad at a relatively late period. The claim of Thebes that Semele was a Theban princess and that the birth took place there, though even violently denied by our author (v. 6), was generally accepted, and indicates that Boeotia was a very early and important centre of the diffusion of the cult (the same conclusion results from the myth of Pentheus in Euripides' *Bacchae*). But even when the story of the blasting of Semele at Thebes was accepted, it was still possible for local cults to claim either that the God was brought up in their land, or else in some far magical country from which he came first to them (see Roscher iv. 609, Malten *ARW.* xii. 1909, 286); for the nurture of the babe by nymphs in a cave is a consistent and probably original part of the legend (see on xxvi. 6). The 'nurses of Dionysus' as well as the 'land of Nysa' are mentioned in the oldest reference, the episode of Lycurgus Z 130 sq.

Divine Names

This seems the proper place at which to state our attitude towards the origin and derivation of Greek divine and heroic names. The first and second hymns are vitally connected with the subject.

From Homer, Hesiod, Euripides, and Plato down to Zonaras, the Greeks had but one principle of derivation, aural similarity of sound. This, now called *Volksetymologie*, still reigns even in technical circles. The determination to explain Greek by Greek, or at all events by Indo-European, and to limit the vocabulary of the first stage of Greek to a native stock, induces living etymologers to follow the ancients in deriving Achilles (and probably Acheron also)[1] from *ἄχος*, Ajax from *αἰαῖ* or *αἶα*, Aeacus also from *αἶα*, and analysing *κένταυρος* into *κεντεῖν αὔραν*.[2] In face of such credulity the individual must fall back on his own judgement.

Myres (*Who were the Greeks?* 310) notices that heroic names resist analysis as Greek, and that too though Agamemnon, Menelaus, Achilles contain elements which resemble Greek. It is still more difficult to treat divine names so palpably un-Greek as Aphrodite, Apollo, or Hephaestus, as Hellenic. Kalinka has told us (*Neue Jahrbücher* 1920 xlv. 401, see also his article in *Klio* xxii. 250 sq.) that Zeus is the only Indo-European God's name. Yet a misguided race-patriotism insists on claiming them for Europe. The Gods' names came with the Gods themselves,[3] but whence we do not yet know nor shall till the Asianic tongues and the languages of Crete and Cyprus have been read. It is admitted on all but every hand that Aphrodite, Artemis, Ares, Apollo, Hephaestus, Leto, Pan, are non-Greek; Eileithyia is meaningless.[4] Even Herodotus (ii. 50) held that most Gods came from Egypt, and the learned half-Asiatic Greeks detected 'barbaric' elements in Greek names, and protested against the attempt to explain them from Hellenic elements: Strabo 321 *καὶ ἀπὸ τῶν ὀνομάτων δὲ ἐνίων τὸ βάρβαρον ἐμφαίνεται,* Κέκροψ *καὶ* Κόδρος *καὶ* Ἄικλος *καὶ* Κόθος *καὶ* Δρύμας *καὶ* Κρίνακος, 607 ἐκαλεῖτο δὲ τότε Σκῆψις, εἴτ' *ἄλλως εἴτ' ἀπὸ τοῦ περίσκεπτον εἶναι τὸν τόπον, εἰ δεῖ τὰ παρὰ τοῖς βαρβάροις ἐν τῷ τότε ὀνόματα ταῖς* Ἑλληνικαῖς *ἐτυμολογεῖσθαι φωναῖς,*

[1] Porphyry ap. Stob. *Ecl.* i. 1. 49 Ἀχέροντα *μὲν διὰ τὰ ἄχη ὡς καὶ* Μελανιππίδης *ἐν* Περσεφόνῃ [fr. 3 Diehl] *καὶ* Λικύμνιος [fr. 2]: ib. 50 Apollodorus derived Styx from *στυγνάζειν*.

[2] The ancients preferred *ὄρρον* (Hesych. *in* Κένταυροι).

[3] As did the names of musical instruments (Strabo 471 *νάβλη, σαμβύκη, βάρβιτος, μάγαδις, καὶ ἄλλα πλείω*) with the instruments. [4] See on *h.Ap.* 97.

Galen v. 213,[1] vi. 380, vii. 348, Procopius *Bell. Goth.* iii. 27 (394).[2]

Διόνυσος to the Greek mind announced its connexion with Zeus, though Dionysus was no more nor less a son of Zeus than Apollo, Ares, Heracles, Hermes and most of the young male Gods. The remainder of the word pointed to a well-known place-name Νύσα,[3] which in the connexion has never been explained. Both elements are the result of mechanical *Volksetymologie*, which occurs as early as Z 133, where Thetis and Lycurgus point to north Greece rather than to Asia, from which (Lydia) the story in the Bacchae brings Dionysus. Modern authorities give no more definite origin to the vine than the Mediterranean basin or Western Asia.

The true origin of the *trieteris* or biennial period in the worship of Dionysus is obscure. That, like the *enneateris* in the worship of Apollo, it is connected with any system of intercalation (Gruppe *Gr. Myth.* ii. 956) is intrinsically improbable, and has no analogy to support it. The view of Rohde (*Psyche* ii. 12), based upon Diodorus iii. 65, iv. 3, and Orph. *h.* liii, that the God's absences in the lower world and subsequent epiphanies occurred at trieteric intervals, is difficult to accept. There is no analogy for celebrating the death and resurrection of a vegetation-god biennially; for obvious reasons such ceremonies are always annual. Further, the theory runs counter to the known facts of Greek cult, for at Delphi Dionysus was annually not biennially present for the three winter months (Plutarch *mor.* 389 C). Farnell (*l.c.* 180 sq.) has

1 ib. 214 ὅτι μὲν ἀλαζὼν ἐστι μάρτυς ἡ ἐτυμολογία, πολλάκις μὲν ὁμοίως μαρτυροῦσα τοῖς τἀναντία λέγουσι τῶν ἀληθῶν, οὐκ ὀλιγάκις δὲ τοῖς ψευδομένοις μᾶλλον ἤπερ τοῖς ἀληθεύουσιν, ἐν ἑτέρᾳ πραγματείᾳ δεδήλωται. He is arguing against Chrysippus. See also Olympiodorus *vit. Plat.* i. 54 Westermann.

2 Asianic originals of Greek divine names that have been so far suggested are Lycian *pldãns* = Apollo, *pulenjda* = Ἀπολλωνίδης Kalinka *Klio* xxii. 254, Lycian *lada* = Leto P.-W. suppl. v. 571, Phrygian ζεμελω = Semele Roscher iv. 665; Artemis is all but literally Lycian, Kalinka *op.c.* 255.

3 But they had other resources; Nonnus ix. 21 νῦσος ὅτι γλώσσῃ Συρακοσσίδι χωλὸς ἀκούει, and Artemidorus *Onir.* ii. 37 says ἔστι γὰρ Διόνυσος παρὰ τὸ διανύειν ἕκαστα. Even Homer's derivation of Odysseus did not satisfy every one; Silenus of Chios (Eust. 1871. 20) preferred ὁδός. Apollo was ὁ μὴ μετὰ πολλῶν συναριθμούμενος, and ἑκατηβόλος because he slew the snake at Pytho ἑκατὸν βέλεσι (Hesych. *in vv.*).

adduced evidence that the festival in alternate years may belong to the original Thracian cult, and has plausibly suggested that this may be connected with the practice of leaving the arable land fallow in alternate years.

Other hymns. The existence of hymns to Dionysus of similar character may be inferred from Menander περὶ ἐπιδεικτ. 6 (Walz *Rh.Gr.* ix. 144) φασὶν . . . ὅτι καὶ χωρὶς τῶν γενεαλογικῶν εἴησάν τινες μυθικοὶ ὕμνοι, οἷον ὅτι Διόνυσος Ἰκαρίῳ ἐπεξενώθη, Aristides iv 28 τοὺς μὲν οὖν τελέους ὕμνους τε καὶ λόγους περὶ Διονύσου Ὀρφεῖ καὶ Μουσαίῳ παρῶμεν καὶ τοῖς ἀρχαίοις τῶν νομοθετῶν. Other poems recorded on the subject are dithyrambs, Pindar *frr.* 79–86, 247; odes, Anacreon *fr.* 2, Castorio *fr.* 1 (*PLG.* iii. 634); elegies, Ion of Chios *fr.* 1 (*PLG.* ii. 251), Eratosthenes and Euphorion ap. Aelian *HA.* vii. 48 fin., Arion *ib.* xii. 45; Orphic hymns xlv, xlvi, xlvii, l, lii, liii, Delphic hymns *BCH.* xvii. 561, xviii. 345; paean, Philodamus ap. Diehl *Anth. Lyr.* ii. 252 sq.; an alphabetic hymn Anth. Pal. ix. 524; Sozomen vi. 252 mentions a hymn by Epiphanius. Fragments of ritual invocations are preserved in Plutarch *mor.* 299 (Elis), 386 (Delphi), Diehl *Carm. pop.* 24(5), 48(8).

1. Δρακάνῳ. This is usually supposed to be the promontory in the island of Icaros (Strabo 639, Paus. ix. 11. 2). Hermann and others therefore held that Ἰκάρῳ could not refer to the island, as the whole would include the part. But, though there were several other places of the name (Pliny *NH.* iv. 23, Steph. Byz. *in v.*), Icaros is here undoubtedly the island near Samos, and Maass is right in identifying Dracanon with a cape of that name in Cos, an island which had some connexion with Dionysus. For this cape see Strabo 657, where it is spelt Δρέκανον. The Dracanon in Theocr. xxvi. 33, Nonn. *Dion.* ix. 16 (mentioned as the birthplace), is also to be taken as in Cos; so also *Anth. Pal.* vii. 651. 3 ἀλλὰ τὰ μὲν Δολίχης τε καὶ αἰπεινῆς Δρακάνοιο | Ἰκάριον ῥήσσει κῦμα περὶ κροκάλαις, where, as in the hymns, the promontory is mentioned as separate from the island. (Doliche is the old name of Icaros, Apollod. ii. 6. 3.)

For the cult of Dionysus in Cos see Ditt. *Syll.* 1012 (D. Thallophorus), 1025 (D. Skyllitas). Two Dionysiac month-names,

Agrionios and *Theodaisios*, occur in the Coan calendar, Paton and Hicks *Inscr. of Cos*, 326 sq.

Ἰκάρῳ. It is from Icaros (not as supposed by Crusius *Philol.* xlviii. 208 from the Attic Icaria) that the God is being ferried by the robbers in the version of the story in *Hymn* vii preserved by Apollodorus iii. 37. For the head of D. as a coin-type in Icaros (c. 300 B.C.) see Head *HN.* p. 602. Tibullus iii. 7. 9 says *cunctis Baccho iucundior hospes* | *Icarus*; the younger Pliny wrote elegies on the Icarian sea and island (*ep.* vii. 4. 3).

2. **Νάξῳ.** The richest and most fruitful of the Cyclades, to which, as the meeting-place in post-Homeric legend of Dionysus and Ariadne, the name Dia was transferred, was specially sacred to the God (Servius *in Aen.* iii. 125), and had the name Διονυσιάς (Diod. v. 52). It possessed a Nysa and a cave in which the babe had been reared (P.-R. 676 n. 2), and a magical spring from which sweet wine flowed (Steph. Byz. in Νάξος). Naxian children were, like Dionysus, born in the eighth month, Asclepiades ap. Steph. *l.c.* For legendary associations of the island with Dionysus, Poseidon, and Hephaestus, see further Plutarch *mor.* 741 A, Ꚃ Theocr. vii. 144, Stesichorus fr. 72. In historical times the importance of the cult is indicated by the fact that the priest of Dionysus was an eponymous official (*CIG.* 2265), and the head of Dionysus was the sole Naxian coin-type from the fourth century onwards (*BM. Cat. Crete and Aegean* 110–12). See further Porphyr. *de antro nymph.* 20, Athenaeus 78 c, *IG.* xii. 5, 45, 46, Kern in P.-W. v. 1025.

εἰραφιῶτα. For the form cf. *σπαργανιῶτα* *h. Herm.* 301, *μηχανιῶτα* 436, *χαριδῶτα* *h.* xviii. 12, *ὑλειῶτα* *Anth. Pal.* vi. 106, *βιοδωτα* *IG.* xiv. 1015, 5, *ὀλβιοδῶτα* *h. Orph.* xxiv. 2, Ἀσκληπιοῦ ὀλβιοδώτα Stob. *Flor.* i. 38, no. 31, *ολβιοτα* Ζευ pap. Goodspeed *JHS.* xxiii. 243 col. vi. 5, Fick *BB.* xx. 179, *ασκληπιωι λιγεωτηι* Ἐφ. Ἀρχ. 1884. 22, *δειραδιώτης* of Apollo Paus. ii. 24. 1, 27. 6, *ἐπιδιώτας* (plural) iii. 17. 9.

The ancients offer a choice of etymologies (Ꚃ A 39 *παρὰ τὸ ἐρέφω, ὅθεν καὶ εἰραφιώτης ὁ Δ. λέγεται, ἐστέφετο γὰρ κισσῷ· ἢ ἀπὸ τοῦ ἐρράφθαι αὐτὸν τῷ μηρῷ τοῦ Διός· ἢ παρὰ τὸ ἐρίφῳ αὐτὸν συν-αναστραφῆναι· ἢ παρὰ τὸ ἐρίῳ αὐτὸν πλέκεσθαι.* Cf. *EM.* 302. 53,

Choerob. ap. Cramer *An. Ox.* ii. 211, 32, Zonaras 627. 7). In literature the sense of the word is *μηρορραφής* (Eur. *Bacchae* 96, Nonnus *Dion.* ix. 23, xlii. 315, Orpheus *h.* xlviii. 2 sq., *h. anon.* 1 = Abel 284). Fick *l.c.* reverts but without probability to *εἶρος ἔρρος*, 'wool', in the sense of 'the shaggy animal'; Wieseler (*Philol.* x. 701) takes the word as equivalent to *ἐρίφιος* preserved by Hesychius and Steph. as a title of D. at Metapontum (to whom kids were sacred); the derivation most in favour is that of Sonne *KZ.* x 103, who compares Sanskr. *ṛshabha*, a bull, cf. Neil ap. Frazer *GB.* vii. 16, where the bull-Dionysus is discussed, Fröhde *BB.* 21. 199, who adds *ἔρραος*, 'ram', Prellwitz *ib.* 22. 99, Meillet *IF.* v. 328 who adduces *ἀρνειός* and Lat. *verres* and thinks the original sense was 'male', Solmsen *ib.* vii. 46 sq., who compares Laconian *εἴρην* and the Macedonian proper name *Ἀρραβαῖος* (Ehrlich *KZ.* 39. 567). The month-name in Amorgos (*εμ μηνι ειραφιωνι IG.* xii. 7. 62, 28) confirms the antiquity of the title. The Aeolic form occurs in Alcaeus *fr.* 90 *ἐρραφεώτου γὰρ ἄναξ.*

3. **ἐπ' Ἀλφειῷ ποταμῷ.** The old and important cult of Dionysus in Elis (Paus. v. 14, 10; 15, 4; vi. 21, 5; 24, 8; 26. 1, Plut. *mor.* 299, 364) seems to have come across the gulf from Delphi (see Weniger in Roscher iii. 2488, Halliday *Greek questions of Plutarch*, 88).

4. On the usual derivation of the word Semele see P.-R. 660 and 664, Kretschmer *Aus der Anomia*, 1890, 17 sq., Fröhde *BB.* xxi. 185 sq., Roscher iv. 665 (Phrygian *ζεμελω*).

τερπικεραύνῳ. The epithet is chosen acc. to Adami (*de poet. scen.* p. 243) to suggest the circumstances of the birth; cf. Eur. *Bacch.* 90 *λιποῦσ' αἰῶνα κεραυνίῳ πλαγᾷ*, Nonnus *Dion.* viii. 319 *νυμφίε τερπικέραυνε.*

5. **ἐν Θήβῃσιν.** The common tradition of the birth at Thebes (on which see Kern P.-W. v. 1014 sq.) is followed in Philodamus' paeans (*BCH.* xix. 393, Diehl *Anth. Lyr.* i. 252) *ὃν Θήβαις ποτ' ἐν εὐίαις | ζη[νὶ γείνατο] καλλίπαις Θυώνα.* Dionysus was washed at a fountain *Κισσοῦσα* near Haliartus *νήπιος ἐκ λοχείας* Plut. *Lysand.* 8.

7. **κρύπτων.** Adami compares Eur. *Bacch.* 98 *κρυπτὸν ἀφ' Ἥρας*, *h. Orph.* xxx. 3, lii. 5.

8. **Νύσῃ.** Ten places called *Νύση* are mentioned by Stephanus

in v., viz. at Helicon, in Thrace, Caria, Arabia, Egypt, Naxos, India, Caucasus, Libya, Euboea (where the miraculous vine, *ante*, p. 97, grew); fifteen by Hesychius (some of the same plus Aethiopia, Babylon, Erythrae, Thessaly, Cilicia, Macedonia, Pangaeum, Syria). The name is as real as any other place-name and several historical events took place in these localities; e.g. Aristodemus, Strabo's teacher, kept his school at the Syrian Nysa (Strabo 650); see the Dict. Geog. As already stated the earliest mention Z 133, where Lycurgus son of Dryas and Thetis are present, suggests the northern Aegean. The frequency of the name had an unfortunate influence on the myth.

The moderns have detected the elements Zeus and Nysa in Dionysus, a procedure worthy of Plato or the *Etymologicum Magnum*, which itself says (66, 19) οὐ δεῖ ἐπὶ τῶν κυρίων ἐτυμολογίας λαμβάνειν. (Plutarch also *Numa* 13 notices attempts to etymologize Italian words as Greek: γλιχόμενος ἐξελληνίσαι τοὔνομα . . . εἴ γε δεῖ πρὸς τὴν Ἑλληνικὴν διάλεκτον ἐξάγειν τὸ ὄνομα. *Ancilia* is not more foreign than διόνυσος.) If the word were Greek it would naturally divide διον-, if we compare Διώνη, Διώνια and the dialectal equivalents διενυσος (Amorgos), δευνυσος (Anacreon 2. 11), δεονυς (Erythrae), δεονυσος (Samos), ζοννυσος (Lesbos), which show a less adapted form. Like most Gods' names (see p. 99) it is non-Greek,[1] and must presumably be looked for in the place of origin of the vine. The author of this hymn, accepting the *Volksetymologie* (ἀπό τε τοῦ πατρὸς καὶ τοῦ τόπου, Diod. i. 15. 5) places Nysa near Egypt, as Diodorus iii. 65 and 68, who quotes Antimachus fr. 70 and other poets. The Νύσιον πέδιον of the Demeter myth (see on ii. 17) was perhaps near the sea.

For the usual view see ante p. 100 and Pearson's notes on Sophocles fr. 255, 959. The Syrian Ῥάφεια (Steph. Byz. *in v.*) ἐκλήθη ἀπὸ τῆς ἱστορίας τῆς περὶ τοῦ Διονύσου.

8. **ὄρος** is supported by *h. Apoll.* 139 ῥίον οὔρεος ἄνθεσιν ὕλης. On the other hand κέρας is used for a peak (German *horn*) in Xen. *Anab.* v. 6. 7, Strabo 395 ὄρη δύο ἃ καλοῦσι κέρατα, cf. also

[1] The Phrygian and doubtless original form is produced from an inscription *Mon. Asiae Min. ant.* i. no. 413 by Calder, *CR.* 1927. 161 (διουνσις).

361, Diod. xiii. 65 τοῖς λόφοις τοῖς κέρασι καλουμένοις, Ar. *Nub.* 597 (Pindar *fr.* 285) ὑψικέρατα πέτραν; the words ὕπατον κέρας of a river occur Ap. Rhod. iv. 282.

ἀνθέον ὕλᾳ occurs in Alcman 58. 1 (ἔνθεον MS.).

11. Etymological explanation of τριετηρίς. The Greeks were peculiarly helpless before words appearing to contain the root τρεῖς. E.g. Hesiod *fr.* 191 πάντες δὲ τριχάικες καλέονται | τρισσὴν οὕνεκα γαῖαν ἑκὰς πάτρης ἐδάσαντο, *fr.* 96. 91 ὥρῃ ἐν εἰαρινῇ ὅτε τ' ἄτριχος οὔρεσι τίκτει | γαίης ἐν κευθμῶνι τρίτῳ ἔτεϊ τρία τέκνα, Aristotle 543 a 5 ἡ δὲ τρίγλη μόνη τρὶς [τίκτει], Diodorus ap. Phot. *Bibl.* 389 b 28 of Triccala Τριόκαλα δὲ αὐτό φασιν ὠνομάσθαι διὰ τὸ τρία καλὰ ἔχειν. Other explanations of τριετηρίς are given by Diodorus iii. 65, iv. 3, Nonnus xlviii 965, Orph. *h.* liii. 4.

In this line μέν is impossible after ὡς. The examples of μέν *solitarium* in K.-G. ii. 272. 2 are not parallel. A verb is required; this is given by reading τάμεν (*secuit*). Examples of the bisection of words are not necessary, but we may quote τὸ μή, τομῇ Hipp. *Acut.* 22, and for the reverse Zonaras 433. 21 γέμεν· ἐγένοντο, which is actually γε μέν Hes. *OD.* 772.

τέμνειν is the normal word for the dismemberment of D. and other personages: σ 339 διὰ μελειστὶ τάμησι, Pindar *Ol.* i. 59 μαχαίρᾳ τάμον κάτα μέλη (of Pelops), Herod. iii. 111 τὰ μέλεα διαταμόντες, Oppian *Cyn.* iv. 281 μελειστὶ τάμεν (of lambs), Manetho vi. 42 διαμελειστὶ ταμόντες (of the embryo): τὸν κατατεμνόμενον Διόνυσον Alexander *de plac. Manich.* c. 4 (Migne xviii 417 B), μεληδὸν διατεμόντες Georg. Acrop. 1668. 21, Theoph. cont. 204. 7, μεληδὸν κατέταμνον Anast. Sinaita, Migne cxxxix. 1424, σῶμα διατεμόντες κατὰ μέλη Evagrius ii. 8, μελειστι διακρεα σειο τα[μειη pap. Mus. Brit. 273. 45 (Album gratulatorium to van Herwerden 1902, p. 137), *membratim sectus* Arnob. *adv. gent.* v. 18,]ετεμον pap. Cunningham Memoirs, R. Irish Academy 1921 vol. art. xii (see Tierney *CR.* 1922. 77 sqq.), κατατμηθῆναι of Apsyrtus Steph. Byz. *in* Τομεύς.

The construction ἔταμε (σε) τρία is normal; Theocr. ix. 27 πέντε ταμὼν (κρέας), Herod. iv. 145 σφέας αὐτοὺς ἓξ μοίρας διεῖλον, Dem. *Symm.* 17 ἑκάστην διελεῖν κελεύω πέντε μέρη, Theoph. *H.P.* ix. 5. 2 διελόντες τρία μέρη, Libanius xxx. 23 πολλὰ μέρη τὸν Ἀλκιβιάδην ἔτεμνον; with other qualifications Euphron com. *fr.* 11. 7 ταύτην ἔτεμε λεπτὰ καὶ μικρά, Aen. Tact. 1497 Schöne ἀστράγαλον τρυπῆσαι εἴκοσι καὶ τέτταρα, Ephippus ii. 262 Kock τὴν βατίδα τεμάχη κατατεμών, Mithaecus ap. Ath. 325 F ταμὼν τεμάχεα; *pass.* Aen. Tact. 1756 χρὴ διατετάχθαι τοὺς ἐν τῇ πόλει μαχομένους τρία μέρη, Plato *Symp.* 191 D τετμημένος ἐξ ἑνὸς δύο.

For σοὶ beginning an apodosis cf. (si tanti est) Isocr. i. 37, and as a verbal coincidence πάντως σοι . . . χρήσεται M. Ant. vi. 42.

The verb elsewhere is in the plural, but the operation, the killing and trisection of a boy, did not require more than one person. Achilles sacrificed Polyxena Philostr. *Heroic.* 329 οἰμωγὴ . . . τῆς κόρης διασπωμένου αὐτὴν τοῦ Ἀχιλλέως καὶ μελειστὶ ξαίνοντος, and in the Hecuba Polymestor killed Polydorus (τεμών 716, διατεμών 782) unaided. Eumaeus ξ 75 cut and spitted two pigs, *ib.* 425 killed a boar with one blow, the others dismembered it. Cotys in Athen. 532 A, suspecting his wife ταῖς αὑτοῦ χερσὶν ἀνέτεμε τὴν ἄνθρωπον, a similar case ib. 415 C. Dionysus was carved, boiled, and roasted on spits Clem. Alex. i. 80 Migne. Lastly Zagreus is found as early as the Alcmaeonis *fr.* 3.

τριετηρίσιν. The reckoning of years being inclusive, it was a biennial festival according to modern computation. A few examples of other than Dionysiac festivals recurring every other year are known (Gruppe *Gr. Myth.* ii. 956), but the *trieteris* was as characteristically associated with the worship of Dionysus as the *enneateris* was with that of Apollo. For theories of its origin, which remains quite obscure, see ante p. 98. For trieteric Dionysiac festivals in Thrace and many parts of Greece, see Farnell v. 307 *Dionysos* ref. nos. 100 a–e.

13. Alternatives, 13–15 and 16, have been supposed, but the similarity largely depends on the alteration of ἐκέλευσε (16) into ἐπένευσε. For the dative with κελεύειν cf. Ψ642 Ω326 μάστιγι κέλευεν. In ἐπ' ὀφρύσι νεῦσε we have a tmesis for ἐπένευσεν ὀφρύσι.

17. ἴληθ': the only Homeric form of the imperative. Cf. ἔλλᾱθι Bacchyl. x. 8. Ἵλαθι Theocr. xv. 143 has α short, and εἰραφιῶτα nowhere shows signs of a digamma. For M's mistake (ἴλαθ'), cf. 19 ἐπιλαθόμενοι. Both forms occur Anth. Pal. xii. 158 ἴλαθ' ἄναξ ἴληθι.

γυναιμανές: of Dionysus Nonnus xvi. 229, 252; so θηλυμανής ib. xvii. 184, xxxvi. 469, χοροιμανής h. Orph. lii. 7; εὔιον ὀρσιγύ-

ναικα μαινομέναις Διόνυσον ἀνθέοντα τιμαῖς ἀνακαλοῦσιν poet. ap. Plut. *mor.* 607 c, 671 c.

18. For the syllable lengthened by position see on *Dem.* 269. For the formula cf. Hes. *Theog.* 48 *ἀρχόμεναί θ' ὑμνεῦσι θεὰς λήγουσαί τ' ᾠδῆς* (codd. *ἀοιδῆς*), *fr.* 192. 4 *ἀρχομενοι δὲ Λίνον καὶ λήγοντες καλέουσιν*, Theognis 1, 2 where *ἀναπαυόμενοι* = *λήγοντες*, Theocr. xvii. 1, Hes. *OD.* 368 *ἀρχομένου δὲ πίθου καὶ λήγοντος κορέσασθαι*, Polybius xxxii. 10. 3 *ἄρχομαι τ' ἀπ' ἐκείνου καὶ λήγω πάλιν εἰς ἐκεῖνον*, Nicom. excerpt. c. 2 (p. 269 Jan) *ἀρχομένου καὶ καταλήγοντος* al.

19. M's *ἐπιλαθόμενοι* points to the dative *ἐπιληθομένῳ* or -*οις*. The same error is clearly found in Ψ767 *νίκης ἱεμένῳ*, where many manuscripts have *ἱέμενοι*. The permutation *οι* = *ωι* is recognized by the scholiast on Eur. *Phoen.* 682 (who refers it to the Euclidean change of alphabet): there the manuscripts read *σοί νιν ἔκγονοι*, which the scholiast corrects to *σῷ νιν ἐκγόνῳ*. For another case cf. Ar. *Rhet.* 1405 a 13, and for the variation in inscriptions Meisterhans 3–24 n., 128.

For the construction cf. E253, Z529 (*ἐλάσασιν* G), O58, Φ185 where the variant is ancient (*κατὰ δοτικὴν αἱ Ἀριστάρχου* with most manuscripts), X110 (*αὐτῷ* most manuscripts), Eur. *Or.* 779, 1657, Herod. i. 19, vi. 103. Ruhnken took the accusative from vii. 59 *σεῖό γε ληθόμενον*.

20. **Διώνυσ'**. On this form (*κατ' ἔκτασιν*) see *EM.* 280. 6 (Herodian).

21. **Θυώνην**. The name is apparently to be connected with *θύειν*, *Θυιάδες* and the festival Thyia. *Θυιάς* appears as a Maenad name, and possibly Thyone was the eponymous heroine of the Thyiades. In some authorities (Panyasis *fr.* 5) Thyone is a nurse of Dionysus. In Euripides *Antig. fr.* 177 *Θυώνη* mother of Dionysus is equated with *Διώνη*; in late authorities only Semele and Dione are identified (Hesych. f. 355. 3 Schmidt *Βάγχου Διώνης· οἱ μὲν βαγχευτρίας Σεμέλης· οἱ δὲ Βάγχου τοῦ Διονύσου καὶ Ἀφροδίτης τῆς Διώνης*). In Sappho (28. 10 Diehl) and in Philodamus' paeans (quoted on v. 5) Thyone is the mother of Dionysus. The turn of phrase here recalls the alternative divine and human names of persons and things in Homer (A 403, B 813, Ξ 291, Υ 74,

κ305, μ61), and the allusion is possibly to the theory that Semele received the alternative name of Thyone upon apotheosis (Apollod. iii. 38, Diod. iv. 25, Charax 103 *fr.* 14, Plut. *mor.* 506, Hygin. *fab.* 251). The Orphics reversed the order; Thyone, an ancient name of Ge, was afterwards called Semele (Diod. iii, 62). The apotheosis of Semele occurs not only in Pindar (*Pyth.* xi. 1, *Ol.* ii. 25), but as early as Hesiod (*Theog.* 942). There were two versions of this occasion; (*a*) apotheosis took place immediately after and perhaps as a consequence of the blasting of Semele by the bolt of Zeus, (*b*) it took place as the result of the action of Dionysus, who descended to the lower world and brought his mother up.

In Rhodes Dionysus was worshipped as Thyonidas (Hesych. in v.); by Latin poets he is called Thyoneus (Ovid. *Met.* vi. 13, Horace *Od.* i. 17. 23, Statius *Theb.* v. 265), and by Oppian (*Cyn.* iv. 285) Thyonaios. See further P.-R. 661, Roscher v. 926 sq.

II

Hymn to Demeter

The myth in literature. The rape and return of Persephone is a frequent theme in classical literature. Homer does not know it (though a *v.l.* on the authority of Agallis or Anagallis ap. ꟅTΣ 483 would put Eleusinian Demeter into Σ 551[a]); we find it first in Hesiod *Theog.* 913, 4. The same author *fr.* 107 mentions a hero Cychrides who received Demeter at Eleusis. Pamphos' hymn is several times mentioned by Pausanias (see Introduction, p. lxxxiv, and on vv. 8, 99, 101); it seems to have been essentially similar to the Homeric hymn, though different in detail, owing no doubt to Athenian influence. Archilochus (Ἰοβάκχοι *fr.* 120), Lasus (*fr.* 1, quoted from Heraclides Ponticus by Athen. 455 C, 624 E ἐν τῷ εἰς τὴν Ἑρμιόνι Δήμητρα ὕμνῳ), Pindar (*fr.* 12 ap. Paus. ix. 23. 2), Panyasis (*frr.* 16, 24), Sophocles (in the *Triptolemus* Nauck p. 28, Pearson ii. 239 with notes), Eumolpus (ἐποποιὸς τῶν πρὸ Ὁμήρου Suid., *in v.*), treated it. Euripides (*Helena* 1301–68) tells the story in a choral song, Carcinus (ap. Diod. v. 5, Nauck p. 620) has left ten lines on it. At Alexandria we find Callimachus' sixth ode,

Nicander *Theriaca* 483–7 (and Σ on 484); later Nonnus vi. 1–168, the Orphic *Argonautica* 1197–1201, and the choriambic hymn of Philicus lately published by Körte, *Hermes* 1931, 445, Gallavotti, *Stud. ital. di fil.* ix. 37. It was popular with the Roman poets: Ovid has two complete accounts, *Fasti* iv. 419–616, *Metamorph.* v. 385–661,[1] Statius *Achill.* ii. 149–51 alludes to the story, Claudian has a whole epic, *de raptu Proserpinae.*

In prose we have a detail of Triptolemus' genealogy in Pherecydes *fr.* 12, a full account in Diodorus v. 3–5 (perhaps from Timaeus), Σ Eur. *Orestes* 964, Nicander *Alex.* 130; later in Hyginus *fabb.* 146, 147, Clement of Alexandria *protr.* ii. 20 (whence Arnobius v. 24), Firmicus Maternus i. 7, Servius on Virg. *Georg.* i. 19 and 163, Lact. Plac. on Ovid *Met.* v. 6. 7, 8.

Local versions besides that of Lasus (quoted above, and in Aristophanes, *Babylonians* fr. 87) are recorded at Argos (Paus. i. 14.2, ii. 14 sqq.), Megara (i. 43.2), Sicyon (ii. 5.8). There is an 'Athenian hymn' in Nonnus xix. 70. There was an elegiac hymn at Paros (I.G. xii. 1229). The ritual hymn was called ἴουλος, Semus ap. Ath. 618 E οὔλους καὶ ἰούλους· δημήτρουλοι καὶ καλλίουλοι, al.

Influence of the Hymn. Extant literature shows little or no trace of imitation of the hymn. Callimachus may have known it, but there is practically no evidence to be extracted from his poem (see on 49 sq.), and he differs from Homer in some particulars (see on 200). Apollonius of Rhodes may have adapted the episode of Demophon (237 sq.) to his account of the childhood of Achilles, but there is nothing in the passage (iv. 869 sq.) which may not be independent. Apollodorus however must have been acquainted with the hymn, as his account of the myth (i. 5) is identical in its main outlines. He disagrees in some details: e.g. Demeter discovers the name of the ravisher from the men of Hermione, not from Helios; Demophon is consumed by the fire; the mission of Triptolemus is narrated. Apollodorus gives Panyasis and Pherecydes as authorities for the genealogy of

[1] On which and their Alexandrian original, see Malten *Hermes*, 1910, 506 sq., and generally Förster *Der Raub und die Rückkehr der Persephone*, 1874.

Triptolemus; he must therefore at least have collated their accounts with the Homeric hymn, and have produced a composite version of the story. Actual citations of the hymn appear in the Orphic papyrus, Philodemus (see on 440) and Pausanias (i. 38. 2 ssq., ii. 14.2, iv. 30.3).

The papyrus alluded to was published in 1907 in the *Berliner Klassikertexte* v. 1 by Schubart and Bücheler. It is no. 44 in the Berlin collection and is ascribed to the first century before Christ by Schubart and Wilcken, to the second by Diels. It was excerpted by Diels, *Fragmente der Vorsokratiker*[3] 173, and reprinted with commentary by Kern, *Orphicorum fragmenta* 1922 119 sqq. It is a very remarkable document for the history of the Orphic rite and creed, and has been treated by Malten, *ARW.* 1909 xii 426 sqq.; but as regards the Homeric hymn, it shows principally that poems of the Homeric corpus were appropriated at this period by the Orphics. The extracts are ascribed to Orpheus (col. ii. 31) and Musaeus (col. iii. 63), and presumably were in the case of the remaining two (vi. 92, vii. 102). This is nothing new; the Iliad and Odyssey were adapted for magical purposes; see Julius Africanus *Ox. pap.* 402, and the magical papyrus Mus. Brit. 121. The passages quoted as from Orpheus or Musaeus show several variants from the text of the hymn given in M, but they do not amount to a new version. There is no reason at all to hold with Diels *l.c.* that the verses have anything to do with those composed 'for the Lycomidae' by Pamphos and 'Orpheus', especially as at v. 108 the passage quoted by Pausanias from Pamphos disagrees with the papyrus. The variants are dealt with at the lines where they occur.

Language. In language the hymn to Demeter resembles that to Aphrodite more closely than any other in the collection (see Comm. on *h. Aphr.*). The author wrote in or after the Hesiodic period: Francke p. 11 collects a large number of words and forms in the hymn which are wanting in Homer but occur in Hesiod. The passages containing the names of the Oceanides coincides with the *Theogony* (see on 417). Forms such as ὄχοισιν, θυσίαισιν, κόρη and words such as ἀδικεῖν, τηρεῖν can only be called post-

Homeric and do not prejudice the age of the hymn.[1] For the evidence of the digamma see p. xcvii.

Integrity of the hymn. A summary of the attempts to disintegrate the hymn (by Matthiae, Preller, Hermann, Wegener, and Bücheler) was given by Gemoll p. 278. A later attempt by Puntoni (*L'Inno omerico a Demetra* 1896) need not be considered. It involved misapprehension of epic usage and even of Greek as a language (e.g. we were told that ἔπειτα v. 47 implied that Demeter made two journeys). The story moves in a simple and straightforward way from beginning to end, and all the episodes fall into their proper places.

Date of the hymn. The archaeological history of the site, now accessible in the admirable publication of Noack,[2] has an important bearing upon the date of the hymn. The precinct of Eleusis consists of an artificial terrace which was more than once enlarged as need required. The earliest terrace belongs to the geometrical period. Though Mycenaean objects and buildings have been found elsewhere at Eleusis, they are of a secular character, and none occur upon the terrace. There is no trace at Eleusis of a Mycenaean palace or of any building, other than the beehive tomb, which there is any reason to believe was sacred. The objects connected with the earliest terrace date its construction as not later than and not much before the eighth century B.C. (Noack pp. 11–15). The terrace formed a *temenos* encircled with a double wall, within which, but not in a separate building (for there is no trace of a contemporary *telesterion*) the mysteries were originally performed in the open air.[3] The first *telesterion*, which was many times enlarged and rebuilt, was probably constructed before the

[1] For fuller lists, see Gutsche *Quaest. de hymn. in Cer.* 1872, 19 sq., Francke *l.c.* 10 sq.

[2] F. Noack *Eleusis, die baugeschichtliche Entwicklung des Heiligtums*, 1927. For criticisms of some of Noack's conclusions see L. Deubner *Attische Feste* 1932, 87 sqq.

[3] Noack suggests that it resembled the *temene* described by Pausanias v. 13. 1, viii. 37. 10, and that the obscure statement of Diod. v. 77 (κατὰ τὴν Κρήτην ἐν Κνωσῷ νόμιμον ἐξ ἀρχαίων εἶναι φανερῶς τὰς τελετὰς ταύτας πᾶσι παραδίδοσθαι) may be explained by a survival in Crete of a similar performance of mysteries *sub divo*.

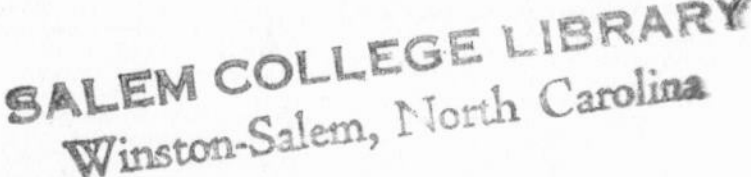

archonship of Solon, for though its general features are those of a building of the late seventh or early sixth century, its measurements appear to have been calculated in Aeginetan not Solonian feet. The change of religious policy implied in the building of a *telesterion* Noack connects with the conquest of Eleusis by Athens. This event he associates with the capture of Salamis, which he dates to 610 B.C. The view he adopts is that the conquest of Eleusis was an incident in the wars with Megara, and occurred in the latter part of the seventh century.[1]

Now in the hymn there is no reference to a *telesterion*, and it is clear that the temple erected and inhabited by Demeter before the mysteries were instituted cannot be an early hall of initiation, which it resembled in neither shape nor position (see on v. 270). This together with the archaeological evidence suggests that the hymn was composed at a date between the construction of the first *temenos* in the eighth century and the building of the first *telesterion*, as a result of the establishment of Athenian control of the mysteries, not long before the beginning of the sixth century.

With this conclusion the internal evidence provided by the hymn is in substantial agreement. The poem contains no mention of Iacchus, whose prominence in the cult at the beginning of the fifth century is attested by a famous passage in Herodotus (viii. 65).[2]

[1] The date of the capture of Eleusis is a difficult matter of dispute. No view which postpones it to a date after Solon is worth consideration, but there are two defensible positions which are argued with violence. One maintains that it represents the last act in what the Athenians called the synoecism of Theseus, and therefore belongs to the period of late monarchy or early aristocracy; the other connects it with the Megarian wars of the seventh century. There is unfortunately no definite evidence upon which the matter can be decided. The most serious argument for the early date is that, since in historical times the *Basileus* was responsible for the Eleusinian cults, Athens must have controlled the mysteries before 681 B.C. (Cambridge Ancient History iii. 592). The argument is not conclusive. If the hymn preceded the conquest, it is more difficult to account for its composition in the eighth century than for the selection of the *Basileus* for these duties at the end of the seventh.

[2] The view that Iacchus first became prominent under the Pisistratean régime is probable. There is, of course, nothing Dionysiac or Orphic about the hymn, but even in historical times the degree of Dionysiac influence

It contains no reference at all to Athens or to Athenians.[1] It has no aetiological reference to any part of the proceedings which took place before the procession from Athens reached Eleusis, the only parts of the historical ritual about which we are relatively well informed. The local colour is markedly Eleusinian. The author knows the topography, and his human actors are all Eleusinian worthies. Triptolemus, who became of cardinal importance in Attic-Eleusinian legend, is here merely an Eleusinian prince. So is Eumolpus. Their brother Diocles bears a name of Megarian not Athenian associations (see on v. 153). To the Kerykes there is no reference. The natural interpretation of all these omissions, which cumulatively justify considerable reliance on the *argumentum ex silentio*, is that the hymn was written before the reorganization of the mysteries under Athenian influence.

Against this view there is only one argument based upon internal evidence which is of any weight. Farnell, who takes the view that the conquest of Eleusis occurred early in the history of Attica, presses very strongly the natural interpretation of vv. 480 sq., that at the date of the composition of the hymn the mysteries were open to all Greeks. Legend, particularly the stories of the initiation of Heracles and the Dioscuri, suggests that at one time participation in the mysteries was open only to Eleusinians. The change from Eleusinian to Panhellenic membership, it is argued, must be the result of a political change, i.e. of the conquest of Eleusis by Athens. On the other hand it is not quite certain, though it is perhaps the natural interpretation, that the phrase 'happy among mortal men is he' necessarily implies, what was certainly later the fact, unrestricted access of all Greeks to the mysteries. But even if this assumption is correct, it is again an assumption that the cause of the extension of the clientèle of the mysteries was the conquest of Eleusis by Athens.

upon the mysteries is habitually exaggerated. Neither Iacchus nor Dionysus had a temple, or priests, or a cult at Eleusis (Kern in P.-W. iv. 273). Foucart's alleged Dionysiac services at the greater mysteries are pure fantasy, resting upon no evidence whatever (Foucart, *Les Mystères*, p. 454 sq.).

[1] The emendation introducing the name in v. 268 is abandoned.

The nature of the evidence does not admit of certainty, but on the whole the archaeological and internal evidence turns the balance of probability in favour of the composition of the hymn before the Athenian conquest and in the latter half of the seventh century.[1] Linguistic evidence (see p. 110) is inconclusive, but does not in the least negative such a date.

The Goddesses of Eleusis. The cults and legends for which Eleusis is famous centre round three divine figures, a mother-Goddess Demeter, a daughter Persephone, and Hades, ruler of the underworld. Of these three Demeter is the most prominent; her daughter in fact but duplicates her functions, and the role of Hades is that of supplying the male partner necessary in a θεογαμία. Further it may be noted that of the names of these divinities Demeter only is used in cult. Persephoneia (the Homeric form), Persephone, Persephassa, etc. (for the various forms see Bloch in Roscher ii. 1287), and Hades or Aidoneus occur only in literature (the only known instance of a cult of Hades—in Elis—is noted by Pausanias vi. 25. 2 as being unique).

The name Δημήτηρ (P.-R. i. 747 n. 6, P.-W. iv. 2713, Roscher ii. 1285) has given rise to as certain a *Volksetymologie* as Διόνυσος (p. 100). As there διο- meant Zeus and the etymologer was left with -νυσος, so it was too much to expect that every Greek should not see μήτηρ in -μητηρ and be left with δη- on his hands. This gave him no trouble; δη = δα = γᾶ = γῆ was the equation, and the howls in Aeschylus ἄλευ ἆ δᾶ *P.V.* 589, οἶ αἶ δᾶ φεῦ *Eum.* 844, 876, ὀτοτοτοῖ ποποῖ δᾶ *Ag.* 1056, which had as much meaning as Hallelujah to a negro Christian, proved it. (Philo *de mundi opif.* p. 90 Pfeiffer τοῖς πρώτοις ἔδοξεν αὐτὴν Δήμητραν καλέσαι τὸ μητρὸς καὶ γῆς ὄνομα συνθεῖσιν.) In modern times δᾶπεδον = γήπεδον has been adduced in spite of the difference in quantity (the real etymo-

[1] Most scholars are in agreement with the view that the hymn is the work of the seventh century. Förster (p. 39) suggests the first half, Duncker (*Griech. Gesch.* iv. 14) the middle. So Francke (*de hymn. in Cer. compositione*, &c. 1881), following Voss (between Hesiod and Solon). The views of Baumeister, who dates the hymn to the period of the Pisistratids, and Fick (*BB.* xvi. 27), who places it between 540 and 504 B.C., may be confidently rejected.

logy acc. to Boisacq is δμπεδον 'au sol de la maison'). The word treated as Greek suggests δῆμος or δημός or the root δαμ- 'overcome', and the Aeolic δωμάτηρ takes us to δῶμα, δόμος (Fick-Bechtel, *Personennamen*, 439). Cf. Hesych. Δαματρίζειν· τὸ συνάγειν τὸν δημητρειακὸν καρπὸν Κύπριοι. The coincidence of the Cyprian king 'Δμήτορι Ἰασίδῃ' ρ 443 with D(o)mater and her lover Ἰασίων ε 125 is suggestive (Iasion was a Cretan, Σ *ad l.*). But δαμητηρ or γαμητηρ is not a Greek compound, unless Γάδειρα means 'neck of land' (τῆς γῆς δειρά Steph. Byz.). There are other expedients; δη- is no longer γᾶ, γῆ, but a Kosewort, like μᾶ 'Mütterchen' (Kretschmer, *Wiener Studien*, xxiv. 525). In the Anglo-Saxon tongues δᾶ (reduplicated) is appropriated to the male parent. Bᾶς (father) has parallels in Afrikaans.

If the unknown language from which Demeter came were Indo-European, the last two syllables may really have meant 'mother', but in Greek the word is as foreign and meaningless as Κυβέλη or Σεμέλη.

Demeter is a Goddess of corn, a power upon whose favour plenty or dearth depends, a Goddess of the underworld and of fertility, a divinity of death and life. The view adopted from Jevons and Frazer (*G.B.* vii. 41 sq.) in the first edition of this work that Demeter and Core were personifications of corn-fetishes, the one representing the sheaf and the other the ear, is certainly based on too narrow a conception of the content of such types of agricultural religion.[1] In its practical application it further lacks the support of any definite evidence (see Farnell iii. 35 sq.). On the whole the most probable explanation of the genesis of Demeter is the view put forward by Farnell (ib. 30 sq.) that the Goddess is a specialized form of Ge, with whom she has a considerable number of cult titles in common. The quite early confusion of Demeter with Rhea-Cybele (see Farnell p. 31) not only supports this view, but also confirms the possibility that the Greek worship of Demeter might readily be assimilated to that of the pre-Hellenic Goddess of fertility and the underworld, who is certainly connected with the Asiatic and Cretan Mother-Goddess of historical times.

The idea that the cycle of birth and death, the annual decay of

[1] The totemistic hypothesis which was fashionable at the time has also been completely exploded by the knowledge since accumulated. There is no evidence of the existence of a totemic system in Greece.

winter, and the resurrection of spring depend for their recurrence upon the union of a male and female divinity of the underworld is not all uncommon among primitive peoples. There are good grounds for believing that it played a prominent part in the religion of Minoan Crete, where, in view of the subordinate role of Hades Plutus, it may be noted that the male partner in the union was obviously of secondary importance. In Greek mythology this idea took the form which is given in the hymn. Here, it is true, we have two Goddesses not one; not Demeter but her daughter is the bride of Hades. For all that the myth seems to be but an elaboration, a beautiful improvement, of the simpler idea of the wedded pair. If Demeter is to be regarded as a differentiated form of Earth, the Maid in turn seems to be a specialized form of Demeter. Core has no functions different and distinct from those of Demeter, and though independent cults of Demeter without Core are frequent, those of Core without her Mother are extremely rare (Farnell 115 sq.).

How early the myth took its characteristically Greek form we cannot say. The silence of Homer, though it is remarkable that he nowhere gives a hint that there is any connexion between Demeter and Persephone, cannot certainly be interpreted as ignorance of the myth, nor can the fact that Hesiod's farmer before ploughing prayed to Zeus Chthonios and Demeter Hagne (*OD.* 463) be taken to prove that in an earlier version Demeter, not her daughter, was the bride of Hades. For Hesiod knew that Persephone was the daughter of Zeus and Demeter, and that Hades carried her off with the cognizance of Zeus (*Theog.* 912)[1].

The religious idea from which this beautiful story sprang has in many parts of the world given rise to ceremonies the general

[1] In Homeric epos Demeter plays no very important part. 'Flowery Pyrasos' is called her *temenos* in the Catalogue (B 695), and the Cretan story of her lying with Iasion in the thrice-ploughed fallow field is mentioned ε 125 (cf. Hesiod, *Theog.* 909). The stock phrase Δημητέρος ἀκτή, common in Hesiod (*OD.* 33, 466, 597, 805, *Scut.* 290) occurs also in the *Iliad* (N 322, Φ 76). Persephone in Homer is the queen of the underworld (I 457, 569, κ 491). She is named the daughter of Zeus (λ 217), but nowhere is there an allusion to her maternal origin. Demeter is catalogued among the mortal loves of Zeus Ξ 326.

character of which the works of Mannhardt and Frazer have made familiar. Their object was to celebrate and thereby ensure the rebirth of vegetation in spring and the continuity of animal and human life. The type of ritual is mimetic. It aims, that is to say, by an emphatic imitation of the desired effect at securing its causation. Thus, for example, to ensure the return of heat to ripen the crops, primitive man will make a fire, or run over the fields with a lighted torch (see on v. 48). Ritual and Myth—which is essentially the explanation of the action (δρώμενα) of Ritual—inevitably react upon each other.[1] A more elaborate or sophisticated form of the simple imitative rite thus arises in the recitation or mimetic representation of a sacred narrative, which religious speculation upon the origin of things has supplied, of how the desired result was brought about in the first instance by the actions of divine or superhuman personages. By their impersonation in the ritual the added efficacy of their divine co-operation is secured.[2]

To this type of ritual drama the subject-matter of the Hymn belongs. In Greek cult it was for obvious reasons particularly frequent in the worship of Demeter, and not only at the mysteries but at most of her major festivals some representation of the rape of the Maid, the Mother's anxious search, and the final promise of the annual return of Core from the lower world was enacted (see below, p. 122).

Now in their more primitive and original forms the object of such ceremonies as we are discussing is communal, to ensure the continuity of life and the fertility both of the human members of

[1] It is a mistake to suppose that myth is purely passive. If it arises as an explanation of why certain ritual acts are performed, the form which that explanation takes has frequently an important influence upon the further development of the rite, as well as upon the content of the conception of the divinity concerned. On this see Rose, *Modern Method in Classical Mythology*, St. Andrews 1930, 1 sq.

[2] Exactly analogous is the familiar 'narrative spell' in magic. Thus, for example, the patient may rid himself of headache by reciting the story of how Jesus once met Headache and banished him into the depths of the sea. See Halliday, *Folklore Studies*, p. 89. Some good examples will be found in Kittredge, *Witchcraft in Old and New England*, pp. 32, 40, and notes.

the community, and of the beasts and plants upon which they are dependent for their subsistence. This remained the object of such rites as those of the *Thesmophoria*. It is not uncommon, however, at a relatively advanced stage of religious development for the analogy of such ceremonies to be applied to the individual, and to be interpreted in terms of hope of a life after death. That the flowers must wither and man die (Z 146, Mimnermus *fr.* 2, Soph. *fr.* 593, Moschus iii. 99) is a reflection common to the human race, but the annual ceremony to ensure that the flowers shall again blossom suggests that for man too death may not be the end of all. He too may come to life again if the necessary religious or magical rites have been performed. Here obviously is an idea of the profoundest spiritual importance, which is capable of development from the notion that ritual participation will magically secure continued existence after death to the conception of the attainment of blessed immortality by ethical and spiritual endeavour. In the cult of Demeter this idea was discovered and developed in the specialized form of worship known as the Eleusinian Mysteries. At the date at which the hymn was composed a relatively advanced stage had been reached. Participation in the holy rites, which, if the usual interpretation is accepted, are no longer confined to the members of the Eleusinian community, is believed to secure for the individual a happiness in the world beyond the grave denied to the uninitiated (vv. 480 sq.)

The Hymn and the Mysteries. Great as is the poetical value of the Hymn, perhaps its chief interest lies in the fact that it is the most ancient document bearing on the Eleusinian mysteries, the foundation of which is ordained in v. 273 and carried out in vv. 473 sqq. Of the actual details of this, the most famous religious ceremony of antiquity, very little is known. About the preliminary proceedings up to the moment of the arrival of the procession of worshippers from Athens at Eleusis we are fairly well informed, but as to what took place at the great service in the *telesterion* we are almost completely in the dark. We are in fact dependent upon conjecture which has no securer foundation than a very few obscure allusions in classical writers, and the equally obscure recriminations which occur in the polemic of Christian Fathers.[1] This latter source is the more uncertain because of its inevitable bias, and the not infrequent doubt as to the reliability of the Christian writer's source of information.[2] The archaeological evidence is of the greatest importance, but its value is mainly negative.

The reason for this lack of information is not obscure. A mystery, a form of worship which in cults of purely Greek origin was restricted to deities connected with the underworld (see on v. 478), consisted of secret rites, the details of which might not be revealed to the uninitiated. Before the great service in the *telesterion* the *hierokeryx* pronounced an injunction of silence (Sopater in Walz, *Rhet. gr.* viii. 118, p. 24 sq.). This prohibition was religiously observed throughout classical antiquity, and, as is shown by the famous incident of Alcibiades, any disregard of it aroused the greatest popular horror and resentment.[3] To this rule of secrecy the writer of the hymn has himself borne witness: σεμνά, τά τ' οὔ πως ἔστι παρεξίμεν οὔτε πυθέσθαι | οὔτ' ἀχέειν. Has he disregarded his own ordinance at least to the extent of referring in his narrative to the reasons for the performance of rites which formed part of the mysteries?

[1] The principal passages throwing light on the ritual of the mysteries at Eleusis are (*a*) classical: Apuleius *Met.* vi. 1, Athenaeus 478c, Proclus *in Tim.* 293; (*b*) patristic: Clem. Alex. *protrept.* ii. 12 sq., Origen *adv. haer.* Migne vi. 3150, Hippolytus *ref. omn. haer.* v. 8. 164, Asterius *hom. in SS. Martyres* Migne xl. 324B, Epiphanius *adv. haer.* iv. 2. 10, Synesius *in Dion.* 52c, Tertullian *ad nat.* ii. 30, Lactantius *div. inst. epit.* 23, Tatian *in Graec.* 8, Gregory Nazianz. *or.* xxxix. 4 (Migne xxxvi. 337).

[2] Thus many scholars attach the greatest importance to the passage in Hippolytus, and regard the announcement of the birth of a divine son and the adoration of an ear of corn as the culminating act of the *epopteia*; others, in view of Hippolytus' gnostic source and suspicious similarities to the known doctrine of the mysteries of Attis, are of opinion that the passage has no evidential value for Eleusinian ritual. See Farnell pp. 177, 183, Halliday, *Pagan Background of Early Christianity*, p. 244, n. 2.

[3] It is for this reason that attempts to interpret scenes upon vase-paintings in terms of the celebration of the inner mysteries are a waste of time and ingenuity. It is inconceivable that any part of the service subsequent to the initiation-preliminaries could have been made public in this way.

Disappointing as the verdict may be, it must be confessed that the only two certain references to the mysteries are the passages announcing their institution. To these we may add the incident of the *kykeon* (208), and possibly the fast (200), which may reasonably be supposed to refer to preliminary rites of initiation (see below, p. 135). The hymn is addressed to Demeter, whose Eleusinian cult contained a number of other festivals, in most of which the sacred drama of the Rape appears to have played a part;[1] to suppose that all references to ritual are necessarily applicable to the mysteries is to make the wish father to the thought.

The story of Demophon quite certainly has no reference to mystery-ritual, but to a domestic rite of infancy (see on v. 237). Of the remaining ritual references most might as well refer to the *Thesmophoria* as to the mysteries, and some are more probably to be assigned to the former than to the latter. The *Thesmophoria* also were mysteries, but two essential differences distinguish them from the Great Mysteries. In the first place the *Thesmophoria* had not emerged from the stage of communal agricultural magic; they had no significance for the individual, nor raised any hopes or fears about the life after death. In the second place, whereas men as well as women were initiated in the Eleusinian mysteries, and the higher officials in their conduct were male, in the *Thesmophoria* the rites were exclusively confined to women. The practice of αἰσχρολογία is common to the *Thesmophoria*, with which Apollodorus explicitly connects the story of Iambe, and to the mysteries; for though the passage in the hymn cannot well be connected with the γεφυρισμός during the procession from Athens, αἰσχρολογία was a feature of the rites of Boedromion 20 at Eleusis (see on v. 195). The carrying of torches, again, is common to the two festivals, though the Eleusinian torch-bearing was not performed by women only. The παννυχίς (v. 292), as is shown by the ignorance of Celeus about the events of the night, is clearly of women only, in this agreeing with the practice of the *Thesmophoria* and similar festivals, but

[1] For the drama as part of the ritual of the *Thesmophoria*, *Scirophoria*, and probably *Haloa*, see Farnell 40 sq., 46, 87.

not with that of the mysteries. There is no evidence that the *Balletys*, to which there is a reference in vv. 265 ff, formed part of the ritual of the mysteries,[1] though it has many analogies in ceremonies connected with festivals of the *Thesmophoria*-type in other parts of Greece. The drinking of the κυκεών (v. 208), however, may be definitely referred to the mysteries, though it belongs to the preliminary rites of initiation and not to the service in the *telesterion*.[2] For it forms one of the four items of Clement's σύνθημα (*protrept.* ii. 21. 2): ἐνήστευσα, ἔπιον τὸν κυκεῶνα, ἔλαβον ἐκ κίστης, ἐργασάμενος ἀπεθέμην εἰς κάλαθον καὶ ἐκ καλάθου εἰς κίστην. The first two items of this declaration may be referred to in the hymn, for although it is improbable that the nine days' fast (47) refers to the ritual of the mysteries, the fast of v. 200, if it is identical with that which Callimachus and Ovid show to have been endured from dawn to sunset, may very probably be assigned to this initiatory rite. The other two actions are not referred to in the hymn, but, except possibly for the detail of the *kalathos*, which may be an addition of Hellenistic[3] date, there is no reason why they should not have formed part of the ritual in the time of the hymn. What was taken from the *cista* and after ritual handling replaced must remain a matter of conjecture. It is doubtful whether Farnell, who adopts Lobeck's emendation ἐγγευσάμενος for the MS. ἐργασάμενος, is right in supposing the objects to be cakes. In view of the ideas in which the whole cult originated, the explanation that the mysterious object was a symbol connected

1 There is no evidence, but the hypothesis has been maintained by Usener *Kl. Schr.* iv. 438 = *ARW.* vii. 301, who is followed by Kern, *Die griechische Mysterien*, 62.

2 The view that the drinking of the *kykeon* was a sacramental act of communion which formed the culminating point of the ceremony has been maintained (e.g. by Diels, *N. Jahrbb.* 1922, i. 244, Rohde, *Psyche* i. 297, Dieterich, *Mithrasliturgie* 170), but cannot be accepted (see Noack p. 227, Farnell p. 195, and below on v. 208).

3 For the view that the *kalathos* is a Hellenistic addition, see Körtel, *Zu den eleusinischen Mysterien*, *ARW.* 1915, xviii. 116 sq. The *cista*, a round receptacle made of wicker, is frequently represented upon earlier monuments referring to the mysteries. See Noack p. 228, Frazer on Paus. viii. 25. 7, Daremberg et Saglio in *Cista mystica*.

with generation and birth is upon the whole more probable.[1] If this supposition is correct, the action is likely to have been a very early feature of the ritual.

All these were preliminary rites of initiation only. As to what took place at the all-night service, which only those who had previously been initiated might attend, we can only guess. That it included some kind of representation of the myth is fairly certain. That this can have been no elaborate theatrical drama is made certain by the architectural features of the *telesterion*, which further prove that in historical times all the action must have been performed by relatively few officials. There was certainly no wandering through chambers containing scenic dioramas of Heaven and Hell, as imagined by Foucart, but probably a succession of pantomimic dances which relied for their effect less upon theatrical illusion than upon crowd-psychology and religious emotion. The tension was doubtless heightened by the alternations of light and darkness as the torches were lighted and extinguished, culminating, perhaps, in some final scene in which the light of the new day was allowed to shine suddenly in through the *opaeon*. Among the matters represented was almost certainly a sacred marriage (see on v. 2). Those who trust the very doubtful authority of Hippolytus will add the announcement of a divine birth and the adoration of an ear of corn.

With regard to the mysteries in the seventh century B.C., what is it legitimate to conjecture? With the possible exception of the superfluous detail of the *kalathos*, there is no reason to reject any of Clement's rites of initiation as necessarily absent. For the rest the main difference will probably have been that the ritual was less systematized. Dances representing the sacred drama will have been enacted, but not on a square central platform open on the four sides in a roofed building packed with a motley crowd. A much smaller and more homogeneous congregation of Eleusinians, with at most a few outsiders, within the ampler space

[1] See Körte, *l.c.*, Dieterich, *Mithrasliturgie* 123, *Mutter Erde* 110, Kern, *Gr. Myst.* 10, Noack 227 sq. It is also upon the whole more probable that the symbol was not a *phallus* but feminine.

enclosed by the walls of the first *temenos* may themselves have played a more active part than the initiated of later days did in the ritual action. Here, probably, was the main difference, and in this, no doubt, the mysteries of the seventh century more nearly resembled other mysteries of Demeter like the *Thesmophoria*, though unlike the *Thesmophoria* they seem never to have been confined to women. This view is perhaps supported by the absence of any sacerdotal influence in the hymn. Even the founder of the Eumolpidae is but one of the Eleusinian princes, aud there is no magnification of the hereditary functionaries who in historical times evidently officiated on behalf of a congregation.

Origin of the Mysteries. The theories which attribute to the mysteries a Thracian origin (P. Gardner, *New Chapters in Greek History*, p. 384) rest solely upon a theory of ancient historians and geographers that Thracians had once occupied central Greece. In accordance with this speculation Eumolpus was said to be of Thracian descent. This learned invention of antiquity rests upon no evidence, and it finds no support in the hymn. It may therefore be dismissed together with its arbitrary elaboration by Ramsay (in the *Enc. Brit.* ed. 4) that the origin was Thraco-phrygian, and that the mysteries came from Asia Minor. Foucart's theory of an Egyptian origin has rightly found no support from any scholar of repute.[1]

More deserving of consideration is the view that the Eleusinian mysteries were a local survival from pre-Hellenic religion—Carian, Cretan, Minoan, Mycenaean or whatever particular label is employed.[2] For this there is a good measure of probability, though

[1] The theory rests upon improbable hypotheses, a misunderstanding of evidence, and a quite unwarrantable exaggeration of Dionysiac elements in the mysteries. These latter were wholly absent at the time of the *hymn*, and were never important. A detailed refutation of Foucart is given by Farnell.

[2] Persson, *Der Ursprung der eleusinischen Mysterien*, *ARW*. xxi. 287 sq., Malten, *Elysion und Rhadamanthys*, *Jahrb. des kais. deutsch. Arch. Inst.* 1913, xxviii. 35 sq., Nilsson, *Minoan Mycenaean Religion*, 539 sq., Evans, *Palace of Minos*, iii. 145 sq.

the evidence is less conclusive than is often supposed. Thus if Evans is right in his interpretation of the 'Ring of Nestor' it suggests no more than that some sort of initiation may have been thought to affect the welfare of Minoans in another world. There is nothing at all at Eleusis which furnishes any analogy to the griffin-headed figures in the ring. Again, the archaeological evidence proves that some of Persson's arguments are from false premisses,[1] and Demeter's fictitious account of herself in the hymn has no evidential value whatever (see on v. 123). But though the case for a pre-Hellenic origin of the mysteries is habitually overstated, the guess may none the less be right. The archaeological evidence, which proves that Eleusis was inhabited in Mycenaean times, but throws no light on the question whether it was or was not then a cult-centre, neither supports nor destroys the possibility.[2] The names of the human personages at Eleusis sound like Greek words,[3] but there is no intrinsic difficulty in supposing that Greek names may have been attached to figures already existing in a pre-Hellenic cult. The early assimilation of Demeter to Rhea-Cybele (see above, p. 115) supports the possibility of her identification with the Minoan Mother-Goddess.[4] The only eponym of a human official in the later cult to be

[1] Since there was no *telesterion* until the seventh century, the dissimilarity of its plan to that of a Greek temple does not prove it to be pre-Hellenic. A building of the seventh century cannot have derived its inspiration from a Minoan theatral area. The alleged Mycenaean palace at Eleusis does not exist.

[2] Some weight may perhaps be allowed to the similarity between the cult vessels called *κερνοί* which were used at Eleusis in historical times and certain similar objects which are fairly frequently found upon Bronze-age sites in Crete and the Cyclades. It should, however, be remembered that the supposition that the Bronze-age examples were used in cult rests solely upon their similarity in shape to the Eleusinian *κερνοί*.

[3] Iambe, and in the non-Homeric versions Baubo, must be excepted. Demeter, Persephone, and Hades are non-Greek names.

[4] Although Kern is unjustified in equating the Demeter of the Cadmea with Demeter Xiphephoros (see on v. 4), the very ancient cults of Demeter in the citadel at Thebes and at Megara do suggest that in these two places the name Demeter may have belonged to a pre-Hellenic citadel-goddess of the type discussed by Nilsson, *Die Anfänge der Göttin Athena*.

mentioned in the hymn is Eumolpus. This may be the name of an office rather than of a man (cf. Keryx), and even a Greek translation of the pre-Hellenic title 'sweet singer'. The name of the village Eleusis is best left untouched. To connect it with ἐλεύσομαι, 'arrival' (Kern, *Die gr. Myst.* p. 8), is worthy of Greeks[1]; to connect it with Eileithyia and Elysion (Malten *op.c.* 49 sq., Persson *op.c.* 294 sq., Jessen in P.-W. v. 2329, Nilsson *MMR.* 447, Bloch in Roscher ii. 1337) is a more surprising effort, and an *obscurum per obscurius*. Demeter was a nurse, but not a midwife. The archaeological evidence certainly indicates that the religion of the Bronze Age was rather specially connected with fertility and the underworld, and that its most prominent object of worship was a Mother-Goddess with whom a subordinate male partner was associated. There are also grounds for believing that the conception of the afterworld embodied in Menelaus' translation to Elysium (ε 561), which is completely inconsistent with the eschatology of the rest of the Iliad and Odyssey, is an inheritance from the religion of pre-Hellenic Crete (Nilsson *MMR.* 541 sq.).

No great reliance can be placed on the argument that the secrecy of mystery-ritual and the *voces mysticae* show that all mysteries belonged to the religion of a conquered people (Kern, *Gr. Myst.* 5, see on v. 478).

If we turn to the site, excavation has shown that the first terraced precinct was not in existence before the geometric period; but an undertaking so considerable for the eighth century as the creation of this walled artificial plateau must have been prompted by the popularity of a pre-existing cult which required more space for the performance of its ceremonial. The motive will have been the same as that which led in later times to the frequent rebuilding of the *telesterion*. The site of the original cult is thought by Noack to have been a cave behind the later Plutonium (*op.c.* p. 14, cf. Kern, *l.c.*).

In short, though the evidence does not justify dogmatism, the most probable theory seems to be that the origin of the mysteries lies in the Bronze Age, and that the name Demeter was that of

[1] Who did not fail to do so: see *EM. in v.*, which also offers κατέλυσεν.

the Goddess in whose honour they were celebrated by the pre-Hellenic inhabitants of Eleusis.

Place of composition. Many critics, since Voss, have attributed the hymn to an Attic writer. If by 'Attic' we mean 'Athenian' there is little to be said for the view. The absence of any Athenian in the story refutes the conjecture of Preller (adopted by Baumeister) that the hymn was composed for recitation at the Panathenaea, and supports the view (above, p. 112 n. 1) that it was written before the Athenian conquest of Eleusis. There is no question that the author is quite familiar with the topography and local legends of Eleusis, and in spite of various critics who have denied the conclusion, there is little doubt that the hymn is Eleusinian (Grote, *Hist. Greece*, II. i. 10, Förster *op.c.* 24). The sole argument to the contrary is the fact that the rape of Persephone, which in the hymn takes place at Nysa, was said by local tradition to have happened at Eleusis itself.[1] But this tradition is not mentioned before Phanodemus and Pausanias (see on v. 17), and may well have been, like other elements in Eleusinian legend (e.g. the story of Eubouleus), a late modification of the original version. When the Athenians became interested in the mysteries they localized the scene in Attica itself (Σ Soph. *OC.* 1590, P.-R. i. 759 n. 1), and this implies that there was no exclusive belief in a καταβασις at Eleusis.

Title. The title as it runs in M inspired Bücheler (ed. p. 3) with the singular idea that there was more than one hymn to Demeter. The same title appears before other hymns and should be read here τοῦ αὐτοῦ ὕμνοι. εἰς τὴν δήμητραν. The form δήμητραν occurs in the title of *h.* xiii in all MSS. except J. It is a variant in Hes. *Theog.* 454, Aristotle *Oecon.* ii. 21, Apollod. i. 4, Paus. ii. 14. 3, and required by the metre epigr. Paus. i. 37. 2 (Preger *inscr. gr. metr.* 202. 2), *orac.* Euseb. *PE.* v.34.

1. ἠύκομον: Archestr. *fr.* iv. 1 ἠυκόμοιο Δήμητρος.

[1] The suggestion of Maass, *Orpheus* 178, that the hymn belongs to North Greece has nothing to commend it; Fick (*BB.* ix. 201) thought that the author, if not an Athenian, was a Parian. The latter conjecture has no probability.

θεάν: for the synizesis cf. 179, xiii. 1 (M, the other MSS. *θεόν*), *orac.* ap. Euseb. *PE.* v. 14. 1 *ἠδὲ Κρόνον καὶ Ῥέαν ἠδ' ἐξείης Ἀφροδίτην*, epigr. Paus. v. 10. 4 (l. 1) *ναὸς μὲν φιάλαν χρυσέαν ἔχει*, *h.* iv. 82 *νεοθηλέαν* (M, *-έος* cet.), *ι* 283 *νέα*, Eur. *El.* 1270 *θεαί*, *Troad.* 969 *θεαῖσι*, *Rhesus* 85 *Αἰνέας*; *ἔαρος* often, K.-B. i. 227.

2. **τανύσφυρον** is quoted by Philodemus *voll. Herc.* vi. col. 7, 157. The rape of Persephone by Hades points to an original annual holy marriage between a God and Goddess of vegetation, instances of which are common in Greece and elsewhere, see Frazer *GB.* ii. 120, vii. 30, 65, viii. 9, Farnell iii. 123. Here as often the marriage is by capture. The presence of Hades suggests an early chthonian triad, Demeter, Core, and Zeus Chthonios (Hades, Pluto): see reff. in P.-W. iv. 2734. There are good grounds for supposing that a representation of a *ἱερὸς γάμος* formed part of the ceremonial of the mysteries (Farnell iii. 176). That this was followed by the announcement of the birth of a divine son, though accepted by many critics as the culminating event of the nocturnal service, rests solely on the doubtful authority of Hippolytus (see p. 119).

3. Hes. *Theog.* 913 *ἣν Ἀϊδωνεὺς | ἥρπασεν ἧς παρὰ μητρός· ἔδωκε δὲ μητίετα Ζεύς.* For the resemblance of Hesiod and the hymn see p. 110. Here, as in Hesiod, the connivance of Zeus at the rape is emphasized (cf. ll. 30, 77). In late versions of the story it is explained that Zeus could not help himself, being in the grip of Moira (Claudian i. 216, cf. *δαίμονος αἴσῃ* Orph. *Arg.* 1195), but according to Greek ideas the assent of Zeus the father was necessary for a legal marriage, and his connivance is therefore essential to the story (Rose, *Handbook*, p. 91). The version of Ovid *Met.* v. 346 (followed by Sil. Ital. xiv. 242 and late Latin mythographers), that the determination of Venus to make even Pluto feel her power was the cause of the rape, is romantic invention, perhaps following an Alexandrian model. It may, however, have some connexion with the Orphic association of Aphrodite with the rape. Aphrodite appears with Athena and Artemis in this context on the Amyclean throne (Paus. iii. 19. 4: see further Bloch in Roscher ii. 1314). **Δῶκεν . . . Ζεύς** is an hyperbaton.

4. **χρυσαόρου**: Hermann thought that the epithet could only have been chosen by an interpolator. Heyne and Boeckh, following a theory of ancient grammarians (Σ E 509, O 256), assumed that ἄορ like ὅπλον might be used of any implement. In this context the epithet was understood to refer to a golden sickle. Nothing is known of the unique cult of Demeter Ξιφηφόρος, in which apparently the cult statue held a sword, beyond its existence in Boeotia (Lycophron 512 with Tzetzes and scholia). Kern's identification of this Goddess with the very ancient Demeter of the Cadmeia at Thebes (P.-W. iv. 2749) rests upon a mistaken interpretation of Paus. ix. 16. 5 and a misunderstanding of Pindar, *Isthm.* vi. 3, where χαλκόκροτος quite certainly refers to the bronze instruments of Demeter Achaea (see Farnell, iii. 71 and ref. no. 7), and not to clashing weapons. The cult attested by Lycophron is without parallel and can hardly have influenced a conventional epithet. Possibly the title may suggest that the Goddess has won her land by the sword and protects her agricultural worshippers (so Kern in P.-W. iv. 2749 comparing Callim. *h. Dem.* 137 φέρβε καὶ εἰράναν, ἵν' ὃς ἄροσε τῆνος ἀμάσῃ); but in any case there is little or no fixity of divine attributes in early literature; the golden sword supplies an epithet to Artemis (*orac.* ap. Herod. viii. 77), Orpheus (Pindar *fr.* 187) and Zeus (Strabo 660, *CIG.* 2730, 2721), as well as to Apollo. See further on *h. Ap.* 395; for the nominative form χρυσάορος, *h. Ap.* 123.

5. Maidens were often carried off while picking flowers, e.g. Orithyia Choer. Sam. 5, Creusa Eur. *Ion* 887, Helen *Hel.* 242–8, the child *Hypsipyle fr.* 754; so the Sicilian version Plut. *aet. phys.* 917 F, P.-R. i. 758 n. 2. It may therefore have no mythological importance. It is, however, more probably to be connected with a ritual custom which may well be older than the legend (Farnell, ii. 124, Roscher ii. 1313). There is some evidence of the existence of a widespread custom of the ceremonial gathering of flowers in spring analogous to the modern Greek May festival of flower-gathering (for which see Frazer on Paus. ii. 22. 1). Ἡροσάνθεια (Hesychius *in v.*) or Ἡροάνθεα (Photius *in v.*) was a Peloponnesian festival of this kind. The practice may have

been connected with different Goddesses in different places. At Argos this may be the explanation of the cult title of Hera Antheia (Paus. ii. 22, 1, cf. *Et. Gud. in* Ἀνθεία, Pollux iv. 78): a similar title was borne by Aphrodite at Cnossus, and at the Carian Aphrodisias ἀνθηφόροι were among her temple officials (see P.-W. i. 2371). A similar flower gathering seems to be associated with Ge in *h.* xxx. 14. Such a festival would easily be connected with the story of the rape. Ἀνθεσφόρια in Sicily (Pollux i. 37) and a flower-gathering festival at Hipponium (Strabo 256) were counted feasts of Core. At Hermione women picked and wore crowns of κοσμοσάνδαλος, a kind of hyacinth (Paus. viii. 37. 4), in honour of Demeter Chthonia (Paus. ii. 35. 5). Artemis and Athena were represented as girls with baskets of flowers on their heads in the temple of Demeter and Core at Megalopolis (Paus. viii. 31. 1: see Hiller von Gaertringen in P.-W. i. 2371). The existence of the alleged *Anthesphoria* in the mysteries at Agra (Svoronos *J. Inst. Arch. Num.* iv. 1901, 235) rests only on a statement of Philostratus (*Her.* 314. 12) that it was an Athenian custom to crown boys of three years old with flowers in the month *Anthesterion*, but it is possible, though far from certain, that Clement's words τὰ ἀνθολόγια καὶ τὸν κάλαθον (*Protrept.* 17) refer to a rite of flower gathering practised at Eleusis in honour of Demeter and Core. The allusion in Σ Ar. *Ran.* 347 = Soph. *fr.* 891 is obscure but may be pertinent, ἄνθη ἀνειμένα τοῖς μύσταις ἐν τῷ πεδίῳ δηλοῖ Σοφοκλῆς.

6. **κρόκον**: cf. Σ Soph. *OC.* 684 κἂν τῇ Νιόβῃ ὁ Σοφοκλῆς τὸν κρόκον ἄντικρυς τῇ Δήμητρι ἀνατίθεται. According to Pearson (on Soph. *fr.* 451) there is no evidence elsewhere of a special connexion between the crocus and Demeter.

ἴα: see on 8.

7. **ἀγαλλίδας**: Hesych. ἀγαλλίς· ὑάκινθος ἢ θρυαλλὶς ἢ ἀναγαλλίς. According to Murr *Die Pflanzenwelt in d. griech. Myth.*, p. 246, it is an iris.

ὑάκινθον: for the hyacinth (*hyacinthus orientalis* Murr) in connexion with Demeter (Chthonia) see Paus. ii. 35. 5. Hyacinths are frequently mentioned among the flowers gathered by Proserpine, e.g. Ov. *Fast.* iv. 437, *Met.* v. 392. Here, however, it is perhaps introduced simply as a common spring flower, as in Ξ 348 κρόκον ἠδ' ὑάκινθον, and often in later poetry, e.g. Mosch. i 65 (a similar list of flowers in the rape of Europa), *h. Pan* 25.

8. **νάρκισσον**: see on 12 and 428. The narcissus was the peculiar flower of the Great Goddesses; cf. Soph. *OC.* 683 and Σ: Hesych. Δαμάτριον· ἄνθος ὅμοιον ναρκίσσῳ. The origin of the connexion is as uncertain as the supposed etymology (νάρκη). This may have been a later explanation; Boisacq remarks 'la plante est sédative'.[1] It was chthonian, being sacred to the Eumenides (Σ Soph. *l.c.* from Euphorion *fr.* 43 Düntzer). It was planted on graves (*Anth. Plan.* App. 120) and was funereal (Artem. *Onirocr.* i. 77). The narcissus was specially mentioned by Pamphos in his version of the rape; Paus. ix. 31. 9 κόρην τὴν Δήμητρος φησὶν ἁρπασθῆναι παίζουσαν καὶ ἄνθη συλλέγουσαν, ἁρπασθῆναι δὲ οὐκ ἴοις ἀπατηθεῖσαν ἀλλὰ ναρκίσσοις. Pausanias' allusion to ἴα refers to the common tradition, Arist. *Ausc. Mir.* 82, Diod. v. 3 (the Sicilian version), Plut. *Aet phys.* 23 = 917 B (the violet grows so thickly on Etna as to make sport impossible), Förster, p. 31. On the violet, which in later times had funereal associations, see Cook *JHS.* xx. 1 sq. In the hymn, however, the emphasis is on the narcissus, and the violet is only one among a number of flowers. Later poets generally include it in their description of the ἀνθολογία: Nicand. *Georg. fr.* 74. 60 ὑάκινθον ἰωνιάδας τε χαμηλὰς | ὀρφνοτέρας, ἃς στύξε μετ' ἄνθεσι Περσεφόνεια, Ovid *Met.* v. 392 *aut violas aut candida lilia carpsit*, Shakespeare *Winter's Tale* IV. iii. 116 *violets dim.*

ὃν φῦσε δόλον: Θ 494 ὄν ποτ' ἐς ἀκρόπολιν δόλον ἤγαγε.

καλυκώπιδι: this epithet not found in Homer; cf. 420, *h. Aphr.* 284, Orph. *h.* lxxxix. 2, καλυκοστεφάνου Ἀρτέμιδος Bacchyl. v. 98.

9. **πολυδέκτῃ**: so 17, 404, 430 πολυδέγμων. The idea of Hades as the 'host of many' is especially Aeschylean: cf. *Suppl.* 157 τὸν πολυξενώτατον Ζῆνα τῶν κεκμηκότων, *PV.* 152 Αἴδου τοῦ νεκροδέγμονος, *Theb.* 860 πανδόκον εἰς χέρσον. Cornutus 35 ἐπονομάζεται δὲ ἐπιθετικῶς καὶ πολυδέκτης καὶ πολυδέγμων καὶ πολύαρχος πολλούς τε δεχόμενος καὶ τῶν λεγομένων πλειόνων ἢ πολλῶν ἄρχων. For references with regard to these titles see Roscher iii. 2561 in *Pleiones.*

[1] Galen xvi. 143, xvii. 1. 479.

12. **τοῦ καί**: cf. A 249 *τοῦ καὶ ἀπὸ γλώσσης*.

ἑκατὸν κάρα: an exaggeration, but the writer was thinking of the *Narcissus tazzetta*, the 'polyanthus' or 'bunch' species, Murr, p. 248 (see on v. 428): cf. Virg. *Georg.* iv. 122 *comantem narcissum*, Soph. *OC.* 682 *καλλίβοτρυς*.

13. Tyrrell's correction is recommended by the fact that it only posits the omission of a syllable (*ζη*); for such omissions see p. xxiii, and *h. Apoll.* 407 (*πρῶτα* for *πρώτιστα* all MSS. but M). For the construction cf. ε 59, ι 210, *Anth. Pal.* vii. 218. 6: for the crasis of *καί* cf. B 238 *χἠμεῖς*, Z 260, N 734, γ 255 *καὐτός*, ζ 282 *καὐτή*, Xenophanes vi. 5 *καὐτοί*, *h. Dem.* 227, Hes. *fr.* 117. 3, Parmenides 51, Cercopes *fr.* 1 *καὐχένος κοὔ*, Hes. *Theog.* 284 *χὠ*, ib. 447 *κἀκ*, *h. Herm.* 173 *κἀγώ*: K.-B. i. 225, La Roche *HU.* i. 283 sq.

14. **ἐγέλασσε**: see on *h. Apoll.* 118.

15. **ἄμφω**: indeclinable, a use not found in early epic; cf. Ap. Rh. i. 165 (gen.), 1169 (dat.), Theocr. xvii. 26 (dat.).

16. **χάνε δὲ χθών**: according to the Eleusinian tradition the chariot disappeared through the opening ground (vase from Eleusis *Ath. Mitt.* xxi. pl. 12, *JHS.* xxii. 3). In some traditions Pluto vanished in a cave (Arist. *Ausc. Mir.* 82); at Enna he ascends through a cave and descends on to the open ground, Diod. v. 3. 4.

εὐράγυια: in Homer of towns only. The epithet is less suitable to *χθών*. G. compares *δίκα εὐρυάγυια* (Terpand. *fr.* 6).

17. **Νύσιον ἂμ πεδίον**: on the places called Nysa see i. 8. To write *Μύσιον* with Malten *ARW.* xii. 288 sq. (though a slight graphical change, Soph. *Aj.* 699 *μύσια νύσια*) is desperate, and his suggestion that the Eleusinian cult derived from the Argive is in itself unlikely. Which particular place the poet intended it is impossible to say. Förster (p. 266) argues for the Carian Nysa, P.-R. (758 n. 3) for the Thracian. Poets generally speak of Nysa as a mountain (Soph. *Ant.* 1130, *hymn* i. 8), but the locality is so uncertain that *πεδίον* may stand, cf. Ap. Rh. ii. 1214 *οὔρεα καὶ πεδίον Νυσήιον*. Hesiod does not localize the myth, but Σ *Theog.* 913 lays the scene by the ocean (hence the Orphic 'island behind Ierne' Orph. *Arg.* 1189, cf. Strabo 168). Various other places

are mentioned: Cyllene, Argos, Hermione (see on 75), Crete (Bacchylides *fr.* 64), Lerna (Paus. ii. 36. 7), Cyzicus (Propertius iv. 22. 4), Crenides = Philippi (Appian *Bell. civ.* iv. 105), Lesbos? (Demades ap. Σ Hes. *Theog.* 914 ἐν νάπαις), Eleusis itself (Phanodemus *fr.* 20, Paus. i. 38. 5, Orph. *h.* xviii, 5) and Attica (see ante, p. 126). See further P.-R. i. 759, Roscher ii. 1313, Förster *l.c.* In later times the Sicilian tradition prevailed (first in Carcinus, Nauck p. 620, cf. Mosch. iii. 128, Opp. *Hal.* iii. 489, Plut. quoted on v. 8, *Timoleon* 8), and often in Latin poetry (Ovid *Fast.* iv. 353, *Met.* v. 385, Lucan vi. 740, Stat. *Ach.* ii. 150, Claudian *de rapt. Pros.* ii. 71). Modern poets have chiefly followed the Romans: *That fair field Of Enna where Proserpine gathering flowers Herself a fairer flower by gloomy Dis Was gathered.*

ὄρουσεν ἄναξ: the trochaic caesura in the fourth foot is rare, except when the caesura is preceded by an enclitic or other monosyllable; see on 248. But the exceptions to the rule in Homer are sufficient to justify the text; see Monro *HG.* § 367. 2, Eberhard *Metr. Beob.* i. 23 sq.

18. πολυωνύμος: first in Hesiod and *h. Apoll.* 82. Preller thinks the epithet appropriate to Pluto, whose titles were numerous, see P.-R. 804, Rohde *Psyche* 192 sq. For the ἐπωνυμίαι of Pluto cf. Paus. ix. 23. 4 (on a hymn to Persephone by Pindar) ἐν τούτῳ τῷ ᾄσματι ἄλλαι τε ἐς τὸν Αἴδην εἰσὶν ἐπικλήσεις καὶ ὁ χρυσήνιος, δῆλα ὡς ἐπὶ τῆς Κόρης τῇ ἁρπαγῇ. On such accumulation of titles see Lobeck *Aglaoph.* i. 401, Gruppe *Culte u. Mythen* i. 553 n. 44, Adami 222 sq., Pfister *Bursians Jahresbericht 1931, Supplementband* 229 p. 200. This may be the right interpretation of the epithet here, but as applied to inanimate objects πολυώνυμος is simply 'famous'; cf. Hesiod *Theog.* 785 (ὕδωρ), Pind. *Pyth.* i. 17 (ἄντρον). That πολυώνυμος in this sense is appropriate is suggested by the very ancient worship of Hades under the euphemistic title Clymenus at Hermione (Farnell iii. 48 sq.), or such cult-titles as Periclymenus (Hesych.), or Εὔκλος and Εὐκλῆς on the Orphic gold tablets from Sybaris (cf. also Hesych. *in* Εὐκλῆς).

19. χρυσέοισιν: cf. Pindar's epithet χρυσήνιος in Paus. quoted above.

20. **ἰάχησε**: so xxviii. 11. Forms from ἰαχέω do not occur in early epic, but cf. xxvii. 7 ἰαχεῖ, Callim. *h. Del.* 146 ἰαχεῦσα.

21. **ὕπατον καὶ ἄριστον** = T 258 (nom.).

23. **ἐλαῖαι**: an early instance of the endowment of nature with hearing. Cf. Eur. *Hipp.* 1074 ὦ δώματ' εἴθε φθέγμα γηρύσαισθέ μοι | καὶ μαρτυρήσαιτ' εἰ κακὸς πέφυκ' ἀνήρ. From Γ 278 and Hesiod *Theog.* 963 downwards nature or things are given sense, especially, as is natural, in drama; Aesch. *PV.* 88, *Ag.* 37, Eur. *Ion* 94, 893, *Phoen.* 1344, *Troad.* 999, *Andr.* 924, *Alc.* 244, Soph. *Aj.* 862 sq., *Phil.* 936 sq., 1453, 1461, Ar. *Birds* 778, Theocr. vi. 74, Bion i. 31 τὰν Κύπριν αἰεὶ | ὤρεα πάντα λέγοντι καὶ αἱ δρύες αἰαῖ Ἄδωνιν, Moschus iii. init., Quintus i. 128, 296 καὶ οἱ συστοναχοῦσι ῥοαὶ πολυηχέος Ἑρμοῦ, Erephanis ap. Ath. 619 C (Clearchus *FHG.* ii. 321) μακραὶ δρύες ὦ Μενάλκα, often in Nonnus (v. 354, etc.). For Latin poetry where it is frequent see Forbiger on Virg. *Ecl.* i. 38, x. 13. In prose cf. Plato *Euthyd.* 303 D, *Phaedr.* 230 D, Lycurgus 150, the Carthaginian oath ἐναντίον ποταμῶν καὶ λειμώνων καὶ ὑδάτων Polyb. vii. 9. 2. In Eusebius *Hist. eccl.* ix. 12 pillars, markets, streets, earth, woods weep; cf. Himerius xx. 5. Olives are a background to every Mediterranean landscape. The flowers were growing among them.

Ignorance of these usages has produced remarkable conjectures.

24. **Περσαίου**: Hecate is daughter of the Titan Perses (= Persaeus here) and Asterie, acc. to Hesiod *Theog.* 411, cf. Apollodorus i. 2. 4, Ap. Rh. iii. 467, Orph. *h.* i. 4, *h. mag.* iii. (Abel, p. 289). Other poets give other genealogies, Σ Ap. Rh. iii. 467, Farnell ii. 502, P.-R. 322, Roscher i. 1899. Hecate is unknown to Homer. The earliest references to her are this passage and the curious panegyric in Hesiod *Theog.* 411–52, the tone of which suggests propaganda in favour of a cult not yet universally accepted. That the Goddess was a relatively late addition to the Greek pantheon from some foreign source is generally agreed, but opinion is divided as to whether she was originally Thracian (Farnell ii. 507) or Anatolian (Nilsson *GF.* 397).

ἀταλὰ φρονέουσα: the derivation of ἀταλός ἀτάλλειν is obscure (see Boisacq and Leismann *Glotta* xv. 163). In usage ἀτάλλειν is either active = τρέφειν, *alere* (e.g. *h. Herm.* 400 ἀτάλλετο for ἀτιτάλλετο), and hardly to be separated from ἀτιτάλλειν; or neuter 'to shelter', as in Hes. *OD.* 130 ἑκατὸν μὲν παῖς ἔτεα παρὰ μητέρι κεδνῇ | ἐτρέφετ' ἀτάλλων μέγα νήπιος ᾧ ἐνὶ οἴκῳ, cf. also Σ 567, λ 39, Hes. *Theog.* 989, Philostr. *Imag.* ii. 3 ἀτάλλει ὑπὸ ταῖς μητράσι. The Greeks took the adj. to mean 'young, soft', much like ἁπαλός. Hesych. Ἀζαλαί· νέαι καὶ ἁπαλαί. Ἀταλά· νήπια, ἁπαλά. Ἀταλοῖς· νηπίοις, ἁπαλοῖς. Ἴτυλος ... ἁπαλός. *IA.* iv. 1. 1 αταλωτατα παιζει of a merry childlike dance. Hence ἀταλὰ φρονέουσα seems to mean 'with kind intent', of Hecate as a nurse or κουροτρόφος.

25. **ἐξ ἄντρου**: cf. Ap. Rh. iii. 1213 κευθμῶν ἐξ ὑπάτων (cf. Hecate). No particular cave is meant. Whether Hecate was originally a moon-goddess or, as Farnell supposes, an earth-goddess, a cave would be appropriate for her home. In this hymn, at all events, she is a moon-goddess, as is shown by the mention of Helios in 26. So Sophocles *fr.* 480 associates Helios and Hecate as sun and moon. Hecate heard the cry, but did not see the rape as it was daytime and she was therefore in her cave; Helios heard (25) and of course saw also (see on 70).

29. **δέγμενος**: the form occurs *h.* iv. 477, B 794, I 191, υ 385, in most cases with an active sense, to which the accent points. It is a proper name Strabo 357. On I 191 there is a variant δέχμενος in 𝔖 A and one MS., and Herodian read δεδεχμένος Θ 296 (δέχμενος· προσδιαδεχόμενος Hesych.). This perhaps favours Cobet's conjecture. For the syncopation cf. ἄρχμενος Callim. *fr.* ix. 56. See Leaf on B 794.

35. **μητέρα** and **φῦλα** are objects, not (as Gemoll) subjects of ὄψεσθαι.

37. **ἔθελγε μέγαν νόον**: cf. M 255 θέλγε νόον. The lacuna is necessary; the change in sense between 37 and 38 and the absence of a protasis to δ' require at least another line. Moreover so important a detail as Persephone's cry (20, 432 ἐβόησα δ' ἄρ' ὄρθια φωνῇ) could not be omitted. See on 432.

38. **ὀρέων κορυφαί** = Alcman 65.

40. **χαίταις**: for the Attic dative cf. 205, 308, 441.

In general cf. the scene of the Mother of the Gods and her daughter, Eur. *Hel.* 1301.

42. **κυάνεον τε κάλυμμα** = Ω 93; see on 182.

43. ἐπὶ τραφερήν τε καὶ ὑγρήν = Ξ 308, υ 98, Oppian *Cyn.* i. 11.

46. οὔτ᾽ οἰωνῶν: the stress on οἰωνῶν is unusual, but G. compares ζώειν *h. Aphr.* 221 with the accent ⏑́ –. The emendations give a colourless verse. Eitrem sees here an allusion to other myths: a bird told Apollo about the faithlessness of Coronis, and a bird told Athene that the daughter of Cecrops had opened the box in which Erechtheus was shut; but here there was none.

47. ἐννῆμαρ: in the present passage this is probably conventional, to express a round number of days with no reference to the actual duration of the fast. A period of nine days or nights is common in Homer: A 53, Z 174, I 470, M 25, Ω 107, 610, 664, 784, η 253, ι 82, κ 28, μ 447, ξ 314; cf. Hes. *Theog.* 722, 724, *h. Apoll.* 91, Callim. *Dem.* 33. This conventional period may have been derived from ancient division of the lunar month into three periods of nine days (see Roscher *Die Enneadischen Fristen*, Abhandl. Sachs. Gesellsch. 1903, xxi. 14 sq.), but Hesiod's month was not of twenty-seven but of thirty days divided either into two periods of waxing and waning moons, or into three decades, a system perhaps connected with the Indo-European decimal system of numeration (see Nilsson *Die griech. Kalender* 30 sq., *Primitive Time-reckoning* 167 sq., Halliday *Folklore* xli. 43). Nine days was the general, though not universal, period of strict mourning after death (Halliday *Greek Questions of Plutarch*, 121 sq.), and of such piacular ceremonies as the extinction of the fire at Lemnos (Philostr. *Her.* xix. 14). The fast of Clytia (Ovid *Met.* iv. 262) is appropriately of nine days.

Roscher and others have supposed that our passage refers to a definite nine days' fast at Eleusis. The necessary period, however, cannot be fitted into the time-table of the festival; the fasting and torch-dances may have extended over the μυστηριώτιδες ἡμέραι, which, though their precise number is unknown, were certainly not as many as nine (see Mommsen *Feste* 230 n. 5). There is more to be said in favour of a nine days' fast at the *Thesmophoria*, with the ritual of which the wandering of Demeter with torches in her hand would equally agree (see on v. 48). The Sicilian *Thesmophoria* (Diod. v. 4, Plato *epist.* 349 D) perhaps consisted of nine days' fast followed by a tenth day's licence. In

Rome the *ieiunium Cereris* of October, which corresponds in date to the *Thesmophoria* of Athens, lasted nine days (Livy xxxvi. 37, Roscher i. 863). In Ovid *Met.* x. 431, the scene of which is laid in Cyprus, the women's fast lasted nine days. Whether, as some scholars allege, Ovid's statement is based upon Athenian practice must remain doubtful. The general fast of the women, as opposed to the special taboos observed by the ἀντλητρίαι, was certainly a prominent feature of the Athenian *Thesmophoria*, ἀλλ' ὡσπερεὶ Θεσμοφορίοις νηστεύομεν (Ar. *Av.* 1519); the last day but one was called νηστεία, and the last, *Kalligeneia*, was a day of rejoicing. Unfortunately the precise duration of the festival in historical times is uncertain. There is, however, pretty clear evidence that originally it was of three days only, and the longer duration may be due in Attica, and also possibly in Sicily, to the incorporation of other festivals (see Halliday *Greek Questions of Plutarch* 143). Nilsson's contention (*GF.* 321) that a nine days' fast can hardly have been a feature of the Attic *Thesmophoria* in their original form must therefore be allowed, though we cannot follow him in supposing the reference to be to the ritual of the Eleusinian mysteries. It will be safer to suppose that the number is purely conventional.

Δηώ: here first, for Δημήτηρ, then often in poetry. The form is usually regarded as hypocoristic, like Ἀφρώ, Εἰδώ, Ὑψώ *E. Gud.* 316. 30, an. Bekk. 857–9, Δωδώ for Δωδώνη Simmias ap. Strab. 364, though Herodian in *EM.* 263. 48 disapproved of this explanation. If Δημήτηρ is non-Greek, *a fortiori* Δηώ.

48. This may refer to that part of the ritual of the mysteries which in historical times immediately followed the arrival of Iacchus and the procession of worshippers on *Boedromion* 20, and consisted of nocturnal torch dances at the Callichoron (Eur. *Ion* 1074, Ar. *Ran.* 340: see further references in Mommsen *Feste* 230). *Tuque Actaea Ceres cursu cui semper anhelo votivam taciti quassamus lampada mystae* (Statius, *Silv.* iv. 8. 50). In this both men and women took part. In the corresponding ritual of *Thesmophoria* (whether Lactantius i. 21. 24 refers to the Mysteries or to *Thesmophoria* or to both is uncertain) the women alone marched ceremoniously over the land with torches (Ar. *Thesm.*

101, 1151). The origin of both rites is mimetic, and their object undoubtedly was to promote the fructifying warmth of the earth. With this may have been combined the notion of the purificatory potency of fire (see Diels *Sib. Blätter* 47 sq., where this aspect is wrongly exaggerated to the exclusion of the fertility-motive), and the intention will then have been both to promote fertility and to cleanse the fields from blight and other noxious influences (see Farnell iii. 103, Frazer *GB*. x. 329).

The idea of thus stimulating the warmth necessary for the crops by the use of fire in ritual appears elsewhere in the cult of Demeter and Core at Argos, where lighted torches were thrown into a pit (Paus. ii. 22. 4), and possibly in the maintenance of a perpetual fire, a practice rare in Greek cult (see Farnell 122 note), in the temple of Demeter and Core at Mantinea (Paus. viii. 9. 2).

Whether the reference in the hymn is to the practice of the *Thesmophoria* or to that of the Mysteries is uncertain. In favour of the former is the fact that only women took part in its ritual. But our problem is complicated because we do not know the form taken by the ritual at Eleusis at the date of the hymn, when there was no *telesterion*, no Iacchus, and no procession from Athens. It is quite possible that the whole ceremonial of the mysteries then more nearly resembled that of the *Thesmophoria* of historical times. In any case it is to agricultural ritual of the type indicated that this passage refers, and not to the prominent use of torch-light in the later service in the *telesterion*, which Sophocles has in mind (*OC*. 1050). Demeter herself holds a torch at Maenalus (Paus. vii. 37. 4), at Stiris (ib. x. 35. 10, Eunapius 90).

49–50. Compare the mourning of Demeter in Callim. *h. Dem.* 17 *αὐσταλέα ἄποτός τε καὶ οὐ φάγες οὐδ' ἐλοέσσω.*

50. **βάλλετο**: the editors quote Λ 536 and other passages where the act. *βάλλειν* has the meaning of 'sprinkle, wet'. No other instance occurs of the middle *βάλλεσθαι* in this sense. Should we read *βάλλε λοετροῖς* (*h. Herm.* 268)?

51. A formulaic line (only here) similar to Z 175 *ἀλλ' ὅτε δὴ δεκάτη ἐφάνη ῥοδοδάκτυλος Ἠώς*, Ω 785 (*φαεσίμβροτος*).

φαινολίς, Ruhnken's correction. Cf. Sappho vii. 1 Lobel ἔσπερε πάντα φέρων ὅσα φαίνολις ἐσκέδασ' αὔως, Moschus iv. 121 ἠὼς δὲ παραυτίκα φαινολὶς ἦλθε (acc. to 'D'), Hesych. φαινόλις· λαμπρά, φωσφόρος. Cf. μαινόλιν Aesch. *Suppl.* 115, Hesych. οἰφόλης and οἰφολίς.

52. **σέλας**: for a torch Ap. Rh. iii. 293, iv. 806. Here it is probably collective, 'torch-light', as the regular attribute of Hecate is a torch in either hand. So δάος = δαίδας in the formula δάος μετὰ χερσὶν ἔχουσαι Ω 647 al. For the attribute of Hecate see Roscher i. 1900, Hesych. Ὑπολάμπτειρα· Ἑκάτη ἐν Μιλήτῳ. Farnell ii. 549 thinks that the torch was originally the symbol of Hecate as a chthonian deity, not as the moon, with which, however, the hymn-writer plainly identified her (see on 25). For the connexion of Hecate with Demeter and Persephone see on 440.

53. **ἀγγελέουσα**: Hecate (or Artemis) was called ἄγγελος at Syracuse (Hesych. *in v.*, and Σ Theocr. ii. 12), but it is unlikely that there is here any allusion to this title.

The news which Hecate 'came to give' is that she heard Persephone's cry, which she thought she was alone in doing. Hence the future stands. Usage admits both future and present. The future is usual with verbs of motion δ 258, 532, 679, χ 434, 496, but we find the present ν 94, π 459, Eur. *Hel.* 1518, both ν 94, ξ 123, Eur. *Phoen.* 1075, *Bacch.* 658, *Andr.* 821, 1071, *Hec.* 187. The present seems usual in prose, e.g. Isocrates i. 33, Plato *Symp.* 175 A ἥκειν ἀγγέλλοντα, Polyb. ii. 63 ἐλθεῖν ἀγγέλλοντα, xxxiii. 12, S. John evang. 20. 18, Polyaenus i. 15 ἔπεμψαν ἀγγέλλοντα and 43, v. 33. 4 καθῆκεν ἀγγέλλοντα, vii. 4 καθῆκε λογοποιοὺς διαγγέλλοντας, viii. 41 ἔπεμψεν θεράπαιναν ἀπαγγέλλουσαν, Polyb. xv. 23. 2, Paus. iv. 12. 9. The tenses are equivalent in Tryphiodorus 212 δὴ τότε κηρύκων ἀπεσκίδνατο λαὸν ἀυτὴ | φεύγειν ἀγγελέουσα, 236 ἤλυθε φήμη | δήιον ἀγγέλλουσα φόβον σημάντορι καπνῷ; they are variants (besides the passages given above) in Musaeus *H. et L.* 105 πολλάκις ἱμερόεσσαν ἑὴν ἐπέκυψεν ὀπωπὴν | νεύμασι λαθριδίοισιν ἐπαγγέλλουσα (-λέουσα) Λεάνδρῳ, Nicander *Alex.* 577 πρῶτον ἀπαγγελέουσα (-έλλουσα) βοᾷ, Dio Prus. xxx. 2 ἀπαγγέλλων (-έλων). No doubt the double lambda assisted the variant.

The sense of pres. and fut. is therefore indistinguishable. It will hardly be believed that the hymn was at one time dislocated owing to the supposed impossibility of the future.

54. **ὡρηφόρε**: the hiatus is legitimate in the bucolic diaeresis, Monro *HG.* § 382 (2). On the epithet 'bringer of the seasons' see P.-R. i. 767, Mannhardt *Myth. Forsch.* 227, who compares *Anth. Pal.* xi. 98. 1 *Δηοῖ λικμαίῃ καὶ ἐναυλακοφοίτισιν Ὥραις.*

55. **θεῶν οὐρανίων**: not Homeric. The Orphic hymn reads *τίς θεὸς οὐράνιος ἠὲ θνητῶν ἀνθρώπων*, *fr.* 49. 102 (Kern). For *θεῶν* cf. *θεοῖσιν* ξ 251, *θεοί* A 18, *θεῶν* Hes. *Theog.* 44, below 259, *θεούς* 325.

57. **φωνῆς γὰρ ἤκουσ'**: the exx. of *γάρ* lengthened by ictus are mostly before *οἱ* or *εὖ*; B 342, Z 38, I 377, δ 826, etc. But in B 39, T 49 *γάρ* before a vowel appears to be established.

58. **ὅς τις ἔην**: parenthetical, cf. 119, *h.* v. 92, *ὅτις γε μέν* Timon ap. Diog. Laert. ii. 10. 107.

ὦκα λέγω νημερτέα: Hecate asseverates the truth of her news by a common formula; cf. 433, λ 137 *τὰ δέ τοι νημερτέα εἴρω*, 'I tell it thee truly'. *Ὦκα* is justified by the content 'and I tell it at once', cf. 171. Hecate spares Demeter disappointment by confessing her ignorance. As, however, the *ἀγγελία* takes the form of a question, the explanation given *JHS.* xvii. 52 (*λέγω σοὶ ὦκα εἶναι νημερτέα*) may be considered; cf. *ἀκριβέα πάντα Iliu Persis* v. 5.

62. **θεῶν σκοπὸν ἠδὲ καὶ ἀνδρῶν**: the idea that the sun sees everything is not uncommon among primitive peoples and frequently finds expression in folk-tales. In Greek poetry it often occurs (e.g. Γ 277, λ 109, μ 323, Soph. *OC.* 899, *Trach.* 101), and hence Helios is *πανόπτης* (Aesch. *PV.* 91, *fr.* 186), *ὁ πάντ' ἐποπτεύων* (Aesch. *Choeph.* 985) or *εὐρύοπα* (Orph. *Lith.* xviii. 58). As he here reveals the rape by Aidoneus, so in θ 271, 302 he discloses the adultery of Ares and Aphrodite. It is because nothing is hid from his eye that Helios is invoked in oaths (e.g. T 197, 258, Ap. Rh. iv. 1019), and as a witness to covenants (Γ 277), and thus acquires an ethical character as the guardian and enforcer of right dealing, e.g. Aesch. *Choeph.* 986, *PV.* 91, Soph. *Aj.* 857, Eur. *Med.* 1252, cf. Orph. *h.* viii. *πανδερκὲς ἔχων*

αἰώνιον ὄμμα (1), *κόσμου τὸ περίδρομον ὄμμα* (14), *πιστοφύλαξ* (17), *ὄμμα δικαιοσύνης* (18). See further Roscher i. 2019 sq.

63. **στὰν δ' ἵππω προπάροιθε** = Ω 286, ο 150.

64. **σύ περ** recurs 116, and Ludwich's conjecture is excellent on palaeographical grounds; cf. *h. Herm.* 308 *ἐνέχωνδὲ* M = *ἔνεχ' ὧδε*. The stroke to denote *ν* in *θεᾶ* (= *θεαν*) was neglected.

65. Pind. *Ol.* vii. 43 *θυμὸν ἰάναιεν*.

66. **κούρην τὴν ἔτεκον**: the antecedent is attracted to the case of the relative, as in K 416, Ξ 75, 371, Virg. *Aen.* i. 573.

67. **ἁδινήν**: the derivation and consequently the meaning are obscure (see Boisacq). The word is often used with verbs or substantives expressing grief, where it seems to mean 'loud' or 'vehement'.

δι' αἰθέρος ἀτρυγέτοιο = P 425. Elsewhere *ἀτρύγετος* is applied to the sea. The derivation and meaning are unknown.

70. **αἰθέρος ἐκ δίης** = Π 365.

καταδέρκεαι ἀκτίνεσσι: cf. *καταδέρκεται ἀκτ.* λ 16. M's *-εται* seems a scribe's error (K 82 *ἔρχεαι, -εται*, 115 *νεμεσήσεαι, -εται*) assisted by λ 16. *ὄπωπεν* followed naturally (*εἴ που ὄπωπας* = γ 93).

74. **Ὑπεριονίδης** without Ἥλιος Nicander *Ther.* 679: Ἠελίου Ὑπεριονίδαο μ 176, Hes. *Theog.* 1011; Ὑπερίων *h. Apoll.* 369.

75. Ovid, who follows the hymn in making Helios announce the rape in *Fasti* iv. 583, in *Met.* v. 504 credits Arethusa with giving Demeter the information. This is purely a literary invention. There were, however, versions which gave the merit of telling the Mother the news to other and human informants (the Gods perhaps were silent for fear of the wrath of Zeus, Claudian iii. 55). Thus the claim was made for the men of Pheneos (Conon 15 Jacoby i. 194), of Hermione (Apollod. i. 29, Σ Ar. *Eq.* 785, Zenobius *Cent.* i. 7; for the hell-gate at Hermione see Paus. ii. 35. 10, Strabo 373), or of Crete (Steph. *in* Πάρος). At Paros Kabarnos, ancestor of the priestly family of Kabarnoi, informed Demeter (Steph. *l.c.*). At Argos Chrysanthis daughter of Pelasgus gave the news, a version connected with the pretension that the Eleusinian cult had an Argive origin (Paus. i. 14. 2). Yet other versions made D. learn the truth at Eleusis from Celeus (Σ Aristid. *Panath.* 181 B, Σ Ar. *Eq.* 698, *Myth. Vat.* ii. 96), or

Triptolemus (Σ Aristid. *l.c.*, Paus. *l.c.*, Claudian iv. 52), or Eubuleus and Triptolemus (Musaeus ap. Paus. *l.c.* 3).

76. **μέγα ἅζομαι**: for the hiatus cf. Hes. *Theog.* 532 *ταῦτ' ἄρα ἀζόμενος*, and sim., Theognis 280 *μηδεμίαν κάτοπιν ἀζόμενοι νέμεσιν* (vulg., *κατόπισθ'* 'A'). On the initial *yod* sometimes assumed in this word see Boisacq in *Ἅγιος*.

77. **οὐδέ** is obviously right, as in the phrases *οὐδέ σε λήσει*, *οὐδέ τί σε χρή*.

79. **θαλερήν**: with *γόνος h. Aphr.* 104, *γάμος* ζ 66, υ 74, *h. Pan* 35; the 'blooming bride' of English ballads.

83. **ἄπλητον**: Simon. Amorg. vii. 34.

83. **οὔ τοι ἀεικὴς γαμβρός**: 363 *οὔ τοι ἐν ἀθανάτοισιν ἀεικὴς ἔσσομ' ἀκοίτης*, *h.* v. 136 *οὔ σφιν ἀεικελίη νυὸς ἔσσομαι*. Similarly Theognis 1344 *οὐ γὰρ ἐπ' αἰκελίῳ παιδὶ δαμεὶς ἐφάνην*, Ovid *Met.* v. 526 *neque erit nobis gener ille pudendus*. The usual expression for a good *parti* is *οὐ μεμπτός*: Paus. ii. 28 *γαμβρὸν οὐ μεμπτόν*, Phoenix 2. 10 *γένοιτο πάντ' ἄμεμπτος ἡ κούρη | κἀφνειὸν ἄνδρα κὠνομαστὸν ἐξεύροι*, Eur. *Phoen.* 425 *οὐ μεμπτὸς ἡμῖν ὁ γάμος*, *Ion* 1519 *τὸ γένος οὐδὲν μεμπτόν*, *Helena* 1424, *Antig. fr.* 168 *ὀνόματι μεμπτὸν τὸ νόθον*, Plut. *Cato* 24 *κηδεστὴν οὐ μεμπτόν*, often in late Greek (Ox. pap. 1083 *fr.* i. 19).

85. **ἀμφὶ δὲ τιμήν**: cf. for the acc. *h. Herm.* 57, vii. 1, xxii. 1, xxxiii. 1. Or is *ἀμφὶ . . . ἔλλαχεν in tmesi*? Hesych. *ἀμφιλήξαντες· ἀμφισβητήσαντες*, Hes. *OD.* 74 *ἀμφὶ δὲ τήν γε | Ὧραι καλλίκομοι στέφον*.

88–9. cf. Hes. *Scut.* 341. 2.

τανύπτεροι of course goes with *οἰωνοί*: Ibycus 10 *τανύπτερος ὡς ὄκα πορφυρίς*. Winged horses occur in Eur. *El.* 466 (G).

92. **νοσφισθεῖσα**: 'avoiding', as *h. Herm.* 562, *orac.* Hendess 119. 7 *νοσφισθεῖσα γέρα προτέρων τιμάς τε παλαιάς* (of Deo).

94. **ἀμαλδύνουσα**: 'wasting', so as to disguise. B. compares Ap. Rh. i. 834, iv. 112; add Bacchyl. xiii. 3 *συμφορὰ δ' ἐσθλὸν ἀμαλδύνει*. She made herself old.

96. **Κελεοῖο**: this is the usual tradition for the king's name; cf. Pamphos in Paus. i. 39. 1, Apollod. i. 5. 3, Σ Ar. *Eq.* 695, Roscher ii. 1026 sq. The Σ Nicand. *Alex.* 130 calls the king Hippothoon (the eponymous hero of the Attic tribe) and his wife

Metanira. For other accounts see Förster p. 12. There was a cult of Celeus and his daughters at Eleusis (Clem. Alex. *protr.* i. 39) and a shrine of Metanira (Paus. *l.c.*).

99. **Παρθενίῳ φρέατι**: for φρέατῐ cf. 101, 248, La Roche *HU.* i. 49, for the local dative Monro *HG.* § 145; it is not harsher than τραπέζῃ φ 35. See also on 308, *h. Aphr.* 173.

For φρέᾰτι cf. ὄνεαρ restored 269. φρέαρ occurs as φρείατα Φ 197 *metri causa*; ὄνειαρ ὀνείατα are exclusive to Homer. Attic comedians make the alpha in φρέατος long, equally to ease their metre. The writer here contrives to use the whole word in its radical form. Cf. στέαρ στέ͡ατος φ 178, 183, στέᾱτι Attic.

The 'Maiden well' is not mentioned again in the hymn; it is probably identical with the 'Flowery well' at which, according to Pamphos, Demeter sat: Paus. i. 39. 1 φρέαρ ἐστὶν Ἄνθιον καλούμενον. ἐποίησε δὲ Πάμφως ἐπὶ τούτῳ τῷ φρέατι καθῆσθαι Δήμητρα κτλ. Frazer *l.c.* thinks it may be the spring called *Vlika*, about a mile and a half west of Eleusis on the road to Megara. This well is not to be confused with the Callichoron, which was close to the precinct of Eleusis (see on 272), Alciphron iii. 69 ἀγαγοῦσα οὖν αὐτὸν ἡ γυνὴ εἰς τὸ Καλλίχορον τὸ ἐν Ἐλευσῖνι φρέαρ ἀπωμόσατο, although the fame of this latter led several ancient writers to identify it with the place where Demeter rested; cf. Callim. *Dem.* 16, Nicand. *Ther.* 486, Apollod. i. 5. 1. In Orph. *Arg.* 729 a river in Asia is called both Parthenius and Callichorus probably in view of this literary tradition. Yet another well was Φιλότης (Hesych. *in* Ἀλόπη). On other sacred sites see on 200. The last hemistich is a formula = η 131, ρ 206.

101. **γρηὶ παλαιγενέι ἐναλίγκιος**: the corn-spirit, in the form of the last sheaf, is often called 'the Old Woman', 'grandmother', etc. (see Frazer vii. 136 sq.), and it has been suggested that in γρηί we have a survival of the otherwise nameless corn-spirit (Jevons 367, 378 sq.). But it is difficult to believe that the Eleusinian Goddesses were nameless until so late a period, nor is there any evidence to support the view that they originated as corn-fetishes (Farnell iii. 35 sq.). The metamorphosis of Demeter into an old woman need have no special significance; some disguise was necessary for the purpose of the story. Compare Pamphos'

account in Paus. i. 39. 1 (γραὶ εἰκασμένην). For a similar disguise cf. Γ 386 of Aphrodite, which shows that the present passage may be due to epic influence.

103. θεμιστοπόλων: Dion. Hal. v. 74 calls the epithet Homeric. It is not in the Iliad or Odyssey. Cf. Hes. *fr.* 7. 3, *PSI* 722. 1.

105. Ἐλευσινίδαο: son of Eleusis the local hero Paus. i. 38. 7, also called Eleusinus Hyg. *Fab.* 147, Servius on Virg. *Georg.* i. 19, al.

106. εὐήρυτον: only here, formed like κοτυλήρυτον Ψ 34 from ἀρύω, which first occurs in Hesiod.

109. Pausanias i. 38. 3 makes a very precise statement about this passage; καλοῦσι σφᾶς (the daughters of Celeus) Πάμφως τε κατὰ ταὐτὰ καὶ Ὅμηρος Διογένειαν καὶ Παμμερόπην καὶ τρίτην Σαισάραν. Cf. Hesych. Σαισαρία· ἡ Ἐλευσὶν πρότερον. The papyrus however supports the text of M, for καλλιοπης τε και κλ[ει]σι[δι]κης και δαμ[ω]ν[ασ]σης is equivalent to καλλιδίκη καὶ κλεισιδίκη δημώ τ᾽ ἐρόεσσα | καλλιθόη τ᾽, especially as δημώ is hypocoristic for δημώνασσα. These catalogues are naturally liable to variant, cf. the Oceanides 418 sq., and the Nereids Σ 39 sq. Pausanias may have made some kind of error, e.g. Ὅμηρος for Ὀρφεύς or Μουσαῖος (as at 154).

111. ἔγνων = the Homeric ἔγνωσαν. So Pindar *Pyth.* ix. 85, ἀνέγνων *Isth.* ii. 23, ἔγνον *Pyth.* iv. 120 (Veitch). Compare ἔβᾰν.

113. παλαιγενέων ἀνθρώπων: a variation of the Homeric τίς πόθεν εἶς ἀνδρῶν, accommodated to D.'s appearance.

115. πιλνᾷς where the verb occurs (πιλνᾷ Hes. *OD.* 510) is transitive, and πίλνασαι is passive Ap. Rh. iv. 952. But πελάζω προσπελάζω are both transitive and intransitive; we therefore keep πιλνᾷς. Cf. Apollonius in *EM.* 672. 7 παρὰ τὸ πιλνῶ ῥῆμα ὃ σημαίνει τὸ προσπελάζω· καὶ γὰρ πιλνᾶταί φησι καὶ συνάπτεται, Herod. iv. 66 κιρνᾶ κίρναται. Of corrections Voss's πίλνασαι is better than Hermann's πιλνᾶ (which rests on δαμνᾶ Ξ 199, called Doric in Σ T).

122. Demeter's pseudonym is unfortunately uncertain. Δώς is a real word. In Hes. *OD.* 356 δὼς ἀγαθή, ἅρπαξ δὲ κακή, θανάτοιο δότειρα, δώς, parallel to ἅρπαξ, looks like an adj. or subst. In Cercidas i. 30 καὶ μετάδως (μεταιδως cod.) μελέτω the word looks

like an abstract. It is recognized together with Σώς as a *κύριον ὄνομα* in *E. Or.* 138. 16, *EM.* 247. 16. But a syllable is wanting after it, and it is difficult to admit the falling out of *μέν* (Brunck). Δωσώ supplies the metre, and feminine names in -σώ are common: Hesych. Εὐδωσώ· Ἀφροδίτη ἐν Συρακούσαις, *ib.* Μορφώ and Περιβασώ also of Aphrodite: cf. Σωσώ Plut. *Arat.* 2, *Anth. Pal.* vi. 216, δοσω on an Attic vase Kretschmer *Vaseninschriften* 202 and Δεξώ, Ἰασώ, Μελλώ, Χρυσώ, Δωρώ, Ἐμβλώ. It is slightly easier to suppose the sequence δωσώ, δωσ͂ω, δωσ, than δὼς μέν, δώς. Other conjectures need not be considered.

123. **Κρήτηθεν**: editors see an allusion to the early worship of Demeter in Crete. For the Cretan cult see Diod. v. 77; the myth of Iasion (ε 125) was localized in Crete Hes. *Theog.* 970. Miss Harrison believed in Cretan influence at Eleusis (*Prolog.* p. 565 sq.). But the explanation is unnecessary, and this fictitious story lacks any evidential value with regard to the origin of the Eleusinian cult. The name of Crete would naturally occur to any one who wished to give a plausible account of his parentage or travels, cf. ν 256, ξ 199, τ 172.

126. **Θορικὸν δέ**: the town and deme of Thoricus (Θερικό) was N. of Sunium with a harbour now called Mandré; Leake *Demi of Attica* 68. It was one of the twelve independent towns of Attica until the time of Theseus (Strabo 397). For its history and remains see Frazer on Paus. i. 31. 3. For the prosody cf. 163 ἡμέτερον δ', 253 πέδον δέ, iii. 28 χέρσον δέ, 119 φόως δέ. M and the other hymn-MSS. have the vulgar accentuation. In the *Iliad* a minority, usually s. x–xi, have δέ independent, as was laid down by Apollonius and Herodian. See Lehrs *qu. ep.* 40, La Roche *H. T.* 221, *Iliad* ed. 1930 prol. p. 220.

κατέσχεθον: the construction *κατασχεῖν νηί* is not Homeric, but occurs in Herodotus and Attic (Franke).

127. A step in the narrative is omitted, cf. ξ 346, ι 85, κ 56, ο 499. A lacuna however does not seem necessary, considering the elliptical style of this hymn (37, 317, 446, and iv. 110, T 80). On the elliptical style of old literature see Galen vi. 106, ix. 760 *ἕπεσθαι δ' οἱ πολλοὶ βραχυλογίᾳ παλαιᾷ μὴ γεγυμνασμένοι λείπειν οἴονταί τινα*, x. 275.

128. **ἐπηρτύνοντο**: the compound is not found elsewhere in the middle, but B 55, K 302 have *ἠρτύνετο βουλήν*.

132. **τιμῆς** (= *ὤνου*) is not Homeric.

137. The key to this passage is *τέων*, of course interrogative. To follow *οἰκτείρατε* it would have to be relative. Rather therefore than write *τέως* (un-Homeric in the sense of 'until') we assume a lacuna containing a verb to govern *τέων*, e.g. *τοῦτο δέ μοι σαφέως ὑποθήκατε ὄφρα πύθωμαι* (on the analogy of 149). The termination would account for the omission. The answer 149 sq. implies a question.

Attempts have been made to make *τοκῆες* trisyllabic, but the synizesis is supported by *βασιλῆες* Hes. *OD.* 263, *ἱππῆες* Λ 151, *ἐπηετανός* *h. Herm.* 113, *OD.* 607.

140. **ἀφήλικος**: not in Homer, cf. *ἄνδρα ἀπηλικέστερον* Herod. iii. 14, Moeris 82 *ἀφηλικεστέραν· πρεσβυτέραν Ἀττικῶς*. In X 490 *παναφῆλιξ* has a different sense.

141. Eur. *Troades* 195 Hecuba has come down to be *παίδων θρέπτειρα*.

144. **δεσπόσυνον**: next in Pindar *Pyth.* iv. 267.

διαθρήσαιμι: Voss' conjecture, based on *ἔργα διδασκῆσαι OD.* 64, gives good sense, but *διδασκήσαιμι* stands in no graphical relation to *διαθήσαιμι*, and involves a second change, *γυναῖκας* for *γυναικός*. It is therefore better to accept Bothe's *διαθ⟨ρ⟩ήσαιμι*, of which the sense 'oversee' is perfect. She will hold the same post as Eurycleia *ἥ τε γυναικῶν δμῳάων σκοπός ἐσσι κατὰ μέγαρ' ἡμετεράων* χ 395. *Ἀθρεῖν* is epic, *διαθρεῖν* occurs Ar. *Clouds* 700 (*ἀντὶ τοῦ ἀνάκρινε καὶ δοκίμαζε* Σ), Epicurus *Epist.* i. 35. 3, Themistius xxiii. 284 c *διαθρῆσαι εἰ δή τινες εἶεν φαρμάκῳ ἀλήλιμμένοι*, Hesych. (emended) *διαθρήσαντα· διιδόντα*, and is corrected from *διαιρεῖν* in Eur. *Alcmen. fr.* 102. 2. Cf. Eunapius 110 and 190 (after Aristophanes).

147–8 = 216–17. Solon v. 64 *δῶρα δ' ἄφυκτα θεῶν γίγνεται ἀθανάτων*, Rhian. ap. Stob. 54 *φέρομεν δὲ θεῶν ἑτερόρροπα δῶρα | ἀφραδέι κραδίῃ*. For *τέτλαμεν* cf. υ 311.

150. For the wording cf. Theognis 171 *θεοῖς εὔχου, θεοῖσιν ἐπικράτος* 'A', *οἷς ἐστι μέγα κράτος* cet.

151. cf. Hes. *Scut.* 165 *ὃς Θήβης κρήδεμνον ἔχει ῥύεταί τε πόλῆα*,

Π 100, ν 388 and the epithet εὐστέφανος, Β 117 πολίων κάρηνα. See also vi. 2.

153 sq. Τριπτολέμου: for Triptolemus and the other princes see 474 sq. According to Paus. i. 14. 2 Triptolemus was the son of Trochilus or (the Athenian version) of Celeus. Apollod. i. 5. 2 calls him the eldest son of Celeus and Metanira, but mentions other genealogies, e.g. that of Panyasis (son of Eleusis and Demeter), and that of Pherecydes (son of Oceanus and Ge). Hyginus *fab.* 147 and Servius in *Georg.* i. 19 give a different parentage (Eleusinus and Cothonea or Cytinia). The comparative insignificance of Triptolemus as merely one of the Eleusinian princes indicates the early date of the hymn. Later, under Athenian influence, his prominence was steadily developed until he became one of the chief figures of Eleusinian legend. On the development of Triptolemus as a culture-hero see P.-R. 770 sq., Roscher v. 1128 sq., Farnell 360, and his ref. no. 228. The derivation of the name presents great difficulty. Neither 'God of the third ploughing' nor 'God of triple ploughing' (Usener *Götternamen* p. 141, Gruppe *gr. Myth.* 49, from τρίς and πολεῖν), nor 'thrice warrior' (Wilamowitz *Aus Kydathen* 132, Kern *Krieg und Kult bei den Hellenen* 6 etc., cl. the name Neoptolemus) can be confidently accepted. Fehrle in Roscher v. 11 sq. follows Kretschmer (*Glotta* xii. 51) in connecting -πτόλεμος with πελεμίζειν, 'he who thrice toils'.

The name of Dioclus or Diocles (the form in 474, 477; Ruhnken compares Ἴφικλος, -κλῆς and other cases), who is here an Eleusinian prince, again points to a time when Eleusis was under the influence of Megara rather than of Athens. For Diocles is a Megarian hero (Ar. *Ach.* 774) in whose honour the festival of Diocleia was celebrated. In a later version he was the Megarian archon of Eleusis conquered by Theseus (Plut. *Thes.* 10). Theocritus (xii. 28) makes him an Athenian exile in Megara, and the scholiast *ad loc.* adds as *aition* of the Diocleia an Alexandrine love story. See Hiller v. Gaertringen in P.-W. v. in *Diokleia* and *Diokles I*, Pfister *Reliquienkult im Altertum* i. 19, n. 44.

Polyxinus and Dolichus may be abstracted from titles of Pluto. For Polyxinus (whose name does not elsewhere occur in connexion with Eleusis), cf. on v. 9 Πολυδέκτῃ. If Meineke's correction (*Philol.* xiii. 551) of Hesychius (*in* Πολύξενος) is right,[1] Polyxenus was one of the hundred names submitted to the Pythia for the selection of the ten Attic tribal heroes (see Höfer in Roscher iii. 2743).

Dolichus (Dolichius) elsewhere is a son of Triptolemus and eponym of Dulichium (Eust. on B 625, Steph. Byz. *in* Δουλίχιον). This represents a relatively late Athenian development of legend, and has doubtless a connexion with the increase of Athenian political interest in the Ionian islands (cf. the similar genealogical mythology discussed in Halliday's *Greek Questions of Plutarch* 81). Herodian π. μον. λέξ. p. 10 quotes a line Εὔμολπος Δόλιχός τε καὶ Ἱπποθόων μεγάθυμος. The reading [πλουτο]νι δ[ολι]χωι in an Eleusinian inscription (Prott *Ath. Mitt.* xxiv. 251) is very problematical and is rejected by Kern P.-W. v. 1282.

154. **ἀμύμονος**: as Paus. in his citation (see app. crit.) expressly says that Homer calls Eumolpus ἀγήνωρ, Ruhnken exchanged the epithets in 154, 155. But Pausanias' quotation is probably a casual error, influenced by the next line.

156. **τῶν πάντων**: resumptive.

κατὰ δώματα π.: a tmesis (Ruhnken).

157. **πρώτιστον**: for this feminine in comparatives and superlatives cf. δ 442 ὀλοώτατος ὀδμή, Hes. *Theog.* 408 (Λητὼ) ἀγανώτατον ἐντὸς Ὀλύμπου, Pindar *fr.* 152 γλυκερώτερος ὀμφά. For exx. in prose see K.-B. i. 554 n.

159. **θεοείκελος**: the Gods even when disguised as mortals often have an air which moves wonder; cf. the disguise of Apollo (iii. 464), of Aphrodite (v. 92), and of Dionysus (vii. 17).

160. **εἰ . . . ἐπίμεινον** = ρ 277.

164. **τηλύγετος**: the derivation and therefore the meaning are unknown.

165. **πολυεύχετος**: only here (= πολυάρητος 220) and in Homer.

166. **ἐκθρέψαιο**: first here except in the v.l. σ 130.

168. **ἀπὸ . . . δοίη**: another tmesis. For θρεπτήρια see on 223.

170. **κυδιάουσαι**: for the occasional retention of the original -αω etc. see Monro *HG.* § 55. Exx. in the hymns are v. 266, vii 14, 41.

[1] viz. Πολύξενος· εἷς τῶν ⟨ρʹ⟩ ἡρώων.

172. ὡς: 'even as', 295, 416.

174. Here and 401 M represents the diphthong ει by η; cf. also iii. 9. Ἦαρος may be a genuine form, or it may result from a confusion with ἦρος, ἠρινός. Homer only uses ἔαρος (Z 148, τ 519).

For the phrase cf. Eur. *Cyclops* 508 ἦρος ὥραις, Philost. *Heroic.* 47 ἐν τῇ τοῦ ἦρος ὥρᾳ (and often in late Greek), Z 148 ἔαρος ὥρη(-ῃ), B 471 ὥρῃ ἐν εἰαρινῇ.

176. This gesture is commonly represented in art from the seventh century, and it is possible that the writer was influenced by works of art (Franke p. 26). The pictorial touch is rather in the manner of a later poet; cf. Ap. Rh. iii. 873 ἂν δὲ χιτῶνας | λεπταλέους λευκῆς ἐπιγουνίδος ἄχρις ἄειρον, iv. 46, 940, Callim. *fr.* 391 ἐλαφρὰ ποδῶν ἴχνι' ἀειράμεναι.

177. **ἀμφὶ . . . αἴσσοντο** = Z 509 (of a horse): cf. also κυδιάουσαι 170 = κυδιόων Z 509, παῖδ' ἐπὶ κόλπῳ ἔχουσα Z 400 = 187.

178. **κροκηίῳ**: only here. For the form cf. κουρήιον also ἅπ. λεγ. 108, for the colour Ovid *Ars amat.* i. 530 *croceas irreligata comas.*

182. **κατὰ κρῆθεν** = Π 548, λ 588, Hes. *Theog.* 574, ἀπὸ κρ. Hes. *Scut.* 7. The covered head and the κυάνεος πέπλος are signs of mourning, cf. Demeter Μέλαινα at Phigalia Paus. viii. 42, P.-W. iv. 2734.

186 = α 333 (στῆ ῥα), al.

187 = ο 469 (in a different sense), ἐπὶ κ. Z 400. For the variation cf. on iii. 18.

188–9. Objection has been needlessly raised to Demeter's miraculous entrance, in spite of which Metanira does not recognize her divinity. She suspects that her visitor is something out of the common (190), as Demeter had seemed θεοείκελος (divine) to the girls (159); but afterwards she accepts D. as a mortal. The case is the same with Anchises' original scruples (*h.* v. 92), and more so with the indifference shown by the pirate captain to a miracle (*h.* vii. introd., notes on *h.* ii. 159, iii. 465). Later mere admiration expresses itself by ascription of divinity, Chariton i. 14 1 κατεπλάγησαν δοκοῦντες θεὰν ἑωρακέναι, v. 9. 1 ἀνέθορε δόξασα Ἀφροδίτην ἐφεστάναι, ii. 3. 6.

μελάθρου κῦρε: = *h.* v. 173. With dative Aesch. *fr.* 154.

Gigantic stature as a sign of the superhuman occurs first in

Δ 443 of Eris: later Callim. *Dem.* 57, Virg. *Aen.* iv. 177 (Fama), x. 767 (Orion).

189. Miraculous light betokens the presence of the Gods *h.* iii. 444 (Apollo), Eur. *Bacch.* 1083 (Dionysus), Ovid *Fast.* i. 94; *infra* 278.

191. **κλισμοῖο**: on the κλισμός see Helbig *HE.* 118, 122. It was more luxurious than the πηκτὸν ἕδος (= δίφρος 198) which Demeter accepted. Matthiae compares Athen. 192 E and τ 55.

193. **φαεινοῦ**: epithet of θρόνος, Λ 645. The κλισμός is πολυδαίδαλος Ω 597 and ποικίλος α 132, i.e. inlaid with silver (ἀργυρόηλος). In Θ 436 the epithet χρύσεος is ideal, of the chairs of the Gods.

194. The last hemistich = *h.* v. 156. Cf. Virg. *Aen.* xi. 480 *oculos deiecta decoros.*

195. The episode of Iambe is narrated by Apollod. i. 5. 1 γραῖά τις Ἰάμβη σκώψασα τὴν θεὸν ἐποίησε μειδιᾶσαι. διὰ τοῦτο ἐν θεσμοφόροις τὰς γυναῖκας σκώπτειν λέγουσι, Nicand. *Alex.* 129 τῷ δὲ σὺ πολλάχι μὲν γληχὼ ποταμηίσι νύμφαις | ἐμπλήδην κυκεῶνα πόροις ἐν κύμβεϊ τεύξας | νηστείρης Δηοῦς μορόεν ποτὸν ᾧ ποτε Δηὼ | λαυκανίην ἔβρεξεν ἀν' ἄστυρον Ἱπποθόωντος | Θρηίσσης ἀθύροισιν ὑπὸ ῥήτρῃσιν Ἰάμβης; Philicus v. 58 (Körte *Hermes* 1931. 447), Iambe speaks: καὶ δὲ σὺ τῆς Ἀτθίδος ὦ δαῖμον Ἰάμβας ἐπάκουσον βραχύ μοι τε κέρδος· | εἰμὶ δ' ἀπαίδευτα χέασ' ὡς ἂν ἀποικοῦσα λάλος δημότις· αἴδεσσαί με . . . 62 οὐθὲν ἐμοὶ τῶνδε παρέστιν γέρας· ἀλλ' εἰ χαλάσεις πένθος ἐγὼ δὲ λύσω. . . . Unfortunately the fragment stops short of what she said or did.

The Σ Nicand. *l.c.*, Diod. v. 4, Hesych. in Θρίαμβος, Ἰάμβη, *EM.* 463. 24, *Gud.* 269. 14 attribute the invention of the iambic metre to Iambe. The derivation is absurd, as that of ἔλεγος from ἐλεγαίνειν (Suid.); like most musical words, ἔλεγος, διθύραμβος, θρίαμβος, παιάν, μάγαδις, etc. *iambos* is non-Greek. Moreover, as Gemoll notes, there is no proof that the Eleusinian raillery was uttered in iambic or any metre. The Σ Nicand. *Ther.* 484 mentions Ambos, a son of Metanira, who laughed at the proceedings and was changed into a lizard. The similarity of the names cannot be overlooked. The story is a variant of that told elsewhere of Ascalabus (see on 208).

For the Orphic version in which Dysaules and Baubo are king and queen of Eleusis, with sons Eubouleus and Eumolpus, and daughters Protonoe and Nisa, see Bloch in Roscher ii. 1318 (ἐξένισεν ἡ Βαβὼ τὴν Δημώ scriptor ap. Suid. *in* Δημώ). In this, Baubo by an exposure (Orph. *fr.* 215 Abel, 52 Kern, cf. Hesych. βαυβάλιον· γυναικὸς μόριον, frag. trag. 136 Nauck βαυβᾶν = κοιμᾶσθαι)[1] caused Demeter to smile. This gesture (ἀνασυραμένη, ἀναστειλαμένη) usually implied contempt, Artemid. *onir.* iv. 44.

A Sardinian parallel to the story of Iambe has been published by Usener (*Rh. Mus.* lix. 625 sq.). The animals came to sympathize with the Virgin Mary upon the death of her Son. At last the frog by a clumsy reference to seven of her own children killed by a cartwheel induced the Virgin to smile and take comfort. This story is connected with a proverb 'non v'ha dolu senza risu', and a ritual at funerals where a buffoon has to make the mourners laugh. Usener, quoting the *scurrae* at Roman funerals, postulates a rite of jesting during mourning in Attica as the origin of the story of Iambe.

Apollodorus (i. 5. 1), however, gives the jesting of Iambe as the explanation of the exchange of obscene badinage (αἰσχρολογία) by the women at the *Thesmophoria*. This practice, which is a very common feature of festivals of fertility, has for its object the stimulation 'of the fertilizing powers of the earth and of the human frame' (Farnell iii. 104; a number of exx. from all parts of the world are collected in Frazer vii. 62, 116, viii. 17). In Greek cult it should be distinguished from the feature of cursing which appears in some rituals (see Farnell, iii. 104 n. *b*). In the cult of Demeter αἰσχρολογία is of frequent occurrence. We hear of it at the *Thesmophoria*, *Stenia*, and *Haloa*, at the festival of Demeter Mysia, at the Sicilian *Thesmophoria*, and in the cult of Damis and Auxesia. Sometimes, as in the *Thesmophoria*, women alone took part, sometimes, as at Eleusis on Boedromion 20, the abuse appears to have been indiscriminately exchanged in a crowd of both sexes.

It is again a difficult question whether the reference is here to the *Thesmophoria* or to the Eleusinian Mysteries. The usual

[1] The name (Babo) appears to remain in Thracian plays as that of an old woman, Dawkins *JHS.* 1906, xxvi. 196, 206.

interpretation (adopted in the first edition), which connects it with the γεφυρισμός of the procession from Athens may quite certainly be ruled out. At the date when the hymn was composed no procession came from Athens across the bridge. Further, whatever its origin, the practice of γεφυρισμός in historical times appears to have assumed the sophisticated form of the lampooning of well-known citizens as they crossed the bridge rather than that of a mutual exchange of abuse; in this ceremony the idea that abuse protects against the evil eye may have played its part. There was, however, αἰσχρολογία at Eleusis on the night of Boedromion 20: χώρει νυν πᾶς ἀνδρείως | εἰς τοὺς εὐανθεῖς κόλπους | λειμώνων ἐγκρούων | κἀπισκώπτων | καὶ παίζων καὶ χλευάζων, Ar. *Ran.* 372.

The epic dignity of the poet of the hymn, who represents all this black man's superstition by the two words πολλὰ παρασκώπτουσα, should be remarked.

199. cf. Ε 879.

200. This has been connected with the tradition that Demeter sat upon an ἀγέλαστος πέτρα Apollod. i. 5. 1, Σ Ar. *Eq.* 782, Suidas *in* Σαλαμῖνος, Hesych. *in v.*, Ovid *Met.* iv. 456 *sedes scelerata vocatur*, *Fasti* iv. 503 *illud Cecropidae nunc quoque triste vocant.* Cf. the rock Ἀνακλήθρα or Ἀνακληθρίς on which Demeter sat at Megara (Paus. i. 43. 2, Methodius in *EM.* 96. 2). This latter name is derived from technical language in which καλεῖν is used of invocation, ἀνακαλεῖν of the invocation of a God or spirit from the underworld (see *ARW.* xxii. 20, 42 sq.). The situation of the Eleusinian stone cannot be identified. Apollodorus places it by the Callichoron, but this has no authority, as he does not seem to follow the local tradition in regard to the resting-place of Demeter (see on 99). The stone is mentioned in a fourth-century inscription (Ἐφ. ἀρχ. 1883. 115); it was possibly near Athens and unknown in the old Eleusinian myth (Svoronos 247 sq.) The word ἀγέλαστος here has no *immediate* connexion with the ἀγέλαστος πέτρα, for Demeter is now sitting ἐπὶ δίφρου in the house.

The last hemistich = δ 788.

ἄπαστος: Callim. (*Dem.* 8), who says nothing of Iambe, makes D. break her fast in the evening, ἕσπερος ὅς τε πιεῖν Δαμάτερα μοῦνος ἔπεισεν. Like Mohammedans at Ramadan the Mystae fasted only until sundown; cf. *quae quia principio posuit ieiunia noctis, | tempus habent mystae sidera visa cibi* Ovid *Fasti* iv. 535, Nonnus vi. 33.

203. **πότνιαν ἁγνήν**: cf. Θεσμοφόρους ἁγνὰς ποτνιάς *Epigr.* Kaibel 774. 3. For πότνια see on 39, for ἁγνή cf. 439, Hes. *OD.* 465, Archiloch *fr.* 120, Moschion *fr.* 6. 24 Nauck, Orph. *h.* xl. 11, 18: as an epithet of Core see on 337.

204. **ἵλαον σχεῖν θυμόν**: Hes. *OD.* 340 ὥς τέ τοι ἵλαον κραδίην καὶ θυμὸν ἔχωσιν. The quantity ἵλᾱος is usual, A 583, Theocr. v 18, Euphorion *fr.* 12, inscr. ap Paus. v. 24. 3, *IG. Ins. Aeg.* ii. 476. -ᾰ- occurs *h.* xxix. 10 (q.v.), Choerob. *in Theod. can.* 252. 21, hιλεϝοι θυμω *IG.* v. 1. 1562. For the three last feet spondees cf. 417, 421, 474, Hes. *Theog.* 48 λήγουσαί τ' ᾠδῆς (ἀοιδῆς codd.). Otherwise the words are usually formulaic: Eberhard *Metr. Beob.* i. 10, La Roche *Wiener Studien* xx. 70.

205. For the σχῆμα καθ' ὅλον καὶ μέρος with the dative cf. A 24, Θ 129, N 82, Hes. *Scut.* 221, Herod. vii. 16.

207. **οὐ γὰρ θεμιτόν**: Σ Nicand. *Alex.* 129 ἡ δὲ θεὸς οὐκ ἐδέξατο, λέγουσα μὴ θεμιτὸν εἶναι πιεῖν αὐτὴν οἶνον ἐπὶ τῇ θλίψει τῆς θυγατρός. Wineless offerings (νηφάλια) were the general rule in the cult of Demeter and Core (Dion. Hal. i. 33, Prott *Fasti sacri* 3, 6 Athens, Paus. v. 15. 10 Olympia, Ziethen *Leg. sacr.* 90 Delos), and the prohibition of wine at the *Thesmophoria* lends its point to the incident of the flagon disguised as a baby (Ar. *Thesm.* 730); but exceptions to the rule are not unknown. The *Haloa*, at which the new wine was ceremonially tasted, was a joint festival of Demeter and Dionysus. Wine was offered to Demeter at Cos (Paton and Hicks 37, 63), and sometimes in Italy (Servius *in Georg.* i. 344); at Andania there was a libation of wine before the oath was taken (Ditt. *Syll.* 736). But in general Demeter's cult was wineless (see Farnell iii. 103). A similar taboo characterized the worship of the Earth Goddess (id. i. 88, ii. 664 n. *a*). Νηφάλια were common in the ritual of the chthonian Gods (Porph. *de antr. nymph.* 18, Diels *Sib. Blätter* 73). Frequently, though not invariably (e g. λ 26), they were offered to the dead (e.g. Eur. *IT.* 632, Porph. *op.c.* 25). They occur in purificatory sacrifices (e.g. Ap. Rh. iv. 712), in magic (Apuleius *Met.* iii. 18), and in

Pythagorean ritual. Wine might not be allowed in the shrine of the hero Eudromos at Delphi (Ziethen *Leg. sacr.* 73). We further find νηφάλια in the worship of Eos, Helios, Winds, Mnemosyne, Selene, Muses, Nymphs, Aphrodite Urania, Attis, Posidon Chamaezelus, Sosipolis, Zeus Hypatos, the daughters of Erechtheus, the Erinyes, and Dionysus in his chthonic aspect. For full references see Wächter *Reinheitsvorschriften im griech. Kult* 109 and Stengel *Kultus-altertümer* 104. Various explanations have been offered. Some particular cases may be covered by the practical motive of preventing drunkenness in a sacred place, but this explanation cannot apply here. The analogy, again, of wine and blood (Pliny *NH.* xiv. 58, and in general Frazer iii. 248) has been adopted by some modern scholars as the reason (e.g. Jevons, 379). But though Demeter's sacrifices were often wineless they were not usually bloodless, not even at Eleusis (see Farnell 186, 190). A possible original motive may have been the primitive fear of the strange daemonic power of wine (see Wächter *op. cit.* 114), but perhaps the most probable reason, though the last mentioned motive may have played a part, is simply that the wineless libation represents the survival of a very early and primitive form of ritual; τὰ μὲν ἀρχαῖα τῶν ἱερῶν νηφάλια παρὰ πολλοῖς ἦν (Porph. *de abst.* ii. 20; cf. Stengel *l.c.*, A. B. Cook *JHS.* xv. 21, Nilsson *GF.* 135). This would explain why it is predominantly in the cult of Nature powers, the dead, the Earth Goddess, and powers connected with the underworld that this form of ritual obtained in historical times.

208. The passage refers to the κυκεών, the institution of which is ascribed to Demeter herself. For the κυκεών in Homer see Λ 641 (ib. 642 it relieved thirst), κ 234. In the latter passage it is called σῖτος, being compounded of ἄλφιτα, but it is always drunk (ἔκπιον κ 237). So Galen ii. 155 ἐξ ἀλεύρων μεθ' ὕδατος οἷον κυκεῶνά τινα, Eust. 870. 65 εἰ καὶ μεταξὺ βρωτοῦ καὶ ποτοῦ ὁ κυκεὼν εἶναι δοκεῖ, ἀλλὰ μᾶλλον οἷα ζωμός τις ῥοφητὸς ὤν, Σ Nicand. *Alex.* 128 (ἔπιε): Hipponax 42. 3 ἀλφίτων . . κυκεῶνα, Polyaenus iv. 3. 32 παιπάλης ἐξ ἀλφίτων πεποιημένης ὡς εἰς κυκεῶνα, Lact. Plac. *in Ovid. met.* v. 7 *polentatam potionem.* It was not necessarily wineless, see Hippocr. *de diaeta* ii (i. p. 674, 13 K) on the kinds of κυκεών,

viz. water, wine, honey, milk; Galen xvii. 2. 333 τροφὴ ἅμα καὶ οἴνῳ. The mixture at Eleusis seems to have included pennyroyal; διδοῖ ποτὸν ὕδωρ ἐμβαλοῦσα γλήχωνα καὶ ἄλφιτον ἐς αὐτό Ant. Lib. xxiv. 1, Ar. *Pax* 712, Herondas ix. 13 γλήχ[ων'] ἐγὼ ['Ελ]ευσῖν' ἤειρα.

With the legend of the institution of the *kykeon* a story is connected, first recorded by Alexandrian writers, of why the lizard hides under stones and has spots on its skin. There was once a boy who laughed at the eager drinking of the Goddess, and she threw the dregs of the *kykeon* at him. He turned forthwith into a lizard, and the marks of the meal are on his hide (Nicander ap. Ant. Lib. xxiv, Ovid *Met.* v. 496, Lact. Plac. *fab.* v. 7). This story of Ascalabus (Ambas in Σ Nic. *Ther.* 484 quoted on 195) is sometimes contaminated with that of Ascalaphus the screech-owl (see on 391). The drinking of this mixture of meal, water, and pennyroyal was one of the ritual actions of initiation into the mysteries as commemorated by Clement of Alexandria (*protrept.* 18). Mommsen (*Feste* p. 231) considers that following the same order of incidents as in the hymn, in which *kykeon* succeeds Iambe, the rite may have taken place on Boedromion 20 immediately after the torch-light dances with their accompanying αἰσχρολογία. It is clear that as an act of initiation the drinking of the *kykeon* was a necessary preliminary to, and therefore did not form part of, the major rites in the τελεστήριον. The view of some scholars that it represented the culminating act of the nocturnal service must therefore be rejected (see above, p. 121). Although the sacramental eating of corn forms a part of the ceremonies of many peoples in many parts of the world (Frazer viii. 48), the apparent analogies are irrelevant. There is no evidence that the Greeks ever ate corn in a sacramental meal, or that the drinking of the *kykeon* at Eleusis was regarded as an act of mystical communion with the Goddess (Farnell, iii. 195). That the action, however important it may have been as an act of initiation, did not form part of the inner and secret ritual which it was impious to reveal to the uninitiated is shown by the fact that the drinking of *kykeon* is depicted on vases (see Farnell iii, plate xv b, 240, Daremberg et Saglio *Dict. des Ant.* ii. fig. 2637).

211. **ὁσίης ἕνεκεν** 'to save the rite', as practised by the mystae.

For the equivalent ὁσίας ἕκατι cf. Eur. *IT.* 1461, Eubulus ap. Athen. 311 D, Ephippus ib. 359 B, Origen *in Cels.* 47, ed. Berol. i. 1104 C; ὁσίας χάριν Marinus *vit. Procl.* 19. The retention of ἕνεκεν involves a lacuna to contain the verb of drinking, e.g. ἔκπιεν, ἡ δὲ λαβοῦσα δέπας θέτο ἔνθεν ἄειρε.

πολυπότνια: not in early epic, but cf. Ar. *Thesm.* 1156, Ap. Rh. i. 1125, Orph. *h.* xl. 16 (of Deo). Other compounds of πολυ- occur vv. 9, 17, 18, 28, 31, etc.

213. **ἐπεὶ οὔ σε κακῶν κτλ.**: cf. v. 132 οὐ μὲν γάρ κε κακοὶ τοιόνδε τέκοιεν, Theocr. xxv. 38 οὐ σέ γέ φημί κακῶν ἒξ | ἔμμεναι οὐδὲ κακοῖσιν ἐοικότα φύμεναι αὐτόν· | οἷόν τοι μέγα εἶδος ἐπιπρέπει, possibly an imitation of this passage. For κακῶν ἄπ' cf. Ξ 472, for ἐπί τοι πρέπει (tmesis) ω 252.

216–17. cf. 147–8.

217. **ζυγός**: in Homer the neuter only. For the phrase cf. Hes. *OD.* 815 ἐπὶ ζυγὸν αὐχένα θεῖναι βουσί, *Theog.* 1023 ὑπὸ ζυγὸν αὐχένα, with gender indeterminate. Callim. *fr.* 467 is the first to certainly use the masc. in the sense of 'yoke', but Plato (*Tim.* 63 B) has it in the sense of 'balance'.

220. **ὤπασαν ἀθάνατοι** = Solon i. 74.

223. **δοίην** is of course right. Metanira will pay the nurse θρεπτήρια when the child grows up. In Hes. *OD.* 188 the word is used of the return made by the child to the parents in their old age, the Homeric θρέπτρα Δ 478, P 302.

227. **κοὔ**: on the crasis see on 13.

κακοφραδίῃσι is a v.l. (τινές) for κακορραφίῃσι β 236.

228–9. Still very uncertain. Ἐπηλυσίη (230, iv. 37) is usually taken = witchcraft (Hesych. ἐπωδὴ φαρμάκων), but in Pollux iv 187 it is a disease, between pleuritis and strangury; perhaps therefore it = 'attack', i.e. a fit, convulsion. (ἐνηλυσία Pollux *l.c.* and Hesych. is a place where lightning falls.)

ἀντίτομον = 'antidote', the act of gathering herbs being expressed by τέμνω Eur. *Andr.* 122, ἀντιτεμών *Alc.* 972; cf. ἀντίτομα (oil) Pind. *Pyth.* iv. 394. Ὑποταμνόν suggested ὀρόδαμνος to Bücheler, but there are many plants of similar terminations, ἴαμνος, ῥάδαμνος, ῥάμνος, θάμνη Herond. vi. 90, *tamnus*, *taminia uva* in Pliny and Columella (ἔκτομον = hellebore in Hippocr. etc.), but none of them suit the equation *ὑλοτόμοιο*. *CR.* 1895. 13 and in the first edition it was suggested that *ὑλοτόμος* and *ὑποτάμνον* (*sic*, participle for substantive as *ἀμείβοντες*, *ἀμφιφῶν*, *ἔμπουσα*, *κελέοντες*, *πρέποντες* 'fishes' Ael. *NH.* ix. 38 and Oppian i. 146, *τελέοντες*) are paraphrases for *ἕλμινς* or *σκώληξ*, widely believed to be the cause of toothache or teething pains. For similar paraphrases or epithets cf. Hesych. *γαφάγας· σκώληξ, ὃν ἡμεῖς γῆς ἔντερον λέγομεν· Συρακούσιοι* (and *EM.* 221. 50 an. Bekk. 230. 39), Aratus 959 *σκώληκες | κεῖνοι τοὺς καλέουσι μελαίνης ἔντερα γαίης*, Strabo 570, Arist. *mir. ausc.* 13 *ξυλοφάγου σκώληκος*, Nonnus vii. 165 *σταφυλητόμον* (*τράγον*), xxi. 97 *γειοτόμοις ἀνέμοισιν*, xxxvii. 400 *ὄμβρου γειοτόμοιο*, whence it appears that the idea of boring or burrowing is expressed by *τέμνω*. Further, in medicine *ὑποτάμνειν* is to 'lance': Hippocr. ii. 70. 11 κ. *φλεβοτομίην ποιεύμενος ἀπὸ βραχιόνων καὶ τὰς ὑπὸ τῶν γλωσσῶν φλέβας ὑποτάμνων*, ib. 672 inf., Aretaeus iii. 24 Hude, *καὶ ὑποτομεῦσι σιδηροῖς* LXX. 2 Regn. 12. 31 ('A'). The pain of toothache, a 'douleur lancinante', is compared to an incision, and the worm is the 'lancer'. The verb is used of food Demetrius *Hieracosoph.* 11.

For the belief see Shakespeare *Much Ado* III. ii. 28 ; for Scotland *County Folklore* iii. 140 (Orkney), for India Crooke *Popular Religion and Folklore of N. India* i. 151 (women of the gipsy-tribes know charms to extract the worm), for Finland Abercromby *Pre- and Proto-historic Finns* i. 328 ; parallels from Germany and China are given by Dyer *Folklore of Shakespeare* 273 sq. ; see also *Notes and Queries* 1876, fifth series, v. 24, 155, 476, vi. 97, 1904, tenth series, 407, 492. Further exx. from different parts of the world are collected in C. S. Myers *Disease and Medicine ERE.* iv. 724, Kittredge *Witchcraft in Old and New England*, 36 and notes. Ailment and remedy occur often in Pliny (*NH.* xxii. 121, xxv. 165, 171, xxvii. 29, 33, 89, xxviii. 45, 95, 178) ; cf. also Sozomen *hist. eccl.* vi. 34. 3. Πτερίς, fern, is a remedy in Theophr. *HP.* x. 20. 5. In the *Geoponica* xii. 27. 35, the same remedies are assigned to worms as to toothache (see Aelian also *NH.* v. 46, viii. 9, ix. 30 on worms in dogs).[1] The same category of charm is suggested by Polemon *Physiognomica* i. 1 (in *Physiognomia* ed.

[1] The mediaeval antidote was the inhalation of the smoke of herbs.

Franz 1780, 171) τὰς δὲ τῶν πανθηρῶν κακίας φυλάττεσθαι ὑποτομαῖς ἐν τοῖς μεγίστοις ἢ τῶν μεγίστων ἐπίσκεψις.

The conjecture οὐλοτόμοιο would be literal, not descriptive, as these names have to be: Cook *CR.* 1894, 381 sq.

231. The story of Demeter nursing Demophon has a parallel in Paus. ii. 5. 5; the children of Plemnaeus, King of Aegialea in Sicyon, died at birth, until Demeter took pity and in the guise of a strange woman reared up a child named Orthopolis. On the close connexion between the growth of children and vegetation see Mannhardt *Myth. Forsch.* 351 sq. For Demeter as a Goddess of healing see Rubensohn *Att. Mitth.* xx. 360 sq. In the hymns Demophon is in no present danger; Demeter only promises to keep him in good health. According to Nicander *Ther.* 485 a lizard had wounded Metanira's child, in Ovid *Fast.* iv. 446 the child Triptolemus is dying.

θυώδεϊ δέξατο κόλπῳ = Z 483 (κηώδεϊ) of Andromache.

232. τ' is in place; D. receives the child in her bosom and her arms, i.e. holds it to her bosom.

234. Apollod. i. 5. 1 follows the same version in making Demophon the child who is placed in the fire, but both he and Hyginus (*fab.* 147) state that when D. was interrupted the child (Eleusis in Hyginus) died in the fire. The reason for this change was no doubt to clear the way for Triptolemus to be able later to receive Demeter's favours. In later legend Triptolemus completely ousted Demophon from the story, and in Ovid *Met.* v. 645, *Fast.* iv. 507, Servius *in Georg.* i. 19. *Myth. Vat.* i. 8, Σ Nic. *Ther.* 484 Triptolemus not Demophon was nursed by Demeter.

236. The abruptness of the text is impossible, and Hermann's supplement is recommended by the homoeoteleuton; cf. iv. 267.

237 sq. For the story of Apollod. i. 5. 1 βουλομένη δὲ αὐτὸ ἀθάνατον ποιῆσαι τὰς νύκτας εἰς πῦρ κατετίθει τὸ βρέφος, καὶ περιῄρει τὰς θνητὰς σάρκας αὐτοῦ, Ovid *Fast.* iv. 487 *inque foco pueri corpus vivente favilla | obruit, humanum purget ut ignis onus.* Similarly Thetis wished to make Achilles immortal, but was prevented by Peleus, Apollod. iii. 13. 6, Ap. Rh. iv. 869 ἡ μὲν γὰρ βροτέας αἰεὶ περὶ σάρκας ἔδαιεν | νύκτα διὰ μέσσην φλογμῷ πυρός· ἤματα δ' αὖτε | ἀμβροσίῃ χρίεσκε τέρεν δέμας ὄφρα πέλοιτο |

ἀθάνατος καί οἱ στυγερὸν χροΐ γῆρας ἀλάλκοι, a passage which as Ruhnken pointed out may be derived from the Hymn. Compare also the story of Medea and her children (Paus. ii. 3. 11) and that of Isis and the infant son of the king of Byblus (Plut. *de Is. et Osir.* 16). These legends are elaborately discussed, with a wealth of analogies from the legends and practices of other people, by Frazer (Apollodorus ii. 311–17, Appendix I, 'Putting children on the fire'). His conclusion that they are connected with the practice of passing children across the fire in order to protect them from the notorious dangers of infancy is almost certainly correct; see also Halliday *CR.* xxv. 1901. 8. The rite corresponding to the legend is that of the *Amphidromia*, and the reference of our story is quite certainly to a domestic rite of infancy and not to any part of the ritual of the mysteries.

238. **καταπνείουσα**: Ovid *op.c.* 540 *iungere dignata est os puerile suo.* | *pallor abit, subitasque vident in corpore vires*: | *tantus caelesti venit ab ore vigor.*

239. **κρύπτεσκε** (*-ασκε* Θ 272): so Apollod. iii. 171 *κρύφα Πηλέως εἰς τὸ πῦρ ἐγκρυβοῦσα*; cf. Medea (Paus. ii. 3. 11) *τὸ δὲ ἀεὶ τικτόμενον κατακρύπτειν αὐτὸ εἰς τὸ ἱερὸν φέρουσαν τῆς Ἥρας, κατακρύπτειν δὲ ἀθανάτους ἔσεσθαι νομίζουσαν.* The meaning of the word is explained by the simile ε 488. Ἠύτε *δαλόν* means 'she hid him in the fire as a log is kept alight in the ashes' (see also on *h.* iv. 238), Sotades Ἐγκλειόμεναι (*fr.* 92. 129 Kock vol. 2) *ἐνεκρύψαθ' ὥσπερ δαλὸν εἰς πολλὴν τέφραν*, Archestratus *fr.* 7. 9 ap. Ath. 278 C *εἶθ' ὑπὸ θερμὴν ὦσον ἔσω σποδόν.* Κρύπτεσκε = *obruit* in Ovid (above).

240. **λάθρᾰ** for *λάθρᾱ* is not stranger than *ἅμᾰ ἁμᾷ, κρύφα κρυφᾷ, δίχα διχᾷ, τρίχα τριχᾷ, σῖγα σιγῇ*, K.-B. ii. 306: it occurs Eur. *fr.* 1117. 28 *εὐνῇ συνελθεῖν λάθρα πως ἠβούλετο* and perhaps *Hel.* 829 *κοινῇ γ' ἐκείνῃ ῥᾳδίως λάθρ' οὐδαμοῦ*, the *γρ.* of 'L'.

241. **προθαλής**: only here, cf. *ἀμφιθαλής* X 496. The last hemistich = Ω 630 (*γάρ*).

242. **ἀγήρων** : see on *h.* v. 214.

244. **ἐπιτηρήσασα** : she watched to see how the nurse made the child thrive, and thus broke the taboo. In Apollodorus an unknown Praxithea, perhaps a nurse, raises the alarm (cf. Σ Nic. *Ther.*

484 φωραθεῖσα ὑπό τινος): in late authorities only (Hyginus, Servius, Lactantius, and *Myth. Vat.* 2) the catastrophe is due to intervention by the father. Curiosity in seeing a forbidden sight is punished in the classical myth of Cupid and Psyche; for other examples of this world-wide motive see Hartland *Science of Fairy Tales* 270 sq.

245. **κώκυσεν**: Ap. Rh. iv. 872 ἧκε δ' ἀυτὴν | σμερδαλέην ἐσιδὼν μέγα νήπιος.

ἄμφω πλήξατο μηρώ: M 162, ν 198.

246. **ἀάσθη**: cf. κ 68 ἄασαν, Λ 340 ἀάσατο δὲ μέγα θυμῷ; in 258 the α is short, as Π 685, Τ 113, 136, *h.* v. 253.

248. **ξείνη σε πυρί**: for the caesura cf. 17; for the quantity of ι see on 99. 𝔓 implies πυρῇ by its relic]λλη. The confusion of πῦρ and πυρά is constant: 287, Ψ 165, 172, 216, η 13, 251, Herod. ii. 39.

253. **ἀπὸ ἕο θῆκε**: ι 461 ἀπὸ ἕο πέμπε, M 205 ἀπὸ ἕθεν ἧκε. Cf. more violently Ap. Rh. iv. 674 τὸν μὲν ἄρ' ἁρπάγδην χαμάδις βάλε κεκληγῶτα.

254. **ἐξανελοῦσα πυρός**: Apollodorus, seemingly following a different tradition, says τὸ μὲν βρέφος ὑπὸ τοῦ πυρὸς ἀνηλώθη. In Ovid's account the mother takes the child from the fire.

κοτέσασα: in Homer κοτεσσαμένη.

256–62. We have two versions of this passage:

(i) *Orphica* 76 Abel 233 Kern:

μηδαμὰ μηδὲν
εἰδότες οὔτε κακοῖο προσερχομένοιο νοῆσαι
φράδμονες οὔτ' ἄποθεν μάλ' ἀποστρέψαι κακότητος
οὔτ' ἀγαθοῦ παρεόντος ἐπιστρέψαι τε καὶ ἔρξαι
ἴδριες, ἀλλὰ μάτην ἀδαήμονες ἀπρονόητοι.

(ii) 𝔓 col. vi. 95:

αφρονες ανθρωποι δυστλημονες [ουτε κακοιο]
[υμμιν επ]ερ[χομενου πρ]ογνωμονες ουτ α[γ]α[θοιο
γ]αρ αβραδι[η]μος πολυπειρατι νυκτος
τη[ ] εκ[ ]α ηρπασεν αγη[
νυν δ ουκ εσθ ως [κεν θα]νατον

In this case Orphica and 𝔓 agree in transposing ἀγαθοῖο and κακοῖο, and in making προγνωμονες and its equivalent φράδμονες adjectival. On the other hand 𝔓 is nearer to the hymn than the Orphica are, and as ἀφράδμονες corresponds to δυστλήμονες in 𝔭 (for which cf. *h.* iii. 191, 532, Pythag. χρυσ. ἔπ. 54–6, Manetho i. 110) there is no need to read φράδμονες in 256. For the correption before φρ cf. ο 444 ἐπιφράσσατ' ὄλεθρον, Hes. *OD.* 655 προπεφραδμένα, *Theog.* 160 ἐπεφράσσατο, *h.* iii. 388, and Ἀφροδίτη regularly, La Roche *HU.* i. 10, Monro *HG.* § 370.

The supplementing of 𝔭 is still quite uncertain; Kern gives previous attempts. Another may be attempted, to give the sense,

> 97 ἣ δὲ γὰρ ἀφραδίῃς ἦμος πολὺ πείρατι νυκτὸς
> τῆκον οἱ νέκταρ ἂψ ἥρπασεν ἀτηρείῃ (or -οῦσα).

258. **μήκιστον** seems intended as a superlative of μέγ' (ἀάσθης). Μήκιστα is an adv. ('last') ε 299, 465; for the sense μέγιστον cf. Eur. *Hipp.* 818 τὰ μάκιστ' ἐμῶν κακῶν (Σ μήκιστα καὶ μέγιστα), Soph. *Phil.* 849 ὅτι δύνᾳ μάκιστον κεῖνο . . . ἐξίδου ὅπως πράξεις (Σ μέγιστον, σύμφορον), Aristides xx. 260 ὦ μήκιστα μηκίστων ἰδὼν καὶ ἀκούσας ἐγώ, xlviii. 340 μέχρι ἂν κορυφωθῇ τὸ μήκιστον, Eusebius ap. Stob. *ecl.* iii. 39. 24 (*fr.* 38 Mullach) εὐχὴ δικαιοτάτη αὕτη ἂν παρὰ πάντων φυλαχθείη ἐπιτηδεία μόνη (corr. to ἐπὶ τῇ διαμονῇ) τοῦ μηκίστου, Galen vii. 673 τέλος ἐπὶ μήκιστον αἴρονται μέγεθος, Philo *quod deus* 443 ἐπιμήκιστα (ἀδικήματα). Al. in the lexx.

259. **ἴστω κτλ.** Cf. Ο 36, ε 184, for the position of ὅρκος before Στυγὸς ὕδωρ Ap. Rh. iii. 714. On the Gods' oath by the Styx see on *h.* iii. 86.

262. **θάνατον . . . ἀλύξαι** = Φ 565, ρ 547, χ 66. Ap. Rh. iv. 872 has γῆρας ἀλάλκοι, but this does not justify alteration.

265–7. The text is sound (with the sole correction of συναυξήσουσ' to συνάξουσ', for which cf. Β 381, Ξ 149, 448, vit. Hom. Suidea 188; συνάξουσ' suggested συναύξω, which was then given its future); 'when Demophon is a man the Eleusinians will always be fighting with one another'. Editors have assumed a lacuna before 265 and after 267, or at all events after the lines. It was supposed that the lost passage or passages referred to the death of Demophon, or to his leadership in the war, or mediation between the parties. This supposition is quite gratuitous; 265 simply marks the time 'when he has grown to manhood', and has no closer connexion with the preceding or succeeding lines. There is no trace in myth or history of an Eleusinian civil war; hence Matthiae (followed by B.) substituted Ἀθηναίοισι for ἐν ἀλλήλοισι, assuming that D. was the leader of the Eleusinians in their war against Athens. The corruption is impossible, not to mention the further difficulty that tradition made Eumolpus not Demophon leader of the Eleusinians (Thuc. ii. 15, Isocr. *Pan.* 19 Apollod. iv. 15. 4, Lycurgus *Leocr.* 24, Paus. i. 38. 3). Creutzer was no doubt right in explaining the lines by reference to the βαλλητύς or sham fight, which is expressly connected with Demophon by Hesychius Βαλλητύς· ἑορτὴ Ἀθήνησιν, ἐπὶ Δημοφῶντι τῷ Κελεοῦ ἀγομένη (cf. *id.* Μόροττον· ἐκ φλοιοῦ πλέγμα τι ᾧ ἔτυπτον ἀλλήλους τοῖς Δημητρίοις). Lobeck *Aglaoph.* 296 quotes an anonymous verse in Artemid. i. 8 ταύροις ἐν Ἰωνίᾳ παῖδες Ἐφεσίων ἀγωνίζονται καὶ ἐν Ἀττικῇ παρὰ ταῖς θεαῖς ἐν Ἐλευσῖνι

κοῦροι Ἀθηναῖοι περιτελλομένων ἐνιαυτῶν,

but it is not clear whether it has any connexion with the βαλλητύς, which according to A. Mommsen and Lenormant took place at the end of the festival. There is no evidence on the point, and the date is quite uncertain. Similar ceremonies in Greek cult were the feasts of *Daulis* at Argos, *Katagogia* at Ephesus, *Lithobolia* at Troezen, *Ballachradae* at Argos, a feast of oriental Artemis at Antioch, and probably the ἀγὼν ἐν σκίλλαις in Sicily (reff. in Nilsson *GF.* 413 sq.; other but less relevant sham fights in Greek cult *ib.* 402). On the meaning of such types of ritual see the discussions in Mannhardt *Antike Wald- und Feldkulte* i. 548 sq., Frazer vii. 98, ix. 173, Eitrem *Opferritus* 290, Usener *ARW.* viii. 297 = *Kl. Schrift.* iv. 435, Rose in *Folklore* xxxvi. 322. Rose points out that neither Usener's explanation that the fight represents the conflict of summer and winter, nor Eitrem's that the object is purification, can possibly account for all the known instances. He suggests that the psychological basis of this type of ritual is the idea that the raising and expressing of excitement creates magical power. In instances of this kind where the object of the rite is agricultural, the magical power or energy is made active for the promotion of fertility.

265. **τῷ γε**, as *τῇ δέ* 390 and *τῇσιν . . . βουσίν* iv. 344 is 'ethic' dative, 'in his case', here perhaps 'in his honour'.

ὥρῃσιν 'at the seasons, as the years revolve', i.e. at the right time in the calendar, cf. *ὥρῃσιν πάσῃσιν* v. 102. Cf also 399, iii. 350.

267. **ἤματα πάντα**: this has its regular meaning 'for ever'; the *βαλλητύς* takes place every year.

268. **τιμάοχος**: only here and *h.* v. 31.

269. The line as given in M lacks connexion between *ἀθανάτοις* and *θνητοῖσιν*. As the former word is made necessary by similar formulae (e.g. 11, 22, 45, 403), a conjunction must be added to the latter (*θνητοῖσιν τ'* or *θνητοῖσι τε*). The line then becomes hypermetrical. The last three words are sound; it follows that *ὄνειαρ* must be reduced to *ὄνεαρ*, a change approved of by Schulze *qu. ep.* 226 and Solmsen *KZ.* xxxii. 92. That the second syllable is always lengthened in Homer is due to metrical convenience and habit, it does not constitute a law, and is of course unoriginal. Other cases are *ἄλεαρ, ἄλειαρ* (Choerob. *orth. An. Ox.* ii. 181, 29), *ἀλείατα* vulg., *δέλεαρ, δελείατος* (Numenius *fr.* 1. 1. ap. Ath. 305 A), *πέαρ* (Hesych. *πέαρ· Γλαυκίας λιπαρόν*), *πεῖαρ* (e.g. *h.* iii. 60 OJKT), *πῖαρ* vulg., *στέαρ, στεῖαρ* (Choerob. i. 381), *ὕφεαρ* 'mistletoe' (see the lexx.), *φρέαρ* (*φρέατι supra* 99), *φρείατα* Φ 199, *ἔαρ εἴαρος, κτέαρ* apparently with -*ε*- always.

ὄνεαρ further involves synizesis of *εα*: this is common in *ἔαρ* (*ἔαρι* Hes. *OD.* 462, *ἔαρ ib.* 492, Mimnermus 2, Chaeremon *fr.* 42), and occurs in *στέαρ*. See on 99, K.-B. i. 471.

For the sentiment cf. Antiphanes *fr.* 1 *ἦν φερέσβιος Δηὼ | βροτοῖσι χάρμα δωρεῖται φίλον.*

270. The revelation of the mysteries is to *follow* the building of a temple devoted to the cult of Demeter, and Demeter is already in occupation of her *νηός before* the institution of the *orgia* (470). Upon other grounds also the temple here mentioned cannot be identified with the *telesterion*, the shape of which is entirely unlike that of a Greek temple, and in which there was no possibility of housing a cult-image. Further, the position of the first *telesterion* does not agree with the description of the site of the temple; if it might be described as *ὑπαὶ πόλιν*, it could not be said to lie Καλλιχόρου *καθύπερθεν*. It is true that no remains of

a temple dating from the seventh century have been found, but Noack has reasonably suggested that it may have been built upon the surface of the rock on the spur (ἐπὶ προὔχοντι κολωνῷ) between the site of the *telesterion* and the modern chapel of the Panagia. This would still be 'below the citadel', and sufficiently far north to be above Callichoron. The complete absence of remains Noack explains by the erection of its successor, for which the foundations were cut deeply into the rock. See Noack 45 sq.

271. **πόλιν αἰπύ τε τεῖχος**: i.e. the acropolis, the fortifications of which (τεῖχος) have been traced on the low hill above the *telesterion*. The actual town lay at the foot of the hill and extended to the sea.

272. **Καλλιχόρου**: see on 99. This well was not discovered till 1892, when excavations showed it to be situated by the Roman propylaea, outside the precinct. The well-mouth is surrounded by concentric circles, no doubt marks for the Eleusinian women who danced round the water in honour of the Goddess (Paus. i. 386). On the discovery see Philios p. 57.

274. **εὐαγέως**: the adv. in Ap. Rh. ii. 699 etc. The adj. is not found in early epic; for exx. in ritual see Dieterich *de hymn. Orph.* 1891, 34 = *Kl. Schr.* 95.

ἱλάσκοισθε: for the opt. cf. ρ 250.

275. **μέγεθος καὶ εἶδος** = *h.* v. 82.

276. **περί τ' ἀμφί τε**: cf. B 305 ἀμφὶ περὶ κρήνην, *h.* v. 271 ἀμφιπεριφθινύθει, Theocr. vii. 142 περὶ πίδακας ἀμφὶ μέλισσαι.

κάλλος ἄητο: cf. Hes. *Scut.* 7 τῆς καὶ ἀπὸ κρῆθεν . . . τοῖον ἄηθ' οἷόν τε πολυχρύσου Ἀφροδίτης.

277. **ὀδμὴ κτλ.** Fragrance is a sign of divinity, *h.* iv. 231, Theognis 9, Aesch. *PV.* 115, Eur. *Hipp.* 1391, Moschus ii. 91, Virg. *Aen.* i. 403, Ovid. *Fast.* v. 375.

278. **φέγγος**: see on 189. Cf. Bacchyl. xvii. 102 ἀπὸ γὰρ ἀγλαῶν λάμπε γυίων σέλας ὥστε πυρός (of the Nereids).

279. **κατενήνοθεν**: no doubt singular, but, as Franke remarks, the writer thought it was plural. On the forms and derivation see Boisacq *in* Ἐνήνοθε.

280. **αὐγῆς**: for this simple correction cf. Soph. *Phil.* 1190 αὐταῖς codd., αὐγαῖς S. Γῆς and τῆς permute *passim*, especially in tragedy.

281. M reads διέκ here with a majority of MSS. at O 124 and other places in the *Iliad*, but 379 δι'ἐκ, and *h*. iv. 158 it has διεκ with ELDB. Cf. the variants on ἀπεκ *h*. iii. 110; ὑπέκ has no variant *ib*. 428; παρέκ has no variant *ib*. 419; at *h*. iv. 547 παρεκ is in ELP, at v. 36 M has παρὲκ (*sic*), the rest παρεκ. Usage in these double prepositions varied, and no principle can be discerned, La Roche *HT*. 333 sq., K.-B. i. 297 b.

282. δηρόν is here adjectival as xxviii. 14, Ξ 206, 305 and often in tragedy (Eur. *HF*. 702, *IT*. 1339, *Orest*. 55, *Heracl*. 69). It is more often absolute, e.g. in the hymns iv. 21, 126 al., Eur. *Andr*. 118, *Hec*. 183.

283. ἀπὸ δαπέδου: Hesych. has ζάπεδον· μέγα ἔδαφος, and the form with ζ- occurs in Xenophanes i. 1, *IGA*. 401 (Kaibel *ep. gr*. 750 a). At λ 598 Aristotle (*Rhet*. iii. 11) read ἐπὶ δάπεδον δέ with some MS. support for the vulgate ἔπειτα πέδον δε. Here therefore ἀπὸ δαπέδου is justified by the original pronunciation. Cf. Solmsen *Rh. Mus*. lx. 500 sq.; on the derivation of the word Boisacq *in v*.

284. ἐλεεινήν: synizesis of εει cannot be proved; on the other hand there is no case of ἐλεινός in epos.

285. εὐστρώτων: only here and *h*. v. 157 ἐς λέχος εὔστρωτον.

289. ἐλούεον: on the form see Schulze *qu. ep*. 65 n. 1, Smyth *Ionic* 535, Solmsen *op.c*. 13, *KZ*. xxix. 98, Jacobsohn *ib*. xlii. 156 n. 1. Ludwich objected to the washing of the child, but the women perform the duty of a nurse (cf. Ap. Rh. iv. 1310) in place of Demeter. It is unnecessary to press the phrase further and to point out that the child was covered with ash, though this is expressly mentioned in a similar passage (of the nymphs and Bacchus) *Anth. Pal*. ix. 331 αἱ Νύμφαι τὸν Βάκχον ὅτ' ἐκ πυρὸς ἥλατο κοῦρος | νίψαν ὑπὲρ τέφρης ἄρτι κυλιόμενον.

291. τροφοὶ ἠδὲ τιθῆναι: Plato *Tim*. 88 D τροφὸν καὶ τιθήνην, Orph. *h*. x. 18 τροφὸς ἠδὲ τιθήνη.

292. The reference is plainly to a παννυχίς or all-night festival confined to women; hence in the morning Celeus' ignorance of what has happened. It follows that there can be no reference to the nocturnal services of the mysteries, which were emphatically not restricted to women. Perhaps it is to the feminine παννυχίς of the *Thesmophoria* that it is to be related.

The prominence of women and the frequent exclusion of men in the ritual of Demeter (see ante, p. 120) has analogies in the agricultural ceremonies of many primitive peoples. See Jane Harrison *Prolegomena* 272, Frazer vii. 113, Jevons 239. Of the theories put forward to account for it, that which represents it as a survival of a matriarchal stage of society may be dismissed. The theory in general finds little favour to-day with anthropologists, and as regards Greece there is no substantial evidence for the existence at any time of a matriarchal system. Others have suggested that in primitive society man is the hunter and woman the farm-labourer, and hence all agricultural rites fall to women. Against this *a priori* hypothesis is to be set the fact that in Greece the divine practitioners of the agricultural art are male heroes not Goddesses, Triptolemus not Demeter. More probable therefore is the explanation based upon the magical quality attributed to members of the female sex by most primitive peoples and the fact, relevant for ritual of this type, that it is women who give birth to new lives (Farnell 106).

293. **δείματι παλλόμεναι**: the same phrase in an oracle ap. Herod. vii. 140 (Hendess 111. 10), Nonnus i. 56.

296. **πολυπείρονα**: Orph. *Arg.* 33 πολυπείρονας οἴμους.

302. **ξανθὴ Δημήτηρ** = E 500, Orph. *Lith.* 594, *fr.* 14 Abel = 263 Kern; ξανθοκόμος Nonn. xi. 395, ξανθοφυής *ib.* vi. 113. It is often suggested that the epithet originally referred to the colour of ripe corn, as the 'hair' of Demeter (cf. 454 κομήσειν ἀσταχύεσσιν, Euseb. *PE.* v. 34 οἱ δὲ ἐκόμων Δήμητρι); but in the hymns Demeter is purely anthropomorphic; ξανθός is the conventional colouring for epic and tragic heroes and heroines. The epithet is further applied not only to Persephone (*Anth. Pal.* vii. 507), who cannot be claimed by the most ardent believer in the corn-fetish theory as representing the *ripe* corn, but to a number of female divine personages, e.g. Aphrodite *AP.* ix. 605. 1, Artemis Anacr. *fr.* 1, Athena Pind. *Nem.* x. 13, *fr.* 34, Dione Theocr. vii. 116, the Charites Pind. *Nem.* v. 54, *AP.* vii. 440. 3.

305. **ἐπὶ χθόνα**: for the accusative see on xxv. 3.

The worship of D. and Core in Triphylia was explained by the alternation of good and bad years (τάχα διὰ τὰς ἐναντιότητας) by

Demetrius of Scepsis ap. Strab. 344. Cf. in gen. Eur. *Helena* 1325 sq.

308. **καμπύλ' ἄροτρα**: Solon i. 48.

ἀρούραις: for the local dative cf. E 137 ἀγρῷ and see on 99.

310. Cf. Hes. *OD.* 180 Ζεὺς δ' ὀλέσει καὶ τοῦτο γένος μερόπων ἀνθρώπων.

312. **θυσιῶν**: so 368. Non-homeric.

314. **Ἶριν . . . χρυσόπτερον** = Θ 398; see on iii. 107: so of Τύχη poeta ap. Stob. *ecl.* i. 135 περὶ σὰν πτέρυγα χρυσέαν. Iris is here employed as messenger to the Gods on earth, Hermes is sent to the underworld (335). Cf. E. Maass Ἶρις *IF.* i. 157. Demeter could not be found; Pan discovered her at Elaeum, Paus. viii. 422.

315. **πολυήρατον . . . ἔχουσαν** = Hes. *Theog.* 908 (ἔχουσα).

316. **ὣς ἔφαθ'**: the use of this formula after an indirect speech is not Homeric, but occurs *infra* 448, Hes. *OD.* 69, Ap. Rh. iv. 236, 1119. See on 127.

317. Cf. *h.* iii. 108.

319. **κυανόπεπλον**: not in Homer, and in the hymns only here, 360, 374, 442 of Rhea, cf. 183. In Hes. *Theog.* 406 it is an epithet of Leto.

321. **ἄφθιτα εἰδώς**: only here, for ἄφθιτα μήδεα εἰδώς *h.* v. 43, where see note.

325. Valckenaer's addition of πατήρ is acceptable as it retains θεούς *in synizesi*, which was probably the cause of the omission. Cf. 345.

328. The alteration ἕλοιτο μετ' ἀθανάτοισι θεοῖσι (on the analogy of 444) does not account for ἑλέσθαι in place of θεοῖσιν. The suggestion βόλοιτο rests on Λ 319, where *e* has δὴ ἐθέλει for δὴ βόλεται. βόλοιτο (ἐθέλοι written above) might have produced ἐθέλοιτο, an impossible form.

331. **θυώδεος**: a favourite word with the writer of this hymn, e.g. 231, 244, 288, 355, 385; of Olympus *h.* iv. 322.

337. **ἁγνήν**: specially an epithet of Demeter (see on 203) and Persephone (λ 386 with the v.l. αἰνή, Orph. *h.* xxiv. 2, xliii. 7, Εὐχή 6, *orac.* Hendess 157. 7, 9, 35). The latter was worshipped

as Ἁγνή in Messenia Paus. iv. 33, 4; cf. the inscr. of Andania. So ἁγναὶ θεαί of both Goddesses *CIG.* 5431, 5643; Rohde *Psyche* 192, Roscher i. 1813, P.-W. iv. 2. 2741, 2754.

ἀπό may be retained, though in the Homeric formula the preposition is ὑπό (Voss): cf. Φ 56 Hes. *Theog.* 653.

339. **μεταλήξειε**: the spelling is philologically correct, as λήγω (σλήγω, see Boisacq in λαγαρός) makes position I 191, θ 87. Aristarchus Σ I 299 read the single liquid at I 157, 261, 299. The vulgate has -λλ-.

344–5. ἐπ' ἀτλήτων gives no sense. To neglect the position τλ also is impossible in early epos. In Homer there is but one case and that doubtful, σχετλίη La Roche *HU.* i. 4, 6; as late as Pindar *Ol.* vi. 38 and Antimachus *fr.* 17 we find ἄτλατος, to say nothing of αἰνοτλήτων Max. π. κατ. 224, 309 (on the other hand there is correption in Empedocles 14, Theocr. xxv. 174, in melos Pind. *Ol.* vii. 20, 77 and often in late Greek, e.g. *Anth. Pal.* vii. 342. 2 Ἀττικίης βαρυτλήτου, epigr. ap. Steph. *in* Θούριοι, Cougny vi. 125. 3, 146. 18). Of the conjectures ἀποτηλοῦ is the best (cf. ἐκ δ' ἄρα τηλοῦ Oppian *Cyn.* iii. 103, and for the sense ἀπάνευθε 355). If miswritten ἀποτληου the resulting word is not worse than M's other corruptions (e.g. ἐπηλσίησι for ἐπηλυσίη 228).

In line 345 an anapaest has fallen out owing to the synizesis of θεῶν (cf. the similar result 325). This may have been τι κακόν as iii. 325ª, or θάνατον as O 349.

347. **κυανοχαῖτα**: the stock Homeric epithet of Posidon. Cf. κυάνεος of Hades, Kaibel *Epigr.* 1046 b 84, and μελαγχαίτας Eur. *Alc.* 439.

348. M's reading requires ἄγειν, ἐξάγειν to mean 'let go, send out'. The parallel passage 335 ff. makes the alteration με easy.

ἀγαυήν: cf. λ 213, 226, 635, Orph. *h.* xli. 5, xliv. 6, xlvi. 6.

349. **Ἐρέβευσφι**: Franke's correction is easy (-ευσφιν, -εσφιν I 572, Hes. *Theog.* 669), but the linguistic characteristics of the hymn are to be preserved (κατενήνοθεν with plural 279, παύσειεν neut. below).

351. **παύσειεν**: the neuter active is rare except in παῦε (e.g. Hes. *Scut.* 449, Ar. *Ran.* 580). But δ 659 there is overwhelming

support for μνηστῆρες . . . παῦσαν ἀέθλων, and cf. *h.* xxxiii. 14 (in *p*), *IG.* iii. 1. 616, Eur. *Hel.*, 1320 ἔπαυσε, *Hec.* 917 καταπαύσας.

352. **χαμαιγενέων ἀνθρώπων** = *h.* v. 108 (note).

357. **μείδησεν . . . ὀφρύσιν.** The usage at *Herm.* 279 ὀφρύσι ῥιπτάζεσκεν of casting glances, and in the *Odyssey* at ι 468 ἀνὰ δ' ὀφρύσι νεῦσεν ἑκάστῳ, μ 194 ὀφρύσι νευστάζων of making signs, seems to show that Hades' 'smile' was conveyed by his eyebrows, not his lips; he did not relax his mouth but *supercilio subrisit*, that is, he raised his eyebrows in private satisfaction. Of the parallels quoted Hermesianax 7. 9 Powell Κωκυτόν τ' ἀθέμιστον ἐπ' ὀφρύσι μειδήσαντα seems good, but Ap. Rh. iii. 1024, Pind. *Pyth.* ix. 16, Ovid *Amores* iii. 1. 33 *limis subrisit ocellis* seem to imply a real smile. Μείδησε δὲ θυμῷ υ 301 is not unlike; the reverse O 101 ἣ δ' ἐγέλασσε | χείλεσιν. For the action cf. Ξ 222, 223.

The last three words occur *IG. Sic. Ital.* 1842, αναξ ενερων *Supp. Epigr.* ii. 615.

358. As ἀπίθησε takes a genitive in this hymn (448), we read the genitive here, i.e. ἐφετμῆς not ἐφετμῇς.

362. **δυσθύμαινε**: post-Homeric, as all compounds of δυσ- and θυμός.

περιώσιον ἄλλων = Pindar *Isthm.* iv. 3.

363. **οὔ τοι . . . ἀεικής**: see on 83.

365. **δεσπόσσεις**: post-Homeric; next in Aeschylus.

366. **σχήσησθα**: as there is no example of the termination -σθα or -θα in a future, while the aorists βάλησθα, πάθησθα, εἴπησθα are Homeric (K.-B. ii. § 209. 3), it seems better to regard σχήσησθα as the subjunctive of the aorist ἔσχησα (cf. the forms σχήσειε Nonnus xvii. 177, *Or. Sib.* 9. 91). The tense is in meaning a future, as in the typical line δύσομαι εἰς 'Αίδαο καὶ ἐν νεκύεσσι φαείνω, μ 383. Cf. on *h. Apoll.* 1. The conjecture σχήσεισθα is called a 'verbildete Form' by Schulze *KZ.* xxxiii. 317. On -σθα in general see Solmsen *ib.* xxxi. 205.

367. **ἀδικησάντων**: the first instance of the verb; ἄδικος is found in Hesiod *OD.* 258, 332. As l. 365 shows, the reference is not to the future life.

371. **αὐτός**: 'in person', not through another.

372. **ῥοιῆς κόκκον ἔδωκε**: Apollod. i. 5. 3 ῥοιᾶς ἔδωκεν αὐτῇ φαγεῖν

κόκκον. In Ovid *Met.* v. 535 Persephone picks the fruit in a garden and eats seven seeds. There is a widespread belief that the living may visit the underworld and return provided that they abstain from the food of the dead. The Finnish hero Wäinämöinen refuses to drink in Manala, the place of the dead (*Kalevala* xvi. 293). In S. Africa there is a similar story; a man visits spirit-land and is warned to return before he meets any one who will give him food (Leslie *Among the Zulus and Amatongas* p. 121). In New Zealand a Maori woman was thought to have come back from the dead, having by her father's advice refused the food which the dead people offered her (Shortland *Traditions of New Zealand* p. 150). The last story is quoted by Tylor *Primitive Culture* ii. 51, who gives a parallel among the Sioux of N. America. Several similar tales are collected by Hartland *Science of Fairy Tales* c. iii. (among the ancient Danes, in the Banks islands, and in the Hervey islands). Hartland remarks that there is the same objection to eating the food of fairies (cf. Rhys *Celtic Folklore* i. 290; see also *Folk-Lore* viii. 380, *County Folk-Lore* iii (Orkney and Shetland) 25, 27). Some other references are given by Frazer on Paus. viii. 37. 7, and in Pinzer-Tawney *Ocean of Story* vi. 133–6; cf. also *Folk-Lore* x. 300 (Japan). The basis of the belief is the idea that a common meal unites the partakers; hence the sanctity of the relation of host and guest. By eating any food in the underworld Persephone established a bond with the dead. But there is also a significance in the particular food, a pomegranate, though its precise meaning has been disputed. According to one view the fruit, from the blood-red colour of the inside, is a symbol of blood and death. According to Artemidorus *Onir.* i. 73 it was unlucky διὰ τὸν ἐν Ἐλευσῖνι λόγον. A pomegranate tree was planted over the graves of Menoeceus, a suicide (Paus. ix. 25. 1), and the unlucky Eteocles (in the latter case by the Erinyes, Philostr. *Imag.* ii. 29, i. 4). It was believed to have sprung from the blood of Dionysus Zagreus (Clem. Alex. *protrept.* ii. 19). The fruit was therefore appropriate to the dead, and as such (ὡς φυτὸν χθόνιον) was taboo in the ἁγιστεῖαι of Attis, Julian *or.* v. 176 A). Probably, however, it is here symbolical of marriage and fertility, from the multitude of its seeds; cf. Herod. iv. 143 ὅσοι ἐν τῇ ῥοιῇ κόκκοι. It was the emblem of Hera, probably as Goddess of marriage, Roscher i. 2090. The fruit expedited birth, Pliny *NH.* xxiii. 107; *ib.* 112 its flowers *sistunt potu menses feminarum.* It was an attribute of Aphrodite (see Murr *Die Pflanzenwelt in d. gr. Myth.* 50 sq.). Pausanias (ii. 17. 4) refuses to discuss the meaning of the fruit in the hand of the Argive Hera. The mystae at Eleusis abstained from eating it (Porph. *de abst.* iv. 16), as did the Thesmophoriazusae (Clem. *l.c.*) and the banqueters at the *Haloa* (Σ Lucian *dial. mer.* vii. 4; see Jane Harrison *Proleg.* 148). The Arcadians would not bring the pomegranate into the temple of Despoina (Paus. viii. 37. 7). In many of these prohibitions (e.g. during the *Haloa*, at Eleusis, in the worship of Attis), the apple, which was undoubtedly regarded as a symbol of fruitfulness or as an aphrodisiac, was coupled with the pomegranate.

According to this view the pomegranate would symbolize not so much Persephone's general union with the dead as her special union with Hades. In actual custom the Greeks made wedding-cakes of sesame (διὰ τὸ πολύγονον, ὥς φησι Μένανδρος Σ Ar. *Pax* 869). The reason for the taboo upon eating pomegranate at these festivals may have been in order to avoid a supposed stimulus to the sexual appetite (Wächter, *Reinheitsvorschriften* 106, 107). This is confirmed by the converse practice of placing herbs supposed to check sexual desire under the beds of the women who observed chastity during the fast of *Thesmophoria* (Pliny *NH.* xxiv. 59), the abstention from garlic at the *Scirophoria* (Philochorus ap. Phot. *lex. in* Τροπηλίς), and the alleged dosing of the hierophant with hemlock (Hippolytus *ref. omn. haer.* v. 8).

For the pomegranate as an attribute of Persephone and Pluto in art see P.-R. 763 n. 2, Bötticher *Baumkultus* c. 38.

It does not appear, however, that the writer of the hymn attached any particular meaning to the pomegranate. Apollodorus does not offer any explanation, and Ovid *Met.* v. 532 simply says *sic Parcarum foedere cautum est.*

373. The sense is obscure owing to the different meanings of νωμᾶν. These fall under two heads (i) 'distribute' = νέμειν, of

food, etc., (ii) 'wield, handle' of (*a*) weapons, etc., (*b*) the mind ='turn over, perceive'. Hermann, taking ἑ from Ruhnken, understood 'dividing it in two', of which parts Hades ate one. But participation by Hades in the food is not mentioned in this or any other account of the myth. Nor is such participation required according to folk-lore; the living have only to eat the food offered by the dead, not share it with them, to prevent their return. It is better to retain ἕ and translate (after Matthiae) 'peering round him', cl. Δ 497 ἀμφὶ ἕ παπτήνας, Ο 241 ἀμφὶ ἓ γιγνώσκων ἑτάρους. For this sense of νωμᾶν cf. Herod. iv. 128 νωμῶντες . . . σῖτα ἀναιρεομένους, Plato *Cratyl.* 411 D τὸ νωμᾶν καὶ τὸ σκοπεῖν ταὐτόν, Eur. *Phoen.* 1255 μάντεις δὲ μῆλ' ἔσφαζον ἐμπύρους τ' ἀκμὰς | ῥήξεις τ' ἐνώμων, where the 𝔖 paraphrase ἐπεσκόπουν καὶ παρετήρουν, perhaps Soph. *Phil.* 716, and in an intermediate construction Eur. *Phoen.* 1563 τάδε σώματα . . . ὄμματος αὐγαῖς σαῖς ἐπενώμας, 𝔖 ἀντὶ τοῦ διεσκόπεις, cf. Aesch. *S. Th.* 25 ἐν ὠσὶ νωμῶν καὶ φρεσίν. This is not more difficult than ἀννείμῃ=ἀναγνῷ Theocr. xviii. 48 Meineke, Hesych. νέμει· ἀναγιγνώσκει (and νέμεις, νέμω), ἀννέμειν· ἀναγινώσκειν, ἐπινεμάτω· ἐπαναγνώτω, Suidas ἀνανέμειν· ἴσον τῷ ἀνάγιγνώσκειν Ἐπίχαρμος, Soph. *fr.* 145 as corr., Parthenius ap. Meineke *An. Alex.* 257, 𝔖 Pind. *Isthm.* ii. 63 ἐν τῇ Ἀρήτῃ τὸ ἄννεμε ἀντὶ τοῦ ἀνάγνωθι, *or. Sibyll.* iii. 423 ἀνανείμῃ, Hesych. Πτερονόμος· τοῖς πτεροῖς νομῶσα καὶ νεμομένη· ὅθεν καὶ τὸ νέμειν ἐπιστροφὴν ἄγειν . . . Ὑπερνέμεις· ὑπερορᾷς: cf. also Strabo 739 ἄλλα καὶ ἄλλα νέμοντες περὶ τῶν αὐτῶν δόγματα. Hades cast furtive (λάθρῃ) glances about him to see if he were observed.

For λάθρῃ cf. ρ 80 and on 413. (The sense is possible σ 216, Hes. *Scut.* 462.)

381. For υ- short cf. Batr. 97, Ap. Rh. iv. 290.

384. **στῆσε δ' ἄγων** = Β 558.

386. **ἠΰτε μαινάς**: cf. Χ 460 μαινάδι ἴσῃ (of Andromache), Ζ 389 μαινομένῃ εἰκυῖα (*id*), *or. Sibyll.* v. 484 μούνη μαινὰς ἄναυδος ἐπὶ ψαμάθοις Ἀχέροντος (of Isis), Xenophon Ephes. v. 13. 2 διὰ μέσης τῆς πόλεως βοῶν ἄθεια ἐοικὼς μεμηνότι ἔθει, Eur. *Hel.* 543 ὡς δρομαία πῶλος ἢ Βάκχη θεοῦ, *Hipp.* 550 ὅπως τε Βάκχαν, Timotheus ap. Plut. *mor.* 22 A, *ib.* 170 A μαινάς of Artemis, Aesch. *Eum.* 502 βροτοσκόπων μαινάδων. There is no reference to

Maenads, and the passage does not imply that there was Dionysiac influence at Eleusis.

The ὄρος . . . δάσκιον ὕλης is the προὔχων κολωνός of 298.

ὕλης is the first example of the plural of ὕλη in the literal sense (woods); cf. Anacreon 39 ὕλης (ὕλη auctores, ὕλαις Ϛ Pind. *Ol.* iii. 52), Hecataeus *fr.* 172 οὔρεα δασέα ὕλῃσι, Moschus iii. 89 Βοιωτίδες ὗλαι, Anacreontea 32. 7 ὗλαι (v.l. ὧραι); it is common in Babrius, the Orphic Argonautica, and Nonnus. In prose the plural does not occur before Lysis ap. Iambl. *vit. Pyth.* 79, Theophr. *CP.* i. 5. 4 ἐν ταῖς ὕλαις καὶ τοῖς ὄρεσι, Dion. Hal. *de Thuc.* 7, Strabo 163 etc. Cf. Zacharias *KZ.* xxxiv. 453. Ἴδη has a regular plural, and γαῖ is more frequent than ὗλαι (*CR.* 1906, 290). As a coincidence cf. δάσκιον ὕλης Nonnus x. 175.

387 ff. For the torn page in M see Introd. p. xxi f. and the facsimile in Goodwin's edition. The supplements, unless the contrary is stated, are due to that editor.

391. In the hymn Persephone herself reveals her action in eating the pomegranate, the consequences of which are automatic and do not depend upon the fact being known. Later versions say that Ascalaphus spied her eating, acted as informer, and was in consequence turned into a screech-owl (Ovid *Met.* v. 534, Servius *in Georg.* i. 39, *in Aen.* iv. 462, and other late Latin mythographers). In Apollodorus (i. 30 and ii. 126) the story has been modified by confusion with the fate of Ascalabus the lizard. In Virgil *Georg.* i. 39 Persephone is well content to stay in Elysium; in Lucan (vi. 741), who must have taken the view that the pomegranate was the fruit of death (see on 372), *contagia passam | noluerit revocare Ceres.*

392. **παυομένη**: M has παομ . . . , but the phonetic exchange of α and αυ is common: cf. ἐπάην, παῆναι (Hermae Pastor *bis*), ἀναπαήσομαι in the lexx., B 867 Νάστης Ναύστης, Λ 578 Φασιάδην Φαυσιάδην, Π 338 καλόν καυλόν, Aratus 668 ἀγήν αὐγήν, Herod. ii. 111, and above 267.

395. The verb νέω 'go' has a doubtful existence (v.l. θ 108, Pindar *fr.* 124 *a* 7, Herod. v. 9 in an epigram, Sophron 19 (fut.)), and therefore Ruhnken's correction is usually accepted. For the supplement cf. Θ 368.

398. **πτᾶσα** occurs Herodian. π. διχρ. 289. 24, cf. Choerob. in Theod. 733, 12 πτάς ἀποπτάς. The simple verb does not occur in Homer. Ἔπτη is found in Euphorion *fr.* 41 Powell, Anacreontea 22–3, Conon ap. Ptol. Heph. 136 a 31, Batr. 208, Bion i. 58, Lucian *Tragoedop.* 218, Nonnus ii. 223, vii. 21, xxxviii. 26, xlii. 537, Heraclit. π. ἀπίστων 9 κάθως εἰώθαμεν λέγειν ἐπὶ τῶν ταχέως τρεχόντων ὅτι ἔπτη: ἔπτης *IG. Sic. Ital.* 2550 and Hesych., πταίην Eur. *Ion* 796, πτῆναι Julian *or.* v. 177 B, ἔπτην *ep.* 193 = 386 C, ἔπτη Heraclit. *l.c.* The compounds are normal in late Greek (ἐξέπτη as early as Hesiod *OD.* 98, Batr. 208, 211, ἐξεπταν Collitz *Dial. Inschr.* 1654). See Veitch *in* ἵπτημι. There is therefore no need to resort to such alterations as ἐπάσω or τι πάσσαο, especially as πάσσατ' 50 and πάσασθαι 413 have survived. 'But if so, back you flit'.

The ellipse of the verb of the second protasis (a kind of σχῆμα ἀναπόδοτον) in a double condition is occasionally found: I 46, 262, strengthened to εἰ δ' οὖν Soph. *Ant.* 722, Nicander *Ther.* 885. In prose it is commoner, Plato *Euthyd.* 285 C, *Symp.* 212 C, *Laws* 759 B, Xen. *Hell.* ii. 3. 16; εἰ δ' ἄρα Strabo 62, cf. 351. 27 inf., εἰ δ' οὖν Hippocr. ii. 538 inf. Kühn, ἀλλ' εἴπερ Plato *Euthyd.* 296 B.

399. Ilgen's ὠρέων is nearest to the MS. and preserves an Ionic form and Homeric synizesis: 406 ἐρέω, 414 Κρονίδεω.

εἰς ἐνιαυτόν. *m*'s substitute can hardly be an invention; for εἰς distributive see LS.[9] III. 3.

The division of time is followed by Apollodorus i. 5. 3 Περσεφόνη δὲ καθ' ἕκαστον ἐνιαυτὸν τὸ μὲν τρίτον μετὰ Πλούτωνος ἠναγκάσθη μένειν, τὸ δὲ λοιπὸν παρὰ τοῖς θεοῖς. The other Alexandrian and later versions divide the year into two equal parts of six months' sojourn and six months' absence (Ovid *Fast.* iv. 614, *Met.* v. 567, Cornutus 28, Hyginus *fab.* 146, Servius *in Georg.* i. 39). A similar alternative version of the period of presence of Apollo is noted in P.-R. 763 n. 3. According to Delian tradition he spent six months in Delos and in Lycia respectively, whereas the Delphians believed him to be present among them for nine months and absent three. The divisions of the year into summer and winter and into three seasons are both primitive systems (see on 47). Two explanations of the meaning of Persephone's absence were current in antiquity. The first, which seems to be orthodox Stoic doctrine, identifies Persephone with the corn, and her absence refers to the sojourn of the corn underground (Cornutus 28, Cic. *de nat. deor.* ii. 66, Σ Hes. *Theog.* 912, Tzetzes in Hes. *OD.* 32, Cleanthes ap. Plut. *mor.* 377 D, Varro ap. August. *de civ. dei* vii. 20, Σ Ar. *Vesp.* 1429). With this theory the rape was placed in the autumn, Orph. *h.* xxix. 14, *fr.* 196 Kern.

A modern and much less probable variation of this view supposes that the descent and ascent of Persephone represent the storing of seed-corn in underground repositories, and its subsequent removal for sowing (Cornford in *Essays and Studies presented to William Ridgeway*, 153 sq.).

The alternative, though certainly wrong, explanation, which was popular with ancient scholars, rested upon the identification of Persephone with the moon (Porph. *antr. nymph.* 18, Servius *in Ecl.* iii. 26, *in Aen.* iii. 13, iv. 51, vi. 118), the disappearance of which was thought to have given rise to the story of Core's absence in the underworld (Ennius ap. Varr. *ling. lat.* v. 68, Plut. *mor.* 942 D, Serv. *in Georg.* i. 39, Fulgentius *Myth.* ii. 16). This identification is late and appears to have come about through the equation of Artemis, Hecate and Persephone, who came to be regarded as three aspects of the triform Goddess (Servius as above and *in Aen.* iii. 7. 3, iv. 511).

401. The pres. ind. with ὁππότε is unusual: cf. Lucian *Toxaris* 46.

403. The construction is broken and a lacuna is necessary.

406. ἐρέω: dissyll. as in Hes. *OD.* 202; without synizesis below, 416.

409. ἐλθεῖν after ἦλθε (407) is not offensive. The construction is as at Λ 715, Ω 194 (Bücheler).

411. αὐτάρ twice cannot be tolerated; Σ 203 αὐτὰρ Ἀχιλλεὺς ὦρτο Διὶ φίλος· ἀμφὶ δ' Ἀθήνη, in several MSS. ἀμφί δ' has given place to αὐτάρ. Ruhnken's εἶθαρ and Ilgen's αὐτίκ' are equally near αὐτάρ; the sense suggests ἤτοι. αὐτὰρ ὁ λάθρῃ = Oppian *Hal.* ii. 413.

413. ἄκουσαν κτλ. In 372 (ἔδωκε φαγεῖν) nothing is said of the compulsion on which Persephone here insists. Hades did not

use force; he gave it her, and she without wanting it (ἀέκουσαν) took it against her will, and found it sweet (μελιηδέ' ἐδωδήν, 'like pomatum', we are told). The pleonasm is traditional, A 430 etc. βίῃ ἀέκοντος.

417 sqq. 𝔭 gives a much more correct list than M; Pausanias's quotation also is accurate. The catalogue coincides with Hes. *Theog.* 349 sq. (cf. also Apollod. i. 11, Hygin. 11 Schmidt, Virg. *Georg.* iv. 336). The writer has taken 16 out of the 41 names in Hesiod, and added Leucippe, Phaeno, Melite, Iache, and Rhodope. Of these Melite is a Nereid Σ 42, *Theog.* 246. Cf. P.-R. i. 552. On Γαλαξαύρη see Kretschmer *Glotta* x. 52, and on variations in names Seneca *de ben.* i. 3.

424. The line is needlessly suspected by Malten. In 5 only the Oceanids are mentioned, naturally, as they form the greater part of P.'s companions. It is no objection that Pallas and Artemis end the list; the list of nymphs in *Theog.* 349–61 is closed with the name of Styx ἣ δή σφεων προφερεστάτη ἐστὶν ἁπασέων. Pallas and Artemis are present in most versions, Eur. *Hel.* 1315, Diod. v. 3, Paus. viii. 31. 2, Stat. *Achill.* ii. 150, Claudian *rapt. Pros.* i. 228, ii. 205 (where they show fight). For ἐγρεμάχῃ cf. *orac.* Hendess 79. 6 Παλλάδι τ' ἐγρεμάχῃ, *IG.* ed. min. i. 573, 576, Orph. Εὐχή 38 (Abel p. 57), ἐγερσιμάχα *AP.* vi. 122. 2. The presence of the Nereids at the rape is the cause of Orphic doctrine expounded in *Orph. h.* xxiv. 9 ὑμεῖς γὰρ πρῶται τελετὴν ἀνεδείξατε σεμνήν. For καί making position see on v. 13.

428. The point of the comparison to a crocus is not clear. The narcissus had a hundred heads from one root (12): in nature the narcissus is usually solitary, while the crocus sends up several flowers from one root. This may be what the comparison implies. Else the crocus is used to denote scent (Hipponax 19 = 41 βακκάρι δὲ τὰς ῥῖνας | ἤλειφεν, ἔστι δ' οἷα περ κρόκος, Athen. 682 c the smell of the crocus is superior to that of the violet, Fronto ad M. Caes. v. *namque ut crocus ita somnus priusquam prope adsit longe praeolet longeque delectat*; on the Cyrenaic crocus cf. Theophr. *HP.* vi. 6. 5), or colour (as of the girls' hair, 178) in Ap. Rh. iii. 855 χροιῇ κωρυκίῳ ἴκελον κρόκῳ. Sibthorp *Flora Graeca* iv. *in v.* quotes Dioscurides 4. 161 (158) as saying that the

Narcissus tazzetta, which is yellow, has a κοῖλον κροκοειδές. Theophr. *HP.* iii. 5 τῆς ἐλάτης τὸ ἄνθος κρόκινον refers presumably to colour. Ib. vii. 7. 1, Aelian *NH.* xvii. 23 are ambiguous.

429. **περὶ χάρματι**: 'for joy', a use not in Homer but frequent in later poetry. To the exx. in LS. add Ap. Rh. iii. 866 ὀδύνῃ πέρι.

431. **ἅρμασι χρυσείοισι**: correption before χρ is rare according to La Roche *HU.* i. 41, who allows only Ψ 186 ῥοδόεντι δὲ χρῖεν as certain. But the shortening is probable in other passages, e.g. Ω 795, θ 353, in the hymns iii. 293, 439, iv. 332, viii. 1 and Orph. *h.* lv. 18 (Agar *CR.* 1901, April).

432. The emphasis laid on Persephone's shriek here, 38 and 57, suggests that it was not idle, but to save the appearance of consent to the abduction. So in the Mosaic code (in the case of rape) Deuteronomy xxii. 24–7 'the damsel . . . cried and there was none to save her'. In other Oriental codes there are similar regulations, but the shriek does not appear. Traces are left in Greek marriage usages: Pollux iii. 42 θυρωρὸς ὃς ταῖς θύραις ἐφεστηκὼς εἴργει τὰς γυναῖκας τῇ νύμφῃ βοώσῃ βοηθεῖν. Cf. Ant. Lib. 11. 11 κατ' ἀνάγκας ἐκλιποῦσα τὴν παρθενίαν πλεῖστα τὴν Ἄρτεμιν ἐπεβοήσατο. Cf. also Gen. xxxix. 14, 18 (Potiphar's wife).

433. Cf. η 297, γ 254.

434. The first hemistich = A 601, the second = X 263, *h.* iv. 391.

435. κραδίην . . . ἴαινον = 65 (ἴηνα). This accounts for the triple repetition of θυμός (-όν).

437. **γηθοσύνας**: the plural of γηθοσύνη is found in Ap. Rh. The emendation is supported by υ 8, *h.* iv. 312.

439. **κόρην**: the form is Aeolic (κόραι Sappho 107. 2) and Attic. Elsewhere the writer uses the Homeric form.

440. Hecate was closely associated with Demeter and Persephone. According to one tradition she was the daughter of Demeter (Eur. *Ion* 1048, Σ Ap. Rh. iii. 467, Σ Theocr. ii. 12). In art she often appears in scenes relating to the mission of Triptolemus, and as ἡγεμόνη in the κάθοδος or ἄνοδος of Persephone; see Roscher 1900, P.-R. 761 n. 1, 763. Farnell ii. 511 thinks that the connexion is due, in part at least, to her chthonian character. This is very probable; it is to be noted, however, that the moon is widely thought to influence vegetation (Frazer

vi. 132), and this belief may have contributed to the association of Hecate, as a moon-goddess, with Demeter or Persephone.

ἄνασσα: Ap. Rh. iv. 147 *ἄνασσαν νυκτίπολον χθονίην*, Orph. *h.* i. 7 *παντὸς κόσμου κληδοῦχον ἄνασσαν*; cf. also Ap. Rh. iii. 861, *epigr.* Kaibel 1036. 3, *h. mag.* iii. 9 Abel.

441. The form *μετάγγελος*, 'intermediary', is found O 144 in a minority of MSS., Ψ 199 in a majority (here Aristarchus read it), in both places with a dative. To read it here gives a genuine construction to *ταῖς*, whereas a tmesis (*μετ' . . . ἧκε*) gives a construction not found in this sense with *μεθίημι*, and Hermann's *μέτ'* is doubtful Greek of motion, notwithstanding Plato's version of Ω 8 2.

442. M's *ἣν μητέρα* rests on the fact that Rhea was the mother of both Zeus and Demeter (Hes. *Theog.* 453); an object *αὐτάς* may be supplied from *ταῖς*, and the subject of *ἕλοιτο* is clear from the context. The conjecture *Δημητέρα* perhaps eases the construction (cf. *h.* xiii title *μητ' . . . ρα, δήμητραν*, Herod. iv. 53. 6 *δήμητρος, μητρός*).

445. **νεῦσε**: the construction if correct is highly elliptical; 'allowed her her daughter in the years' circuit one-third part beneath the night, two-thirds with her mother and the other immortals'.

446. Compare the triple division of the year in the case of Adonis, Apollod. iii. 185 *μίαν παρ' ἑαυτῷ μένειν τὸν Ἄδωνιν, μίαν δὲ παρὰ Περσεφόνῃ . . . τὴν δ' ἑτέραν παρ' Ἀφροδίτῃ.*

ἠερόεντα: cf. the dative superscribed 464.

448. **ἀπίθησε . . . ἀγγελιάων.** Alterations like Ruhnken's *ἀγγελίῃσιν* are impossible, and the justification of the genitive by the *σχῆμα νησιωτικόν* of Lesbonax is equally absurd. Hermann's *ἀμέλησε*, in itself equally preposterous, suggests the right solution. *Ἀπειθεῖν* takes a gen. on the model of verbs of obeying and neglecting K.G. i. p. 359 n. 6, e.g. 358, Eur. *IA.* 726 *πείθεσθαι . . . σέθεν*, Herod. i. 126 *ἐμέο πειθόμενοι*, vi. 12 *μὴ πειθώμεθα αὐτοῦ*, Thuc. vii. 73 *σφῶν πείθεσθαι*, K 57 *κείνου γάρ κε μάλιστα πιθοίατο* (minority *κείνῳ*), Galen xvii. 1. 20 *μὴ πειθόμενος Ἱπποκράτους*. These are analogous to *ἀκούειν*. Cf. Aesch. *Septem* 875 *ἄπιστος φίλων*, Plato *leg.* 632 B *εὐπειθέσι τῶν νόμων*.

450. According to Herodian (*π. μον. λέξ.* 35, Σ BLiTA 56,

an. Bekk. 693. 11, Arcad. 200. 22, Choerob. *in Theod. can.* 27) ραρος (and therefore its derivatives) should be written with *spir. lenis* ῥάρος. For the word Ῥαρία or Ῥάριον see Hermesianax *fr.* 719 Powell Ῥάριον ὀργειῶνι νόμῳ διαποιπνύουσα | Δήμητρα, Plut. *mor.* 144 B, Hippolytus *c. haer.* v. 7. 5 ἢ Ῥαρίας Διάλου οἰκιστῆρ' Ἐλευσίς, inscr. in Ἐφ. ἀρχ. 1883 119 sq., *Marmor Parium* 25. Ῥαρίδος Δηοῦς is quoted by Herodian *l.c.*, Ῥάριον πεδίον ἐν Ἐλευσῖνι καὶ Ῥαρία γῆ καὶ Ῥαριὰς ἡ Δημήτηρ Steph. Byz.

For the place cf. Paus. i 38. 6 τὸ δὲ πεδίον τὸ Ῥάριον σπαρῆναι πρῶτον λέγουσι καὶ πρῶτον αὐξῆσαι καρπούς, καὶ διὰ τοῦτο οὐλαῖς ἐξ αὐτοῦ χρῆσθαί σφισι καὶ ποιεῖσθαι πέμματα εἰς τὰς θυσίας καθέστηκεν. 'The plain Rharium seems to have been in the immediate vicinity of Eleusis, but on which side it would be difficult to determine', Leake *Top. Ath.* ii. 149. Rarias is attested as a cult-title of Demeter at Eleusis by Steph. Byz. (above) and Suidas, who also give the story of the reception of Demeter by Rar or Raros the eponym of the Rarian plain.

450. **φερέσβιον**: also in Hes. *Theog.* 693. Apollodorus in Σ Genev. on Φ 319 gives the word as παρ' Ὁμήρῳ. See Introduction p. lxxiii. On the word see Solmsen *op.c.* 20 sq.; cf. also xxx. 9.

οὖθαρ ἀρούρης = I 141.

451. **ἔκηλον**: 'idle'; cf. Ap. Rh. iv. 1247 εὐκήλῳ δὲ κατείχετο πάντα γαλήνη.

453–6. Two seasons are described: spring, when the ears are green, and harvest time when the rich furrows are laden with ripe ears, cut and lying on the ground, while other ears (τὰ δ') have already been bound into sheaves (Franke). G. quotes Hes. *Scut.* 288 οἵ γε μὲν ἤμων | αἰχμῇς ὀξείῃσι κορωνιόωντα πέτηλα | βριθόμενα σταχύων, ὡσεὶ Δημητέρος ἀκτήν, | οἱ δ' ἄρ' ἐν ἐλλεδανοῖσι δέον, but the original is rather Σ 552 δράγματα δ' ἄλλα μετ' ὄγμον ἐπήτριμα πῖπτον ἔραζε, | ἄλλα δ' ἀμαλλοδετῆρες ἐν ἐλλεδανοῖσι δέοντο. In the latter passage, as in the hymn, there are two distinct scenes in the harvesting: (1) reaping, (2) binding; but in the hymn the completion of each operation is described, whereas in the *Iliad* the operations are still in progress. Cf. also Nonnus ii 78, xxxvii. 385 δαπέδῳ πέσε καρπὸς ἀώριος, xlvii. 125 χθονὶ πῖπτε.

454. **κομήσειν**: κομᾶν tropically first here: cf. Plut. *Eumen.* 6 τῶν πεδίων κομώντων, Suid. *in* Ἄλσος . . . τοῦ χώρου κομῶντος, Ael. *NH.* v. 46 al., and passages in the lexx.

455. **ἦρος**: the form is found in Alcaeus *fr.* 45 and other lyric poets.

456. On ἐλλεδανοῖσι cf. Solmsen *Untersuchungen*, p. 244.

458. **κεχάρηντο**: the Homeric form is κεχάροντο.

459. **λιπαροκρήδεμνος**: of Hecate 438 and 25 (q.v.), of Rhea in Orph. *Arg.* 627, of Charis Σ 382, *Anth. Pal.* vi. 61. 5, and of the nymphs and Charites *Cypria* 5. 3.

471. For the gifts of husbandry and religion imparted by Demeter to Attica cf. Hippocr. iii. 771, Isocr. iv. 28, Diod. v. 68. 2, 3, Diogen. 517, *EM.* 147. 36 (Ἀρόη). Phytalus received Demeter when the fig first appeared, Paus. i. 5. 2, Cougny iii. 24.

476. **δρησμοσύνην**: recognized by Hesych. and *EM.*, who gloss it θεραπεία, ὑπηρεσία. Cf. δρηστοσύνη ο 321. M's χρησμοσύνη may be right = χρῆσις, 'working'; see Bywater on Heraclitus *fr.* xxiv, where χρησμοσύνη is interpreted as = διακόσμησις (L.S.). But the variant may be graphical.

Pausanias' πᾶσι is to be preferred to καλά (M). Πᾶσι naturally leads to another enumeration of names, and excuses the repetition in 477; after καλά, σεμνά (478) would be very awkward. There is perhaps an echo in an inscr. Ἐφ. ἀρχ. iii. 81 ὄργια πᾶσιν ἔφαινε βροτοῖς.

478. **παρεξίμεν**: 'transgress', e.g. Soph. *Ant.* 60, a strengthened form of παριέναι (to the exx. of which may be added an inscr. ap. Hoffmann *Ion. dial.* 65. 4 εαν δε τι]ς τι τουτων παριη[ι φηνατ]ω ο θελων); Ruhnken's παρεξέμεν, 'divulge', is given by ἀχέειν 479, and παρεξίημι is not used tropically.

πυθέσθαι: Paus. i. 38. 6 τοῖς οὐ τελεσθεῖσιν, ὁπόσων θέας εἴργονται, δῆλα δήπου μηδὲ πυθέσθαι μετεῖναί σφισιν.

479. **ἀχέειν**: 'divulge', the later μηνύειν (e.g. Andoc. i. 10). The existence of this word was maintained by Buttmann (*Lexilogus* Eng. tr. p. 178) here and in *h. Pan* 18 (where the MSS. give ἐπιπροχέουσα χέει). It is apparently defended by Hes. *Scut.* 93 ἦν ἄτην ἀχέων, Ion *fr.* 39 ὕμνον ἀχέων (MSS. ἀχαιῶν), Eur. *Phoen.* 1040 αχαι ℙ Oxy. 224 (ἰαχά ἰαχᾶ MSS.) Hesych. μέγ' ἀχήσεται· μέγα βοήσει, Moschion 187 ἀχήσεται. Zenodotus

read the same form instead of ἰάχων Σ 160, apparently as equivalent in sense (though the $ understands 'grieving'). See generally Schulze *KB*. xxix. 247, who reads ἀχέει in *h. Pan* but not ἀχέειν here.

The injunction to silence was proclaimed to the initiates at the mysteries by the hierokeryx, and was religiously observed (see ante, p. 119). A mystery was a secret form of worship not freely open to all members of a social group. The centre of interest in its ritual was not, as in other forms of religious service, a sacrifice, but a δρᾶμα μυστικόν. (Δρᾶμα, δρᾶν, δρησμοσύνη (476) are technical terms). In this the initiate was shown certain sacred actions and objects, the meaning of which was explained by a ἱερὸς λόγος. Nearly all ritual of the type in ancient Greece was connected with the worship of powers of the earth, or of death and the underworld. It may have been the particular and awful holiness of these powers that led in the first place to the precautions of elaborate purifications and secrecy (Farnell 129 sq.). Others have less probably explained the secrecy of the ritual as due to the fact that the mysteries belonged to a conquered race which thus attempted to guard their rites from the conquerors (Gardner *New Chapters* 383, Kern *Gr. Myst.* 5). Others suggest that 'to tell will break the spell', and to speak of what had been done in the rites would rob them of their effect (Ramsay in *Enc. Brit.* ed. 9 under *Mysteries* p. 125); cf. Strabo 467 ἡ κρύψις ἡ μυστικὴ τῶν ἱερῶν σεμνοποιεῖ τὸ θεῖον. See also Jevons p. 360, who believes that the silence imposed on the initiated was not for concealment but to prevent pollution.

480. This is the earliest allusion to the happiness of the initiated after death; cf. Pindar *fr.* 137 ὄλβιος ὅστις ἰδὼν κεῖν' εἶσ' ὑπὸ χθόν'· οἶδε μὲν βίου τελευτὰν | οἶδεν δὲ διόσδοτον ἀρχάν, and *frr.* 129, 143, Soph. *fr.* 753 (N.) ὡς τρισόλβιοι | κεῖνοι βροτῶν οἳ ταῦτα δεχθέντες τέλη | μόλωσ' ἐς Ἅιδου· τοῖσδε γὰρ μόνοις ἐκεῖ | ζῆν ἐστί, τοῖς δ' ἄλλοισι πάντ' ἔχει κακά, Eur. *HF.* 613, Ar. *Ran.* 455, Isocr. *Pan.* 28, Plato *Phaed.* 69 C, *Axioch.* 371 D, Cic. *leg.* ii. 14, Aristid. *or.* xiii, *ib.* xix., Galen iii. 576, iv. 361. For the phrase (ὄλβιος κτλ.) cf. Solon 13. 1, *h.* xxv. 4.

For other reff. see Lobeck *Aglaoph.* i. 69, Foucart *Recherches*

53, Dieterich *Nekyia* 64. In this passage, as in Pindar, Sophocles, Euripides, and others, it seems distinctly stated that initiation procures happiness in a future state; nothing at all events is said about the necessity of a virtuous life. Foucart (p. 65) thought that the object of the mysteries was essentially practical; the mystae were taught how to avoid the dangers which beset the soul in its descent to Hades. But it is a most improbable hypothesis that the ἀπόρρητα at Eleusis provided a kind of 'guide to Hades', and this theory has been decisively refuted by the archaeological evidence, which shows that no architectural arrangements such as he postulates existed or were possible in the *telesterion*. It is clear that in the general opinion of the early mystae actual communion with the deities of the underworld was the main, if not the only, essential to salvation. That this belief persisted is evident from the remark of Diogenes, τί λέγεις, ἔφη, κρείττονα μοῖραν ἕξει Παταικίων ὁ κλεπτὴς ἀποθανὼν ἢ Ἐπαμεινώνδας ὅτι μεμύηται; (Plut. *mor.* 22 A). Serious and educated thinkers, at least in later times, believed that initiation in the Eleusinian or other mysteries was an incentive to virtue (Andoc. *de myst.* 31 μεμύησθε . . . ἵνα τιμωρήσητε μὲν τοὺς ἀσεβοῦντας, σῴζητε δὲ τοὺς μηδὲν ἀδικοῦντας, Diod. v. 49.) For a discussion of the ethical influence of these mysteries see Farnell iii. 165–8, and on the moral value of ancient mystery religions in general, Halliday *Pagan Background of Early Christianity* 274 sq.

ὄπωπεν: the word suggests the ἐποπτεία, but probably refers generally to all sights seen by μύσται and ἐπόπται alike (if this distinction is as old as the hymn).

486. **μέγ' ὄλβιος κτλ.**: cf. xxx. 7.

489. The figure of Plutus belongs primarily to folk-lore custom, in which he is the half-personified symbol of Plenty. Thus at the rite of the 'Expulsion of Famine' at Chaeronea, a type of ceremonial rendered familiar by the works of Mannhardt, Frazer, and Usener, the people cried ἔξω βούλιμον, ἔσω δὲ πλοῦτον καὶ ὑγίειαν (Plut. *mor.* 693 F); cf. the Eiresione-song *vit. Hom. Herod.* 469 αὐταὶ ἀνακλίνεσθε θύραι· πλοῦτος γὰρ ἔσεισι | πολλός, σὺν πλούτῳ δὲ καὶ εὐφροσύνη τεθαλυῖα | εἰρήνη τ' ἀγαθή· ὅσα δ' ἄγγεα μεστὰ μὲν εἴη κτλ.

The association of Plutus with Demeter is intelligible enough. He is son of D. and Iasion, Hes. *Theog.* 969. Cf. the scolium Athen. 694 Πλούτου μητέρ' Ὀλυμπίαν ἀείδω | Δήμητρα στεφανηφόροις ἐν ὥραις, | σέ τε παῖ Διὸς Φερσεφόνη. The name of Plutus follows those of Demeter and Core in a prayer, Ar. *Thesm.* 296. D. is πλουτοδότειρα in Orph. *h.* xl. 3. See further Eisle in Roscher iii. 2573, and for representations of P. in art, usually as a boy with corn-basket or cornucopia, ib. 2576. For the representation of P. on the so-called Mystery-vases, see Kern *Gr. Myst.* 64, Farnell iv. 252. It is most improbable, however, that any of the secrets of the service in the *telesterion* would be broadcast upon vase-designs, and the theories which, accepting the doubtful authority for the announcement of the birth of a divine son being the culminating moment of the *epopteia* (see ante, p. 119), proceed to identify this divine child with Plutus, Iacchus, or Plutus-Iacchus, cannot be accepted. For the connexion of Plutus and Pluto, the common later name for Hades, not found in Homer or the Homeric hymn, see Pearson on Soph. *fr.* 273.

ἄφενος: neuter, as in Homer (A 171: in Ψ 299 there is a variant ἄφενον acc.). Only here in the *Hymns*.

490. For confusions caused by ἄγ' or ἄγε cf. H 299, Ξ 314, *h.* iii. 165.

491. The cult of Demeter at Paros is attested by the title Δημητριάς applied to the island (Nicanor ap. Steph. *in* Πάρος). The island was colonized from Crete, one of the oldest centres of her cult (see on 123). From Paros it was said to have been carried to Thasos by Cleoboea (Paus. x. 28. 3). According to Σ Ar. *Av.* 1764 Archilochus composed a hymn to the Parian Demeter. The cult is also known from an inscr. at Paros (*Ath. Mitth.* xvi. 6 = *IG.* xii. 227) δημητρι θεσμοφορωι και κορηι και ευβουλει και βαβοι (= βαυβοῖ). Eubuleus is the husband of Persephone, Cougny ii. 377. 10. Cf. also Boeckh *CIG.* 2557, and *BCH.* i. 135. 54. An ear of corn and the head of D. are common types on the coinage, Head *HN.* 488 sq.

See further P.-W. 2722, Roscher ii. 1302.

Ἄντρωνα (Ἀντρῶνας Demosth. x. 9, cf. Strabo 432, Scylax 63, Ἀντρώνιος ὄνος Pherecrates 15): a Thessalian town, in the Catalogue

(B 697), opposite Oreus in Euboea, not elsewhere mentioned for the worship of Demeter. (It produced stone for millstones, *EM.* 114. 55, *An. Ox.* i. 84.) But B 696 the neighbouring Pyrasus is called Δήμητρος τέμενος (cf. Strabo 435), so that the cult prevailed along the Pagasean gulf in very early times (as at Anthela, Herod. vii. 200). See further P.-W. i. 2642, iv. 2714.

494, 5 = xxx. 18, 19; cf. the endings of vi, x, xxv, xxxi, Choerilus *fr.* 1 a 1 ἡγεό μοι λόγον ἄλλον, Theocr. xv. 135 σέθεν δ' ἐγὼ ἶσα καὶ ἄλλων | μνάσομαι ἡιθέων.

ᾠδῆς: the contracted form occurs also *h.* iii. 20.

ὀπάζειν: this correction of ὄπαζε (cf. Φ 217 ῥέζε, ῥέζειν, Π 92, Χ 259, Ap. Rh. iv. 1600, Hes. *OD.* 611 ἀπόδρεπε, -εν, -ειν) is slighter than to write πρόφρων δ' for πρόφρονες (on the analogy of xxx. 18, xxxi. 17). For the infinitive in liturgy see Adami *de poet. scaen.* 243 and Smyth *Greek Melic Poets* 500, who compares Soph. *Ant.* 1144 and the song of the Elean woman ἐλθεῖν ἥρω Διόνυσε. Cf. also ἔνθα σὺ ῥέζειν *orac.* ap. Phlegon iv. p. 92, 10 Keller, μεμνημένος εἶναι *ib.* p. 93, ἐφαρμόζου, -ειν poet. ap. Clearch. ap. Athen. 317 A, σὺ δὲ σώζειν μὲν . . . Μεσσηνίους, σώζειν δὲ καὶ σαυτόν Paus. iv. 21. 10. For the word cf. Bacchyl. xvi. 132 ὄπαζε ἐσθλῶν τύχαν. On the Homeric use of the infin. for imper. see Hentze *BB.* 1902, 106.

495. **σεῖο**: the writer returns to Demeter the subject of the hymn, though the previous lines include Persephone in the invocation.

III

Hymn to Apollo

Date and place. The hymn to Apollo is the oldest in the collection, and its age can be fixed with some exactness. The date and authorship are mentioned by the scholiast on Pindar *Nem.* ii. 2 on the authority of Hippostratus (see the passage, p. lxxvi), who attributes the hymn to Cynaethus of Chios 'who first recited the poems of Homer at Syracuse in the sixty-ninth Olympiad' (504 B.C.). This is the same kind of evidence as that on which the dates and birthplaces of the poets of the Cycle (e.g. of Arctinus and Lesches) rest, and there is no reason to suspect Hippostratus' statement. The year, however, is far too low, and it is generally agreed that the figure has been miscopied (p. lxxvii).

The argument for an early date is also usually made to rest on the Ionian assembly, and though this is not in itself conclusive (p. 194 sq.) it has weight. The panegyris must have been famous as early as the beginning of the eighth century B.C., when the Messenians sent a sacrifice and a choir of men to Apollo at Delos in the reign of Phintas, before the first war with Sparta, for which embassy a prosodium was written by Eumelus of Corinth (Paus. iv. 4. 1.). Eumelus' floruit is ol. iv. 2, and he 'coincided' with Archias the founder of Syracuse (Kinkel *EGF.* 185, 6). There is therefore nothing to prevent the first portion of the hymn belonging to this century and being contemporary with the older of the Cyclic epics. At this time the Ionians on the coast of Asia Minor and on the islands attained the height of their prosperity. Their art is attested by the excavations on the site of the temple at Ephesus conducted by David Hogarth.

A further argument for putting the hymn in the eighth century is that it describes a state of things earlier than the Cimmerian invasion about 700 B.C. This is not conclusive. The invaders, though they ravaged a great part of Asia Minor, did not reach the islands, and the festival was not apparently interrupted. Its splendour was even increased in the period of Polycrates and Pisistratus. It was not till the defeat of the Ionians by the Persians that it declined in prestige, till it was revived by the Athenians at the beginning of the Peloponnesian war. History therefore would allow the first part of the hymn any date between the eighth century (or even earlier) and the time of Pisistratus. But the lower limit is impossible on other grounds; the hymn is treated as Homeric by Thucydides and Aristophanes, and the first part therefore must be considerably older than the fifth century, since Thucydides, though a poor literary critic, would not have used a sixth-century document as Homeric. This conclusion is supported by archaeological evidence, which points to a date not later than 600 B.C. (see p. 199 f.).[1]

The age of the second part, though uncertain, seems equally high. The episode of Typhaon has been thought later than Stesichorus, as he and not the author of the hymn is mentioned in the *EM.* 772. 50 in connexion with Typhaon's birth. This argument is worthless; the hymns are constantly obscured by melic literature (see p. lxx, and note on 306). On the ground that the digamma is somewhat more often observed in the second than in the first part of the hymn[2] Fick *BB.* xvi. 21 was led to the singular conclusion that Cynaethus took the second part as his model. Few models have less resembled their copy in theme and treatment. An early date for the second part is required by the absence of the name Delphi and any mention of chariot-races (ignored in 270, 271); the *terminus ad quem* is 586 B.C., when these races were instituted (see further on 542). The temple built by Trophonius and Agamedes was standing in the poet's time (299); it was burned in 548 B.C. (Paus. x. 5. 8). The episode of the Cretan priesthood, of which there is barely another mention in history, is ancient (especially if the present tense be read in 394); the serpent and Typhaon, in later accounts fused into one, are discriminated. The 'Pythian' part on this evidence cannot be later than the beginning of the sixth century, and may be very much older. The early date of the whole hymn accounts for the omissions in the description of both sites, the show places at Delos, and 'the chasm, the tripod, the omphalos, the crowds of worshippers, the priestess herself' (Verrall) at Delphi: see Oppé *JHS.* xxiv. 214 sq. Pylos is the Alphean, not the Messenian. The language shows the mixed Ionic dialect which was the consecrated epic language, but betrays its age by the admission of several un-Homeric words and forms. Everything conspires with Hippostratus' statement that the hymn was by

[1] The dedicatory inscriptions found at Delos (collected by Hoffmann *Der Ion. Dialekt* i. 19, 20, 30, 31) appear to go back to 600 B.C.

[2] The figures, as given in our first edition, were—

	observances	neglects
Part I	23	8
Part II	59	14

Cynaethus who first recited Homer in Syracuse, surely not long after its foundation in 733 B.C.

He was coeval with Arctinus of Clazomenae, Antimachus of Teos, Eumelus of Corinth. His hymn belongs to the period of the older poems of the Cycle and that of the Hesiodean theogony. Philodemus (p. lxix) quotes him in the same breath as Orpheus. His account of both the sacred places is simple, a characteristic of the early period of all religions. Elaboration and pomp come with time, as we see in the case of cults whose later history is known.

Unity of the Hymn.

External evidence. Thucydides iii. 104 cites lines 146–50 as ἐκ προοιμίου Ἀπόλλωνος, and adds ἐτελεύτα τοῦ ἐπαίνου ἐς τάδε τὰ ἔπη (quoting 165–72). The ἔπαινος obviously means not the whole hymn but that part of it which contains the eulogy of the Delian women. Aristides, however, ii. 558 quotes 169 sq. using the words καταλύων τὸ προοίμιον, and if he quoted at first hand this would be a clear proof that in the second century after Christ there was a hymn to Apollo which ended with the invocation of the Delians by the blind Chian. Against this Hermann argued that Aristides was quoting from Thucydides, not from Homer (both authors use the word προοίμιον), and took τοῦ ἐπαίνου in Thucydides to mean τοῦ προοιμίου. The probability that Aristides did not use the hymn at first hand is increased by the fact, observed in connexion with the Ἀθηναίων πολιτεία, that all his quotations from Solon are found in that treatise (ed. Sandys, p. liv). He only followed the inveterate habit of the ancients of copying their predecessors quotations and all.[1] Moreover, that the hymn was

[1] Later historians, such as Strabo (43, 211, 300 Ἡσίοδος μάρτυς ἐν τοῖς ὑπ' Ἐρατοσθένους παρατιθεμένοις ἔπεσιν, 302, 320, 452, 460), Plutarch, Pausanias, (e.g. ix. 38. 6, Chersias through Callippus), Athenaeus, often but by no means always name their immediate source. Pliny prefixes his sources to his books, cf. praef. § 21 *in his voluminibus auctorum nomina praetexui. est enim benignum ut arbitror et plenum ingenui pudoris fateri per quos profeceris . . . scito enim conferentem auctores deprehendisse me a iuratissimis et proximis veteres transcriptos ad verbum neque nominatos.* The practice of giving detailed references became more general though not universal among the Christians and is seen in Galen and Stephanus of Byzantium.

a single document in the time of Aristides is proved by the citations of his contemporaries, e.g. Pausanias (x. 37. 5 Ὅμηρος ἔν τε Ἰλιάδι ὁμοίως καὶ ὕμνῳ εἰς Ἀπόλλωνα) and Athenaeus (22 C, quoting v. 515 with Ὅμηρος ἢ τῶν Ὁμηριδῶν τις ἐν τῷ εἰς Ἀπόλλωνα ὕμνῳ).[1] Later writers (Steph. Byz. *in* Τευμησσός· Ὅμηρος ἐν τῷ εἰς Ἀπόλλωνα ὕμνῳ, Eust. 1602. 25) confirm the earlier authorities.

There is therefore nothing in the language of Thucydides to suggest that he knew of a 'Delian' hymn ending at v. 178; and as Gemoll observes, if he had been acquainted with more than one hymn to Apollo he would hardly have written τοῦ προοιμίου Ἀπόλλωνος. As the so-called 'Pythian' hymn is certainly much older than Thucydides the conclusion from this evidence only is that the unity of the document extends to the fifth century at the latest. Aristophanes, as Gemoll further suggests, seems to quote both the first and the last parts of the hymn (see on 114 and 443) and therefore recognized a single composition. The argument in itself is of little value, as Aristophanes might have quoted from two hymns as well as from one; but it may be conceded that if Thucydides was unaware of the existence of separate Delian and Pythian parts, his contemporary and fellow-countryman was equally ignorant. Gemoll further notices that in hymn xxvii there are reminiscences of both parts of the Apollo-hymn; and hymn xxvii is almost certainly older than Thucydides.

Verbal parallels to Thucydides' expression are Demosthenes *Erot.* 32 αὐτοῦ καταλύσειν μοι δοκῶ τὸν ἔπαινον, followed by twenty-four chapters, Dion. Hal. τεχν. ῥητ. v. 2 κατακλείσεις δὲ τὸ ἐγκώμιον εἰς τοῦτο ὅτι κτλ., *comp. verb.* 216 εἰρηκὼς δὴ καὶ περὶ τούτων . . . αὐτοῦ κατακλείσω τὸν λόγον, Plut. *Flamininus* 16 ᾄδουσι παιᾶνα πεποιημένον οὗ τἆλλα διὰ τὸ μῆκος παρέντες ἀνεγράψαμεν ἃ παυόμενοι τῆς ᾠδῆς λέγουσι. . . .

Internal evidence. Since Ruhnken's time it has been thought self-evident that the hymn to Apollo consists of two hymns put together in a clumsy manner. Editors from Wolf to Abel printed and even numbered the two hymns thus obtained separately, to the complete confusion of references. Gemoll first obliterated

[1] On a false reading ὕμνοις, an argument, quoted even by Gemoll (p. 114), was based for the existence of two separate hymns in the Antonine age.

the distinction, and the Oxford edition of 1896 put Dionysus and Demeter in their proper position before Apollo and not after Aphrodite.

The interference with the Apollo-hymn was due to two causes; misunderstanding of the language of the hymn, and misconception of the circumstances and character of the post-Homeric period of Greek literature. All the operations ascribed by critics to unseen late hands may be safely given to Cynaethus.

If we read the hymn as it stands it gives the following picture: the writer will celebrate Apollo born together with his sister in Delos; his worship is universal, on land and on the islands of the Archipelago (21); hills and peaks of mountains, rivers, coasts and harbours are his (22–4); in all of them he might be sung, but the poet chooses his birth at Delos, whence his universal sovereignty started (29); his mother looked for a place to bear him in on both sides of the Aegean and on the islands, without success; finally Delos heard her prayer; there Apollo was born, and the island burst into golden scrub (135); from Delos Apollo began his wanderings o'er land and sea, where he has temples and groves, and where he loves all hills and peaks of mountains, rivers, coasts and harbours; his greatest joy is in Delos; here the Ionians and their families come to a fair, a great sight, and a greater the Deliades, and lastly the poet himself, who will celebrate these women on his journeys through all populous towns (140–76); he will not stop here, however (*οὐ λήξω*), he continues his praise of Apollo; Apollo possesses Lycia and Maeonia and Miletus, Delos also especially, and he goes making music to Pytho in immortal raiment, from Pytho to Olympus, where the younger gods give a concert and Zeus and Leto look on; how then shall the poet continue to sing the universally singable (*πάντως εὔυμνον* 207)? He gives the audience a choice; shall he follow Apollo in his amours, in the families he founded? (and the descendants of Coronis and 'the wife of Leucippus', and the others of whom the poet gives a concise Gotha, mysterious to us, might have preferred this, to judge from Pindar's clients), or shall he take the foundation of the first oracle (214)? he decides on this, and brings Apollo from Olympus through a series of places in North

Greece, across the Euripus, past the site of Thebes, and along the later pilgrims' way to Delphi; here the god founded his temple; Trophonius and Agamedes built the floor, and countless tribes of men laid the stone; there he killed the serpent by the well; priests were wanting; he found a Cretan cargo-boat on its way to the Alphean Pylos, and in the guise of a dolphin compelled it to encircle the Peloponnesus till the high hill of Ithaca appeared in the clouds and the boat made Crisa in the vast gulf which cuts off the Peloponnese; at Crisa he revealed himself to the crew, installed them in their office, and laid down the rule of Delphic administration σφάζειν αἰεὶ μῆλα.

Where is divided authorship here? where Ionian and Dorian poet? where enmity between races and centres of religion? Delos and Pytho were Apolline long before Cynaethus' time. Apollo was consulted by Agamemnon (θ 79–81 Πυθοῖ ἐν ἠγαθέῃ, ὅθ' ὑπέρβη λάϊνον οὐδὸν | χρησόμενος) before the first Dorian showed his face in Greece. Ulysses (λ 580) saw Tityos in hell serving his punishment for laying hands on Leto on her way by Panopeus to Pytho. The later politics of Delphi do not concern the hymn, and were the result of its geographical position, surrounded by North-Greek tribes and accessible from the Peloponnese by water.

Comparisons between the two parts of the hymn, usually to the disadvantage of the latter part, are insecure, and in any case do not establish two authors. The poet we are told left out the glories of Delphi. What did he not leave out at Delos? The Hyperboreans and all the historical sights. Where are the wheel-shaped pond and the altar of horns? Delphi has at least as good treatment; the serpent (at very great length),[1] the Cretan priesthood, and the instructions given them were more vital in the history of the oracle than the acrobats and boxers at Delos. Whether we find the connexion between the two parts skilful or not is a matter of feeling. Epos is not on the same level throughout. The connexions in the *Iliad* (B and Θ) are mechani-

[1] Owing largely to the opportunity of bringing in Hera Queen of heaven, and analysing her feelings, a *morceau* not to be neglected by a virtuoso like Cynaethus, who had endless material to pick from.

cal. The poet lost his sense of proportion when he brought the Deliades and (in the true *m'as-tu vu*? spirit) himself into the picture, and had (according to our notions) some difficulty in picking up his thread.

There is no rivalry between Delos and Delphi expressed in the hymn. Even in history the oracle at Delos was not important. It never had the vogue of Delphi, Ammon, or Dodona. To perceive in this document competition of shrines and rivalries of races is to strain the historical imagination. The omissions themselves put the date of the hymn back. Time at both centres produced elaboration.

To go into detail:

(1) It is assumed by the separatists that vv. 165 sqq. are the end of one hymn, and 179 sqq. part of another. The reasons given are as Gemoll said not conclusive. The 'farewell' to the Deliades (χαίρετε δ' ὑμεῖς πᾶσαι 166) marks the close of a digression in the poem, not the end of the whole hymn. Cf. Hesiod *Theog*. 963, where a similar formula (ὑμεῖς μὲν νῦν χαίρετ' Ὀλύμπια δώματ' ἔχοντες . . . νῦν δὲ θεάων φῦλον ἀείσατε ἡδυέπειαι | Μοῦσαι) marks a transition to a new subject. Again vv. 177, 178 αὐτὰρ ἐγὼν οὐ λήξω κτλ. are not a formula of conclusion, though they have been so taken. 'I will not cease' means 'I will continue', in other words 'to resume'. See the note.

(2) Wherever Apollo came from, and wherever in Greece his worship first found a shrine, we have, when our evidence opens, Apollo resident both at Pytho and at Delos. Πυθὼν πετρήεσσα in the Phocians' territory (B 519) is in Achilles' mouth the repsoitory of proverbial wealth behind its 'stone threshold' (I 404); the oracle and the gifts of its worshippers are implied. Agamemnon, as mentioned above, consulted it (θ 79–80). In the same generation Ulysses says (ζ 162) that he and his people on their way to Troy saw a palm tree growing by the altar of Apollo at Delos. Excavation has identified the position of the palm tree.

The later history of Delos is well known. It had an oracle, but one not more prominent than, or as prominent as, the innumerable oracles of Apollo in other places in Asia and Europe. It no more rivalled Delphi than it rivalled Dodona. Therefore when one finds a sub-epic document in which the origins of both shrines are celebrated (and in their proper spheres, Delos as the birthplace, Delphi as the oracle), and a glance is given at other of Apollo's exploits, there is no prima facie reason to doubt the unity of the work. When 'Hesiod' and 'Homer' competed in celebrating Apollo son of Leto in 'new hymns', the place where they did so was Delos (Hesiod *fr.* 265); and the Boeotian poet, though piety and etiquette may have compelled him to dwell on the birth at Delos, cannot have omitted the marvels and authority of Delphi (he won). It is therefore a modern misapprehension and a false exercise of historical fancy to deny that a Chian poet of the eighth century (on the date see above) could embrace the two seats of Apolline worship in one hymn. The hymn was not written for Delian use exclusively, in fact Cynaethus' bargain with the Deliades is that he will carry their praises all over the world. Cynaethus was a touring artist like Arion and Simonides (Phaedrus iv. 22), and the Dorian Syracusans, to whom he introduced Homer, would have been surprised if the wandering blind man's account of Apollo had stopped short at Delos. He may have left out his appeal to the Deliades when he performed afield, but there is no reason to suppose that the description of Delos and the Ionians, natural in a Chian poet, was found offensive in the Peloponnese or the west. Pilgrims made their way to Delos, to see exactly these sights and more, from all parts, even Messenians with a hymn from Dorian Corinth. Eumelus of Corinth, Cynaethus' exact contemporary, beside furnishing this προσόδιον, declared that Zeus himself was a Lydian (*fr.* 18). The Megarian Theognis (776 sq.) prays that the Megarians ἐν εὐφροσύνῃ | ἦρος ἐπερχομένου κλειτὰς πέμπωσ' ἑκατόμβας | τερπόμενοι κιθάρῃ καὶ ἐρατῇ θαλίῃ | παιάνων τε χοροῖς ἰαχῇσί τε σὸν περὶ βωμόν; he is addressing Phoebus. There was therefore no declared enmity between Delos and Delphi in these centuries.[1] States which might have

[1] There were no doubt Delphian accounts of the Apollo-story. Leto in the *Odyssey* λ 580 'on her way to Pytho' may have been going there with Apollo in her arms (see on 214). From Heraclides ἐν τῇ συναγωγῇ τῶν ἐν μουσικῇ (ap. Plut. *de mus.* 1132 A) we learn Φιλάμμωνα τὸν Δελφὸν Λητοῦς τε καὶ Ἀρτέμιδος καὶ Ἀπόλλωνος γένεσιν δηλῶσαι ἐν μέλεσι, καὶ χοροὺς πρῶτον

been jealous of Delos were Ephesus and Rhodes. Cynaethus lived at the end of the Heraclid dynasty in Lydia, before the advent of the Mermnadae. Gyges and before him Midas sent offerings to Delphi (Herod. i. 14), the reputation of which was therefore established in Asia by 700 B.C. If, what we deny, 'harmonization' had been needed, Cynaethus, an international performer, who exported the Ionian Homer to Sicily, was himself the man to have made it.

If this is admitted, criticism of the hymn reduces itself to the appreciation of the skill with which Cynaethus combined the parts of his theme. This is legitimate, and there is no reason why we should expect or pretend to find perfect or even great art in him. Homer with all his mastery was not at his best in composition, and Cynaethus like Homer was hampered by tradition, in his case religious tradition amounting to dogma. The merit of the hymn is a matter of private feeling, but there can be no doubt that the Delian part has been overestimated at the expense of the Delphian, and that the awkwardness of the connexion, being misunderstood, has been exaggerated. The Delphian story is told with a gravity which befits the theme and place, and if the poet yielded to temptation in the *παρέκβασις* about the serpent he is not without precedents. He omitted, as we have noticed, in the Delian part as well as in the Delphian, many features famous in later times. This is partly in the epic manner, partly a sign of antiquity.[1] The cheerfulness of the Delian part is not inherent in the story, it is due to Cynaethus' satisfaction at the festival of his own race at which he himself appeared.

Further, if the poet of the second half was as the current view goes a Boeotian, perhaps a Hesiodean, it is to be observed first that Delphi is not in Boeotia; it properly belonged to the Phocians, natural enemies of Boeotia; later it was internationalized. Secondly, what position does Boeotia hold in the hymn? Apollo passes through it like a pilgrim to his own shrine, his route is defined by a mention of some of the places on it. But where

περὶ τὸ ἐν Δελφοῖς ἱερὸν στῆσαι. He is mythical, being the father of Thamyris. Presumably the later nomes bore his name.

[1] Oppé, *l.c.*

are Abae, Ptoon, Tegyra, the Tanagraean Δήλιον? The antiquity of Delphi is shown at the expense of Thebes; the only Boeotian worship mentioned, that at Telphusa, is punished and exterminated. The argument to a Boeotian origin resembles the proof of an Athenian edition of the *Iliad*, in which Athens and Attica make all but no appearance.

Cynaethus, seated at the centre of post-Homeric epos, had before him (or in his memory) the Homeric poems, Hesiod's *Works and Days*, perhaps the first poems of the Cycle, e.g. the *Cypria* and the *Aethiopis*. His debt to his master is obvious, but there are abundant coincidences with the *Theogony* and probably the *Catalogi*. We use the word coincidence advisedly. The productions of the Hesiodic school cannot be dated more nearly than to the end of the eighth century, and this is to give them the highest antiquity they can claim. Cynaethus belonged exactly to this period, and it is therefore an open question if the *Hymn to Apollo* or the *Theogonia* be the older. At all events agreement in language between the Hymn and the surviving Hesiodea is no proof of a Boeotian origin of the Pythian portion. Cynaethus, who amplified Homer with new lines (probably from Hesiod, see *Origins*, p. 203 sqq.), would have had no scruple *à prendre son bien où il le trouvait*. These coincidences are 62 (*Theog*. 404), 81 the word χρηστήριον (Hes. *fr*. 39. 6, 48), 93 the mention of Rhea and Themis (*Theog*. 135), 121 ἁγνῶς καὶ καθαρῶς (*OD*. 337), 241 quoted as from Hesiod (not from the *OD*.). The resemblances evidently do not go for much, and only one (121) can be called borrowing.

There is therefore no need to bring the hymn down to a period when a 'harmonization' of the different sites was taken in hand. Such schematizations are found in Ephorus, who (Strabo 373, 374, Paus. ii. 33. 2) says that Delos and Pytho originally belonged to Posidon, who gave Delos to Leto in exchange for Calauria, and Pytho to Apollo in exchange for Taenarum. This method is quite unlike the narrative in the Hymn.[1]

[1] Since this introduction went to press there has appeared *Die archäische Mythenerzählung* by F. Dornseff; in this book the unity of the hymn to Apollo is maintained, but the attempt to bring the date down to 580 B.C.

Subject of the Hymn: (*a*) *Apollo Delius and the Delian Festival.*

The origin of the cult of Apollo, who is indubitably a late comer into the Greek Pantheon, is a matter of dispute: the two main rival theories derive his worship from some country north of Greece direct overland or from the east.[1] The Homeric Apollo possesses features which appear foreign to the early legend and cult of Delphi: on the other hand there is rather strong evidence in favour of the view that the cult passed direct to Delphi from the north, down the line of the Sacred Way. A third possibility may be suggested, viz. that Apollo Delius who, like the Homeric Apollo, is particularly closely associated with two feminine deities, a mother Leto and a sister Artemis, may have come to Greece from Asia Minor, while Apollo Pythius came direct overland from the original northern home of the God. But however that may be, Apollo, unlike Dionysus, had entered the Greek pantheon before Homer, to whom both the oracle at Pytho (Β 519, Ι 404, θ 79) and the cult at Delos are known. The visit of Odysseus to the famous palm tree attests by implication the existence of the birth legend at Delos in the time of the Trojan War (ζ 162), and the crime of Tityus (λ 580) an equally early connexion of Apollo Letoides with Delphi (above, p. 189). These passages indicate first that the Delian cult anteceded the Ionian migration and cannot therefore have been founded in the course of that movement: secondly, that even if the differences between Apollo Pythius and Apollo Delius justify the hypothesis that their cults arrived in Greece from distinct sources, a harmonization of the two cults had taken place in pre-Homeric times, and long before the *Hymn* was written. In fact, throughout their history there was never rivalry or jealousy between the two cults. The *Hymn*, after narrating the birth legend, describes the annual festival of the God, which was the occasion of musical and poetical contests and, like similar

and to connect it with Stesichorean melos rests, naturally, on no evidence. The views of F. Jacoby *Proceedings of the Prussian Academy* 1933, xv. 682 sq. do not require us to alter what we have written.

[1] For the northern theory see Farnell iv. 103: for the oriental theory Wilamowitz *Greek Historical Writing and Apollo* 28, *Hermes* xxxviii. 575; Nilsson *GF.* 102. On the name Apollo see Kalinka *Klio* 1929, xxii. 254.

medieval festivals, provided a fair. *Panegyreis* of this type were probably common. We possess, for example, an account by Asius of an analogous festival of Hera at Samos, *Tonaia*, to which similarly long-robed Ionians flocked with golden grasshoppers in their hair (Asius *fr.* 13 ap. Athen. 525 F). Neither the Samian nor in the first instance the Delian festival had probably any political significance. The story that Eumelus wrote a hymn for the Messenian theoria to Delos (above, p. 184) shows that the Delian festival existed in the eighth century. The connexion of Prasiae, whose importance as a port belongs to the flourishing days of the amphictyony of Calauria, with the Attic *theoria* suggests a very early date indeed both for the festival and for Athenian participation therein. The Delian month Γαλαξίων and the cult of Apollo Γαλάξιος in Boeotia suggest another very early link with central Greece. Thucydides, who (iii. 104) quotes the hymn as evidence of the antiquity of the feast, says that it had formerly been patronized by islanders and Athenians, but misfortunes had brought about its decay until its splendours were revived by Pisistratus. Pisistratus used this revival to support Athenian pretensions to hegemony in the Cyclades. The festival was again revived by Pericles, with the wider aim of asserting the claim of Athens to be the motherland and natural leader of the Ionian race.

The probable date of the festival presents grave difficulty.[1]

[1] See Nilsson *GF.* 144, Farnell iv. 28, Homolle ap. Daremberg et Saglio in *Delia*, Stengel in P.-W. iv. 2433. Inscriptions record two festival names, *Apollonia* and *Delia*. Some following Robert accept these as two festivals, placing an annual *Apollonia* in *Thargelion*, and a pentaeteric *Delia* in *Hieros*. Others argue that *Apollonia* is the Delian name, *Delia* the foreign name for the same festival, which they place in *Hieros*. That the festival took place in the spring is stated by Theognis 775 (above, p. 191). Dion. *Perieg.* 526 and Virgil (*Aen.* iv. 143) clearly associated it with the close of the ἀποδημία in Lycia, which lasted (Serv. *ad l.*) the six winter months. For *Thargelion* 7 as the God's birthday, see Diog. Laert. iii. 2, Plut. *qu. conv.* viii. 1. 2, anon. *vit. Plat.* p. 6 Didot. *Thargelion* 7 also fits in with the possible time-table of Theseus' movements. He left Attica on *Munichion* 6, which would leave time to kill the Minotaur and reach Delos in time to crown the victors in the Delian contest (Paus. viii. 48. 3). The month Δάλιος in Rhodes, Cos,

Under Athenian auspices there were two festivals, an annual celebration and a *pentaeteris* which was first instituted by Pisistratus in the third year of the Olympiad. The original festival was probably annual. That it took place in spring is certain. Of the two possible dates *Thargelion* 7, the reputed birthday of the God, may be thought more likely than a day in the month *Hieros*, February to March, which is very early in the year for an assembly of *theoriae* coming by sea.

Of the sacred sights which in later days were shown to pilgrims our author apparently knows only the palm tree. The olive and laurel which shared the connexion with the birth-story (see on 117) are not mentioned. Apollo is promised βωμὸς καὶ τέμενος, which may be the equivalent of the temple asked for by Delos (80),[1] but there is no mention of the Letoon hard by the palm tree,[2] the oval pond,[3] or the altar of horns.[4] Perhaps these, like the famous colossal statue of the Naxians,[5] were not there when Cynaethus wrote. The celebrated *Geranos* or crane dance appears

and Calymna corresponds to *Thargelion*. Against the acceptance of *Thargelion* is the argument that it is curious that the greatest local festival should not occur in the month called Holy, but in one called after another festival, which moreover has a gloomy and apotropaic character.

[1] The extant remains of the great temple date only from the fourth century B.C., Homolle *Les Fouilles de Délos, Monuments grecs* p. 33.

[2] Strabo 485. It has been identified by excavation, *BCH.* xxix. 449, num. 144.

[3] This artificial cistern is first mentioned by Theognis 5 Φοῖβε ἄναξ ὅτε μέν σε θεὰ τέκε πότνια Λητὼ | φοίνικος ῥαδινῆς χερσὶν ἐφαψαμένη | ἀθανάτων κάλλιστον ἐπὶ τροχοειδέι λίμνῃ, later by Aeschylus *Eum.* 7 λιπὼν δὲ λίμνην [τὴν στρογγύλην 𝔖] Δηλίαν τε χοιράδα, Herod. ii. 170 λίμνη τέ ἐστι ἐχομένη λιθίνῃ κρηπῖδι κεκοσμημένη καὶ ἐργασμένη εὖ κύκλῳ καὶ μέγαθος ὡς ἐμοὶ ἐδόκεε ὅσηπερ ἡ ἐν Δήλῳ ἡ τροχοειδὴς καλεομένη, Eur. *Ion* 161, 170, *IT.* 1103, Callim. *Del.* 261, *Apoll.* 59. This tank, upon which in antiquity the sacred swans of Apollo floated, and the fish of which were leased by the temple (*BCH.* xiv. 392), has often been described by travellers, e.g. Tozer *Islands of the Aegean* 12.

[4] The βωμὸς κεράτινος or κερατών, of which relics were discovered in 1884 (*BCH.* viii. 417), is first mentioned in Callim. *Apoll.* 58 (for later mentions see Polyb. xxvi. 10. 12, Plutarch *Thes.* 21, *de soll. an.* 983 E, Ovid *Heroid.* xxi. 81, Martial *Spect.* i. 4).

[5] Set up about 600 B.C. For the well-known inscription του αϝυτου λιθου ειμι see Röhl *IGA.* 409.

to have been danced in honour of Aphrodite and, if so, was not germane to the theme of the hymn.[1] Very remarkable, however, is the total omission of any reference to the Hyperborean maidens. For although the legend of the Hyperborean maidens and the ritual of the offerings of the first-fruits wrapped in straw were probably borrowed from Delphi, they must have been very early established at Delos. Olen brought Eileithyia from the Hyperboreans to assist at the divine birth and mentioned the mysterious maidens. Two Mycenaean tombs were pointed out as being their graves, and were spared as holy when Pisistratus cleansed the island.[2]

(*b*) *Apollo Pythius and the foundation of the Delphic oracle.*

The second part of the hymn, apart from the Homeric references, provides our earliest evidence about the Delphic oracle. In many ways it is perplexing; more significant than the statements are some of the omissions, not all of which can be due to accident. There is no mention of Dionysus, who shared with Apollo the chief honours at the historical Delphi. There is no reference to the *omphalos*, to the Pythia, or to the fabled temples of beeswax, feathers, and laurel, which were said to have preceded the building attributed to Trophonius and Agamedes (see on 296). None of these omissions, however, are necessarily significant. The poet had no special call to mention Dionysus, or the *omphalos*; though there was opportunity, it was not necessary to his theme to mention the early temples or the Pythia.[3] Hiller von Gaertringen P.-W. iv. 2527) certainly goes too far in assuming that the Pythia did not deliver oracles at the date of the hymn and that ἐκ δάφνης (396) necessarily implies the existence of a tree oracle like that of the oak of Zeus at Dodona. The name Delphi, which occurs in *hymn* xxvii. 14, is not mentioned in the poem nor elsewhere in

[1] This dance, which took place round the κερατών, is depicted on the François vase. For what reason Bruchner (P.-W. iv. 2468) connected its evolutions with the wanderings of Leto is unknown. Tradition alleged that it represented the mazes of the labyrinth, and was instituted by Theseus in honour of Aphrodite (see Nilsson *GF.* 380, and references there given).

[2] See Nilsson *GF.* 207, where the references are collected.

[3] The Pythia appears first in Theognis 807. †

literature before Heraclitus *fr.* 93 ap. Plut. *mor.* 404 c. No conclusion, however, can safely be drawn from this omission. The first half of the poem explains the origin of the name Pytho, the second clearly intends to suggest that the name Delphi is connected with Apollo Delphinios, a theory not confined to Cynaethus (cf. Σ Eur. *Phoen.* 232, Tzetzes on Lyc. 208, and the dolphin as a canting coin of Delphi, Head *HN.*[2] p. 340). By implication, therefore, the place-name Delphi, unknown apparently to Homer, was probably known to the author of the hymn.

There is no mention of a chasm or of vapour issuing from it which provided the physical cause of the Pythia's inspiration. This theory, which was widely held in later classical antiquity, has been challenged by Oppé (quoted p. 185), who maintains that the theory originated first in the Alexandrine period and that it was from the first a learned theory based upon no physical fact. The excavations have revealed no chasm or fissure, and geological considerations are against the theory that a fissure, subsequently closed by earthquake, had ever existed on the site occupied by the successive temples. If the geological evidence is as definite as stated, it is of course conclusive. At the same time it is a little peculiar that the theory should have been invented and have gained general acceptance without any basis of fact. It may be noticed further that the story of the derivation of Pytho from the putrescent dragon belongs to a type fairly widely distributed in the Greek world, which invariably was attached to places remarkable for the escape of sulphurous fumes, or for the existence of sulphurated streams (see the references collected in Halliday *Greek Questions of Plutarch* 86–7).

In the first part of the hymn Apollo approaches Delphi through Boeotia via Onchestus and Telphusa, and not by the Sacred Way from Tempe. He finds Pytho unoccupied by any other divinity though a female snake guards the spring. There is no hint at all of a succession of preceding oracular cults of Ge, Themis, and Posidon, which appear in the orthodoxy of the fifth century B.C. (Aesch. *Eum.* 1 f., Eur. *IT.* 1260). The snake is not in any way represented as the guardian of an oracle, or as the servant of any other divinity, but is a bane to mortals, like Sphinx or Echidna or the dragon which Cadmus slew at Thebes. The list of successive cults established for the fifth century has the appearance of theological speculation rather than of genuine tradition. The evidence of the hymn at any rate lends no support whatever to it, nor to the far-reaching speculations of modern scholars which have been based upon it.

Similarly the advent of the Cretan priests of Apollo Delphinios in the second part of the hymn, though it may represent an historical event, lends no support to modern theories of the existence of a cult at Delphi in the Bronze Age. A cult may well have existed at so remarkable a natural site, but we possess no evidence. The indeterminate Mycenaean remains which have been discovered and recorded tell us only that the place was inhabited in the Bronze Age. It is quite illegitimate to combine their existence with the tradition of the Cretan priests as the basis of a theory of a pre-Hellenic cult, seeing that the cult of Apollo Delphinios belongs not to the Bronze Age but to the first period of Greek colonization.

To return to the dragon, there are remarkable omissions which incidentally attest the very early date of the hymn. The name Python, it is true, is late (see on 371). But undoubtedly the slaughter of the dragon early acquired a religious importance in the Delphic cult, which is completely absent from the hymn. There is no mention whatever here of the doctine of purification, early established at Delphi, with which the dragon-slaying was associated. The God, who came as we have noticed through Boeotia and not along the Sacred Way, has no apparent need of purification from blood-guilt, and does not repair to Tempe to obtain it. There is no hint of any ceremony like that of the festival *Septerion*, an obviously ancient rite which was interpreted, though probably wrongly, by later times in terms of the slaying of Python and the subsequent purification of the God (see Halliday *Greek Questions of Plutarch* 67).

Finally, it is clear from 264 f. that Pythian Games at which chariot-racing took place had not yet been instituted. This makes it certain that the hymn must have been written before 586 B.C. For it was at the conclusion of the First Sacred War that the Pythian festival was made pentaeteric instead of enneaeteric, and, according to some authorities, chariot-racing, which certainly formed a part of subsequent celebrations, for the first time added to a programme of musical contests.

The hymn in relation to later literature.

While the other Homeric hymns were generally neglected by ancient authors, the hymn to Apollo seems to have been known and appreciated from early times. It served as a model for two of the shorter hymns (see on xxvii and xxviii). In the sixth century Theognis shows the influence of at least the Delian part (see on 117, 118). Pindar has possible reminiscences, but they are doubtful (see on 73, 189). By the end of the fifth century it had become a classic: Thucydides treated it as historical evidence, and Aristophanes assumed that it was familiar to his audience. The Alexandrian poets made free use of it; Callimachus was the chief debtor, in his hymns to Apollo and Delos (see on 19, 119, 135, 383, 396), but Apollonius and Theocritus utilized it (see on 119, 487). Theocritus' seventeenth idyll is clearly inspired by the Delian part.

A considerable number of hymns to Apollo are recorded, some by early writers, which are no longer extant, e.g. by Olen (Paus. v. 7. 8), Boeo (*ib.* x. 5. 7), Eumelus (*ib.* iv. 33. 2), Herophile the Sibyl (*ib.* x. 12. 2), Melanopus of Cyme (*ib.* vi. 7. 3), Philammon (Heraclides ap. Plut. *de mus.* 1132 A), Tynnichus of Chalcis (Plato *Ion.* 534 D, see above, p. cviii), Cleochares (Dittenberger *Sylloge* 450), Aristonicus (*ib.* 662), an Eretrian ἐγκώμιον (*IG.* xii. 9. 913), the Spartan poetess Myia (Suidas in Μυῖα).

Among hymns extant, whole or in part, are Callim. *h. Apoll.*, a Tenian hymn *IG.* xii. 5. 893, Orph. *h.* xxxiv, anon. *h.* ii (Abel *Orph.* p. 285), hymn. mag. i, ii (*ib.* pp. 281, 289), hymns 1 and 2 in Jan, *Script. mus. graec.* suppl. pp. 12, 23, Ox. pap. 1792, Pindar *frr.* 87, 88, *paeans* iii, iv, v, vi, Alcaeus *frr.* 2–4, Ananius *fr.* 1, Archilochus *fr.* 27, Terpander *fr.* 2, Simonides *fr.* 2, scolia 4 (*PLG.* iii. 644).

1. As Apollo approaches the seated Gods he strings his bow to test it, and produces the same panic that Ulysses did by the same action among the suitors (υ 409).

μνήσομαι οὐδὲ λάθωμαι. For this construction (fut. and aor. subj.) cf. B 488, δ 240 οὐκ ἂν ἐγὼ μυθήσομαι οὐδὲ λάθωμαι, ζ 126 πειρήσομαι ἠδὲ ἴδωμαι, μ 383, ν 215.

3. **ἐπὶ σχεδὸν ἐρχομένοιο,** i.q. σχεδὸν ἐπερχομένοιο *in tmesi*, as χ 205 ἐπ' ἀγχίμολον . . . ἦλθεν. This decides against ἐπισχεδὸν (ὑφ' ἓν) first found in Apollonius.

5. On Leto and the Lycian *lada*, often accepted as the etymology, see the reff. in P.-W. *Supplementbd.* v. 571.

μίμνε, 'was sitting', imperf. of accompaniment, but virtually an aorist as ἔτικτεν 13. It is wrong to over-distinguish tenses.

8. **πρὸς κίονα πατρὸς ἑοῖο,** i.e. the pillar where his father sat. Arete sat κίονι κεκλιμένη ζ 307, and so Demodocus θ 65, Odysseus ψ 90.

11. 'And next the other deities sit down there', ἔνθα is local, as in P 529 ἔνθα δ' ἔπειτ' ἀφίει μένος ὄβριμος Ἄρης.

14–18. Nothing is more natural than to salute the Mother before celebrating the Son, and to include Artemis. Homer (A 9, 36, Π 849 al.) and Hesiod (*Theog.* 918) were aware of Leto's offspring, but neither refers to the birth-story, though the mention of the palm tree at Delos (ζ 162) implies it.

μάκαιρ' ὦ Λητοῖ: the inversion is somewhat formulaic, cf. Eur. *Bacch.* 565 μάκαρ ὦ Πιερία, Ar. *Nub.* 1205 μάκαρ ὦ Στρεψιάδες, Orph. *h.* iii. 12 μάκαιρ' ὦ νύξ, *Anth. Pal.* vi. 239. 1 ἀγρονόμ' ὦ Πάν.

16. = Orph. *h.* xxxv. 5.

Ὀρτυγίῃ: hardly the Syracusan Ortygia as Fick supposed (*Odyssee*, p. 281), though this place was associated with Artemis (Pind. *Nem.* i. 1, *Pyth.* ii. 7, Diod. v. 3). 'Quail island' is appropriate enough for any of the Cyclades, and it was often applied to Delos itself (Σ Ap. Rh. i. 419, Athen. 292 D, Callim. *h. Ap.* 59, *Anth. Pal.* vi. 121, Virg. *Aen.* iii. 125, Hesych. *in* Ὀρτυγία, Eust. 1558. 8). Here Ortygia and Delos are distinguished as in *Anth. Pal.* vi. 273 Ἄρτεμι Δᾶλον ἔχουσα καὶ Ὀρτυγίαν ἐρόεσσαν. Strabo 486 therefore identified Ortygia with Rheneia, which agrees with the position given it ο 404. For further reff. see P.-R. 297, Farnell ii. 433. The word was used as a title of

Artemis (Soph. *Trach.* 213, cf. Ar. *Av.* 870, where Leto is called Ὀρτυγομήτρα).

Later Delian tradition distinguished the births of Apollo and Artemis by time as well as by place. Artemis was born on 6th Thargelion, the day before Apollo's birth, at which she rendered expert assistance (Serv. on *Aen.* iii. 72, Apollod. i. 42, *Vat. Myth.* 37, Bode i. 13).

Apollo first appeared in the Greek world at Delos, and hence was held to have been born there according to the principle in Herod. ii. 146. So Aphrodite appeared at Cythera, Hes. *Theog.* 192. Other claims to be the birthplace were made by Lycia (Hagnon in Σ A 101, 119, Semus ap. Steph. Byz. *in* Τέγυρα), Tegyra near Orchomenus, where the epithet Πτῷος was explained by Leto's fright at a boar (Σ Lyc. 265, Plut. *Pelop.* 16, *def. or.* 412 B, Aelian *VH.* v. 4), Ptoon (Steph. *in* Ἀκραιφία), in Attica by Zoster (Hyperides *Del. fr.* 67, Paus. i. 31. 1, Steph. *in* Τέγυρα) and Hymettus (a late and worthless story based upon an etymology of the cult-epithet Κύννειος, see Suid. *in* Κυνήειος), by Amphigeneia in Triphylia (Steph. *in v.*), and Ephesus (Strabo 639, 640, Tac. *Ann.* iii. 61). The secondary character of these claims is shown by the fact that most are derived from explanations of local cult-titles and by the frequent introduction of reminiscences of the Delian story. At Ephesus there was a *lucus Ortygia* and the olive clasped by Leto (see on 117) was shown; at Tegyra there was a mountain called Delos and two streams, Phoenix and Elaea, between which the birth took place.

17. The view adopted in the first edition that the birth took place on the mountain is abandoned. The site is securely fixed by the palm tree, one of the most famous sights of antiquity, from Homer to Pliny (see on 117). In historical times this was shown below the mountain against which Leto leaned, near the Letoon. It is indeed against nature that a palm tree should have grown on the bare granite top of Mt. Cynthus. Further, it now appears that the cave sanctuary hailed by Lebègue as the first astronomical observatory of the ancient world, the birthplace of Apollo and the site of the Delian oracle, is but a pseudo-antique of Alexandrian construction built in honour of Heracles, ancestor of Ptolemy II

(Plassart, *Exploration archéologique de Délos* xi. 228 sq.). There is, therefore, no need to discover a discrepancy between Cynaethus and Theognis and later writers. Our poet, like those of later date, thought of the birth as taking place at the foot of Cynthus, where the Inopus issued from the hill.

Cynthus, a granite hill clothed only in scrub, is the most striking natural feature of the island for which Cynthia is often used as a synonym. Its summit, upon which traces of pre-Hellenic occupation have been found, was occupied in classical times by a temple of Zeus Kynthios. Although Apollo and Artemis had no temples on the hill they shared this cult-epithet with Zeus and Athena (P.-W. ii. 57, iv. 2473, xii. 42). For the archaeological remains on Cynthus see Plassart as above.

18. ὑπ', 'by': cf. B 616 ὑφ' Ὑρμίνῃ (a minority of MSS., ἐφ' vulg.), Φ 87 ὑπὸ Σατνιόεντι codd., ἐπὶ Strabo 605 (but ὑπὸ 619); it is a v.l. Π 719 ῥοῇς ἔπι (ὑπὸ L[10]) Σαγγαρίοιο, ι 284 ἐπὶ (ὑπὸ L[8]) πείρασι γαίης; cf. also Eur. *Heracl.* 355 ὑπὸ ζυγοῖς, Ap. Rh. ii. 794 ὑφ' εἰαμεναῖς Ὑπίοιο; in prose Strabo 346, *IG. Sept.* 53. 6, and other exx. in the lexicon.

Inopus, first identified by Ross, whose view has been confirmed by an inscription (*BCH.* vii. 329), had but little water during most of the year (Strabo 485); its ebb and flow was thought to be connected with the movements of the Nile (Call. *Dian.* 171, *Del.* 206, 263, Lycophr. 569, Pliny *NH.* ii. 229, Paus. ii. 5. 2, Rufus ap. Orib. *coll. med.* v. 3. 24. For other exx. of the supposed subterranean connexion of rivers see Halliday *Greek Divination* 120 n. 1.) An official called ἰνωποφύλαξ or κρηνοφύλαξ occurs in inscriptions (*BCH.* xiv. 487, vii. 330).

The name has the termination and accentuation of many rivers, Ἀσωπός, Εὐρωπός, etc. Attempts have been made to derive it (Meister *KZ.* xxxii. 136 from ἰνάω), but it is doubtless non-Greek, like Κύνθος.

19. Callim. *Apoll.* 30 οὐδ' ὁ χορὸς τὸν Φοῖβον ἐφ' ἓν μόνον ἦμαρ ἀείσει, | ἔστι γὰρ εὔυμνος, Aristides xl. 1 πάντων δὲ πολυύμνητος εἶ.

19–24 are a prooemium stating the universality of Apollo's sphere, and choosing out of it Delos in particular for celebration.

20. **νομὸς βεβλήαται ᾠδῆς**: the MSS. appear to give a case of the Ionic perf. pl. taken for a singular, as Hippocr. i. 485 K. καρδίη περιβεβλέαται χιτῶνα λεῖον. In Π 243 Zenodotus read οἶος ἐπιστέαται, on which Aristarchus remarked ἀγνοεῖ ὅτι τὰ τοιαῦτα ῥήματα πληθυντικά ἐστι. In γ 438 several MSS. have θεὰ κεχαροίατ' ἰδοῦσα, in Λ 660 one reads βεβλήαται μὲν ὁ Τυδείδης. Cf. the v.l. νεκρός Ψ 197, Herod. iv. 166; Aratus 817 has καὶ μᾶλλον μελανεῦσα καὶ εἰ ῥηγνύατο μᾶλλον. Conversely we have in the plural κεχείμανται φρένες Pind. *Pyth.* ix. 56, κέκρανται συμφοραί Eur. *Hipp.* 1255, ἐπικέκρανται ἕτεραι Aretaeus vii. 1. 4. There is further a doubt whether we should accept the MS. reading νομός or alter to νόμος. The latter word occurs first in Alcman *fr.* 25 ὀρνιχῶν νόμως: the oxytone form occurs in Υ 249, Hes. *OD.* 403 ἐπέων νομός, and should prevail.

For βάλλεσθαι, 'lay', cf. Pind. *Pyth.* iv. 245, vii. 4, *Nem.* i. 8; for ᾠδῆς Hes. *Theog.* 48, *h. Dem.* 495.

21. **πορτιτρόφον**: cf. Bacchyl. xi. 30 of Metapontum. The alternative παντοτρόφον occurs in Aeschylus *fr.* 186. 4.

22. Θ 557, Π 299 ἐκ δ' ἔφανεν πᾶσαι σκοπιαὶ καὶ πρώονες ἄκροι (Μ 282 πρώονας ἄκρους). σκοπιαί are look-out posts, sometimes fortified with towers from which warning was given of the approach of pirates. Thus κ 30 as Odysseus' ship approached Ithaca beacons were lit upon the hills (Ormerod *Piracy in the Ancient World* 41 sq.).

23. **ποταμοὶ ἅλα δὲ προρέοντες**: Ε 598, κ 251. On the accentuation ἅλα δέ and 28 χέρσον δέ see ante p. lxi.

24. ν 234 ἦέ τις ἀκτὴ | κεῖθ' ἁλὶ κεκλιμένη.

26. **Κύνθου**: Steph. Byz. explicitly says Κύνθος· καὶ θηλυκῶς καὶ οὐδετέρως, but it is difficult to suppose that the same writer could use it in two declensions, here as a neuter and 141 (Κύνθου παιπαλόεντος) as masculine, without any metrical necessity. Antimachus *fr.* 101, 102 used the word Πύδης in two declensions, but that was a mere matter of metaplasm. Moreover ὄρος in Homer is construed with a genitive.

27. **Δήλῳ ἐν ἀμφιρύτῃ** = inscr. in *Mon. grecs* 1879, p. 45. ἑκάτερθε suggests its small size.

28. **λιγυπνοίοις**: only here; δ 567 Ζεφύροιο λιγὺ πνείοντος. On

the lengthening -οι- see Solmsen *Untersuchungen zur griech. Laut- und Verslehre*, p. 114.

29. No lacuna is necessary if we put a full stop at ἀνάσσεις. The sense is abrupt, but the connexion at the end of the narrative (τόσσον ἔπ' . . .) is certain. The asyndeton is the rule, cf. M 19, Ω 544; the latter passage was in the writer's mind, cf. ἐντὸς ἔχει with ἐντὸς ἐέργει Ω 544 and Μάκαρος ἕδος 37 with the same line.

30. The cult of Apollo is attested in practically all the cities mentioned of which anything is known (see geographical registers of cults of Apollo in P.-W. ii. 72 sq. and Farnell iv. 433), and it has been suggested that they were named for this reason. But the list is more probably geographical only, and is compiled to show the extent of Leto's wanderings round the coasts and islands of the Aegean. This is indicated (i) by the orderly sequence (modified by the claims of metre) in which the places are enumerated (the most serious lapse from a continuous if erratic itinerary is in 35, where Leto returns to Scyros from Ida before approaching Phocaea), (ii) by the omission of important centres of the cult of Apollo Delius such as Rhodes, (iii) by the inclusion of sailors' landmarks like Pelion, Athos, and Ida in preference to states; not Erythrae but the two capes of its peninsula are mentioned.

In Nonnus xxvii. 269–77 Peneus, Dirce, and Asopus refused her; she was conducted by Athena, Aristides ii. 13, xiii. 97, xvii. 250.

Κρήτη: Crete, Athens, and Delos are connected by the legend that Theseus, on his return from killing the Minotaur, instituted the festival of Apollo at Delos; cf. Paus. viii. 48. 3, Plut. *Thes.* xxi. Cretans were among those who danced round the altar of Delian Apollo, Virgil *Aen.* iv. 146. The participation of Athens in the Delian festival is very early (see ante p. 195). According to the Athenian story, Leto passed direct from Attica to Delos (Hyperides *fr.* 70). But although these associations may have been known to Cynaethus, the mention of Crete and Athens here is due to geographical rather than to mythological reasons.

31. Spondaic lines are rare. La Roche *Wiener Studien* xx. 68 admits χ 175 = 192. The others usually quoted (A 130, Ψ 221, ο 334, φ 15) can be resolved.

32. **Αἰγαί** is a common name, and considerable confusion

reigned between the synonyma: Steph. Byz. Αἰγαί· πόλεις πολλαί, Κιλικίας (Dio Prus. xxxiv. 10), Μακεδονίας, ἥτις καὶ μηλοβότειρα ἐλέγετο, τῆς Θρᾳκησίων Χερρονήσου, καὶ ἡ ἐν Μυρίνῃ ἐν τῇ Αἰολίδι, καὶ Λυδίας καὶ Λόκριδος καὶ Αἰτωλίας καὶ Εὐβοίας, ἃς Ὅμηρος ἐν τῷ Ν′ [21]. The best known was that in Achaea mentioned together with Helice *l.c.* and Θ 203. This is out of the question here, as the required Aegae must be in N. Greece. This is provided by Hesychius Αἰγαί· νῆσος πρὸς τῇ Εὐβοίᾳ, ἱερὸν Ποσειδῶνος (cf. also 𝕾 N 21 Νικοκράτης ἐν τῷ περὶ τοῦ ἐν Ἑλικῶνι ἀγῶνος οὐ ταύτας φησὶ τὰς Αἰγὰς [sc. τὰς τῆς Εὐβοίας] λέγειν τὸν ποιητὴν ἀλλ᾽ ἑτεράν τινα νῆσον ἐν τῷ Αἰγαίῳ πελάγει, 𝕾 Ap. Rh. i. 831, 𝕾 Pind. *Nem.* v. 67, Eust. 708. 38).

There were other forms of the name: ἡ περὶ Κανὰς Αἴξ 𝕾 Ap. Rh. i. 1165 (Αἰγά = Καναία Strabo 123), an Αἰολικὸν πολισμάτιον Plut. *Sol.* 25, a cape Αἰγᾶ Strabo 615, πολυαι[.]γαν among islands belonging to Cimolus inscr. Collitz 3277, αιγεαν in a list of Thracian and Macedonian places *ib.* 3286. 15, Aegae a rock between Tenos and Chios Pliny *NH.* iv. 51, an Aegae on the Pythicus above Myrina Agathias p. 9 ed. Bonn. (the same as in Steph. above), Αἰγάτης Steph.

One ancient derivation took the name from αἶγες, 'waves' (Hesych., Artemid. *onir.* ii. 12), but this and the identification of the place in the present passage are quite uncertain.

The reading of *HJ* implies a v.l. Κύδνη for Αἰγαί. Steph. Κύδνα· πόλις Μακεδονίας· Θεαγένης ἐν Μακεδονικοῖς [*FHG.* iv. 509 *fr.* 5] ἣ κατὰ παραφθορὰν Πύδνα λέγεται, Mela ii. 3. 1. There was a Κύδνα in Lycia also (Ptol. *Geogr.* v. 3, Πύδναι Stadiasm. 248). Possibly here an identification was made, as at v. 40. Pydna was also known as Κίτρον Strabo vii. *fr.* 22.

Εἰρεσίαι: Pliny *NH.* iv. 23 mentions an island Irrhesia on the Thermaic gulf, which suits Peparethos and Athos. Livy xxxii. 13 mentions Iresiae as an inland town on the borders of Thessaly and Dolopia. The name occurs *EM.* 303. 14 as a town in Boeotia. There is therefore no need to alter to Piresiae, a town in Magnesia (Ap. Rh. i. 37, 584). Lists of places are never in geographical order; cf. 35, 217, 218, 240 sq., 419 sq. and the Homeric Catalogue. Nonnus iv. 331 sq. is much worse.

Strabo 27, 376 notices the epic habit ὁ δὲ ποιητὴς ἔνια μὲν χωρία λέγει συνεχῶς ὥσπερ καὶ κεῖται . . . ἄλλοτε δ' οὐχ ὡς ἔστι τῇ τάξει.

ἀγχιάλη: of an island Soph. *Aj.* 135 Σαλαμῖνος ἀγχιάλου. For the variant ἀγχιάλῄ, -ος, cf. B 697 ἀγχίαλόν τ' Ἄντρωνα (ἀγχιάλην Zen.), and in the hymns iii. 181, 251, iv. 124, 209, 272, 412, v. 39, 50; Lobeck *Paralip.* 474, K.-B. § 147.

33. Cf. Soph. *fr.* 237 Θρῇσσαν σκοπιὰν Ζηνὸς Ἀθῴου.

35. **Αὐτοκάνης**: the MS. tradition is vindicated by the legend ΑΥΤΟΚΑΝΑ on coins (Head *HN.* 552); the head of Apollo sometimes occurs. For Κάνη or Κάναι, a mountain-range opposite the S. point of Lesbos, see Strabo 615, P.-W. i. 2597. Autocane seems to have been the port of Canae. Similar names, doubtless non-Greek, are Αὐτολέων (αὐδ- coins) Diod. xx. 19, Αὐταριάται Strabo vi. 4 (*aud-* Justin, Diod.), Αὐτόμαλα Strabo 123, Αὐτομάλαι and Αὐτόμολοι Steph. See Kretschmer *Einleitung* 247.

36. **εὐκτιμένη**, quadrisyllable, cf. εὔσκοπος v. 262: εὐκτιμένης below 102, which Hermann wished to retain.

ἀμιχθαλόεσσα: only here and Ω 753 in the same phrase. The derivation and meaning are obscure (Boisacq). Antimachus *l.c.* read μιχθ-. The dactylic caesura (*Dem.* 17) is excused by the proper name.

37. See on 29 above. Paus. x. 38. 2 Μάκαρος τοῦ Αἰόλου. For legends connected with him see Roscher *in v.*

38. η 44 ἀπόπροθεν εἰν ἁλὶ κεῖται, ι 25 πανυπερτάτη εἰν ἁλὶ κεῖται, Callim. *Del.* 3 νήσων ἱερωτάτη εἰν ἁλὶ κεῖται. The epithet λιπαρωτάτη is applied here only to land. From Φαναία, a cape in Chios, Leto saw Delos, Steph. *in v.*

39. **Μίμας**: opposite Chios, in the Erythraean peninsula: cf. γ 172. Callim. *Del.* 157 Iris watched on Mimas to prevent the islands from receiving Leto.

Κωρύκου: the southern cape of the Erythraean peninsula. Κώρυκος ὄρος ἀρσενικῶς λεγόμενον ὑψηλὸν πλήσιον Τέω τῆς Ἰωνίας καὶ Ἐρυθρῶν ὡς Ἑκαταῖος Ἀσίᾳ. καὶ λιμὴν ὁμώνυμος καὶ νησίον ὁμώνυμον Steph. *in v.*

40. The Byzantine identification (cf. p. lxxxii) in the margin of Π seems to refer to Κλάρος (perhaps to Μίμας). Malagina or

Mela is, as Mr. J. G. C. Anderson informed us, a town in the theme Ὀψίκιον (Obsequium). See Ramsay *Hist. Geog.* 204. It is not clear what ground the Byzantine geographer had for moving the places in this verse so far north.

For Claros (not in Homer) see ix. 5. It had a temple and oracle of Apollo. See Frazer on Paus. viii. 3. 1. The meaning of the epithet αἰγλήεσσα is not clear. In Homer it is only applied to Olympus, and therefore may = 'bright', as Nic. *Ther.* 958 Κλάρου νιφόεσσα πολίχνη, where νιφόεσσα = 'bright', as in *Ther.* 291, 881 *Alexiph.* 252. Aristides xiii. 787 compares the atmosphere of Athens to light; γνοίης δ' ἂν αὐτὴν [τὴν πόλιν] ἐπὶ τῇ πόρρωθεν ὥσπερ αὐγῇ τῷ ὑπὲρ κεφάλης ἀέρι, and xx. 261 the γάνος of Smyrna to a light that never was on land or sea. On the other hand the epithet may be conventional, as in xxxii. 9 of horses, Theocr. xxviii. 3 πόλιν εἰς Νειλέος ἀγλαάν of Miletus; or lastly it may indicate a white stone town; cf. xix. 12 ἀργινόεντα οὔρεα. In Pollux ix. 20 ὑπερλάμπουσα occurs among epithets of towns ἐν ὄρει.

Αἰσαγέης: elsewhere only in Nicander *Ther.* 217

ἢ καὶ ἐρυμνὸς
Αἰσαγέης πρηών (v.l. αἰγαγέης)

Σ Βουκάρτερος καὶ Αἰσαγέης καὶ Κέρκαφος ὀνόματα εἰσὶν ὀρῶν τῆς Ἀσίας. Somewhat similar names are Αἴγιγες· ὄνομα ἔθνους Suid., Ἀγχαλέη· τόπου ὄνομα παρ' Ἱππώνακτι [*fr.* 99] Hesych., Αἰγανέη *Anth. Pal.* vii. 390, Αἰσαγένης *IG.* v. 2. In Scylax 100 εἶτα λιγαία πόλις εἶτα χελιδονίαι, λιγαία might represent αἰγαία or αἰγάγα.

41. Samos is called ὑδρηλή from the abundance of its streams; Callim. *Del.* 48 νήσοιο διάβροχον ὕδατι μαστὸν Παρθενίης, οὔπω γὰρ ἔην Σάμος; Pliny *NH.* v. 37 names several rivers and fountains on the island.

Μυκάλης . . . κάρηνα = B 869 (following Miletus 868).

42. **Μερόπων ἀνθρώπων**: the Meropes were the ancient inhabitants of Cos (not of Miletus, whence πόλεις in *p* is a mistake; the same variant occurs Υ 60). They are mentioned by Pind. *Nem.* iv. 26, *Isthm.* v. 31, Herondas ii. 95, Hesych. *in v.*, Eust. 97. 40:

the singular is a proper name B 830; cf. also Call. *Del.* 160 ὠγυγίην δήπειτα Κόων Μεροπηίδα νῆσον | ἵκετο. Meropis = Cos *IG* xiv. 1. 293 A 23. The ancient statue of Apollo and the Charites at Delos was said to be the work τῶν καθ' Ἡρακλέα Μερόπων (Plut *de mus.* 1136 A). The Homeric formula μερόπων ἀνθρώπων (of unknown derivation and meaning) suggested the addition of ἀνθρώπων here; the usage is not Homeric but is found below 398, 424, Ap. Rh. ii. 677. Homer, however, uses ἄνδρες in the same combination A 594, ζ 3.

43. Cnidos is not in Homer. The Cnidians worshipped the Triopian Apollo as well as Aphrodite (Head *HN.* 615), and Κνίδιος is found once (in an inscription) as a title of the God. See P.-W. ii. 57. There was a temple of Apollo at Carpathos, *IG.* xii. 977.

44. **Ῥήναιά**: the form is found in Theocr. xvii. 70, Suid. in v. (who also gives Ῥηνία), Ῥηναία (parox.) in Steph., but the usual and probably correct form is Ῥήνεια, which Lobeck *Paralip.* 302 would restore. Attic inscriptions support -εια, *CIA.* i. 283, ii.[2] 814, but Ῥηναιεύς occurs *ib.* 813. Steph. gives also the forms Ῥήνη, Ῥηνίς. Neither Paros nor Rhenaia are in Homer.

46. σοι is a misdivision.

γαιέων. The plural of γαῖα occurs θ 284, μ 404, ξ 202. We find γεῶν in Herod., γέας in Democritus, but γαῖ, γᾶς are not frequent before Aristotle; see LS[9]. *in v.*

θέλοι is a necessary correction. θέλω occurs o 317, ii. 160, iv. 274, v. 38.

47 = H 151. The reason for this reluctance to become the birthplace of the God is fear of the wrath of Hera. In Callimachus *Del.* Hera dreads the birth of a son whom Zeus will love more than Ares. Ares and Iris are sent to prevent the reception of Leto by any land or island. Only the floating Delos, which has lain hidden in the Euripus, comes forward and welcomes Leto. A late version given by Hyginus *fab.* 140 makes Python Hera's agent. Hera swore that the birth should not take place where the sun's rays penetrated. Boreas rescued Leto and took her to Posidon, who covered Ortygia with waves under which the birth took place. Apollo when four days old slew Python. A third

variant connected with the title Λυκογενής (Δ 101, 119) and with a bronze statue of a she-wolf, which was shown at Delphi, brought the pregnant Leto in the shape of a wolf in twelve days from the Hyperboreans to Delos (Aristotle *NH.* 580 A, Philostephanus ap. Σ Ap. Rh. ii. 123, Antig. Caryst. 61, Aelian *NA.* iv. 4, x. 26, Plut. *qu. nat.* 38, Apostolius 1084 = paroemiogr. ii. 510). Tegean legend recorded that Apollo and Artemis punished the places which refused to receive their mother (Paus. viii. 53. 1).

49. **ἐβήσετο**: for the variant -ε- and -α- cf. Γ 262 (Ar.) ἐδύσετο, μητίσετο ii. 345. The MSS. are about equally divided.

51. **εἰ γάρ κ' ἐθέλοις**: the apodosis is not expressed.

53. **ἄλλως** was thought of, and has some manuscript support, but is unnecessary.

λήσει: Agar's conjecture (*CR.* x. 388) has settled this line. It is supported by S. οὐδὲ σὲ λήσει is a common threat Ψ 326, Ω 563, λ 126, and there are similar *v. ll.* λ 102, υ 85, *Batr.* 93, Theognis 20, Herod. iii. 2, *Anth. Pal.* vii. 513. 3.

54. σε ἔσεσθαι: Spitzner compared Τ 288, ζ 151 for the hiatus.

55. πολλήν, though an interesting alternative, is the weaker reading. The accentuation οἰσεῖς is due to scribes who had been copying Theocritus.

οὔτ' ἄρ φυτὰ μυρία φύσεις: Delos is quite treeless at the present day.

57. **ἑκατόμβας.** In historical times the hecatomb sacrifice was specially associated with Apollo, who sometimes bore the title *Hecatombaios*, and in whose honour the festival *Hecatombaia* was celebrated. From the festival the month-name *Hecatombaion* came, usual in the calendar of Ionian communities; Nilsson *GF.* 43, 138, 174.

59. The key to the reconstruction of this line was given by the *x* family; and the problem therefore was beyond the older editors. Stoll in 1849 neglected the indication δηρ̂ον, out of which Cobet extracted δημοῦ (this indeed had suggested itself to Baum., ἀναΐξει apparently first to Schneidewin). Stoll added the wanting syllable in βοσκήσεις, which future is recommended by ἀγινήσουσι and ἀναΐξει. The sense 'you shall feed those who

own you from alien hands' is supported by the case of Delphi (536–7). Hollander, p. 13, explained *περί τας* in *ET* as = *περὶ τὰ σ'*, denoting the size of the lacuna, but this is false palaeography.

60. **πῖαρ ὑπ' οὖδας**: ι 135 *ἐπεὶ μάλα πῖαρ ὑπ' οὖδας*. Buttmann is right in considering *πῖαρ* a substantive here, as it is Λ 550, P 659 *βοῶν ἐκ πῖαρ ἑλέσθαι*, Solon 25. 7 *πρὶν ἀνταράξας πῖαρ ἐξεῖλεν γάλα*, 'there is no fatness beneath the ground'. *πῖαρ* or *πεῖαρ* (*x* and M at v. 31) is the lengthened form of *πέαρ* (Hesych. *πέαρ· Γλαυκίας λιπαρόν*). For the acc. with *ὑπό* cf. Γ 371, Τ 259, *β* 181 al.

62. **Κοίοιο**: cf. Hes. *Theog.* 404, Pindar *paean* vii. 22, *fr.* 88. 2, *Κοιογένεια* Ap. Rh. ii. 710, *Κοιηίς* Callim. *Del.* 150, *Κοιαντίς* Orph. *h.* xxxv. 2, *Κοίου κόρας* Aristonous 5 Diehl. *Κρόνοιο* is a singular corruption: cf. Θ 383 *μεγάλοιο Κρόνοιο*.

63. **γονὴν . . . δεξαίμην**: Lucian *dial. mar.* 10 *ἥ τε γῆ πᾶσα οὐκ ἂν δύναιτο ὑποδέξασθαι τὰς αὐτῆς γονάς* (Matthiae).

64. **δυσηχής**: 'ill-sounding', in Homer only of *πόλεμος* and *θάνατος*.

68. **πρυτανεύσεμεν**: the verb and its cognates are not in Homer (but *Πρύτανις* is a Lycian E 678).

71. *ἴδης* (*x*) is of course wrong; *ἀτιμήσω, -σῃ* seem corrections made when the construction was lost, and further require a conjunction in 73. The two participles *ἀτιμήσας, καταστρέψας* are genuine: cf. M 113 sq., Hes. *Theog.* 521 sq. (*δήσας* is well attested), Ar. *Nub.* 937, *Ran.* 281, Eur. *Or.* 656, Herod. iv. 22, viii. 105.

72. On the division and accentuation of *ἐπειη* (82, v. 195) see La Roche *HT.* 267; *ἐπείη* or *ἐπειή* is the vulgate, but the MSS. of the Iliad give *ἐπειῆ* and *ἐπεὶ ῆ* fairly frequently, e.g. A 156 (*Iliad* 1931, *proleg.* 235).

κραναήπεδός: only here; cf. *κραναά* of Delos 16, 26, Pind. *Isthm.* i. 3, Orph. *Arg.* 1357.

73. **καταστρέψας**: 'overturning' or 'upsetting' Delos and so making it a reef. G. supposes a reference to the story of the floating island, and wrongly thinks that Pindar *fr.* 87, 88 had this passage in mind. There is no reference in the hymn either to the

floating island or to the change of name associated with it. The idea of a floating island appears in the home of Aeolus κ 3. For the common story that Asterie or Ortygia was a floating island, which after the birth of the God was anchored by four pillars and received the name Delos, the earliest authority is Pindar. Once anchored it was believed that Delos remained immune from earthquakes (Herod. vi. 98, Thuc. ii. 8, Pliny *NH.* iv. 16, Macrob. iii. 6. 7). The name Delos given after this change of condition was variously interpreted. According to Callimachus the floating Asterie had a way of disappearing from the mariner's ken by sailing up the Euripus; once anchored it was οὐκέτ' ἄδηλος (*Del.* 51). Others explained the name from the oracular God, δηλοῦσα γὰρ ἦν τὰ δυσεύρετα (Steph.). Compare also Aratus ἐν τοῖς κατὰ λεπτόν ap. Strab. 486 ὦ Λητοῖ σὺ μὲν ἤ με σιδηρείῃ Φολεγάνδρῳ | δειλὴ ἢ Γυάρῳ παρελεύσεαι αὐτίχ' ὁμοίην, and of another island visited by Apollo, Ap. Rh. ii. 679 ἡ δ' ὑπὸ ποσσὶν | σείετο νῆσος ὅλη, κλύζεν δ' ἐπὶ κύματα χέρσῳ.

ἁλὸς ἐν πελάγεσσιν = ε 335.

77. Cf. ε 432 πουλύποδος θαλάμης ἐξελκομένοιο.

78. **οἰκία ποιήσονται** = Μ 168 (-ωνται).

ἀκηδέα: cf. Φ 123 αἵ μ' ἀπολιχμήσονται ἀκηδέες. The word amounts to ἕκηλος.

The reading of *p* seems an attempt by a Byzantine reader to fill the space occupied by ἀκηδέα ἄχη τεϊλάων, based on δ 404 φῶκαι νέποδες καλῆς ἁλοσύδνης. The form is obviously barbarous, being formed mechanically from the Alexandrian νέπους.

79. Cf. ε 178, κ 343.

81. **χρηστήριον**: not in Homer (Hes. *fr.* 134. 6).

The oracle at Delos was of no importance in historical times, and its existence has been doubted. The references in late classical writers (Diod. v. 58, Lucan vi. 425, Lucian *bis accus.* 1, Serv. on *Aen.* iv. 143, Himerius xviii. 1, Max. Tyr. xli) are of a loose and general character; no evidential weight can be attached to the divine voice heard by Aeneas (*Aen.* iii. 90), or to etymological explanations of the name Delos (see on 62). The cave oracle of Lebègue has turned out to be neither old nor connected with Apollo (see on 17, 18). Bouché-Leclercq (*hist. de la divina-*

tion iii. 13) from the reference to οἱ τῶν Δηλίων μάντεις of Semus *Delias* ap. Athen. 331 maintained that there was no oracle and that χρηστήριον referred loosely to unattached diviners who drew inspiration from Brizo or Glaucus. But a single inscription (*c.* 280 B.C.) has proved alike the existence and the insignificance of the oracle. In the accounts recorded in *IG.* xi. 2. 165 v. 44 there is the entry και τας επι του μαντειου π[. . . ; *unam hanc deliaci oraculi mentionem in titulis nostris novi* is the comment of the editor Durrbach.

Hermann's lacuna is necessary to give the sense 'let him first make a temple here, and then he may build temples among all men, for', etc.

82. **πολυώνυμος**: see on *Dem.* 18.

83. **θεῶν μέγαν ὅρκον** = β 377 (89 = β 378).

The oath by the Styx occurs in *Dem.* 260 and *Herm.* 519. In Homer Styx is the river of the underworld Θ 369, and the form of oath in the Homeric poems seems to be by Earth and Sky (O 36), or Earth and Sea (Ξ 271), and the river of the underworld. In the latter passage Hera touches earth and sea with either hand, making the Titans underground witnesses to her oath (see on 332 below). The original purpose of the invocation of Styx seems the same as that of the Erinyes, to bring in the powers below to sanction the oath.

In Hesiod the passage *Theog.* 775 sq. represents a later ritualistic, probably Orphic, conception. The water *per se* has magical power, and is fetched for the purpose by Iris in a golden jug. It works on the principle of a poison-ordeal (see Frazer on Paus. viii. 184, Halliday *Greek Divination* 108; its effect upon divine perjurers is described Hes. *l.c.* 793; cf. Serv. on *Aen.* vi. 565).

In Hesiod the river, which is a branch of Ocean, flows over a lofty cliff (μακρῇσιν πέτρῃσι κατηρεφέ' 778, cl. 786), and this consistent feature of the imaginary river may have led to the identification of the Arcadian waterfall with Styx. Of this in Homer there is no hint. In the *Iliad* the earthly overflow of Styx is Titaressos (B 755). The personified Styx was the eldest of the Oceanides (Hes. *l.c.* 361), and as such made her appearance in the company of Persephone (*Dem.* 423).

84–6. Cf. O 36–8, ε 184–6.

86. **ὅρκος** is here not the oath (as in 83) but the object sworn by; so B 755, Hes. *l.c.* 400, 784, and often.

87. **θυώδης βωμός**: cf. v. 59, *orac.* ap. Hendess 19. 1 *βωμούς τε θυώδεις.*

90. **γόνῳ**, 'seed' = *γονήν* 63. These pairs of words are constant.

92. **ἔνδοθι**: ε 58 *τὴν δ' ἔνδοθι τέτμον ἐοῦσαν*, Hes. *fr.* 76. 4 *ἔνδοθι νήσου*, Callim. *Del.* 222 *Λητώ τοι μίτρην ἀναλύεται ἔνδοθι νήσου.*

93. **ὅσσαι ἄρισται ἔσαν**: the first syllable of *Διώνη* is usually short (E 370, Hes. *Theog.* 17, 353, Theocr. xv. 106); *ἔσαν* may have come from *ἔσαν* 92 or *ὅσσοι ἄριστοι ἔσαν* P 377. G. retains *ἔσαν*, comparing *Dĭana* in Latin, Schulze *qu. ep.* 156 n.

The choice of the Goddesses here named is remarkable; they probably represent older Titanic deities. Rhea and Themis are mentioned together as Titans by Hesiod (*Theog.* 135) and Apollodorus (i. 3) who adds Dione. Athena is found on a pyxis from Eretria Ἐφ. ἀρχ. 1902, 130 (Stais), Eilithyia and Lachesis are in Pindar, *paean* Ox. pap. xv. no. 1792.

94. **Ἰχναίη τε Θέμις**: cf. Lycophron 129. The title is connected with the place-name Ichnae in Macedonia (Steph. *in* Ἴχναι, Hesych. *in* Ἰχναίην) and Thessaly (Strabo 435), where the name Themisto and the month *Themistios* testify to the importance of the cult of Themis, for which there is also epigraphical evidence (reff. in Roscher v. 590). Macedonian Ichnae possessed an oracular cult of Apollo, and Phyllus, the site of the cult of Apollo Phyllius, was near Thessalian Ichnae. The title Ichnaia, 'the tracker' (cf. Ἰχναίη παρθένος of Nemesis in *Anth. Pal.* ix. 405. 1), is appropriate to the Goddess of Law, but there is some evidence that the original form of the place-name was Achnae, an apparently pre-hellenic name attested also for Boeotia and the Cyclades. It is therefore uncertain whether Themis derived the epithet from the place or the place owed its form to an original epithet of Themis (see Weniger in Roscher *l.c.*). For titles derived from place-names cf. Δ 8 Ἥρη τ' Ἀργείη καὶ Ἀλαλκομενηὶς Ἀθήνη. In Nonnus vii. 162 Θέμις εἰλείθυια helps Aphrodite at the birth of Beroe. Themis (Orph. *h.* 79. 6) taught prophecy, *ἣ καὶ Φοῖβον ἄνασσα θεμιστοσύνας ἐδίδαξε.*

ἀγάστονος Ἀμφιτρίτη = μ 97 : πολύστονος 'A. Quintus xiv. 644. She was present at the birth of Athena (relief of Gitiadas, Paus. iii. 17. 3) and of Aphrodite (base of statue of Olympian Zeus by Phidias id. v. 11. 8). She was unimportant in cult except at Teos, Nilsson *GF.* 81.

96. This line fell out in M E T from homoearchon with 98. For exx. of the *former* line of a pair being omitted cf. below 344, 345, iv. 215, 216.

97–9 seem adapted from N 521–4. Virgil (*Aen.* xii. 792) has a similar expression (*Iunonem*) *fulva pugnas de nube tuentem.*

97. **μογοστόκος Εἰλείθυια** = Π 187, Τ 193, in the plural Λ 270. On the forms of the word see Schulze *qu. ep.* 259 sq., Kretschmer *Vaseninschriften* 157. Derivation and meaning are quite unknown. Account should be taken of Theophrastus' statement *CP.* v. 4. 4 τὰ ἐκ τῶν ξύλων ἐκφυόμενα καὶ μάλιστα ἐκ τῶν ἐλατίνων ἃ καλοῦσιν οἱ μάντεις εἰλειθυίας (sim. *HP.* v. 9. 8).

98. **νέφος** and νεφέλη generally make position in Homer, but not P 243, 372, N 523 ἀλλ' ὅ γ' ἄρ' ἄκρῳ Ὀλύμπῳ ὑπὸ χρυσέοισι νέφεσσι.

99. **φραδμοσύνῃς** : the reading of M, which does not use iota subscript. For the plural B. compares *Theog.* 626, 884, 891, *OD.* 245. The singular first occurs in Ap. Rh. ii. 649.

100. **ὅτ'** : generally held to be for ὅ τε, not ὅτι, La Roche *HV.* i. 122, Monro *HG.* § 269.

102 f. Eilithyia occurs sometimes as an independent goddess of childbirth, sometimes as a cult epithet of Hera or Artemis. It is the view of Farnell not only that her association with Hera is primary (in Λ 270 the plural Eilithyiae are daughters of Hera, and Eilithyia is daughter of Zeus and Hera in Hesiod, *Theog.* 922, cf. Pind. *Nem.* vii. 2, Apollod. i. 3. 1), but that the name was originally 'an epithet of Hera and then detached from her and treated as the name of a separate divinity' (ii. 608). It is more probable, however, that Eilithyia is a pre-Hellenic goddess of childbirth who became identified with Hera and Artemis because of this special aspect of their functions. (Artemis delivered Leto, Apollod. i. 21.)

The presence of Eilithyia at the divine birth was brought into line with the Hyperborean cycle of Delian legend (see p. 197 above). Olen's hymn, in which she is called εὔλινος and is the mother of Eros, brought her to Delos from the Hyperboreans (Paus. i. 18. 5, viii. 21. 3, ix. 27), and her worship is associated by Herodotus (iv. 35) with the Hyperborean maidens, Hyperoche and Laodice. Hence her name may be to be sought in the Balkan tongues, as Paus. i. 18. 5 suggests when he says τοὺς δὲ ἄλλους παρ' αὐτῶν [τῶν Ὑπερβορέων] φασι τῆς Εἰλειθυίας μαθεῖν τὸ ὄνομα.

Eilithyia was the object of cult at Delos in historical times, and the island was said to be the centre from which her worship had spread in the Cyclades (Paus. i. 18. 5 : for cult in Paros and Teos *IG.* xii. 5 index, Amorgos *IG.* xii. 7, 84, 85, 420, Thera *IG.* xii. 3, 326, and Anaphe *IG.* xii. 3, 192). For the cult of Eilithyia in Greece generally see Farnell ii. 608, and Roscher i. 1219, where references will be found for the cult in Crete, Boeotia, Attica, Argos, and the Peloponnese.

In Homer, Eilithyia is under the direct control of Hera, who, in the parallel instance of Alcmena, prevents her attendance and so retards the birth of Heracles (T 119, cf. Anton. Lib. 29, Ovid *Met.* ix. 285). The details of the story of the magical retarding of the birth of Heracles by crossing the fingers (see Halliday, *Greek and Roman Folklore*, p. 28) explain the representation of Eilithyia in ancient art with an open hand of which the fingers are extended (discussed by Weinreich, *Antike Heilungswunder* p. 9 f.).

102. **Ἶριν**: the Delians sacrificed to Iris (Semus ap. Athen. 645 B) on the Ἑκάτης νῆσος, an islet off Delos (Harpocr. and Suid. *in v.*), and it is possible that the archaic statue called the Nike of Archermus really represents Iris (Sikes *Nike of Archermus*, see Gardner *Greek Sculpture* i. 117). But the introduction of Iris in the hymn may be due to epic influence. In the hymn of Callimachus Iris together with Ares acts in the contrary role, as Hera's agent, watching from Mimas to see that no island receives Leto.

104. **χρυσείοισι λίνοισιν ἐερμένον.** Barnes, by assimilating this line to σ 296, eliminated its meaning. λίνον is the thread or cord on which beads, stones, etc. are strung. Strabo 777 fin.

χρυσός τε ὀρυκτὸς γίνεται παρ' αὐτοῖς οὐ ψήγματος ἀλλὰ βωλαρίων χρυσοῦ καθάρσεως οὐ πολλῆς δεομένων, μέγεθος δ' ἐχόντων ἐλάχιστον μὲν πυρῆνος, μέσον δὲ μεσπίλου, μέγιστον δὲ καρύου· τρήσαντες δὲ ταῦτα ἐναλλὰξ λίθοις διαφανέσιν ὅρμους ποιοῦνται διείροντες λίνον, περιτίθενται δὲ περὶ τοὺς τραχήλους καὶ καρπούς. In temple-inventories the word is constant: *BCH.* x 164 ορμους χρυσους συν τωι λινωι και τοις επηρτημενοις, *IG.* xi (2) 161 B. 43, 94, 162. 18, 31, 42, 203. 49, 50, 283. 14, etc. συν τωι λινωι, συν τοις λινοις, *ib.* 85, 287 B 16 χρυσια ανειρμενα επι λινου; Apollodor. epit. i. 14 λίνον είρ αντι, Galen ii. 668 K. βελόνην καμπύλην λίνον ἔχουσαν al. There are various equivalents for λίνον, *IG. l.c.* 203. 61 συν τωι σπαρτωι, συν τω ιμαντι, Herod. iv. 190 ἐνειρμένων περὶ σχοίνους, Origen *c. haer.* iv. 96 (Migne vi. 3095) σανίδα λεπτὴν σχοινίῳ λεπτῷ περιειλήσαντες. Cf. also Galen *lex. Hippocr.* in Ῥαφίῳ . . . τοῦ λίνου διέρσει, Aen. Tact. 31. 18 ὅταν τινα θέλης ἐν αὐτοῖς τίθεσθαι λόγον λίνῳ διείρειν (διαιρεῖν cod.) . . . , ἐὰν θέλης αινειαν δηλοῦν τῇ διέρσει (διαιρέσει cod.) τοῦ λίνου . . . δίειρον πάλιν, παρεὶς δὲ τούτου τὰ ἐχόμενα . . . δίειρον τὸ λίνον, καὶ οὕτω τὰ ἐπίλοιπα τοῦ λόγου ἀντιγράφων ἔνειρον (-ρε cod.) εἰς τὰ τρυπήματα κτλ., Hippocr. ii. 243 inf. διέρσας διὰ τοῦ κύαρος τὸν λίνον, Zenob. iv. 92 τῷ διὰ τοῦ κοχλίου λίνον διείραντι . . . λαβὼν δὲ τὸν λίνον διειρμένον, Pollux ix. 116 διὰ τοῦ τρήματος διεῖρται σχοινίον, sim. i. 88, 94, 146, 147, 148, vi. 54 (περοναῖς), Hesych. περίδρομος· τοῦ δικτύου τὸ διειρόμενον σχοινίον, Galen xiii. 778 διείραντα λίνῳ, xiv. 780 λίνον λεπτὸν διείροντες.

Epic εἴρειν corresponds to ἀν-, δι-, ἐν-, συν-είρειν of later Greek. Aristophanes wished to read it for πείροντες κ 124, sc. ἰχθῦς δ' ὣς εἴροντες ἀτερπέα δαῖτα φέροντο, 'stringing them like fish'. The primitive also occurs: Hesych. Πανσικάκη· μηχάνημα τροχῷ ἐοικὸς δι' οὗ τὸν τράχηλον εἶρον (ἧρων MS.), Συνείροντες· συνάπτοντες, εἴρειν γὰρ τὸ ὁμοῦ συνάπτειν, *mantissa proverbiorum* (paroem. ii. 775) τὸν ἐν κάλυξι καθήμενον εἴρειν χρὴ στεφάνους, and often in later Greek: Oribasius *coll. med.* iv. 49. 23. 8 εἴρεται διὰ τοῦ τρήματος, sim. 10, 12; 13 οὗτοι οἱ κάλοι εἴρονται, and cf. the part. ἐρτός. The tropical usage in connexion with words or notes is common. In ο 460 χρύσεον ὅρμον ἔχων μετὰ δ' ἠλέκτροισιν ἔερτο the ὅρμος or chain was hung with amber beads or pendants, here the necklace is strung on gilded thread. The latter explanation is supported by *ορμος χρυσους επι ταινιδιωι* *BCH.* vi. 50, *ταινια περιηργυρωμενη* *ib.* 32. 'At Asine the Swedes found necklaces of gold and glass paste strung on thread [*Bull. Soc. R. des Lettres de Lund* 1924–5, p. 90], Schliemann found amethyst beads strung on bronze wire, *Mycenae* figs. 206–8. At Mycenae I found a string of white crystal beads round the neck of a skeleton, but no sign of how it was threaded. I therefore presume it was on a flaxen string' (letter from Mr. A. J. B. Wace).

107. **ποδήνεμος ὠκέα Ἶρις** = E 368. This epithet, taken together with *χρυσόπτερος* Θ 398, Λ 185, shows that Homer conceived of Iris as actually flying, but with foot-wings, such as are generally found in archaic monuments of the winged female type. Flying figures were at first represented by Greek artists in the attitude of striding, *βῆ ῥα θέειν*.

108. **τὸ μεσηγύ** : cf. *Dem.* 317.

109. Cf. E 367, 368.

110. **ἀπό** seems preferable to *ἀπέκ* (Quintus iv. 540), which is not found in Homer, though *διέκ*, *ὑπέκ* are common. See on *Dem.* 379.

114 = E 778 *αἱ δὲ βάτην τρήρωσι πελειάσιν ἴθμαθ' ὁμοῖαι. ἴθμαθ'* recurs Call. *Dem.* 59. Cf. Hesych. *ἐξίθν(?μ)η· ἔξοδος*. Of the v. ll. (which occur also in E), *ἴσμαθ'* is recommended by Marx *Rh. Mus.* 1907, 620, *ἴσθμαθ'* by Jacobsohn *Hermes* 1910, 201.

One of the few places in the hymns to which ancient authors refer; Ar. *Birds* 575 *Ἶριν δέ γ' Ὅμηρος ἔφασκ' ἰκέλην εἶναι τρήρωνι πελείῃ*, on which Σ Rav. *ὅτι ψεύδεται παίζων· οὐ γὰρ ἐπὶ Ἴριδος ἀλλ' ἐπὶ Ἀθηνᾶς καὶ Ἥρας*, and quotes E 778. The Σ Ven., however, remarks *οἱ δὲ ἐν ἑτέροις ποιήμασιν Ὁμήρου φασὶ τοῦτο γενέσθαι· εἰσὶ γὰρ καὶ ὕμνοι*. *Knights* 1016 *διὰ τριπόδων ἐριτίμων* seems a quotation from 443 below.

117. Cf. Theognis 5 *Φοῖβε ἄναξ ὅτε μέν σε θεὰ τέκε πότνια Λητὼ | φοίνικος ῥαδινῆς χερσὶν ἐφαψαμένη*, Callim. *Del.* 208 *ἀπὸ δ' ἐκλίθη ἔμπαλιν ὤμοις | φοίνικός ποτε πρέμνον*. The palm in the precinct of Apollo is mentioned ζ 162; it was reputed to be alive in the time of Cicero (*Leg.* i. 1) and Pliny (*NH.* xvi. 89). It was one of the types on Delian coins (Head *HN.* 485). Three trees, a palm, an olive, and a laurel were shown at Delos as associated

with the birth. Of these the palm appears to be the oldest and best attested, and the laurel may be a late addition. All three are given by Eur. *IT.* 1097; palm and olive, grasped by Leto in either hand, *Hec.* 458, *Ion* 919, Eust. 1558. 2. The names of the two streams at Tegyra (see on 16) show an adaptation there of the version of palm and olive. The olive alone occurs in the Ephesian claim to be the birthplace (Tac. *Ann.* iv. 61, cf. Strabo 639, 640), and in Limenius ap. Diehl ii. 307 ὃν ἔτικτε Λατὼ μάκαιρα πα[ρὰ λίμνᾳ] κλυτᾷ χερσὶ γλαυκᾶς ἐλαίας θιγοῦσ' ὄζον ἐν ἀγωνίαις ἐριθαλῆ. Cf. also Callim. *Del.* 262, *Iamb.* 279, Aelian *VH.* v. 4, Hyg. *fab.* 140, Catull. xxxiv. 7. Finally, Tzetzes on Lycophr. 401 gives laurel and palm, Servius on *Aen.* iii. 91 two laurels. Hera was born in Samos παρὰ τῷ Ἰμβράσῳ ποταμῷ καὶ ὑπὸ τῇ λύγῳ τῇ ἐν τῷ Ἡραίῳ κατ' ἐμὲ ἔτι πεφυκυίᾳ Paus. vii. 4. 4.

It has been suggested that the legend has some connexion with a modern Greek custom of grasping an olive branch sacred to St. Eleutherios or Panagia Vlastike (Bent *Cyclades* 182, Rodd *Customs and Lore of Modern Greece* 141). Cf. the holding of a venerated twig by Swedish women, Mannhardt *BK.* 51, Frazer ii. 68. There is, however, no evidence that palm or olive were supposed in antiquity to assist delivery. It is more probable that the kneeling Leto grasped the palm or other trees for support.

γοῦνα δ' ἔρεισε: the kneeling position was commonly adopted by Greek women, as it is among many peoples, though it was not recommended by Greek medical science (Samter *Geburt Hochzeit und Tod* 6 sq.). Hence such kneeling statues of Goddesses of fertility as Αὔγη ἐν γόνασιν at Tegea (Paus. viii. 48. 5), or Damia and Auxesia in Aegina (Herod. v. 82). Beside the kneeling marble figure from Sparta discussed by Samter *l.c.* a number of similar statues, most of which are probably to be interpreted as representations of birth or of Goddesses of birth, have been collected by Baur *Philologus* viii, *Supplem.* 481 sq.

118. **μείδησε δὲ γαῖ' ὑπένερθεν**: Pindar *paean* xii (Ox. pap. 1792) ἔλαμψεν δ' ἀελίου δέμας ὁπότ' ἀγλαὸν ἐς φάος ἰόντες δίδυμοι παῖδες πολὺν ῥόθον ἵεσαν ἀπὸ στομάτων Ἐλείθυιά τε καὶ Λάχεσις, Theognis 9 ἐγέλασσε δὲ γαῖα πελώρη, γήθησεν δὲ βαθὺς πόντος ἁλὸς πολιῆς.

For ἐγέλασσε cf. Τ 362 γέλασσε δὲ πᾶσα περὶ χθὼν χαλκοῦ ὑπὸ στεροπῆς. In the present passage, as often in later Greek, smiling nature is personified; e.g. *Dem.* 14 (q.v.), Aesch. *P.V.* 90, Theocr. xvii. 64, Ap. Rh. i. 880, iv. 1169. Compare also Limenius 7 πᾶς δὲ γάθησε πόλος οὐράνιο[ς ἀννέφελος ἀγλαὸς ν]ηνέμους δ' ἔσχεν αἰθὴρ ἀ[ελλῶν ταχυπετ]εῖς [δρό]μους κτλ., Philodamus 8 (Diehl ii. 352) πάντες δ' [ἀστέρες ἀγχ]όρευσαν, πάντες δὲ βροτοὶ χ[άρησαν σαῖς] βάγχιε γένναις. Other exx. in Adami *de poet. scaen.* 232 sq.

119. **ἐκ δ' ἔθορε πρὸ φόως δέ**: see on *Herm.* 12. The cock was present Ael. *NH.* iv. 29. For the day of the month v. Hesiod *OD.* 770. For ἐκ δ' ἔθορε cf. Hes. *Theog.* 281, Callim. *Del.* 255, *h.* iv. 20, Panyasis *fr.* 5 καί ῥ' ὁ μὲν ἐκ κόλποιο τροφοῦ θόρε ποσσὶ Θυώνης.

For the accent φόως δέ cf. ii. 163. The hymn-MSS. have no trace of Aristarchus' reading φώως δέ.

θεαὶ δ' ὀλόλυξαν: Frazer on Paus. ix. 11. 3 gives examples of cries at birth uttered by women probably to announce the birth. So Theocr. xvii 64 Κοώς δ' ὀλόλυξεν at the birth of Ptolemy. The whole passage (58–79) and Callim. *Del.* 255–8 show acquaintance with the hymn.

120. **ἤϊε**: only here and Ο 365, Υ 152. The derivation is unknown (Boisacq).

λόον: on λόω, λοέω, by-forms of λούω, see Veitch *in* Λόω, Schulze *qu. ep.* 65 n., Smyth *Ionic* 535, Solmsen *Untersuch.* 13. The common form (unmetrical) has invaded the text here, as Ar. *Nub.* 838 and the variant in Ο 393 ap. Σ T. Add λόει Praxilla *PLG.* iii. 650, λοηται *IG.* xii. 569. 5.

121. **ἁγνῶς καὶ καθαρῶς** = Hes. *OD.* 337, *orac.* ap. Hendess 1. 14, 54. 3.

123. **θήσατο**: here only of the mother. In Homer and *h.* ii. 236 it is of the child. Cf. the uses of θηλάζω.

124. Themis, in a tradition attributed to Musaeus, acted as nurse to Zeus, Hygin. *astr.* ii. 13, Σ German. 156, cf. Ovid *Fast.* vi. 158. In a hymn on the birth of Athena (Galen *de Hipp. et Plat. dogm.* v. 351) Themis similarly takes charge of Athena after she emerges from the head of Zeus. For the treatment compare that of Demophon (*h.* ii. 236), who is denied the

breast and human food but grows miraculously as the result of an external application of ambrosia. The babe Aristaeus is fed on nectar and ambrosia and so made immortal, Pind. *Pyth.* ix. 63.

125. **ἐπήρξατο**: 'offered', as γ 445 χέρνιβά τ' οὐλοχύτας τε κατήρχετο. In Homer with δεπάεσσι of the libation, to which the suckling of the child is compared.

127. Apollo, like Hermes *h.* iv. 15, shows his divinity by precocious strength and talent. In later accounts he kills the dragon while still a babe in arms (see on 214). At four years old he built the κερατών Callim. *Ap.* 58. The idea of divine precocity (cf. of Zeus Callim. *Zeus* 56 ἀλλ' ἔτι παιδνὸς ἐὼν ἐφράσσαο πάντα τέλεια) is common in folk-lore, see below, p. 269.

129. **δεσμά**: this without variant is the plural of δεσμός in the hymns (iv. 157, 409, vii. 12, 13); in Homer the form is δέσματα. This and the force of the repetition of σε turn the scale in favour of δεσμά.

131. Callim. *Ap.* 44 Φοίβῳ γὰρ καὶ τόξον ἐπιτρέπεται καὶ ἀοιδὴ, | κείνου δὲ θριαὶ καὶ μάντιες.

φίλη: predicative, not epithetic.

132. **χρήσω**: for the active cf. χρείων θ 79.

133. **ἀπό**: 'on', i.e. he left the ground, got up upon it, as Ε 13 τὼ μὲν ἀφ' ἵπποιιν ὁ δ' ἀπὸ χθονὸς ὤρνυτο (and the common ἀφ' ἵππων on horseback), Ξ 153 Ἥρη δ' εἰσεῖδε χρυσόθρονος ὀφθαλμοῖσι | στᾶσ' ἐξ Οὐλύμποιο ἀπὸ ῥίου, 349 (ὑάκινθον) ὃς ἀπὸ χθονὸς ὑψόσ' ἔεργε (esp. with Zenodotus' reading ἵν' ἀπὸ χθονὸς ἀγκαζέσθην), τ 389 ἷζεν ἀπ' ἐσχαρόφιν (v. l. ἐπ'), χ 72 οὐδοῦ ἄπο ξεστοῦ (v. l. ἔπι), *orac.* Sibyl. iv. 10 ὃν ἰδεῖν οὐκ ἔστιν ἀπὸ χθονός, sc. οἶκον, Theocr. xiv. 68 ἀπὸ κροτάφων πελόμεσθα | πάντες γηραλέοι, *IG. Ins. Aeg.* iii. 449 ευμαστος με αηρεν απο χθονος ho κριτοβουλου, and in geometry = on a line (e.g. Plato *Meno* 82 E ἀφ' ἧς τὸ ὀκτώπουν χωρίον γενήσεται).

ἐβίβασκεν: βιβάσκων is a v. l. on βιβάσθων Ν 809, Ο 676; cf. inscr. at Corinth *AJA.* 1919 331.

135. **χρυσῷ**: the idea is amplified by Callim. *Del.* 260 χρύσεά τοι τότε πάντα θεμείλια γείνετο Δῆλε | χρυσῷ δὲ τροχόεσσα πανήμερος ἔρρεε λίμνη | χρύσειον δ' ἐκόμησε γενέθλιον ἔρνος ἐλαίης | χρυσῷ δ' ἐπλήμμυρε βαθὺς Ἰνωπὸς ἑλιχθείς, | αὐτὴ δὲ χρυσέοιο ἀπ' οὔδεος

εἴλεο παῖδα. The island is suddenly covered with golden scrub, i.e. the natural scrub burst into flower. Cf. 223 and the miracles at the birth of Athena Pind. *Ol.* vii. 34. On the flowering shrubs on islands and capes see Beloch[2] i. 64.

136–9. This is the clearest case of the alternatives which are assumed in the text of the hymns, since here the MSS. distinguish them. 136–8 are found only in *y*, i.e. in the margins of E L T (in Π they have accidentally been copied into the text). Of the two versions perhaps 136–8 is the later, since *εἵλετο* c. gen. 'preferred to' is un-Homeric (Soph. *Phil.* 1100). For *γηθοσύνη* subst. see Lobeck *Pathol.* 232; for *ὡς ὅτε* without a verb M 132, for the language i. 8 *ἀνθέον ὕλῃ*.

140. **αὐτὸς δ'**: resumptive after 134–9. See on 181.

142. **ἂν νήσους**: D'Orville's correction (also made by Ilgen) appears to be necessary. *ἠλασκάζες* might perhaps govern the acc. *νήσους* on the analogy of 175 *στρεφόμεσθα πόλεις*, but the construction can hardly be extended to *ἀνέρας*. For the corruption cf. B 198 *ὃν δ' αὖ*, Eust. *ὃν δ' ἄν*.

The expression *νήσους τε καὶ ἀνέρας* means the whole world, 'islands and mankind (elsewhere)': cf. Pind. *Ol.* vi. 10 *οὔτε πὰρ ἀνδράσι οὔτ' ἐν ναυσὶ κοιλαῖς*, Athen. 184 C *ἐποίησε πλήρεις τὰς νήσους καὶ πόλεις ἀνδρῶν γραμματικῶν κτλ.*, Libanius i. 183, 188, 224 *περὶ οὗ ποία πόλις οὐκ ἀκήκοε τῶν ἐν ἠπείροις ἢ νήσοις*; Theocr. xvii. 77 *μυρίοι ἤπειροί τε καὶ ἔθνεα μυρία φωτῶν*, Quintus xii. 10 *νήεσσι καὶ ἡμῖν*, Theognis 247 *καθ' Ἑλλάδα γῆν στρωφώμενος ἠδ' ἀνὰ νήσους*.

144, 145 = 22, 23: see on 20–24.

146. On the variants in this passage between the MSS. and the quotation by Thucydides and Aristides see Introd., p. lxvi. There is not much doubt that the two versions are independent (Gemoll). We have followed the MS. text except in 165 and 171, where graphical corruption has taken place.

ἀλλὰ σύ: this suits the context better than *ἀλλ' ὅτε* of the Thucydidean version. With *ἀλλ' ὅτε* the passage would mean 'but when your heart most rejoices in Delos, then the Ionians gather', a way of saying that the Ionians gather at the time of the feast of Apollo at Delos. *ἔνθα* would thus be apodotic and demonstrative; in the text of the MSS. it is relative, 'where'.

On Apollo's ἀποδημίαι at Delos and Miletus cf. Menander in *rhet. gr.* ix. 140.

147. Cf. Ἰαόνες ἑλκεχίτωνες N 685. Long robes and extravagance were a characteristic of the Ionians: see Thuc. i. 6. 3, Democritus of Ephesus *FHG.* iv. 383, Hippias *ib.* 431 (on Erythrae and Chios), Asius *fr.* 13 (on Samos), Bacchyl. xvii. 2, ἁβροβίων Ἰώνων, id. *fr.* 32, Xenophanes iii. 1 ἁβροσύνας δὲ μαθόντες ἀνωφελέας παρὰ Λυδῶν | . . . ἤισαν εἰς ἀγορὴν παναλουργέα φάρε' ἔχοντες | . . . αὐχαλέσιν χαίτῃσιν ἀγαλλόμεν' εὐπρεπέεσσιν | ἀσκητοῖς ὀδμὴν χρίμασι δευόμενοι, Strabo 466.

148. **αὐτοῖς σὺν παίδεσσι**: Hermann's αὐτοῖσιν παίδεσσι is idiomatic and easy (cf. λ 359 πλειοτέρῃ σὺν χειρί codd., πλειοτέρῃσιν χερσίν Aristoph., and for the reverse *Herm.* 94, where Demetrius corrected φὰς συνέσευε for φασὶν ἔσευε) but unnecessary, cf. M 112, Ξ 498, ν 118.

The Thucydidean σὴν ἐς ἄγυιαν is curious. It, of course, cannot mean a procession as Baumeister thought, and Pind. *Ol.* ix. 51, *Nem.* vii. 92 do not prove that it is a poetic synonym of πόλις. Perhaps it is the *place* before the temple where the contests took place.

Cf. the five-yearly panegyris at Palaepaphos ἄνδρες ὁμοῦ γυναιξὶν συνιόντες Strabo 683.

149. **ὀρχηθμῷ καὶ ἀοιδῇ** = Theognis 791. Both ὀρχηθμός and ὀρχηστύς are found in Homer.

151–2. Thucydides leaves us here. Martin's divination has established 152. ἐπαντιάζειν is ἅπ. λεγ., but more suitable than ἀπ-, ἐν-, or ὑπ-. οἵ, which has to be altered to ὅς to suit the verbs, seems due to ἰαόνες after the intermediate syllables had become gibberish. Martin further conjectured ἀθάνατος, which is the reading of M, and possibly connected with ἀνήρ of *x*. But the expression is hyperbole (Θ 538 εἰ γὰρ ἐγὼν ὣς | εἴην ἀθάνατος καὶ ἀγήρως ἤματα πάντα); it is the Ionians who look like Gods. (For the variant cf. Ω 499 αὐτούς, αὐτός.)

151. Cf. M 323 αἰεὶ δὴ μέλλοιμεν ἀγήρω τ' ἀθανάτω τε ἔσσεσθ'.

155. **αὐτῶν**; almost pleonastic as β 154 ἤιξαν διά τ' οἰκία καὶ πόλιν αὐτῶν.

κτήματα πολλά: indicates a fair such as in all times and countries tends to grow up at religious gatherings (Homolle, Daremberg and Saglio ii. 55 n. 16). An event at one is recorded by Maximus of Tyre xxi. 2 ἐν τῇ τῶν Ἰώνων ἀγορᾷ ἐν Πανιωνίῳ [πανίω MSS.] ἐκόμιζεν τίτθη βρέφος. ὁ δὲ Ἀνακρέων βαδίζων μεθύων ἄκων ἐστεφανωμένος σφαλλόμενος ὠθεῖ τὴν τίτθην σὺν τῷ βρέφει κτλ.

156. ὅου κλέος οὔποτ' ὀλεῖται = B 325, cf. *orac.* ap. Paus. x. 6. 7. On the form ὅου see Monro *HG.* § 98, and for the accentuation *EM.* 614. 34 (Herodian), Ϭ α 70.

157. κοῦραι Δηλιάδες: for this chorus see Homolle *BCH.* xiv. 501, εἰς τογ χορον τογ γυναικων τογ γενομενον τοις ἀπολλ[ωνίοις]. The Delian chorus took part in several festivals, Apollonia, Letaea, Artemisia, Britomartia, Aphrodisia, and on the occasion of θεωρίαι from Cos, Rhodes, Siphnos, and Carystos. Cf. Dion. *Perieg.* 527 ῥύσια δ' Ἀπόλλωνι χοροὺς ἀνάγουσιν ἅπασαι [sc. αἱ Κυκλάδες] ἱσταμένου γλυκεροῦ νέον ἔαρος. Cratinus' play the Δηλιάδες may have had to do with this choir. Eur. *HF.* 687 calls their song a paean, παιᾶνα μὲν Δηλιάδες ὑμνοῦσ' ἀμφὶ πύλας τὸν Λατοῦς εὔπαιδα γόνον εἱλίσσουσαι καλλίχορον: *Hec.* 463 σὺν Δηλιάσιν τε κούραισιν Ἀρτέμιδός τε θεᾶς χρυσέαν ἄμπυκα τόξα τ' εὐλογήσω; compare the chorus of Λυδῶν κόραι at Ephesus Ar. *Nub.* 599, Ion *fr.* 22, Diog. *fr.* 1, Strabo 639, Aelian *VH.* xii. 9, at Sardis Dion. *Perieg.* 839.

θεράπναι = θεράπαιναι first here: cf. θεραπνίς.

160. After melic prooemia to the local Gods they give a melic hymn on national history, heroes, heroines, κτίσεις, etc., the κλέα ἀνδρῶν of Homer. These are extant in Pindar and Bacchylides: cf. *h.* xxxi. 18, xxxii. 18. The passage is important for the meaning of the word προοίμιον.

162. κρεμβαλιαστύν: the alternative βαμβαλιαστύν is not elsewhere found, but it may be justified by βαμβαίνων K 375, -ει Bion vi. 9, βαμβαλύζω Ϭ K *l.c.* The two words have the same meaning, castanets or bones. Cf. κρέμβαλα in the worship of Artemis *carm. pop.* 3 (in Dicaearchus *FHG.* ii. 239). During the song there was no doubt a dance, the hyporcheme: this was sacred to Apollo and was kept up at Delos in the time of Lucian (*de salt.* 16 παίδων χοροὶ συνελθόντες ὑπ' αὐλῷ καὶ κιθάρᾳ οἱ μὲν

ἐχόρευον, ὑπωρχοῦντο δὲ οἱ ἄριστοι προκριθέντες ἐξ αὐτῶν). Whether the boys had taken the place of the women, or continued in the second century A.D. together with them, it is impossible to say.

163. The hyporcheme was mimetic (Athen. 15 D), but the accomplishment ascribed to the Deliades is that of singing in dialect. Dialects in antiquity had the dignity of languages. The Pythagoreans recommended their disciples to keep their native speech (Iambl. *vit. Pyth.* 241) though the school inclined to Doric. Shows were given in dialect: Suet. *Iul.* 39 *ludos [edidit] etiam regionatim urbe tota et quidem per omnium linguarum histriones*, sim. *Aug.* 43. Recitations in dialect are to be met with in Italy to-day. The accomplishments of the Delian women suggest the powers of Helen δ 278 sq. (as a φωνόμιμος she was called Ἠχώ Ptol. Heph. i. 149 b 3) or Crassus (Quintilian xi. 2. 50), or of Cleopatra (Plut. *Ant.* 27 τὴν γλῶσσαν ὥσπερ ὄργανόν τι εὐπετῶς τρέπουσα καθ' ἣν βούλοιτο διάλεκτον), who spoke seven languages including those of the Troglodytes and the Jews.

Religious centres appear to have been polyglot. Compare the Dorian of the Delphic oracle and the inscriptions of Dodona, and the priest at Ptoeum who ordinarily speaking Aeolic fell into Carian to answer Mys (Plut. *Aristid.* 19, *def. or.* 412). From Plut. *Nicias* 3 we learn that pilgrims to Delos brought their choir with them, as the Messenians did to sing Eumelus' prosodion (which from the quotation Paus. iv. 4. 3 was in Doric): Pronomus of Thebes wrote one for the Chalcidians (*id.* ix. 12. 5). Apollo answered pilgrims in their own dialect and with their own music. This made D'Orville (J. Ph. xxv. 250) think of the gift of tongues, *fere idem praedicatur de Apostolis in Actis.*

165. In this verse the Thucydidean tradition is clearly better than that of the MSS. -λήκοι suggested ληποι, λητω to scribes full of the legend. Cf. Dion. *Perieg.* 447 ἀλλ' ὁ μὲν ἱλήκοι. The verb in the second person is common.

Ἀπόλλων Ἀρτέμιδι ξύν = ο 410. The two divinities were closely connected at Delos as at many other places. Their temples were side by side and they had common offerings. Reff. in Farnell ii. 577, P.-W. i. 33. For their common cult at Delphi see on xxvii. 13.

166. Here he leaves the Gods and compliments the Deliades with a view to his own recommendation. Professional *ἀοιδοί* periodically met in competition at Delos (e.g. Homer and Hesiod, Introd. p. lxxxviii). The Deliades therefore had material for judgement.

171. **εὖ μάλα πᾶσαι**: Theocr. xxv. 9 *εὖ μάλα πᾶσι.*

ὑποκρίνασθ' ἀμφ' ἡμέων: Marx *Rh. Mus.* 1907. 620 has settled this passage, and the less said about previous interpretations the better. For the omission of *μ* before *φ* in inscriptions cf. *αφι* = *αμφι*, *νυφη* = *νυμφη* in the index to Kretschmer *Vaseninschriften*; in MSS. *ἀμφασίη, ἀφασίη* P 695, *ἀμφίς, ἀφείς* Φ 162, *ἀμφίσταμαι, ἀφ-, ἐφ-*, Soph. *El.* 192. The MSS. M L_1 Π At Dz turn out to be nearest to the truth, next ET and *p*, furthest off Thucydides. For the phrase cf. Aesch. *Suppl.* 615 *ἀμφ' ἡμῶν λέγων*, Babrius *fr.* 18, p. 200 Crusius *ἀ(μ)φ' ὑμέων κοκύῃσι καθημένη ἀρχαίῃσι.*

172. For the reference of the poet to himself and his country cf. Hesiod *OD.* 639, *Theog.* 23, *fr.* 227.

παιπαλοέσσῃ: of Chios γ 170. This line was the origin of the tradition that Homer was blind and a Chian (the latter belief occurs as soon as Simonides *fr.* 85), as 174 was of that which made him travel (Paus. i. 2. 3 *ἀποδημήσας ἐπὶ μακρότατον*). Thamyris and Demodocus also were blind; it was natural that the blind should become *ἀοιδοί*, as the lame, like their God Hephaestus, became blacksmiths (Bergk). Brugmann *IF.* iii. 257 n. compares Servian epos.

173. **ἀριστεύουσιν**: the present is correct; the poet claims that his songs are famous as soon as he has sung them (*μετόπισθεν*). His merits are recognized in his lifetime (170). To alter to the future would make the women prophesy. Cf. Theognis 22, 23.

174. **ὑμέτερον** is clearly correct. He makes a bargain with the Deliades, as the minstrel *vit. Herod.* 439 with the potters, and Ulysses η 332, θ 496, ρ 418, cf. τ 333.

175. **στρεφόμεσθα**: 'roam round'; not elsewhere with acc., but cf. the compounds *γαῖαν ἀναστρέφομαι* ν 326, *ἐπιστρωφῶσι πόληας* ρ 486 (Hermann). Not unlike is *ποῖ στρέφει;* Ar. *Thesm.* 230, 610. The statement suits the rhapsode in general (Homer,

Thamyris, Arion) and Cynaethus in particular. Cf. in general Hegemon 6–9. Cf. also the Anglo-Saxon poet Widsith (Chadwick *Heroic Age*, p. 81).

177. Here the poet returns from the Deliades and himself to Apollo, his proper theme. He announces himself as continuing, which he does 179 sq. Οὐ λήξω has nothing to do with the epilogic formula ἀρχόμενοι λήγοντές τε (I 97 *h. Dion.* 18), it is in fact the contrary of it. The verb is used in its natural sense (θ 87 ἦ τοι ὅτε λήξειεν ἀείδων θεῖος ἀοιδός, I 191 δέγμενος Αἰακίδην ὁππότε λήξειεν ἀείδων); he makes a virtual apology for intercalating a personal episode into his proper theme.

179–206 hold together, repeat the ubiquity of Apollo already dwelt on in 142–3, and take him to Pytho and Olympus, where he and his mother are in glory. 179–81 give a short recapitulation of the previous theme and continue. They add Lycia and Maeonia to the places mentioned at the beginning. The resumption of the hymn proper is marked by an invocation (ὦ ἄνα). The poet then falls back into the third person (182), which he had previously used: he changes again into the second 207–8. The list of Apollo's haunts shows his wide acceptance; it is not meant that he went to Pytho directly after being born at Delos. Moreover, it was only after the foundation of the oracle and the death of the serpent that Apollo would approach Pytho making music. From Pytho, it being northerly, he naturally passes to Olympus, to direct the heavenly concert.

After this completion of the God's habits and haunts, poet considers which of his feats and adventures he shall sing (207 sqq.).

179. Cf. ὦ ἄνα Λητοῦς υἱέ Theognis 1, Orph. *fr.* 49.

Λυκίην: on the Lycian Apollo see P.-W. ii. 58, Farnell iv. 113, P.-R. i. 254. Apollo was thought to spend six months in summer at Delos, the other six at Patara (Serv. on *Aen.* iv. 144, Hor. *Carm.* iii. 4. 65). According to another tradition he absented himself from Delphi during the three winter months (Pind. *Pyth.* iv. 5, Plut. *de EI* 9).

Μῃονίην ἐρατεινήν: cf. Γ 401, Σ 291. For the Lydian cult (especially at Magnesia near Sipylos), P.-W. ii. 82.

180. **Μίλητον**: for the cult of Apollo Διδυμεύς at Branchidae near Miletus see P.-W. ii. 49, P.-R. i. 283.

ἔναλον: cf. Pind. *Ol.* ix. 150 εἰναλία Ἐλευσίς, Critias i. 6 ἔναλος πόλις of Chios.

181. **αὐτός**: unemphatic, 'and you': cf. 155.

περικλύστου: Archestr. *Hedyp. fr.* 27 ἐν περικλύστῳ | Δήλῳ.

184. **τεθυωμένα**: τεθυώδεα is a *vox nihili*. Barnes' conjecture is supported by *Cypria fr.* ii. 8 τεθυωμένα εἵματα ἕσται. Pierson's εὐώδεα is about equally similar to τεθυώδεα.

185. **καναχὴν ἔχει**: so Π 105, 794, βοὴν ἔχον Σ 495.

186. **ὥς τε νόημα**: for the simile see on *Herm.* 43.

189. Cf. A 604, ω 60. For later references see P.-W. ii. 38, P.-R. 279. Compare especially the dance of the Muses to the sound of Apollo's phorminx in Hes. *Scut.* 201, Pind. *Nem.* v. 22, and the inscr. on the chest of Cypselus Μοῦσαι δ' ἀμφ' αὐτὸν χαρίεις χορὸς αἶσι κατάρχει Paus. v. 18. 4, μουσάρχῳ Λατοῦς υἱεῖ *carm. pop.* Diehl 49. 3. See also on iv. 450.

190. **δῶρ' ἄμβροτα**: i.e. immortality (Franke).

191. Cf. Archilochus 7. 6 θεοὶ γὰρ ἀνηκέστοισι κακοῖσιν | ὦ φίλ' ἐπὶ κρατερὴν τλημοσύνην ἔθεσαν.

192. **ἀφραδέες**: *h.* ii. 256 νήιδες ἄνθρωποι καὶ ἀφράδμονες, Nonnus v. 349 ἀφράδεες ζώουσι.

194. For the connexion of the Charites with Aphrodite see n. on v. 61, for the Horae n. on vi. 5. With the line cf. Panyasis *r.* 13. 1 Χάριτές τ' ἔλαχον καὶ εὔφρονες Ὧραι, Xen. *Symp.* vii. 5 (dance of Charites, Horae, and Nymphs). For the conjunction of Charites and Muses cf. Hes. *Theog.* 64, Sappho *fr.* 22 δεῦτέ νυν ἄβραι Χάριτες καλλίκομοί τε Μοῦσαι. The Charites are associated with Apollo in literature (Pind. *Ol.* xiv. 10, *fr.* 122, with the Muses also) and art (Paus. ix. 35. 1 of the Delian Apollo). The very ancient statue at Delos, the dedication of which was attributed to the Meropes of Cos, represented the God with a bow in his right hand, and in his left the three Charites, each with a different musical instrument, Plut. *mor.* 1136 A. Similarly the Horae appear in art with Pan and Apollo (Paus. viii. 31. 3 at Megalopolis), and Apollo has such titles as ὡρομέδων (hymn of

Tenos *IG.* xii. 5. 893), ὡρίτης Lycophr. 352, ὡρεσιδώτην *Anth. Pal.* ix. 525. 25 (Abel *Orph.* p. 285).

εὔφρονες : the Horae are invariably good to mankind, πολυγηθέες Φ 450, ἀληθεῖς Pind. *fr.* 30. 6. The Hesiodic Horae are Eunomia, Dike, Eirene. See P.-R. 477.

196 = Σ 594.

197. Cf. ζ 107, where Artemis is conspicuous among the nymphs; *h.* xxvii. 15 she leads the Muses and Charites in the dance.

μεταμέλπεται : the Goddess sang as she danced, cf. Π 182 μελπομένῃσιν ἐν χορῷ Ἀρτέμιδος. So the Phaeacian girls sang as they played ball ζ 100 f. For the v. l. οὔτ' ἐλάχεια, οὔτε λάχεια cf. ι 116, κ 509.

199. Cf. ix. 2.

201. **παίζουσ'**, sc. ὀρχοῦνται, as θ 251, ψ 147, *h.* v. 120, Diodorus v. 49. 1 at the marriage of Cadmus and Harmonia Ἀπόλλωνα μὲν κιθαρίσαι, τὰς δὲ Μούσας αὐλῆσαι.

202. **καλὰ καὶ ὕψι βιβάς** = 516. Apollo keeps time to his own music; cf. his title ὀρχηστής Pind. *fr.* 125, and perhaps σκιαστής in Laconia, which Σ Lycophr. 561 explains as 'the dancer'. High stepping was characteristic of tragic dance: ἄνθρῳσκε Soph. *fr.* 422, πάλλε πόδ' αἰθέριον Eur. *Troad.* 325, and cf. Ar. *Wasps* 1492, 1524. For religious ritual we may compare 2 Samuel vi. 16, where David leaps and dances before the Ark. Apollo was called Αἰγλήτης in Crete, Strabo 484.

203. **μαρμαρυγαί**: of feet only here and θ 265 μαρμαρυγὰς θηεῖτο ποδῶν.

204. For Leto's pride in her children cf. ζ 106, *h.* iii. 12, 125.

θυμὸν μέγαν : cf. *h.* ii. 37 μέγαν νόον of Demeter, I 496 θυμὸν μέγαν of Achilles, and the ordinary μεγαλήτορα θυμόν; for the acc. *h. Pan* 45 πάντες δ' ἄρα θυμὸν ἔτερφθεν.

205 expands the pronoun, and hardly deserves the name of hyperbaton.

207. The poet proceeds to deal with other episodes in Apollo's career, and hesitates between his parentages and his founding of Delphi. He elects the second.

πῶς τ' ἄρ' and **ἠέ** (ἢ) occur in 19, 25, and are therefore no peculiarity here.

208. Our materials do not allow the complete elucidation of this catalogue. Several of the legends which were before Cynaethus did not come down to the logographi and mythographers. As Servius says (on *Aen.* ix. 361) it is *locus unus . . . de sic relictis ut nobis per historiae ignorantiam liquide non intelligantur.* One difficulty is this; does every rival (ἅμα) imply a new μνηστή? as 209, 210 Coronis is μνηστή and Ischys is rival, and 212 Leucippus is rival and Daphne (presumably) μνηστή. Were, in 211, Phorbas and Ereutheus rivals for Coronis as well as Ischys, or does each imply a new μνηστή?

The Dotian plain was the home of Coronis (*h.* xvi): Triopas, of whose blood Phorbas was, came to Rhodes from Dotion (Dieuchidas *FHG.* iv. 389 *fr.* 7), and returned from the Cnidian peninsula to Dotion, Diod. v. 61. Phorbas therefore being a neighbour may have been another rival for Coronis; and therefore Ereutheus (or Erymanthus or Amarynthus) also. Leucippus seems to imply Daphne, but then the wife, the chariot and Triops are unintelligible. It must be Phorbas who οὐ Τρίοπος ἐνέλειπεν, fell not short of his ancestor. Then perhaps it was all one transaction, all were suitors to Coronis.

μνηστή, absolute (= Homeric μνηστὴ ἄλοχος), appears first here, then in Theognis 1202, Ap. Rh. i. 780. In Procopius (*Bell. Goth.* iii. 1, p. 286 fin., *anecd.* 34. 22, 104. 11, 12 ed. Bonn) and Byzantine law it = sponsa, fiancée; e.g. *Synopsis Basilicorum* ed. Z. v. Lingenthal M. xv. 11, διὰ νόσου τοῦ μνηστῆρος ἢ τῆς μνηστῆς (13, 15, 17, 21 etc.). Cf. also κουριδίη subst. Quintus v. 445, x. 265, 312, 472, κουρίδιος x. 434.

209. **μνωόμενος** is Martin's brilliant conjecture. We may suppose that μνωόμενος first lost the initial μ, and ὅππως became ὅπποσ (cf. the variants on 19), when α was added to give the necessary syllable: cf. ἀνεμόμενοι νεμόμενοι Plat. *rep.* 401 C.

Ἀζαντίδα: the next line makes it almost certain that the reference here is to Coronis, for whom Ischys son of Elatos was Apollo's rival (Hes. *fr.* 125, Pind. *Pyth.* iii. 55, etc.). Elsewhere however, Coronis is called the daughter of Phlegyas (xvi. 2, and see reff. in Roscher and P.-W.). Phlegyas is usually a Lapith of Thessaly, but according to one version (Paus. ix. 36. 3, and see on 173) he was a Phocian. Hence Ἀβαντίδα has been suggested, but the first vowel in this word is short. According to another version of the birth of Asclepius his mother was not Coronis but Arsinoe, whose father Leucippus was descended from Atlas (Apollod. iii. 118, cl. 110, Paus. ii. 17). This might support M's reading Ἀτλαντίδα, were it not that Ischys is associated only with Coronis and not with Arsinoe. Martin read Ἀζανίδα, i.e. Arcadian, and Ἀζαντίδα, daughter of Azan, similarly places Coronis among the figures of early Arcadian genealogy (see P.-R. 520 n. 3). Phlegyas is not known to have been connected with Arcadia, but if we may assume a lost version of the legend in which Coronis was daughter of Azan its origin may so far be accounted for by a confusion between Elatus father of Ischys and Elatus who is an important figure in Arcadian genealogy (for reff. see Roscher *in v.*).

210. **Ἐλατιονίδῃ**: son of Ἐλατίων (= Ἔλατος): Hes. *l.c.* Εἰλατίδης. For the ῑ cf. Ταλαϊονίδαο Β 566, Solmsen p. 58.

211. The person intended by τριόπω γένος of the MSS. might be another μνηστή, in which case γένος would be objective acc., 'child' (an echo of which might be τριόπεω γόνον the reading of one MS. Callim. *Dem.* 24). But as Phorbas was the son of Triopas (Paus. viii. 26. 12, Hyg. *Astr.* ii. 14), γένος is certainly acc. of respect 'by birth', for which cf. Ε 544, 896 etc. The two words therefore balance Ἐλατιονίδῃ in 210, and the dative of a patronymic form must be extracted from τριόπω or τριοπόω. The latter points to a synizesis, and the conditions are satisfied by Τριοπέῳ, dative of Τριόπεος formed direct from Τριόψ (= Τριόπας Hellanicus ap. Steph. in Τρίοπιον, Apollod. i. 53 Τρίοπα, Τρίοπος gen.), since the adj. from Τριόπας in use is Τρίοπειος, *CI. Sic. et Ital.* 1890 no. 1389. This would be parallel to Δεινομένειε παῖ Pind. *Pyth.* ii. 18, Οἰνῆιδε Τυδῆ Antim. fr. 7: cf. Leo *BB.* iv. 1–21 *Die homerische Vaternamen*, K.-B. ii. § 294, Zacher in *Diss. Phil. Ital.* 1878, p. 59. The name seems on the whole Asianic.

Phorbas is here the rival of Apollo; acc. to Hyg. *l.c.*, Plut. *Num.* 4 he was his eromenos.

Ἐρευθεῖ: nothing is known of an Ereutheus in this story

(δῖον Ἔρευθον is a Greek in Quintus ii. 239). *y*'s ἀμαρύνθῳ has nearly all the elements of ἅμ' ἐρευθεῖ, but no connexion of Apollo and Amarynthus is otherwise known. It is as easy to conjecture Ἐρυμάνθῳ (παῖς Ἀπόλλωνος Ptol. Heph. 146 b 41). D'Orville conjectured Ἐρεχθεῖ (as M), but this is not supported by any known myth of Erechtheus.

212. ἅμα Λευκίππῳ: the allusion is to Daphne, who was courted by Leucippus and Apollo. Paus. viii. 20. 3 says that Apollo was angry with Leucippus, who disguised as a woman ἐς φιλίαν ἰσχυρὰν ἐπάγεται τὴν Δάφνην; Daphne and her companions discovered his sex and killed him. To give δάμαρ its proper sense of 'wife' there must have been another version; the word is remarkable.

213. Owing to the obscurity of 212 it is not clear if a new achievement of Apollo is intended by the words πεζὸς, ὁ δ' ἵπποισιν, which seem to refer to a contest between Apollo on foot and a rival in a chariot. Schneidewin's idea that this contest was between Apollo and Idas for Marpessa does not suit the words οὐ μὴν Τρίοπός γ' ἐνέλειπεν. He thought that ἐνέλειπεν or ἐνέλιπεν was a scribe's note to indicate an omission. But they said λείπει, not even ἐλλείπει. The Greek as it stands means 'he came not short of Triops'.

214. Apollo starts from Olympus (where he had been received 186) in search of an oracle for mankind. He had already visited Pytho on his way from Delos to Olympus (183). In the later accounts it was on this first journey that he founded Delphi (Pindar *fr.* 286), landing at Tanagra (this has been thought an error for Tegyra, but Pindar referred to the district Δήλιον on the Tanagraean coast, cf. Thuc. iv. 76, Paus. ix. 30. 1, which was a religious colony from Delos, Strabo 403, and had a festival to the Delian Apollo *IG.* Sept. 20). According to Aeschylus *Eum.* 9 and Limenius (Diehl i, p. 307) Apollo landed at Athens; thence he travelled along the sacred way of the θεωροί (see on 280), Ephorus *fr.* 70, P.-R. ii. 239 n. 1, P.-W. i. 24.

In the hymn Apollo's age at the founding of the oracle is indefinite. In later times he was a child, or was even carried to Delphi in his mother's arms (Eur. *IT.* 1250, Clearchus *fr.* 46: cf. λ 580); he slew Python when four days old (Hyg. *fab.* 140), or when still a youth (Ap. Rh. ii. 70): in Paus. ii. 7. 7 Apollo and Artemis together killed it.

216. Πιερίην: the acc. is necessary, the gen. (x) and dative (p) seem corrections. Cf. Ξ 225 λίπεν ῥίον Οὐλύμποιο | Πιερίην δ' ἐπιβᾶσα καὶ Ἠμαθίην ἐρατεινὴν κτλ., ε 50. Pieria strictly speaking is N. of Olympus. In Ξ the geography is right, as Hera was going to Thrace.

217. Λέκτον τ' ἠμαθόεντα: no Λέκτος is known in Europe, and the Trojan promontory is out of the question. Αὐτοκάνη however iii. 35 shows how place-names last in MSS., and therefore we neglect B.'s Λάκμον, the best of the conjectures. Lectus may have been a town or harbour, or even a river, and therefore ἠμαθόεντα may stand, in spite of Matthiae's Ἠμαθίην τε, which rests on Ξ 226. The same critic with greater certainty emended Αἰνιῆνας out of ἀγνιῆνας, μαγνιῆνας, μαγνηίδας. Cf. Hes. *OD.* 394 ἀγνῇ MSS., αἰνῇ a quotation, Herod. vi. 127 πάγου παίου, Ap. Rh. i. 757 αἰνυμένοιο ἀγν-, Aesch. *Suppl.* 226 ἂν ἀγνεύοι, ἀναινεύοι. The form Ἐνιῆνες is found (but with variations) B 749, Herod. vii. 132; cf. Strabo 442 and Ἔπιον Αἴπιον; add Αἰνιέων Kaibel *ep. gr.* praef. 856a 2. In the historical period and probably at the time when the hymn was written the Aenianes were at the sources of the Spercheus. The Perrhaebi were at Larissa (see *Catalogue*, p. 132). Hence it is correct that Apollo should pass through them between Olympus and Iolcus. The poet inverts the order for metrical reasons, following a universal principle. See on 32.

On the wanderings of Aenianes see Plut. *quaest. graec.* 293 F Halliday, *Catalogue* above.

218 ff. Here the geography is more accurate. From Iolcus Apollo passes, either along the coast of Phthiotis or across the gulf, to Cenaeon, a cape at the extreme N.W. of Euboea (Soph. *Trach.* 752). He thus reached the Lelantine plain, between Chalcis and Eretria. Eretria was unhealthy, Diog. Laert. ii. 133. This is the first mention of the Euripus.

223. This mountain is Messapius opposite Chalcis; see Aesch. *Ag.* 284, Strabo 405, Paus. ix. 22. 5. The epithet χλωρόν and vv. 225–8 indicate the writer's view of the primeval condition of the country, pale with flowering shrubs and unbroken forest

('lentisk and holly-oak', Frazer on Paus.). Cf. Beloch quoted on 135. There is nothing singular in the omission of the name. Panopeus is omitted 278. Μεσσάπιος would have required a different line. There is not the slightest reason to make χλωρόν into a proper noun (with Ulrich *Reisen* etc. 1840, and Oldfather *AJA*. xx. 71).

224. **Μυκαλησσόν**: a town at the foot of Messapius, in ruins by the time of Pausanias (ix. 19. 4). Frazer *ad loc.* identifies it with the modern Rhitzona. Between this place and Teumessos was Harma, where πυθαϊσταί allowed θυσίαι to proceed to Delphi or prevented them according to the results of divination by lightning (Strabo 404).

Τευμησσόν: the modern Mesovouni, a village on the slopes of a low hill about five miles from Thebes, Paus. ix. 19. 1. The hill is bare and rocky (Τευμησιάδες τ' ἄνετοι σκοπιαί 𝔓 Berol. 9775 v. 6, Diehl i. 310), and the epithet λεχεποίην seems inappropriate. Frazer thinks the ancients extended the name to include the hills on the south (now called Mount Soros) which are less bare. Statius (*Theb.* i. 485) and Nonnus v. 59 follow our author in calling Teumessos grassy and wooded. Antimachus *fr.* 2 more truly called it ἠνεμόεις ὀλίγος λόφος, though Strabo 409 disagreed. The variant Τελμησσόν occurs in the MSS. of Eur. *Phoen.* 1100, Strabo 409, 412, Dion. *Perieg.* 859 (also τερμ-), Plut. *mor.* 988 A. Attempts at etymology will be found in *KZ.* xxviii. 121, *BB.* xxvi. 148.

226. The poet claims a greater age for Pytho than that of Thebes, itself reputed a very ancient town. Tradition, however, held that there were towns in Boeotia before the foundation of Thebes; Ap. Rh. i. 736 ἀπύργωτος δ' ἔτι Θήβη κεῖτο πέλας, Conon Διηγήσεις in Phot. *bibl.* 137 b 27, Nonnus iv. 354 οὔ πω γὰρ ἐν οἰνοφύτοισιν ἀλωαῖς | ἁβρὸς ἀεξομένης ἀνεφαίνετο καρπὸς ὀπώρης. In historical times Apollo Ἰσμήνιος was worshipped as an oracular God at Thebes: Herod. i. 52, 92, viii. 134, Paus. ix. 10.

228. **ὕλη** for **ὕλην** is an admirable conjecture of Barnes. The accusative came from the tendency to be influenced by the nearest apparent construction, cf. N 104.

230. **Ὀγχηστόν**: the precinct of Posidon at Onchestus was

famous from early times: B 506 Ὀγχηστόν θ' ἱερὸν Ποσιδήιον ἀγλαὸν ἄλσος, Hes. *fr.* 41, Alcaeus *fr.* 10, Pind. *Isthm.* i. 33, iv. 19, *fr.* 104 D 58. Strabo 412 speaks of the grove as bare and treeless in his day, Pausanias (ix. 26. 3) saw the ruins of the town, temple (with the statue of Posidon still standing), and precinct. On the site see Frazer *l.c.* The lake produced a φοβερὸν ἦχον Aelian *VH.* xii. 5. It was feverish, Dicaearchus *fr.* 59. 25.

The grove, which lay halfway between Thebes and Orchomenus and was shared by both (P.-R. 573), was the centre of the Boeotian league (Strabo 412, cf. *IG.* iv. 1. 98 [election of league-officials], Ditt. *Syll.* 366 [oath in a treaty between Phocians, Aetolians, and Boeotians, *c.* 269 B.C.]).

The prosody of the word Ὀγχηστος varies in the MSS.

B 506 ὄγχηστόν (followed by an enclitic) vulg.
ὀγχηστόν nine MSS.

h. iii. 230 ὄγχηστον codd.

h. iv. 88 ὀγχηστόν codd.
186 ὀγχηστὸν D, ὄγχηστόν Π, ὀγχηστόν cet.
190 ὀγχηστοῖο codd.

Pindar *Isthm.* iv. 33 ὀγχηστόν codd.

Strabo 412 ὀγχηστός, -οῦ codd., -ῷ Paus. i. 39. 5.

Paus. ix. 26. 5 ὀγχηστοῦ, but the oecist Ὄγχηστος.

Zonaras 1423. 18 ὀγχηστός.

The tendency on the whole is oxytone. There is no ancient dictum. The paragraph in Herodian i. 223. 29 Lentz is the composition of Lentz.

231–8. The custom at Onchestus is puzzling, as the account in the hymn is obscurely worded, and is our sole authority. The passage is discussed in *JHS.* xvii. 274 (T. W. A.), *JHS.* xix. 39 (E. E. Sikes), Farnell iv. 15, Nilsson *GF.* 70. Many scholars have followed Böttiger in explaining the custom as a mode of divination: if the horses entered the ἄλσος the omen was favourable; see Bouché-Leclercq *Hist. Div. Ant.* i. 150. This and similar views, however, depend on Barnes' emendation ἄγωσιν, which cannot be accepted (see on 235). In any case the chariot drives into the grove, and then the driver jumps off: it is not a question of whether the chariot enters the grove or not. Ilgen suggested a connexion with Poseidon ταράξιππος: a bolting or shying horse was often thought to be panic-stricken by that God (Dio Prus. xxxii. 76, Paus. vi. 20. 15 with Frazer's note). It has then been suggested that the custom was 'a rule of the road'. Poseidon was offended at wheeled traffic passing his grove. If the horses bolted and broke the carriage, the driver had to leave the wreckage in the precincts. This explanation is in every respect improbable. So inconvenient a rule is unlikely; the phrase νεοδμὴς πῶλος is literal, and would not apply to old horses. Obviously the procedure is not one which happens casually, but takes place upon some specific occasion. Alternatively it is supposed that Poseidon, God of horses, might object to his sacred animals bearing the yoke. The newly broken colts were passed before the God: if they drew the carriage safely through, they might be driven by men: if they broke the chariot, Poseidon claimed them for his own. The owners indeed could retain them, but not for the indignity of the yoke; the chariot was left in the grove, as being marked by Poseidon's displeasure. It is fatal to this theory that there is no indication that the horses which are retained by the owners could not subsequently be driven in harness. What happened? The chariot is driven into the grove and the driver then jumps off. The test then is whether the chariot is broken among the trees or not. If it is, the horses are groomed, the chariot is set up on end or propped against the temple wall (κλίναντες), and left in the grove as the property of the God to whom a prayer is offered. The horses clearly remain in their owner's possession. Obviously the custom is not a race; equally obviously it is not a casual custom but a specific rite performed almost certainly upon some specific occasion, possibly at the meeting of the Boeotian league (see on 230). If Γαιήοχος is genuinely the cult-title of Onchestian Poseidon, it is probable that horse-races were held in his honour (see on *Herm.* 186). If so, the custom may be connected with the dedication of their chariots by the winners of races at the Onchestian festival: for dedication of victorious chariots cf. Euagoras at Olympia (Paus. vi. 10. 8) or Arkesilas at Delphi (Pindar, *Pyth.* v. 35 f.). In any case Nilsson (*GF.* p. 70) is probably right in his explanation of the essential character of the procedure as a means of discovering whether the offering (of the chariot) is acceptable to the God or not. 'Bei Opfern ist es sehr gebräuchlich dass die Gottheit irgendwie veranlasst wird, ihren Willen kund zu thun.'

Several Hesychian glosses seem to bear upon the subject:

Ἱπποδέτης· Ἡρακλῆς ὁ ἐν Ὀγχηστῷ τιμώμενος.

Περρησιππίαν· τὴν ἀνατρέπουσαν ἵππον.

Στ(ε)ρηναῖα ὁδός . . . ἀπειθής, ἀπὸ τῶν στρηνιώντων ἵππων.

Ταράξιππος· οὕτως ὑπ' ἐνίων Πέλοψ ἱστορεῖται.

231. **ἀναπνέει**, 'breathes again', that is, halts, as Aesop 298.

232. **ὁδὸν ἔρχεται**: Martial iv. 55. 23 *et sanctum Buradonis ilicetum per quod vel piger ambulat viator* has a verbal resemblance.

234. **κείν' ὄχεα κροτέουσιν** = O 453 (where we find M's *κρατέουσιν*), and cf. Λ 160, Hes. *Scut.* 303, Lycophr. *Alex.* 42, 43 (at Olympia).

The MSS. with *κείν'* give the usual method of accenting an elided oxytone. Another was to put a circumflex on the parateleuton. This took place, perhaps by conjecture, in S. M's *κεῖνον* seems the result of a third method, omission of any accent except that on the vanished syllable, viz. *κειν*ˆ: the accent was then mistaken for the syllabic compendium *ον*, and the resultant *κεινον* given its proper accent. Examples of all three methods are found at O 453. See in general Chandler §§ 908, 909 (Herodian's dictum varied), KB. i. 332, Postgate 301, *Iliad* ed. 1931 *proleg.* 236.

ἀνακτορίην, 'mastery, authority', not in Homer, but *ἄναξ* = master occurs; for the general sense cf. Ap. Rh. i. 839, verse in Paus. x. 12. 6, Parthenius *epigr.* 14. 1, v. 6.

235. **ἀγῆσιν**: this is practically the MS. reading, and is required by the dative and *ἐν*, Paus. vi. 20. 15 *τὰ ἅρματα καταγνύουσιν ὡς ἐπίπαν.*

236. **κομέουσι**: this verb means 'groom' Θ 109, 113, but more generally to 'keep', ρ 310, 319, *Anth. Pal.* vii. 717. 3.

κλίναντες: the carriage was propped against a wall, Θ 435, δ 42 *ἅρματα δ' ἔκλιναν πρὸς ἐνώπια παμφανόωντα.*

238. The chariot was confiscated, and became an *ἀνάθημα* or was sold. The sale of duplicate or damaged objects from temple

treasuries is known from inscriptions, Homolle in Daremberg and Saglio *Donarium* p. 381, 2. (In this case one may imagine the owner bought his vehicle in.)

240. The geography here is difficult. Haliartus lies between Onchestus and Ocalea, and the Cephissus or Melas flowed across the northern part of lake Copais, and would not be crossed by the road from Thebes to Panopeus. The writer, like the author of the Catalogue, was indifferent to the order of places on a route (cf. 30 sq., 422 sq.), and may be allowed to have transposed Haliartus and Ocalea, but it is hard to imagine him making the stream which separates Onchestus and Haliartus (mentioned without a name by Nonnus xiii. 71, and usually identified with the Lophis) into the Cephissus. By the date of the hymn the old Minyan system of drainage will have broken down and Copais have become, as it remained till not long ago, in the winter a sheet of water, in the summer a swamp intersected by rivers and canals. It may therefore be suggested (1) that the writer meant by Κηφισός the lake, as in 280 he situates Panopeus Κηφισίδος ἐγγύθι λίμνης while it was in reality near the river. So the φοβερὸς ἦχος at Onchestus (see on 230) is stated to be made by the λίμνη not by a river (it must refer to a broken drain or katavothra), (2) that the entire system, rivers and canals, was considered to be branches of the Cephissus, and that the southernmost canal with its tributaries (which came close to Haliartus and Onchestus, and joined the Melas at the N.W. corner of the lake) was known by that name. Strabo 407 says distinctly that the Melas flowed through the country of Haliartus. There was much confusion of names in this submerged country. Even a resident antiquary like Plutarch (*Sulla* 20, *Pelop.* 19) mistook the Cephissus for the Melas; Strabo 412 accuses Alcaeus of misplacing Onchestus and misspelling the name of a river, and (407) explains that when Homer (E 708) speaks of Cephissus he means the Ὑλικὴ λίμνη. Hesiod *fr.* 38 describes the course of the Cephissus proper. Cf. Frazer Paus. x, vol. v, 110 sq., and his map. The extension of names in the Venetian lagoon (Brenta nuova etc.) seems parallel.

241. The line is quoted by Σ B 523 as from Hesiod (*fr.* 37):

ὁ δὲ Κηφισὸς ποταμός ἐστι τῆς Φωκίδος, ἔχων τὰς πηγὰς ἐκ Λιλαίας, ὥς φησὶν Ἡσίοδος ὅς τε Λιλαίηθι προίει καλλίρροον ὕδωρ Eust. *ad. loc.*, who quotes the line with προχέει. The Homeric scholia ignore the Hymns; we must suppose the line stood both in Hesiod and the Hymn. For Lilaea and the source of the Cephissus see Frazer on Paus. x. 33. 5.

242. **Ὠκαλέην**: B 501; it was near the lake Copais and 30 stadia from Haliartus, Strabo 410.

πολύπυργον: only here. Cf. εὔπυργος of Troy H 71, εὔπυργον Πανοπῆα *or. Sibyl.* xi. 315. Even a small town if walled may have many towers; Guérande (Loire inférieure) has ten remaining out of eleven, Menneton (Loir-et-Cher) very many. Barnes' alteration therefore is needless.

244. **Τελφούσης**: here and in 247, 256, 276, the MSS. vary between the forms τελφοῦσα and δελφοῦσα. Other spellings are found. Steph. Τέλφουσα· πόλις Ἀρκαδίας . . . Λυκόφρων (1040) δίκης ἐάσει τάρροθος Τελφουσία. ἔστι καὶ Βοιωτίας Τελφούσιον. Στράβων ἐνάτῃ (411 and 413), Ἔφορος δὲ (*fr.* 67) Τιλφωσέων ὄρος ἐν Ἀλαλκομενίᾳ. Πίνδαρος δὲ (*fr.* 198, quoted in Athen. 41 E) καὶ Κηφισίδα καλεῖ ταύτην (Strabo *l.c.* Π. δὲ καὶ Κ. καλεῖ ταύτην, παρατίθησι γοῦν τὴν Τιλφῶσσαν κρήνην ὑπὸ τῷ Τιλφωσσίῳ ὄρει ῥέουσαν πλησίον Ἁλιάρτου καὶ Ἀλαλκομενῶν . . . αὐτοῦ δὲ καὶ τὸ τοῦ Τιλφωσσίου Ἀπόλλωνος ἱερόν). ἔστι δὲ καὶ Βοιωτίας Τίλφωσσα κρήνη καὶ ὄρος ἀπὸ Τιλφούσης. Ἡρωδιανὸς δὲ καὶ Τιλφῶσσα φησίν. Theopompus *fr.* 240 and Demosth. xix. 141, 148 say τὸ Τιλφωσσαῖον. Apollod. iii. 7. 4, 3 says Τιλφοῦσσα, Paus. ix. 33. 1 Τιλφοῦσα, Τιλφούσιον ὄρος. In Arcadia Θέλπουσα was the name of a town and nymph (Paus. viii. 35), coins bear the legend ΘΕΛ Head *HN.* 456. These forms are perhaps connected with the root θαλπ-, sc. θερμὰ λουτρά (Pott *KZ.* viii. 416). There is no evidence for a local form in δ, but Androtion *fr.* 2 speaks of Δελφοῦσα in Arcadia. The interchange of τ and δ is not common (δρύφακτος, τρύφακτος, δάπιδες, τάπητες Kretschmer *KZ.* xxxiii. 467).

The spring has been identified at the foot of the mountain, 'a spur of Helicon which advances to within a few hundred paces of what used to be the margin of the lake', Frazer on Paus. *l.c.* For the remains of a temple see Bursian *Geog.* i. 234.

ἀπήμων, 'safe'. Cf. νόστος ἀπήμων δ 519, Hes. *OD.* 670 (πόντος).

250. **ἔχουσιν** . . . 251 **κάτα** is a delayed tmesis for κατέχουσιν, KG. i. 531 n. 1; cf. Hesiod *Scut.* 149 and for the reverse (preposition first, verb after) η 69.

Πελοπόννησον: as a single word here first in extant literature, but Hesiod (*fr.* 213) used it acc. to Σ I 246 (τὴν ὅλην Πελοπόννησον οὐκ οἶδεν ὁ ποιητής, Ἡσίοδος δέ): *Cypria* 6. 3 νῆσον ἅπασαν | Ταντολίδου Πέλοπος, Tyrtaeus 2. 4 εὐρεῖαν Πέλοπος νῆσον, Arion 12, *epigr.* Kaibel 47 (s. iv B.C.) Πέλοπος γᾶν. On compounds in -νησος see Strabo 618, Fick *BB.* xxii. 29.

251 (291). **Εὐρώπην**: the first appearance of this name. Hes. *Theog.* has the nymph. Here it seems to mean north Greece. Hegesippus of Mecyberna (*fr.* 6 *FHG.* v. 422) ἀφ' ἧς (sc. Europe the nymph) ἡ ἤπειρος πᾶσα ἡ πρὸς βορέαν ἄνεμον Εὐρώπη κέκληται, Sozomen *hist. eccl.* iii. 14 Θρᾴκιοι δὲ καὶ Ἰλύριοι καὶ ὅσοι τὴν καλουμένην Εὐρώπην οἰκοῦσι. In Aeneas of Gaza (Migne lxxxv. 1312) Europe with Macedonia I and II, Hellas and both Scythias is included in the bishopric of Thessalonica. Stephanus *in v.* gives the form Εὐρωπία from Soph. *fr.* 36 and Eur. *fr.* 382. There were towns called Εὔρωπος, one in Macedonia (Thuc. ii. 100), one in Syria, one in Caria (a mistake for Euromos). There were also two rivers Εὐρωπός (oxytone) in Thessaly. In the course of time the connotation of the word widened, as in the case of Asia and Hellas. Attempts to find an Indo-European derivation (Brugmann *KZ.* xxvii 591, Aly *Glotta* v. 63, Grimme *ib.* xiv. 17, Prellwitz xv. 135) fail. Hesychius Εὐρώπη· χώρα τῆς δύσεως ἢ σκοτεινή implies a Semitic origin (*ereb*, 'sunset', i.e. West) as Asia = 'rising', East. These terms suggest Crete as the central point. The sense of continent appears first in Pindar *Nem.* iv. 114, Herod. viii. 133, 135.

253. **θεμιστεύοιμι**: concessive optative 'I would prophesy'. vv. 252, 253 = 292, 293, where M has ἄρ', the rest ἄν. For the word cf. Himerius xviii. 1 of Apollo at Delos θεμιστεύειν ἐκεῖθεν τοῖς Ἕλλησι.

254. **διέθηκε**: not in Homer or Hesiod, nor in poetry at all before the *Birds* 439 (middle).

255. **διηνεκές**: unhomeric as adverb (*διηνεκέως*). In 295 *x p* have *διαμπερές*.

257. **ἔπος τι κτλ.** = T 121.

262. I.e. the traffic on the important thoroughfare.

265. **κτύπον**: for this zeugma cf. ι 167 (*ἐλεύσσομεν*) *καπνόν τ' αὐτῶν τε φθογγήν*.

ὠκυπόδων κτλ.: cf. K 535.

269. **Παρνησοῖο**: Steph. *Παρνασσός . . . ἔνιοι δέ φασιν ἀπὸ Παρνασσοῦ Παρνασσὸν τὸ ὄνομα λαβεῖν, ὃν καὶ μαντεύσασθαι Πυθοῖ πρῶτον, ὡς Ἀλέξανδρος φησὶν ἐν τῷ περὶ τοῦ ἐν Δελφοῖς χρηστηρίου.*

270. This line seems to prove that the hymn is older than the foundation of the Pythian games. Ante p. 199, and see on 540.

272. **Ἰηπαιήονι**: here and in Ap. Rh. ii. 704 a title of Apollo; in 500, 517 below it is applied to the song. Cf. Aristonous Diehl ii. 297 *ἰὴ ἰὲ Παιάν, ὦ ἰὲ Παιάν*, Timotheus *Pers*. 218, *fr*. 25 *ἴε παιάν*. Cf. the similar history of the Linus-song, the hymenaeus and the iobacchus. On *Παιάν* and *Παιών* see P.-R. 241 n. 2, 277 n. 2, P.-W. ii. 62; on the very doubtful etymology Clearchus *fr*. 46, Boisacq *in v*., Mrs. Macurdy *CR*. 1912, 249, *CQ*. 1915, 65.

273. **ἀμφιγεγηθώς**: lit. 'all round, on both sides', and so 'exceedingly'; cf. A 103 *μένεος δὲ μέγα φρένες ἀμφὶ μέλαιναι | πίμπλαντ'*, P 83, 499, 573. The compound verb is supported by Γ 442 *ἔρως φρένας ἀμφεκάλυψεν*, Z 355 *πόνος φρένας ἀμφεκάλυψεν*.

275. Cf. a Rhodian inscr. *IG*. xii. 1. 737 *σαμα τοζ ιδαμενευς ποιησα hινα κλεος ειη*.

278. The godless Phlegyae (or Phlegyes Eust. 933. 15) resemble the Cyclopes, ι 275 *οὐ γὰρ Κύκλωπες Διὸς αἰγιόχου ἀλέγουσιν*. Here Apollo killed Tityos Ephorus *fr*. 70, who had attacked Leto λ 581, Nonnus iv. 331. But the Phlegyan hostility to Apollo is historical; the tribe attacked Pytho, from which they were repulsed by the God, only a few escaping to Phocis, Paus. ix. 36. 2, x. 7. 1, Pherecydes *fr*. 102 A, Σ Pind. *Pyth*. x. 55. For their city Panopeus see Strabo 423, Paus. x. 4. 1 (Frazer). It lay 20 furlongs W. of Chaeronea.

280. **Κηφισίδος λίμνης**: lake Copais is so called E 709, Pind. *Pyth*. xii. 27. Paus. (ix. 24. 1) says that the lake was called by

both names, he himself prefers Cephisis. The road from Athens to Delphi by Panopeus seems to have been a sacred way; cf. on 214 and Herod. vi. 34, $ Plat. *Phaed.* 58 B (θεωρὶς ὁδός). Cf. the Πυθιὰς ὁδός from Tempe, Aelian *VH.* iii. 1. It was liable to brigandage, Diog. Laert. ii. 136. Cf. also the road from Elis to Olympia.

281. **προσέβης**: with a direct acc. 520, *h.* iv. 99 and in Homer.

θύων: of the God's quick pace.

282. **Παρνησὸν νιφόεντα**: cf. Panyasis *fr.* 15, Callim. *Del.* 93. The situation of Crisa is correctly described, Strabo 418 ταῦτα γάρ ἐστι τὰ ἑσπεριώτατα μέρη τῆς Φωκίδος.

283. Cf. μ 81 πρὸς ζόφον . . . τετραμμένον, τ 389 ποτὶ δὲ σκότον ἐτράπετ' αἶψα, *Hes. OD.* 594, 727.

284. For πέτρη, πέτρος cf. Π 411 Eust., Hes. *Theog.* 778, 792.

285. **τεκμήρατο** with infin. is post-Homeric: Ap. Rh. iv. 559.

287–93 = 247–53.

292. **ἄρ'**: ἄν is only found in *x* and cannot be defended by 252, where κ' was a conjecture.

293. νηῷ, βωμῷ: the same variant ζ 162, A 39, Ap. Rh. i. 403, iv. 1471. Here νηῷ with χρέων ἐνί is necessary, βωμῷ may be due to ζ.

294. Building of the temple. On Delphi and the temple see Strabo 419 sq., Paus. x. 5. 5 sq., Homolle *BCH.* xx. 641, 677, 703, xxi. 256, xxv. 457, xxvi. 641, Courby *Fouilles de Delphes* ii. 92 (1927), Pomtow *Rh. Mus.* li. 259, Philippson and Hiller von Gärtringen in P.-W. iv. 2517.

Of the first temple, burned ol. 58. 1 (= 548 B.C.), and rebuilt by the Alcmaeonidae (P.-W. *l.c.* 2550), no traces have been found, nor sign of a conflagration.

295 = 255. The families have each diverged, M writing καλά for μακρά, *x p* διαμπερές for διηνεκές. In μ 436 καλοί for μακροί was read by Apoll. *lex.*

296. This passage, not the *Telegonia* of Eugammon (Homer ed. Ox. v., p. 109), is the first mention of Trophonius and Agamedes as builders; see Kern in P.-W. i. 719. For other accounts of them see Plato *Axiochus* 367 C, Strabo 421, Paus. ix. 37. 3, Charax ap. $ Ar. *Nub.* 508 = *FHG.* iii. 637. They occupy a position in

architecture similar to that of Daedalus in sculpture. Buildings attributed to them were the wooden temple of Posidon (Paus. viii. 10. 2), the thalamos of Alcmena (id. ix. 11. 1), the golden treasury of Augeas or Hyrieus at Elis (ib. 37. 5), and, to Trophonius, his own shrine at Lebadia (Charax).

According to Strabo *l.c.* it was the second, according to Paus. x. 5. 13 the fourth temple that was built by the pair. The hymn-writer knows nothing of the Delphian legend (Paus. *l.c.*, Philostr. *vit. Apoll.* vi. 10. 11) that the first temple was of laurel-wood, the second of beeswax and wings, and the third of bronze.

296. The οὐδός built by the sons of Erginus is here distinguished from the νηός built by 'the tribes of men'. The οὐδός may therefore be the *adytum*: Steph. Byz. Δελφοί· ἔνθα τὸ ἄδυτον κατεσκεύασται ἐκ πέντε λίθων, ἔργον Τροφωνίου καὶ Ἀγαμήδους. More probably the architects laid the first courses (οὐδός) of the whole building, which was finished by other workmen. λαινὸς οὐδός θ 80, I 404 is certainly the threshold. Cf. also Pindar *frr.* 2 and 3, Plato *Axioch.* 367 C, Cicero *Tusc.* i. 47.

297. **Ἐργίνου**: another Erginus was the Argonaut king of Orchomenus (Apollod. i. 113 al.).

φίλοι ἀθανάτοισι θεοῖσι: their pay from Apollo (seven days feasting and death in their sleep) is narrated by Plutarch and Cicero.

298. **ἔνασσαν**: only here = 'build': the causal is confined to the aorist, δ 174 καί κέ οἱ Ἄργεϊ νάσσα πόλιν. ἀμφὶ . . . ἔνασσαν is perhaps *in tmesi*.

299. **κτιστοῖσιν**: possibly = 'wrought, founded, deep-laid': Hesych. Ἀκταία· . . . ἡ ἐκ τοῦ ἀκτίστου λίθου κατασκευασθεῖσα τοῦ Πεντελικοῦ (the word has been altered). Empedocles 139, Pind. *Pyth.* v. 89 use κτίζειν of trees; cf. Strabo 206 αὐλῶνες εὖ συνεκτισμένοι, Anaxandrides *fr.* vi. 2 ἐν πυρικτίτοισι γᾶς; of bodily organs, Hippocr. iii. 196 κύστις τε γὰρ καὶ γοναὶ καὶ ἀρχοῦ τὸ χαλαρὸν ἐν τούτῳ ἔκτισται, Pseudo-Hipp. *Ep.* iii. 802. 5 K. ἄργυρον κτίζοντα καὶ χρυσόν. Of the conjectures ξεστοῖσιν and ῥυτοῖσιν are impossible, τυκτοῖσιν is nearer (Orph. *Arg.* 611 λάεσσι δ' εὐτύκτοις, Eur. *Troad.* 814 τυκτίσματα, κτίσματα, Hesych. Ἀποτυχισθείς· . . . τὸ ἀποτυχισθὲν ἐπὶ τοῦ ἀποπελεκῆσαι τὸν λίθον ἀπὸ τῶν

τύχων. ἔστι δὲ λιθοξοικὸν σιδήριον). Possibly κνιστοῖσιν (= ξεστοῖσιν, 'scraped'): Aristophanes *fr.* 908 λάχανα κνιστὰ ἢ στέμφυλα, Lucr. v. 1267 *levia radere tigna.* The stone came from Cyzicus *Anth. Pal.* vi. 342. 7.

ἀοίδιμον ἔμμεναι αἰεί: the temple therefore was standing in the writer's time.

300–74. The slaying of the serpent. This episode, usually condemned, is one of Apollo's greatest exploits and was a necessary measure for the foundation of the oracle. It was, therefore, rightly inserted here by Cynaethus. Part of the wickedness of the serpent was that she 'brought up' Typhaon; he therefore also is mentioned. Both were enemies of Zeus and Apollo his prophet. The episode is at least as germane as the section on the Deliades and the author, or the punishment of Telphusa. The length of the passage, which cannot be denied, is due to the opportunity of introducing Hera and analysing her feelings.

Snakes played a large part in the early Greek imagination: Strabo 19 κεραυνὸς καὶ αἰγὶς καὶ τρίαινα καὶ λαμπάδες καὶ δράκοντες καὶ θυρσόλογχα τῶν θεῶν ὅπλα μῦθοι καὶ πᾶσα θεολογία ἀρχαική. We have, e.g. in epic and later literature, the δράκων ἐπὶ νῶτα δαφοινός which came out of the altar at Aulis and ate the birds B 308, the semi-human Echidna αἰόλος ὠμηστής Hesiod *Theog.* 300, the δεινὸς ὄφις which guarded the golden apples *ib.* 334, the δεινὸς ὄφις κατὰ νῶτα δαφοινός *ib. fr.* 96. 91 (of which it is said ὅτε τ' ἄτριχος οὔρεσι τίκτει | γαίης ἐν κευθμῶνι τρίτῳ ἔτεϊ τρία τέκνα) killed by the shafts of Zeus, another at Phocis χρυσέαις φολίδεσσι Orph. *Arg.* 929, the two δράκοντες that destroyed Laocoon and one of his sons *Iliu persis* in Proclus epit. (p. 107 Hom. ed. Ox. v); Lamia or Sybaris at Cirphis, Ant. Lib. 8, the same Ptol. Heph. ap. Phot. *Bibl.* 190, p. 147. 23 (δράκοντα γηγενῆ), the story of Elera or Elara in Pherecydes *fr.* 5 ap. Et. Flor. *in* Ἐλέρα, Eudoc. *in* Ἐλάρη, Σ Ap. Rh. i. 761, Σ Pind. *Pyth.* iv. 160, Apollod. i. 41, Eust. 1581. 54; Hesych. *in* Κρίσαμις Κῷος· τούτῳ φασὶν ἔγχελυν ἐπιφαινομένην κατ' ἔτος τὸ κάλλιστον τῶν προβάτων ἁφαρπάζειν; Ar. ap. Apollon. *hist. mir.* 39 ὄφις ὤφθη ἐν Πάφῳ πόδας ἔχων δύο ὁμοίους χερσείῳ κροκοδείλῳ.

Modern zoologists assure us that there were no Pythonidae in Greece in the historical period.

The Pythian serpent is often mentioned. The Delphic version (which he condemns) is given by Plut. *def. orac.* 417 F, 421 C. In the Sicyonian version (Paus. ii. 77) and on the chest of Cypselus (*id.* iii. 18. 16) Apollo and Artemis together kill the python (Tityos): so Lucian *dial. mar.* 10. 2, *Anth. Pal.* iii. 6 Pytho prevented Leto from founding the oracle (prevented Leto bearing her children, Lucian *l.c.*) and was killed by Apollo (by Leto, Apollo and Artemis, Paus. x. 11. 1). Tityos assaulted Leto, epigr. Cyzic. 14, Quintus iii. 392. Macrobius i. 17. 17 and 52 relates how the snake attacked Apollo and Artemis in their cradles. An ἐπιτάφιος over the dragon was written by Eunomus of Locris, Clem. Alex. *protr.* i. 2. There are allusions to the story in Simonides 26 A Bergk, Ovid *Met.* i. 4. 38, Prop. iv. 6. 35 (*imbelles quem timuere ferae*). For statues of the personages see Pliny *NH.* xxxiv. 59, 70. Lastly we may quote Hesych. Ἑκατηβόλος· . . . τινὲς δὲ ἐπεὶ ἑκατὸν βέλεσι τὴν ἐν Πυθοῖ δράκαιναν ἀνεῖλεν Ἀπόλλων.

Here the δράκαινα and the monster Typhaon son of Hera are distinct. In the later versions the monster whether Typhoeus or Tityos is masculine. The discrimination points to the age of the hymn. See p. 185.

The dragon is very generally supposed to represent an earlier Pythian cult dispossessed by Apollo. The supposition, however, rests upon no evidence whatever. The succession of cults preceding that of Apollo at Delphi appears first in the fifth century B.C. (Aesch. *Eum.* 1, Eur. *IT.* 1245). The oracle was originally that of Gaia, it passed from her to Themis and then to Phoebe, whom Apollo succeeded. This has the appearance of theological speculation rather than of genuine tradition, and the Hymn, the earliest evidence for the foundation of the oracle, knows nothing of it. That the snake was in any way oracular, or a representative of the Earth Goddess, or a guardian of the oracle, is modern speculation based upon analogies of dubious relevance. In this, the simplest and probably original form of the story, the nameless female dragon is the guardian of the spring, and the tale, like that of the snake which Cadmus killed (Eur. *Phoen*. 657, 931, Ap. Rh. iii. 1180, Plut. *de fluv*. ii. 1), belongs to a type very common in Greece and elsewhere (see Frazer on Paus. 10. 5 and Hartland *Legend of Perseus*).

The name Python for the dragon does not occur before the Euhemeristic version of Ephorus. Variations on the story of how Python assisted in the ill-treatment of Leto, or how he was slain by Apollo as an infant, or by Apollo and Artemis, are late inventions. Remarkable, however, in our account is the complete absence of any reference to the purification of Apollo after the slaughter of the snake, for the development of the doctrine of purification in Apolline cult must have been relatively very early. In later times the festival *Septerion* (on which see Halliday *Greek Questions of Plutarch* 67) was supposed to commemorate the killing of Python by the God, though it is difficult to fit the facts known about the ritual to this interpretation. But, even if originally unconnected with the *Septerion*, the flight to Tempe of the boy impersonating Apollo and his processional return after being purified were probably early. This ritual appears to have had some connexion with the Pythian games, at which the victor's wreath is said to have been made out of laurel brought back by the boy from Tempe (arg. Pind. *Pyth*. iii). But the hymn is earlier than the institution of the Pythian games (see on 270).

300. The identification of the fountain is not clear. The editors assume that it is the Castalian spring (on the situation of which see Frazer on Paus. x. 8. 9), and the fame of this makes it probable that it was considered the scene of the conflict. Frazer, however, identifies it with the spring, called Cassotis by Paus. (x. 24. 7), just above the temple, or with another below the temple (see his notes *l. c.* and 12. 1). There were other identifications: Hesych. Τοξίου βουνός· . . . *βέλτιον δὲ ἀκούειν τὴν ἐν Δελφοῖς Νάπην λεγομένην· ἐκεῖ γὰρ καὶ ὁ δράκων κατετοξεύθη.* ℨ Pind. *Pyth*. 1 praef. ἐκαλεῖτο δὲ τὸ πρότερον Νάπη, εἶτα Πετρήεσσα, εἶτα Κρίσσα, εἶτα Πυθώ. Steph. *in* Δελφοί calls the fountain Δελφοῦσσα.

δράκαιναν: the feminine form is not Homeric. The poet

follows what is doubtless the original myth, in which Apollo like St. George kills a nameless 'dragon' or 'worm'. In Eur. *IT.* 1245, Paus. x. 6. 5 the reptile is unnamed but its sex has changed to male. The confusion of sex persisted when names were given to it in later times. The usual name was Πύθων (first in the Euhemeristic version of Ephorus *fr.* 70, cf. Paus. x. 6. 5), as in Apollod. ii. 318, Clearchus *FHG.* ii. 318; for other reff. see P.-R. i. 239 n. 2. Other names were Δελφύνη (fem.), Δελφύνης (masc.): in Ap. Rh. ii. 703, Nonnus xiii. 28 the gender is doubtful: possibly the masc. is a fiction of grammarians; see Kern in P.-W. *in* Δελφύνης. According to Σ Ap. Rh. *l. c.* Callimachus (*fr.* 364) used the fem., which the Σ thinks is more correct; so Dion. *Perieg.* 442.

306. **Τυφάονα**: so 352, but in 367 Τυφωεύς. The two names vary in Hes. *Theog.* 306 (Typhaon), 821, 869 (Typhoeus). Τυφώς and Τυφών are other forms; Philodemus (Philippson *Hermes* 1920, 254), if the restoration of]ωνεα is right, used the form τυφωνεύς as M at 367. See P.-R. 63 and on 367. For his parentage *EM.* 772. 50 Ἡσίοδος αὐτὸν γῆς γενεαλογεῖ [Ant. Lib. 28 Γῆς υἱός], Στησίχορος δὲ Ἥρας μόνης κατὰ μνησικακίαν Διὸς τεκούσης αὐτόν. It is to be noticed that the *EM.* quotes Stesichorus, not the hymn. So Σ Ap. Rh. iv. 1310 quotes Stes. as the first to describe the birth of Athena full-armed; he neglects *h.* xxvii. On the connexion of Hera and Typhoeus see Farnell i. 183, who rightly explains it as due to the character of Hera, the jealous Goddess in epos. She is not here a chthonian deity. Hera nourished (θρέψε) the Lernaean hydra and the Nemean lion in her wrath with Zeus (Hes. *Theog.* 314, 323). There was a Τυφαόνιον near Thebes, Hes. *Scut.* 32.

308. ἦνεκ' in M, which the scribe saw was a mistake, is for ἡνίκα, as χ 198.

309. The birth of Athena from the head of Zeus is Homeric (E 875, 880). It is true Homer does not mention the head, but ἐπεὶ αὐτὸς ἐγείναο E 880 almost certainly refers to the myth. It is in the Homeric manner to pass over the grotesque and primitive.

311 = Θ 5, T 101.

θέαιναι: in Homer only in this phrase, Θ 20, θ 341.

312. Cf. θ 308 ὡς ἐμὲ χωλὸν ἐόντα . . . αἰὲν ἀτιμάζει.

313. **πρῶτος**: apparently for πρότερος, as ἄρξωσι πρότεροι Δ 67.

316. **ἠπεδανός** = Θ 311.

317. **ῥικνός**, not Homeric: cf. Ap. Rh. i. 669, ii. 198. The lameness of Hephaestus is accounted for by Servius on *Aen.* viii. 414 *quia per naturam nunquam rectus est ignis.* In point of fact as smiths are often lame the divine smith was lame too, as in the case of the Norse Völundur, the Teutonic Wieland, and the Berkshire Wayland.

ὃν τέκον αὐτή: not 'whom I bore by myself', as in Hes. *Theog.* 927 she is his sole parent, for in that case she would have been even with Zeus without the birth of a monster (Franke); but 'my very own son', i.e. not the son of any other Goddess or woman. So Ξ 338, θ 312. On the birth of Hephaestus see Usener *Rh. Mus.* 1901, 180.

After this line a lacuna, as Demetrius saw, is required. The construction is impossibly harsh, and Γ's emendation δέ for ἀνά gives up the problem. A new line αἶσχος ἐμοὶ καὶ ὄνειδος ἐν οὐρανῷ ὅν τε καὶ αὐτή was suggested *JHS.* xv. 278. There are two versions again of the fall of Hephaestus; A 591 he is thrown down by Zeus, Σ 395 by Hera, in disgust at his lameness; this is followed by Paus. i. 20. 3, *Mythogr. graec.* Westermann p. 372, and here.

319. In Σ 398 he is saved by Eurynome and Thetis. The line is repeated by Matro *Conv. Att.* 33 (ἦλθε δέ).

321. **χαρίσσασθαι**: the aorist is more appropriate than the present, and -σσ- is common, e.g. φράσσασθαι 415; an inscr. in Preger 126. 3 has ἐχαρίσσατο (saec. v).

322. **σχέτλιε ποικιλομῆτα** = ν 293.

μητίσεαι is supported by 325 a, *h.* ii. 345, and is Homeric. μήσεαι is a graphical error, ΜΗ[ΤΙ]ϹΕΑΙ; ἔτι was added perhaps from λ 474 by *p.* μητίσατο occurs Parmenides 13, Plato *Symp.* 177 B, Orph. *Arg.* 22, μητίσαιτο Maximus π. κ. 406, μήσεαι in *or.* Hendess 14. 4 τί νυ μήσεαι ὦ Ζεῦ; the reverse process occurs K 52, the same variants Eur. *Hipp.* 592.

324 sq. Cf. Ovid *Fasti* v. 239 sq. with new details.

325. Demetrius and the second hand of Γ corrected ἦ to ἦν 3 pers. 'she would have been called yours'. But ἄν or κεν is required. Therefore with Matthiae we read ἦα ῥ', 'I was'. Cf. Δ 60, Σ 365 οὕνεκα σὴ παράκοιτις | κέκλημαι.

325a was omitted in all MSS. except the margins of *x*, perhaps owing to the resemblance of νῦν μή τοί and νῦν μέντοι. This is enough to decide in favour of M's καὶ νῦν μέντοι, between which and *p*'s καὶ νῦν τοι γάρ there is little to choose. Cf. X 358 φράζεο νῦν μή τοί τι θεῶν μήνιμα γένωμαι.

330. **οὖσα**: cf. οὔσας *h.* iv. 106, ὤν xix. 32 and xxix. 10. These *testes linguae* are not to be disturbed. **ἀπὸ σεῖο τηλόθεν οὖσα** = νόσφι Διός 338, 344. She will make shift without Zeus.

μετέσσομαι: she did not cut herself off from the other Gods, and had relations with Ge, Uranus, and the Titans.

331. **χωομένη περ**: we have the particle in its original non-adversative sense. Cf. Ψ 79 γεινόμενόν περ, ρ 13, 47 (Σ H τὸ πέρ ἀντὶ τοῦ δή), Ω 504 ἐλεεινότερός περ, A 416 μίνυθά περ.

333. **χειρὶ καταπρηνεῖ** = Π 792, ν 164.

ἔλασε χθόνα: for this method of invoking chthonian deities or ghosts cf. I 568, Ξ 272, Aesch. *Pers.* 674, Eur. *Troad.* 1293, Plat. *Crat.* 423 A, Plut. *mor.* 774 B, Philostr. *v. Soph.* ii. 1. 10, Diog. Laert. vii. 26, *Anth. Pal.* vii. 117, Coluth. 47, Cic. *Tusc.* ii. 25. 60, Livy vii. 6. 4, Macrob. iii. 9. 12; Sittl *Gebärden* iii. 9. 12, Rohde *Psyche* 111, 693: 'the action was practised by the Zulus in divination, and by a Highlander of the last century, appealing to the dead Lovat', A. Lang in his translation.

334. For μοι with κλύειν, cf. E 115, K 278, Ω 335, Theognis 4, 13, Solon 13. 2, epigr. *vit. hom. Herod.* 417; with ἀκούειν Π 515.

335. For etymologies of Τιτῆνες see Assmann *Babyloniaca* 1912, vi. 236, Nehring *Glotta* xiv. 153.

τοὶ . . . ναιετάοντες. As explained *CQ.* 1931, 146 τοὶ is the article. The article in the τ-form, common in later Greek, occurs Ω 687

σεῖο δέ κε ζωοῦ καὶ τρὶς τόσα δοῖεν ἄποινα
παῖδες τοὶ μετόπισθε λελειμμένοι.

On this passage there are no Σ, but Eustathius says ἀντὶ τοῦ οἱ ἔτι ζώοντες, τοῦ $\overline{\text{τοι}}$ δωρικῶς λεχθέντος ἀντὶ τοῦ $\overline{\text{οι}}$ προτακτικοῦ πληθυντικοῦ ἄρθρου, εἰ μὴ ἄρα ἐγκλιτικῶς γράφουσι παῖδές τοι. That is, he recognizes a variant τοι, actually given by a minority of MSS. The passage demands the article, which occurs for the second time in the line before us, and further in Λ 535, Υ 500 without a participle ἄντυγες αἱ περὶ δίφρον, where the MSS. vary between αἱ (majority) and αἳ, and in Φ 353 ἰχθύες οἱ κατὰ δίνας (οἳ majority of MSS.). Cf. also Ξ 274.

336. **τῶν ἐξ**: on the absence of accent on ἐξ in this position see Lehrs *qu. ep.* 98, Chandler § 913. The MSS. accent it as at ε 335; at E 865 they vary.

Cf. Orph. *h.* xxxvii. 1 Τιτῆνες Γαίης τε καὶ Οὐρανοῦ ἀγλαὰ τέκνα | ἡμετέρων πρόγονοι πατέρων; on the common parentage of Gods and men Hes. *OD.* 107, Pind. *Nem.* vi. 1.

339. **ἔστω** is nearest to M's ἐστιν. The variants in the other MSS. are curious: cf. K 41 ἔσται ἐστι εἴη, Λ 366 ἐστι εἴη ἦ.

340. **ἵμασε**: B 782 γαῖαν ἱμάσσῃ, I 568 γαῖαν πολυφόρβην χερσὶν ἀλοία, Hes. *Theog.* 857 αὐτὰρ ἐπεὶ δή μιν [Briareos] δάμασεν πληγῇσιν ἱμάσσας.

341. **φερέσβιος**: not in Homer, though quoted as παρ' Ὁμήρῳ by Apollodorus ap. Σ Gen. Φ 341. It occurs Hes. *Theog.* 693 and five times in the hymns.

ἡ δὲ ἰδοῦσα: M allows for the digamma while the other MSS. obscure it. At 255, however, all have ἐσιδοῦσα.

346. **εἰς θῶκον** is after ἐφεζομένη, αὐτῷ depends on φραζέσκετο.

347, 348. Cf. *h. Dem.* 28, 29.

349 with μῆνες = λ 294, ξ 293, a *hysteron proteron*. **νύκτες** read in *xp* here is less effective, introducing the unessential contrast of light and dark. Cf. the similar formula Hes. *Theog.* 58.

351. For δέ *in apodosi*, cf. 480.

The assonance of 351 and 352 did not produce omission. It did so however at 231, 232, and 537, 538.

354. **κακῷ**: sc. the δράκαινα.

356. **φέρεσκέ μιν**: this use of φέρειν with ἦμαρ is more meta-

phorical than in Homer, where κῆρες literally carry their victim off, e.g. B 302, I 411, ξ 207.

357. This is the first instance of πρίν with the indicative, Sturm *Beiträge zur hist. Syntax* ii. 47.

358. Archilochus 104. 2 χαλεπῇσι θεῶν ὀδύνῃσιν ἕκητι | πεπαρμένος δι' ὀστέων, *hymn. Delph.* Diehl i, p. 305 ὅτε τ[εοῖσι βέλεσιν ἔτρ]ησας αἰόλον ἑλικτὰν [φύαν ἔσθ' ὁ θὴρ συχνὰ] συρίγμαθ' ἱεὶς ἀθώπ[ευτ' ἀπέπνευσ' ὁμῶς].

360. **ἀνὰ δρυμὰ πύκνα καὶ ὕλην**: as the dragon in Hes. *fr.* 96. 93.

361. **λεῖπε δὲ θυμόν**: Pind. *Pyth.* iii. 180 τόξοις ἀπὸ ψυχὰν λιπών (Matthiae), Virg. *Aen.* iii. 140 *linquebant dulces animas.*

362. **φοινόν**: Π 159 παρήιον αἵματι φοινόν, Δ 524, Ν 654 θυμὸν ἀποπνείων, Virg. *Aen.* xi. 349 *purpuream vomit ille animam* (Ilgen): 'she left her red life, breathing it out'. The blood is the life.

363. **ἐνταυθοῖ νῦν**: cf. Φ 122, σ 105, υ 262: so ἐνταῦθα νῦν Aesch. *PV.* 82, Ar. *Vesp.* 149, *Thesm.* 1001, *Plut.* 724.

364. **ζωοῖσι** adjectival, as ζωὸς βροτός ψ 187. Cf. the uses of θνητός.

367. **δυσηλεγέ'**: θάνατον χ 325, πόλεμος Υ 154, δεσμοῦ Hes. *Theog.* 652, Βορέας *OD.* 506, connected acc. to Boisacq *in* Ἀλέγω with ἄλγος.

τυφωνεύς: τυφ]ωνεα Philodemus (Philippson *Hermes* 1920, 254), Hesych. Τυφωνεῖ· ἑνὶ τῶν γιγάντων. For the different forms see on 306.

368. **Χίμαιρα**: daughter of Typhaon and Echidna, Hes. *Theog.* 306, 319. G. suggests that the δράκαινα may therefore be Echidna.

369. **ἠλέκτωρ Ὑπερίων** = T 398; ἠλέκτωρ alone Z 513, Empedocl. 263 = fire; cf. Ἠλέκτρα, ἤλεκτρος, -ον. Derivation and meaning are quite unknown (see a choice in Boisacq).

371. **κατέπυσ'**: this etymology recurs in Paus. x. 6. 5. Others, regardless of quantity, connected Pytho with πυθέσθαι, e.g. Soph. *OT.* 603, Strabo 419 (he notices the quantity), Plut. *de EI* 2. Mommsen *Delph.* p. 4 compared the Swiss *Faulhorn*, but this supposes that the word is Greek. Others again connected the word with πείθειν, Philo *de post. Cain.* 278.

Snakes have a rapid decomposition, more rapid than that of fish, hence stories of a rotting monster (or of the festering wounds of giants or Centaurs), e.g. Strabo 281, 346 fin., 427, Paus. v. 5. 9, 10 were frequently attached to localities at which there were sulphurous exhalations or sulphurous streams (Halliday *Greek Questions of Plutarch* 86, 87). This is interesting in view of the explanation current in late antiquity that the Pythia derived her inspiration from a gas rising from a cleft under the tripod. Oppé (*JHS.* xxiv. 214) declares that this idea is not earlier than Alexandria, and that archaeology and geology prove that there was never a gaseous cleft. If this is correct it is decisive, but it remains at least curious that later centuries believed in some sort of natura emanation of gas, and that our earliest record tells a tale of a type usually associated with natural phenomena of the kind. But the whole story may have been invented by etymologers.

ἱερὸν μένος: *ἵμερος* is not an adjective, and its iota is long. The Homeric phrase, therefore, has to be inserted. Cf. Aeschin. *FL.* 10 *ἱερείας, ἱμεραίας.*

373. **Πύθειον**: we can hardly admit *Πύθῑον* (in spite of Danielsson p. 58 n.): for the termination *-ειος* cf. *βωμὸς δέλφειος* 496, *Αἰάντειον . . . βωμόν* Pind. *Ol.* ix. 112, *Anth. Pal.* x. 17, *EM.* 696. 21 *Πύθεια καὶ Πυθαῖος· ὄνομα ἑορτῆς,* Suid. *Πυθεῖον· τὸ μαντικόν.* It may be restored in Pind. *Ol.* xiv. 16, where *πύθιον* corresponds to *κόλποισι* (Farnell). In prose *Πύθιος* is the regular title P.-W. i. 65. See Schulze *qu. ep.* 254 (*πυθεῖον*).

κεῖθι | αὐτοῦ. Cf. κ 271 *σὺ μὲν αὐτοῦ τῷδ' ἐνὶ χώρῳ,* *h.* iv. 169 *αὐτοῦ τῇδε.*

374. **μένος ὀξ. Ἠέλ.** = Hes. *OD.* 414.

376. **ἐξαπάφησε**: she wished to retain her own pilgrims and not lose them to Delphi. For her punishment cf. Paus. viii. 53¹, Menecrates *fr.* 2 *FHG.* ii. 243 *ἐπὶ δὲ τὴν κρήνην αὖτις ἐξίκετο* (Leto) *δίκην ἐπιβαλοῦσα τοῖς ἐξελάσασιν αὐτὴν βουκόλοις.*

380. **προρέειν**: the cognate use is established by Ap. Rh. iii. 225 *ἡ δ' ἄρ' ὕδωρ προρέεσκε,* Orph. *Arg.* 1137, and of the simple verb by *IG. Ins. Aeg.* 96 *ο λαρναξ ουτος ρει τοις διψωσιν υδωρ ποτον,* and other exx. in the lexx. Else Barnes's *προχέειν* is supported by 241 and Φ 219, and is a v.l. Φ 366.

383. **πέτρῃσι προχυτῇσι**: dat. of circumstance, 'with a shower of stones' (Matthiae): so Fick *BB.* xxvi. 113 and *JHS.* xvii. 250. Cf. Callim. *Del.* 133 ἀλλά οἱ Ἄρης | Παγγαίου προθέλυμνα καρήατα μέλλεν ἀείρας | ἐμβαλέειν δίνῃσι, ἀποκρύψειν δὲ ῥέεθρα. Frazer on Paus. ix. 33. 1 identifies Telphusa with a spring which issues from the foot of the mountain; the overhanging cliff called Petra is very steep. Cf. 244.

388. For ἐφράζετο see on *Dem.* 256.

389. The prose form is ὀργεών, -ῶνος except in a Lemnian decree, *IG.* xii. 8. 19 οργειωσι, οργειωνικον. Ὀργεών also occurs in Aeschylus *Mysi* 140; but Antimachus *Lyde fr.* 2 (*PLG.* ii. 289) has ὀργίωνας (or ὀργεῶνας in another source) at the end of a hexameter, Hermesianax ap. Athen. 19 has Ῥάριον οργιωνα (sic). The manuscript spellings do not go for much. It is usual (Headlam *CR.* 1901, 403, Schulze *qu. ep.* 255, Fick *BB.* xvi. 27) to write ὀργείονας; but ῑ is frequent in Greek (e.g. πέαρ, πεῖαρ, πῖαρ), so we follow the MSS. On the other hand there seems no reason why the accent should shift beyond the parateleuton.

391. M's remark was perhaps caused by the unintelligible ἠμαθοήν.

393. **Κρῆτες ἀπὸ Κνωσοῦ**: the writer expressly localizes the home of the cult of Apollo δελφίνιος in Crete. A temple of the God as δελφίνιος is known at Cnossus (*CIG.* ii. 2554 Γ 98), and Cretan inscrr. at Delos call him δελφιδιος (*BCH.* iii. 293, iv. 355). There was a Cretan month Delphinius (*BCH.* iii. *l.c.*, *CIG.* 2448), and a Delphinion at Drerus in Crete (*Rh. Mus.* 1856, 393). See P.-R. i. 257 n. 4, P.-W. ii. 47, Wide *Lakon. Kulte* 87. See further on 495.

394. The present ἀγγέλλουσι is established by M *x*, and the change of ῥέζουσι to ῥέξουσι is almost imperceptible and constant in MSS. of the *Iliad.* The lines 393–6 therefore are an hyperbaton (Gemoll compares α 23, 24). The function of the Cretans is mentioned by anticipation; they preceded the Pythia as mouthpieces. The hymn, therefore, goes back to this period, when the Cretan priesthood, though after a political change, still announced Apollo to mankind.

395. **Φοίβου Ἀπόλλωνος χρυσαόρου** = Ε 509. On the form

χρυσαόρου see on 123. In later times Apollo has not usually a sword, but the view (Σ A on O 256) that *ἄορ* means the belt or even the lyre of Apollo has no foundation. Apollo has a sword in his contest with Tityos and in scenes from the Gigantomachy, e.g. on the vase of Aristophanes and Erginus (*Wiener Vorlegebl.* i. 5); other reff. in P.-W. ii. 111. In the early period the attributes of the Gods were less stereotyped than later; even Demeter has the sword (*Dem.* 4).

396. **ἐκ δάφνης**: Callim. *Del.* 94 *ἀπὸ δάφνης*. The allusion may be doubted. Perhaps the tripods (see on 443) are meant; Σ Ar. *Plut.* 39 *οἱ τρίποδες δάφνῃ ἦσαν ἐστεμμένοι*. Ilgen with more probability saw an allusion to the laurel-tree which was said to have grown in the temple: cf. Ar. *Plut.* 213 *Πυθικὴν σείσας δάφνην*, Σ ib. *φασὶν ὡς πλησίον τοῦ τρίποδος δάφνη ἵστατο ἣν ἡ Πυθία ἡνίκα ἐχρησμώδει ἔσειεν*; Aristonous *paean* 10 *χλωρότομον δάφναν σείων*. But this does not justify the view of Hiller von Gärtringen (P.-W. iv. 25, 27) that the Delphic oracle at this time was a tree-oracle, the laurel taking the part of the oak at Dodona. The first temple at Delphi was built of laurel (Paus. x 5. 5); there were branches at the entrance (Eur. *Ion* 80, 103) and laurel-trees in the *τέμενος* (ib. 76). The priestess chewed laurel before delivering the oracle (Lucian *bis acc.* 1, Tzetzes *in Lycophr.* 6), and fumigated herself with burning laurel before descending into the cavern (Plut. *de EI* 2). See further P.-W. ii. 110, P.-R. 285, 291, Mannhardt *BK.* 296, Pearson on Soph. *fr.* 897, Halliday *Folk-Lore* xli. 129.

γυάλων ὕπο Παρνησοῖο: Hes. *Theog.* 499 (*γυάλοις*), Aristonous *Παρνασσοῦ γυάλων*.

398. The Triphylian Pylos is meant, as appears from 424.

400. **δελφῖνι ἐοικώς**: stories of animals guiding people to a new town or country are very common, see Frazer on Paus. x. 6. 2. For Apollo's connexion with the dolphin see on 495.

402. We have to decide between *οὔ τις . . . ἐπεφράσατο* of M and *ὅστις . . . ἐπιφράσσαιτο* of the other MSS. It is hard to understand how the sailors did not see the dolphin, which lay on the deck, and the contrary is stated 415 sq. This disposes of Matthiae's *ἐπεφράσατ' οὐδ' ἐνοήσε*. We therefore accept *ὅστις*

ἐπιφράσσαιτο, 'whoever thought to observe': for the infinitive cf. ε 183 ἐπεφράσθης ἀγορεῦσαι, Callim. *Hec.* 34. 28 ἐπεφράσσαντο τελέσσαι. ἀνασσείασκε means 'shook up, shook to and fro', the object is the offender (ὅστις); 'whoever thought to mark him he shook him and rattled the ship's timbers'. The offender was flung about as the ship reeled.

For the form in -ασκε cf. κρύπτασκε Θ 272, ῥίπτασκον Ο 23, ῥίπτασκε θ 374.

405. The sailors in 414 wanted to stop the ship, but in 405–6 they were too afraid to lower the sails. λύον (ο 496, more elaborately below 487) = ἀνέλυον (Aratus 374, Libanius viii. 3 τὸν αὐτῆς ἱστὸν ἀναλυούσης). Baumeister's ἕλκον would give the opposite sense.

406. **λαῖφος**, 'sail'; in this sense not Homeric, but in Alcaeus 18. 7.

407. **κατεστήσαντο**, 'fixed it down'; there seems no parallel.

408. For ἔπλεον see La Roche *HU.* 3.

Ruhnken's ἔπειγε is a slight alteration, and the verb is frequent in this connexion, e.g. Soph. *Phil.* 1443, Ap. Rh. iv. 1769. ἐγείρειν (and compounds) in later Greek usually means to erect, build; but Herod. vii. 49 ἐγειρομένου χειμῶνος, Ap. Rh. i. 1159 ἐγρομένοιο σάλου, iii. 296 (σέλας) ἀνεγρόμενον, *Anth. Pal.* vi. 21. 7 πρασιὴν διψεῦσαν ἐγείρειν, Quintus ix. 271 (κῦμα) ὅτ' ἐξ ἀνέμοιο διεγρόμενον φορέηται seem to justify the use here of the effect of wind on a quasi-animate object like a ship.

410 sq. **πὰρ δὲ . . . ἷξον** = παρῖξον δέ *in tmesi*; for the verb cf. Pind. *Pyth.* vi. 43 παρῖκε, Orph. *Arg.* 392 ἐξῖκε; for the tmesis μ 2 ἀπὸ δ' ἵκετο. The πτολίεθρον is the peninsula ending in Taenarum, as in ω 377 the word is applied to Nericus, ἀκτὴ ἠπείροιο. 'They went past the Laconian land, sea-girt country, and past Taenarum': cf. παρέστιχες 217, παρενίσατο 430. On Taenarum town and cape see Pherecydes *fr.* 88, Strabo 360, Paus. iii. 25. 9, Ptol. iii. 14. 32, Procop. *bell. Vand.* i. 13. It occurs in the story of Arion, Herod. i. 23, and in that of the Corcyraeans, ib. vii. 168 (Ταίναρον γῆς τῆς Λακεδαιμονίων). The epithet ἁλιστέφανος is true of the Taenarian peninsula, as ἁλιερκέες ὄχθαι of Cumae, between two seas, Pind. *Pyth.* i. 18. The

nearly identical ἀλιστεφής is common in late verse, Orph. *Arg.* 145, 186, 1208, Nonnus xiii. 455.

411. τερψιμβρότου Ἠελίοιο = μ 269, 274.

412. There is no other record of sacred flocks at Taenarum, but there were cults of Helios in various parts of Laconia, e.g. at Taleton where horses were sacrificed, Paus. iii. 20. 4. Other reff. in Wide *Lakon. Kulte* 215 sq. Herodotus ix. 93 mentions flocks belonging to Apollo at Apollonia in Epirus. The author had in mind the herds and flocks of the Sun in Thrinacia μ 128. The subject is discussed by O. Müller *Proll.* 224, 368, H. D. Müller *Myth.* ii. 338, Wilamowitz *Hom. Unters.* 168, Tümpel *Lesbiaka* i in *Philologus* N.F. ii. 124 (quoted by Wide), P.-R. 430. The meaning of the flocks or herds of the sun has exercised commentators from the time of Eustathius and Σ on μ 129, who give Aristotle's explanation that they are an allegory of the lunar year.

414. For the harbour see Frazer on Paus. iii. p. 396, Weil *Ath. Mitth.* i. 160.

416. δαπέδοισι, 'floor'; neither the plural nor the meaning 'deck' are Homeric.

417. πολυίχθυον: not Homeric.

ἀμφὶς ὀρούσει: ἀμφίς with verbs of motion occurs M 434 ἀμφὶς ἀνέλκει, Ψ 393 ἀμφὶς ὁδοῦ δραμέτην, Hes. *Theog.* 748 ἀμφὶς ἰοῦσαι (gl. χωριζόμεναι). For the sense 'apart' cf. also χ 57, ω 218, Ap. Rh. iii. 1070, orac. ap. Herod. i. 85. αὖθις or αὖτις is too common to have been miscopied.

418. Cf. Theognis 458 πηδαλίῳ πείθεται.

419. παρὲκ . . . ἔχουσα: probably *in tmesi* = παρεξέχουσα, 'leaving on one side', as παρεξάγω, παρέξειμι, παρεξελαύνω, παρεξέρχομαι. This gets rid of the difficulty of taking ἔχουσα attributively. On παρ' ἐκ see on ii. 281.

The Cretans' journey 'with Peloponnesus on one side' was made by Telemachus on his return to Ithaca (ο 295–300), attempted by Jason in the Argo (Herod. iv. 178), and by Rhodine and her brother (Stesich. *fr.* 44 ap. Strab. 347). The list of Nestor's towns in the Catalogue (B 591–4), many of which were on or near the coast, and his stories of his youth (H 133–6,

Λ 711 sq.), provide further information. Cf. also Pherecydes *fr.* 87 and Strabo 337 sqq. Strabo, who successfully proved the Nestorian to be the Triphylian Pylos (wherein Didymus Σ Pind. *Pyth.* vi. 35, and the source of Σ T Λ 726 agreed with him), is much taken up with identifying Homeric sites. This district was described in 1831 in the *Expédition de Morée* (Blouet), from whose results and from Boutan *Archives des Missions Scientifiques* 1865, 219 sq., and, following Strabo, Victor Bérard (*Les Phéniciens et l'Odyssée* 1902, i. 61 sq.) convincingly asserted the claims of Triphylia. His results were confirmed by Dörpfeld's excavations in 1907 (*Ath. Mitt.* 1907, 1908). See *Catalogue* 75 sq.

The list of names here mostly nearly resembles that in the *Odyssey.* The order, as we might expect from 30 and 240, is misleading. Pylos, Cruni, and Chalcis were S. of the Alpheus, but the writer mentions them after Thryon; Dyme, which is N. of Elis, appears after it. As Strabo observes, poetical order does not always agree with fact; see on 32. Argyphea is new. The disappearance of the old names and the oblivion of Pylos was due to political circumstances, see p. 275 f. They would supply a *terminus ad quem* to the Apollo hymn as to that to Hermes, but their evidence is unnecessary.

A voyage in the reverse direction, from Cephallenia to Messenia, took one day (Polyb. v. 5).

422. **Ἀρήνην**: cf. B 591, Λ 723. It was the home of Lynceus and Idas, Ap. Rh. i. 152, Simonides *fr.* 216. Strabo 346 identifies it with Σάμος or Σαμικόν; the other school (as early as the poet Pisander ap. Σ Ap. Rh. i. 471) with Ἔρανα in Messenia; cf. τινές in Strabo 348, 361.

423 = B 592.

Θρύον: Strabo 349 καλεῖται δὲ νῦν Ἐπιτάλιον (Polyb. iv. 80) τῆς Μακιστίας χωρίον. As he says, it is identical with the Θρυόεσσα πόλις of Λ 711. The singular mistake εὐκτίμενον for εὔκτιτον is found in several MSS. B 592, Quintus xii. 91.

Αἶπυ: Strabo 349 discusses views on Αἶπυ, whether it is a noun or an adjective, and if it was the actual Μαργάλα (or Μαργάνα) in Amphidolia, or Epitalion. It is usually identified with Αἴπιον or Ἔπιον which occurs in the later lists (Herod. iv.

148, Polyb. iv. 77, 80). It remained in the name of a district, ἐν τῇ χώρᾳ τῇ νῦν Αἰπασίᾳ καλουμένῃ Strabo 346.

424. The Pylos mentioned here, 398, B 591, *h.* iv. 398 is naturally the Alphean or Triphylian. Strabo 344 explains the epithet ἠμαθόεντα by the nature of the coast below the Triphylian Pylos: θινώδης δὲ καὶ στενός ἐστιν ὁ τῆς θαλάσσης αἰγιαλός, ὥστ' οὐκ ἂν ἀπογνοίη τις ἐντεῦθεν ὠνομάσθαι τὸν Πύλον (cf. Σ Ap. Rh. i. 152 ἀμμώδης ἀπὸ τοῦ παραρρέοντος ποταμοῦ). On the quicksands at Samicum see Paus. v. 5. 7, 6. 3 (διὰ χωρίου τὰ πλείονα ὑποψάμμου), and for the actual condition of the coast Bérard and Frazer *Paus.* vol. iii, pp. 473, 481.

425. Strabo in two places (350, 447) speaking of Telemachus' return journey from Pylos to Ithaca quotes a line βὰν δὲ παρὰ Κρουνοὺς καὶ Χαλκίδα καλλιρέεθρον (in 447 πετρήεσσαν). As Strabo ignores the Hymns and says (341) that Δύμη is not in Homer he can hardly allude to the present line; it is possible that he read it in the *Odyssey*, where, as ο 295, Barnes replaced it after Casaubon had noticed the omission. At the same time the omission in all MSS. of the *Odyssey* without apparent cause is singular.

For Κρουνοί and Χαλκίς see Strabo 343, 351, where he calls them ὀχετοί rather than rivers (as he calls the Iardanus of H 135 a ποτάμιον 342). They were small streams (Chalcis was also a κατοικία) in the district of Macistia S. of the mouth of the Alpheus, and seem to have been obliterated by the lagoon which now stretches from the Alpheus past Macistus, part of which (that formed by the Anigrus at Arene) is mentioned by Strabo 347. See Frazer *Paus.* vol. iii. 478.

Δύμην: this town is first mentioned here, and out of its place.

426, 427 = ο 298, 297. In the *Odyssey* they are in the right geographical order, and ἡ δέ takes the place of εὖτε, and ἐπειγομένη of ἀγαλλομένη.

426. **Ἐπειοί**: the Homeric name for the inhabitants of Elis (B 619, Δ 537, Λ 688, 694, Ψ 630, 632) and Dulichium (N 686, 691, O 519). It is still used of the Eleans by Justin xxvi. 14 (v.l.). By Hellanicus and Damastes (*fr.* 5, 6) it was applied to Aetolians also.

427. **φεράς**: in ο 297 the MSS. have Φεράς, but Aristarchus acc. to Σ H 135 read Φεαῖς, and Strabo quotes Φεάς 350, Φεάν 351. It is usual to print Φεάς in the *Odyssey*, but to do so here would increase the poet's inaccuracy, seeing that Phea is S. of Elis. Pherae is a frequent place-name; there was one in Aetolia (Steph. *in v.*), and a Pharae in Achaea (Strabo 388, Polyb. ii. 41, Paus. vii. 23) not far east of Dyme and not further from the sea than Elis. The writer may well refer to this place. The quantity in the word varies: B 711 Φεράς, 763 Φηρητιάδαο. Moreover Pherecydes and Didymus read Φηρᾶς for Φειᾶς H 135. For other confusions produced by Φειά see on ο 297.

With ἐπιβάλλω in this sense a dative is usual: φεαῖς Ar. H 135, νήσοις ὀξείῃσι καὶ Ἀρτεμίτῃ ἐπέβαλλον Rhianus *fr.* 39. L[1]'s reading Φερᾶς suggests this.

εὖτε is asyndetic (see on 115), and καί marks the apodosis as in ν 79.

428. Ithaca is visible from Patrae (Frazer *Paus.* vol. iv. 144) and therefore from Pharae (if that place is intended). Even if Φεάς be read the statement holds good. According to Frazer (ib. iii. 475) Cefalonia is visible from the coast near Lepreum, and even from a hill above Cyparissia, much further south (ib. 463).

429 = α 246, ι 24, π 123. The line is formulaic. Zante is much nearer than Ithaca. Dulichium was argued (*Catalogue* 82), after Bunbury and Vollgraff, and in agreement with Stürmer, to be Leucas, and the view was accepted by Bury.

Same was held by Apollodorus and Strabo 452 to be Cephallenia. A modern town in Cefalonia is called Samos. The form varies between Σάμη and Σάμος in the *Odyssey*: Σαμαῖοι (Thuc.), *Samaei* (Livy) is the name of the population.

430. **παρενίσατο**: the aor. of νίσσομαι does not occur in Homer, but the tense is better than the imperfect.

431. **ἐπὶ Κρίσης**: as the whole Corinthian gulf is meant (below), ἐπί = 'in the direction of' as γ 171 νήσου ἐπὶ Ψυρίης, 'towards', Strabo 249 ἐπὶ δὲ Ῥώμης Κασίλινον ἵδρυται, 378 τὸν ἐπὶ Μαλέας πλοῦν, Herod. vii. 115 κόλπον τὸν ἐπὶ Ποσιδηίου, and Γ 5, Ε 700, Λ 546, Ψ 374. The epithet ἀπείρων suits the gulf of Corinth, not the bay of Crisa, which cannot be said to 'separate Peloponnesus'.

431. **κατεφαίνετο**: for the compound cf. Ap. Rh. iv. 1231, Theocr. iii. 8, vi. 37, vii. 10, Lucian *Menipp.* 10, *Icarom.* 4–12.

434–5. Cf. ο 293–4.

435. **ἀνύσειε**: δ 356 ὅσσον νηῦς ἤνυσεν, *h.* iv. 337 πολὺν διὰ χῶρον ἀνύσσας.

436. **ἄψορροι**: for the variation between adj. and adv. cf. Ω 330, Hes. *Theog.* 659. Between ἀντίος and ἀντίον it is constant in Homer.

438. On Crisa and Cirrha see O. Davies 'Two North-Greek mining towns', *JHS.* 1929, 89.

439. For the repetition of ἐς cf. *h.* v. 58–9, ἐν Λ 479–80, Χ 503–4, Ω 614–15.

ἐχρίμψατο: the first example of this correption within the word, La Roche *HU.* 10.

441–2. Cf. Δ 75 οἷον δ' ἀστέρα ἧκε Κρόνου παῖς ἀγκυλομήτεω | ἢ ναύτῃσι τέρας ἠὲ στρατῷ εὐρέι λαῶν | λαμπρόν· τοῦ δέ τε πολλοὶ ἀπὸ σπινθῆρες ἵενται· | τῷ ἐικυῖ' ἤιξεν ἐπὶ χθόνα Παλλὰς Ἀθήνη. Sparks flew from both, each was 'like' (εἰκυῖα, εἰδόμενος) a star.

443. **διὰ τριπόδων ἐριτίμων**: Ar. *Eq.* 1016 ἴαχεν ἐξ ἀδύτοιο διὰ τριπόδων ἐριτίμων; see on 114, Introd. p. lxxviii. The plural shows that the oracular tripod is not meant. Tripods, i.e. caldrons on feet, were arranged in front of the temple, Bacchyl. iii. 18 τριπόδων σταθέντων πάροιθε ναοῦ, or in it. In Aristophanes the voice comes through them, perhaps in Aristonous 9 also, ἔνθ' ἀπὸ τριπόδων θεοκτήτων χλωρότομον δάφναν σείων μαντοσύναν ἐποιχνεῖς, unless Aristonous confused τρίπους and votive τρίποδες, or used pl. for sing. On the vessels forming the wealth of Apollo at Delphi and elsewhere see Wieseler *Fleckeisens Jahrb.* 75, 692, P.-R. 291, Pind. *Pyth.* xi. 4 *cum* Σ (of gold, at Thebes), Eur. *Suppl.* 1197, *h.* iv. 179 (other reff. in Wieseler).

444. **πιφαυσκόμενος τὰ ἃ κῆλα** = Μ 280 (of snow). In Hes. *Theog.* 708 the κῆλα of Zeus are thunder, lightning, and the thunderbolt. The rays of the sun are appropriate to Phoebus.

447. **μέγα γὰρ δέος ἔμβαλ' ἑκάστῳ**: cf. Λ 11 μέγα σθένος ἔμβαλ' ἑκάστῳ. The alternative εἷλεν ἕκαστον is equivalent.

448. **ἆλτο πέτεσθαι**: cf. *h.* ii. 389 ἆλτο θέειν. The infin. is not Homeric.

449 = Π 716 (εἰσάμενος).

450. Cf. *h.* vii. 4.

452–5 = γ 71–4, ι 252–5. Here πόθεν supplanted τίνες in all MSS. So *h. Dem.* 411 αὐτάρ supplanted ἤτοι or αὐτίκ', *Herm.* 453 ὧδε in M supplanted ἄλλο.

453. **κατὰ πρῆξιν**: cf. 397 ἐπὶ πρῆξιν, θ 162 πρηκτῆρες. For the question cf. Thuc. i. 5.

456. **ἧσθον τετιηότες**: cf. 487 κάθετον λύσαντε, 501 ἵκησθον, *h.* iv. 504. Zenodotus, Eratosthenes, and Crates (Σ A Ω 282) admitted the use of the dual for the plural in Homer (e.g. A 567, Δ 407, E 487, Θ 74, O 347), Aristarchus denied it. As the dual disappeared early from the κοινή these false duals were considered as literary equivalents of the plural: so in later poetry Aratus 968, 1023, Ap. Rh. iii. 206, perhaps i. 384, orac. ap. Herod. vii. 140, epigr. *vit. hom. Herod.* 181, *h.* vi. 12. So Monro *Odyssey* ii, p. 438. The explanations in K.-G. i, § 368 are artificial. Cf. Debrunner *Glotta* xv. 16.

463. **Κρητῶν ἀγός**: Orion 46. 22, *EM.* 255, 18, Tzetzes *in Lycophr.* 208 call him Castalius, Serv. on *Aen.* iii. 332 Icadius.

466. The combination of ἐπεί and γάρ is remarkable.

466–72. Cf. ω 402, 403, ν 233, α 182, ι 261, M 225 (αὐτὰ κέλευθα).

475. **ἀμφινέμεσθε**: imperf., as τὸ πρίν shows. Cf. ἀμφινέμοντο B 521, 634.

487. On the dual see on 456, Ap. Rh. iii. 206 κατειλύσαντε βοείαις.

488. **ἀν' ἐπ'.** The hiatus ἐπὶ ἠπείρου is not tolerable. For ἀν' cf. 506.

489. **ἔντεα**: un-Homeric (= ὅπλα).

491. In 509 δ' is connective; here where the operations are simultaneous it is unnecessary.

495. The cult of Apollo δελφίνιος is certainly old, but its home is uncertain. Some critics, ancient and modern, have derived it from Delphi; others, among whom was the author of the hymn, from Crete. A. Mommsen, on the other hand, thought it was Chalcidic. The connexion with Delphi rests on two foundations:

(1) a supposed etymological link between Delphi and Delphinios, (2) the prominent part played by Delphi in Greek colonization, for Apollo Delphinios was the God who led the ships of merchant adventurers (see on 496). That the title had its origin in Delphi is most improbable. Whether the author of the hymn is correct in making Crete, an important centre of the cult, its first home must remain uncertain. The cult seems to have developed in the seafaring states, probably in the islands, and thence to have come back, a return wave as it were, to mainland Greece (Farnell iv. 145). If so, it may be noted that the Mycenaean remains found at Delphi are quite irrelevant to the story in the hymn, which if historically true belongs not to prehistoric but to early historical times. The motive of the story no doubt was to provide an *aition* for the name Delphi, as the first part of this section of the hymn provided one for Pytho. The name Delphi itself, however, does not occur in the hymn.

ὁ βωμός: Paus. x. 5. 5 does not mention an altar, and there appear to be no remains. In literature there are two stories resembling the hymn: (1) Plutarch *de soll. animal.* 984 A = c. 36 καὶ μὴν Ἀρτέμιδός γε Δικτύννης Δελφινίου τ' Ἀπόλλωνος ἱερὰ καὶ βωμοὶ παρὰ πολλοῖσιν εἰσὶν Ἑλλήνων· ὃν δ' αὐτὸς ἑαυτῷ τόπον ἐξαίρετον ὁ θεὸς πεποίηται . . . Κρητῶν ἀπογόνους οἰκοῦντας ἡγεμόνι δελφῖνι χρησαμένους· οὐ γὰρ ὁ θεὸς προενήχετο τοῦ στόλου μεταβαλὼν τὸ εἶδος, ὡς οἱ μυθογράφοι λέγουσιν, ἀλλὰ δελφῖνα πέμψας τοῖς ἀνδράσι ἰθύνοντα τὸν πλοῦν κατήγαγεν εἰς Κίρραν. He then tells a story how two persons in the time of Ptolemy Soter, who were driven by a storm off Malea, ἐν δεξιᾷ Πελοπόννησον ἔχοντες (the same route as the Cretans), were led by a dolphin to Cirrha, where they offered an ἀναβατήριον (on the βωμός?). Plutarch's μυθογράφοι may be writers who borrowed from the hymn, or may stand for the hymn itself.

(2) The story of Icadius son of Apollo and the nymph Lyceia: *inde cum Italiam peteret naufragio vexatus delphini tergo exceptus dicitur, ac prope Parnassum montem delatus patri Apollini templum constituisse, et a Delphino locum Delphos appellasse: aras deinde Apollini tanquam patri consecrasse, quas ferunt vulgo patrias dictas*, Servius on *Aen.* iii. 332. For the altar on the shore cf. Ap.

Rh. ii. 659, where the Argonauts erect a βωμὸς ἐπάκτιος on the island where Apollo appeared.

The metrical difficulties which beset δελφίνιος (δελφῖνιος, δελφῑνῑος) are too great for it to be entertained, especially after δελφῑνίῳ in the line before. To this it probably owes its existence.

δέλφειος does not occur elsewhere, but is supported by ὄρος τὸ καλούμενον Δέλφ(ε)ιον Arist. *Mir. Ausc.* 839. 1, a Thessalian inscription τες βελφαιο (= τα ες δελφαιου) *Ath. Mitt.* xxi. 249; the termination -ειος by Πύθ(ε)ιον 373, Αἰάντειον βωμόν Pind. *Ol.* ix. 112, ἠιὼν ἀλιτενὴς Αἰάντειον Strabo 595, τέμενος Αἰάνειον ib. 425, τοῦ τῶν Κορείων (-ίων MSS.) ἀγῶνος ib. 425, and other cases in Paus. i. 19. 3, ii. 2. 6, 7. 6, ii. 14. 4, iv. 1. 3 al. See Farnell on Pindar *l.c.* and on *Ol.* xiii. 108, and note on 373. Cf. vit. Eugenii p. 368 Westermann περὶ τῶν τεμενικῶν ὅπως προφέρεται οἷον Διονύσειον Ἀσκληπιεῖον.

496. On Apollo Delphinius see P.-R. *l.c.*, P.-W. ii. 47, iv. 2513. The title is rightly connected with the dolphin. As the patron of sailors and colonization Apollo travelled over many seas as a dolphin, cf. Artemid. ii. 35. Dolphins tumbling in front of a vessel are a familiar sight in southern waters: Ap. Rh. iv. 933, *Anth. Pal.* ix. 83. 1 νηὸς ἐπερχομένης ὠκὺν δρόμον ἀμφεχόρευον | δελφῖνες.

ἐπόψιος: Hesych. Ἐπόψιος· Ζεὺς καὶ Ἀπόλλων, Ant. Lib. 6. 2, Orph. *Arg.* 1035 Δία ἐπόψιον, Dittenb. *Syll.*[2] 870. 2 δι εποψιω, Soph. *Phil.* 1040 θεοὶ ἐπόψιοι, Fränkel *KZ.* xlv. 164. Similar titles are ἐπόπτης: Hesych. Ἐπόπτης· Ζεύς (of the Sun, *CIG. addend.* 4699), Ἐπωπέτης· Ζεὺς παρὰ Ἀθηναίοις, Ἐπωπίς· Δημήτηρ παρὰ Σικυωνίοις, Paus. viii. 30. 1 Ποσειδῶνος Ἐπόπτου ναός. So Artemis ἐπίσκοπος, Callim. *Dian.* 38, 259, at Elis Plut. *qu. graec.* 47. Cf. also Φοῖβε Κεφαλλήνων λιμενόσκοπε *Anth. Pal.* x. 25, Πᾶνα τὸν εὐόρμων τῇδ' ἔφορον λιμένων *ib.* x. 10. Apollo is προσόψιος Paus. i. 32. 2.

499. Cf. ω 489 (σίτοιο μελίφρονος ἐξ ἔρον ἕντο).

500. **ἰηπαιηόν'**: see on 272. The paean was the germ of the later Pythian games. Before the first Sacred War it was sung every eighth year at a competition of cithara-players: Strabo 421,

Paus. x. 7. 2, Pind. *Pyth. arg.*, Censorinus *de die nat.* 18, Mommsen *Delphika* 153.

501. For this variant (εἰς ὅκε, εἰς ὅτε) cf. τ 144, ω 134, Ap. Rh. ii. 857, *h.* xxviii. 14. For εἰσοκε either ἐν παραθέσει or ἐν συνθέσει see *E. Gud.* 174. 3, *Iliad proleg.* 245.

503 sq. Compare A 433 sq. (504 = A 434, 505 = A 437). Ꝑ 53 of the *Iliad* shows a version of A 484–6 which resembles the Hymn (*Origins* 207).

505. On βαῖνον, βῆσαν see Debrunner *IGF.* 1921, 202.

507 = A 486 (ὑπό for παρά).

ἕρματα, 'shores', B 154, Hes. *OD.* 624 νῆα δ' ἐπ' ἠπείρου ἐρύσαι πυκάσαι τε λίθοισι | παντόθεν.

515. On the variants of this line see pp. xxvi, xxxix. ἀγᾰτόν, which was long printed, does not exist, and was a correction of the singular lacuna in *x* (it is a v.l. for ἀγητόν Theocr. i. 126).

516. **καλὰ καὶ ὕψι βιβάς** = 202.

ῥήσσοντες, 'beating time'; cf. Σ 571 τοὶ δὲ ῥήσσοντες ἁμαρτῇ . . . ἕποντο, Ap. Rh. i. 539 with an object πέδον ῥήσσωσι πόδεσσιν. On the derivation see Boisacq *in* Ῥάσσω.

518. **οἷοί τε Κρητῶν παιήονες**: the paean was pre-Dorian. It was sung by the Achaeans to Apollo (A 472) and as a general triumphal hymn (X 391). Later it is found at Sparta and Delphi and in Crete, connected with the cult of Apollo.

520. **ἄκμητοι**: also in Nicander *Thes.* 737.

523. **ἄδυτον ζάθεον** (*y*) is perhaps the better reading, but the alternative αὐτοῦ δάπεδον, if αὐτοῦ is superfluous, is possible: Preger *inscr. metr. gr.* 89 νῦν δέ με Λητοίδου θεῖον ἔχει δάπεδον.

524 = υ 9 (τοῦ).

528. **βιόμεσθα**: O 194, X 431 several MSS. have βίομαι, the vulgate βείομαι. Aristarchus almost certainly read βι- (so Ꞩ B on X 431; Ꞩ A is itacistic). Schulze *qu. ep.* 246 n. and Fick on π 852 prefer βι-. See also Solmsen *l.c.* 91, 92. Cf. βίονται orac. ap. Phleg. *mir.* 2. 8.

The barren soil of Delphi was a stock reproach to the priests; cf. the story of Aesop Ꞩ Ar. *Vesp.* 1446, *Pax* 129 ὅν φασιν ἐλθόντα ποτε εἰς τοὺς Δελφοὺς ἀποσκῶψαι αὐτοὺς ὅτι μὴ ἔχοιεν γῆν ἀφ' ἧς ἐργαζόμενοι διατρέφοιντο, ἀλλὰ περιμένοιεν ἀπὸ τῶν τοῦ θεοῦ θυμάτων διαζῆν, Himerius xiii. 5. Cf. also Ox. pap. 1800, pap. Ross.-Georg. 18, Callim. *Iambi* 172, Aelian *fr.* 203, Macarius 325 (paroemiogr. ii. 155), Diogen. 487 (ib. i.) Δελφὸς ἀνὴρ στέφανον μὲν ἔχει δίψῃ δ' ἀπόλωλεν: in general Lucian *Phalaris* ii. 8 (a Delphian speaks) ὅτι μὲν δὴ ἐν κρημνοῖς τε οἰκοῦμεν αὐτοὶ καὶ πέτρους γεωργοῦμεν οὐχ Ὅμηρον χρὴ περιμένειν δηλώσοντα ἡμῖν, ἀλλ' ὁρᾶν πάρεστι ταῦτα, καὶ ὅσον ἐπὶ τῇ γῇ βαθεῖ λιμῷ ἀεὶ συνῆμεν ἄν· τὸ δὲ ἱερὸν καὶ ὁ Πύθιος καὶ τὸ χρηστήριον καὶ οἱ θύοντες καὶ οἱ εὐσεβοῦντες ταῦτα Δελφῶν τὰ πεδία, ταῦτα ἡ πρόσοδος, ἐντεῦθεν ἡ εὐπορία, ἐντεῦθεν αἱ τροφαί . . . καὶ τὸ λεγόμενον ὑπὸ τῶν ποιητῶν ἄσπαρτα ἡμῖν καὶ ἀνήροτα φύεται τὰ πάντα ὑπὸ γεωργῷ τῷ θεῷ. As in Homer Πυθῶνα τε πετρήεσσαν B 519 and Πυθοῖ ἔνι πετρηέσσῃ I 405 are the only mentions of Delphi Lucian must refer to this passage.

529. **ἐπήρατος** followed by τρυγηφόρος, 'it is not desirable as vineland or pasture': the construction is supported by ν 246 αἰγίβοτος δ' ἀγαθὴ καὶ βούβοτος, ι 27 τρηχεῖ' ἀλλ' ἀγαθὴ κουροτρόφος, Hes. *OD* 783 ἀνδρογόνος δ' ἀγαθή, Solon *fr.* 43 λιπαρὴ κουροτρόφος, Dicaearchus i. 13 καὶ ἱπποτρόφος δὲ ἀγαθή (of Thebes), Theophr. *HP.* viii. 28 καὶ γὰρ εἶναι σιτοφόρον μὲν καὶ ἐλαιοφόρον ἀγαθήν, ἀμπελόφορον δὲ μετρίαν (*CP.* ii. 42. 4, 5. 10 al.), Strabo 837, Diod. ii. 48. 9, v. 17. 2, xix. 98 ἀγαθὴ δ' ἐστι φοινικόφυτος, Lysias i. 7 οἰκονόμος δεινὴ καὶ φειδωλὸς ἀγαθή.

530. **καὶ ἅμ' ἀνθρώποισιν ὀπηδεῖν**, 'and accompany mankind', sc. to the oracle. The priests introduced the inquirer to Apollo: for ἅμα ὀπηδεῖν see Ebeling (e.g. η 165, 181 ὅς θ' ἱκετῃσιν ἅμ' αἰδοίοισιν ὀπηδεῖ of Zeus). This is the view of Franke.

532. Cf. *Dem.* 257 in 𝔭 αφρονες ανθρωποι δυστλημονες, and 191 above.

μελεδῶνας: the MSS. of the Hymns here and *Herm.* 447 imply a nom. μελεδών. At τ 517 the MSS. are divided. Eust. *ad l.* recognized both declensions.

534. Cf. λ 146.

535. **μάλα** is not elsewhere found with ἕκαστος, but often with πολλοί, πάντες, etc.

536. For the sacrifice of sheep at Delphi cf. Pind. *Pyth.* iii. 27 ἐν δ' ἄρα μηλοδόκῳ Πυθῶνι, Bacchyl. vii. 39 Πυθῶνα μηλοθύταν,

Eur. *Ion* 228; Croesus sent 2,000, Herod. i. 50. The usage produced comment and satire; cf. the lines on Delos 59–60 above, and for Delphi and other temples Eur. *Ion* 323 βωμοί μ' ἔφερβον οὑπιών τ' ἀεὶ ξένος, *IT.* 1274, *Andr.* 1138 βωμοῦ . . . δεξίμηλον ἐσχάραν, *Phoen.* 633 θεῶν τε δεξίμηλ' ἀγάλματα, *Andr.* 1149, Achaeus *frr.* 12, 13, Aristophanes *frr.* 560, 684, and the story of the death of Neoptolemus at Delphi Pind. *Nem.* vii. 50, where the Σ says φασὶ τοῦ Νεοπτολέμου θύοντος τοὺς Δελφοὺς ἁρπάζειν τὰ θύματα ὡς ἔθος αὐτοῖς: cf. also Pindar *paean* vi. 117, Eur. *Orest.* 165, Pherecydes *fr.* 98, Strabo 421, Paus. i. 4. 4, 13. 9, iv. 17. 4, x. 24. 4, Justin xvii. 3. 7, com. anon. Kock iii. *fr.* 460 Δελφοῖσι θύσας αὐτὸς ὀψωνεῖ κρέας, Tryphiodorus 640, Callim. *iamb.* 171; append. prov. 94 (*paroemiogr.* i. 393) Δελφικὴ μάχαιρα, Zenob. 147, Diog. 146 τὸ Αἰσώπειον αἷμα (from Aristotle ἐν τῇ Δελφῶν πολιτείᾳ, ap. Miller *Mélanges* 369; Arist. was perhaps the source of the other stories).

The flesh actually was given to the inhabitants, inscr. Collitz 2652. For the wording cf. Bacchyl. v. 109 σφάζε τε μῆλα, α 92, Eur. *Ion.* 228 ἐπὶ δ' ἀσφάκτοις | μήλοισι δόμων μὴ πάριτ' ἐς μυχόν, *Plisth. fr.* 630 μηλοσφαγεῖ τε δαιμόνων ἐπ' ἐσχάραις.

538. **προφύλαχθε**, 'be sentry to', the first instance of the verb. The omission of the reduplication is not explained. ἄνωχθε somewhat resembles it.

539. Either the end of the line is corrupt or a verse has fallen out. ἰθύν is a good word, 'direction', locally or tropically (Z 79, δ 434, π 304); so the second expedient recommends itself. If the missing line began εἰρομένων the omission would be due to homoearchon, and the sense 'who gather here and ask my direction before everything', i.e. they do not come κατὰ πρῆξιν. The emendations neglected μάλιστα. The rest of the line contained a threat, e.g. ἀλλ' εἴ τι παρεκβήσεσθε θέμιστα, where the rhyme again helped the omission. Misconduct of Delphians to pilgrims is mentioned by Aelian *VH.* xi. 5.

540. ἠέ . . . ἠέ are disjunctive particles, following the verb thus supplied. There follows a prophecy after the event of an infraction by the Cretans of the ordinance, with the result that though they remained priests (as they are 393 sq.) 'other governors

were set over them'. Presumably they taxed pilgrims, as the Crisaeans did in later days (Strabo 418 fin. εὐτυχήσαντες γὰρ οἱ Κρισαῖοι διὰ τὰ ἐκ τῆς Σικελίας καὶ τῆς Ἰταλίας τέλη πικρῶς ἐτελώνουν τοὺς ἐπὶ τὸ ἱερὸν ἀφικνουμένους καὶ παρὰ τὰ προστάγματα τῶν Ἀμφικτυόνων), and the Amphissians after them (καὶ χείρους ἦσαν περὶ τοὺς ξένους τῶν πάλαι Κρισαίων). So the *baroni di campagna* plundered the pilgrims to the threshold of the Apostles and caused the *via Appia antica* to be deserted. We know nothing about the history of Delphi in the eighth century, as Strabo says 420 τὰ πάλαι μὲν ἀγνοεῖται, and his account begins with Acrisius, who organized the Amphictyonic system. This was the result of the first Sacred War, of which the date (B.C. 586) is known (Paus. x. 7. 2, 37, 5). There can be no reference here to these events, which happened a hundred and fifty years after the date of the hymn. A tradition of the original worship remains in Strabo 421 ἀγὼν δὲ ὁ μὲν ἀρχαῖος ἐν Δελφοῖς κιθαρῳδῶν ἐγενήθη παιᾶνα ᾀδόντων εἰς τὸν θεόν· ἔθηκαν δὲ Δελφοί (Paus. x. 7. 2 ἀρχαιότατον δὲ ἀγώνισμα γενέσθαι μνημονεύουσι καὶ ἐφ' ᾧ πρῶτον ἆθλα ἔθεσαν ᾆσαι ὕμνον ἐς τὸν θεόν). The Amphictyony added horse-races, athletics, and instrumental music. It may also be mentioned that in Hesiod *fr.* 99, which comes from the Catalogi and is more or less contemporary with this hymn, Apollo himself is the Delphic prophet, and is said not to understand the will of Zeus which he gives out.

τηΰσιον: Hesych. ταύσιμον· μάταιον. On the derivation see Boisacq.

IV

Hymn to Hermes

1. *Subject.*

For the cult and mythology of Hermes see Farnell v. 1, Nilsson *GF.* 388, P.-R. 385, P.-W. viii. 738. Roscher i. 2342 is useful for the references which it contains, but the discussion is vitiated by the untenable assumption that Hermes is a wind-god.

Many critics have postulated a single theme of which the hymn is the elaboration. Some have supposed it in honour of the God in his thievish aspect; other suggestions have been the cunning of the infant God in acquiring Olympian recognition (Ilgen, Gemoll), or the aspiration of Hermes to the privileges of Apollo (Baumeister). The mere fact that a variety of answers can be defended with equal plausibility suggests that the search for a single theme giving unity to the hymn is a mistake. It has been undertaken owing to an unfounded belief in the unity of each hymn, a theory first started by Matthiae. This canon rests on arbitrary aesthetic opinion. The hymn to Pan (xix) certainly does not conform to it, nor among the longer hymns the hymn to Apollo, unless indeed the old bisection of it into Delian and Pythian is retained. In the hymn to Hermes there is nothing not justified by the Unity of Time. The poet takes, as it were, a 'day in the life of Hermes', and shows how in a few hours the new-born child showed his precocious genius, becoming a musician, a cattle-lifter, a diviner, a match for Apollo, and finally winning recognition and a place in Olympus for his mother and himself.

Hermes, like the trickster Gods of other mythologies (e.g. Loki), is a divine character of great versatility and of many aspects, and so far from its being true that any single one of these is emphasized in the hymn to the exclusion of the rest, only two of his major aspects do not receive recognition. Of these one, which he shares with Apollo, his patronage of the palaestra (see Farnell v. 28), is relatively late; its omission is due to the fact that the hymn was written before organized athletics had gained prominence in Greek life. The other is old, but was appropriate neither to the theme nor the temper of the hymn, namely the function of Hermes as God of the dead and of the underworld In the hymn, on the other hand, we find the God of flocks and herds (567), the rogue and patron of thieves (14, 577), the God of inventions who makes the first fire-drill (108), and fabricates strange shoes to conceal tracks (79), the God of music, inventor of the lyre, the first *keryx* (331), who ordained the ritual of sacrifice (115), the God of luck (the finding of the tortoise is the first *ἕρμαιον*, 35) the giver of profit (*ἐριούνιος* 3, 28, 551), the patron of minor divinations by the lot (552), of skill in bargaining and in forensic eloquence (see P.-W. viii. 782). The principal episodes of the hymn are the theft of the cows, the reconciliation with Apollo and exchange of gifts, the invention of the lyre and the institution of burnt sacrifice.

The idea of a trickster-God is one which appeals to the primitive mind. Among the Greeks, prone to give cleverness more than its due among the talents, this aspect of Hermes is established by the earliest literary evidence (Ω 24, τ 395, Hes. *OD.* 67, 78). Additional force is given to stories of cheating and lying when the rogue is a new-born babe or otherwise insignificant; Andrew Lang well remarks 'the poet chiefly revels in a very familiar subject of savage humour (notably among the Zulus), the extraordinary feats and tricks of a tiny and apparently feeble and helpless person or animal, such as Brer Rabbit' (Lang *Homeric Hymns*, p. 36). Again a very familiar subject of folk-tale is the precocious child, such as Krishna in India, the boy Cadi in the Arabian Nights, the divine child Seragunting among the Dyaks, Vali in Norse legend, who goes out to avenge the death of Balder the first night after his birth (see Crooke *Folk-lore* xi. 9. This idea occurs elsewhere in Greek mythology, see on 214 and *h.* iii. 127). There is nothing therefore in the theme of the quick-witted infant rogue (which is found in primitive societies elsewhere and is old in Greece) to necessitate a late dating of the hymn. Nor is the burlesque tone other than primitive. It occurs frequently in folk-tale and it early made contribution to Greek mythology (e.g. the legends of Heracles, on which see Nilsson *Mycenaean Origin of Greek Mythology* 202). The over-ingenious efforts of Eitrem (*Philologus* lxv. 275), who sees sophisticated humour in the hymn, which he assigns to the fifth century B.C. and endeavours to interpret in terms of Aristophanic comedy, are based upon a misapprehension. There is an element in common between the temper of the hymn and that of Old Comedy, but it consists in the circumstance that both were written by Greeks. The humorous attitude towards divine persons in the hymn is an earlier manifestation of the same national temperament.

The theft of the cattle is followed by a contest of litigious minds, and the reconciliation of Hermes and Apollo by an exchange of gifts. This supplies a mythological explanation of the many points of contact between Hermes and Apollo. Both were patrons of flocks and herds (Apollo rather God of cattle, Hermes of sheep). Both were Gods of music, both of divination, though in these two fields Hermes rather represented the humbler forms of art, in music the shepherd's pipe and the house-lyre rather than concert-instruments, and in divination the simpler modes of telling the future by fortuitous utterances or the chances of the lot.[1] Both as patrons of youth became patrons of the palaestra and athletic contests. Both were guardians of the house, in front of which stood images of Hermes Pylaeus and Apollo Agyieus (see Farnell v. 19). In mythology the two Gods were rivals for Akakallis (Σ Ap. Rh. iv. 149). In many cults they were associated or received joint honours, and they frequently appeared together in art (see reff. P.-W. ii. 37, viii. 781).

2. *The theft of the cows of Apollo.*

The myth was very ancient, and by the 'solar' school of mythologists was assigned to the stock of Indo-European stories belonging to the undivided Aryan race. (Compare the Vedic parallel, in which Ahi steals the cattle of Indra, P.-R. 394 n. 1. For representations of the theft in art see Roscher i. 2429.) It is known to have been related by Hesiod in the Μεγάλαι Ἠοῖαι, but no fragment is preserved. Alcaeus handled the same story in a hymn to Hermes, of which only one stanza is extant (*fr.* 5; cf. Horace *Od.* i. 10).

Since the first edition of this book about 400 lines of a satyr-play by Sophocles called Ἰχνευταί have been published by A. S. Hunt from a papyrus of s. ii. p. C. See *Oxyrhynchus papyri* ix, no. 1174, and the reprint with commentary by A. C. Pearson *Fragments of Sophocles* i. 224 sq. (where the literature down to 1917 is referred to). It may be said at once that the *Ichneutae* throws no light on the hymn, and the account of the events

[1] Apollo did not completely surrender these minor modes of divination. For *thrioboly* at Delphi see on 552, on Apollo as patron of *kledones* at Thebes Paus. ix. 11. 7.

it gives differs from the Homeric and agrees more with that of Apollodorus. How much Sophocles invented, how much he took from Hesiod's Ἠοῖαι and the hymn of Alcaeus we cannot tell. The satyr-play is about as near to the hymn as the *Cyclops* is to the *Odyssey*. The differences are, to quote Mr. Pearson (p. 226), '(1) the theft of the cows here [in the play] precedes, but in Homer follows, the invention of the lyre: (2) the cows are concealed on Mt. Cyllene itself and not in the neighbourhood of Triphylian Pylos: (3) Cyllene [a nymph] and not Maia has charge of the infant: (4) the informer, to whom later writers gave the name of Battus, is displaced by the satyrs, an essential modification in view of the dramatic requirements'. The papyrus ends before Apollo is informed of the discovery of his oxen, and we therefore lose its aid at the moment when it might have been of use. There are verbal coincidences between the two documents collected by Pearson, p. 228, but they come to little.

In later Greek the most important version of the myth is in Apollodorus iii. 10. 2. He presents an account much resembling the hymn. The events are the same though not in the same order. He differs from the hymn in the following respects: (1) Hermes eats some of the flesh: τὰς μὲν βύρσας πέτραις καθήλωσε, τῶν δὲ κρεῶν τὰ μὲν κατηνάλωσεν ἑψήσας, τὰ δὲ κατέκαυσε (2) Hermes steals the cows before he finds the tortoise. He makes the strings of the lyre ἐξ ὧν ἔθυσε βοῶν, not from sheep-gut, as in the hymn. (3) Apollo inquires at Pylos, not Onchestus. (4) Apollo discovers the thief ἐκ μαντικῆς. (5) Maia shows Hermes to Apollo. (6) Apollo desires the σῦριγξ as well as the lyre, and takes it in exchange for ἡ διὰ ψήφων μαντική.

Apollodorus names no authority, and how much he owed to the hymn is disputed. The general view was that he used the hymn and supplemented it from an unknown source. This source is now obvious. He is nearer in several respects to Sophocles than he is to the hymn.

The version of Antoninus Liberalis 23 is confined to the incident of Battus. Hermes steals twelve πόρτιες, a hundred βόες ἄζυγες and a bull from Apollo, and ties branches (ὕλη) to the tail of each, ὡς ἂν τὰ ἴχνη τῶν βοῶν ἀφανίσῃ. Battus, who was paid by Hermes not to tell, proved false and was changed into a stone. Ovid *Met.* ii. 676 and Philostratus *Imag.* 26 mention the story. The popularity of the myth is shown by the list of sources quoted by Antoninus: Νίκανδρος ἑτεροιουμένων α', Ἡσίοδος ἐν μεγάλαις Ἠοίαις (*fr.* 153), Διδύμαρχος Μεταμορφώσεων γ', Ἀντίγονος ἐν ταῖς Ἀλλοιώσεσι, καὶ Ἀπολλώνιος ὁ Ῥόδιος ἐν ἐπιγράμμασιν on the authority of Pamphilus ἐν α'. The geographer Philostephanus, a disciple of Callimachus, dealt with the subject in his περὶ Κυλλήνης (*FHG.* iii. 28), a book which might have given us much information. Another Alexandrian, Eratosthenes (doubtless ἐν τῷ Ἑρμῇ, Σ Ap. Rh. iii. 802, where φωρίαμος is derived from φῶρ) narrated the birth of Hermes and his theft of his mother's and her sister's clothing (Σ Ω 24), and interpreted the Homeric Ἑρμείας ἀκάκητα. Nonnus i. 337–40 has a brief allusion to the theft and the exchange. The hypothesis to the Pythian odes (Drachmann ii, p. 1) contains a rationalizing account: ἔρχεται τοίνυν εἰς Δελφοὺς Ἀπόλλων Πύθωνι τὰς βοῦς νέμων, Ἑρμῆς δὲ χέλυν εὑρὼν τετράχορδον λίνα ἀντὶ χορδῶν ἐνημμένην ἐπειδὴ οὔπω τῶν νεύρων ἡ χρῆσις εὕρητο, καὶ ἁλοὺς τὰς Ἀπόλλωνος βοῦς κλέπτων, ἀντὶ τῆς κλοπῆς τὴν χέλυν δίδωσι τῷ Ἀπόλλωνι, λαβὼν παρ' αὐτοῦ τὰ κηρύκια κτλ. The λίνα explain Λίνος (p. 2). Cf. also Σ Dion. Thrac. *an. Bekk.* ii. 752. 10 εἴρηται δὲ λύρα λύτρα τις οὖσα· φασὶ γὰρ ὅτι ποτὲ Ἑρμῆς ἐν Ἀρκαδίᾳ ἀναστρεφόμενος εὗρε χελώνην καὶ διακόψας ἐποίησε κοιλίαν λύρας. ἡνίκα δὲ τοῦ Ἡλίου βοῦς κλέψαι ἠβουλήθη καὶ διὰ τὸ μαντικὸν τοῦ θεοῦ οὐ δεδύνητο, ἀνελήφθη. εἰδὼς δὲ καὶ τοῦ θεοῦ τὸ μουσικὸν δέδωκεν ὑπὲρ ἑαυτοῦ τὴν λύραν λύτρον καὶ ἠλευθερώθη τοῦ ἐγκλήματος. Cf. also Lact. Plac. *in Ovid. Met.* ii. 11. Cumont, *Les mystères de Mithra* 1913, 135, draws a parallel to Mithras βουκλόπος, wrongly it would seem.

The geography of the several versions of the raid is different. In the hymn Hermes drives the oxen from Pieria (70, 85, 191) along a sandy sea-beach (79, 341); when this was passed and hard earth began (354), he came to Onchestus (88, 186), whence 'over many dark hills and windy valleys and blooming plains' he came to the river Alpheus (101, 139, 398), where the oxen of themselves went to the stall or cave (401) and the troughs. In the *Ichneutae* the passage (20–3) is fragmentary: what is preserved (ε]πειτα [δε | τ]α Θεσσαλων ..... ε] πετου θ[ην] | Βοιωτιας τε γ[ης .....]ς πολεις, and v. 24]ς Δωρικο[ ) does not contradict the hymn. Antoninus, however, gives a long itinerary: Apollo being in Magnesia, Hermes attacked his herd, *αἳ δὲ ἐνέμοντο ἵναπερ ἦσαν αἱ Ἀδμήτου βόες* (sc. at Perea, where Admetus' son Eumelus kept his horses B 766). He drove them *διά τε Πελασγῶν* (sc. Pelasgiotis) *καὶ δι' Ἀχαίας τῆς Φθιώτιδος καὶ διὰ Λοκρίδος καὶ Βοιωτίας καὶ Μεγάριδος, καὶ ἐντεῦθεν εἰς Πελοπόννησον διὰ Κορίνθου καὶ Λαρίσης* [? Argos] *ἄχρι Τεγέας, καὶ ἐντεῦθεν παρὰ τὸ Λύκαιον ὄρος ἐπορεύετο καὶ παρὰ τὸ Μαινάλιον καὶ τὰς λεγομένας Βάττου σκοπιάς.* Battus promised silence, *ἐπεὶ δὲ αὐτὰς Ἑρμῆς ἔκρυψεν ἐν τῷ πρηῶνι παρὰ τὸ Κορυφάσιον εἰς τὸ σπήλαιον εἰσελάσας ἄντικρυς Ἰταλίας καὶ Σικελίας* (Methone was a frequent port of call), he returned to Battus and, finding him false, turned him into stone.

In this account also the earlier part does not differ from the hymn, except that the place where the cows were kept is defined as *ἵναπερ ἦσαν αἱ Ἀδμήτου βόες.* Admetus was king of Pherae, Boebe, Glaphyrae, and Iolcus (B 711); his son kept his horses, as was said above, at a place called in the Homeric vulgate Pieria, but which from some manuscripts, ancient testimony, and an inscription is known to have been called *Πηρείη.* Therefore it is a possible conclusion that as *Πιερίῃ* (and other forms) overlaid *Πηρείῃ* in the *Iliad*, Pieria in the hymn is unoriginal also. The discrepancies in the later part of the journey are even more striking: there is no mention of Onchestus, the episode is transferred to the *Βάττου σκοπιαί* near Maenalus in Arcadia, and the cave where the oxen are stowed is carefully defined as at Coryphasium (i.e. at the Messenian Pylos). This last variation is natural, seeing that as early as about 500 B.C. the existence of the Triphylian Pylos was forgotten (see on *h. Apoll.* 424). The view, therefore, that an actual cave at Coryphasium contained stalactites resembling hides (O. Müller in *Hyperbor.-Röm. Stud.* p. 310 quoted by Baumeister: we have not seen the book) falls to the ground.[1] Hermes' route was by the sea-shore as far as

[1] The cave is described by Frazer on Paus. iv. 36. 2, and the phenomenon is known; in the caves at Cheddar there is a stalagmitic formation which closely resembles a curtain; at Adelsberg (Austria) there are stalactites

possible, i.e. from Olympus (if we keep Pieria; sand under Olympus is testified to by Polyb. iii. 55, Leake *NG.* iii. 1. 30) or Perea along the gulf of Volo past the Spercheus as far as where the road turned away into Boeotia: here 'on the hard ground' the track was lost (353), and the old man at Onchestus had to enlighten Apollo; at Pylos there was once more sand and therefore footprints (218). There was a cave at Samos belonging to the Atlantids, Strabo 346, and another belonging to the Ἀνιγρίδες, Paus. v. 11. 5; there were many Ἑρμεῖα about the mouth of the Alpheus, Strabo 343. At Lepreum (Paus. v. 5. 5) was the tomb of Caucon, τούτῳ δὲ καὶ ἐπίθημα ἄνδρα ἐπεῖναι λύραν ἔχοντα. This may be an echo of the story. Oxen were driven by the same route by a Pylian prophet, τὰν ἀγέλαν χὡ μάντις ἀπ' Ὄθρυος ἆγε Μελάμπους ἐς Πύλον, Theocr. iii. 42, *o* 225 sq.; the cave where he stalled them was shown at the Elean Pylos, Paus. iv. 36. 3.

3. *Place of Composition.*

There is no tradition on the subject. The dialect shows more singular forms than that of the other hymns, but without a definite bearing. See Introduction, p. cvii. Boeotian influence is suggested by ἀθρόᾶς 106, the elision of ι in περ' ἰγνύσι 152, θᾶττον 255, perhaps φύζαν 114, οὔ χ' 284 (see note); Euboean perhaps by φύζαν 114 and θεμούς (if this emendation for θεούς is accepted) 531. This would agree with the numerous coincidences with Hesiod (10, 19, 30, 36, 67, 76, 80, 98, 106, 110, 120, 124, 236, 243, 415). Fick *BB.* xxii. 272 called the author a Euboean Ionian.

On the other hand οὔσας 106, φιλῶ 382, ἀντιτοροῦντα 283, ὄρῃ 95, ἀπονοσφισθῶσι 562, ἐδύνω 405, ἔρχῃ 156, seem late: ἐμάρανε 140 is un-Ionic. But our knowledge of the early history of the Greek dialects is almost non-existent, and it is impossible to say when or where these forms began.

The part played in the hymn by Onchestus, which does not

in form of drapery. However, Pausanias *l.c.* § 5 admits the country is not suitable for cattle. The cave is mentioned without qualification Orph. *Lithica* 18 and 55. Later accounts, as in Acron on Horace *carm.* i. 10, combined the story with Apollo's penance, which consisted in herding Admetus' cattle.

appear in the other versions, suggests the Hesiodic school; the legal usage in 372 points nowhere in particular.

4. *Date.*

The date is equally uncertain. The evidence of the digamma (Introduction, p. civ.) would make this hymn later than the other three long ones. As Hermann (*Orph.* p. 689) and Baumeister observed, there is no living digamma, though hiatus often remains owing to the disappearance of the sound. Cf. Eberhard *die Sprache der hom. Hymnen* ii, p. 34 sq., and n. on 92.

Definite evidence has been found in the mention of the seven-stringed cithara (51), the invention of which is often ascribed to Terpander (who died, an old man, ol. 26 = 676 B.C.). This ascription, however, is apocryphal, and the tale, like others of the same type, has no evidential value at all (see P.-W. xiii. 2482). That the seven-stringed lyre was in use in Crete in the Bronze Age is shown by the Hagia Triada sarcophagus; and as Gemoll remarks (p. 193), the writer could not have attributed the seven strings to Hermes had not the cithara been long established in that form.

Other factors in the date may be derived from two different sources.

The Pylos to which Hermes drives the cattle is the Alphean or Triphylian Pylos (398). Now it is common knowledge that, in the later Greek period, of the three Pyloses only two were left, the Elean and the Messenian, and the Homeric or Nestorian Pylos was claimed by both (see on the whole subject the note on *h. Apoll.* 419). Accordingly if the period at which the Triphylian Pylos was forgotten can be found, a *terminus ad quem* would seem to be provided for this hymn. Strabo 355 says that at the end of the last Messenian war (which took place in the seventh century) συνέπραξαν καὶ οἱ Λακεδαιμόνιοι μετὰ τὴν ἐσχάτην κατάλυσιν τῶν Μεσσηνίων συμμαχήσασιν αὐτοῖς [τοῖς Ἠλείοις] τἀναντία τῶν Νέστορος ἀπογόνων καὶ τῶν Ἀρκάδων, συμπολεμησάντων τοῖς Μεσσηνίοις, καὶ ἐπὶ τοσοῦτόν γε συνέπραξαν ὥστε τὴν χώραν ἅπασαν τὴν μέχρι Μεσσήνης Ἠλείαν ῥηθῆναι καὶ διαμεῖναι μέχρι νῦν, Πισατῶν δὲ καὶ Τριφυλίων καὶ Καυκώνων μηδ' ὄνομα λειφθῆναι. καὶ αὐτὸν δὲ τὸν Πύλον τὸν ἠμαθόεντα εἰς τὸ Λέπρεον συνῴκισαν, χαριζόμενοι τοῖς Λεπρεάταις κρατήσασι πολέμῳ, καὶ ἄλλας πολλὰς τῶν κατοικιῶν κατέστασαν. Pylos and all but all the other Homeric Triphylian villages disappeared at this moment.

The same result comes from the story of the Minyae in Herodotus iv. 148; he says οἱ γὰρ πλεῦνες αὐτῶν ἐτράποντο ἐς τοὺς Παρωρεάτας καὶ Καύκωνας, τούτους δὲ ἐξελάσαντες ἐκ τῆς χώρης σφέας αὐτοὺς ἓξ μοίρας διεῖλον, καὶ ἔπειτα ἔκτισαν πόλιας τάσδε ἐν αὐτοῖσι, Λέπρεον Μακίστιον Φρίξας Πύργον Ἔπιον Νούδιον. τουτέων δὲ τὰς πλεῦνας ἐπ' ἐμέο Ἠλεῖοι ἐπόρθησαν. Of these six κατοικίαι only one, Ἔπιον, perhaps corresponds to the Homeric Αἶπυ. The rest are new. Pylos, Arene, etc., are not mentioned. The events in Herodotus lead up to the colonization of Cyrene, which took place in 640–631 B.C.

Further, in the story of Rhadine in Stesichorus *fr.* 44 the heroine sails from Samos (the same as Samicum) for Corinth. This place, therefore, was alive as a port in Stesichorus' time (flor. 611 B.C.). On the other hand Pisander the poet, whose floruit according to some was 648 B.C., identified the Homeric Ἀρήνη with Ἔρανα in Messenia (Σ Ap. Rh. i. 471), and Pindar *Pyth.* v. 94 makes Pylos = Messenia.

We see, therefore, that the heroic series of hamlets and ports disappeared from the world in the seventh century, and had a precarious existence with the poets between 648 and 611. The hymn to Hermes, therefore, in which the coast south of the Alpheus is a real place to which cattle from north Greece might naturally be driven, is not later than the seventh century.

Further, the hymn does not approach the childishness of the *Batrachomyomachia* (attributed to Pigres about 480 B.C. by Plutarch and Suidas), nor to the comic effects of fourth-century parody. Still less is it Alexandrian. It is excellent racy literature of an early period, and its free cynical style makes it unique. The moral tone is perhaps low judged by modern feeling, but not as low as that of the Lay of Demodocus (see introd. *h. Aphr.*). The writer is no critic of religion like Euripides, nor scoffer like Lucian. His Hermes is far removed from the diffuse gaiety of the *Ichneutae* or the sorry figure of the *Plutus*.

5. *Influence on later literature.*

The hymn made little or no impression on later literature, and it is rarely quoted even where a reference might be expected. Pausanias, who quotes the hymns to Demeter and Apollo, ignores this one, and referring to the myth of cattle-lifting mentions only Alcaeus (viii. 20. 4). The *Ichneutae* owes little to it. The silence of Apollodorus is still more significant. The account of the invention of the cithara was equally neglected. Euripides speaks of the lyre as the gift of Hermes to Apollo, but it does not follow that he used the hymn (see on 416). In Alexandrian times Aratus and Nicander mention the myth, but their accounts seem independent of the hymn, and the scholia on Nicander do not refer to it. Callimachus, who certainly knew the hymn to Apollo, owes nothing to the style or language of this. The direct citation of a line (51) by Antigonus of Carystus (s. iii–ii B.C.) is exceptional.

6. *State of the text.*

The usages of its language and the absence of similar surviving literature make the hymn very difficult. Several verbal corruptions have taken place. Not one line, however, need be omitted or transposed, and the ingenuity of the commentators, who have been particularly active in dissecting the document, is wasted. In several places the interruption of sense seems to demand small lacunae, a remedy more probable on graphical grounds than assumptions of interpolation or transposition.

(R. = Der homerische Hermeshymnus von L. Radermacher 1931.)

1–9. These lines with a few unimportant variations are the first nine lines of *h.* xviii.

1. Ἑρμῆν: only this contracted form is found in this hymn. It occurs also Υ 72, ε 54, ξ 334, ω 1.

Μαιάδος: so ξ 435, Simon. *fr.* 18, Semon. *fr.* 20, Anacreon 112 etc., Μαίη Hes. *Theog.* 938; Μαῖα is not Homeric except as a v.l. α 38 (R.).

2. Κυλλήνης: for the Cyllenian cult of Hermes see Farnell

v. 2, P.-R. 389, Roscher i. 2342, P.-W. viii. 743, Immerwahr *die Kulte und Myth. Arkad.* i. 73. The theory of the last-mentioned that the Messenian and Elean cult was prior to that of Arcadia is mistaken (Farnell *CR.* x. 256). Though Arcadian Cyllene was generally accepted as the birthplace of the God, other claims were made in Arcadia by Pheneus, where the stream was shown in which the nymphs had washed the infant (Paus. viii. 16. 1), and Daseae, where he was said to have been brought up (*ib.* 36. 10). Outside Arcadia Tanagra, an old and important centre of his cult, claimed that he had been born there on Mt. Kerykion (Paus. ix. 20. 3, 22. 2), and some birth-story seems to have been put forward by Thebes (*ib.* viii. 36. 10) and Olympus (Philostr. *Imag.* 26).

6 = xviii. 6 ἄντρῳ ναιετάουσα παλισκίῳ. ναίειν here governs the accusative, as often in Homer, and ἔσω is to be taken absolutely, 'within', cf. Theocr. *epigr.* xi. 5 ἄντρον (v.l. -ου) ἔσω στείχοντες, and for ἔσω = ἔνδον with a verb of rest N 553, η 13, σ 96, φ 229. Cf. also Herod. v. 103 ἐκπλώσαντες ἔξω τὸν Ἑλλήσποντον, vii. 58 ἔξω τὸν Ἑλλήσποντον πλέων. Zen. on η 13 denied the use.

For caves in these stories cf. *Ichneut.* 264 . . . λήθῃ τῆς βαθυζώνου θεᾶς. | [κατὰ σπέ]ος δὲ παῖδ' ἐφίτυσεν μόνον, Antimachus *fr.* 3 ἄντρον ἐνὶ σκηνῇ τευ μήσατο ὄφρα κεν εἴη | Φοίνικος κούρη κεκυθημένη, ὥς ῥά ἑ μήτις | μηδὲ θεῶν ἄλλος γε παρὲξ φράσσαιτό κεν αὐτοῦ.

7. **νυκτὸς ἀμολγῷ**: meaning and derivation are quite obscure.

8. **ὄφρα**: the sense is obviously 'while', usually expressed by the indicative, often by the subjunctive, here only by the optative.

10. **ἐξετελεῖτο**: the same tense of the same verb A 5, *Cypria fr.* 1. 7, Hes. *Theog.* 1002, *h.* iii. 351.

11. **δ'** marks the apodosis, as in iii. 349; cf. also 108, 116.

μείς: μής was read in the Chia at T 117 and is found in the MSS. O² V¹⁶ ss., and in the Heraclian tables *IG.* xiv. 645. 11, Solmsen *KZ.* xxix. 61.

ἐστήρικτο: T 117 τῇ δ' ἕβδομος ἑστήκει μείς. Moon and month are the same (R.).

12. **εἴς τε φόως ἄγαγεν**: not of the mother: the subject is Zeus, as T 118 ἐκ δ' ἄγαγε πρὸ φόωσδε of Hera interfering at the

birth of Eurystheus. If we insist on Maia being the subject καὶ τότ' ἐγείνατο παῖδα 13 is a tautology.

14. **ἡγήτορ' ὀνείρων**: for Hermes as a dream-god cf. Ap. Rh. iv. 1732, Σ Orph. *Lith.* 20, and see the introduction to *h.* xxix.

15. **ὀπωπητῆρα**: from ὀπωπεῖν: *epigr.* Kaibel 1032 οπωπ[ητηρα, Orph. *Arg.* 183, 1022. The thief-god is ἡμερόκοιτος (Hes. *OD.* 603).

πυληδόκον: only here: cf. ὁδοιδόκος Dio Prus. iv. 95, θεαραδόκος and καυλοδόκος in the lexx.

17. **ἐγκιθάριζεν** implies an audience, viz. Maia and her women (ἀμφίπολοι 60); so *h.* iii. 201 of Apollo 'playing among' the Gods. To make μέσῳ ἤματι depend on the verb (with LS. and R.) seems singular.

19. i.e. the fourth of the month. B. noticed that the month is here bipartite; the triple division into decades would require πρώτῃ for προτέρῃ. Cf. Hes. *OD.* 785 ἡ πρώτη ἕκτη. This, however, has no special significance, for Hesiod uses quite indifferently three methods of numeration, (1) by the days of the month up to thirty, (2) the tripartite division into decades, (3) the dual division of waxing and waning moons. In Hesiod the fourth and seventh are lucky days, as are the fourth and seventh in each decade. The seventh is definitely associated with the birth of Apollo, but the fourth is not in Hesiod explicitly associated with Hermes, and whether it was originally a lucky day and so associated with the birth of Hermes, or the belief that the God was born on that day gave it its lucky character, is an insoluble problem. The polemical tone of Hesiod *OD.* 819 suggests that the luckiness of four was not then universally accepted, like that of seven, and there is evidence of the contrary view that the fourth was unlucky (see Halliday *Folk-lore* xli. 143). However that may be, in historical times the fourth of the month was lucky, and it was Hermes' birthday (Plut. *mor.* 738 F). Cakes were regularly offered to Hermes upon the fourth (Ar. *Plutus* 1126 and Σ), upon the fourth the superstitious man spent the day crowning his Hermaphrodites (Theophrastus *char.* xvi. 10). According to Proclus (on Hes. *OD.* 798) Aphrodite and Hermes were both born upon the lucky fourth, which was διὰ

τοῦτο πρὸς συνουσίαν ἐπιτηδεία. (This has a bearing on the difficult question of the origin of Hermaphroditus, but it is obscured by the fact that neo-Platonic doctrine here seems to disagree with Pythagorean, see Halliday *l.c.*) On the fourth in historical times it would seem to have been the custom to hold convivial parties with jocular improvisations (see on 55, 56). Again we find Hesiod an uncertain guide; the analogous social entertainments in the *Works and Days* (788) take place on the sixth of the month.

Why the fourth was specially lucky, or why, if this is the source of its luckiness, Hermes was born upon the fourth, is unknown. The accumulation of references by Roscher i. 2370, 2386 to show that the fourth day prognosticates the weather for the rest of the month are irrelevant, since his argument rests upon the absurd assumption that Hermes was a wind-god. Baumeister's theory of a connexion between the God's birthday on the fourth and the τετράγωνον σχῆμα of Hermes is fanciful.

21. ἱερῷ ἐνὶ λίκνῳ: *Ichneut.* 269 πρὸς σπ]αργάνοις μένουσα λικνῖτιν τροφήν. The infant Hermes sitting up in the *liknon* looking at the stolen cows is represented on a r. f. *kylix* in the Vatican (*JHS.* xxiii. 294, fig. 1). For the use of the *liknon* as a cradle and the cult of Dionysus Liknotes see J. E. Harrison *l.c.* 292.

24. The *Ichneutae*, Eratosthenes *Catast.* 24, and Apollod. iii. 10. 2 make the episode of the tortoise follow the theft of the cows, which provided Hermes with strings for his lyre: καὶ εὑρίσκει πρὸ τοῦ ἄντρου νεμομένην χελώνην. ταύτην ἐκκαθάρας εἰς τὸ κύτος χορδὰς ἐντείνας ἐξ ὧν ἔθυσε βοῶν καὶ ἐργασαμένος λύραν εὗρε καὶ πλῆκτρον. According to Paus. viii. 17. 5 the tortoise was found on Chelydorea, a mountain near Cyllene; but this is merely an inference from the name, like Κηρύκιον and Πόλος at Tanagra (*id.* ix. 20. 3), and the etymology of Tanagra itself. Tortoises were actually found at Parthenius and Soron, Paus. viii. 23. 9. In Lucian *dial. deor.* 7. 4 the tortoise is dead: it appears in the Egyptian version in Isidore iii. 22. 8.

Polyphemus in Lucian *dial. mar.* 1. 4 used a κρανίον ἐλάφου.

25. The repetition in 24, 25 is characteristic of the writer. So

12, 13. For the expression cf. the hymn of the Delphian Boeo (Paus. x. 5. 7) πρῶτος δ' ἀρχαίων ὕμνων τεκτάνατ' ἀοιδάν (of Olen), Sappho iv. 1. 12 Lobel ἄοιδον λιγύραν χελύνναν, *fr.* 1 (45 Bergk) ἄγε χέλυ δῖα μοι λέγε φωνάεσσα δὲ γίνεο, Nicander *Alex.* 560 (quoted on 47), Menander *fr.* 314 ἑπτ]άφωνε οὐρεία χέλυς, Hesych. χελοπὴ κιθάρα· ἀπὸ γὰρ ὀστράκων χελώνης ἡ κιθάρα γίνεται.

26. **ἐπ' αὐλείῃσι θύρῃσι** = σ 239, ψ 49. Maia's cave is fitted up like an Homeric house: cf. μεγάροιο 146, προθύροιο 158, μεγάλοιο δόμοιο 246. It has an αὐλή in front like the cave of Polyphemus ι 462.

27. Cf. Ξ 347 νεοθηλέα ποίην.

28. **σαῦλα**: of a horse, Simon. Amorg. 18 καὶ σαῦλα βαίνων ἵππος ὡς κορωνίης: of women, Anacr. 55 Διονύσου σαῦλαι Βασσαρίδες, so Eur. *Cycl.* 40 ἀοιδαῖς βαρβίτων σαυλούμενοι, Aristoph. *Vesp.* 1173 σαυλοπρωκτιᾶν, *fr.* 624 διασαυλούμενον: 'mincing', of the deliberate movement of a tortoise's feet: Hesych. σαῦλα· κοῦφα, ἥσυχα, τρυφερά.

30. **σύμβολον**: an omen which a person meets on his road. See Bouché-Leclercq, *Hist. de la Divination* i. 121, Halliday *Greek Divination* 173, Pearson on Soph. *fr.* 148. Hermes, God of luck, found the first ἕρμαιον. On these see P.-R. 403 n. 3.

οὐκ ὀνοτάζω, sc. δέχομαι: for the verb cf. Hes. *OD.* 256, Aesch. *Suppl.* 11 (middle), ὀνοτα⟨σ⟩τόν *h.* v. 254. On the acceptance of oracles see Halliday *l.c.* 47.

31. **φυὴν ἐρόεσσα**: of course ironical. The appearance of a live tortoise is described Philostr. *imag.* 10 ἡ χέλυς μέλαινα μέν, διηκρίβωται δὲ κατὰ τὴν φύσιν καὶ λαγαροὺς περιβέβληται κύκλους ἄλλον ξυνάπτοντας ἄλλῳ ξανθοῖς τοῖς ὀμφαλοῖς. Cf. Hesych. ὀροφηφόρον· ζῷον πᾶν ὀστρακόδερμον. For modern Greek views of the appearance of a tortoise see R. p. 65.

χοροιτύπε: R. rightly restores the paroxytone, altered by Matthiae: 'that beatest the dance', i.e. marks the time. Though dead the reptile works. For the accent cf. the variants in 56, and n. on xix. 11.

δαιτὸς ἑταίρη: cf. ρ 271 (φόρμιγξ) ἣν ἄρα δαιτὶ θεοὶ ποίησαν ἑταίρην, θ 99 φόρμιγγός θ' ἣ δαιτὶ συνήορός ἐστι θαλείῃ: π]ηκτίδα δ' οὐρανίαν ἑτάρην θαλίης τε χορῶν τε *epigr.* Kaibel 1025⁸, Πανὸς ἑταίρη of the syrinx Nonnus x. 389, of echo Lucian *epigr.* 29, βολβίτου κασιγνήτη Hipponax 70 A, συνέστιε δαιτός *Anth. Pal.* vi. 248. 3, of a lagynus *id.* ix. 229 (ἀρχαίη σύνδειπνε), λιγύφωνον ἑταίρην *infra* 478: νυκτὸς ἑταῖρε *infra* 290 of Hermes: Tryphiodorus 503 νυκτὸς ἑταίρη (ἡσυχίη), Pindar *fr.* 212 κενεοφρόνων ἀνδρῶν ἑταῖρος (φθόνος), Plut. *qu. conv.* 712 F γνωρίμη τῆς δαιτός (κιθάρα).

32, 33. **ἕσσο**: conjectured and given up by Matthiae, was revived by Tyrrell. It suits the tone of the hymn, and might easily have been corrupted, especially in the neighbourhood of ἕσσῃ 34. For the neglected digamma cf. Γ 57 λάϊνον ἕσσο χιτῶνα. The awkward construction induced Hermann to take τόδε = *huc.* καλὸν ἄθυρμα is acc. in apposition with αἰόλ. ὄστρ. The word ὄστρακον occurs in the *Ichneutae* 303 and perh. 307: *ib.* 295 ποικίλῃ δορᾷ. Here καλόν is again ironical.

36 is hyperbatic. The proverb occurs Hes. *OD.* 365; another common to Homer and Hesiod is found ρ 352, *OD.* 317. It is here paradoxical, in keeping with φυὴν ἐρόεσσα. The tortoise supplied many proverbs: Suid. *in* Εἰς λατομίας· ἢ οἶκος φίλος οἶκος ἄριστος (part of this was used by Cicero *ad Att.* xv. 16 a), append. prov. 415 (paroemiogr. i. p. 438), Babrius ed. Crusius p. 226; Plut. *conj. praec.* 142 D τὴν Ἠλείων ὁ Φειδίας Ἀφροδίτην ἐποίησε χελώνην πατοῦσαν, οἰκουρίας σύμβολον ταῖς γυναιξὶ καὶ σιωπῆς, cf. *Is. et Osir.* 75, Aesop. *fab.* 154, Cercidas *fr.* 2 Powell τᾶς ῥικνᾶς χελώνας μναμόνευ'· | οἶκος γὰρ ἄριστος ἀλαθέως καὶ φίλος, *PLG.* iii. 662 χέλει χελώνη τί ποιεῖς ἐν τῷ μέσῳ; The marginal note in some MSS. shows that the reader considered the hymn older than Hesiod.

37. With the line cf. *h.* ii. 230.

ἔχμα is a certain correction: cf. Hesych. αἴχματα· ἔχματα, κωλύματα, Ap. Rh. iv. 201 αἶχμα (with ε written above), Ξ 410 in 'D', Φ 259 in 'O[8]', and the echo (ν)αίχι, ἔχει Callim. *ep.* 30.

For the tortoise as a charm cf. Plin. *NH.* xxxii. 4 *terrestrium* (sc. *testudinum*) *carnes suffitionibus propriae magicisque artibus refutandis et contra venena salutares produntur*: headache, toothache, and other complaints were cured by the blood, flesh, or gall of tortoises (see P.-W. i. 77). These beliefs refer to the reptile when dead; for the protective power of a live tortoise (as here) cf. *Geoponica* i. 14. 8 (from Africanus) where it is a charm against hail; it is carried on its back in the right hand round the vineyard, and left alive in the same position in the centre of the yard.

38. *Ichneutae* 292 καὶ πῶς πίθωμαι τοῦ θανόντος φθέγμα τοιοῦτον βρέμειν; πιθοῦ, θανὼν γὰρ ἔσχε φωνήν, ζῶν δ' ἄναυδος ἦν ὁ θήρ. Pearson *ad loc.* gives a quotation from Pacuvius *Antiope fr.* iv.

41. **ἀναπηλήσας**: in the other accounts a constant moment is the *turning* of the reptile *over*: *Ichneutae* 280 ἐξ ὑπτίας κ[ ]ανήσατο, Babrius 115. 8 ὑπτίην δ' ἄρας, Paul. Aegin. v. 24 ὕπτιον ἀντρέψειν (of the χελώνη θαλασσία), Oppian *Hal.* v. 397, 404 ἀντρέψῃ, Nicander *Ther.* 701

ἤτοι ὅταν βροτολοιγοῦ ὑπὲκ πόντοιο χελώνην
αἰγιαλῶν ἐρύσωσιν ἐπὶ ξερὸν ἀσπαλιῆες
τὴν δ' ἀνακυπώσας κεφαλῆς ἀπὸ θυμὸν ἀράξαι κτλ.

Σ ὁ νοῦς ἅπας οὕτως· ὅταν ἐπὶ τῆς χέρσου τις ἀπὸ τῆς θαλάσσης ἐκβάλῃ χέλυν, ἀνάστρεψον αὐτὴν ὑπτίαν . . . ταύτην ἀνακυπώσας τουτέστιν ὑπτίαν ποιήσας καὶ ἀναστρέψας ἐπὶ νῶτον κτλ. Apostolius 217 of a fox ἀνατρέπει αὐτοὺς καὶ κλίνει ὑπτίους. Demetr. *Hieracosoph.* 27 τοῦ ὀστράκου γυμνωθεῖσαν ὑπτίαν (χελώνην).

This in the present passage is conveyed by ἀναπηλήσας, which must come from ἀναπηλεῖν a by-form of ἀναπάλλειν. Lobeck Ῥηματικόν p. 149 *interdum detractionem liquidae comitatur trope vocalis* θάλλω θηλέω, δάλλει (κακουργεῖ Hesych.) *et* δηλέω, πάλλω πηλέω, *si* ἀναπηλῆσαι *in H. H. in Merc.* 41 *luxando vicinam habet significationem laxandi solvendique.* The meaning here is rather 'toss up, throw up', as of Galba's head, Plut. *Galb.* 27 περιπείραντα περὶ λόγχην καὶ ἀναπήλαντα πρεσβύτου πρόσωπον. An equivalent is ἀνακινεῖν, Herod. iv. 94 ἄλλοι δὲ διαλαβόντες τοῦ ἀποπεμπομένου τὰς χεῖρας καὶ τοὺς πόδας ἀνακινήσαντες αὐτὸν μετέωρον ῥίπτουσι ἐς τὰς λόγχας; Paus. vii. 24. 11 of an earthquake ἀναπάλλειν = ἀνακινοῦσαν *ib.* 12.

The emendations are useless, except perhaps Agar's (ἀπειλήσασα of an intention, Theocr. xxiv. 16); peculiarly absurd is πιλεῖν, 'pound', of a tortoise, notoriously resistant to pressure (κραταιρινοῖο

Herod. i. 47, δυσριγότερος χελώνης Macarius 341 in *Paroemiogr.* ii. 159, Alciphron *fr.* iv. Wagner οἷα πάσχεις μετ' ἐκείνης καθεύδων τῆς χελώνης). πιλεῖν is used of pounding the flesh of a sepia or polypus to make it soft enough to eat (Zenobius 3. 24 ὁ πολύπους θηρευθεὶς τύπτεται πολλάκις πρὸς τὸ πίων γενέσθαι): Plato com. *Phaon fr.* 173. 16

πουλύποδος πλεκτὴ δ' ἂν πιλήσῃς κατὰ καιρὸν
ἑφθὴ τῆς ὀπτῆς ἣν ᾖ μείζων πολὺ κρείττων,

Eubulus *fr.* 150. 7 = Ephippus Γηρυόνῃ *fr.* 3. 10

πιλοῦν τε πολλὰς πλεκτάνας ἐπιστρεφῶς,

Aristophanes Δαιδάλῳ *fr.* 191

πληγαὶ λέγονται πουλύπου πιλουμένου.

The sepia is the food of the people in Mediterranean countries, and is almost inedible unpounded. No one eats a tortoise's inside, and Hermes shows no wish to do so.[1] The smell of roasting meat racked him. The operation of killing the reptile is either omitted with the usual brachylogy (Galen x. 275 al.) or it is covered by ἐξετόρησεν. The real method we learn from Galen xiii. 1022 σφάζεται δὲ ἡ χελώνη κατὰ τὴν κατακλεῖδα καλάμῳ ἀποξανθέντι ἀμφότερα τὰ μέρη.

42. **αἰῶν' ἐξετόρησεν**: 'scooped out' the marrow. For the verb cf. 119, Aratus 269 Ἑρμείας ἐτόρησε, Galen xii. 821 διαστήσας κατατίτρα λεπτῷ τρυπανίῳ. In the other accounts the action is denoted by ἐκκαθάρας (Apollodorus), ἐκδεῖραι (Pausanias): cf. Nicander *Alex.* 56 σαρκὸς νόσφισσε χέλειον, Lucian *dial. mar.* 1. 4 κρανίον ἐλάφου γυμνὸν τῶν σαρκῶν, *ver. hist.* ii. 37 of a colocynth κοιλάναντες αὐτὴν καὶ ἐξελόντες τὴν ἐντεριώνην. In the case of the tortoise its flesh is called by analogy 'marrow'. For αἰών = marrow cf. Hesych. αἰών· . . . τινὲς δὲ τῶν νεωτέρων τὸν νωτιαῖον μυελὸν [μέλος MS., corr. Musurus] ἀπέδωκαν, ὡς Ἱπποκράτης [*Epidem.* vii. 7, p. 705 K.] τὸν αἰῶνά τις νοσήσας ἑβδομαῖος ἀπέθανε, *EM. in v.*, Erotian p. 49 Klein. So it was taken T 27 ἐκ δ' αἰὼν πέφαται (Σ D ἤτοι ἀνῄρηται ὁ βίος . . . ἢ ὡς οἱ γλωσσο-

[1] The proverb would have been a warning: ἢ δεῖ χελώνης κρέα φαγεῖν ἢ μὴ φαγεῖν. See the paroemiographi.

γράφοι αἰὼν ἔφθαρται ὅ ἐστιν ὁ νωτιαῖος μυελός). Pindar *fr.* 111 αἰὼν δὲ δι' ὀστέων ἐραίσθη almost certainly has this meaning, and probably Hippocr. π. ἀγμῶν ii. 21 ἢν σφακελίσῃ τὸν αἰῶνα πάντα ἀντισχεῖν τὰ νόστιμα (though Galen paraphrases it τὸν ὅλον βίον), iii. 268, 291 κίνδυνος ... σφακελίσαντα τὸν αἰῶνα πρήγματα παρέχειν: possibly also ε 152 κατείβετο δὲ γλυκὺς αἰών, Plut. ap. Stob. *ecl.* iii. 6. 53 μεθύουσιν εἰς ἀναισθησίαν, λαγνεύουσιν εἰς αἰῶνα, καθεύδουσιν εἰς ἔργα. It is a case of concrete from abstract, as *vitalia*, 'vitals', and in Italian *vita* = back, waist; for the extension to articles of dress cf. in Greek θώρηξ, ἐπωμίς, and perhaps αἰών itself, Sappho 30, Bacchyl. xvi. 112.

43. For the simile cf. O 80 ὡς δ' ὅτ' ἂν ἀΐξῃ νόος ἀνέρος ὅς τ' ἐπὶ πολλὴν | γαῖαν ἐληλουθὼς φρεσὶ πευκαλίμῃσι νοήσῃ | ἔνθ' εἴην ἢ ἔνθα; for the abbreviated ὡς εἰ ... νόημα η 36, Hes. *Scut.* 222, *h.* iii. 186, 448, Theogn. 985: ἅμα νοήματι Plut. *Alex.* 35, Epicurus ap. DL. x. 48. 2, 61. 23, Artemidorus i. 2, ἅμα νοήσει Dion. Hal. *comp. verb.* 25, θᾶττον νοήματος Aristaenetus i. 5, Longinus iii. 30, θᾶττον πτεροῦ καὶ νοήματος Themistius xviii. 221, τάχιστος νοῦς, διὰ παντὸς γὰρ τρέχει Thales ap. DL. i. 35, πτηνοῦ δίκην Julian *ep.* 183.

44. **θαμιναί** is well established: θαμεινός is recognized by Choeroboscus *epit. Orthogr.* in *an. Ox.* ii. 180. 6, cf. Arcad. 195. 11 (οἱ ποιηταὶ δὲ πολλάκις ἐκτείνουσι): e.g. Nicander *Ther.* 239 αἱ δὲ θαμιναί (χαμηλαί one MS.), Callim. *Aetia* 9. 36 Pf. ᾧ τε θαμινοί. Prose is less cogent, but the MSS. give θαμειναί Xen. *Anab.* iv. 1. 16, θαμινά, -εινά id. *de re equestr.* x. 7, κρανάινα, -ηνα, -εινα id. xii. 12, ὑδατειναί Hipp. *aer.* 15. 19, ὑδατίνους Matro 79, Ἀμαντίνην ᾤκισαν Ὠρικίην ap. Σ Ap. Rh. iv. 1175, Steph. *in* Ἀβαντίς· ἐρεβινθινὸς Διόνυσος com. anon. iii. *fr.* 862 Kock. Ruhnken quoted forms in -ρινος (ὀπωρινός, γυρίνων Aratus 947, ὀρθρινά Ap. Rh. *fr.* 5. 1 Powell), but these are in a different class. Cf. however δωτίνη and perhaps ἐνδίνων Ψ 806, Schulze *qu. ep.* 253.

The stem contains -ε-; cf. θαμέως (Alcaeus 45. 5) as well as θάμα.

45. **ἢ ὅτε**: this reading involves a double comparison to illustrate one aspect, whereas in Homer accumulated similes usually express different pictures or views, e.g. B 144, 455–83, Hes. *Scut.* 402–5. But passages like T 374, Ψ 366, η 36, Ap. Rh.

iv. 877, 1298 (ἢ ὅτε), 1452 (ἢ ὅτε), Quintus x. 66, show that alternative similes can refer to the same aspect.

For the 'twinkling of an eye' cf. 1 Cor. xv. 52 ἐν ῥιπῇ ὀφθαλμοῦ, for the wording Oppian *Cyn.* iii. 3390 ἀπ' ὀφθαλμῶν ἀμαρυγαί, Sappho 27. 18 ἀμάρυγμα.

46. Cf. T 242 αὐτίκ' ἔπειθ' ἅμα μῦθος ἔην τετέλεστο δὲ ἔργον, Ap. Rh. iv. 103 ἔνθ' ἔπος ἠδὲ καὶ ἔργον ὁμοῦ πέλεν ἐσσυμένοισιν, Herod. iii. 134. 6 ταῦτα εἶπε καὶ ἅμα ἔπος τε καὶ ἔργον ἐποίεε, Zenob. 77 ἅμ' ἔπος ἅμ' ἔργον· ἐπὶ τῶν ταχέως καὶ ὀξέως ἀνυομένων.

47–51. Invention of the lyre. See Th. Reinach in Daremberg et Saglio iii. 1438, Abert in P.-W. xiii. 2479. The principal passages on the construction of the lyre in ancient authorities are Sophocles *fr.* 36, 238, 244 (on which see Pearson's notes), Σ Ar. *Ran.* 231, Pollux iv. 62. Greek stringed instruments were of two main types, the λύρα and the κιθάρα, the first an instrument used in education and in the house, the second a concert instrument. In construction the principal differences were that the cithara had a sounding-board made of wood or metal prolonged into its broad arms, which were hollow and resonant, and in fact formed a continuous part of the sounding-board. The lyra on the other hand had a sounding-board constructed of a tortoise-shell (even when another material was used, e.g. box-wood, or in later times ivory, the shape and decoration of the sounding-board imitated the original shell), and the arms were horns or solid wooden rods fastened on to the sounding-board instead of forming its lateral continuations. It is a general view that the cithara was a late development of the lyre, and that it came into use about the time of Pindar. There is, however, no reliable evidence as to the origin and relation of the two types. In Homer two words are used for stringed instruments, φόρμιγξ and κίθαρις. They are probably alternative names for the same instrument (φόρμιγγι λιγείῃ ἱμερόεν κιθάριζε Σ 569); about its construction there is no evidence. In later literature the words φόρμιγξ and κίθαρις belong solely to poetic diction. λύρη, which occurs once in the hymn (423), is not Homeric. The earliest other literary reference for the word is Archilochus *fr.* 51, 47 Diehl. Some confusion has been caused about the construction of the lyre by variation in the use of technical terms. Thus the bridge, which was originally made of reed but afterwards of horn, was called both *δόναξ* and *κέρας*. The arms of wood or horn were called *πήχεις* and *ἀγκῶνες*, or often *κέρατα*.

The account of the making of the lyre in the hymn is quite straightforward.

For Hermes' invention cf. the fragments *Ichneutae* 302 sqq., Nicand. *Alex.* 560 *ἄλλοτε δ' οὐρείης κυτισηνόμου, ἥν τ' ἀκάκητα | αὐδήεσσαν ἔθηκεν ἀναύδητόν περ ἐοῦσαν | Ἑρμείης. σαρκὸς γὰρ ἀπ' οὖν νόσφισσε χέλειον | αἰόλον, ἀγκῶνας δὲ δύω παρετείνατο πέζαις*, Arat. *Phoen.* 268 *καὶ χέλυς ἥ τ' ὀλίγη, τὴν γάρ τ' ἔτι καὶ παρὰ λίκνῳ | Ἑρμείας ἐτόρησε, λύρην δέ μιν εἶπε λέγεσθαι.* Neither account need have been taken from the hymn, and the versions in Lucian *dial. deor.* vii and Orpheus *Arg.* 383, as Apollo there plays on the lyre before Hermes finds the tortoise (cf. Paus. iv. 26. 7, Diod. iv. 59), are independent. Other variations are to be found in Eratosth. *Catast.* 24, Philostr. *Imag.* 10, Bion ix. 8 *ὡς χέλυν Ἑρμάων, κίθαριν ὡς ἄνυσ' Ἀπόλλων*: in Callim. *Del.* 253 Apollo invents the seven-stringed lyre (cf. also Diod. v. 75, Macrob. i. 19. 15). For representations in art see Roscher i. 2432. Nicomachus *excerpta* 1 gives the succession of the lyre from Hermes to Terpander.

48. **πειρήνας διὰ νῶτα διὰ ῥινοῖο χελώνης.** The appearance of two identical prepositions with different cases in one line seemed awkward, and in the 1911 text *κατὰ νῶτα* was printed on the supposition that the second *διά* had expelled *κατά* (as in K 54, 141, 298), to mean 'behind', as *κατὰ νῶτον* Hes. *Scut.* 167, *κατὰ πυθμένα τρήσειν* Hippocr. ii. 379. 8. (R. found no difficulty in the two *διά*.) But *πειρήνας διά* appears to be a tmesis for *διαπειρήνας*, and this removes the difficulty. For the reversed or post-positive tmesis see *CQ.* 1932. 85, e.g. P 522 *ἶνα τάμῃ διὰ πᾶσαν*, M 195, Ξ 7 *θερμήνῃ καὶ λούσῃ ἄπο βρότον*, O 343 *ἐνάριζον ἄπ' ἔντεα*, P 91 *εἰ μέν κε λίπω κάτα τεύχεα καλά*, Φ 57, ι 17 *φυγὼν ὕπο νηλεὲς ἦμαρ*, σ 257 *λιπὼν κάτα πατρίδα γαῖαν*, Hesiod. *fr.* 96. 59 *μεῖξαι κάτ' ἀπείρονα γαῖαν.* Compounds of *δια-* usually govern an accusative, e.g. 146, 421, *h. Apoll.* 254.

The verb *διαπε(ι)ραίνω* exists tropically in Attic, literally in

Manetho *Apotel.* ii. 106 οἱ δὲ δύω τοί πέρ τε πόλῳ διαπειραίνουσι, Aretaeus ii. 8. 2 περήνασα and διαπερήνασα c. acc. = 'piercing'. περαίνω act. appears to mean primarily 'pierce, thrust, push':[1] 133 περῆν' ἱερῆς κατὰ δειρῆς, Hippocr. iii. 343. 10 K. οὐδὲν γὰρ χαλεπώτερον ἤπερ προβάτου διειρομένου τὸν δάκτυλον μεταξὺ τοῦ δέρματος καὶ τῆς σαρκὸς περαίνειν, where περαίνειν = ὦσαι in 342. 1 μέσον τὸν σπόγγον ὦσαι κατὰ τῆς ἕδρης ὡς προσωτάτω; perhaps in Aratus 24 καί μιν [τὸν οὐρανὸν] πειραίνουσι δύω πόλοι ἀμφοτέρωθεν, the poles pierce the firmament (cf. ii. 470 τρυπῆσαι πέρην τρυπάνῳ περητηρίῳ). Moreover the passages given by LS[9]. under II belong to this verb (= τρυπᾶν): cf. Demetr. ap. Stob. *ecl.* iii. 8. 20, Dion. Hal. π. σχημ. ii. 11, often in Artemidorus. διὰ ῥινοῖο is clearly authentic, Oppian *Cyn.* iv. 390 διὰ ῥινοῖο τέτανται.

51. On Antigonus' variant θηλυτέρων see Introd. p. lxvii. It is an easy extension of the Homeric use to apply it to animals. συμφώνους in the literal sense occurs here for the first time, next in *Ichneutae* 319, *Birds* 221, 659, Ion of Chios 3. 2; the verb in Machaon com. *fr.* 2. 10. Apollodorus substituted the entrails of the cows, see on 24.

The invention of seven strings is attributed to Hermes by Lucian (*dial. deor.* vii. 4) and Ovid (*Fasti* v. 106), to Orpheus by Lucian *astrol.* 10, to Apollo by Callim. *Del.* 253, to Amphion by Paus. ix. 5. 7. According to Timotheus *Persae* 233 Orpheus invented the χέλυς, Terpander the ten-stringed lyre. Diodorus v. 75. 3 harmonizes.

52. **αὐτὰρ ἐπεὶ δὴ τεῦξε** = Σ 609, θ 276. φέρων is expletive, Hermes did not move his instrument when he had made it. For the use cf. 159, Soph. *fr.* 324, Theocr. xxiv. 94, with Herod. viii. 87, Aeschin. iii. 82 in K.-G. ii. p. 86 n. 6; often in later Greek. In 63 the participle has its natural force.

53, 54. Cf. 419, 420 and 501, 502.

53. μέρος is not Homeric, and in the two places where the phrase recurs (419, 501) the MSS. have μέλος; this therefore has the balance of evidence. Strabo 83 in an obscure note distinguishes between the two words (καθάπερ ἡ κατὰ μέλος τομὴ τῆς

[1] Hesych. περαίνει· ἐπὶ πέρας ἄγει, πληροῖ, ἀνύει, though tropical, shows the original meaning. Cf. also Aelian NA. xi. 15 δι' ἀμφοτέρων θάτερον πείρας τοῖν κεράτοιν.

ἄλλως κατὰ μέρος διαφέρει). On the lengthening see Hartel *Hom. Stud.* 35, 38, Eberhard *Metr. Beob.* ii. 26.

54. **σμερδαλέον**: so all the MSS. in 420, and M in 502 (the rest ἱμερόεν), often with verbs of sound (see the passages in Ebeling). On the derivation and primitive meaning see Boisacq.

55. **ἠύτε**, 'even as', i.e. as readily as. The words ἠύτε . . . κερτομέουσιν are an hyperbaton. We may perhaps think of the meetings sacred to Hermes on the fourth of the month; Hesych. τετραδισταί· σύνοδος νέων συνήθων κατὰ τετράδα γινομένη.

56. **παραιβόλα**: usually considered equivalent to παραβλήδην 'sidelong, malicious' (Δ 6 κερτομίοις ἐπέεσσι παραβλήδην ἀγορεύων, Ap. Rh. ii. 60, 448, iii. 107), but better taken by R. as = παράβολα, 'bold, impudent', of the repartees at the θαλίαι. For the custom the editors compare Pind. *Ol.* i. 22, Herod. vi. 129, Ap. Rh. i. 458 (quoted on 454).

58. Unless we can either (i) call ὅν an internal accusative with ὠρίζεσκον, sc. ὄαρον, cl. *h.* xxiii. 3 ὀάρους ὀαρίζει, and further support the omission of the masculine accusative by the proverbs ὁ λαγὼς τὸν περὶ τῶν τριχῶν τρέχει sc. δρόμον ap. Zenob. iv. 85, Diogen. vi. 5, Plut. *non posse suaviter* c. 2 καὶ τὸν περὶ τῶν κρεῶν ἐπάξειν, Synesius *ep.* 5 τὸν ὑπὲρ ψυχῆς θέομεν, and other cognates such as Plato *Laws* 739 A, 820 C κινήσω τὸν ἀφ' ἱερᾶς sc. πεττόν, perhaps Soph. *El.* 1075 τὸν ἀεὶ πάρος στενάχουσ' sc. στόνον, Theocr. xviii. 11 ἦ ῥα πολύν τιν' ἔπινες sc. πότον, Soph. *fr.* 592, or (ii) assume the all but perfect anagrammatismus ὁππόσ' ἄρ', the line is hopeless, for ὅν could not supplant ὡς or even οἵ (which is awkward). Moreover, the contraction ὠρ. = ὀαρ. does not appear elsewhere in epos. R. demands a lacuna, which is equivalent to giving the passage up. (As a coincidence we may mention ὃν πάρος Nonnus ii. 269.)

Hitherto the evidence of M has not been taken into account. M reads

ὃν πάρος ὠρίζεσκον καὶ ἑταιρείῃ φιλότητι,

the rest

ὃν παρὸς ὠρίζεσκον ἑταιρείῃ φιλότητι.

M is hypermetrical, and there is no explanation of the presence of *καί*. If *καί* was original, *ὠρίζεσκον* must have been shorter. LS send us to Hesychius *ὠρίζει· ὑπνοῖ, ὁμιλεῖ, φροντίζει, μεριμνᾷ, ἀδολεσχεῖ*. As Schmidt remarks, the first interpretation is defended by *ὦρος somnus* in *EM*. 117. 16, Callim. *fr*. 150. If here we read *ὃν πάρος ὤριζον καὶ ἑταιρείῃ φιλότητι* we get a real construction for *ὅν*, 'whom they used to put to sleep with friendly affection', that is Zeus, who visited Maia not as a bull or a swan, or in thunder and lightning, but in human form, and was given a night's rest by Maia and her household. Maia, who had been put *dans ses meubles*, inhabited a *μέγας δόμος* with three cupboards full of gold and silver, meat and drink, and Maia's wardrobe (247 sq.). She had servants (*ἀμφίπολοι* 60). On Zeus' visits Maia *λέχος πόρσυνε καὶ εὐνήν*. This gives a meaning to *ἑταιρείῃ* 'even with friendly affection'; the maidservants were well disposed to the master. Of Maia only the epithet would be otiose. *καί* is emphatic.

This interpretation makes the relative refer to the further antecedent only, as in 428 (there the number, here the gender, assists the reference); cf. also *ι* 222, 223, *ο* 345 for a kind of hyperbaton.

To explain M's reading we suppose that *ὤριζον* was altered by some one who did not understand it to *ὠρίζεσκον*, which became the vulgate: then a reader corrected M's predecessor by writing
ζεσκον
the vulgate over the line *ὤριζον καί*, which M reproduced as *ὠρίζεσκον καί*.

59. For the repetition cf. *δ* 278 *ἐκ δ' ὀνομακλήδην Δαναῶν ὀνόμαζες ἀρίστους*.

60. **ἀμφιπόλους**: Calypso in her cave *ε* 199 had *δμῳαί*.

61. **ἐπηετανούς**: the meaning seems 'perennial, constant'; see Boisacq.

62. Cf. *β* 92, *ν* 381, *σ* 282 *νόος δέ οἱ ἄλλα μενοίνα*. As Hermes sang the idea of taking the oxen occurred to him. So he put the lyre down (63). In Philostratus *vit. Ap. Tyan.* c. 15 = 200 the Horae *ἐς ἔρωτα* [*τὸν Ἑρμῆν*] *τῶν τοῦ Ἀπόλλωνος βοῶν κατέστησαν*, telling him *ἐν σπάργανοις ὄντι* the story of the *βοῦς* which spoke to the man about itself and the world.

64. **κρειῶν ἐρατίζων**: of a lion Λ 551, P 660.

65. **ἆλτο, ὦρτο.** The same variant Υ 62 (for ὦτο cf. N 125, Ξ 522, O 694).

εὐώδεος: Pind. *Ol.* vii. 32 εὐώδεος ἐκ μεγάροιο.

66. δ 843 φόνον αἰπὺν ἐνὶ φρέσιν ὁρμαίνοντες.

67. The spelling φη- is the property of *xp*; in 175, however, these families also read φι-. The word is not Homeric. In Hesiod *OD.* 375 the MSS. are divided; Phot. lex., *EM.* and Gud. have φηλ- in the series φη as well as φιλ- in the series φι. Elsewhere the iota prevails (Archil. *fr.* 46, Aesch. *Cho.* 999, Soph. *fr.* 848, *Ichneut.* 332, Eur. *Rhes.* 217, Callim. *Hec.* 34. 56); Aesch. *Ag.* 497 has ἐφήλωσεν (and the Σ says ἐξ οὗ καὶ ὁ φηλήτης ἐν δυσὶν η̄). This is the result not only of itacism but of the dicta of Herodian and Trypho (ap. Choerob. *an. Ox.* ii. 271, cf. Σ P 3 on I 643 *ib.* iii. 75, Et. Gud. 532. 53). The word is paraphrased and derived by Plutarch on Hes. *OD.* 1 (vii, p. 70 Bern.). The etymology and hence the true spelling are uncertain (Seneca *ep.* v. 11. 13 *latronum more quos* φιλήτας *Aegyptii vocant*), cf. Hesych. βροτόφηλος. Hermes is called βοῦκλεψ by Soph. *fr.* 927 Nauck. In the Rhesus *l.c.* he is φηλητῶν ἄναξ, cf. *CIG.* 2299 (Kaibel *ep. gr.* 1108) Ἑρμῆν τὸν κλέπτην τις ἀφείλετο; θερμὸς ὁ κλέπτης | ὃς τῶν φηλητέων ᾤχετ' ἄνακτα φέρων.

70. On Pieria and the earlier Perea see introd. p. 273.

θέων: the variant θεῶν perhaps came from θεῶν 71, but may = θεῖα, cl. 551, Υ 53 (where there is the same variant), ω 67, Theocr. xxvii. 4. However, Hermes' haste is marked throughout this part of the hymn.

71. The writer calls the cows indifferently the property of the Gods (ὑμέτεροι 276, 310) or of Apollo (18, 22 etc.). On the analogy of the Vedic hymns (introd. p. 270) it might appear probable that in the oldest form of the myth the cattle belonged to the Sun, afterwards to Apollo as Sun-god. In Homer Apollo has no herds; the oxen slaughtered by Odysseus' men (μ 127) belong to Helios. In Apollodorus the ownership is vague (κλέπτει βόας ἃς ἔνεμεν Ἀπόλλων); Σ Dion. Thrac. (ann. Bekk. i. 752) the Sun is specified. See on *h.* iii. 412.

ἄμβροτοι, 'divine', as often of divine property, not 'immortal'.

72. **ἀκηρασίους**: ι 204 *οἶνον . . . ἡδὺν ἀκηράσιον θεῖον πότον* apparently from *κεράννυμι*; here the word seems connected with *ἀκήρατος* (found with *κᾶπος, λειμών*), on which see Boisacq.

73, 74. For the double gen. cf. 82 in *x p*, B 685.

75. **πλανοδίας**: adj., cf. Hesych. *πληνοδίᾳ· τῇ πεπλανημένῃ τῆς ὀρθῆς ὁδοῦ.* For lengthening of *α* see Schulze *qu. ep.* 187.

76. **ἴχνι' ἀποστρέψας**, 'turning their footprints round', cf. X 197, χ 173, 190, *h.* v. 168 (so R.).

δολίης δ' οὐ λήθετο τέχνης = Hes. *Theog.* 547, cf. δ 455, 529, *Theog.* 560

77. He drove the cattle backwards, fore-hooves behind, hind-hooves in front; he himself walked the reverse way (to them), viz. straight forward. The stratagem was well known in antiquity: cf. the story of Cacus Virg. *Aen.* viii. 210, Livy i. 7, auct. orig. gent. vi. 2, Ovid *Fasti* i. 550, Prop. iv. 9. 12, Mart. v. 65. 6, Dion. Hal. *ant. rom.* i. 38. Ilgen compared the behaviour of Commodus Herodian v. 6. Cf. also the *ὀπισθονόμοι βόες* of Herod. iv. 183, Aelian *NA.* xvi. 33, *ὀπισθοφανῶς* of Noah's sons Genesis ix. 23, Pliny's hippopotamus (*NH.* viii. 95) *ex agro ferentibus vestigiis ne quae revertenti insidiae compararentur*, and the hare (Aelian *NA.* vi. 47) *ἐς τὴν κοίτην τὴν συνήθη οὐ πάρεισιν πρὶν ἢ ταράξαι τὰ ἴχνη.* We have now the confirmation of *Ichneut.* 110 *παλιστραφῆ τοι ναὶ μὰ Δία τὰ βήματα· | εἰς τοὔμπαλιν δέδορκεν αὖ· τάδ' εἴσιδε· | τί ἐστὶ τουτί; τίς ὁ τρόπος τοῦ πράγματος; | εἰς τοὐπίσω τὰ πρόσθεν ἤλλακται, τὰ δ' αὖ | ἐναντί' ἀλλήλοισιν ἐμπεπλεγμένα. | δεινὸς κυκησμὸς εἶχε τὸν βοηλάτην.* The backward march of the cattle was called *παλιμπυγηδόν* Aristotle 559 a 57, 659 a 20. Autolycus (Hesiod. *fr.* 112) camouflaged the animals he stole (*ἐνήλλασσε τὰς χροιὰς αὐτῶν*), to which Sisyphus replied by scratching his monogram under his cows' hooves (Hyginus cci, Σ Soph. *Aj.* 190, comm. in Arist. *Rhet.* vol. xxi, p. ii, p. 284), or the words *Αὐτόλυκος ἔκλεψεν* (Polyaenus vi. 52). Cf. also Hesych. *Ἄμη· . . . σκάφη εἰς ἣν ἐβάλλοντο ἐρίφων πόδες πρὸς τὸ μὴ βαίνειν.*

In the case of horses, reversal of their shoes to avoid pursuit is found as far afield as Servia and Wales, and is frequent in Border literature. The best-known case is the New Forest story of Tyrrell who shot William Rufus. See *Notes and Queries* 1931, pp. 244, 323, 359, *History of Hampshire* by Westwood, Wilks, and Lockhart iii. 35.

79. The MSS. give two finite verbs (ἔριψεν, διέπλεκε) without connexion. To introduce this, αὐτίκα, omitted in *x*, has been attacked. The omission is clerical, and gives no ground for suspicion. ἔριψεν is difficult to explain, for Hermes is putting his shoes on, not taking them off as 139. Matthiae's ἔραψεν is identical with διέπλεκε. Postgate's emendation supplies a word suitable to the context and suppresses the first verb (the Homeric form is ῥίπεσσι ε 286; it is sufficiently rare to make corruption easy, cf. ῥιψί, ῥίπει Herod. iv. 71). These *skis* had a particular use on the sandy coast between the mouth of the Alpheus and the Triphylian Pylos (on this district see *h.* iii. 424). On his return Hermes threw them into the Alpheus (139). R. strangely invents two pairs of shoes.

80. **θαυματὰ ἔργα** = 440, *h.* vii. 34, Hes. *Scut.* 165. The word is not Homeric.

81. Cf. K 467 συμμάρψας δόνακας μυρίκης τ' ἐριθηλέας ὄζους.

μυρσινοειδέας = μυρσίνους; -ειδέας is otiose as in ψαμαθώδεα 75, ἠεροειδέι iii. 493, δονακώδεα Νεῖλον Bacchyl. *fr.* 30 al.

Eitrem (*Philologus* 1906, lxv. 248 sq.) refers to the wooden ξόανον of Hermes in the temple of Athena Polias at Athens ὑπὸ κλάδων μυρσίνης οὐ σύνοπτον (Paus. i. 27. 1), to Myrtilus son of Hermes, and to Myrtous and Myricaeus, cult titles of Apollo. This is the misplaced ingenuity of erudition. Hermes uses the materials which he found to hand.

82. M's reading νεοθηλέαν ἀγκαλωρήν (not -ής, as the reader may see for himself in the facsimile which the Leiden authorities were good enough to send us) suggested to Hermann to substitute ὥρης for ὕλης, but since the second α in ἀγκαλωρήν cannot by any method be lengthened, we read ἀγκάλῳ ὥρην. This reading and that of *x p* are much on a level, but with M ἀγκάλῳ (masc. or neut.) ceases to mean 'bundle' and = 'arm'. The sister-form ἀγκάλη = 'arm' only, though in papyri αγκαλων = δεσμῶν is common (*P. Oxy.* 935, 18 η μεταφορα των αγκαλων). ὥρην seems a better word than ὕλην, and is used in this sense by Aeschylus *fr.* 43. 6, perh. *Eumen.* 109, Eur. *Phoen.* 786, Xenophon *Hell.*

ii. 1. 1. For the metaplasm from 3 decl. to 2 decl. cf. Aesch. *Eum.* 453 νεοθηλοῦ (sic), implying νεοθήλεος, and ἀτελής ἀτέλεος (Galen iv. 624 ἀτέλεον ζῷον), μελάνεον (= μέλαν) Galen xix. 121 (v.l.). Similar is σύνοχος for συνεχής, which Galen disapproves (x. 603 συνόχους ὀνομάζουσι τοὺς τοιούτους πυρετούς, οὐχ Ἑλληνικῷ μὲν ὀνόματι χρώμενοι, σολοικίζειν ἑλόμενοι), but uses *ib.* 708, 756 al.[1] Lastly, we save one genitive (though two are defended by 73).

83. Inexplicable suspicion has fallen on ἀβλαβέως ('without hurt', i.e. to himself, that is 'fast, firmly'). The compounds of βλάβος, as Galen says (ii. 349 K.) are ὀνόματα τῆς ἐνεργείας τε καὶ τοῦ πάθους κοινά (so other negatives, ἄκοπος, ἄλυπος, ἄνατος, ἀπήμων, ἀργός, ἀσινής). The adverb is more often passive, e.g. Theognis 1154 ζώειν ἀβλαβέως μηδὲν ἔχοντι κακόν, Maximus π. καταρχῶν 10 ἀβλαβέως, Polyb. ii. 9. 6, v. 96. 3, Arrian *fr.* 85 Roos in a context similar to ours οἱ δὲ κύκλους ἐκ λύγων τοῖς ποσὶ προσαρμόσαντες αὐτοί τε ἀβλαβῶς ἐπήρχοντο κατὰ τῆς χιόνος πιεζομένης ὑπὸ τῶν κύκλων (first cited by Pierson), Musonius ap. Stob. *ecl.* iv. 271, Themistius xxii. 220; but sometimes as here may be called active; Sosiades ap. Stob. *ecl.* iii. 1. 173 χαρίζου ἀβλαβῶς, Polyb. vi. 10. 12 ἀβλαβῶς συνεστήσατο τὴν πολιτείαν, Libanius *or.* xlii. 23 ἀβλαβῶς ὑπηρετῶν, Galen x. 689 τούτους μὲν οὖν οὐδ' ἐν ταῖς παρακμαῖς ἀβλαβῶς ἂν τρέφοις, xii. 588 Artemidorus *onir.* ii. 12 λέοντα . . . προσιόντα ἀβλαβῶς. See also on 393.

Hermes wished to disguise his track (222), and at the same time skate over the sand: cf. Lucian *Anach.* 27 ψάμμῳ βαθείᾳ ἔνθα οὔτε βεβαίως ἀπερεῖσαι τὴν βάσιν οὔτε ἐπιστηρίξαι ῥᾴδιον ὑποσυρομένου πρὸς τὸ ὑπεῖκον τοῦ ποδός.

85. **ὁδοιπορίην ἀλεείνων**, 'avoiding wayfaring', i.e. the fatigue of walking on sand: Gods usually flew. Cf. Nonnus xxv. 551 ἁρμονίῃ πέλε μορφῇ, ποσσὶν ὁδοιπορίῃ, 'walking'; *epigr.* Kaibel 711. 2 δηναίης ἀποθοῦ φόρτον ὁδοιπορίης, Xen. *Cyrop.* i. 2. 10 γυμνάζει . . . ὁδοιπορίαις καὶ δρόμοις. This, or the avoidance of snow, ice, and mud was the intention of other arrangements, e.g. crampons and toboggans Strabo 506, the shoeing of cattle with σπαρτός Galen vi. 502; cf. also Theophanes p. 604, ed. Bonn

[1] Among substantives cf. ὄσχη ὄσχεον -ος, γάστραν, Δήμητραν, θήραν = θῆρα Aelian *NA.* xv. 18, xvii. 12. Further, δυήπαθος δυηπαθής (486).

ὑπερβὰς μετὰ κυκλοπόδων τὰς χιόνας τῶν Καυκασίων, Hippocr. iii. 239. 15 ἀρβύλαι . . . αἱ πηλοπατίδες καλεόμεναι. τοῦτο γὰρ ὑποδημάτων ἥκιστα κρατέεται ὑπὸ τοῦ ποδός, ἀλλὰ κρατέει μόνον. Other reff. in R. pp. 82, 247. On the way back to Olympus (320) Hermes (and Apollo) did without them.

86. The syntax of the line is fixed by Xen. *Anab.* i. 5. 91 σπεύδων πᾶσαν τὴν ὁδόν, Demosth. xix. 165 τὴν αὐτὴν ὁδόν . . . καθήμενοι . . . ὅτε δὲ . . . ἐπειγόμενοι, *Anth. Pal.* ix. 83. 1 νηὸς ἐπειγομένης ὠκὺν δρόμον. The first four words of the line therefore go together.

δολιχήν: 143 δολιχῆς ὁδοῦ, he had a long journey before him.

The remarkable words **αὐτοτροπήσας** and αὐτοπρεπὴς ὥς must not be abandoned. Compounds of τροπ- are frequent: ἀτρόποισι ἔπεεσι Pind. *Nem.* vii. 151, ἀτροπίης Theognis 218, ἀτροπίῃσιν Ap. Rh. ii. 246, ἐναντιοτροπή D.L. (Heraclitus) ix. 1. 7, ἀλλοτρόπως Arist. π. φυτ. 818 a 23, ἑτερότροπα Nonnus ii. 699, vii. 7, -ον Ar. *Thesm.* 724, ἐντροπίη Democritus *fr.* 57, μετάτροπα Hes. *Theog.* 89, ὁμότροπα Herod. viii. 144, Menander Περικ. *fr.* 391, Aen. Tact. *pass.* As verbs we find ἀλλοιοτροπεῖν Hippocr. π. τῶν ἐντὸς παθῶν 37, Galen xix. 75 (these I take from the new LS), ἀλλοτροπῆσαι Hesych., ἑτεροτροπεῖν Cyril *in Ioann.* 15, 19, p. 875 (from Steph.), κακοτροπέει Hippocr. ii. 655. 5; further, ἀρχαιότροπα Thuc. i. 71, -πία Plut. *Phocion* 3, ἰδιότροπος id. *non posse* 1098 F, Strabo 823, -ως Diod. iii. 29. 2, πραΰτροπον Plut. *amor. prol.* 493 D. Τοιουτότροπος and μονότροπος are common.

To these αὐτοτροπεῖν clearly belongs, and means to have one's own τρόπος or character, to be original or unique. Compounds of αὐτο- are familiar: αὐτοδίδακτος, αὐτόδιον, αὐτοετές, αὐτάγρετα, Αὐτόλυκος, αὐτογνωμονεῖν (Xen. *Hell.* vii. 3. 6). The invention of these unheard-of shoes (πέλωρα, αἰνά 225, 226) justified the epithet.

The alternative reading αὐτοπρεπής has much the same sense, 'like oneself, unique', cl. ἀρχαιοπρεπής, δουλοπρεπής, ἱεροπρεπής Menander Δυσκόλῳ 3, Strabo 405, 417, ξενοπρεπές Hippocr. i. 80. 4, but the unnecessary ὥς suggests a corruption from the other word; cf. ἂν διαπρέψειεν, ἀντρέψειεν Plato *Sophist.* 219 C, θεότρεπτα, -πρεπτα Aesch. *Persae* 907.

87. The old man's occupation is more specifically stated, 90 ὅς τε φυτὰ σκάπτεις and 207 ἔσκαπτον περὶ γουνὸν ἀλωῆς

οἰνοπέδοιο. His work was something like that of Laertes ω 227, λιστρεύοντα φυτόν, i.e. he was digging about his vines in bud (ἀνθοῦσαν), clearing the rows and loosening the roots. This process was called γύρωσις by Greek agriculturists, e.g. Xen. *Oec.* xx. 20, Aratus 9, *Geopon.* v. 20 γυρώσομεν δέ, τουτέστι περισκάψομεν, iv. 1. 5, 13. 1 etc., and v. 25 σκάπτειν δὲ χρὴ πρὸ βλαστοῦ προβολῆς, Aelian *NA.* ix. 32 περισκάπτουσι μὲν γύρους καὶ ὑποκινοῦσι τὰς ῥίζας, Strabo 502 ἄσκαφοι δὲ ἄμπελοι μένουσαι διὰ τέλους, Cato *de r.r.* 33, Pliny *NH.* xvii. 188, Nonnus xvii. 83, xlviii. 69, Theophr. *HP.* ii. 5. 1 γύρους προσρύττειν, *CP.* iii. 4. 1 κατασκάπτειν κτλ., al., Alciphron iii. 13. 77, Philostr. *Heroic.* 61. A later time for this operation is given by Columella iv. 28 *pubescentem vero et quasi adulescentem convenit religare foliisque omnibus nudare, tum et crebris fossionibus implere* (*circumfodere* Seneca *ep.* 1. 12, *circumfossa* Pliny *NH.* 21. 21 of roses). These passages amply justify M's ἀνθοῦσαν (for which αἴθουσαν vulg. is mere nonsense). Add Hesiod *OD.* 570–2, Pallad. iv. 7, v. 20, Aeschines ii. 156, Menand. *Georg.* 64, Moschus iv. 100, Theocr. xxv. 27, Luke xiii. 8.

The word δέμων (for which again the vulgate δόμων is nonsense) may very well be used of this work, building up a vineyard, to which the epithet ἐυκτιμένη is applied ω 226. Herodotus uses δέμειν of road-making. Cf. σ 359 αἱμασίας τε λέγων καὶ δένδρεα μακρὰ φυτεύων, ω 224.

88. On the site of Onchestus see *h.* iii. 230. The place appears only in this version of the story : see introd. p. 273.

90. **ἐπικαμπύλος ὤμους** : ω 242 ἦ τοι ὁ μὲν κατέχων κεφαλὴν φυτὸν ἀμφελάχαινε. Ruhnken quotes Lucian *Tim.* 7 σκάπτει δὲ οἶμαι ἐπικεκυφώς. M's reading ἐπικαμπύλα ξύλα is unmetrical; it may point to a variant ἐπικαμπύλα κᾶλα = Hes. *OD.* 427. κᾶλα occurs 112 *infra.* The 'bent wood' would be the crooked woody stem of the vine Eur. *Cycl.* 572 τὸ ξύλον τῆς ἀμπέλου.

91. **πολυοινήσεις** : Ilgen's conjecture based on M is certain. For compounds of οἶνος cf. Plut. *qu. conv.* iv. 661 αἱ ἀλλοινίαι λεγόμεναι τάχιστα μεθύσκουσι, Hippocr. ii. 293 ἀοινεῖν, ἐξοινεῖν, Strabo 516, 637 ἐξοίνους, 512 εὐοινεῖν, 73 εὐοινίᾳ, 231 εὐοινοτάτην, 234 τόποι εὔοινοι, 241, 268, 269, Hippocr. ii. 328. 2 ἡδυοινίην,

Geopon. v. 2, 43 tit. *κακοοινία*, 2. 19 *καλλιοινία*, Hipp. iii. 8 *μίσοινοι*, Strabo 637 *χρηστοινεῖν*. *παροινεῖν* is common.

φέρῃσι: neut. 'bear' is well attested. Hermes makes a promise, 'there will be plenty of wine when the vines bear if . . .' The condition is continued in 92. We therefore require a principal verb to govern *εἶναι*, and an assonance to account for the omission of the line. This was supplied with great ingenuity by Evelyn-White. Tucker and R. taking *εἶναι* as imperative do without the lacuna. Eitrem (*l.c.*) compares *IG*. xii. 2. 476, an inscription on a Hermes set up in a vineyard, *ὅπως ἀσινῇ διὰ παντὸς | ἄμπελος ὡραῖον καρπὸν ἔχῃ βοτρύων*. But there is no authority for the worship of Hermes Phytalmios to which Eitrem refers, and the God was not specially connected with vegetation (see on 410).

92. The inconsistency shows that the digamma was not felt in *μὴ ἰδών*, and there is a real hiatus in *τε ἰδών*.

For the expression cf. Aesch. *PV*. 463, *Sept*. 246, Polybius xii. 246 *βλέποντος μὴ βλέπειν*, Plaut. *Mil. Glor.* ii. 6. 91, Demosth. xxv. 89 *οἱ μὲν οὕτως ὁρῶντες τὰ τῶν ἠτυχηκότων ἔργα ὥστε, τὸ τῆς παροιμίας, ὁρῶντες μὴ ὁρᾶν καὶ ἀκούοντες μὴ ἀκούειν*, Plut. *de lib. educ.* 13 E. The positive occurs M 442 *οὔασι πάντες ἄκουον*, Plut. *Lysand.* 27, *Gaius Marc.* 38. For the policy of discretion cf. Eur. *Ino fr.* 417.

93. **τὸ σόν** is certainly subject: Eur. *Phoen.* 990 *μὴ τὸ σὸν κωλυέτω*, Aristides xlix. 360 *εἰ μὴ τὸ σὸν κωλύει*, 'saving your own interest', Lysias viii. 19 *τὸ μὲν οὖν ἐμὸν οὐκ ἐμποδὼν ὑμῖν ἔσται*, Galen vi. 296 *εἰ μηδὲν ἕτερον κωλύοι*, xv. 665 *ἢν μή τι τῶν ἀπὸ σπλάγχνων κωλύῃ*, xvi. 267 *εἰ μηδὲν ἕτερον κωλύῃ*. Cf. also Dionysius Chalcus i. 5 *τὸ σὸν εὖ θέμενος*. For the verb cf. Xen. *Cyrop.* i. 6. 18 *τὸν δέ γε ἐργάτην στρατηγὸν ἀναδέχομαι ἢν μή τις θεὸς βλάπτῃ*, Aesch. *PV*. 789 *εἰ μή τις βλαβή*.

94. **συνέσευε**: an excellent conjecture. Hesych. *συσσοίη· ἡ ἀνεμπόδιστος φορά*; cf. *id.* *εὔσους· . . . καὶ εὐκίνητος, εὔφορος, εὐσοία*, Soph. *OC*. 390, *fr.* 119. Hesych. *μηλοσόη ὁδός· δι' ἧς τὰ πρόβατα ἐλαύνεται. Ῥόδιοι.* Hermes now drives the cows in a body, not straggling: cf. *συνέλασσεν* 106. The reversed pacing ceased when the going became hard. *βοῶν ἴφθ. κάρ.* = Ψ 260.

95. **αὐλῶνας**: not in Homer, who also does not use κελαδεινός of places.

97. **ἐπίκουρος**, 'accomplice', cf. Γ 11.

This night, like the night in K, was well filled. Hermes stole the cows at sundown, after a long journey came to the Alpheus at moonrise (99), and after killing two cows and inventing fire 'all night long' (141) came to Cyllene at dawn (143). This, however, is nothing against the integrity, still less the consideration that the moon would not rise in the early morning on the fifth of the month. This astronomical fact has no bearing on literature. In Wolfe's poem *The Burial of Sir John Moore* the line 'By the struggling moonbeam's misty light' is inaccurate, as the moon was invisible at the time of the burial (Ball *Story of the Heavens* p. 51).

98. **ἡ πλείων**: cf. K 252 παρῴχηκεν δὲ πλέων νύξ.

ὄρθρος: not in Homer, but in Hes. *OD.* 577, Ibycus *fr.* 7.

δημιοεργός: cf. Hes. *OD.* 580 ἠώς, ἥ τε φανεῖσα πολέας ἐπέβησε κελεύθου | ἀνέρας, Callim. *Hec. fr.* 34, 54 Pf., Aratus 6, poet. ap. Plut. *mor.* 722 D, Orph. *h.* lxxviii. 6, Virg. *Aen.* xi. 183, Ovid. *Met.* iv. 663. Hesychius' gloss δημιουργός· ὁ ἥλιος ὅτι πάντα πέσσει καὶ θέρει cannot refer to this place.

100. This genealogy occurs only here: in Hes. *Theog.* 371 Selene is the daughter of Hyperion and Theia.

With regard to Pallas, G. rightly rejects a connexion with Arcadian myths in the person of Pallas founder of Pallantium (Paus. viii. 3. 1). This hero was son of Lycaon (Apollod. iii. 8. 1) and could hardly be related to Selene. The Hesiodean Pallas (a Titan) was son of Crius (*Theog.* 375) and grandson of Uranus (*ib.* 134). His brother Perses was father of Hecate (*ib.* 377, 409), and G. suggests that if Pallas is related to Hecate he may also be connected with Selene. This is likely enough, though the two Goddesses are distinct in Hesiod. Of Megamedes, who takes the place of the Hesiodean Crius, nothing else is known, but he is entitled to exist; see Mayer *Die Giganten* 67, on the form Lobeck *Paralip.* 45.

101. The description is elliptical. Hermes first drives the cows to the river (i.e. to the ford at Thryon or Epitalion, 398),

thence to Pylos (first named at 216). On his return he threw his shoes, when they ceased to be useful, into the river (139). The mention of the Alpheus fixes Pylos as the Triphylian or Lepreatic. See *h.* iii. 424.

103. **ἀδμῆτες**: not 'unyoked' (δ 637), sc. to the plough or cart, that is, having done no work (*nullum passa iugum curvique immunis aratri* Ovid *Met.* ii. 11), a quality irrelevant to the situation and introducing an affected construction. How the kine came to the stalls is evident: *Anth. Pal.* vii. 173 αὐτόμαται δείλῃ ποτὶ ταὔλιον αἱ βόες ἦλθον, Theocr. xi. 12 ταὶ ὄϊες ποτὶ τὠλίον αὐταὶ ἀπῆνθον, Ovid *l.c.* 634 *incustoditae Pyli memorantur in agros processisse boves*, Virg. *Ecl.* vii. 11 *huc ipsi potum venient per prata iuvenci* ('*ipsi*' *id est sponte sua* Servius), Tibullus i. 3. 45 *ultroque ferebant obvia securis ubera lactis oves*, Aelian *NA.* xvi. 16 (ἑκόντα). They strayed of their own will to the byre and the troughs. For the contrary cf. Ovid *Fast.* i. 323 *quia non veniant pecudes sed agantur*. The writer used ἀδμής in a slightly unusual sense, justified etymologically. The conjecture ἀκμῆτες is absurd; the kine after being driven backwards from Pieria to Pylos were exhausted, and as Seneca says *de tranqu. an.* 11 *pecoribus fatigatis velocior domum gradus est.*

αὔλιον: un-Homeric.

104. **ληνούς**, 'troughs', first here, next in Hippocr. *Mochl.* 38. On the derivation (unknown) see Boisacq.

106. **ἀθρόας οὔσας**: ἀθρόᾰς resembles κοῦρας ὁμόφρονας Hes. *Theog.* 60, τροπᾰ̀ς ἠελίοιο *OD.* 564, and other cases in Hesiod, *OD.* 675, *Theog.* 267, 401, *fr.* 190 etc. See introd. p. cvii.

οὔσας: this form occurs also *h.* iii. 330.

107. B 776 λωτὸν ἐρεπτόμενοι ἐλεόθρεπτόν τε σέλινον.

108. The first **δ'** here, and **δ'** 116, are apodotic, as *Aphr.* 235.

ἐπεμαίετο: tropical with acc. is established by 511 σοφίας ἐκμάσσατο τέχνην as against the Homeric use with gen., K 401 δώρων ἐπεμαίετο θυμός. M's τύνη is unexplained.

This is the earliest mention of the method of making fire by the drill. It is described by Σ Ap. Rh. i. 1184 (on the line τοὶ δ' ἀμφὶ πυρήια δινεύεσκον)· τὸ δὲ δινεύεσκον ἀντὶ τοῦ ἔστρεφον, παρέτριβον· τὰ γὰρ ξύλα παρέτριβον καὶ ἀπ' αὐτῶν πῦρ ἔλαβον. πυρήια γὰρ ταῦτα φησὶ τὰ προστριβόμενα ἀλλήλοις πρὸς τὸ πῦρ ἐγγενᾶν, ὧν τὸ μέν ἐστιν ὕπτιον ὃ καλεῖται στορεύς, θάτερον δὲ παραπλήσιον τρυπάνῳ, ὅπερ ἐπιτρίβοντες τῷ στορεῖ στρέφουσιν. (Hesychius *in* Στορεύς inverts the names of the parts and must be either confused or corrupt: στορεύς· γαληνοποιός, καὶ τὸ ἀντὶ τοῦ σιδήρου τρύπανον ἐμβαλλόμενον ξύλον ῥάμνου ἢ δάφνης. Can σιδήρου, which is senseless, be an echo of σιδήρῳ 109?) This detailed account agrees with what we know of the actual habits of primitive peoples, see Kuhn *Die Herabkunft des Feuers* 1859, Planck *Die Feuerzeuge der Griechen und Römer* 1884, Tylor *Primitive Culture* ii. 251 etc., Henry Balfour and others *Notes and Queries* 1892, ii, pp. 47, 114, 231, 314.

In scientific writers the first and best account is in Theophrastus *HP*. v. 9. 6 (=*frag*. i. 9. 63: *sim*. v. 4. 4, *CP*. i. 21. 7, *frag*. iii. 3. 29) πυρεῖα δὲ γίνεται μὲν ἐκ πολλῶν, ἄριστα δὲ ὥς φησι Μενέστωρ ἐκ κιττοῦ· τάχιστα γὰρ καὶ πλεῖστον ἀναπνεῖ. πυρεῖον δέ φασιν ἄριστον μὲν ἐκ τῆς ἀθραγένης καλουμένης ὑπό τινων· τοῦτο δ' ἐστὶ δένδρον ὅμοιον τῇ ἀμπέλῳ καὶ τῇ οἰνάνθῃ τῇ ἀγρίᾳ. ὥσπερ ἐκεῖνοι καὶ τοῦτο ἀναβαίνει πρὸς τὰ δένδρα. δεῖ δὲ τὴν ἐσχάραν ἐκ τούτων ποιεῖν, τὸ δὲ τρύπανον ἐκ δάφνης. οὐ γὰρ ἐκ ταὐτοῦ τὸ ποιοῦν καὶ πάσχον, ἀλλ' ἕτερον εὐθὺ δεῖ κατὰ φύσιν, καὶ τὸ μὲν δεῖ παθητικὸν εἶναι, τὸ δὲ ποιητικόν. οὐ μὴν ἀλλὰ καὶ ἐκ τοῦ αὐτοῦ γίνεται, καὶ ὥς γέ τινες ὑπολαμβάνουσιν οὐδὲν διαφέρει· γίνεται γὰρ ἐκ ῥάμνου καὶ πρίνου καὶ φιλύρας καὶ σχεδὸν ἐκ τῶν πλείστων πλὴν ἐλάας . . . ἀγαθὰ δὲ καὶ τὰ ἐκ ῥάμνου· ποιεῖ δὲ τοῦτο καὶ τὴν ἐσχάραν χρηστήν· πρὸς γὰρ τῷ ξηρὰν καὶ ἄχυμον εἶναι δεῖ καὶ μανοτέραν ἵν' ἡ τρίψις ἰσχύῃ, τὸ δὲ τρύπανον ἀπαθέστερον. δι' ὃ τὸ τῆς δάφνης ἄριστον, ἀπαθὲς γὰρ ὂν ἐργάζεται τῇ δριμύτητι. Hence Pliny *NH*. xvi. 40. 76. Cf. also Seneca *qu. nat*. ii. 22 *videamus quemadmodum apud nos fieri soleat ignis: duobus modis, uno si excitatur sicut ex lapide percusso, altero si attritu invenitur, sicut quum duo ligna inter se diutius trita sunt.* It is alluded to by Plato *rep*. 435 A; Theocr. xxii. 33 and Ap. Rh. (above) make the Argonauts use it: Phoenix Coloph. ap. Athen. 530 E, l. 5 οὐ παρὰ μάγοισι πῦρ ἱερὸν ἀνέστησεν | ὥσπερ νόμος ῥάβδοισι τοῦ θεοῦ ψαύων (text uncertain), Lucian *ver. hist*. i. 32 τὰ πυρεῖα συντρίψαντες, Xen. *Cyrop*. ii. 2. 15 ἐκ σοῦ πῦρ ῥᾷον ἄν τις ἐκτρίψειεν ἢ γέλωτα ἐξαγάγοιτο, Soph. *Phil*. 36 πυρεῖα, *fr*. 638 ἀχάλκευτα τρύπανα.

Fire was also produced by the flint: Seneca above, Soph. *Phil.* 296 ἐν πέτροισι πέτρον ἐκτρίβων μόλις | ἔφην' ἄφαντον φῶς, Galen vii. 625 ξύλον ἢ λίθον παρατρίβων ἐφάψεις ποτὲ πῦρ, cf. iii. 2. 658, Nonnus ii. 493 ὡς λίθος ἀμφὶ λίθῳ φλογερὴν ὠδῖνα λοχεύων | λάινον ἠκόντιζε πολυθλιβὲς αὐτόγονον πῦρ | πυρσογενὴς ὅτε θῆλυς ἀράσσεται ἄρσενι πέτρῳ, xxxvii. 56 ἔνθα πυρὸς χρέος ἔσκε . . . (Faunus) πυρσοτόκους λάιγγας ὀρειάδος ὄργανα τέχνης | ἤγαγεν ἐκ σκοπέλοιο καὶ . . . | λείψανα θεσπεσίου πυρὸς ἤγαγεν ὥς κεν ἀνάψῃ | πυρκαΐην φθιμένοιο· διοβλήτῳ δὲ θεείῳ | ἀμφοτέρων ἔχρισε λίθων κενεῶνας ἀλείψας | πυρσοτόκων· καὶ λεπτὸν Ἐρυθραίοιο κορύμβου | κάρφος ἀποξύσας διδυμάονι μίγνυε πέτρῳ· | τρίβων δ' ἔνθα καὶ ἔνθα καὶ ἄρσενι θῆλυν ἀράσσων | ἔγκρυφον αὐτολόχευτον ἀνείρυε λαΐνεον πῦρ); and by the burning-glass or crystal (Blaydes on Ar. *Nub.* 768): this was used particularly for sacred fire, Orpheus *Lith.* 184.

In the hymn it is plain that the δάφνης ἀγλαὸς ὄζος is the τρύπανον, and the unnamed object ἄρμενον ἐν παλάμῃ (Σ 600, ε 324) is the στορεύς (torus), ἐσχάρα or πάσχον, which required to be held steady in the hand. The τρύπανον, far from being held steady, was twisted or revolved (in real life by means of a strap: in antiquity also, Crates ap. Stob. *ecl.* iii. 4. 50 Κράτης ἀπείκαζε τοὺς ἀνοήτους τῶν ἀνθρώπων τοῖς τρυπάνοις· ἄνευ γὰρ δεσμοῦ καὶ ἀνάγκης μηδὲν ἐθέλειν τῶν δεόντων ποιεῖν, cf. ι 385, al. in the lexx. The strap was called τρυπανία). It is also plain that the word σιδήρῳ applies to neither of these objects, and means as usual tool or knife (Theophr. *HP.* ix. 4. 4 τὸν λιβανωτὸν . . . ἀποξύειν σιδήροις, *CP.* iii. 2. 2 τὰ μὲν σιδήροις τὰ δὲ ταῖς χερσί, *frag.* ii. 7. 43 ἔνιοι δὲ λίθοις ἄλλοις γλύφονται, σιδήροις δ' οὐ δύνανται, Plut. *inst. Lac.* 287 B καλάμου τὰ ἄκρα ταῖς χερσὶν ἄνευ σιδήρου κατακλάσαντες, Athen. 51 B κνίσαντες σιδηρίῳ). σιδήῳ is one of Ludwich's bad conjectures (its quantity is doubtful).

Therefore, taking the vulgate as it stands, we translate 'he took a fine stick of laurel and trimmed it with his knife', that is to say, removed the bark from the end and pointed it. ἐπιλέπω = trim to a point; the simple λέπω (A 236, unless this is a tmesis for περιλέπω, as περὶ . . . λέψαιο Nicander *Ther.* 587, and Josephus *Ant. Iud.* xvii. 183 of an apple, where μαχαιρίῳ = σιδήρῳ) and ἀπολέπω, ἐκλέπω (e.g. τὰ ᾠά) mean to peel off, peel entirely.

This force of ἐπί may be illustrated from ἐπικόπτειν, ἐπιτέμνειν, ἐπικνίζειν, ἐπικάειν.

M's variant ἐνίαλλε is impossible, no 'dashing on' is required in the process. Postgate's suggestion that it is an anagrammatismus for λείαινε is likely; it would be a synonym of ἐπέλεψε; cf. Quintus xii. 136 οἱ δ' ἄρ' ἀπ' ὄζους | λείαιναν πελέκεσσι, Plut. *praec. ger. reip.* 802 B ὄζους τινας ἐν ξύλῳ καὶ διπλόας ἐν σιδήρῳ μαλάσσων καὶ καταλειαίνων, Theophr. *HP.* v. 4. 6, Philostr. *Imag.* 16 (393).

Accordingly, if ὄζον and ἄρμενον denote different things, and if, as all anthropologists have seen, the process of friction is omitted, the lacuna demanded by Kuhn must be allowed. It contained the equivalent of στορεύς (perhaps κισσός or δάφνη) in apposition with ἄρμενον, and a verb such as τρίβειν or τρυπᾷν.

110. **παλάμῃ**: παλάμῃσιν Σ 600, ε 234.

ἄμπνυτο: the correct quantity (Schulze *qu. ep.* 324) shows the superiority of M over the other MSS.

θερμὸς ἀυτμή = Hes. *Theog.* 696. On the quotation *ap.* Ṡ Σ 222 see p. lxxvi, note 1.

111. The line is formulaic, as 25. Both enounce the God's achievements. **τοι** is resumptive.

ἀνέδωκε, 'gave forth', as ἀνέκαιε 115, not 'gave back', for there is no allusion to Hes. *OD.* 50. According to the usual tradition Prometheus gave men fire, or restored it when it was hidden by Zeus. The present line does not necessarily imply a different tradition. Hermes did not discover fire, he invented a new method (τέχνην) of making it by 'fire-sticks'. This invention was also ascribed to Prometheus (Diod. v. 67, Sikes and Wilson on Aesch. *PV.* xvi). ζώπυρα were ascribed to Anacharsis by Ephorus *fr.* 76; the invention of fire by the Argives to Phoroneus (Paus. ii. 19. 5).

113. **οὖλα** is sound, though the meaning is not certain. The Homeric sense of οὖλος is 'close, thick', but it is applied to wool or hair only: in later Greek it is used of plants or trees. Here it might mean ἐπηετανά, 'in thick bundles', or possibly 'bushy', with leaves, twigs and all. On the derivation (the root of *lana*) see Boisacq.

ἐπηετανά: with synizesis, as Hes. *OD.* 607, Orph. Ἔργ. καὶ Ἡμ. 11, 10; in Maximus π. καταρχῶν 465 we find ἐπητανὸν ὄλβον; cf. βασιλῆες *OD.* 263, τοκῆες *h.* ii. 137. The word has open vowels in 61.

114. φῦσαν is Valla's correction, repeated by Clarke and Hemsterhuys, first printed by Ernesti. **φῦζαν** must be original: no scribe of any period could have conjectured it. Mr. R. McKenzie informs us that it may be a Cretan form, since σ or σσ takes the form ζ in Cretan (Bechtel *Gr. Dial.* ii. 694, 967). Cf. Hesych. Ἐφύζα· ἐφύσα, Ἐχεφύζα· ἐφύσα, εἶχε φυγεῖν (sic). On the etymology of φῦσα (φυτyα) see Boisacq and Solmsen *Beiträge zur gr. Wortforschung* i. 247.

116. **ὑποβρύχιας**: elsewhere the adj. means 'submerged', but as the verbs ὑποβρυχάομαι and ὑποβρύχω exist in the sense of 'roaring', the adj. may have the same meaning. The hypsilon in βρυχάομαι and cognates is, however, long, and hence there is some probability in Ludwich's ὑποβρύχους—unless indeed -ιας is *in synizesi.*

119. The action, if pleonastically expressed (ἐγκλίνων means much the same as ἐκύλινδε), is clear. The cows being on their backs (118) Hermes 'turned them round and rolled them over' in order to reach their αἰῶνες or backbones. These he pierced with his γλύφανον, a process not unlike modern methods; cf. P 520, Quintus i. 264 κόψας αὐχενίους τένοντας, Babrius 37. 12, Galen v. 239 τοὺς κατὰ τὸν πρῶτον σφόνδυλον ὁσημέραι διατεμνομένους (bulls). For ἐγκλίνων act. cf. Galen xii. 654 κλίναντα τὸν ἄνθρωπον ἐς τὸ οὖς, Ael. *NA.* vi. 24 κλίναι ὑπτίαν, poet. ap. Plut. *mor.* 462 F κλίναι . . . κάπρον. The beasts' throats were not cut, hence ἀγκλίνων (Orph. *Arg.* 314 σφάζον ἀνακλίνας κεφαλήν, Polyaen. viii. 46 παρακλίνασα τὸν τράχηλον εὐκόλως ἀπέσφαξεν) = ἄνω τρέπων Soph. *Aj.* 293 is unsuitable. M's ἐκκρίνας can hardly be given a meaning.

τετορήσας. This form and τετορήσω (Ar. *Pax.* 381 εἰ μὴ τετορήσω ταῦτα καὶ λακήσομαι) appear to imply a present τετορῶ with reduplication like τετρεμαίνω τετραίνω. On the other hand ἀντιτοροῦντα 283, ἀντιτορήσων 178, ἀντιτορήσας K 267 imply ἀντιτορεῖν. ἀντετόρησεν E 337, Oppian *Hal.* iii. 55 can be explained on either assumption. ἔτορε Λ 236, τέτορεν· ἔτρωσεν, τετόρῃ· τρώσῃ in Hesychius, σὺν δ' ἐτόρησεν Oppian *Hal.* iv. 545 point to a form τόρω (-έω). Hence the name to be given to τετορήσας is uncertain. If we are moved by τετορήσω, the forms in 178, 283, K 267 must be emended to ἀντε-, the similarity to the preposition ἀντί (which as Leaf observed on K 267 has no particular meaning in the compound) causing the error. See Fick *BB.* xxii. 269. The word is usually called a reduplicated aorist like ἀμπεπαλών.

Further δι . . . τετορήσας appear to be *in tmesi.* Suidas has διατορηθῆναι ἀντὶ τοῦ διακοπῆναι, τρυπηθῆναι, and as the compounds of δια- in the great majority of cases govern an accusative and not a genitive (e.g. 48 πειρήνας διὰ νῶτα), this may turn the balance in favour of αἰῶνας of M *x*. The sense also is more direct, 'piercing the spines' rather than 'piercing them through the spine'.

122. **γεράσμια**, not in Homer.

'The meat, the saddles, and the puddings, and this (τὰ δ') was left there in the place.'

124. Here Apollo found them 403. D'Orville (see *J. Ph.* xxv. 254) first suggested that these were actual skins, preserved as relics. As Gemoll notes, the skins were probably exhibited outside the cave. A long list of such relics will be found in Pfister *Der Reliquienkult im Altertum* i. 331. In the ordinary ritual of sacrifice the skins of the victims either became the perquisite of the priests or were sold. The proceeds, sometimes called δερματικόν, were used for religious expenses, Stengel *Kultusaltertümer* 116. The skins were also sometimes dedicated; cf. the story in Dio Prus. i. 53 καταλαμβάνω (between Heraea and Pisa) λίθους τε τινας εἰκῇ συγκειμένους, καὶ δέρματα ἱερείων κρεμαμένα, Longus ii. 30. 5 κρεμάσας ἀπέδειρε καὶ τὸ δέρμα ἀνέθηκε, 31. 3 τὸ δὲ δέρμα κέρασιν αὐτοῖς ἐνέπηξαν τῇ πιτύι πρὸς τῷ ἀγάλματι ποιμενικὸν ἀνάθημα ποιμένι τῷ θεῷ, Σ T X 159 καὶ νῦν Οἰταῖοι Ἡρακλεῖ πεντετήριον ἀγῶνα ποιοῦντες βύρσας διδόασιν.

καταστυφέλῳ: first here and Hes. *Theog.* 806. Hesych. κατάστυφλον· κατάξηρον.

125. The line was hopeless until O. Müller (*Hyperbor. Röm.*

Stud. 310 quoted by B.) accepted M's *μέτασσα*. The neut. plur. *μέτασσα* is recognized in the Epimerismi of O 8 in Μέτασσα *an. Ox.* i. 280: *ὥσπερ παρὰ τὴν ἐπὶ γίνεται ἔπισσα* [*ἔπισσαι* Hecataeus in *EM.* 596. 22] *οὕτω καὶ παρὰ τὴν μετὰ μέτασσα*. The fem. occurs ι 221 *χωρὶς μὲν πρόγονοι χωρὶς δὲ μέτασσαι*. See Smyth *Ionic* 305 n. 3, Schulze *KZ.* xxix. 263. The neuter may be used adverbially as *μέσσα* Nicander *Alex.* 366 with the meaning 'thereafter'.

126. **ἄκριτον**: adverbial, as 577 *τὸ δ' ἄκριτον*, *h.* xix. 26 *ἄκριτα*. The sense is 'without bounds', i.e. endlessly. Cf. Virgil *Georg.* iii. 476 *nunc quoque post tanto.*

127. **χαρμόφρων**: preserved by Hesych. *χαρμόφρων· ὁ Ἑρμῆς.*

πίονα ἔργα: elsewhere of fields, M 283, δ 318.

128. **πλαταμῶνι**, 'slab', first here, defined by Hesych. as *τόπος πλατὺς καὶ μέγας ὑποθαλάττιος, οἱ δὲ λεωπετρία*; Strabo 224, vii. *fr.* 35, 538 a place-name, Hippocr. iii. 412. 7. Here it served as a butcher's block. Cf. *τραχών* Strabo 180, 756.

δώδεκα μοίρας: this was taken to refer to the twelve Olympian Gods. See R.

129. Eitrem *l.c.* 258 supposes that Hermes cast lots to decide which God should get which portion, and himself as the God of lots gets the best. *Ἑρμοῦ δὲ κλῆρος ἡ πρώτη τῶν κρεῶν μοῖρα* Pollux vi. 55, cl. Ar. *Pax.* 365. This speculation is not justified by any words in the text.

κληροπαλεῖς: only here.

γέρας: cf. 122 *νῶτα γεράσμια*, and δ 66 where the back is the portion of honour. The word was technical, Dittenberger index in v., Stengel *Kultusalt.* 32, 40, 106.

131. **ὀδμὴ . . . ἔτειρε** = δ 441.

132. *ἐπεπείθετο* M: cf. β 103.

The view of Robertson Smith (*Rel. Sem.* ed. 3, p. 306) that this passage together with the epithet *βουφόνος* (436, where see note) refers to the origin of sacrifice in the sanctity of the divine animal is mistaken. The sanctity would be violated by killing as well as by eating the oxen, whereas Hermes has no scruple in killing, and only refrains from eating. Another explanation has been suggested, that there is here an allusion to a local ritual of bloodless sacrifice to Hermes. It is true that the ritual of Hermes varied, in some cults animal oblations being offered, in others bloodless sacrifice (see references in Farnell v. 30, P.-W. viii. 763). Although the latter may possibly have been the older form of sacrifice, animal offerings to Hermes were certainly common in the Homeric period (ξ 422, τ 393). At Cyllene (Gemin. *elem. astr.* i. 14) animal victims were offered. It is probable that the bloodless ritual was more usual in the cult of Hermes under his chthonian aspect, which in this hymn is not mentioned at all. It is also difficult to imagine that if the allusion were to a local ritual prohibition of animal sacrifice, Hermes should perform the full rites of sacrifice short of himself eating the meat. The passage appears only to allude to the institution of sacrifice to the twelve Gods, with particular reference to the inclusion of Hermes in the number (see on 128). Farnell v. 36 has brought it into connexion with works of art depicting Hermes in his capacity of divine *keryx* performing sacrifice to other divinities. For the duties of *kerykes* in the ritual of sacrifice see Stengel *l.c.* 50; cf. ὅτι δὲ σεμνὸν ἦν ἡ μαγειρικὴ μαθεῖν ἔστι ἐκ τῶν Ἀθήνησι κηρύκων· οἵδε γὰρ μαγείρων καὶ βουτύπων ἐπεῖχον τάξιν Athenaeus 160 A, and Hermes' connexion with cooking and carving ο 319. With the scenes on these vases Farnell compares Vedic ritual in which Agni the Fire God wafts the savour of sacrifice to heaven. In Greece this function was not performed by Hephaestus or Hestia, but by Hermes the cook and sacrificial attendant.

For the language cf. Plato *Laws* 782 C οὐδὲ βοὸς ἐτόλμων γεύεσθαι.

133. **περῆν, πέρην'** point to parts of περαίνω, πειραίνω, 'shove, push', i.e. περῆν' (R.), see on 48. Other expressions are λαυκανίης καθέηκα Ω 642, κατὰ λαιμὸν ἱείη Τ 209, τροφὴν διὰ φάρυγγος ἀφῆκε M. Ant. ix. 26, διὰ δέρης ἐδέξατο *Orestes* 41, *Ion* 1037, Nicand. *Alex.* 131.

134. There has been some doubt about Hermes' arrangement, but it is clear that the two cows were divided into three parts: the skins were left outside on the hard rock (124); the flesh, chines, and puddings (122), which had been cooked on spits and divided into twelve portions, were brought into the cave and put

away (134): lastly the heads and feet were burned, τὰ μέν is answered by ἐπὶ δέ (136).

135. **μετήορα κτλ.**: Hermes stowed the portions high up in the cave (on a shelf of rock? πέτρῃ ἐπ' ἠλιβάτῳ 404), 'proof of his recent theft'.

136. **φωρῆς**: this neat emendation depends on 385, where M (wanting here) alone has φωρήν.

ἀείρας: is obviously right. Hermes lifted, i.e. piled, fresh wood upon his old fire. The fire was allowed to burn down to embers before the meat could be roasted (121), as it was held over the fire on spits (cf. I 213): a blazing fire was now needed to burn the heads and feet.

137. **οὐλόποδ' οὐλοκάρηνα.** There was nothing now left of the cows except the heads and feet, Ruhnken is therefore right in understanding these words as substantival, 'all the feet and heads'. G. compares ὁλόπτερος, ὁλόσχοινος, ὁλοκαυτῶ; i.e. οὐλο- here is from οὖλος = ὅλος, although τ 246 οὐλοκάρηνος means 'with curly hair'. Cf. οὐλομελής, the Hippocratean οὐλομελίη (see the lexx.), οὐλαοπλάσμαθ' (*sic*) Orph. *Arg.* 957.

138. **κατὰ χρέος**: Ap. Rh. iii. 189.

140. **ἐμάρανε**: for the alpha cf. Φ 347 ἀγξηράνῃ (Lobeck *Paralip.* 22). The word is used properly of a fire that dies down; Arist. *de Coelo* iii. 7. 4 δύο δὲ τρόπους ὁρῶμεν φθειρόμενον τὸ πῦρ, ὑπό τε γὰρ τοῦ ἐναντίου φθείρεται σβεννύμενον, καὶ αὐτὸ ὑφ' αὑτοῦ μαραινόμενον.

ἀμάθυνε: apparently = 'dusted, sanded', from ἄμαθος. Aesch. *Ag.* 815 πόλιν διημάθυνεν it = 'levelled'. Cf. Philostr. *Gymnast.* 56 μέλαινα δὲ καὶ ξανθὴ κόνις γεώδεις μὲν ἄμφω καὶ ἀγαθαὶ μαλάξαι τε καὶ ὑποθρέψαι.

141. P 650 ἠέλιος δ' ἐπέλαμψε, but M's κατέλαμψε, though un-Homeric, is preferable. It is frequent of the sun: Hippocr. i. 192. 3 ἦμος ἠέλιος νεωστὶ καταλάμπει, 530. 12 ὁ γὰρ ἥλιος κωλύει ἀνίσχων καὶ καταλάμπων (but 531. 12 ὁ γὰρ ἥλιος πρὶν ἄνω ἀρθῆναι οὐκ ἐπιλάμπει), Plut. *aet. rom.* 284 F τοῦ ἡλίου καταλάμποντος ἡμᾶς, Diod. i. 73 τοῦ περὶ τὸν ἥλιον πυρὸς καταλάμψαντος, Dio. Prus. xl. 38, Lucian βίων πρ. 26, Alciphron iii. 1 οἷος . . . ὑπὸ τῶν ἀκτίνων τῶν ἡλιακῶν ὁ πόντος καταλαμπόμενος φαίνεται, Julian *or.* iv. 146 A

τὸν βασιλέα τῶν ὅλων Ἥλιον ἀθρόως καταλάμποντα: of the moon, Plut. *sept. sap. conv.* 160 F ἡ σελήνη κατέλαμπεν εἰς τὴν θάλασσαν; of lightning, Lucian *Tox.* 20, Theophr. *fr.* vi. 43 ἐὰν ἅπαντα καταλάμπῃ μέγαν χειμῶνα σημαίνει: cf. also *h.* ii. 70 καταδέρκεαι ἀκτίνεσσι, Lucian *ver. hist.* i. 10 φωτὶ μεγάλῳ καταλαμπομένην, *Hipp.* 70 fin. On the other hand ἐπιλάμπει of the moon Galen ix. 904, Max. π. καταρχ. 8.

144 = ι 521, *h.* v. 35; cf. A 339.

145. **Διὸς . . . Ἑρμῆς**: for the gen. cf. B 527 Ὀιλῆος ταχὺς Αἴας, Hipponax *fr.* 21 A Κυλλήνιε Μαιάδος Ἑρμῆ, Soph. *Aj.* 172 Ταυρόπολα Διὸς Ἄρτεμις, *ib.* 1302, *Anth. Pal.* vi. 334. 3 Μαιάδος Ἑρμᾶ, *Anth. Plan.* i. 11. 3 Μαιάδος Ἑρμᾶν.

146. The temple of Hermes on the summit of Cyllene was in ruins in the time of Pausanias (vi. 17. 1): ashes were found there, Plut. *mor.* vii. *fr.* 150 (p. 180 Bern.), Geminus *elem. astr.* xvii. 3 (ed. Teubner, p. 180). There is no record of the cave.

δοχμωθείς: 'turning sideways', cf. δοχμός, δόχμιος M 148, Ψ 116; of a boar turning suddenly Hes. *Scut.* 389. The passage is a reminiscence of δ 802 ἐς θάλαμον δ' εἰσῆλθε παρὰ κληῖδος ἱμάντα, 836 παρὰ κληῖδα λιάσθη. There the subject is an εἴδωλον, here δοχμωθείς and ἦκα ποσὶ προβιβῶν show that Hermes kept his bodily shape: ἠύτε, 'like', i.e. as easily as. Fairies pass through keyholes, *Notes and Queries* 1888, 237, R. p. 102. The passage gives no support to the theory that H. was a wind-god. διὰ . . . ἔδυνεν is *in tmesi.*

147. ζ 20 ἡ δ' ἀνέμου ὡς πνοιὴ ἐπέσσυτο (of a dream), A 359 ἠύτ' ὀμίχλη (of Thetis), and the double comparison Ap. Rh. iv. 877 αὐτὴ δὲ πνοιῇ ἰκέλη δέμας ἠύτ' ὄνειρος (also of Thetis); generally Athanasius *vit. Anton.* 40 (Migne xxvi. 901 B) διὰ τῆς θύρας ὥσπερ καπνὸς ἐξερχόμενος ἐφάνη, *ss. Macariorum apophthegm.* 3 (Migne xxxiv. 240 C) ὅτε ὁρᾷ με στρέφεται ὡς ἄνεμος, the same with ἀνέμῃ Migne lxv. 261 B: *more animae* Juv. iii. 261, ὥσπερ δὲ ὀμίχλη δρόσου ἀφανὴς ἐγένετο Job xxiv. 20. The comparison is frequent in Nonnus (xxviii. 102 φυγὰς εἴκελος αὔραις, 150, 282, xi. 226, xxxii. 256, viii. 107 ὅμοιος ἔσσυτο καπνῷ) and Quintus (εἴκελος αὔρῃ sim.) iii. 781, iv. 111 etc., *epigr.* Kaibel 322. 4.

148. **ἰθύσας** is a real past and recapitulates: 'he made straight

for the cave and . . .', cf. 12 and 13, 24 and 25, 34 and 35. The νηός was the inner part, the *cella*.

For the genitive cf. O 693, α 119, γ 17, Babrius 95. 42 θύρης κατιθύς.

149. **ὥς περ ἐπ' οὔδει**: 'as (might be expected) on a floor': cf. the prose use of ὡς, e.g. οὐδὲ ἀδύνατος ὡς Λακεδαιμόνιος λέγειν. The name for the sound of a foot was νοῦθος, Herod. π. μον. λέξ. 42, quoting Hes. *fr.* 43. Cf. Ovid *Amores* iii. 1. 52.

151. Asyndeton (a characteristic of this hymn, 17, 25, 111, 237, 438, 447, 478, 482, 512) evidently occurs here, for εἰλυμένος is true of κεῖτο and certainly not of ἐπῴχετο.

152. **περ' ἰγνύσι**, sc. περί. Cf. Theocr. xxv. 242 περ' ἰγνύῃσιν ἕλιξε κέρκον. The elision of περί, well-established in Hesiod (*Theog.* 678, 733) and Pindar (*Ol.* vi. 38, *Pyth.* iii. 52, iv. 265, *Nem.* xi. 40, *fr.* 122) and even in Aeschylus (*Ag.* 1147, *Eum.* 634), is, like ἀθρόᾱς 106, one of the linguistic peculiarities of the hymn. Inscriptions from Megara (*CIG.* 1064) and Delphi (1688) show it, and Hellanicus read it at O 651 (Αἰολικῶς). See La Roche *HU.* i. 121, Schulze *qu. ep.* 133 n. 7, K.-B. i. § 53.

λαῖφος ἀθύρων: λαῖφος = σπάργανα, not bed-clothes (δέμνια) unnecessary for a swaddled child in its cradle; the word elsewhere = a sail, or clothing, but not 'sheets'. Hermes was a νεοσπαδής (Hesych. νεωστὶ τὰ σπάδη περικείμενον, ἅ ἐστι σπάργανα). A child with its hands free would pull at the σπάργανα round its legs. Hephaestus in Lucian *dial. de or.* vii. 2 is told that he will see his πυράγρα ἐν τοῖς σπαργάνοις τοῦ βρέφους. Similar gestures of persons in bed are rendered by ἐψηλάφα, ἔτιλλε, ἔγλυφε, ἐτριχολόγει, ἐκροκυδολόγει Hippocr. iii. 509. 12, 656. 10, κροκυδίζει καὶ καρφολογεῖ Galen viii. 227, 330.

The derivation and specific meaning of ἀθύρειν are unknown (it may well mean 'to finger', e.g. in 485, cf. Hesych. ἐναθύρσας· ἐμπλέξας). Its construction is usually with the accusative, e.g. Pind. *Nem.* iii. 78 ἔργα, *Isthm.* iii. 57 ἀρετάν, *h. Pan* 15 μοῦσαν, *epigr.* Kaibel 325. 9 χορὸν εὐρύν, Philostr. *Imag.* 5 περὶ τὸν Νεῖλον οἱ πήχεις ἀθύρουσι παιδία ξύμμετρα τῷ ὀνόματι, Nonnus xlv. 244 ἀγήνορα κόμπον, in the passive this hymn 485. Only one example of the dative is given in the lexx. (Alexandrian). The same is the case with *παίζειν*,[1] *προσπαίζειν*, *γελᾶν*, *ludere*. Some of the accusatives may be called 'cognate', others are not. Our modern constructions '*jouer de*, play with' should not influence us.

153. 'Keeping it on the left of his hand,' i.e. between his arm and the edge of the cradle. Cf. ε 277, Pind. *Pyth.* vi. 19, Aratus *Phaen.* 278 (M. & R.).

155. **τίπτε . . . πόθεν**: double question, an extension of the Homeric *τίς πόθεν*; cf. Eur. *Hel.* 86, 873 *τί τἀμὰ πῶς ἔχει*; 1543 *πῶς ἐκ τίνος*; *Alc.* *τίς ἂν πῶς πᾷ*; *Hec.* 1076 *ποῖ πᾷ*; *IT.* 77, 1360, *Troad.* 291, *Auge fr.* 278 *ποῖ πῶς δὲ λήσει*; Soph. *Trach.* 707 *πόθεν γὰρ ἀντὶ τοῦ*; *Philoct.* 1090, *h.* ii. 113.

τόδε, 'hither': cf. α 409 (where one MS. has *τάδε*, as the vulg. here), *ἐς τόδ'* Eur. *Heracl.* 393. So Apollonius took it *adv.* 591.

156. **ἀναιδείην ἐπιειμένε** = A 149, I 372.

158. **Λητοΐδου**: neither word nor genitive is Homeric, but were found on an 'ancient blade' dedicated at Delphi, quoted by Phaenias *FHG.* ii. 297 = Preger *inscr. metr. gr.* 89.

159. It is possible to take **φέροντα** in the sense of 'raiding, plundering', since *φέρειν* and *ἄγειν* are used in this sense without an object (see the lexx.), but the alternative *λαβόντα* would be an obstacle. As Tucker saw, *φέροντα* is expletive; cf. 52 and in late Greek Aelian *frr.* 10, 69, Porph. *vit. Plot.* 24, Philostr. *vit. Apoll.* iii. 4, Lucian *Tim.* 26, *dial. mort.* 6. 3, *de merc. cond.* 9, 24, 39, *Icarom.* 10, 13. LS. assert that *λαμβάνω* also is expletive, but their examples do not bear examination; *βαλών*, however, is expletive in Epictet. ii. 20. 10 *βαλὼν ἐκάθευδε*, iv. 10. 29 *τί οὖν οὐ ῥέγκω βαλών*; and with this gentle metathesis the two readings confirm one another.

μεταξύ, 'by whiles' (Soph. *fr.* 206), explained by 287.

For wooded hills as the resort of brigands, cf. 287, Dicaearchus i. 8, *Anth. Pal.* vii. 544, Juvenal iii. 307 Mayor.

160. **πάλιν**: 'go back', i.e. whence you came; ii. 398 *πτᾶσα πάλιν*.

163. To translate this passage we must take the middle in the sense of *ποιεῖς*, as *τιτύσκει* may be taken in Antimachus *fr.* 44,

[1] esp. Empedocles 100. 9 Diels *ὥσπερ ὅταν παῖς | κλεψύδρην* (v.l. *-αις*) *παίζῃσι δι' εὐπετέος χαλκοῖο*.

Aratus 418, Oppian *Hal.* ii. 99, *epigr.* Kaibel 1035. 24 (προ-), more in the lexx. τιτύσκεσθαι is twice used tropically in Homer in the sense of 'reflect' (N 558, θ 556), derived from the original sense 'aim', but there is no case of an acc., to say nothing of a double acc. On the other hand Pierson's δεδίσκεαι, supported by the similar passage Υ 200 (μὴ δή μ' ἐπέεσσί γε νηπύτιον ὣς | ἔλπεο δειδίξεσθαι, ἐπεὶ σάφα οἶδα καὶ αὐτὸς | ἠμὲν κερτομίας ἠδ' αἴσυλα μυθήσασθαι) is made improbable by the fact that δ and τ are not graphical exchanges, and there was no reason to alter a fairly familiar word with a clear meaning like δεδίσκεαι to τιτύσκεαι.

164. **ὃς . . . οἶδε** is an anticipatory hyperbaton.

παῦρα and **αἴσυλα** are the best readings, supported by the Homeric passage above, where Σ B gives the correct sense, αἴσυλα τὰς παρὰ τὸ καθῆκον λεγομένας ἀπειλάς, 'improper threats'. M's πολλὰ . . . ἄρμενα would state much the same thing conversely, but the negative παῦρα is more effective, 'little wickedness, few bad words'.

165. **ταρβαλέον**: first here (Hesych. ταρβαρέον· δεινόν, φοβερόν).

167. **βουκολέων**: this correction may be accepted: at Ξ 445 𝔭[10] has βου(κο)λεοντι. The attempts to make βουλεύων take an accusative or to make it absolute, ἐμέ following ἐπιβήσομαι, are impossible. For the metaphor cf. ποιμαίνω Pind. *Isthm.* iv. 12, Aesch. *Eum.* 91, and the reverse εἰ τὸν παῖδα . . . ἀποβουκολήσαιμι Xen. *Cyrop.* i. 4. 13, ἀβουκόλητον Aesch. *Suppl.* 940.

168. Of the two readings **ἄλιστοι** is the better. Hermes and his mother were not ἄπαστοι with their stores of nectar and ambrosia (248). For the single λ cf. πολύλιστος.

169. **αὐτοῦ τῇδε**: Herod. vii. 141 αὐτοῦ τῇδε μενέομεν (Matthiae), id. vii. 10, ix. 11, *vit. Hom. Herod.* 139, αὐτοῦ ταύτῃ often.

172. For the gen. cf. Π 825 πίδακος ἀμφ' ὀλίγης, θ 267 ἀμφ' Ἄρεος φιλότητος. *H. Dem.* 85 the acc. stands in the same phrase.

173. **κἀγώ**: for the crasis see on *h.* ii. 13.

174. Cf. A 324 εἰ δέ κε μὴ δώῃσιν ἐγὼ δέ κεν αὐτὸς ἕλωμαι. Schmidt suggests that Hesychius (μὴ δώησ[ο]ι· μὴ δῷ) quotes this line.

175. The quantity of φηλητέων (φιλ-) requires the omission of δέ (inserted when the verb was treated as related to φίλος): the

editors from Demetrius to Franke punctuated *πειρήσω· δύναμαι φηλητέων ὄρχ. εἶναι*; since then *δύναμαι* has been taken parenthetically. Asyndetic parenthesis is almost limited to *οἶμαι, οἶδα, ὁρᾷς*; *φημί* (549), see KG. ii. 353; but cf. Eur. *IT*. 1073 *φθέγξασθε*, Cephisodorus i. 800. 2 Kock (Ath. 553 A) *ἄγαμαι*, Paus. vi. 14, 12 *γένος ἀνδρὸς ἐξ Ἀβδήρων*, viii. 8, 4 *ὁποῖον οὐ μνημονεύουσιν*.

178. **ἀντιτορήσων**: see on 119. Here and 283 we should perhaps correct to *ἀντετορήσων*.

179 = ν 217: 181 = Θ 471, ω 511; cf. Δ 353. On the wealth of Delphi see 335, *h*. iii. 536.

186. For the accent of Ὀγχηστος and the precinct of Posidon see *h*. iii. 230.

187. **γαιηόχου**: this title, common in poetry, is rare in cult. Except for Posidon Erechtheus Gaeeochus at Athens (Dittenberger *Syll*. 790, *IG*. iii. 276) the only certainly attested cult of Posidon Γαιάϝοχος was in Laconia, at Gythium and Therapne (Hesych. *in* Γαιήοχος, ann. Bekk. i. 229. 8, Paus. iii. 21. 8). The Laconian, like the Onchestian God, was a patron of horses, and races were run in his honour (Paus. iii. 20. 2, Xen. *Hell*. vi. 5. 20, *IG*. viii. 1. 213; see further, Nilsson *GF*. 65).

187. **ἐρισφαράγου**: not in Homer; cf. Bacchyl. v. 20 *Ζηνὸς ἐρισφαράγου*, poeta ap. *EM*. in Ἀσφάραγος· *ἐρισφάραγος πόσις Ἥρης ἔσται*, Eust. 1636. 8.

188. 'He found an old man grazing his brute, the stay of his vineyard, beside the road.' Κνώδαλον usually connotes some kind of monster (e.g. a serpent, *κυρίως τὰ θαλάσσια θηρία* Hesych.), but is used of animals in general ρ 317, Hes. *Theog*. 582, of beasts of burden or draught-animals Aesch. *PV*. 478, Pind. *Pyth*. x. 36, of large game Oppian *Hal*. i. 17, of a lion Theocr. xxv. 183, of butcher's meat generally *Anth. Pal*. vi. 101. 1, even of human beings Cratinus *fr*. 233. It is in keeping with the racy style of this hymn to apply it to the old man's donkey, no doubt a poor donkey, like the *ὄνος βαλανέως ξύλα καὶ φρύγανα κατακομίζων* of Plut. *de. cup. div*. 525 E (Alciphron iii. 20 *οἶσθά με ἐπισάξαντα τὴν ὄνον σῦκα καὶ ἀσπαλάθας*), or the *ὀνάριον* of Diphilus *fr*. 89 *ἓν ὀνάριον ἐξ ἀγροῦ μοι καταβαίνει | καθ' ἕκαστον ἐνιαυτὸν ἀγαπητῶς | ὥσπερ κανοῦν μοι πάντ' ἐνεσκευασμένον | σπονδὴν ὀλὰς ἔλαιον ἰσχάδας*

μέλι, and that in com. anon. ap. Stob. *ecl.* iv. 15. 28. 20 ὀνησίφορα γένοιτο, τοῦτο γίνεται | ὃ γὰρ φέρει νῦν οὗτος εἷς ὄνος φέρει, Virg. *Copa* 25 *lassus iam sudat asellus*, Strabo 659 ἡμίονον ξυλοφοροῦντα, Babrius 55. 6 τίς ἄξει τῷ γέροντι τὰ σκεύη; 129. 659.

ἕρκος ἀλωῆς (lit. Moschus iv. 100) is a parody of the Homeric ἕρκος Ἀχαιῶν of Ajax, and similar expressions (ἕρκος Ὀλύμπου of Ares *h.* viii. 3, ἕρκος ἀρούρης of the lesser Ajax, Christodorus *Ecphrasis* 210, ἕρκος ἐτύχθη πατρὶ τέκος *Anth. Pal.* ix. 446, 5; Plut. *Aem. Paul.* 6 τὸ Λιγύων ἔθνος ὥσπερ ἕρκος ἢ πρόβολον ἐμποδὼν κείμενον τοῖς Γαλατικοῖς κινήμασιν: cf. also ἕρμα Ψ 121, Plut. *praec. ger. reip.* 814 C ἕρμα τῆς πολιτείας βέβαιον, *epigr.* Kaibel 452. 11, Hippocr. *Epist.* 13 (iii. 779) τοὺς ἀγαθοὺς ἄνδρας ἐρύματα ἑωυτῶν: κίονες Archilochus 17. 2; τείχεα γαίης of kings Oppian *Hal.* v. 45; πύργος Alcaeus 23, Theognis 233, of Achilles Theocr. xxii. 220). πίονα ἔργα 127 also is parodic.

The conjectures principally attack κνώδαλον, with the result that νέμοντα must govern ἕρκος ἀλωῆς in the literal sense, and as you cannot graze a hedge νέμοντα is written δέμοντα. But the old man is called βατοδρόπε, and brambles are not plucked from hedges, they are encouraged to grow. He dug them out of the vineyard (207). The donkey was his 'support', it removed the weeds with a cart or baskets. In the meantime it grazed by the side of the road, as the swine grazed by the hedge υ 164, and as Lucius did as an ass (Lucian *Asin.* 43), εἶτε ἐκεῖνος μὲν καὶ ἔσκαπτε καὶ ἐφύτευε καὶ τὸ ὕδωρ τῷ φυτῷ ἐπῆγεν, ἐγὼ δὲ ἐν τούτῳ ἑστήκειν ἀργός; cf. in general Libanius *or.* l. 23 καὶ τί δεινὸν ἐξιόντα τὸν ὄνον φορτίον ἕτερον οὐκ ἔχοντα τοῦτο φέροντα ἐξιέναι; lv. 24 ὅστις ὄνος ἐστὶ λεοντῇ κεκαλυμμένος ἀθλιώτερος . . . ἢ εἰ σιγᾶν ἐγνώκει καὶ ποιεῖσθαι τὸν βίον ἀπὸ τοῦ λίθους τοῖς οἰκοδομοῦσι φέρειν.

190. **βατοδρόπε**: cf. Laertes ω 230 χειρῖδάς τ' ἐπὶ χερσὶ βάτων ἕνεκ'.

192. **κεράεσσιν ἑλικτάς**: apparently = the Homeric ἕλικας.

196. **ὃ δὴ . . . τέτυκται**: Σ 549 τὸ δὴ περὶ θαῦμα τέτυκτο.

197. **καταδυομένοιο**: on the ῡ see Schulze *qu. ep.* 136.

202. **ἴδοιτο**: for the omission of τις cf. N 287, X 199, ω 108, Hes. *Theog.* 741, and with a participle *OD.* 12, v.l. 291, *h.* xxix. 6, Ξ 58 (γνοίη Aristoph.), see KG. § 352 g, LS. *in* τις. In later Greek cf. Theocr. xvii. 41, Xen. *Symp.* i. 8, *Rep. Ath.* i. 10.

203. ὁδίστης, to which E's correction points, is not found; ὅδισμα exists.

205. M repeats πρήσσουσιν from 203.

206. **πρόπαν . . . καταδύντα**: a common formula, A 601 etc.

208. **ἔδοξα** (in Homer ἐδόκησα) is qualified by the parenthetical σαφὲς δ' οὐκ οἶδα.

209. **ὅς τις** κτλ. Cf. 277, 311, *h.* ii. 58, 119, often in Attic poetry (Blaydes on Ar. *Nub.* 883): Lucian *Somn.* 5 ἀναπεμπάζῃ τὸν ὄνειρον τίς ποτε ὁ φανείς σοι ἦν, Strabo 625 τὴν Ἀπολλοδώρειον αἵρεσιν . . . ἥτις ποτ' ἐστί. For the expression cf. Babrius 59. 50 οὐκ εἶδον εἶπε, τῷ δὲ δακτύλῳ νεύων | τὸν τόπον ἐδείκνυ' οὗ πανοῦργος ἐκρύφθη, Max. Tyr. xxxii. 1 ὁ δὲ ποιμὴν οὐκ ἔφη εἰδέναι, καὶ ὁμοῦ λέγων τὴν χεῖρα ἀποτείνας ἔδειξε τὸ χωρίον (Aesop 10 and 399).

210. **ἐπιστροφάδην**, 'from side to side', following the oxen; Hippocr. iii. 284 ὁδοιπορέουσι δὲ περιστροφάδην ὡς βόες, ib. 214 ἥ τε ὁδοιπορίη περιφοράδην τοῦ σκέλεος ὥσπερ τοῖς βουσί, ib. 225 σαλεύουσιν ἐν τῇ ὁδοιπορίῃ ἔνθα καὶ ἔνθα.

211. **ἔχεν**: kept them facing him. He 'saw him driving them to Pylos' 354, and Apollo, without being told, went forthwith to Pylos. Perhaps the bird indicated the direction.

213. It is clear from the epithet that an actual feathered fowl is intended, which informed Apollo that Hermes was the thief. So Apollod. iii. 10. 2, 5.

216. The first mention of Pylos: the Alpheus, mentioned in the account of the actual journey, shows that it was in Triphylia.

217. For the wording cf. Π 360. For the concealment cf. E 186, Π 790.

219. Cf. N 99, O 286, Υ 344, Φ 54.

222. This verse and 345 give the first appearance of βῆμα. It occurs as a v.l. θ 192, and *Ichneut.* 112 (παλινστραφη τοι ναι μα δια τα βηματα | εις τουμπαλιν δεδορκεν αυ).

224. On the centaurs see Roscher *in v.* (and an absurd etymology in *Glotta* x. 50). This verse leaves the question open whether the writer regarded the centaur as a hairy wild man, with nothing equine in form (probably the original and Homeric conception, see Mannhardt *AWF.* 79), or as having two human

and two equine legs (as on the chest of Cypselus), or with four horse's legs (the fifth-century type).

ἔστιν ὁμοῖα (*xp*): *Batr.* 170 *b* κενταύρων μεγαλαύχων ἦσαν ὁμοῖοι is a reminiscence.

225. **βιβᾷ**: cf. 149 προβιβῶν, *h.* iii. 133 ἐβίβασκεν, Pind. *Ol.* xiv. 25 βιβῶντα. In Γ 22, Η 213 Aristophanes restored the forms from βιβάς for the vulgate βιβῶν.

226. **αἰνὰ . . . αἰνότερα.** These adjectives refer to Hermes' βήματα, for Apollo recognized the cows' ἴχνια as cattle-tracks, although they pointed the wrong way. Hermes wearing his skis floundered (ἐπιστροφάδην 210) from one side of the road to the other; for the gen. cf. Herod. ii. 176 ὁ μὲν ἔνθεν ὁ δ' ἔνθεν τοῦ μεγάλου, Xen. *Cyrop.* vi. 1. 30 ἔνθεν καὶ ἔνθεν τῶν τροχῶν, *ib.* 33, vii. 1. 31; with ἔνθα 357 ὁδοῦ τὸ μὲν ἔνθα τὸ δ' ἔνθα, Hippocr. ii. 238. 2 ἔνθα τῆς γῆς . . . ἔνθα δὲ οὔ, iii. 456 ἡ μὲν ἔνθα ἡ δὲ ἔνθα τῶν σπονδύλων, Aristotle 400 b 4 παρέτρεψε δὲ τοῦ φλογμοῦ τὸ μὲν ἔνθα τὸ δ' ἔνθα, Orph. *Arg.* 559 τοίχων ἔνθα καὶ ἔνθα. A lion's spoor is somewhat similarly described Aelian *NH.* ix. 30.

228. **καταειμένον ὕλῃ** = *h.* iii. 225.

229. **κευθμῶνα**: first in ν 367 μαιομένη κευθμῶνας ἀνὰ σπέος, Stesich. iv. 3 ἐν κευθμῶνι πέτρας.

230. **ἀμβροσίη** = ἄμβροτος Hom.

ἐλόχευσε: not in Homer.

231. It is uncertain whether the writer refers (1) to Maia's fire (Calypso had one ε 59), or (2) to a miraculous scent betokening a deity (see on *h.* ii. 27 and R.), or (3) the natural smell of crops and flowers; cf. Theognis 830 πένθει δ' εὐώδη χῶρον ἀπολλύμενον, Ap. Rh. iii. 291, *Ichneutae* 215 τονδε χλοερον υλωδη παγον ενθηρον (Cyllene was fertile, Theophr. *HP.* iii. 2. 5). Cf. a hill at Carthage Arist. *Mir. Ausc.* 113, Philostr. *Heroic.* 12 ὡς ἀμβροσία ἡ ὀσμὴ τοῦ χωρίου, *vit. Ap. Tyan.* ii. 1 προσιόντας τῷ Καυκάσῳ εὐωδεστέρας τῆς γῆς αἰσθέσθαι, Moschus i. 92 λειμῶνος ἐκαίνυτο λαρὸν ἀυτμήν, Martial iii. 65, 4 *gramina quod redolent quae modo carpsit ovis*, 7 *gleba quod aestivo leviter cum spargitur imbre*, Antyllus ap. Orib. *coll.* vi. 21. 16 οἱ [περίπατοι] ἐν λειμῶνι συμπληρωτικοί εἰσι κεφαλῆς διὰ τὴν εὐωδίαν. Equally ambiguous are ἄντρῳ ἐν εὐώδει *h.* xxvi. 6, θυωδέος Οὐλύμποιο below 322.

234. **αὐτὸς Ἀπόλλων**: formulaic and unemphatic, as *h.* iii. 181, Moschus iv. 13; ἐκηβόλος αὐτὸς Ἀπόλλων *h.* v. 151 is emphatic.

236. **χωόμενον περὶ βουσίν** = Hes. *Scut.* 12 (χωσάμενός).

238. ὁλοσποδός is one of M's corruptions (see p. xxiv), possibly due to οὐλόποδ' οὐλοκάρηνα 137. **ὕλης σποδός** is original. σποδός is 'dust' generally; therefore the defining gen. material is not otiose. Cf. Galen. xiv. 521 ἄνθρακα δρυός, 295 χάρτου σποδοῦ = χάρτου κεκαυμένου, xii. 356 καρκίνων τέφρα, 939 χελιδόνων σποδοῦ, xix. 743 σποδὸς φύλλων ἐλαίας, Herod. iv. 35 μηρίων σποδόν, Charito i. 3. 2 οἴνου πηλόν, Plut. *coh. ir.* 463 A, Geopon. ii. 27. 6 τέφραν κληματίδων δρύος (= vi. 5. 6 διὰ σποδοῦ κληματίνης), v. 32. 2 μυρίκης μὲν μάλιστα εἰ δὲ μὴ οἱουδήποτε ξύλου τέφραν, vii. 21. 2 τέφρας κληματίδων μελανῶν ἐμβαλλομένης (= κληματόεσσαν τέφρην Nicander *Alex.* 539), ix. 25. 3 ἄνθρακας πεπυρωμένους ἐλαίνου ξύλου, x. 7. 35 τὴν τούτων τέφραν, 8. 2 τὴν τέφραν τῶν σικυηλάτων (with prepositions τὴν ἀπὸ σιδήρου σποδόν Demetr. *Hieracosoph.* 44, sim. 252, Aristides xxv. 315 πίτταν ἐξ οἴνου, Suet. *Tib.* 74 *cinis e favilla et arboribus*). The phrase therefore = τῇ ξυλίνῃ σποδῷ in Strabo 269. In 140 the fire is extinguished with ordinary dust, κόνις μέλαινα. The simile resembles ε 488, where Odysseus keeps up his spark of life in a covering of leaves, as a man hides a smouldering log under a heap of ash. Cf. *h.* ii. 239, Theocr. xi. 5, xxiv. 88, Ap. Rh. iii. 291, Callim. *ep.* 45. 2, of cooking Hippocr. ii. 544, 654 ἧπαρ ὄϊος ἢ αἰγὸς ἐς τέφρην κρύψαι.

239. **ἀνεείλε' ἓ αὐτόν**: the MS. ἀλέεινεν is impossible, and the sense 'hid' cannot be read into it on the strength of Hesych. ἀλεάζειν· κρύπτειν. ἀλέαινεν 'warmed' is unsuitable, and more so ἀλέγυνεν, which means to prepare. The required sense is given by ἀνειλεῖν 'roll up': cf. Aelian *NA.* vi. 5. 4 μέλλων ἁλίσκεσθαι ἑαυτὸν συνειλήσας ἄληπτον ἐργάζεται, 64 τὸ σκληρὸν τῆς μαλάχης φύλλον ᾧ τὰ ἄλλα συνειλοῦσιν, Plato *Symp.* 206 D συσπειρᾶται . . . καὶ ἀνείλλεται (v.l. ἀνειλεῖται). For the uncontracted form cf. κατεκόσμεε Δ 118, μετεφώνεε θ 201 (-ει Ar.), π 354, προσεφώνεε π 308, ᾤκεε Hes. *fr.* 74.

240. **συνέλασσε**, 'huddled' head, hands, and feet in a small space.

241. **φῄ**: this brilliant emendation of Barnes (who accented it

φῇ) is confirmed by θῆρα in *y*. It will occur first here, next in Callim. *Hec.* 34, 49. Zenodotus wished to introduce it into Homer, Bergk conjectured it in Hipponax 15. 2. On the derivation see Boisacq.

νεόλλουτος: apparently = new-born child, in the racy style of this author. Literally νεόλουτος is frequent in Hippocrates of a *puerpera* (i. 535. 1, 574. 11, 577. 14, 817 *inf.*, 829. 6, iii. 10. 36). The formation with νεο- is frequent in the author, νεοβρῶτι ii. 35. 10 al., νεορρόφητον 63. 1, νεοπυρίητος, νεόξαντα, νεότρωτοι, νεόποτον. In other authors cf. νεόπλυτα ζ 64, νεόπλ[ο]υτον Anacr. 54. 4, νεόπλυτα Orph. *Lith.* 708, νεόκαυστος Theophr. *CP.* vi. 17. 7.

For compounds of -λουτ- cf. ἀλουτία Eupolis 251, ἡμίλουτοι Cratinus 416, ἀλούτησον Epict. iii. 22. 73, ψυχρολουτεῖ Plut. *amat.* 752 A, θερμολουτοῦσι 789 F, Jakobsohn *KZ.* 42. 160.

For the practice Martin (*varior. lect.* ed. 2. 1755) quotes Theocr. xxiv. 3, Lycophron 321, Callim. *Del.* 6, *Jov.* 16, Plautus *Amphitr.* v. 1. 50; cf. also *h.* iii. 120, Nonnus viii. 406, 413.

The variant in *y* νέον λοχάων suggests the Latin *recens ab*, 'fresh from his birth' (λοχόαις· γεννήσεσι Hesych.), but there is no case of a gen. after νέος, as after ἐλεύθερος etc. K.-G. i. p. 401. We may see in it a compound of -λοχ-, such as are ἐλλοχᾶν (Alciphron ii. 3 [τοῦ Νείλου] ἐλλοχωμένου τοσούτοις κακοῖς) and συλλόχεια (Hippocr. i. 458 κατὰ τὰς συλλοχείας). Can we invent νεολλοχεών, on the analogy of ἀπατεών, κωπεών, λυμεών etc.? For the sense cf. νήπιος ἐκ λοχειας Plut. *Lysand.* 8.

ἤδυμον: the form recurs *infra* 449. At *h.* v. 171, xix. 16 the MSS. give νήδυμον. In the MSS. of Homer νήδυμος prevails, but there is some authority for ἤδυμος B 2, δ 793, μ 311. Here and 449 the form is proved by the metre. Both forms occur as proper names. On the derivation see Boisacq.

242. In this line Martin made ἄγρης· εἰν- into **ἐγρήσσων**, for which cf. Hipponax 89 Ἑρμῆ μάκαρ καθ' ὕπνον οἶδας ἐγρήσσειν. For the confusion of ἀγ-, ἐγ- cf. P 660, υ 53. **ἐτεόν** also is certain; the word is corrupted Υ 255. A plausible sense is thus obtained. What R. prints is unintelligible.

243. **γνῶ δ' οὐδ' ἠγνοίησε** = Hes. *Theog.* 551.

245. **παῖδ' ὀλίγον δολίῃς εἰλυμένον ἐντροπίῃσι.** The word ἐντροπίη

occurs elsewhere in Hippocr. π. εὐσχημ. i. p. 67 Kühn ἀκμάζοντες δὲ δι' ἐντροπίην ἱδρῶτας τίθενται βλέποντες, 'by attention, anxiety'. It seems the same as the more common ἐντροπή, which from Hippocrates and Sophocles downwards means 'respect, consideration', e.g. Hipp. ib. 70, Ioseph. *Ant. Iud.* xiv. 375 κατ' αἰδῶ καὶ πολλὴν ἐντροπὴν προπεμφθέντες, xv. 370 ἐντροπῆς διὰ τὸν Πολλίωνα τυχόντες, xvi. 1. 187 δι' ἐντροπῆς; and this is the sense of the middle verb, e.g. *ib.* 288 οὐ γὰρ ἐντραπέντες οὐδ' ἀρνησαμένοι τὴν πρᾶξιν. This sense does not suit Hermes, who is 'wrapped in crafty ——'. Perhaps we may give ἐντροπίῃσι the more primitive sense of 'attention, care, plot', to which Pindar *Pyth.* i. 92 μὴ δολωθῇς ὦ φίλος κέρδεσιν ἐντραπέλοις (Σ τῇ ἐχθροτάτῃ φιλοκερδείᾳ), and Theognis 400 ἐντράπελ' ἀθανάτων μῆνιν ἀλευάμενος are not unlike. The word will here refer to Hermes' 'precautions', reversing the cattle, making snow-shoes, etc.

246. **ἀνά**: for this preposition with παπταίνειν cf. M 333 (v.l. ἄρα), Ap. Rh. iii. 1284; for the direct acc. see Δ 200. In general cf. Orph. *Lith.* 18 ἐς πολυήρατον ἄντρον ἐσελθέμεν Ἑρμείαο | ἔνθ' ὅγε παντοίων ἀγαθῶν κατέθηκεν ὅμιλον, and *ib.* 55.

247. **ἀδύτους**: only here masc. In Homer E 448, 512, Pind. *Ol.* vii. 59 the gender is doubtful, but presumably neuter.

252. **ἐξερέεινε**: cf. μ 259 πόρους ἁλὸς ἐξερεείνων.

253. **Λητοΐδης** (158): un-Homeric, and among the Hymns only in this one. It is Hesiodic (*Scut.* 479, *fr.* 125. 3), and appears on the Chest of Cypselus (λατοιδας Paus. v. 18. 4). It is perhaps a sign of locality.

255–7. Cf. Θ 12 sq.; *infra* 466 = Θ 40. At this point Hermes stole Apollo's bow according to Philostr. *Imag.* 26.

θᾶττον: the form ἐλαττον occurs in the Oropian inscription, which also has ηχοι, εντοθα, αφικνεμενων. The -ττ- here is also probably local: cf. καλοῦσι δὲ Βοιωτιακῶς Μυκαληττόν Strabo 404. On ττ = σσ in Boeotian see Meister *die gr. Dial.* i. 264.

256. **λαβών**: Ilgen's metathesis seems necessary, cl. Θ 13 ἤ μιν ἑλὼν ῥίψω, *h.* iii. 318 ῥίψ' ἀνὰ χερσὶν ἑλοῦσα.

259. **ὀλίγοισι**: Hermes will play the leader among 'little men', men of his own size. The word is usually applied to children, 245, 456, *Anth. Pal.* vii. 632. 1 ὀλίγον βρέφος, Theocr. i. 47

ὀλίγος τις κῶρος, Rhianus ap. Stob. *ecl.* iii. 33. For children in Hades cf. Virg. *Aen.* vi. 427, Lucian Κατάπλ. 5, 6, Dieterich *Nekyia* 151. For ἀνδράσι cf. ἀνδράσι πυγμαίοισι Γ 6.

μετά and ἐν are equally good: for the latter cf. Plato *rep.* 474 C.

263–4 = 363–4 (οὐδέ κε for οὐκ ἄν).

263. **ἄλλου μῦθον ἄκουσα**: cf. γ 94, δ 224, ψ 40: an echo *Batr.* 147–8.

264. **μήνυτρον**: first here; μηνυ[τρ *Ichneutae* 88.

265. **οὐδέ** for οὔτε is a slight change, and sufficient. The repeated negatives produced some confusion. Line 264 repeated 364 opens with οὐδέ κε.

266. **πάρος**, 'hitherto, formerly' of time.

272 = ἅμα βουσίν Aphr. 78; 'that a newborn child should come through the yard with cattle of the field', viz. driving them: Apollo expected to find them in the cave.

275. For μή with the indic. in oaths cf. K 330, O 41.

277. Cf. B 436 δὲ κλέος οἷον ἀκούομεν.

279. **ὀφρύσι ῥιπτάζεσκεν**: he 'tossed about with his eyebrows', i.e. wagged his head from side to side. The verb is intrans. in Hippocr. *Acut.* ii. 18 of patients tossing in bed, passive or middle of the mind Plut. *de lib. et agr.* 6 ῥιπταζόμενος ἐπὶ πάντα καὶ ψηλαφῶντι προσεοικώς; ῥιπτεῖν is intrans. Theognis 176, Eur. *Hec.* 1325, ἀναρριπτεῖν Lucian *Hermot.* 28. For ὀφρύσι cf. μείδησεν . . . ὀφρύσι *Dem.* 357. The action is described by Aristaenetus i. 22 ἐφ' ἑκάτερα παρακινοῦσα τὸ βλέμμα, 24 ὑποκινοῦσα σὺν τοῖς ὤμοις τὸ βλέμμα.

ὁρώμενος ἔνθα καὶ ἔνθα = Hes. *fr.* 188. 2 (-ον).

280. **ἀποσυρίζων**: to show his indifference: Lucian *merc. cond.* 10 ὑπὸ θυρωρῷ κακῶς συρίζοντι . . . ταττόμενον (unless this means to speak bad Syrian), Juv. x. 22 *cantabit vacuus coram latrone.*

ἅλιον τὸν μῦθον ἀκούων: an extension of E 715 ἅλιον τὸν μῦθον ὑπέστημεν Μενελάῳ, 'hearing his words as nothing'. For a further predicate with ἀκούω see 443: a similar use with χαίρω is called Oropian; *EM.* and Suid. *in* χαίρω· χαίρω σε ἐληλυθότα. 'Ορωπικοὶ οὕτως λέγουσιν: Eur. *Hipp.* 1339 τοὺς γὰρ εὐσεβεῖς θεοὶ | θνῄσκοντας οὐ χαίρουσι. ὡς, added as a gloss to explain the construction, made its way into the text of some MSS. and expelled τόν in M. R.'s odd conjecture ἅλιόν τως introduces a new enclitic and rests on *Ichneutae* 296, where the real reading is ἦθ' ὥς.

283. **ἀντιτοροῦντα**: we should perhaps write ἀντετοροῦντα. See on 119.

284. The necessary future is given by Tucker's very neat χ' ἕνα: cf. Theognis 83 οὔ χ' εὕροις, *IG.* vii. 3467 ος χ αδαν πιε (R.).

ἐπ' οὔδεϊ φῶτα καθίσσαι is proverbial: Wisdom of Sirach LXX xi. 5 πολλοὶ τύραννοι ἐκάθισαν ἐπὶ ἐδάφους, Ar. *Rhet.* ii. 21 (iii. 11 Eust. 395. 39) οὐ δεῖ ὑβριστὰς εἶναι ὅπως μὴ οἱ τέττιγες χαμόθεν ᾄδωσιν, *Anth. Pal.* vii. 723 οἰωνοὶ δὲ κατὰ χθονὸς οἰκία θέντες μύρονται | μήλων δ' οὐκ ἀίουσι λύκοι, Eur. *fr.* 188. 6 ἐξ ὧν κενοῖσιν ἐγκατοικήσεις δόμοις of Sparta; Theocr. i. 51 ἐπὶ ξηροῖσι καθίζειν 'on the cold ground'.

285. **σκευάζοντα**, 'packing', as συσκευάζεσθαι, σκευωρεῖσθαι (Plut. *Caes.* 51 τὴν Πομπηίου οἰκίαν).

288. The alternatives are equivalent.

289. **πύματόν τε καὶ ὕστατον** = X 203, υ 116.

290. **νυκτὸς ἑταῖρε**: see on 31. Νυκτὸς δὲ φίλη καὶ ἑταίρη poeta ap. Orig. *in haer.* 72 (*PLG.* iii. 682), *furibus apte* Ovid *Fast.* v. 104, τῶν φηλητέων . . . ἄνακτα Cougny v. 24. 2.

295. **ἀειρόμενος**: Herod. ii. 162 ἐπαείρας ἀπεματάισε (Maximus xci. 880 Migne). The verb αἴρειν whether act. or mid. is often intransitive: ν 83, 84, Herod. iv. 150, Eur. *Hypsip. fr.* 754. 1, Xen. *Anab.* i. 5 ταῖς πτέρυξιν αἴρουσα, Quintus xi. 268: more often in composition: Evangelius *FCA.* iii. 376, v. 10 ὥστε τὸν δειπνοῦντ' ἐπαίρειν ἥν τι βούληται λαβεῖν, Apollonius *hist. mir.* c. 18 μέχρι θανάτου οὐκ ἐπαίρουσιν (*nec se sublevat*): Hesych. ἐξᾶραι· οὕτως λέγεται ὅταν τι τῶν ὀρνέων εἰς μετέωρον ὕψος αἴρεται (Strabo 196): perhaps Solon 10. 5; καταίρειν, 'settle', of birds Plut. *quom. qu. suos* 78 E. Ἀπ- δι- κατ- αίρειν are nautical.

Hermes would not submit to violence; he therefore replied by 'two omens', the first of which is not elsewhere in Greek an omen, but finds parallels in the Middle Ages (see R.); the second (sneezing) is well known (Halliday *Greek Divination* 175 sq.). Apollo took it in the sense given by Hesych., ἐπιπτάρ(ν)υμαι· μετακαλῶ, κατέχω· ἐπισχετικὸν γὰρ ὁ πταρμὸς πολλάκις. Apollo dropped him both on this account and for the reasons expressed in Ar. *Plutus* 698 (R.). Sneezes also were not good between midnight and noon (Aristotle *Probl.* 33. 11).

296. **ἀγγελιώτην** : elsewhere Callim. *Hec.* 34. 6, Nonnus xiii. 35.

299. He had dropped the child; he left the next move to it.

303. **οἰωνοῖσι**: Hesych. ξυμβόλους· τοὺς διὰ τῶν πταρμῶν οἰωνισμοὺς ἔλεγον : Archiloch. 46 σύμβολον ποιεύμενος.

304. **Κυλλήνιος** of Hermes occurs in Homer only in ω 1; of Otus, referring to the Elean Cyllene, O 518.

305. **σπουδῇ** : the words ἐσσυμένως (320) σπεύδοντε (397) show that this word here = quickly, as in B 99, ν 279, ο 209 (where the ancient interpreters were divided between μόγις and ἐν τάχει); cf. Soph. *Ant.* 223 τάχους v.l. σπουδῆς, *fr.* 237 τάχος . . . σπουδῆς.

Hermes' action here is described by Apollo 360 πολλὰ δὲ χερσὶν | αὐγὰς ὠμόργαζε (Ilgen for ὠμάρταζε), and this seems modelled on σ 199 τὴν δὲ γλυκὺς ὕπνος ἀνῆκε | καὶ ῥ' ἀπομόρξατο χερσὶ παρειάς. 'Wiping the eyes' is slightly less forcible than 'wiping the cheeks'. It was a habit of the Emperor Claudius, Suet. *Claud.* 8 *solebant et manibus stertentis socci induci ut repente expergefactus faciem sibimet confricaret.* Hence it seems that in this passage we have a tmesis for παρεώθει χερσὶ τὰ οὔατα, 'pushed his ears back', a more vigorous equivalent of ἀπομόρξατο αὐγάς or παρειάς. A similar emotion was expressed by a similar gesture: Hesych. ὀφρύκνηστον· ἐρυθριῶντα. οἱ γὰρ ἐρυθριῶντες κνῶνται τὰς ὀφρῦς, i.e. they cover their faces and scrape their eyebrows. Cf. also Philostr. *vit. Ap. Tyan.* iv. 20 τὸ δὲ μειράκιον ὥσπερ ἀφυπνίσαν τοὺς ὀφθαλμοὺς ἔτριψε, Callim. iii. 71 θεμένη ἐπὶ φάεσι χεῖρας of fright, Strabo 602 παρατρίβεσθαι τὸ πρόσωπον. A milder expression τ 361 γρηῢς δὲ κατέσχετο χερσὶ πρόσωπα. Yet another metaphor, of kissing: Hesych. παρακονᾶν· τὸ ἐν τῷ ἀσπάζεσθαι παρατρίβειν τὸ γένειον καὶ τὰς παρειάς, Phot. *lex.* παρακονᾶν· τὸ ἐν τῷ φιλεῖν διατρίβειν.

With this sense the construction σπάργανον ἀμφ' ὤμοισιν ἐελμένος becomes legitimate. Otherwise if we render ἐώθει τὸ σπάργανον παρὰ τὰ οὔατα, the construction (with σπάργανον taken ἀπὸ κοινοῦ) is intolerable, and has produced the inadmissible alteration of nominative to accusative (this amongst other reasons disproves Eitrem's view (v. p. 269) that H. covered his ears to avoid hearing the omen (!); it would have been too late). For the syntax cf. 151, Paus. v. 27. 8 ἐπικείμενος τῇ κεφαλῇ κυνῆν, Eur. *IT.* 442 ἀμφὶ χαίτᾳ δρόσον αἱματηρὰν ἑλιχθεῖσα; for part of it Herod. i. 171 περὶ τοῖσι αὐχέσι τε καὶ τοῖσι ἀριστεροῖσι ὤμοισι περικείμενοι; for the compound verb Hippocr. iii. 165 ἅμα δὲ ὠθεῖν τἀναντία ἐφ' ἑκάτερα καὶ παρωθεῖν ἐς χώραν, tropically Plut. *de tuen. san. praec.* 125 D ἡμῖν οὔτ' ὄψον παρωσαμένοις μετεμέλησεν οὔθ' ὕδωρ ἀντὶ Φαλερίνου πιοῦσιν.

308. **ὀρσολοπεύεις**: cf. Hesych. ὀρσοπολεῖται· διαπολεμεῖται, ταράσσεται· Αἰσχύλος (*Pers.* 10); Anacr. *fr.* 74 ὀρσόλοπος of Ares, tropically Max. π. καταρχῶν 108 (μύθῳ ὀνειδείῳ). The derivation is unknown (Fröhde *BB.* xx. 222, Schwyzer *Glotta* xii. 21). Müller-Strübing's (*Wiss. Monatsbl.* 1879 no. 5 ap. Gemoll) suggestion (ὄρρος and λοπεύω) would suit the humour of the hymn: cf. Hesych. ἐλέπουν· οἷον ἐλέπιζον τύπτων καὶ μαστιγῶν, an insect ὀρσοδάκνη Ar. *HA.* v. 19, 21, Hesych.

311 = 277 (αἵ τινες αἱ βόες εἰσί· τὸ δὲ κλέος).

313. **διαρρήδην**: first here. Hesych. φανερῶς, σαφῶς.

ἐρέεινον, 'asked about, questioned' as 487, 533, ἐξερεείνῃ 483, -ειν 547, ἐξερέεινε 252 'searched'; they had questioned one another 254, 307.

314. **οἰοπόλος**, 'shepherd', 570 sq., by anticipation.

315. The words as handed down give no connexion: the conjectures have no probability (φωρήν may be defended by the variant φωρήν, φωνήν 385, but the resulting double accusative is impossible: moreover νημερτέα φωνήν, 'true word', gives excellent sense.) We therefore assume a lacuna facilitated by φωνήν Ἑρμῆν: it will have contained a participle (ἱείς).

316. **οὐκ ἀδίκως** = Simonides 89. 3, *epigr.* Kaibel 38. 2.

320. i.e. they went back.

322. **τέρθρον**: properly a nautical term (Hesych. ὁ λεγόμενος ἀρτέμων· ἔνιοι δὲ τὸ ἄκρον τοῦ κέρως, καὶ στέγη οἰκίας. τινὲς δὲ τὸ ἔσχατον καὶ ὑψηλόν, Erotian 366 τέρθρον ἔλεγον οἱ παλαιοὶ τὸ ἔσχατον καὶ ἐπὶ τέλει) = τέρμα Eur. *fr.* 372, of the tip of the nose Emped. 346. First here. On the derivation see Boisacq.

θυώδεος Οὐλύμποιο = *h.* ii. 331.

324. δίκης . . . τάλαντα, 'the scales of justice': Bacchyl. xvii. 25 δίκας ῥέπει τάλαντον, Aesch. *Ag.* 250 δίκα ἐπιρρέπει, *Anth. Pal.* vi. 267. 4 ἐκ Διὸς ἰθείης οἶδε τάλαντα δίκης. In Homer, Zeus weighs κῆρε θανάτοιο Θ 69, X 209, balances the scales T 223, his ἱρὰ τάλαντα are recognized Π 658. See further Roscher ii. 1142 *in* Κῆρες. The wording of the present passage resembles Σ 507 κεῖτο δ' ἄρ' ἐν μέσσοισι δύω χρυσοῖο τάλαντα, but τάλαντα there were 'deposits'.

325. The key to εὐμιλίη or εὐμυλίη has not been found. The following attempts have been made to interpret either of the two forms: (1) -μυλ- is connected with μὺ μῦ Ar. *Eq.* 10, μυλιόωντες Hes. *OD.* 530, μύω, μοιμύλλειν, etc., of a muttering sound produced by closing the lips. The sense would be 'a pleasant buzz, a hum' of conversation, part of the morning meeting. They were exchanging the matutinal χαίρειν ὑπὸ τὴν πρώτην ἔντευξιν Lucian *pro laps. in. sal.* 2, and for once not shouting διανομὰς διανομάς· ποῦ τὸ νέκταρ; ποῦ τὸ νέκταρ; ἡ ἀμβροσίη ἐπέλιπεν, ἡ ἀμβροσίη ἐπέλιπεν· ποῦ αἱ ἑκατόμβαι; ποῦ αἱ ἑκατόμβαι; κοινὰς τὰς θυσίας *Jup. Trag.* 13. (2) Radermacher saw μύλλειν, *mola*, *mill* in the word, and thought the whole meant food. But ambrosia was not ground, and they had nothing else (οὐ . . . σῖτον ἔδουσ', οὐ πίνουσ' αἴθοπα οἶνον E 341); even the parodist Archestratus 6 does not state as much, θεοὶ εἴπερ ἔδουσιν | ἄλφιτ' ἐκεῖθεν ἰὼν Ἑρμῆς αὐτοῖς ἀγοράζοι. (3) ὅμιλος is now explained as ὁμο-μιλος (Sansk. *milati*, Latin *miles*), see Boisacq *in v.* From this stem εὐμιλίη would not be impossible, with obvious sense. Or (4) it is perhaps simpler to see in εὐμιλίη a graphical fault for οὐμιλίη (Є = O), and in οὐμιλίη an Ionicism like οὐδός, οὔνομα, δούνακος, etc. 'There was company in Olympus'; or perhaps οὐμιλίη has the sense of 'good company, sociability' which sometimes belongs to ὁμιλία: Galen xviii. 1. 316 ὁμιλεῖν ἔλεγον οἱ παλαιοὶ τοὐπίπαν οὐκ ἐπὶ τοῦ διαλέγεσθαι καθάπερ νῦν οἱ πολλοί, τὸ συνιέναι δὲ ἀλλήλοις . . . ταύτῃ προσηγόρευον τῇ φωνῇ, e.g. Socrates ap. Stob. *ecl.* iii. 1. 87 οὔτε συμπόσιον χωρὶς ὁμιλίας οὔτε πλοῦτος χωρὶς ἀρετῆς ἡδονὴν ἔχει, Lucian *conv. sept. sap.* 15 ἤδη δὲ καὶ ἐς τοὺς ἄλλους συνεχῶς περιεσοβεῖτο ἡ κύλιξ καὶ φιλοτησίαι καὶ ὁμιλία, Plut. *Ages.* 34 ἐπαιδαγώγει

ὁμιλίᾳ τὸν πότον, *Philop.* 8 ὁμιλίᾳ καὶ πρᾳότητι, sim. *Marcell.* 22, *Flamin.* 2; Machaon ap. Ath. 578 C φωνῇ δ' ὁμιλίᾳ τε κεχορηγημένη, Philodem. *de victu deorum* vi. c. 18 καὶ φωνῇ δὲ χρῆσθαι ὁμειλίᾳ τῇ πρὸς ἀλλήλους ῥητέον.

The metre and formation (of εὐμιλίη) resemble κλαιωμιλίη, γελοωμιλίη Ammonianus *Anth. Pal.* ix. 573.

The alterations are either violent or introduce common words (e.g. εὐμελίη) which would not have been miswritten. D'Orville's στωμυλίη grasped the situation.

326. **ἄφθιτοι**, 'the deathless immortals', as θνητοὶ βροτοί γ 3 (G.).

μετὰ χρυσόθρονον ἠῶ: agrees with A 497, ε 1 where the Gods assemble in the morning. This seems better than the alternative.

331. **φυὴν κήρυκος**: the writer anticipates Hermes' functions, as with οἰοπόλος 314.

332. **σπουδαῖον τόδε χρῆμα**, 'this is a fine thing', ironically. The adj. and χρῆμα in this sense are not Homeric. Cf. Hes. *OD.* 344, Soph. *Ichneut.* ii. 17, vi. 4, ix. 14, poeta ap. Plut. *brut. rat.* 988 A μέρμερον χρῆμα, Xen. *Cyrop.* i. 4. 8 καλόν τι χρῆμα καὶ μέγα (ἔλαφον), Theocr. xv. 83, 145: often in late Greek (λάλον χρῆμα ὁ Φαβωρῖνος Philostr. *vit. soph.* 232 al., Lucian *dial. mar.* 6. 1); see R. It is called an Attic construction Σ *Clouds* 2.

335. **φιλολήιος**: with reference to the wealth of Delphi as 179, 495, Lycophr. 208 Δελφινίου παρ' ἄντρα κερδῴου θεοῦ (B.).

336. **διαπρύσιον**: apparently 'piercing, penetrating', cf. πρυμνός, πρύτανις (Boisacq): cf. *h.* v. 19 of a piercing noise, and διάτορος. Homer has the adverb. The gloss in Π φανερὸν κλέπτην is mistaken.

337. **πολύν, κτλ.**: in tmesi, cf. Hes. *OD.* 635 πολὺν διὰ πόντον ἀνύσσας, Theognis 511.

338. **κέρτομον**: first in Hes. *op.c.* 788 for the Homeric κερτόμιον. The meaning is obviously 'impudent'.

339. **λησίμβροτοι**: only here.

γαῖαν: is better than γαίῃ. Cf. H 446, δ 417, η 382, ρ 386, ψ 371, Eur. *Alc.* 896, Theocr. xxii. 128.

342. **εὐθύ**: first here and 355 (εὐθύς) for the Homeric ἰθύ. The participle ἐλάων also is not Homeric except as a v. l. μ 398 (ἐλόωντες).

The vulgate εὐθυπόρον δ' is an adverb from εὐθυπόρος, 'direct', which does not occur before fourth-century prose (add Callistr. *Ecphr.* 1 αὐλῶνας εὐθυπόρους). Line 355 εἰς Πύλον εὐθὺς ἐλῶντα supports εὐθὺ Πύλον δ' ἐλάων here.

δοιά: δῖα *p* is an itacism; Herondas i. 64 δῖα, δ 526 δοιά, one MS. διά. Theocr. xii. 12 δοιώ is wrongly altered to δίω. Barnes's τοῖα rests on 349, but there and in 225 the word has not been altered. The sense is 'there were two footprints, wonderful', i.e. those of the cows (μέν 344) and of Hermes (δ' 346).

342, 345. Commentators have been exercised to know how Apollo knew that Hermes' object was Pylos, as Battus did not give him this information. Pylos was the port of export on the W. coast of the Peloponnesus, and a trade in cattle was done between it and the islands. A cattle-thief who went south from Pieria would in all probability be making for Pylos. So Melampus ο 235 ἤλασε βοῦς ἐριμύκους ἐς Πύλον ἐκ Φυλάκης. Apollo treats Hermes as an ordinary cattle-thief. Or, as suggested on 211, the 'long-winged bird' may have indicated Hermes' direction.

344. **τῇσιν μὲν γὰρ βουσίν**: 'ethic' dative as ii. 265, 'in the case of the cows the black dust held and showed their footprints facing towards the meadow', as 221 πάλιν τέτραπται ἐς ἀσφοδελὸν λειμῶνα. For ἀντία ἐς cf. ἐναντίον πρός Plat. *Phaed.* 60 B, and εἰς after ἄχρι and πέραν. Possibly this is not the construction, and ἀντία = 'reversed', as 77 ἀντία ποιήσας ὁπλάς. On κόνις see Schweizer *IF.* x. 205 n.

346–7. **αὐτὸς δ' οὗτος ὅδ' ἐκτὸς ἀμήχανος, οὔτ' ἄρα ποσσὶν**
οὔτ' ἄρα χερσὶν ἔβαινε διὰ ψαμαθώδεα χῶρον·

Since neither ἕκτος *sixth*, ἑκτός from ἔχω, nor ἐκτός *outside* can be entertained, the syllables must be run together. The apparent sense wanted is a compound of ὁδός (e.g. ὅδιος, ἐνόδιος), but ὁδαῖος (Ludwich), ὁδουρός are too far from the tradition. Radermacher in *Festschrift für R. Kretschmer* 1926, 151 suggests ὅδακτος (in the sense of ὁδηγός) on the strength of the entry ὁδανός· ὁδηγός in Hesychius; but Guyet corrected ὁδανός to ὁδαγός, and ἄδεκτος (Hesych. ἄδεκτον· ἄπιστον and ἄζετον· ἄπιστον Σικελοί) would be as good, and recommended by ἀμήχανος (ὅδ' ἐκτὸς = ἄδεκτος with ο written above the α). The negative has also suggested other negatives, such as Hermann's ᾇκτος (ἄικτος· ἀπρόσιτος Hesych.), or J. P. Postgate's ᾇστος (= ἄικτος ἐκτός).

347. **χερσὶν ἔβαινε**, 'walked on all fours', like an infant or a very decrepit old man; Aesch. *Eum.* 37 τρέχω δὲ χερσίν, οὐ ποδωκείᾳ σκελῶν (τετραποδηδόν Σ on 34) Levit. xi. 27; but of swift magical motion of disembodied powers in the oracle to Glaucus Herod. vi. 86 ἀλλ' Ὅρκου πάις ἐστὶν ἀνώνυμος, οὐδ' ἔπι χεῖρες | οὐδὲ πόδες, κραιπνὸς δὲ μετέρχεται.

348. As G. saw, διέτριβε means 'wore tracks', the *skis* wore ruts in the sand 'as extraordinary as if...' On the short syllable -ετρ- see La Roche *HU.* i. 9, ἀπέκρυψε 394.

349. **δρυσί**: the instrumental dative requires no alteration, cf. 346, 347, M 207 πέτετο πνοιῇς ἀνέμοιο, υ 67, Solon xi. 5 ἀλώπεκος ἴχνεσι βαίνει, Hippocr. iii. 214 inf. τῷ ποδὶ εἴσω βαίνειν al., Galen ii. 347 ποῦς . . . ᾧ βαίνομεν, Strattis *fr.* 66. Hermes seemed to be walking on 'young trees' (81).

352, 353: for the repetition στίβον στίβος, cf. 340, 342 (ἐλαύνων, ἐλάων), 365 (ἄρ' twice), 385 (ποτ', ποτί), 398, 399 (ἷξον, ἐξίκοντο).

354. **κρατερόν**, 'hard', as ψ 46 κραταίπεδον οὖδας (Ilgen).

356. κατέρεξε is obviously wrong with ἐν ἡσυχίῃ, and Apollo did not know of the slaughter: so E 650 ἔρξαντα ῥέξαντα, I 535 ἔρξ' ἔρεξ' ῥέξ'.

357. **διαπυρπαλάμησεν**, 'juggled', practised his extraordinary step. Apollo was unaware that H. had thrown his sandals into the Alpheus, and imagined him striding ὁδοῦ τὸ μὲν ἔνθα τὸ δ' ἔνθα.

Ilgen united the preposition to the verb (παλάμησε is a signal case of M's excellence). The uncompounded verb and adjective are attested: Hesych. πυρπαλάμης· πυρπαλάμους ἔλεγον τοὺς διὰ τάχους τι μηχανᾶσθαι δυναμένους καὶ τοὺς ποικίλους τὸ ἦθος; Suetonius ap. Miller *Mélanges* 420, Phot., Suid., Eust. 513. 20 connect it with πῦρ (οἱονεὶ διὰ πυρὸς ἰέναι), obviously a Volksetymologie. Neither meaning nor derivation is known, Stolz *Wiener Studien* 1903, 251, Boisacq *in* Παλάμη.

358. Cf. A 47 ὁ δ' ἤιε νυκτὶ ἐοικώς, swift and menacing, like the descent of night in the Mediterranean; the phrase δύσετο δ' ἠέλιος

σκιόωντο δὲ πᾶσαι ἀγυιαί is taken to refer to the absence of twilight (Zenodotus, however, in the *Iliad* read ἐλυσθείς, 'wrapped').

360. **λάων**: cf. the v.l. N 344 γηθησ]ειε λ[αων (νιδ[written above) 𝔓[16], which implies λάειν = βλέπειν, τ 230 ὁ μὲν λάε νεβρὸν ἀπάγξας, where the 𝔖 give a choice of meanings, οἱ μὲν ἐπεβλέπετο, οἱ δὲ ἀπολαυστικῶς ἤσθιεν, Hesych. λάετε· σκοπεῖτε, βλέπετε, and *in* λάε gives a further interpretation (οἱ δὲ ἐφθέγγετο). Boisacq compares λεύσσω.

361. **αὐγάς** = 'eyes' is first found here (B.).

ὠμόργαζε: a brilliant emendation based on σ 199 τὴν δὲ γλυκὺς ὕπνος ἀνῆκε | καὶ ῥ' ἀπομόρξατο χερσὶ παρειάς. Cf. 305.

ἀλεγύνων: for the variants cf. 85, 557. In Homer it occurs only in the *Odyssey* of preparing a meal.

362. **ἀπηλεγέως ἀγόρευεν**: cf. I 309, α 373. Like δυσηλεγής it is derived from ἀλέγω: 'carelessly': see Boisacq in 'Αλέγω.

365: π 213 ὣς ἄρα φωνήσας κατ' ἄρ' ἕζετο.

367. **δείξατο**, 'made plain', i.e. directed his remarks to, T 83 Πηλείδῃ μὲν ἐγὼν ἐνδείξομαι· αὐτὰρ οἱ ἄλλοι | σύνθεσθ' Ἀργεῖοι.

θεῶν σημάντορα πάντων = Hes. *Scut.* 56.

369. **νημερτής**: of persons δ 349, 384 al., Hes. *Theog.* 235.

370. **ἐς ἡμετέρου**: the gen. in this expression occurs with varying MS. support β 55, η 301 (where Aristarchus read it), ρ 534; also in the MSS. at Herod. i. 35, vii. 8. Cf. the reverse ἐκ Πεισάνδροιο σ 299.

372. Apollo had not complied with legal requirements. The writer models heaven on his own πόλις, which however is not indicated, as the law of φωρά was probably universal in Greece, in Italy, and even in Indo-European countries generally: cf. Plato *Laws* 954 A. Hermes was an *abigens* Digest 47. 14. 1. It must also be remembered that Apollo had no presumption. He had committed a 'heartless trespass' νηλέα φωρήν. R. compares Dem. *Mid.* 78 sq.

373. **μηνύειν**: on the quantity ⏒ see Schulze *qu. ep.* 340.

375. **φιλοκυδέος**: only here and 481. Cf. Hes. *Theog.* 988 τέρεν ἄνθος ἔχοντ' ἐρικυδέος ἥβης.

379. Hermes is disingenuous. He had driven the cattle off, but not to his home, and he had not crossed the threshold.

381. He wishes to covertly disarm the Sun, who sees all things. Else the mention of him is pointless.

383. **ἐπιδαίομαι** and *ἐπιδεύομαι* point to an older corruption *ἐπιδέομαι* which remains in L²Π. Barnes' *ἐπιδώσομαι* is too familiar to have crumbled, and the meaning of *ἐπιδώμεθα* X 254 is uncertain. Herwerden's *ἐπιμαίομαι* is not used in this connexion. It was suggested, *JHS.* xv. 291, that the original was *μέγαν δ' ἐπὶ ὅρκον ὀμοῦμαι*, and that *ὅρκον* being omitted and added at the end of the line gave *δεπιομουμαι ορκον*, out of which *δ' ἐπιδέομαι ὅρκον* arose. If we cling to the letters *μέγαν δ' ἄρ' ἐπαιδέομ' ὅρκον* might be possible. For *ἐπαιδεῖσθαι* see the lexx.

384. The oath 'by the splendid porticoes' seems parodic. He intended to live there.

385. **ποτ'** is *ποτε*, with natural elision and position (*ρ* 249, *h.* iii. 305, v. 48), there is no need to invent another Aeolic elision. Then after *τίσω* we may take *ποτί* from M with *τίσω in tmesi*: for this figure cf. Ξ 396 *οὔτε πυρὸς τόσσος γε ποτὶ βρόμος αἰθομένοιο*, viz. *προσαιθομένοιο* (*CQ.* 1931, 33). *προστίνω* is new, but *προστιμᾶν* is a legal term: 'I will repay him with interest his cruel trespass some day'. In any other sense *ποτί* is meaningless (*ποτί* = *ποθι* = *που*, which Hermann conjectured).

φωρήν (un-Homeric) is oxytone here and in Bion ix. 6, paroxytone in Nicander *Alex.* 273. Hesych. *φωρᾶν· τὸ τὰ κλεψιμαῖα ζητεῖν, καὶ φωριᾶν, φώρην δὲ τὴν ἔρευναν.* There is no ancient dictum on the subject: it is unnecessary, as Schneider on Nicander remarks, to erect two substantives with different accentuations and meanings. The oxytonesis is guaranteed by the Sanskrit according to Boisacq *in v.* As between *φωρήν* and *φωνήν* the quality of M is evident.

387. **ἐπιλλίζων**: σ 11 *οὐκ ἀίεις ὅτι δή μοι ἐπιλλίζουσιν ἅπαντες*, Ap. Rh. i. 486, iii. 791, *κατιλλώπτοντι Anth. Pal.* v. 199. 3: the primitive *ἰλλός* (Hesych. *στρεβλός, στραβός, διεστραμμένος*) Ar. *Thesm.* 846, *ἰλλότερος* Sophron *fr.* 158 (see Boisacq).

389. As he laughed at Apollo, Eur. *IT.* 1274.

391. **ὁμόφρονα θυμὸν ἔχοντας**: formulaic, X 263, *h.* ii. 434, Theognis 81, 765.

392. **διάκτορος**: connected with *κτέρεα, κτερίζω* by Solmsen

IF. iii. 90. For other views see Oestergaard *Hermes* 1902, 333, Cook *CR.* 1903, 177.

393. **ἐπ' ἀβλαβίῃσι νόοιο**, 'subject to, on the condition of, innocency of intent, purpose'. Hermes was not to steal nor Apollo offer violence. The words are paraphrased 391 *ὁμόφρονα θυμὸν ἔχοντες*. *ἐπί* conveys the terms of Zeus' sentence and is juridical, as R. remarks (though his interpretation of the word is wrong); cf. *ἐπ' ἀρθμῷ καὶ φιλότητι* 524, *Ζεὺς αὔτ' ἔπαυσ' ἐπ' ἀβλαβείᾳ* (v.l., Σ *ὥστε μὴ ἕτερον βλαβῆναι*) Aesch. *Ag.* 1009, *οὔτ' ἐπὶ βλαβῇ φρενῶν* Eur. *Hipp.* 511. *ἀβλάβεια* is translated *innocentia* by Cicero *Tusc.* iii. 8. 16, and *Ἀβλαβίαι* evidently in this sense are personified inscr. Dittenb. *Syll.* 600. 38, *Ἀβλάβιος* is a proper name (Pape, Synes. *ep.* 61). Equivalent Latin terms are *absque dolo, absque ulla fraude.* On the word, with its active and passive meaning, see on 83 and the article in LS., who (after Stephanus) correctly explain it as there active (it is passive in Eur. above). Thucydides quotes it from treaties v. 47 *ἐμμενῶ τῇ ξυμμαχίᾳ κατὰ τὰ συγκείμενα δικαίως καὶ ἀβλαβῶς καὶ ἀδόλως*, 18 *σπονδὰς . . . ἀδόλους καὶ ἀβλαβεῖς*, and similar phrases occur in the index to *IG.* i, ed. min.; Charondas ap. Stob. *ecl.* iv. 2, p. 153 Hense *βλασφημείτω δὲ μηδεὶς ἐπὶ ἀδίκῳ βλαβῇ περὶ μηδένος*, *PSI.* 392. 13 (s. iii. B.C.) *χρειαν εχοντες αβλαβως*. In later jurisprudence it seems not to occur. Equivalents are *ἄνευ δόλου καὶ ἐπιβουλῆς* Polyb. vii. 9. 8, *χωρὶς δόλου καὶ ἀπάτης id.* xxxvi. 6. 50, Epicurus *κυρ. δοξ.* 34 *ὑπὲρ τοῦ μὴ βλάπτειν ἄλληλα μηδὲ βλάπτεσθαι*, *ib.* 33, 35; the reverse of *ἐπὶ βλαβῇ* Isocr. iv. 13, viii. 72, Artemid. i. 22, iv. 70.

A further sense of *ἐπί* c. dat. may be found in Plutarch *de tranq. an.* 466 D *αὐτόπυρον* [*ἄρτον*] *ἐπ' ἐλαίαις ἢ καρδαμίδι* 'aux olives'.

394. **ἀπέκρυψε**: cf. *ἐνέκρυψε* ε 488, La Roche *HU.* i. 9.

397. *σπεύδοντο* entails *δ' ἐπ'* in 398 (B.), but the middle is only found in the future until the Attic period.

400. **ἠχοῦ** was brilliantly restored by Fick (*BB.* xxii. 271) from the disjointed elements of the MSS. It was suggested to him by *ηχοι* in an Oropian inscription (*IG. Sept.* i. 235, Dittenb. *Syll.* 589, Hoffmann p. 16, Solmsen *inscr. gr. dial.* 1903, 95); this is in the Eretrian dialect, to which Fick referred *ἠχοῦ* and the hymn. But the formation belongs to common Greek (*ἀλλαχοῦ*, *διτταχοῦ*,

ἐνιαχοῦ, μοναχοῦ, ὀλιγαχοῦ, πανταχοῦ, πολλαχοῦ). The word survives in Hesychius ἦχου [*sic*]· ἐνθάδε. Cf. the commoner ἦχι and ἠχῇ Heph. *ench.* i. 8 (ἡ χή, ἠχή MSS.) = ὥσπερ.

χρήματα, 'goods, chattels', usual in later Greek, Hesych. κτήνεα· χρήματα, βοσκήματα.

ἀτάλλετο is a necessary correction of ἀτιτάλλετο the common word; see on *h.* ii. 24.

401. **παρά**, 'along', i.e. right into.

403. **ἀπάτερθεν**, 'aside', Theognis 1059 ἀπάτερθεν ὁρῶντι. This word and ἀπάνευθεν are confused E 445.

405. **ἐδύνω**: the form occurs first here.

407. **θαυμαίνω**: the verb occurs θ 108, *h.* v. 84. *Ichneut.* 271 ὁ δ' ἀ]ύξεται κατ' ἦμαρ οὐκ ἐπεικότα | ἄπαυ]στος ὥστε θαῦμα καὶ φόβος μ' ἔχει.

κατόπισθε: adv. 'afterwards', past or future according to context. 'I admire, looking back': χ 40 'thereafter'. The preposition always = 'behind'.

409. Baumeister's lacuna is necessary (*a*) to indicate the intention of the δεσμά, (*b*) to provide ταί in 410 with an antecedent.

(*a*) It has been supposed that Apollo intended to tie Hermes up, either to prevent his doing more mischief or to stop his growth (407, 408). But no withies would have held Hermes, any more than the φᾶρος and στροφοί held Apollo (*h. Ap.* 128), the λυγοί Dionysus (*h.* vii. 13), or the 'seven green withes' Samson[1]. Hephaestus it is true forged chains which were able to hold Ares, but Apollo was not a smith and ἄγνος is not metal. Still less could he expect to stunt Hermes, whose divinity he had recognized. Vv. 407, 408 are jocose. Moreover, what would have become of the sentence of Zeus, the ἀβλαβίαι νόοιο, and the injunction ὁμόφρονα θυμὸν ἔχειν?

Apollo's preoccupation was to recover his remaining ten cows. To get them back to Pieria he began to halter them or to tie them one to the other by the horns or necks, or even heads and tails

[1] Some God tried to tie up Hermes in his sleep, Lact. Plac. in Stat. *Theb.* ii. 64.

in a file, as is done with camels now in Egypt. As he did so the withies 'grew into the ground beneath their feet', covering the cows in a mesh, so many jacks-in-the-green, and of course preventing them from moving[1]. If Apollo had begun by tying Hermes, how should the chains have spread to the cows?

For tying oxen, either to drive them or to break them in, see Columella vi. 2. 3 *cannabinis funibus cornua iuvencarum ligabo* . . . 4 *manu producantur ita ut aliquis ante et a tergo complures qui sequantur retinaculis eos contineant*, Virgil *Georg.* iii. 166 *ac primum laxos tenui de vimine circlos* | *cervici subnecte.* The Berlin Thesaurus offers Gregory of Tours *Iul.* 31 *tauros qui* . . . *alligati funibus ducebantur.* Add Parthenius vii: Antileon after killing the tyrant δρόμῳ ἵετο καὶ διέφυγεν ἂν εἰ μὴ προβάτοις συνδεδεμένοις ἀμφιπεσὼν ἐχειρώθη . . . καὶ νόμος ἐγράφη μηδένα ἐλαύνειν τοῦ λοιποῦ πρόβατα συνδεδεμένα, Soph. *Ajax* 62 τοὺς ζῶντας αὖ δεσμοῖσι συνδήσας βοῶν, Eur. *Cyclops* 224 ἄρνας . . . στρεπταῖς λύγοισι σῶμα συμπεπλεγμένους, Ant. Lib. 20. 4 ἐκλύσαντες τῶν δεσμῶν τοὺς ὄνους, ι 427 Ulysses tied three sheep at a time εὐστρεφέεσσι λύγοισι, Plut. *Lucull.* 24 (βοῦς) καταβαλοῦσα τὴν κεφαλὴν ὥσπερ αἱ δεσμῷ κατατεινόμεναι. A single beast σχοίνῳ δεθεὶς κέρατα Babrius 37. 7, Hesych. *in* Κερασβόλα . . . οἱ περὶ τῶν κεράτων βοῶν δεσμοί, *in* Κερατεσσεῖς· οἱ τοὺς ταύρους ἕλκοντες ἀπὸ τῶν κεράτων· καλοῦνται δὲ καὶ κεραελκεῖς; a proverb βοῦς ἐπὶ δεσμά *in* Κυὼν ἐπὶ δεσμά. See on 103. On preparing willow *ad vitium ligamina* see Columella xi. 292; sim. Frontinus i. 5. 21 *ex vimine silvestri catenas conseruit*, Hesych. Κερασός . . . σχοινίον δὲ ποιεῖ ὁ φλοιὸς αὐτοῦ μεθ' οὗ ἀντὶ νεύρων δεσμεύουσιν.

(*b*) The missing word must be feminine and therefore is λύγοι. Cf. vii. 13, Athen. 671 F ὁ γὰρ τῆς λύγου στέφανος ἄτοπος, πρὸς δεσμοὺς γὰρ καὶ πλέγματα ἡ λύγος ἐπιτήδειος, Pliny *NH.* xxiv. 59 *Graeci lygon vocant alias agnon*, Amerias ap. Ꙏ Theocr. i. 97 λύγος· ῥάβδος, ἄγνος, Paus. iii. 14. 7 ἡ δὲ ἄγνος λύγος καὶ αὐτὴ κατὰ ταὐτόν ἐστι τῇ ῥάμνῳ, *Geopon.* ii. 4. 1 λύγοι αἱ ὑπό τινων λεγόμεναι ἄγνοι, Longus ii. 1. 2 λύγου ξηρᾶς πληγαῖς κατεξασμένης, 13. 3 λύγον χλωρὰν μακρὰν στρέψαντες ὡς σχοῖνον, Hesych. Λύγοισι·

[1] In the story of Antiope, Apollod. iii. 43, the fetters fall off, τῶν δεσμῶν αὐτομάτων λυθέντων.

φυτῷ τινι ἱμαντώδει ὃ ἡμεῖς κύτινον λέγομεν. Λύγος . . . ἱμαντῶδες φυτόν. Μόσχος . . . λύγοι δὲ εἰσὶ τὰ ἱμαντώδη φυτά; cf. the story of a βρέτας supposed to have run away, tied up in a θωράκιον of λύγος—τοὺς εὐμηκεστάτους τῶν κλάδων ἑκατέρωθεν ἐπισπασαμένους περιειλῆσαι πάντοθεν Athen. 672 D. So chicory was used Theophr. *HP*. vii. 11. 3.

Hence we may supplement βοῦς ἕλικας δῆσαι μεμαὼς κρατεραῖσι λύγοισι. Matthiae, Hermann, and Franke took this view.

410. With this miracle Eitrem (*Rh. Mus.* lxiv. 333), who supposes Hermes to have been bound with the withies, compares Hermes Polygios (equivalent in his view to Πολυλύγιος, cl. Artemis Lygodesma) at Troezen, against whose image Heracles leaned his club. It miraculously took root and grew into a tree (Paus. ii. 31. 10). His further speculations about Hermes as a healer of the diseases of dogs are irrelevant, nor is he right in thinking that Hermes was worshipped as Phytalmios or in general as a God of vegetation (see on 91). The title Hermes Epikarpios at Amorgos *IG*. xii. 7. 252 is unique. In both passages the miracles have no reference to the general characteristics of the God.

411. **ἐμβολάδην**: only here, 'graft-like', cf. ἐμβάλλω, ἐμβολάς, ἔμβολος. M's ἀμβολάδην occurs 426 in an entirely different sense and would leave ἀλλήλῃσι without construction.

412. **ῥεῖά τε καὶ πάσῃσιν**: Hes. *Theog*. 87 αἶψά τε καὶ μέγα νεῖκος ἐπισταμένως κατέπαυσε (G.).

414. **θαύμασεν**: the first occurrence of the aorist.

415. B.'s second lacuna also is necessary, for (1) Hermes' action in 415 has no assignable motive, (2) ἐγκρύψαι μεμαώς requires an object, (3) a mention of the lyre is required to supply an object to λαβών (not however if we accept the conjecture ἄθυρμα for M's λύρην in 418). What the missing line was depends on what we think Hermes wished to hide. The only objects susceptible of concealment were the βοεῖαι on their lofty stone, which Apollo had already seen (403), and the δημὸς καὶ κρέα πολλά of 135. These were the 'proof of his theft', σῆμα νεῆς φωρῆς (136), and to avoiding irritating Apollo by reminding him that two oxen had been prepared for food and roasted, H. tried to

cover them up. We therefore invent *βόθρῳ ἔνι κρέα πολλὰ βοῶν καὶ πιόνα δημόν*. We have had the *βόθρος* 112; cf. Orpheus *Lithica* 733 *τὰ δὲ λείψανα γαῖα καλύπτοι* after a meal, Paus. x. 32. 14 the remains of the previous sacrifice *κομίζουσιν ἐς τὸ αὐτὸ ἀεὶ χωρίον καὶ κατορύσσουσιν ἐνταῦθα*. The homoeoteleuton of *δημόν υἱόν* produced the omission.

ὑποβλήδην: apparently 'askance': A 292 *τὸν δ' ἄρ' ὑποβλήδην ἠμείβετο*.

πῦρ ἀμαρύσσων: Hes. *Theog.* 827 *ὑπ' ὀφρύσι πῦρ ἀμάρυσσε*, Quintus viii. 28.

416. Ꙃ Dion. Thrac. (*anecd. Bekk.* ii. 752) connects *λύρα* and *λύτρα* (*ἡνίκα δὲ τοῦ ἡλίου βοῦς κλέψαι ἠβουλήθη, καὶ διὰ τὸ μαντικὸν τοῦ θεοῦ οὐ δεδύνητο, ἀνελήφθη· εἰδὼς δὲ καὶ τοῦ θεοῦ τὸ μουσικὸν δέδωκεν ὑπὲρ ἑαυτοῦ τὴν λύραν λύτραν*). So *E. Gud.* 375. 6, Boissonade *anecd.* iv. 459 quoting Eur. *Antiope fr.* 190 *λύραν βοῶν ῥύσ(ι)α ἐξερρύσατο*.

418. Whether the lyre was mentioned in the lacuna after 415, or in the present line M's *λύρην* has displaced *ἄθυρμα* (as a gloss), *xp's χειρός* having come from 419 and a recollection of 499, no expression of the object is necessary.

ἐπ' ἀριστερὰ χειρός = 499: cf. *ἐπωλένιον* 433. The shell rests 'on the arm', 'to the left of the hand' which holds it. See on 153.

419, 420 = 53, 54, and with variations 501, 502. Line 420 resembles ρ 542 *σμερδαλέον κονάβησε· γέλασσε δὲ Πηνελόπεια*.

422. The omission of this line in all MSS. except M is accidental and due to *ἐρατὴ . . . ἐρατόν*. For *ἰωὴ ἐνοπῆς*, cf. ρ 261 *ἰωὴ φόρμιγγος*, Π 127 *πυρὸς δηίοιο ἰωήν*, etc. (LS.).

426. **ἀμβολάδην**: not 'boiling, bubbling', as Φ 364 of a seething cauldron, a style which would not have captivated Apollo, but 'preluding', making a *προοίμιον* (as *ἀναβάλλεσθαι, ἀναβολή*), as Pindar *Nem.* x. 33 (LS.).

427. **κραίνων**: the nom. is right, *ἐρατὴ . . . φωνή* being hyperbatic. Hesychius has *Κραίνειν· τιμᾶν, Κραίνουσι· πληροῦσι, παρέχουσι, τιμῶσι, Ἔκραινον· ἐτίμων*, on the ground of which Maurophrydes *KZ.* vii. 346 gives the sense 'celebrate' to the word here, 531 and 559. This is uncertain, but the writer seems to use the word

in an unusual sense here and in 559, probably for γεραίρειν. In Empedocles 462, 463 φάρμακα δ' ὅσσα γεγᾶσι κακῶν καὶ γήραος ἄλκαρ | πεύσῃ, ἐπεὶ μούνῳ σοι ἐγὼ κρανέω τάδε πάντα, the word seems = ἀείδειν; there are possible ambiguities in τ 567, Eur. *Ion* 464.

γαῖαν ἐρεμνήν = ω 106. Hermes sings a cosmogony; cf. Hes. *Theog.* 1–21, Ap. Rh. i. 496, Virg. *Ecl.* vi. 13.

429. Mnemosyne is mother of the Muses Hes. *l.c.* 53.

430. **λάχε**, 'drew' i.e. obtained; for the expression cf. Ψ 79, Pind. *Ol.* viii. 15, Ar. *Eccl.* 999, Theocr. iv. 40, Ap. Rh. ii. 258, Callim. *Apoll.* 43, Oppian *Hal.* v. 378, and more in LS., Matro *fr.* vi. 4 ὃν ἀθάνατον λάχε γῆρας.

431. **πρέσβιν**: Plato *Legg.* 855 D κατὰ πρέσβιν ἱζέσθω, 924 C (Matthiae). On the word see Johansson *KZ.* xxx. 404, n. 2.

433. **ἐπωλένιον**: Ap. Rh. i. 557 (of a baby); at 510 the MSS. give ὑπωλ-.

436. **βουφόνε**, 'butcher': the subst. first here, the verb H 466 βουφόνεον δὲ κατὰ κλισίας καὶ δόρπον ἕλοντο, the adj. Aesch. *PV.* 546 θοίναις βουφόνοις; cf. the word πρόσφατος fresh killed, and Aesch. *Sept.* 44 καὶ θιγγάνοντες χερσὶ ταυρείου φόνου. In all these places the word means 'kill, slaughter' without further implication. The idea that βουφόνος here expressed the sanctity of oxen in early times, supported by the modern interpretation of the ritual of the Attic *Buphonia*, in which the priest was called ὁ βουφόνος (Frazer on Paus. i. 24. 4), rests on more than dubious speculation. (The name Βουφόνια finds parallels in the Ταυροφόνια at Mylasa, Le Bas *Asie mineure* 404, and the Ταυροφονήα at Anaphe *IG.* xii. 3. 249, 23.)

μηχανιῶτα: only here. See on i. 2.

πονεύμενε: the participle has a substantival sense as E 831 τοῦτον μαινόμενον, a use natural in hymnal style, among attributes; cf. Orph. *h.* 14. 8 ὀβριμόθυμε, | ψευδομένη, σώτειρα, 51. 7 φαινόμεναι, ἀφανεῖς; Nonnus almost *passim*, e.g. ii. 570 ψευδόμενε, σκηπτοῦχε, viii. 200 ἑζομένης δὲ Ἥρης ψευδομένης.

437. Apollo hints at an accommodation.

μέμηλας: *lusisti*, only here in act. with acc., otherwise in the part. μεμηλώς c. gen. But we have the middle μέλομαι c. acc.

Anacr. 65. 2, Anacreont. 53. 2 (corrected from μέλπομαι, which the metre forbids), the passive ταὶ μέλονται πρός τινος in a lyric poet quoted by Favorinus π. φυγῆς pap. Vat. 11 (1931). 11. 6, μεληθέν *Anth. Pal.* v. 200. 31. Cf. also the Hesychian glosses μεμελημένως· πεπονημένως and μεμήλω· φροντίζω.

438. υ 180 νῶι διακρινέεσθαι ὀίω.

440. **ἐκ γενετῆς**: cf. Ω 535, σ 6 (Hermann), Ar. *Eth. Nic.* vi. 13. 1; vii. 14. 4.

443. **νεήφατον**: only here, cf. παλαίφατος. For the predicative adj. (**θαυμασίην**) with ἀκούω cf. 280.

447. **μοῦσα ἀμηχανέων μελεδώνων**: the hiatus may stand in the trochaic caesura of the third foot, Eberhard *Metr. Beob.* ii. 10. The genitive is objective (Franke): Eur. *Troad.* 609 μουσά θ' ἣ λύπας ἔχει, Theocr. xiv. 52 φάρμακον . . . ἀμηχανέοντος ἔρωτος.

ἀμηχανέων is fem. pl. from ἀμήχανος: for feminines of adjectives in ἀ- privative cf. in Homer ἄβροτος, ἀεικέλιος, ἀθάνατος, ἄνιπτος (Zen. Z 266), ἀπειρέσιος, ἄσβεστος. Hesiod has ἀκαμάτῃσι *Theog.* 519, cf. *h.* v. 133, Mimnermus 6. 1 ἀργαλέων μελεδώνων. For the sentiment cf. Hes. *Theog.* 55, *Cypria* 10, *Ichneut.* xiii. 1.

448. **τρίβος** (not in Homer) apparently = τριβή; see the passages from Hippocrates quoted by Foës, e.g. iii. 53. 8 μήτε ἐν τρίβῳ μήτε ἐν ἔργῳ, 143. 7 ἡ δὲ κεφαλὴ τοῦ βραχίονος ἤδη τρίβον ἑωυτῇ πεποιημένη, 223. 5 ὅταν τρίβον λάβῃ τὸ ἄρθρον ἐν τῇ σαρκί, 305. 7 τὸ ἔθος τρίβον ποιεῖ, though Galen takes the second passage literally; on the third he says κατὰ μεταφορὰν εἴρηκε τρίβον ἀπὸ τῶν τετριμμένων χωρίων ὑπὸ τῶν ὁδοιπορούντων; and on the first (xviii. i. 836) says τρίβον μὲν οὖν καλεῖ καθ' ὃ τρίβεταί τι μέρος τοῦ σώματος. These pairs of words (masc. and fem.) in many cases retain the same sense, see Ϛ B T Σ 551, *EM.* 261. 14, K.-B. i. 501, e.g. οἶμος οἴμη below.

449. **ἔρωτα.** The first case of this acc. = Homeric ἔρον. ἔρως however occurs Γ 442 (v.l. φρένας ἔρος), Ξ 294 (v.l. ἔρος).

450. **ὀπηδός** is not in Homer, though ὀπηδεῖν is frequent Cf. Dion. Hal. *ars rhet.* i. 1 ὅσοι γε δὴ Μουσῶν καὶ Ἀπόλλωνος ὀπαδοί.

According to the present hymn Apollo and the Muses had known only the flute (452) until Hermes invented the lyre; *h.* iii. 131 Apollo claims the lyre as his own in his childhood.

According to a third version Apollo and Hermes fought for the lyre, e.g. in a group at Helicon, Paus. ix. 30. 1 (*BCH.* xv. 399). For other representations of this version cf. *Monumenti* 1830, pl. ix. 2. According to the author of the *Europa* and Myro ap. Paus. ix. 5. 8 Hermes gave the lyre to Amphion.

451. Cf. Orpheus *fr.* 259 Abel (38 Kern) *οὐδέ τι λήθονται Μουσέων βροτοί, αἳ γὰρ ἔασι | κοίρανοι αἶσι μέμηλε χορὸς θαλίαι τ' ἐρατειναί.*

οἶμος ἀοιδῆς: it is doubtful if *ὕμνος ἀοιδῆς* (*θ* 429, Nonnus xvii. 374) should not be preferred. For the metaphor in *οἶμος* cf. Pind. *Ol.* ix. 47 *ἐπέων οἶμον λιγύν*, Callim. *Jov.* 78 *λύρης εὖ εἰδότας οἴμους.* The form is not found in Homer, who uses *οἴμη.*

454. **νέων θαλίῃς**: Ap. Rh. i. 458 *οἷα τε πολλὰ νέοι παρὰ δαιτὶ καὶ οἴνῳ | τερπνῶς ἑψιόωνται*, frag. trag. adesp. 327 *θαλίαι τε νέων*, above 55 *ἠύτε κοῦροι ἡβηταὶ θαλίῃσι παραιβόλα κερτομέουσιν.*

ἐνδέξια, 'clever', only here in this sense; cf. *δεξιός, ἐπιδέξιος.* Perhaps we should read *θαλίῃς ἐν δεξιά*, as Ptol. Asc. divided *ἐνδέξια* into *ἐν δεξιά* I 236; but *δεξιός* also in this sense is non-Homeric.

456. **οἶδας** occurs *α* 337, *οἶσθα* above 382. See Solmsen *KZ.* xxxix. 207.

457, 458. The omission of these lines in *xp* is due to the homoearchon of 456, 458.

457. **ἶζε** is right; Δ 412 *τέττα σιωπῇ ἧσο ἐμῷ δ' ἐπιπείθεο μύθῳ*, cl. H 115, Ϛ Plat. *Theaet.* 146 A in a game *ὄνος κάθου, ἐπὶ τῶν ἐν πράγματι ἡττωμένων.*

For the rest we accept Ruhnken's easy metathesis (e.g. O 94, Ϛ Ap. Rh. ii. 1219, iii. 98), with the second dative demanded by Epaphroditus on Σ 313 (*Πουλυδάμαντι δ' ἄρ οὔ τι* [*ἐπῄνησαν*] for *τις*, with some MSS.), and found in the v.l. *σ* 167 *πάντα μνηστῆρσιν ὑπερφιάλοισιν ἐπαινεῖν* (for *ὁμιλεῖν*); the dative of the person only occurs in inscrr., Meisterhans 172. 37.

460. Achilles swears by a sceptre A 234: cf. Aesch. *Septem* 829, and for parallels to swearing on a spear R., p. 154.

κρανέινον: this form appears to be correct, cf. the variants Herod. vii. 92, Xen. *Hipp.* 12. 12, Strabo 570; -*αἴνας ῥάβδους* Hippocr. iii. 113 inf., *ῥάβδοι κρανίης* 306. 6, *κόμμα μελαγκράινον* (codd.)

Philetas *fr.* 17 Powell. On the wood see Theophr. *HP.* iii. 12. 1 τὸ δὲ ξύλον τῆς κρανείας ἀκάρδιον καὶ στερεὸν ὅλον, ὅμοιον κέρατι τὴν πυκνότητα καὶ τὴν ἰσχύν.

ἀκόντιον: not in Homer. The MSS. here and apparently everywhere else make this word proparoxytone (although it is a diminutive) according to the rule in Theognostus 123. 4 (*an. Ox.* ii). See Postgate *British Acad. Proc.* xi. 14 and 18.

Apollo carries the spear as a fighter rather than as a herdsman, though Eumaeus used one ξ 531 (G.), and cf. *Anth. Pal.* vi. 177. 3 (Theocr. *ep.* ii).

461. Unless ἡγεμονεύσω can = ἡγήσομαι *ducam* it is impossible. Hermes is ἡγεμόνιος Ar. *Plut.* 1159, Arrian *Cyneg.* 34. 3, so perhaps an equivalent of ἡγεμόνα ἱδρύσομαι is wanted. Tyrrell's εἴσω is nearest to this.

464. **περιφραδές**: more likely vocative, when it is complimentary, than adverbial.

467. Cf. βουλῇ καὶ μύθοισι καὶ ἠπεροπηΐδι τέχνῃ quoted by Strabo 17, 601 as from Homer (perhaps γ 130 *a*).

468. **θαάσσεις**: 172 θαασσέμεν and in Homer there is no variant. The grammarians however preserve θοάζειν (Hesych. θοάζει· κάθηται, Σ Aesch. *Suppl.* 595, Soph. *OT.* 2, Ap. Rh. ii. 1026). The original of θῶκος was θόϝακος (Hesych. θάβακον· θᾶκον), Schulze *qu. ep.* 434.

471. **καὶ τιμὰς σὲ δέ φασι** (M): this is the earliest example of καὶ . . . δέ separated, see *KG.* ii. 253, n. 3. The next apparently is Aesch. *PV.* 1005. This is obscured by the γέ of the other MSS. The sentence runs on to θέσφατα πάντα, which recapitulates, as θαυματὰ ἔργα 80, 440, vii. 34, ἐνδέξια ἔργα 454. To make a gnome of Διὸς πάρα θέσφατα πάντα (sc. ἐστί) would be too pompous for Hermes.

473. The two ends of this line are sound, the centre and the sense are lost. The *pâté* παιδαφνειον is unmetrical. A kind of vulgate was arranged by writing σε for γε (but αὐτὸς ἔγωγε is too frequent to be altered), thus τῶν αὐτὸς ἐγώ σε [ ] ἀφνειὸν δεδάηκα, 'in which I myself understand you are rich'. Here αὐτὸς ἐγώ is inert. Further, it has been supposed that a request for prophecy

(refused in 533) took place here. To this view δεδάηκα lends itself singularly little, and the view is false (see on 533). The text as far as τῶν νῦν αὐτὸς ἔγωγε . . . δεδάηκα goes reads 'of which I myself have learned', but παΐδαφνειον resists; παιδ- easily = πεδ- (one of the commonest exchanges)[1], and our old conjecture πεδάφνειον (= μετάφνειον, Hesych. μεταίφνιος· ἐξαπίνης) is as good as another: 'I have suddenly (recently) learned about them', i.e. since I was born. πεδ- = μετ- is frequent in Aeschylus (πεδάρσιος, πεδαίχμιος, πεδάοραι, πεδοίκου *fr.* 52), and Euripides (πεδαίρουσ' *HF.* 872, *Phoen.* 1027), and in a document which has ἀθρόᾶς, περ'(ι) and θᾶττον is not out of place.

474. **αὐτάγρετόν**: π 148 εἰ γάρ πως εἴη αὐτάγρετα πάντα βροτοῖσι.

475. **ἐπιθύει**: with infin. Σ 175, Schulze *qu. ep.* 340.

477. **δέγμενος**: see on *h.* ii. 29: a proper name Strabo 357.

479. **ἐπιστάμενος**: for the metre cf. Ap. Rh. i. 725 ἠέλιον ἀνιόντα, 1361 εὐρεῖαν ἐσιδέσθαι. See in general Monro *HG.* § 375. This is a good conjecture of Barnes for ἐπισταμένως, due to a desire to help the metre and which gives no copula. Apollo already 'knew to sing'.

480. **φέρειν**: infin. = imper. after a principal verb. For the wording cf. Hes. *OD.* 671 εὔκηλος τότε . . . ἑλκέμεν (B.).

481. **φιλοκυδέα**: cf. 375 φιλοκυδέος ἥβης. φιλομειδέα though an excellent word has in epos -μμ-, and may be explained as a graphical (μ = κ) and itacistic change.

κῶμον: not in Homer or Hesiod.

483. **ἐξερεείνῃ**, 'invites'.

485. **συνηθείῃσιν**, 'habituation', one may render 'gentle practice'. The lexx. offer Plato *Legg.* 65 D, Polyb. i. 42. 7.

ἀθυρομένη: pass., see on 151.

486. 'Avoiding (denying itself to) painful working', painful that is to the instrument. For such personification cf. Plat. *rep.* 531 B σὺ μὲν τοὺς χρηστοὺς λέγεις τοὺς ταῖς χορδαῖς πράγματα παρέχοντας καὶ βασανίζοντας, ἐπὶ τῶν κολλόπων στρεβλοῦντας· ἵνα δὲ μὴ μακροτέρα ἡ εἰκὼν γίγνηται πλήκτρῳ τε πληγῶν γιγνομένων καὶ κατηγορίας πέρι

[1] Pindar fr. 124 c ap. Ath. 641 B καὶ περι παιδα φθονον MS. = καί περ πεδ' ἄφθονον βοράν 'after', Alcman fr. 33. 5 παῖδα τὰς τροπάς, corr. πεδά.

καὶ ἐξαρνήσεως καὶ ἀλαζονείας χορδῶν, παύομαι τῆς εἰκόνος, *Gorg.* 482 B ἀναρμοστεῖν τε καὶ διαφωνεῖν.

ἐργασίην, 'practice': the word applies to all arts, *Gorg.* 450 C πασῶν τῶν τεχνῶν τῶν μὲν ἐργασία τὸ πολύ ἐστι καὶ λόγου βραχέος δέονται, Isocr. xv. 291 μελέτῃ κατεργασθέν, Dion. Hal. *de Lysia iud.* 11 εἴτε φύσεως αὐτὴν δεῖ καλεῖν εὐτυχίαν εἴτε πόνου καὶ τέχνης ἐργασίαν, and among them to music, Eur. *Andr.* 476 τεκτόνοιν θ' ὕμνοιν ἐργάταιν δυοῖν | ἔριν Μοῦσαι φιλοῦσι κραίνειν, Plato *Phaedo* 60 E μουσικὴν ποίει καὶ ἐργάζου, Aristotle *part. an.* 660 b 3 πρὸς μὲν τὴν τῆς φωνῆς ἐργασίαν ἄχρηστον τὰ πολλὰ τὴν γλῶτταν ἔχει, 802 b 15 τῶν χορδῶν . . . βέλτισται καὶ . . . τὴν κατεργασίαν ἔχουσι πάντοθεν ὁμοίαν, of the flute *Pol.* viii. 6 ἐπεὶ δὲ τῶν τε ὀργάνων καὶ τῆς ἐργασίας ἀποδοκιμάζομεν τὴν τεχνικὴν παίδειαν . . . διόπερ οὐ τῶν ἐλευθέρων κρίνομεν εἶναι τὴν ἐργασίαν ἀλλὰ θητικωτέραν. Not unlike is Longinus τέχν. ῥητ. 559 εἰ τοίνυν τὸ μουσικὸν . . . ξύμμετρόν τε καὶ ξυμμελὲς ἐξεργάσαιο, Juvenal vi. 383 *quo [pectine] tener Hedymeles operas dedit.*

For **μαλακῇσιν** (485) cf. *Anth. Pal.* x. 23 πρηείης ἄρχεται ἐκ μελετῆς of a rhetor, Hesych. σταδαῖον μέλος· τὸ πρᾷον, Hippocr. iii. 391. 3, 409. 11, πρηέως ἀρχόμενοι, πρηεῖα ἴησις frequently (as ἠρέμα, etc.), μειλιχόμειδε of Sappho Alcaeus 55. 1. Estienne quotes S. Basil *hom. in 1 psalm.* (ed. 1721, p. 91) βίαιον μὲν γὰρ μάθημα οὐ πέφυκε παραμένειν, τὰ δὲ μετὰ τέρψεως καὶ χάριτος εἰσδυόμενα μονιμώτερόν πως ταῖς ψυχαῖς ἡμῶν ἐνιζάνει. Cf. also Euryphamus ap. Stob. *ecl.* iv. 39 (p. 916 Hense) λύρα πᾶσα χρῄζει τριῶν τούτων τυχέν, ἐξαρτύσιος, συναρμογῆς, ἐπαφᾶς τινος μωσικᾶς . . . ἐπαφὰ δὲ μωσικὰ ἁ κατ' ἀρετὰν καὶ νόμως τούτων σύγκρασις, Antig. Caryst. 169 εἶναι δ' αὐτῶν τὴν ἁφὴν ἐν τῇ χρείᾳ σκληράν, Nicomachus *enchir.* 4 τῇ γὰρ πολλῇ λειποτονήσαντι παραπομπῇ τὸ πνεῦμα ἐξίησιν εἰς τὸν πέριξ ἀέρα καὶ δυσεμφάτως αὐτὸν πλήσσει καὶ κινεῖ.

The singular variant φθέγγουσα is a correction (cf. ἐπιδεύομαι, -δέομαι 383, στρεύγεσθαι, στρέγγεσθαι μ 351), thought suitable to the subject, of φεύγουσα, φέγουσα, φέγγουσα. For φεύγειν of things cf. Soranus iii. 29. 1 μήτραν . . . ἃ μὲν φεύγουσαν, ἃ δὲ διώκουσαν, 5 μήτρα . . . τερπομένη μὲν τοῖς εὐώδεσι, φεύγουσα δὲ τὰ δυσώδη, iv. 36. 11.

δυήπαθος occurs only here: δυηπαθής, -εια are Alexandrian.

488. **μετήορα**, 'high', i.e. off the note, perhaps 'sharp'. The word has an unfavourable connotation in medicine and rhetoric, but is not applied elsewhere to musical notes.

θρυλίζοι: the corruption *θρυαλίζοι* points to *θρυλλίζοι*, a constant variant.

489 = 474. The repetition is a characteristic of the hymn, cf. 25, 111.

491. **ὄρεος** and **πεδίοιο** depend on *νομούς*; *κ* 159 *ἐκ νομοῦ ὕλης*. *νομοὺς . . . νομεύσομεν* as *βουλὰς βουλεύων*, etc., *KG*. i, p. 320, 3 *a*. *βουσί* is dat. commodi. Who is responsible for the interpretation of *νομεύειν* = *depascere* with *βουσί* dat. instr. (LS.) we have not discovered.

494. **μίγδην**: first here, for the Homeric *μίγδα*.

495. **κερδαλέον**, 'avaricious', fond of property, as 335.

497. **ἔχων**: not more otiose than *ἔχουσα* 345. D'Orville's *ἔχειν* does not account for *ἔχων*.

501, 502 = 53, 54 and 419, 420 with variations.

M's *ὑπὸ νέρθεν* (R.) = *ὑπὸ χειρός* 419. The *καλόν* of the other MSS. came from 502. For Apollo's action cf. Diod. iii. 59. 2 (he had given up music after the death of Marsyas v. 75. 3).

σμερδαλέον: see on 54.

503. **ἐτραπέτην** may be either act. or med., and the MSS. provide for both voices (*βόας*, *βόες*). **βόες** gives a stronger sense (the cows went home of themselves, as to the troughs in 103), and another case of dual = plural is obtained; see on iii. 456.

The oxen gone home and the bargain clinched by the passing of the cithara from one to the other, Hermes consoled himself by the invention of the syrinx, and gave a further undertaking to Apollo to respect his property and his strong house. Apollo on his side engaged to hold no God nor son of Zeus dearer than Hermes (making the lyre a public token of the undertaking), and gave him the caduceus. At this point he became pontifical, denied him prophecy, 'about which he had asked', on the ground that he could not reveal the mind of Zeus, and enlarged shortly on the policy of Delphi. After doing so he offered Hermes the divination of the *σεμναί*. The topics are rather packed,[1] and we

[1] Like the list of Apollo's amours *h*. iii. 208 sq.

may if we please suppose that there was a fuller tradition of them which the writer epitomised; but the whole is a natural completion of the definition of the provinces of the two Gods. To scent interpolation is the result of subjective prepossession, and false prepossession at that. What do we know of the 'unities' of the seventh century? and at a later period who was likely to insert these highly compressed and obscure details? The only discrepancy even imagined between this passage and the earlier part of the hymn rests on a mistranslation of Greek (533).

507. **καὶ τὰ μέν**: either this or *τὸ μέν* (β 46) = 'firstly' It is very remarkable that the alteration *ὁ μέν*, which introduces an opposition between persons, has been printed from Ruhnken down to Ludwich.

508. **ὡς ἔτι καὶ νῦν**: cf. 125 *ὡς ἔτι νῦν*, Ξ 234, Theocr. ii. 61 (R.). The expression refers to the close connexion between the cults of the two Gods in various parts of Greece; see introduction, p. 270.

509. **σήματ'**: sc. *σήματι*. The elision of iota is frequent; Γ 349 *ἀσπίδ' ἐνὶ κρατερῇ*, Δ 259 *ἐν δαίθ'*, Ε 5 *ἀστέρ' ὀπωρινῷ*, cf. Monro *HG.* § 375 (3). The dative is of 'reason or occasion' (*ib.* § 144), 'with a token', i.e. the lyre, which had passed hands, was the visible sign of the compact, as it were a *σφρηγίς*; cf. *σῆμα νέης φωρῆς* of the hides 136; M's superiority is again manifest. *Σήματ' ἐπεὶ* = *ἐπεὶ σήματι* as Ζ 474, ξ 175 (B.).

510. **ἱμερτὴν δεδαώς**: the position of *ἱμερτήν*, if we took it with *δεδαώς*, would be strange. With Ludwich's punctuation *δεδαώς* refers to Apollo, 'he learned it and played it' (ρ 519 *ἀείδῃ δεδαώς*). It is implied that the learning was immediate, 474 *σοὶ δ' αὐτάγρετόν ἐστι δαήμεναι ὅττι μενοινᾷς*.

ἐπωλένιον: the conjecture is necessary, the form occurs without variant 433, and the lyre rested on the arm.

512. For the abruptness cf. 25, 111. On the invention of the pipe see Apollod. iii. 115 *Ἑρμῆς δὲ ταύτας νέμων σύριγγα πάλιν πηξάμενος ἐσύριζεν. Ἀπόλλων δὲ καὶ ταύτην βουλόμενος λαβεῖν τὴν χρυσῆν ῥάβδον ἐδίδου ἣν ἐκέκτητο βουκολῶν.* This was the invention of a symmetrical mythographer, lyre for cattle, syrinx for caduceus. The syrinx had nothing to do with Apollo; it is found as the

property of Hermes' son Pan. Hermes made it to suit his new occupation of *νόμιος*.

τηλόθ' ἀκουστήν: sc. by the cattle and sheep. Roscher sees the whistling wind in it, but it is the natural instrument of the shepherd; Plato *rep.* 399 D *κατ' ἀγροὺς τοῖς νομεῦσι σύριγξ ἄν τις εἴη*, Ant. Lib. 22. 2 *σύριγμα ποιμενικὸν ἐν τοῖς ὄρεσι.*

515. For *ἀνακλέψῃς* cf. a Dodonaean inscr. Collitz ii. 2 no. 1586 p. 12. 4 *ανε[κλεψεν]*, Hesych. *ἀνακλέπτεσθαι· ἀναχωρεῖν.* For the variant cf. *γ* 276 *ἀναπλέομεν* Zen., *ἅμα πλ.* codd. The theft of the bow is mentioned by Horace *Od.* i. 10. 11, perhaps after Alcaeus, and Lucian *dial. deor.* vii. 1.

516. **ἐπαμοίβιμα**: well restored by Wolf and Ludwich from M's *ἐπ' ἀμοίβημα*: cf. Δ 381 *παραίσιμα, -ια*, Z 62 *αἴσιμα, -ια.* The expression is an euphemism.

518. Cf. *ε* 178, *κ* 343, *h.* iii. 79 (*θεά*).

θεῶν μέγαν ὅρκον: the oath taken by Gods, as *κ* 299. Otherwise *β* 377.

κατόμνυμι which the v.l. implies does not occur before saec. v.

519. Alternatively, with a nod (as Zeus A 524) or on the Styx: the construction *ἐπί τι* does not elsewhere occur (the simple acc. is Homeric). R. compares *ἐπόμνυμι* c. acc.

524. **ἐπ' ἀρθμῷ καὶ φιλότητι**, 'on the understanding of', legal language as 393. For the words cf. Aesch. *PV.* 207, Callim. *fr.* 199 (*φιλίαν*). The v.l. *ἀριθμῷ* is frequent, H 302, *π* 427, Ap. Rh. ii. 755, Syrian. *in* Ar. *Metaph.* M 4, 891 B: the ancients saw an etymological connexion Stob. *ecl.* i. 2.

526. **ἄνδρα**, 'human, mortal'.

An omission has evidently taken place. The line to be supplied must give a tmesis (*ἐκ*), provide an object to which *σύμβολον* is predicate, and account for the 1st pers. *ποιήσομαι. τέλειον* suggests *ἐπιτελέα ὅρκον ποιέειν* in the Hippocratean oath; *ὅρκον* therefore may start the line. Verbs beginning with *ἐκ* and meaning 'ratify' are few; *ἐκποιεῖν* has another meaning; perhaps *ἐκπίπλημι.* The *σύμβολον* (whether masc. or neut. only of things, here = a token shared by parties, e.g. Soph. *Phil.* 403, Σ Eur. *Med.* 613) can only be the *χέλυς*, as in 30, and the only synonym of χέλυς which suits the metre is ἄθυρμα (32 and perhaps 418). So we get

> ὅρκον πέπληκεν· φάτο δ' αὖ τόδε καλὸν ἄθυρμα
> σύμβολον ἀθανάτων ποιήσομαι κτλ.,

'a token for immortals and every one together'. It had been called a σῆμα 509. Lyre and caduceus are exchanged. For ἅμα πάντων cf. φ 230 ἅμα πάντες (R.).

The attempt to justify the transition from 3rd to 1st person (and dispense with a lacuna) fails: Δ 303, Ψ 855 are after verbs of command, O 348 is no case.

529. **ῥάβδον**: not the μάστιγα φαεινήν (497) given to Hermes as herdsman, but the staff afterwards called κηρύκειον, which puts men to sleep or wakes them, Ω 343, ω 2; hence the epithet χρυσόρραπις ε 87, κ 277, 331. There is no adequate ground for supposing that the κηρύκειον was borrowed either from Phoenicia (Hoffmann) or from Phrygia (Ramsay); see Farnell v. 90.

530. **τριπέτηλον**: explained by Preller (*Philol.* i. 518) as 'with three branches', one forming the handle, the other two springing from it and uniting at the top. See also Roscher 2401, J. E. Harrison *Proleg.* 46.

ἀκήριον: pass. 'unharmed', as Phocyl. *gnom.* 105. For the order cf. υ 47 διαμπερὲς ἥ σε φυλάσσω, ψ 56 κακῶς δ' οἵ πέρ μιν ἔρεζον.

531. The line ascribes unheard of virtues to the caduceus and gives an impossible genitive. πάντας ἐπικραίνουσα seems solid, cl. O 599 πᾶσαν ἐπικρήνειε (Θέτιδος ἐξαίσιον ἀρήν). A word is wanted to justify the genitive: πάντας implies]ους, and the word is perhaps θεμούς. θεμός is recognized by *EM.* 445. 17 ἐκ τοῦ [τίθημι] γίνεται θεμὸς καὶ θεσμὸς καὶ θέσμις καὶ θέμις, *Gud.* 258. 6 ἐκ τοῦ θεμὸς ὃ σημαίνει τὸν νόμον γίνεται θέσμις καὶ ἀποβολῇ τοῦ σ̄ θέμις. Hesych. θεμούς· διαθέσεις, παραινέσεις. Its reality is guaranteed by θέμωσε δὲ χέρσον ἱκέσθαι ι 486, 542, and the proper names θεμοθεος, θεμανδρος Bechtel *KZ.* 1913, 45, 149 from Eretria[1].

[1] One would be inclined to read ἀθέμως instead of the unmetrical ἀθέσμως Aesch. *PV.* 150, but that Hesychius quotes ἀθέτως (ἀθέτως· ἀθέσμως ἢ (οὐ) συγκατατεθειμένως. Αἰσχύλος Προμηθεῖ Δεσμώτῃ). The sense of ἄθετος,

The accent is the same as that of θεούς, the rarity of the word accounts for the omission of μ. Translate 'accomplishing all the laws of good words and deeds that I say I have learned from Zeus' voice'. Hermes effects the bidding of the Delphic oracle. This is intelligible, though as was said it gives Hermes' wand a new office. Perhaps it comes under his function of ἄγγελος ἀθανάτων.

The conjecture is the property of Arthur Ludwich (*Hymnenbau* p. 145); it was independently made *CQ.* 1931. 25. On the strength of the coincidence we have put it in the text.

533. μαντείην δὲ . . . ἣν ἐρεείνεις. It would appear that Groddeck in 1786 invented the meaning of 'claim, demand' for ἐρεείνεις to support his view that this part of the hymn is an addition. Barnes was sound (*sciscitaris*), but Hermann (1806) seems to imply this meaning when he says 'possit aliquis colligere scribendum esse ἣν ἐρεείνῃς quod nihil tale dixerit Mercurius', in spite of the formal warning of Ilgen (p. 468) 'at vero quid est quod *preces* quae antecesserint nos intelligere cogat? ἐρεείνειν nunquam est *precibus contendere* sed *interrogare*, *quaerere*, sic *Iliad.* κ 558 ἵπποι δ' οἵδε γεραιὲ νεήλυδες οὓς ἐρεείνεις Θρηίκιοι, ubi Nestor simpliciter interrogavit de equis eosque laudavit'. Stephanus does not know of the meaning, but LS. admit it, one may wonder from whom. Of recent editors Gemoll denies it. Any one who looks at the § in Ebeling will see that ἐρεείνω without exception means 'ask about, mention', never 'demand'. Hence the assertion that Apollo refuses a claim which Hermes had made and which does not appear in the hymn falls to the ground. Hermes 'mentioned' prophecy 471, and here is the reply. There is no other reason to condemn 503–80.

534–5. Apollo shelters himself behind Zeus. In Hesiod *fr.* 96. 82 he is even said not to understand his father's will. For the negative cf. Aesch. *PV.* 536 τοῦτ' οὐκ ἂν οὖν πύθοιο μηδὲ λιπάρει.

541–9. To assign these lines to Hermes is truly extraordinary, and that objections should have been raised to the future

ἀθέτως (Eustathius *or.* xxiii. 26 Tafel, Plut. *qu. conv.* vii. 10. 2 = 715 B πρὸς σκέψιν ἀθέτως ἔχειν διὰ τὸν οἶνον, Dio Prus. viii. 26 = f. 284 Reiske, v. l. ἀθλίων) is quite different.

δηλήσομαι. Apollo will do as he has done. The passage is a statement of the position of Delphi with regard to the inquirer, an official vindication of the God in his dealings with men, Bouché-Leclercq *Hist. de la Divination* iii. 82, 99. Stress is laid on the observance of the proper ritual, without which inquirers approach the God at their own risk. If they are duly accredited with the right omens a true answer is obtained. Cf. (of Dodona) Hesiod *fr.* 134. 9 ἔνθεν ἐπιχθόνιοι μαντήια πάντα φέρονται, | ὃς δὴ κεῖθι μολὼν θεὸν ἄμβροτον ἐξερεείνῃ | δῶρα φέρων τ' ἔλθῃσι σὺν οἰωνοῖς ἀγαθοῖσιν; the attitude of Hecate to her worshippers Hes. *Theog.* 416, 442–3, 447; Apollo's ignorance of the intention of his own oracle Hes. *fr.* 96. 82 (above); Ezekiel xiv. 7–9, xx. 25; Soph. *fr.* 707; this hymn *infra* 563; Aratus 768 πάντα γὰρ οὔπω | ἐκ Διὸς ἄνθρωποι γινώσκομεν ἀλλ' ἔτι πολλὰ | κέκρυπται, Xen. *Cyrop.* i. 6. 46 τῶν συμβουλευομένων ἀνθρώπων οἷς ἂν ἵλεῳ ὦσιν προσημαίνουσιν ἅ τε χρὴ ποιεῖν καὶ ἃ οὐ χρή· εἰ δὲ μὴ πᾶσιν ἐθέλουσι συμβουλεύειν, οὐδὲν θαυμαστόν· οὐ γὰρ ἀνάγκη αὐτοῖς ἐστιν ὧν ἂν μὴ θέλωσιν ἐπιμελεῖσθαι. The Muses say Hes. *Theog.* 27 ἴδμεν ψεύδεα πολλὰ λέγειν ἐτύμοισιν ὁμοῖα, | ἴδμεν δ' εὖτ' ἐθέλωμεν ἀληθέα γηρύσασθαι: cf. also vit. Sibyll. (Westermann Βιογρ. p. 85) εὑρίσκονται καὶ οἱ στίχοι ἀτελεῖς καὶ ἡ διάνοια σκάζουσα· εἴτε καὶ κατ' οἰκονομίαν θεοῦ τοῦτο γέγονεν, ὡς μὴ γιγνώσκοιντο ὑπὸ τῶν πολλῶν καὶ ἀναξίων οἱ χρησμοὶ αὐτῆς. Schoemann *Gr. Alt.*[3] ii. 318.

542. **πολλὰ περιτροπέων**: cf. ι 465 πολλὰ περιτροπέοντες ἐλαύνομεν (μῆλα), Ap. Rh. ii. 143 ἄσπετα μῆλα περιτροπάδην ἐτάμοντο. Apollo drives men like silly sheep, bewilders them. Men on their part 'beguile' (παρατρωπῶσι) the Gods by sacrifice, prayers, and wine and steam I 500.

544. The variants are equal. The datives are equivalent to σύν in Hes. *fr.* 134 above.

τελῃέντων, 'fateful, significant', the opposite of μαψίλογοι. Cf. β 181 ὄρνιθες δέ τε πολλοὶ ὑπ' αὐγὰς ἠελίοιο | φοιτῶσ', οὐδέ τε πάντες ἐναίσιμοι, Callim. v. 123 γνωσεῖται δ' ὄρνιθας ὃς αἴσιος οἵ τε πέτονται | ἤλιθα, καὶ ποίων οὐκ ἀγαθαὶ πτέρυγες. For human disregard of birds cf. Hector's utterance M 237 sq.

549. **φήμ'** (φῆμ', φημ', φήμ' MSS.): on the accentuation see *Iliad* ed. 1931, prol. p. 220.

ἐγὼ δέ κε δῶρα δεχοίμην: payment is not by result, the fee is not returned. The declaration seems in reply to we know not what public opinion. B 420 of Zeus ἀλλ' ὅ γε δέκτο μὲν ἱρά, πόνον δ' ἀμέγαρτον ὄφελλε. The Delphian point of view in general is expressed by Ion in Euripides: 226 εἰ μὲν ἐθύσατε πέλανον πρὸ δόμων | καί τι πυθέσθαι χρῄζετε Φοίβου | πάριτ' ἐς θυμέλας, ἐπὶ δ' ἀσφάκτοις | μήλοισι δόμων μὴ πάριτ' εἰς μυχόν, and again 374 εἰς γὰρ τοσοῦτον ἀμαθίας ἔλθοιμεν ἂν | εἰ τοὺς θεοὺς ἄκοντας ἐκπονήσομεν | φράζειν ἃ μὴ θέλουσιν ἢ προβωμίοις | σφαγαῖσι μήλων ἢ δι' οἰωνῶν πτεροῖς· | ἂν γὰρ βίᾳ σπεύδωμεν ἀκόντων θεῶν | ἀνόνητα κεκτήμεσθα τἀγάθ', ὦ γύναι, | ἃ δ' ἂν διδῶσ' ἑκόντες ὠφελούμεθα. Zeus refuses what he is asked according to ritual Γ 276 (and cf. H 478), O 378, Π 250, Σ 328, ι 553, Athena Z 311, γ 145, the Spercheus Ψ 149.

552. 'There are certain reverend women, three of them.' The allusion cannot be to the σεμναί (θεαί) of Athens, and the variant μοῖραι (probably inspired by τρεῖς) is obviously wrong. Hermann, from the allusion to divination by pebbles in the account of Apollodorus iii. 15 and Philochorus *fr.* 196 (to which add Pherecydes in Cyril *lex.*, *an. Par.* iv. 183), first identified the sisters with the Thriae. These (for whom see Weniger in Roscher v. 866, Wilamowitz *Der Glaube der Hellenen* 379) are the eponymous nymphs of the θριαί or divining pebbles: μαντικαὶ ψῆφοί εἰσιν αἱ θριαί· λέγεται δὲ αὐτὰς εὑρῆσθαι ὑπό τινων τριῶν νυμφῶν. διὰ τοῦτο καὶ θριαὶ ὠνομάσθησαν, οἱονεὶ τριαί Σ Callim. *Apoll.* 45, Steph. Byz. *in* Θρῖα, Hesych. *in v.*, *EM.* 455. 34, *E. Gud.* 266. 6. The etymology is unknown.

The method of divination by stones is world-wide, and must have existed in Greece from time immemorial; see Frazer on Paus. vii. 25. 10, Bouché-Leclercq *Divin. dans l'antiquité* i. 192. Its antiquity (αἱ πρῶται μάντεις Hesych.) is attested by the word ἀναιρεῖν = 'decide' of oracles, which Lobeck *Aglaoph.* ii. 814 explained as *sortes tollere.* Cicero *de div.* i. 34 suggests the early employment of a similar method at Dodona as well as at Delphi, where it remained in use for subsidiary purposes, e.g. to decide the order of inquirers (Bouché-Leclercq *l.c.*). The Thriae elsewhere are described as nymphs of Parnassus and τροφοί of Apollo.

The connexion with Athena alleged by some authors (e.g. Zenobius v. 75, Steph. Byz. *l.c.*, *an. Bekk.* 265) is unreal, being due to an attempt to find an explanation for the names of the Attic deme Thria and the Thriasian plain (Wilamowitz *l.c.*).

554. **πεπαλαγμέναι ἄλφιτα λευκά**: the canephori powdered their hair with flour, Ar. *Eccl.* 732 ὅπως ἂν ἐντετριμμένη κανηφορῇς (Σ σμηχθεῖσα), Hermippus Θεοί *fr.* 26 ὥσπερ αἱ κανηφόροι | λευκοῖσιν ἀλφίτοισιν ἐντετριμμένος (-οις MSS.), Ar. *Telmiss. fr.* 533 ἀλφιτόχρωτος κεφαλῆς, Hesych. ἀλφιτόχρως· λευκή, πολιά, Eust. 868. 37, 976. 53.

The words then are to be taken literally, and not as a paraphrase for 'white-haired'. The three hags wore as it were white wigs. Ilgen thought the expression implied bees covered with pollen.

556. The Thriae taught the humbler kind of divination, used by peasants (ἐπὶ βουσί) ἀπάνευθε, 'apart' from me, viz. not at Delphi.

557. **ἀλέγιζεν**: an evident correction, 'my father recked not', i.e. allowed it. Cf. the v.l. at 361, Quintus ii. 420.

558. **ἄλλοτε ἄλλῃ**: this correction is made probable by δ 236, Phocyl. *fr.* 15, Solon 13. 76, Hesiod *OD.* 713, *Theognis* 157, 232, 318, 992, where τ' or similar fillings are found to avoid the hiatus.

559. Honey gave inspiration: hence the Pythia was called μέλισσα Pind. *Pyth.* iv. 60 (Mnaseas of Patara *ib.*), see also *Ol.* vi. 47, Ar. *Ran.* 1274 μελισσονόμοι, Ox. pap. 1802 col. ii, Cook *JHS.* xv. 7. Cf. also Josephus *Ant. Iud.* v. 6 Δεβώρα προφῆτις, μέλισσαν δὲ σημαίνει τοὔνομα, Robert-Tornow *de apium mellisque signif.* 1893, Frazer on Paus. x. 5. 7, Usener *Rh. Mus.* 1902 lvii. 2. 179, Jane Harrison *Prol.* 91. It is uncertain whether the poet intended aged women who changed themselves completely into bees, or winged women with bees' bodies. The latter view is supported by representations of a winged woman with the body of a bee from the waist on plaques from Camirus (see Cook p. 12, Roscher v. 870). Cf. also Sittig *KZ.* lii. 205, 209. Cf. τ 567 οἵ ῥ' ἔτυμα κραίνουσι (ὄνειροι), Eur. *Ion* 464 μαντεύματα κραίνει.

560. **θύσωσι** *p*: the omission of ι in the diphthong υι is common: at Λ 180 only nine older MSS. have θυῖεν, in Hesiod papyri

in some places keep the iota, in others omit it, cf. *OD.* 621, *Theog.* 109, 131, 848, 874. For inscriptions see Meisterhans 46.

563. The reading of *y* is evidently preferable, δονέουσι (well corrected from δενέουσαι by B.) is appropriate to bees: δ[ονει *Ichneut.* 282, μυρία φῦλ' ἐδονεῖτο πολυσμήνοισι μελίσσαις Choerilus ap. Herod. π. μον. λέξ. 13.

565. *Ichneut.* xiv. 6 τέρπου φρένα; Mimnermus 7. 1 σὴν αὐτοῦ φρένα τέρπε.

568. A lacuna here again is necessary to provide a main verb. The subject can hardly be other than Zeus (G.).

Hermes, to whom and the nymphs Eumaeus made offering (ξ 435), was the God who gave increase to the herds; Hes. *Theog.* 444 of Hecate ἐσθλὴ δ' ἐν σταθμοῖσι σὺν Ἑρμῇ ληίδ' ἀέξειν, | βουκολίας δ' ἀγέλας τε καὶ αἰπόλια πλατέ' αἰγῶν, | ποίμνας τ' εἰροπόκων ὀΐων, θυμῷ γ' ἐθέλουσα | ἐξ ὀλίγων βριάει καὶ ἐκ πολλῶν μείονα θῆκεν. He was peculiarly God of sheep-farming (μηλοσσόε Μαιάδος Ἑρμᾶ *Anth. Pal.* vi. 334. 3); hence the cult-titles ἐπιμήλιος and κριοφόρος (see Farnell v. ref. nos. 5, 6a–d, P.-W. viii. 756, 758). The claim here made for Hermes' sway over the animal world beyond domestic herds seems to go beyond common usage. It is paralleled in the sculpture found at Delos (s. i B.C.) in which the God appears together with goat, dog, horses, cock, panther, and dolphin (*BCH.* xiii. 375).

572. **τετελεσμένον ἄγγελον**: Demosth. xiii. 19 στρατηγὸς τελεσθῆναι.

573. The line must refer to Hades; Hermes was not ἄδοτος, 'implacable'. It is possible that the γέρας is Hermes' office, but this was presumably in the gift of Zeus along with Hermes' other privileges. Otherwise the 'present' must be death, as in the story of Cleobis and Bito, and of Agamedes and Trophonius, Plato *Axioch.* 367 C.

576. M's νομίζων is a graphical mistake for νομιλει.

577, 578 recapitulate Hermes' nature. See on 541. Of Zeus B 420 quoted on 549 πόνον δ' ἀμέγαρτον ὄφελλε, Aesch. *Choeph.* 812 of Hermes ἄσκοπον δ' ἔπος λέγων | νύκτα πρό τ' ὀμμάτων σκότον φέρει, | καθ' ἡμέραν δ' οὐδὲν ἐμφανέστερος, in general id. *frr.* 294, 295.

V

Hymn to Aphrodite

The germ of the story is found in the Iliad; B 820 Αἰνείας, τὸν ὑπ' Ἀγχίσῃ τέκε δῖ' Ἀφροδίτη | Ἴδης ἐν κνημοῖσι θεὰ βροτῷ εὐνηθεῖσα, E 313 (Ἀφροδίτη) ἥ μιν ὑπ' Ἀγχίσῃ τέκε βουκολέοντι: Hes. *Theog.* 1008 Αἰνείαν δ' ἄρ' ἔτικτεν ἐυστέφανος Κυθέρεια | Ἀγχίσῃ ἥρωι μιγεῖσ' ἐρατῇ φιλότητι | Ἴδης ἐν κορυφῇσι πολυπτύχου ὑλῃέσσης: among later poets we find it in Theocr. xx. 34, Prop. ii. 32. 35, Nonnus xv. 210. In prose Acusilaus *fr.* 26 is the best authority; he makes Anchises elderly (ἤδη παρηκμακότι συνῆλθεν), next Apollodorus iii. 142, who adds another son, Lyros, to Aeneas. He shows no signs of using the hymn (*ib.* 141 he makes Ganymede carried off by an eagle, not as in the hymn by a whirlwind), which is not quoted by any ancient writer. It seems strange to us that such brilliant literature made little or no impression on subsequent readers.[1] In Hyginus *fab.* 94 Anchises is punished for indiscretion (see on 228). A parallel story is that of Eryx in Diod. iv. 8. 3 Ἔρυκά φασιν υἱὸν μὲν γενέσθαι Ἀφροδίτης καὶ Βούτα βασιλέως τινος ἐγχωρίου δόξῃ διαφέροντος.

The hymn has often been compared to the lay of Demodocus on the loves of Ares and Aphrodite θ 266 sq. There are coincidences in language (see on 58, 234). But the tone of the hymn is higher than that of the *Odyssey*. B. (p. 250) was wrong when he called Aphrodite *vulgivaga*, and G. (p. 238) replied with justice that Aphrodite feels shame, and that her passion has been imposed on her by Zeus. Her position is not unlike that of the epic Helen. The adventure is treated with frankness but without loss of dignity, and the raciness of Demodocus is entirely absent.

The poem has sometimes been unduly depreciated. There may be inelegance in the repetition of ἔργον five times in vv. 1–15, but this and similar blemishes, collected by Suhle,[2] do not justify his preposterous verdict *permediocris poeta*. MM. A. and M. Croiset

[1] For coincidences between this hymn and that to Demeter, see below, p. 350 *ad fin.*

[2] *de hymno Homerico iv*, 1878, 23.

(*Greek Literature*, Eng. tr. i. 590) thought the poem too long for the subject, but the laws of 'composition' troubled the ancients, especially early poets, very little (Ar. *Poetics* 6, 1405 a 37). There is not room for originality in a style which follows the Homeric language so closely (see below), but credit is due to the artist who caught the spirit of epos. The narrative is direct and sensuous [1]; though the subject is simple, variety and additional interest are given it by the three short 'hymns' at the beginning (to Athene, Artemis, and Hestia), and the introduction of Ganymede, Tithonus, the nymphs and the Sileni at the end.

The poet's conception of Aphrodite is simple. She is mistress of the animal world (2–6), but there is no hint of a deity who inspires the whole Cosmos, an Aphrodite Urania by whose agency

ἐρᾷ μὲν ἁγνὸς οὐρανὸς τρῶσαι χθόνα,
ἔρως δὲ γαῖαν λαμβάνει γαμοῦ τυχεῖν

(Aesch. *fr.* 41). Such an idea of a universal love-goddess grew up, as Farnell remarks (ii. 699), on eastern soil. In Greek literature we do not find it till Euripides *fr.* 89 and the Orphic hymns (e.g. lv. 4).

The *date* of the hymn is naturally uncertain. Its language usually inclines critics to find it old. As many as twenty verses come from Homer with little or no variation; and the poem abounds in epic hemistiches and formulae. On the other hand there are a number of non-Homeric words and usages.[2] These moved Suhle *l. c.* to the extraordinary view that the author was a contemporary of the Pisistratidae, or even of Sophocles! There are also coincidences with Hesiod (see on 5, 14, 29, 108, 258), and, what is more remarkable, with the hymn to Demeter. The two hymns have in common several words and expressions not found, or not in the same sense, elsewhere: 31 τιμάοχος (Dem. 268), 157 εὔστρωτος (Dem. 285), 257 βαθύκολπος of nymphs (Dem. 5), 284 καλυκῶπις (Dem. 8, 420), 156 κατ' ὄμματα καλὰ

[1] Farnell *Pindar* ii. 474 'the secular voluptuous tone of the Homeric Hymn'.

[2] See on 13, 19, 29, 31, 32, 52, 74, 84, 86, 90, 104, 108, 127, 135, 189, 197, 199, 204, 246, 259, 262.

βαλοῦσα (Dem. 194), 173 μελάθρου κῦρε κάρη (Dem. 188). There are coincidences with Sappho also (iv. 1 Lobel); see on 13, 228, 234, 235. The passage on Tithonus may have been Sappho's model. The forms ἐκγεγάονται (197), τεκεῖσθαι (127) are of uncertain origin. On the whole the hymn can hardly be dated later than 700 B.C.

The place of composition is no less obscure. On the strength of the title Κύπρις (2), the phrase Κύπροιο ἐυκτιμένης μεδέουσα (292), and the word σατίνη (13), the hymn as late as Fick (*BB.* ix. 200) was said to be Cyprian. But Κύπρις and Κυθέρεια are stock epithets (e.g. vi. 2, 18, x. 1), and the origin of σατίνη is more likely Asiatic, and Sappho, Anacreon, and Euripides use it. Again it was supposed to have been composed in honour of a descendant of Aeneas. But it bears no trace of having been written on a definite occasion, or for a particular person. The allusion to the revived Trojan kingdom 196 sq. is vague and merely follows the Homeric tradition. But the mention of the Trojan nurse in Phrygia (113) clearly implies Asia, as well as the distinction between the Trojan and Phrygian languages. The author may have been an Aeolian or a Lesbian, e.g. Lesches.

To see in the hymn a contamination of the Greek Aphrodite and the Asiatic Cybele is unsound. It is true that in the Troad Aphrodite was probably another form of Cybele (Farnell ii. 641), but the hymn-writer follows the Homeric conception and for Homer Aphrodite is far removed from Cybele. As G. observes, Aphrodite is called daughter of Zeus, and her train of beasts is a reflection of the animals which follow Circe (see on 69).

The unity of the hymn is so obvious that it has suffered comparatively little from criticism. Groddeck and Ilgen thought fit to suspect the description of the nymphs 260–72. The lines are perhaps the most interesting in the poem.

For cults and legends of Aphrodite see Farnell ii. 618, Nilsson *GF.* 362, Roscher i. 390, P.-W. i. 2729, P.-R. 345. Other hymns to her are Orph. *h.* iv, Proclus *h.* ii (Abel, p. 278), v (Abel, p. 280). Chrysostom iii. 1, p. 211 (vol. li Migne) mentions a hymn to Aphrodite at marriage.

1. **μοῦσά μοι ἔννεπε**: α 1 ἄνδρά μοι ἔννεπε Μοῦσα.

3. All living things are the conquest of love, Theognis 1526–9, Soph. *fr.* 941, Eur. *Hipp.* 447, 1269, Lucr. i. 1.

4. **διιπετέας**: the paroxytonesis helps to identify this with the Homeric διιπετής, of rivers that 'fall from heaven', i.e. are fed by rain (Strabo 36, 693 τοῦ τ' ἐκπίπτοντος ἐκ Διὸς καὶ τοῦ ποταμίου). Of birds it = 'that fall from the sky', swoop and settle on the ground. Cf. ἀεροπετής (LS.).

5. **πολλὰ τρέφει**: cf. Hes. *Theog.* 582 κνώδαλ' ὅσ' ἤπειρος πολλὰ τρέφει ἠδὲ θάλασσα, *Cypria* vii. 12 θηρί' ὅσ' ἤπειρος αἰνὰ τρέφει.

6. Proclus *h.* iv. 13 πᾶσιν δ' ἔργα μέμηλεν ἐρωτοτόκου Κυθερείης (Matthiae).

8. This 'hymn' to Athena agrees with *h.* xxviii in nothing but the epithet γλαυκῶπιν. In the reference to ἀγλαὰ ἔργα it coincides with xx. 2.

γλαυκῶπιν: so α 156, Hes. *Theog.* 13, 888, *h.* iii. 314, xxviii. 2 without variant: γλαυκώπιδ(α) is found Θ 373, *h.* iii. 323.

10. Hes. *Theog.* 926 πότνιαν ᾗ κέλαδοί τε ἅδον πόλεμοί τε μάχαι τε. For cults of Athena as Goddess of war see Farnell i. 308, and for the probably correct theory of her origin as the palace-goddess of the Mycenaean king Nilsson *Anfänge der Göttin Athene.*

12. For Athene as patron of crafts see xx introd., Farnell i. 314 (cults of Athene Ergane, Calliergos, Machanitis, etc.).

τέκτονας: for dedications to Athena by τέκτονες cf. *Anth. Pal.* vi. 204, 205. Athena gave men τὴν τεκτονικὴν τέχνην Diod. v. 73; as early as Hesiod (*OD.* 430) the plough-builder is Ἀθηναίης δμῶος.

13. **σατίναις**: this word occurs elsewhere in Sappho ii. *fr.* 2 Lobel σατίναις ὑπ' εὐτρόχοις, Anacr. xxi. 12 σατινέων, Eur. *Hel.* 1311, Herod. π. διχρ. 291. 25, Hesych. σατίναι· αἱ ἁμάξαι. It is derived by G. Meyer (*Alban. Stud.* ii = Sitzungsb. d. Wiener Ak. 125, p. 51 Anm. 1): 'das Wort stammt aus Vorderasien, und gehört zu ai. sátrŭs "Feind", air. cath "Haupt", gall. caturgies, ahd. hadu, agr. heado'. Solmsen *KZ.* xxiv. 38 and 69 adds the Phrygian Κότυς, and the Thracian tribe Σάτραι, Σατροκένται. These are very doubtful speculations. A Phrygian or Armenian origin is preferred by Boisacq. The quotations in literature (in

Anacreon the word is part of a description of eastern luxury, in Euripides it represents Cybele's car) seem to make *σατίνη* a Grecized Asian, perhaps Phrygian, word.

καὶ ἅρματα π. χ.: Δ 226, Κ 393 *καὶ ἅρματα*, Κ 322 *τε καὶ ἅρματα*. Hence perhaps Ruhnken on *Dem.* 275 was right in writing *τε καί* throughout.

14. Cf. Hes. *OD.* 519 *παρθενικῆς ἀπαλόχροος*, Σ 567, λ 39, xxx. 14 *παρθενικαί*, η 20 *-κῇ*, Tyrtaeus *fr.* 612 *δεσποσύνοισι=δεσπόταις*.

Athena's connexion with womens' handiwork, especially weaving, is shown by the story of Arachne and conventional phrases such as *ἡ δ' ἐς Ἀθηναίης ἔργα νόῳ τρέπετο IG.* vii. 3, *Suppl.* 1271. 4, *ἥδε γὰρ ἀθανάτων προφερεστάτη ἐστὶν ἁπασέων | ἱστὸν ἐποίχεσθαι ταλασήϊά τ' ἔργα πινύσσειν* Orph. *fr.* 135 Abel = 178 Kern. Athena is *ἱστοπόνος Anth. Pal.* vi. 247. 2.

16. The section has nothing in common with *h.* xxvii except these epithets.

χρυσηλάκατον κελαδεινήν: = Π 183, Υ 70, xxvii. 1. Hesych. is probably right in explaining *χρυσηλάκατος* = *καλλίτοξος· ἠλακάτη γὰρ ὁ τοξικὸς κάλαμος*. Cf. *ἄτρακτος* = *οἰστός*. This was the view of D'Orville *JP.* xxv. 257, who compared Soph. *Trach.* 636. The epithet *κελαδεινή* is a further argument, of the Goddess calling on the hounds; Σ A Π 183 *παρὰ τὸν γιγνόμενον ἐν τοῖς κυνηγεσίοις κέλαδον*. So probably Bacchyl. xi. 37 *Ἄρτεμις ἀγροτέρα χρυσηλάκατος . . . τοξόκλυτος*. Other poets, Pindar (who uses the epithet of Amphitrite *Ol.* vi. 104, and Leto *Nem.* vi. 36, *fr.* 139), Nonnus (i. 367 *δυσηλακάτου Μοίρης*), understood it of the distaff: so Bacchyl. himself viii. 1.

17. **φιλομειδής**: frequent in this hymn only (and in the *Il.* and *Od.*). *φιλομμηδής* Hes. *Theog.* 200 (there etymologized *ὅτι μηδέων ἐξεφαάνθη*) is perhaps the Boeotian form, Eust. 439. 36 (*βοιωτικῶς*).

18. **οὔρεσι κτλ.** = Φ 485; cf. also Callim. *Dian.* 2 *τῇ τόξα λαγωβολίαι τε μέλονται | καὶ χορὸς ἀμφιλαφὴς καὶ ἐν οὔρεσιν ἑψιάασθαι*. M's reading may point to the omission of a line owing to homoeomeson between 18 and 18 *a*, e.g. *καὶ γὰρ τῇ ἅδε [παρθενίη μέν τ' ἀγαμίη τε πουλύχρυσα δὲ] τόξα κτλ.*

19. **διαπρύσιοι**: only the adverb in Homer. On the word see *h.* iv. 336.

For the musical character of Artemis cf. xxvii. 18, Farnell ii. 471.

20. **δικαίων τε πτόλις ἀνδρῶν**: for Artemis as a lover of justice cf. Callim. *Dian.* 122 ἀλλά μιν εἰς ἀδίκων ἔβαλες πόλιν. Her social and political side was not very prominent. See P.-W. 1350, Farnell ii. 467. The epithet πολιήοχος given her, Ap. Rh. i. 312, does not occur in actual cult. Although Zeus promises her 'thirty cities to cherish no other God but thee, and be called by the name of Artemis' (Callim. *Dian.* 34, and cf. 225 πολύπτολι), these cities as Farnell points out are not Greek cities proper, or are unknown to us. Her titles Βουλαία and Βουληφόρος at Athens and Miletus show some connexion with civic life; at Olympia she was worshipped as Ἀγοραία. Cf. Anacr. i. 4 ἤ κου νῦν ἐπὶ Ληθαίου δίνῃσιν θρασυκαρδίων ἀνδρῶν ἐσκατορᾷς πόλιν. At Metapontum (Bacchyl. v. 115) she was δέσποινα λαῶν. But the ordinary conception of Artemis is expressed by Callim. *Dian.* 19 σπαρνὸν γὰρ ὅτ' Ἄρτεμις ἄστυ κάτεισιν· οὔρεσιν οἰκήσω κτλ.

πτόλις though a conjecture seems required by the metre: cf. the same word and πτόλεμος in Homer. Otherwise πόνος is easier in the singular.

21. This 'hymn' has nothing in common with *h.* xxiv.

22. The Ionic form ἱστίη has survived here in the greater part of the MSS.; in *h.* xxiv. 1 and xxix. 1 ἑστίη is invariable, but at xxix. 6 ἱστίη is read by all copies but two. In the four places where the word occurs in the *Odyssey* ἱστ- is the vulgate, but in all except υ 231 the common form has crept into some copies. At B 537 Ἱστίαιαν does not vary. In Hesiod *OD.* 734 ἑστίῃ is the vulgate, *Theog.* 454 ἑστίην is only found sporadically.

23. Cronus (Hesiod *Theog.* 495) disgorged his children in an order inverse to that in which he had swallowed them. Hestia, the eldest child, was swallowed first and disgorged last. She therefore had a second birth, as much as Dionysus, who was born again from the thigh of Zeus. The mention of Hestia as 'eldest and youngest' is perhaps connected with the custom of making libation to her at the beginning and end of a feast. See xxix. 5.

24. The wooing of Hestia by Posidon and Apollo is not

mentioned elsewhere. There is no ground for supposing, with Preller and B., a physical meaning, nor with Mommsen *Delphika* 2 that this is specifically a Delphic legend (see P.-W. viii. 1269). There was a group of Posidon, Amphitrite, and Hestia at Olympia (Paus. v. 26. 2), a conjunction of deities which may have a physical origin but has nothing to do with the present myth.

25. **στερεῶς ἀπέειπεν** = I 510.

For Hestia see introduction and notes to *h.* xxiv. Hestia and Ge are the least completely anthropomorphic deities of the Greek pantheon, and Hestia, seldom represented in art in human form, is never completely dissociated from her embodiment in the hearth. Whatever was the case with houses of historical times, the hearth in the Homeric house was in the centre of the *megaron*. This central position (v. 30, cf. Orph. *h.* lxxiv. 2 ἣ μέσον οἶκον ἔχεις πυρὸς ἀενάοιο) throughout colours the cult of Hestia. Hence Delos, the centre of the Cyclades, is called ἱστίη ὦ νήσων εὐέστιε (Callim. *Del.* 325), and hence the importance of the hearth of Delphi, which was the centre or navel of the earth. In philosophical speculation this was pushed further in the identification of Hestia with the Earth, the centre of the universe, or the fire which is its vital element (see further on *h.* xxiv). In so far as she was personified Hestia was regarded as a virgin: μετὰ γὰρ τὸ καταλυθῆναι τὴν τῶν Τιτάνων ἀρχὴν τὸν Δία δεξάμενον τὴν βασίλειαν ἐπιτρέπειν Ἑστίᾳ λαβεῖν ὅτι βούλοιτο. τὴν δὲ πρῶτον μὲν παρθενίαν αἰτῆσαι, μετὰ δὲ τὴν παρθενίαν ἀπαρχὰς θυομένων αὐτῇ νέμεσθαι πρώτῃ παρὰ ἀνθρώπων (Σ Ar. *Vesp.* 846 quoting Aristocritus; for the second boon see on *h.* xxix. 5). For her virginity cf. also Porphyry ap. Eus. *praep. ev.* iii. 11, Cornutus 28, Ovid *Fasti* vi. 288, Artemidorus *onir.* i. 83.

29. Cf. Hes. *Theog.* 585 τεῦξε καλὸν κακὸν ἀντ' ἀγαθοῖο. Here and *OD.* 63 we find κᾰλόν, which is not Homeric.

30. **πῖαρ** (πεῖαρ): Λ 550 βοῶν ἐκ πῖαρ ἑλέσθαι. On the word see on *h.* iii. 60.

31, 32. Cf. xxix. 1–3.

τιμάοχος: only here and *h. Dem.* 268.

32. **πρέσβειρα**: not elsewhere before Euripides (*IT.* 963).

34. **πεφυγμένον**: this passive perfect with active sense occurs

Z 488, X 219 (with dative of the person), α 18 (with gen. of the thing), ι 455 (with acc. of thing vulg., but gen. v.l.).

35 = ι 521. For the sentiment cf. Soph. *Ant.* 788, *fr.* 856. 8 sq., Eur. *Hipp.* 1274–81.

36. K 391 παρὲκ νόον ἤγαγε. For the sense cf. Eur. *Troad.* 948, Moschus i. 76.

42–4. Modelled on Δ 58–61.

43. **ἄφθιτα μήδεα εἰδώς**: cf. Ω 88, Hes. *Theog.* 545, etc.; Ζεὺς ἄφθιτα εἰδώς *h. Dem.* 321.

47, 48. For the sequence εἴη -εἴπῃ cf. E 567, O 598, Π 650–1, Σ 308, Ω 654, δ 692, μ 156. At E 567, μ 156 there are v.ll. There is no discernible difference of sense between the moods.

52. **ἀνέμιξε**: the MSS. give συνέμιξε 39, 50, συνέμιξα 250 without variant, and would have kept συνέμιξε here had it been original. ἀναμίσγεσθαι is distinguished from μιχθῆναι Herod. i. 199, but the derivatives of μίγνυμι are often synonymous, e.g. συμμίσγεσθαι = 'associate with' Herod. vi. 13. 8, Eratosthenes *Catast.* 28, Libanius *ep.* 473. 1, 736. 1; compare ἀνεμίσγετο Procop. *anecd.* 9, p. 60, οὐδ' ἀνεμίσγετο ταῖς λοιπαῖς παρθένοις (of Daphne) Parthenius 15. 10, Ῥοδίοις τισι βαλαντιουργοῖς ἀναμιχθείς Alciphron i. 2, with ἀναμιχθῆναι ξυλίνῃ βοΐ Palaephatus 2. 27. 17, συμφύντες ἀλλήλοις ἀναμιγῶμεν Xen. Ephes. iv. 9; the word has both senses Plut. *coni. praec.* 143 A καὶ σώματα καὶ χρήματα καὶ φίλους καὶ οἰκείους ἀναμιχθῆναι. In the hymn variety dictated ἀνέμιξε; συμμῖξαι is opposed to συγγενέσθαι Strabo 505. The compound συναναμίγνυμι occurs.

54. **ἐν ἀκροπόλοις ὄρεσιν** = E 523, τ 205.

πολυπιδάκου: the form was condemned by Aristarchus; Σ A Ξ 157 τὸ δὲ διὰ τοῦ ῡ γράφειν τελέως ἄγροικον. It is given however in the *Cypria* 5. 5; cf. Strabo 602 πολυπίδακον δὲ τὴν Ἴδην ἰδίως οἴονται λέγεσθαι, La Roche *HT.* 343. For the double form cf. φύλαξ φυλακός, μάρτυς μάρτυρος.

57. **ἐκπάγλως**: A 268, ἔγπαγλα φίλησα Γ 415, E 423 (-σε).

58–63 = θ 362–5 with the addition of Ξ 169 (= 60) and 172 (= 63). The lines are not literally identical (θ 362 runs ἡ δ' ἄρα Κύπρον ἵκανε φιλομειδὴς Ἀφροδίτη and θ 363 has θυήεις not θυώδης), and in 63 Ξ 172 has ἑδανῷ not ἑανῷ as the hymn-MSS. As ἑάνῳ cannot be an adj., and in Ξ 172 p[10] Athen. 688 E and $ Ξ 346 have ἑανῷ, it is probable that here ἑδανῷ was original. See on 63.

59. For the repetition of ἐς see on *h.* iii. 439.

βωμός τε θυώδης after *θυώδεα νηόν* draws attention to the incense, a feature of the Paphian worship, Virgil *Aen.* i. 416.

ἔνθα δέ is the vulgate θ 363, *ἔνθα τε* is a v.l.

60. **θύρας ἐπέθηκε φαεινάς** = Ξ 169, φ 45, cf. ζ 19, E 751. 'Put to'.

61. In E 338 the robe of Aphrodite is the work of the Charites, *Cypria* 4 it is woven by the Charites and the Horae. Aphrodite shares the dance with the Charites σ 194, *h.* iii. 194. Nymphs, Charites, and Aphrodite sing on Ida *Cypria* 5. The connexion is old, though we cannot assert it to be primitive, see Farnell ii. 625. At Elis Pausanias (vi. 24. 5) saw statues of the Charites with emblems of Aphrodite and remarks *Χάριτας δὲ Ἀφροδίτῃ μάλιστα εἶναι (θεῶν) οἰκείας.* Cf. also θ 364, Hes. *OD.* 73, Mosch. i. 71, Coluth. 16, and other reff. in Roscher i. 875.

62. **οἷα . . . ἐόντας**: *οἷα* is not the simple adverb used with the participle (K.-G. ii. 97), but the generalizing relative 'things which', as (with *τε*) ι 128, λ 536, of which passages the latter (*οὔτ' ἄρ βεβλημένος ὀξέι χαλκῷ οὔτ' αὐτοσχεδίην οὐτασμένος οἷά τε πολλὰ γίγνεται ἐν πολέμῳ*) is the best parallel. (Ameis on ι 128.) That the hyperbaton comes after a singular is unessential.

ἐπενήνοθεν: neither the meaning nor the derivation is known (Boisacq).

63 = Ξ 172. The writer who combined the passages in Ξ and θ was not offended by *ἀμβρότῳ . . . ἀμβροσίῳ*, which he probably regarded as synonymous. Compare *ἄμβροτα . . . ἀμβροσίῳ* at two lines' distance σ 191, *νυμφάων . . . νυμφῶν infra* 97, 98, *οὕνεκα . . . ἕνεκα* 198, 199, *ᾠδῆς . . . ἀοιδῆς Dem.* 494, 495. The repetition is made more tolerable by the hyperbaton.

ἑδανῷ: as *ἑανός* is a substantive, and the identical adjective has ᾱ, Clarke's conjecture is inevitable. In Ξ 172 *ἀμβροσίῳ ἑανῷ* crept into three authorities (see on 58) from *ἀμβρόσιον ἑανόν* 178. The meaning of *ἑδανῷ* may be 'sweet', as Apollonius and Herodian took it, but the derivation is unknown; see Meyer *Griech. Et.* i *in v.*, Solmsen *Untersuch.* p. 283, Boisacq *in v.* Cf. Hesych.

ἰδανή· τρυφερά, εὐπρεπῆ. ἰδανόν· εὐειδές καὶ τὸ ἡδύοσμον, καὶ ἀχίλλειον ῥιζίον, Callim. *fr.* 535 ἰδανάς.

66. **ἐπί**: c. gen. 'towards', cf. Γ 5, Ε 700, *h.* iii. 49.

εὐώδεα: suggested by Ξ 171, where Hera anoints herself (G.).

68 = Θ 47 (ἵκανεν), Ξ 283 (ἱκέσθην).

μητέρα θηρῶν: μητέρα μήλων Β 696, Ι 479, Λ 222, *h.* xix. 30.

69. The passage resembles the episode of Circe κ 212, where wolves and lions fawn not on Circe but on Odysseus' men. Ap. Rh. i. 1144 wild beasts fawn on Rhea, iii. 383 on Artemis, iv. 672 on Circe. Cf. Soph. and Lucr. quoted on v. 3. In Hesiod *Theog.* 194 the advent of the Goddess is accompanied by vegetable not animal increase: ἐκ δ' ἔβη αἰδοίη καλὴ θεός, ἀμφὶ δὲ ποίη | ποσσὶν ὕπο ῥαδινοῖσιν ἀέξετο. Cf. also Nonnus xv. 210 εἴκελος Ἀγχίσῃ ῥοδοειδέι τοῦ ποτε Κύπρις | ἀργεννὴν ἐνόμευεν ὀρεσσινόμων στίχα ταύρων | κεστὸν ἐλαφρίζουσα βοοσσόον.

71. **παρδάλιες**, πορδάλιες. The Paris family give the Aeolic form, which was in common use, e.g. Strabo 613, 619. In Homer (Ν 103, Ρ 20, Φ 573, δ 457) the MSS. are divided, and so in Quintus i. 480, 541, v. 19 al., Nonnus v. 296. In Nonnus πορ- is normal. Aristarchus read παρ-.

δόρξ, δορκάς is a sufficient parallel to πρόξ, προκάς.

74. **σύνδυο**: not in Homer, but cf. σύντρεις ι 429.

The effect of the line recalls Aristotle's dictum (*Poet.* 1460 a 12) of the difference between epos and drama: μᾶλλον ἐνδέχεται ἐν τῇ ἐποποιίᾳ τὸ ἄλογον . . . διὰ τὸ μὴ ὁρᾶν εἰς τὸν πράττοντα, cf. Dion. Hal. *de comp. verb.* c. 16 κρεῖττον γέγονεν ἀκουσθῆναι λεγόμενα ἢ ὀφθῆναι γενόμενα, Plato *Hippias maj.* 299 A.

76. **σταθμοῖσι**: for the locatival dative cf. θ 66 μέσσῳ δαιτυμόνων (θῆκε), Υ 22 πτυχὶ Οὐλύμποιο ἥμενος, especially with names of places as ζ 8, 162, etc. For exx. in the hymns see *infra* 173, *h.* ii. 99, xx. 4.

77. **θεῶν ἄπο κάλλος ἔχοντα** = θ 457 (ἔχουσα), ζ 18 Χαρίτων ἄπο κάλλος ἔχουσαι (= Hes. *fr.* 94. 6), 12 θεῶν ἄπο μήδεα εἰδώς.

84. θάμβαινεν *p* is found in one MS. of Pind. *Ol.* iii. 32 (where the others have θαύμαινε, θάμαινε, θαύμαζε).

86. **φαεινότερον πυρὸς αὐγῆς** = Σ 610 (θώρηκα).

87. **ἐπιγναμπτάς**: only here, but the verb ἐπιγνάμπτω is not un-

common; ἕλικας κτλ. cf. 163, Σ 401. According to Helbig *HE.* 279–82 the ἕλικες were spiral brooches, but the more probable interpretation is that they were spiral bracelets, see Iwan Müller *Griech. Privatalt.* 87, P.-R. 290, n. 2.

The κάλυκες were probably ear-rings in the shape of flower-buds; Ś A B Σ 401 give a choice of meanings, rings, ear-rings, and spirals for the hair (cf. P 52).

90. Various solutions have been offered of ὅρμοι followed by ἐλάμπετο: (1) schema Boeoticum: this occurs in Hesiod, but not in Homeric epos; Dem. 279 is no case: (2) that the subject is Aphrodite; but she is too far off, and you could not say of a woman ἐλάμπετο ἀμφὶ τοῖς στήθεσιν, and it is the jewels, not Aphrodite, which were θαῦμα ἰδέσθαι: (3) ἐλάμπετο is impersonal. This use is limited to meteorological words, e.g. συνεσκόταζε, K.-G. i. § 352, and σελήνη makes such a construction additionally impossible. In X 319 ὡς αἰχμῆς ἀπέλαμπ' εὐήκεος the subject is ἀστήρ, 'spark', in ι 143 οὐδὲ προὐφαίνετ' ἰδέσθαι the subject is θεός, 'he did not appear in sight', Hes. *Scut.* 72 (166) πῦρ is subject: (4) 89, 90 have been placed between 87 and 88. But we cannot ease grammar by moving lines about.

ἐλάμπετο seems to be a case of attraction to the number of the nearer substantive. See exx. in K.-G. i. 75, 76, e.g. Herod. ii. 15 αἱ Θῆβαι Αἴγυπτος ἐκαλέετο, Strabo 639 ὑφόρμων ὧν ὁ κάλλιστος Ἱστοὶ λέγονται, Plato *rep.* 485 D αἱ ἐπιθυμίαι . . . εἰς τἆλλα ἀσθενεστέραι [εἰσὶν] ὥσπερ ῥεῦμα . . . ἀπωχετευμένον, where Plato if he had followed the hymn might have said ὡς δὲ ῥεῦμα ἀπωχετευμένον ἐστι, and the poet had metre allowed ὥσπερ σελήνη λαμπομένη. The attraction of gender is more frequent.

92. Cf. ζ 149: with 97–9 cf. ζ 123–4. For ἥτις κτλ. see *Dem.* 119.

94. Themis is καλλιπάρῃος O 87, ἀγλαόμορφος Orph. *h.* lxxix. 7, καλυκώπιδα κούρην *ib.* 2. Cf. the youthful Themis as Pythia on vase paintings Roscher v. 579.

95. In Homer the Charites are mainly associated with Aphrodite (see on 61), although Charis is the wife of Hephaestus Σ 382, and Hera promises Hypnos one of the Charites in marriage Ξ 267, 275. In later times they were connected with various

deities, e.g. Apollo, Artemis, the Muses, Hermes, Dionysus, and Hera. For references see P.-R. 482.

97, 98. Here (as in 62, 63 *ἀμβρότῳ, ἀμβροσίῳ*) the repetition *νυμφάων, νυμφῶν* has been a ground for assuming two recensions, but in each case the second line introduces a fresh item of description, and the redundancy does not involve more than a poverty of art or careless ear. *Νυμφάων, νυμφῶν* has the exact parallel of *ᾠδῆς, ἀοιδῆς* *Dem.* 494, 495. Lines 97, 99 = Υ 8, 9 (ζ 124) (*οὔτ' ἄρα* for *ἤ τις*). With 98 cf. ζ 123 *νυμφάων αἳ ἔχουσ' ὀρέων αἰπεινὰ κάρηνα.* Oreads are mentioned in Z 420 *νύμφαι ὀρεστιάδες* and in the *Odyssey*. See on 258.

99. **πηγὰς ποταμῶν**: sc. *νηϊάδες* ν 104 (*νηΐς* Z 22).

102. **ὥρῃσιν πάσῃσι**: cf. *h. Dem.* 399, xxvi. 12 (G.).

103. Z 476 *δότε δὴ καὶ τόνδε γενέσθαι* | *παῖδ' ἐμὸν ὡς καὶ ἐγώ περ ἀριπρεπέα Τρώεσσιν.*

104. **εἰσοπίσω**: first here, then in Soph. *Phil.* 1105. The lexx. give *εἰσόπιν χρόνου* from Aeschylus.

105. **ζώειν κτλ.** = κ 498.

108. **χαμαιγ. ἀνθρ.**: for the phrase cf. Hes. *Theog.* 879, *h.* ii. 352.

109 = π 187 (*ἀθανάτοισιν*).

111. Γ 186 Otreus is a chief of the Phrygians, from whom the town Otroea took its name, Strabo 566.

112. **εὐτειχήτοιο**: *ἅπ. λεγ.*

113. Homer is aware that the Trojan host contained several languages (B 804, Δ 437), and that the Carians (*βαρβαρόφωνοι* B 867) did not talk Greek, but this is the first passage where a difference between Trojan and Phrygian is asserted, and where a native of Phrygia being on Mt. Ida thinks it necessary to account for having a knowledge of Trojan. This was noticed by Schliemann in *Ilios*, p. 120, Sayce *ib.*, p. 704, Kretschmer *Einleitung*, p. 182. The realization of the difference between adjacent Asiatic tongues points to an Asiatic, perhaps Aeolic, origin for the hymn. In later days the difficulty of foreign tongues was admitted (Solon 24. 10–12, Aesch. *Ag.* 1034, 1046, 1253, Eur. *Phoen.* 391 c. schol., *Rhesus* 294, 295, Gorgias *Palamedes* 7, Timotheus 157 sq., Ovid *Her.* 3. 2, Max. Tyr. viii. 8, Xen. Ephes. iii. 1. 2 *καὶ γὰρ ὁ Ἱππόθοος ἐμπείρως ἔσχε τῆς Καππαδοκῶν*

φωνῆς), and even the difference of Greek dialects (Aesch. *Choeph.* 563 ἄμφω δὲ φωνὴν ἥσομεν Παρνησσίδα | γλώσσης ἀυτὴν Φωκίδος μιμουμένω, Soph. *Aj.* 1263). In Homer there is no interpreter.

118 = Π 183 (ἐν χορῷ). In Eur. *Hel.* 44 Hermes carries off Helen.

120. **ἀπείριτος ἐστεφάνωτο** = κ 195 (πόντος) of an island, Hes. *Scut.* 204 (ὄλβος). For a crowd round dancers cf. Σ 603.

121. **χρυσόρραπις**: see on *h.* iv. 529.

123. **ἄκληρόν**, 'undivided'.

ἄκτιτον, 'uncultivated', the opposite of εὐκτίμενος ι 130, ω 336. For the omission of γῆν cf. Ξ 308, υ 98, *h.* ii. 43, iii. 529, and the phrase πουλὺν ἐφ' ὑγρήν K 27, δ 709, Hes. *Theog.* 440 al.

125. 'I thought I should never feel ground', i.e. stop. The present would mean 'I thought I was not touching ground', but the Gods and persons they conveyed flew, Hera Ξ 228, Aeneas Υ 335, Hermes ε 49, Persephone *h.* ii. 383, Iphigenia Eur. *IT.* 29, Memnon Quintus ii. 569 (τυτθὸν ὑπὲρ γαίης).

126. **καλέεσθαι**: the fut. καλέω occurs four times in Homer, cf. Soph. *El.* 971, K-B. ii. 108 n. 6. For the word cf. η 313 (αἲ γὰρ) ἐμὸς γαμβρὸς καλέεσθαι.

127. **τεκεῖσθαι**: only here, but regularly formed from the short stem. A stranger form is τεξείεσθε Aratus 124.

130. **κρατερὴ κτλ.** = κ 273.

132. Cf. δ 64 ἐπεὶ οὔ κε κακοὶ τοιούσδε τέκοιεν, which supports κε. For the exchange of κε and τε cf. O 224. For the sense cf. *h.* ii. 213.

133. For negative adjectives with three terminations see on *h.* iv. 447, for other adjectives on *h.* iii. 32. Cf. ἀεικελίη 136, 136 a.

135. **ὁμόθεν**: un-Homeric, but in Hes. *OD.* 108.

136, 136 a. These lines, like Quintus i. 369, 370, are incompatible. They do not seem corruptions either one of the other or of a common original. Both must have been in the archetype of *p* for homoeomeson to take place. Flach (*Das nachhes. Digamma*, p. 36 n.) preferred 136 a on the ground that ἀλλ' εἰκυῖα neglects F. For the expression cf. Ovid *Heroid.* v. 83 *non tamen ut Priamus nymphae socer esse recuset* | *aut Hecubae fuerim dissimulanda nurus* (D'Orville), and see on *h.* ii. 83.

139. **χρυσόν κτλ.** = ν 136, π 231.

140. **ἄποινα** apparently means the presents given to a bride by her parents as a dowry, called *μείλια* I 147, and cf. X 51.

141. Cf. *γάμου ἱμερόεντος* Phocyl. 2. 8.

147. **ἀθανάτου δὲ ἕκητι**: for M's retention of the digamma cf. *h.* iii. 341. Where *ἕκητι* occurs in Homer the digamma is observed (ο 319, τ 86, υ 42), but in the last passage there is a variant *τ' ἀέκητι*. In xxvi. 5 it is neglected.

148. Cf. *h.* iv. 292 *κεκλήσεαι ἤματα πάντα.*

150. **σχήσει πρὶν . . . μιγῆναι**: cf. P 502 *οὐ γὰρ ἐγώ γε Ἕκτορα . . . σχήσεσθαι ὀίω πρὶν . . . βήμεναι ἵππω*, and the infin. without *πρίν* P 182 *σχήσω ἀμυνέμεναι.*

154. Cf. *Hero and Leander* 79 *αὐτίκα τεθναίην λεχέων ἐπιβήμενος Ἡροῦς* (B.), and E 685, η 224.

156. **κατ' ὄμ. κ. β.** = *h. Dem.* 194.

163 = Σ 401.

165. **ἐπὶ θρόνου ἀργυροήλου** = η 162 al.

168. **ἀποκλίνουσι**, 'turn back', as *ἀποστρέψας*, 'turning round', *h.* iv. 76.

173. **κλισίῃ**: for the locative dative cf. *σταθμοῖσι* 76 and on *h. Dem.* 99. The passage is very abrupt, a rhetorical asyndeton with a kind of climax, K.-G. ii. 340. Various attempts have been made to introduce a copula. Estienne printed *πάρ* for *ἄρα*, and this was long believed to be a manuscript reading.

μελάθρου κῦρε κάρη = *h. Dem.* 188. The substitutes for *κῦρε* in all MSS. except M show the exchange between *η* and *κ* which we find in the early period of minuscule. There is no resemblance between the later forms of these letters when both had become semi-uncial.

175. **ἐυστεφάνου**: this epithet recurs in this hymn at 6 and 287 without variant and in θ 267, σ 193, and later poets. *ἰοστέφανος* appears first in vi. 18 (with variant in *p*), Solon *fr.* 7, 4, Theognis 250 and later. Cf. *ἰόπλοκος, ἰοπλόκαμος, ἰοβλέφαρος.*

176. Cf. K 138.

177. Cf. *h.* iv. 289.

179. For the correption *τὸ πρῶτον* cf. 131, 187 and Homeric

examples in La Roche *HU.* i. 9. On the other hand cf. τὰ πρῶτα 185.

180. Cf. K 162 ὁ δ' ἐξ ὕπνοιο μάλα κραιπνῶς ἀνόρουσε, ξ 485 ὁ δ' ἄρ' ἐμμαπέως ὑπάκουσε.

181. Cf. Γ 396 καί ῥ' ὡς οὖν ἐνόησε θεᾶς περικαλλέα δειρὴν | στήθεά θ' ἱμερόεντα καὶ ὄμματα μαρμαίροντα.

182. Cf. π 179 ταρβήσας δ' ἑτέρωσε βάλ' ὄμματα μὴ θεὸς εἴη.

187. The first instance of πρός c. gen., J. A. Scott *Classical Philology* ii. 324.

188. G. suggests a debt to the story of Circe κ 301 μή σ' ἀπογυμνωθέντα κακὸν καὶ ἀνήνορα θείῃ and ib. 341. The danger there arises, however, from the fact that Circe is a malevolent sorceress. In Homer the lovers of Goddesses have to fear the jealousy of the Gods, not danger from the Goddesses themselves. Calypso, who is not married to a God, does no harm to Odysseus. But Artemis and Zeus kill Orion and Iasion the mortal lovers of Eos and Demeter (ε 121). In folk-lore the same notion appears in the jealousy with which the fairies regard one of their number who has loved a mortal. In modern Greek superstition Nereids are apt to take cruel punishment from those who spy upon them, and a Melian peasant who came unexpectedly upon some of them and underwent their entertainment suffered the fate dreaded by Anchises (Lawson *Modern Greek Folk-lore* &c. 139). But as a rule union between a Nereid and a mortal, which is not at all uncommon, is followed by no physical calamity to the husband, though fairy brides are fickle and seize the first opportunity to escape.

Probably the fears of Anchises here are based upon a vague dread of the supernatural, like the belief that 'no man may see God and live'. In northern Europe the love of a nymph or giantess was thought to bring death or misfortune to a mortal (Elton-Powell *Saxo* lxiv): the natives of New Caledonia think that intercourse with a supernatural being is deadly (see Lang in Kirk's *Secret Commonwealth* xxxi and other exx. in his transl. of the *Hymns* 42). Istars' lovers came to an unhappy end: Gilgamesh therefore rejects her overtures (Jastrow *Religion of Babylonia* 482), a story which Frazer (*GB*[3]. ix. 371) interprets in terms of the union of a divine pair of which the male died every year. (Plut. *def. orac.* 417 E Molus *νύμφῃ πρὸς βίαν συγγενόμενος ἀκέφαλος εὑρεθείῃ*, Charon in *EM.* 75. 36 *ἐπιζήμιον μὲν ἔλεγεν εἶναι τοῦτο.*) Rose (*CQ.* 1924 xviii. 11) supposes that the consequences here dreaded by Anchises point to the Anatolian origin of the story, and that it is connected with the cult of the fertility-Goddess and her subordinate lover, who like Attis is called upon to sacrifice his virility. He interprets Virgil Aen. ii. 647 *iam pridem invisus divis et inutilis annos* | *demoror* as referring to a version in which Anchises when smitten by a thunderbolt (see on 288) became impotent. But even if this, rather than paralysis, be the meaning of the passage, it would most probably be accounted for by a recollection of the language of the hymn. The ingenious theory of Professor Rose has very little substantial foundation.

189. **βιοθάλμιος**: only here. Cf. *ζωθάλμιος* Pind. *Ol.* vii. 20, where there is a variant *ζωοφθάλμιος* similar to *βιοφθάλμιος* here, and *πολυθάλμιος* Orph. *h.* lxviii. 1.

193 = δ 825 (*πάγχυ* for *σῆσι*).

194. **δέος** always makes position in Homer.

195. **ἐπεὶ ἦ**: see on *h.* iii. 72. The MSS. here give *ἐπειή*.

196–7. Cf. Υ 307 *νῦν δὲ δὴ Αἰνείαο βιὴ Τρώεσσιν ἀνάξει* | *καὶ παίδων παῖδες τοί κεν μετόπισθε γένωνται.* For the tradition that the kingdom of the Troad passed after the destruction of Troy to Aeneas and his descendants see P.-W. i. 2752, Farnell ii. 638, who points out that the character of Aeneas and the prophecy about him imply that Homer knew of the tradition. Strabo (607, 608) states on the authority of Demetrius of Scepsis that the descendants of Aeneas survived in that town for many generations and were called kings (*ἔχοντές τινας τιμάς*, probably priestly functions). See also Hellanicus *fr.* 31 Jacoby, Menecrates *FHG.* ii. 343, Acusilaus *fr.* 39 J., Conon *fr.* 46 (Jacoby i. 268).

197. **ἐκγεγάονται**: if this word is sound it is a fut. perf. as Buttmann (*GG.* ii. 137) supposed. For this form *ἐκγεγάασθε* *vit. Hom. Herod.* 505 and *ἐκγεγάαντο* *Anth. Pal.* xv. 40. 20 only are quoted. B.'s ingenious alteration *ἐκγεγάοντες* would have

given ἐκγεγαῶτες or -ότες as the Aeolic perfect participles in Homer have done.

For the dat. παίδεσσι with ἐκγίγνομαι see the exx. in LS.

198. **αἰνόν**: the significance of a name is Homeric: cf. Ὀδυσσεύς and ὀδύσσομαι α 62, τ 407–9. Ἀχιλλεύς from ἄχος (Ἰλίου or λαοῦ) is not in Homer but is given by 𝕾 Α 1. For such etymologies in tragedy see the comm. on Eur. *IT.* 32 and Aristophanes' excellent parody (*fr.* 357) Θόας βραδύτατος ὢν ἐν ἀνθρώποις δραμεῖν.

199. Σ 85 ἤματι τῷ ὅτε σε βροτοῦ ἀνέρος ἔμβαλον εὐνῇ.

The conjunctional use of ἕνεκα, 'because', appears in Ap. Rh. iv. 1521, Bion xii. 7, Callim. *fr.* 187. In Pindar *Isthm.* viii. 33 it = ὅτι. Apollonius *conj.* 503. 5, *adv.* 553. 20, and Dion. Thrax 643. 5 ap. Lehrs *qu. ep.* 110 call it a σύνδεσμος αἰτιολογικός. The repetition οὕνεκα, ἕνεκα is not worse than νυμφάων, νυμφῶν 97, 98.

200 sqq. Ganymede and Tithonus occur in the genealogy of the house of Troy given to Achilles by Aeneas Υ 206 sqq.

201. The legend occurs in Υ 234 τὸν καὶ ἀνηρείψαντο θεοὶ Διὶ οἰνοχοεύειν | κάλλεος εἵνεκα οἷο ἵν' ἀθανάτοισι μετείη. Cf. also Ε 266. He is son of Laomedon *Il. Parv.* 6. 4. Here Zeus instead of the Gods carries off Ganymede, apparently in a whirlwind (cf. 208), like the daughters of Pandareus υ 66. The eagle is a later invention, see P.-R. 499, and the articles in Roscher i. 1595, P.-W. vii. 737. The name appears as *Catmite* in Etruscan, Eva Fiesel *Namen des gr. Mythos im Etruskische* 67. The variants ἐπιοινοχοεύειν . . . τετιμένον . . . ἀφύσσειν in M (the second confirmed by the conflation τετιμένονος = τετιμένον with ος written above in *x*) are remarkable for consistency, but the change from ἵνα with the opt. to the infin. is very violent, and a copula requires insertion in 206. As B. says, the infin. may be due to Υ 234 οἰνοχοεύειν.

204. **ἐπιοινοχοεύοι** does not seem distinguishable from οἰνοχοεύοι. The adj. ἐπιοίνιος occurs in Theognis 971. Cf. α 143 κῆρυξ δ' αὐτοῖσιν θάμ' ἐπῴχετο οἰνοχοεύων.

211. **ἀρσίποδας** = ἀερσίποδας Γ 327 al. For the horses given to Tros see Ε 265. In another version, *Il. parv. l.c.*, Laomedon, not Tros, was the father of Ganymede, and received a golden vine, not horses, in return. 𝕾 λ 521 the vine is given to Tros. In Serv. *in Aen.* i. 489 it is given to Memnon, father of Tithonus.

214. **ὡς ἔοι**: for the constr. cf. ω 237 εἰπεῖν ὡς ἔλθοι.

ἀγήρως: ἀγήρων *h.* ii. 242, ἀγήραον 260, ἀγήρως ἀγήραος Θ 539, ἀγήραον ἀγήρω Β 447, sim. ε 136, ἀγήραον only η 257. Aristarchus and Aristophanes read the trisyllable.

ἶσα θεοῖσιν (= λ 304) is stronger than ἤματα πάντα, which may have come from 209.

215 nearly = ε 150.

217. Simonides 19 ἀελλοπόδων . . . ἵππων.

218. On Tithonus see the collection of passages in Schmidt's article Roscher v. 1021, Kakridi *Wiener Studien* 48 (1930). Compare the rape of Cleitus ο 250 ἀλλ' ἤτοι Κλεῖτον χρυσόθρονος ἥρπασεν Ἠὼς | κάλλεος εἵνεκα εἷο, ἵν' ἀθανάτοισι μετείη, and of Cephalus Eur. *Hipp.* 455, Apollod. iii. 181, Paus. i. 31, and of Selemnus Paus. vii. 23. 2. Tithonus according to Homer was son of Laomedon and brother of Priam Υ 237; according to others (Ctesias ap. Diod. ii. 22, Clearchus *frr.* 20, 21, Demetrius *FHG.* ii. 100, Strabo 720, Athen. 548 F, Zenob. 618) he came from farther east and was the father of Memnon. His name (*Tinthun* in Etruscan, v. Schmidt *l.c.*, Eva Fiesel p. 59) is eastern and seems to correspond to Ταντάνης in Constantine Manasses 1367 ed. Bonn.: τὸν οὖν Ταντάνην τῶν Ἰνδῶν Πρίαμος ἱκετεύει | καὶ μετὰ πλήθους στέλλεται Μέμνων ἀπειραρίθμου, | ὃ δὲ στρατὸς ἦσαν Ἰνδοὶ πάντες μελανοχρῶτες. Tantanes King of Assyria occurs also in Cyril *in Iulian.* 11 D Aubert. Memnon has a monument in Phrygia Hes. *fr.* 252.

The legend of the eternal old age of Tithonus does not occur in Homer, where (Λ 1, ε 1) he is still the consort of Eos (Hieronymus ap. Σ B Λ 1). Sappho, however, has it (iv. 1), and Mimnermus (iv. 4). Eos also bore Zephyrus, Boreas, and Notos to Astraeus a Titan, Hes. *Theog.* 378, Servius *in Aen.* i. 132.

223. **νηπίη κτλ.** Cf. Β 38, Υ 264, Χ 445, Hes. *OD.* 40.

224. **ξῦσαί τ' ἄπο γῆρας**, *in tmesi*, 'scrape off', Ι 446 γῆρας ἀποξύσας, *Nosti* 6. 2 γῆρας ἀποξύσασ', *Anth. Pal. ep. christ.* 14. 1, 2 γῆρας . . . ξύσεν. Literally Lucian *navig.* 45 τὴν πολλὴν κορύζαν ἀποξύσας, *conv. seu Lap.* 33 ἀπεξύετο ἐκ τῆς κεφαλῆς τὸν ἄκρατον, 'wiped', Alciphron i. 2 init. νύκτωρ ὑπὸ λαμπάσι τὸν βυθὸν ἀποξύουσι, 'sweep'; sim. Eunapius 173 fin. δεσποίνη

νεοπλούτῳ καὶ τὸ γῆρας ἀπεξεσμένῃ, metaph. Alciphr. iii. 40 τὴν αἰδῶ τοῦ προσώπου ἀπέξυσται. Cf. (literally) ἀναξύσαι Antiphon *Herod.* 45. γῆρας = πολιαὶ ἔθειραι. To 'smooth wrinkles' is ῥυτίδας ἐκτανύειν Lucian *Epigr.* 38. 2.

For the form **ὀλοιόν** see Solmsen *Untersuchungen* 114.

225. The beauty of Tithonus was proverbial: Tyrtaeus *fr.* 9. 5 οὐδ' εἰ Τιθώνοιο φυὴν χαριέστερος εἴη: other reff. in Roscher v. 1022.

εἷως: this form may stand in the hymn, though the earliest instance of it appears to be in a Thasian inscr. of the end of the fifth century B.C. (Herwerden *lex. graec. suppl.* in v.).

227. Cf. ἔσ]χατα γᾶς φέροισα Sappho iv. 1. 20.

228. Cf. πολιαὶ κατέχυ]ντο τρίχες ἐκ μελαίναν Sappho ib. 1. 14: Prop. ii. 18. 7 sqq. (who makes Eos kinder): of Endymion *Anth. Pal.* vi. 58 πολιὴ γὰρ ὅλου κρείουσα καρήνου | οὐ σώζει προτέρης ἴχνιον ἀγλαΐης. Hesychius Τιθωνοκόμον ἔθνος· μέλαν μὲν τὸ ὅλον σῶμα, λευκὸν δὲ τὰς κόμας: Tithonus was conceived as an aged negro, κυανόχρως *or. Sibyll* xi. 68. Anchises dedicates his last black hair *Anth. Pal.* vi. 76. Glaucus in the story Σ Eur. *Or.* 364 al. γέγονεν ἀθάνατος ἀλλ' οὐκ ἀγήραος, ἐφ' ᾧ κατεπόντισεν ἑαυτόν.

229. **εὐηγενέος**: the η may be due to false analogy with such words as εὐήνωρ. Cf. Λ 429, Ψ 81, where as in this passage it has been corrupted into εὐγενής. (At Ψ 81 Aristophanes and Rhianus read εὐηφενέων, now confirmed by inscriptions, see Schulze *qu. ep.* 34, Herwerden *lex.* in ἄφενος; this is impossible here.) Cf. εὐγενῆ παρηΐδα Eur. *Ion.* 242, εὐγενῆ δέρην *Hel.* 135.

233. **κατὰ γῆρας ἔπειγεν** = Ψ 623 (ἐπείγει). Cf. Mimnermus 4 Τιθωνῷ μὲν ἔδωκεν ἔχειν κακὸν ἄφθιτον ὁ Ζεὺς | γῆρας ὃ καὶ θανάτου ῥίγιον ἀργαλέου, Sappho *l.c.* 13]ντα χρόα γῆρας ἤδη. It is *in tmesi.*

234 = θ 298 (ἦν for δύνατ'). Sappho 15 γόνα δ' οὐ φέροισι.

235. This line is followed by a new main verb with asyndeton ι 424, λ 230; by an infin. Β 5, Κ 17, Ξ 161, Hes. *fr.* 79. 1. In Sappho 17 Eos says ἀ]λλὰ τί κεν ποείην;

236. ἐπὶ τῷ γήρᾳ καθεῖρκται Clearchus *l.c.* 20. He was hung in a cage, ἐν θαλάμῳ κρέμαται ib. 21, κρεμαστός Athen. 548 E, ἐν ταλάρῳ ἢ καρτάλῳ Suetonius in Miller *Mél.* 423, Eust. 1527.

64; he became a τέττιξ Hellanicus *fr.* 142, Clearchus *l.c.*, Serv. *in Aen.* iv. 585, Achill. Tat. i. 15. 8 οἱ ᾠδοὶ δὲ τέττιγες καὶ χελιδόνες· οἱ μὲν τὴν Ἠοῦς ᾄδοντες εὐνήν . . ., and others ap. Schmidt: a type of the garrulity of old age Longinus ix. 13, Demetr. π. ἑρμ. I. 7; cf. Juvenal vii. 35 *facunda senectus.*

237–8. Cf. λ 393–4, Λ 669, φ 283.

237. **ῥεῖ ἄσπετος**: cf. Σ 403 ῥέεν ἄσπετος, which defends ῥεῖ. Other coincidences with Σ occur 86, 87. Cf. for the sense A 249 ῥέεν αὐδή, Hes. *Theog.* 39 ἀκάματος ῥέει αὐδὴ | ἐκ στομάτων ἡδεῖα, 84 τοῦ δ᾽ ἔπε᾽ ἐκ στόματος ῥεῖ μείλιχα. His voice 'flows ceaselessly' like the rattle of the cicada. Rapp's derivation, however, of the cicada story from v. 237 (Roscher i. 1263) is rightly rejected by Schmidt (*ib.* v. 1025).

κῖκυς: λ 393, Aesch. *fr.* 226, *Et. Gud.* (321. 53) κικύω. σημαίνει τὸ ἰσχύω. ἄκικυς adj. is commoner.

244. **τάχα γῆρας**: Quintus iii. 614.

γῆρας ὁμοίιον = Δ 315. ὁμοίιος is an epithet of γῆρας, νεῖκος, πόλεμος, and θάνατος. It has no connexion with ὁμοῖος. The derivation and meaning are uncertain; the Sanskrit *amiva*, 'suffering', has been proposed (Boisacq). From the other side, cf. of Marpessa ἡ δὲ δείσασα ὡς ἂν μὴ γηρῶσαν αὐτὴν Ἀπόλλων καταλίπῃ τὸν Ἴδαν εἵλετο ἄνδρα Apollod. i. 61.

245. **νηλειές**: the form occurs also in Hes. *Theog.* 770; see Schulze *qu. eq.* 290.

ἔπειτα, 'thereafter'.

246. **καματηρόν**: first here.

248. Cf. Π 499 ἔσσομαι ἤματα πάντα διαμπερές (κατηφείη καὶ ὄνειδος).

252. Martin's στόμα χείσεται is still the best correction of στοναχήσεται. Cf. Λ 462 ὅσον κεφαλὴ χάδε φωτός. Buttmann's ἀχήσεται gives no construction.

254. **οὐκ ὀνοταστόν**, 'not to be made light of, serious'; Clarke's correction is certain. The verb occurs ὀνοτάζω *h.* iv. 30, Hes. *OD.* 258, μή με κατονοσθῇς Herod. ii. 136, οὐκ ἐπιμωματόν, μηδεὶς τὰ θεῶν ὀνόσαιτο Theocr. xxvi. 38, οὐκ ὀνοτὴν γαῖαν *Anth. Pal.* vii. 393. 2, δῶρα μὲν οὐκέτ᾽ ὀνοστά I 164, etc. ap. Ebeling. See on *h.* ii. 83. The etymology is doubtful (Boisacq). The secondary

sense of οὐκ ὀνομαστόν, 'unmentionable', does not occur before Ap. Rh. iii. 801.

257. For μιν after τὸν cf. π 78 (B.).

ὀρεσκῷοι: of uncertain derivation (Boisacq), applied to animals *h.* iv. 42, xix. 43, goats ι 55, centaurs A 268. Nymphs nurse Dionysus *h.* xxvi. 3.

βαθύκολποι: in Homer κόλπος = bosom, not robe. No allusion to luxuriant vegetation need be seen with Mannhardt *AWF.* 7. The ocean nymphs are βαθύκολποι *h.* ii. 5.

258. It is difficult to distinguish between ὀρειάδες and δρυάδες. Originally perhaps the ὀρειάδες were tree-spirits like the δρυάδες, for in a mountainous and wooded country like Greece the largest class of δρυάδες would be ὀρειάδες. The latter, however, were also called ἀντριάδες (cf. 263). Z 420 the Oreads (νύμφαι ὀρεστιάδες) plant trees on a grave.

ὄρος . . . τε = Hes. *Theog.* 2.

259. **ἕπονται**, 'go with', i.e. belong to. There is no parallel to this use.

260. **δηρὸν μὲν ζώουσι**: Hes. *fr.* 171 ἐννέα τοι ζώει γενεὰς λακέρυζα κορώνη | ἀνδρῶν ἡβώντων· ἔλαφος δέ τε τετρακόρωνος· | τρεῖς δ' ἐλάφους ὁ κόραξ γηράσκεται· αὐτὰρ ὁ φοῖνιξ | ἐννέα τοὺς κόρακας· δέκα δ' ἡμεῖς τοὺς φοίνικας | νύμφαι εὐπλόκαμοι κοῦραι Διὸς αἰγιόχοιο, Paus. x. 31. 3 τὰς νύμφας δὲ εἶναι πολὺν μέν τινα ἀριθμὸν βιούσας ἐτῶν, οὐ μέν τοι παράπαν γε ἀπηλλαγμένας θανάτου ποιητῶν ἐστὶν ἐς αὐτὰς λόγος, Aristotle ap. Serv. *in Aen.* i. 372, Ap. Rh. iii. 479, Nonnus xiv. 209, Hesych. *in* Μακρόβιοι.

261. **ἐρρώσαντο**: only here with cognate acc.

262. **Σειληνοί**: see Kuhnert in Roscher in v. *Satyros*, p. 504 sq. The word is Thraco-Phrygian, Lagercrantz in Boisacq. It first occurs here, then in *Ichneutae* 148 Pearson, cf. Paus. vi. 24. 8. The cognate σάτυροι appears first in Hes. *fr.* 198. The sileni are frequently lovers of nymphs on vases, and on coins of Thasos (Head *HN.* 264). For Hermes and the nymphs cf. xix. 34 and often P.-R. i. 399, ii. 720, P.-W. viii. 774.

264. This passage is the first to contain a definite statement that the life of tree-nymphs is bound up with the tree. In later poetry the belief is common: Pind. *fr.* 165 ἰσοδένδρου τέκμαρ

αἰῶνος λαχοῖσαι, Σ Ap. Rh. ii. 478, Callim. *Del.* 83 ἦ ῥ' ἐτεὸν ἐγένοντο τότε δρύες ἡνίκα νύμφαι; | νύμφαι μὲν χαίρουσιν ὅτε δρύας ὄμβρος ἀέξει, | νύμφαι δ' αὖ κλαίουσιν ὅτε δρυσὶν οὐκέτι φύλλα, Ap. Rh. iii. 481 μὴ ταμέειν πρέμνον δρυὸς ἥλικος, Nonnus ii. 92 ἁδρυάδες δὲ | ἥλικες ὠδύροντο λιπόσκια δένδρεα νύμφαι, xiv. 212 συμφυέες μελίαι δρυὸς ἥλικος, xvi. 245, xlviii. 641, Ovid *Met.* viii. 738–878. Similarly in Czech and German folk-lore the life of the Moosleute, Elfen etc. depends on that of the tree; Mannhardt *AWF.* 4, *B.-K.* 75, Bötticher *Baumkultus*, Frazer ii. 12.

264. The same pair of trees occurs Eur. *Phoen.* 1515, *Bacchae* 110. They are perhaps representative. On the other hand the Dryad was extended to trees in general: Paus. x. 32. 6 ἐφύοντο (νύμφαι) ἀπό τε ἄλλων δένδρων καὶ μάλιστα ἀπὸ τῶν δρυῶν. The sanctity of the oak is perhaps due to the connexion of that tree with the Aryan God of the sky, and this in turn to the fact that the oak is more liable than other trees to be struck by lightning (Warde Fowler *Roman Essays and Interpretations* 37).

267. Cf. Xenophanes 17 ἑστᾶσιν δ' ἐλάτης ⟨βάκχοι⟩ πυκινὸν περὶ δῶμα. The asyndeton is natural to introduce details in the description.

ἠλίβατοι: derivation and proper meaning are unknown. In Homer it is limited to πέτρη, and so in Hes. *Theog.* 675, *h.* iv. 404, xix. 10; it is applied to a cave Hes. *Th.* 483, to Tartarus Stesich. 83, to a tree as here *Scut.* 421 ὡς ὅτε τις δρῦς ἤριπεν ἢ ὅτε πεύκη (one MS. for πέτρη) | ἠλίβατος. Cf. also an epigram ap. Plut. *T.Q. Flamin.* 9 Ἀλκαίῳ σταυρὸς πήγνυται ἠλίβατος. It is used of a town by Abydenus ap. Euseb. *PE.* ix. 14, a goat Aristoph. *fr.* 13, fire Hanno *peripl.* 16, evil Damascenus com. *fr.* 2. 22, and with almost any noun by Nonnus (i. 164, 285, ii. 129, 371, 549, iii. 205, vi. 335).

ἑ as a plural occurs only here and in B 197 if with Zen. we read βασιλήων in 196; cf. ἑάς of a plural subject *Batr.* 161, ἑᾶς Pindar *Pyth.* iv. 187, and the normal ἑαυτῶν, ἑαυτοῖς, ἑαυτούς. The original pronoun of the 3rd pers. early lost its number and its person. For the verse-ending cf. δ 355 Φάρον δέ ἑ κικλήσκουσιν.

268. **ἀθανάτων**: not the nymphs, who are mortal, but the Gods

to whom the groves belong. Cf. the nymphs in the grove of Demeter (Callim. *Cer.* 36) and of Ceres (Ovid *Met.* viii. 738).

272. The scribes intended δέ κε by δέχ', as οὔχ' *Herm.* 284 for οὔ κε. So it is better to turn λείπει into λείποι than δέχ' into δέ θ'. The statement of the dryad's death is less precise than the drying up of the tree, the withering of the bark, and the falling off of the boughs.

274. In ο 363 sq. Eumaeus narrates how Anticlea brought him and Ctimene up together, αὐτὰρ ἐπεὶ ῥ' ἥβην πολυήρατον ἱκόμεθ' ἄμφω Ctimene was given in marriage, αὐτὰρ ἐμὲ χλαῖνάν τε χιτῶνά τε εἵματ' ἐκείνη | καλὰ μάλ' ἀμφιέσασα ποσὶν δ' ὑποδήματα δοῦσα | ἀγρὸν δὲ προΐαλλε, a time of life which agrees with 277 here, τὸν μὲν ἐπὴν δὴ πρῶτον ἴδῃς θάλος ὀφθαλμοῖσι, | γηθήσεις ὁρόων ... | ἄξεις δ' αὐτίκα νιν ποτὶ Ἴλιον ἠνεμόεσσαν. Therefore if πολυήρατος ἥβη is governed by this usage it would seem that 274–5 and 276–8 are two versions of the same incident. But the writer uses θάλος of the five-year-old, and may therefore use ἥβη of an earlier age; and this is not contradicted by Ω 728, where Neoptolemus is still in arms. The moment of the first presentation may be that when the child leaves its σπάργανα and begins to walk, nine months after birth in Mediterranean countries; or perhaps when it is weaned (ἀπογαλακτισμός Genesis xxi. 8, at two years Orib. *syn.* v. 5. 3). The nymphs show him to prove Anchises' paternity and the child's age. The second presentation is made by the mother, when the boy is five years old, a θάλος, and ready to leave the women (πρῶτον goes with θάλος, which is predicative). Nymphs are Goddesses μ 131, xxvi. 3, 7. The Persians (Herod. i. 136) παιδεύουσι τοὺς παῖδας ἀπὸ πενταέτεος ἀρξάμενοι . . . πρὶν δὲ ἢ πενταέτης γένηται οὐκ ἀπικνέεται ἐς ὄψιν τῷ πατρί, ἀλλὰ παρὰ τῇσι γυναιξὶ δίαιταν ἔχει (quoted by Roscher *Die Enneadischen Fristen* 75), and so the Liburnians *Paradoxogr. Vat.* 47 Keller. The usual Greek age was seven, Plato *Alcib.* 121 E, *Laws* 794 C, *Axiochus* 366 D. Ἥβη in Ar. *Pol.* viii. 47 and 49 means seven years or thereabouts.

280. νιν: the only example of this acc. in Homer or the *Hymns*; otherwise in Theognis 364, then Herondas iii. 33. 96, Theocr. iii. 16 v.l. The alteration to μιν is easy (Σ 64 𝔭[11] has νιν with μ above), but the peculiarity should be left. Smyth *Ionic* p. 445, K.-B. i. 592.

284. Matthiae imported φάσθαι from ι 504, but μυθεῖσθαι 283 gives the imperative here. Anchises is not to deny paternity, but to say 'they say he is the offspring of a beautiful nymph': cf. φασίν of the same child Υ 105, and μήτηρ μέν τ' ἐμέ φησι τοῦ ἔμμεναι αὐτὰρ ἐγώ γε | οὐκ οἶδ'· οὐ γάρ πώ τις ἑὸν γόνον αὐτὸς ἄνεγνω α 215 and δ 387. Anchises cannot identify the mother.

For nymphs as mothers of a race, see Agroetas ά Λιβυκῶν *FHG*. iv. 294.

καλυκώπιδος: *h. Dem.* 8.

285. ὄρος κτλ. = ν 351.

288. In Soph. *fr.* 373, Hygin. *fab.* 94 (*inter sodales per vinum est elocutus*) Anchises boasted of his fortune and was struck by lightning and blinded (Servius on *Aen.* i. 617) or paralysed (*id. ib.* ii. 649).

290. Cf. λ 251 and ε 146.

291. ἠνεμόεντα: only here as an epithet of the sky.

VI

Hymn to Aphrodite

This slight hymn was composed for a contest (19, 20), but there are no distinctive marks either of date or locality. The voyage of the Goddess across the sea to Cyprus in the ἀφρός is already in Hesiod's *Theogonia*; the dressing and adornment of Aphrodite by the Horae is told at some length, but corresponds to fragments 4 and 5 of the *Cypria*. This latter poem it must be remembered was by a Cypriote, Hegesias or Stasinus (see *Origins* p. 62), and the hymn may be so also.

There is no clear trace of a debt to the longer hymns to Aphrodite, but there are coincidences with Ξ (see on 8, 14) and Hesiod (see on 1, 3, 5, 19).

1. Cf. Hes. *Theog.* 193 ἔνθεν ἔπειτα περίρρυτον ἵκετο Κύπρον. | ἐκ δ' ἔβη αἰδοίη καλὴ θεός (for the sequence χρυσοστέφανον καλήν *ib.* 17), Orph. *fr.* 101 Abel = 127 Kern παρθένον αἰδοίην of Aphrodite. The epithet suits a Goddess whose cult as Farnell ii. 668 observes is on the whole austere: see also P.-R. 377, 378.

2. **Κύπρου κρήδεμνα**: an extension of the Homeric usage of this word with a city (Τροίης, Θήβης, πόληος). It must mean here 'walls', i.e. fortified towns.

λέλογχεν: *hymn. mag.* iii. 11 (in Abel *Orphica* p. 289) καί τ' ἔλαχες δεινὰς μὲν ὁδοὺς κτλ., Orph. *Arg.* 2.

3. **μένος ὑγρὸν ἀέντος**: cf. *Theog.* 869, 870.

The Goddess was carried from Cythera to Cyprus (by the west wind) Hes. *Theog.* 190. For other reff. to Aphrodite ἀφρογενής see Farnell ii. 748. The ludicrous Hesiodean etymology was accepted by Anacr. 54. 13, Plato *Crat.* 406 D and generally. For other ancient and modern derivations see P.-W. i. 2773. In Homer Aphrodite is the daughter of Zeus and Dione E 312 (and in some later poets, e.g. Eur. *Hel.* 1098, Phaeth. *fr.* 781. 15, Theocr. xvii. 36). Later speculation, e.g. in Plato *Symp.* 180 D, used the two birth stories to account for the two aspects of Aphrodite, Urania being born from the foam, Pandemos from Dione.

5. The connexion of Aphrodite with the Horae is similar to that of the Charites, with whom she is more often mentioned (see on *h.* v. 61); cf. *h.* iii. 194, Aristoph. *Pax* 466 Ἑρμῇ Χάρισιν Ὥραισιν Ἀφροδίτῃ Πόθῳ. In functions the Charites and Horae are almost identical. Compare the adornment of Pandora, by the Charites with golden chains, by the Horae with flowers Hes. *OD.* 73, Cypria *fr.* 4 εἵματα μὲν χροὶ ἕστο τά οἱ Χάριτές τε καὶ Ὧραι | ποίησαν καὶ ἔβαψαν ἐν ἄνθεσιν εἰαρινοῖσιν | οἷα φοροῦσ' Ὧραι κτλ., and *fr.* 5. For the flowered robes of the Horae, cf. Ovid *Fasti* v. 217, Orph. *h.* xliii. 6, and for the number of the Horae see on 12.

χρυσάμπυκες: cf. 12 and Pindar *fr.* 30. 6 τὰς χρυσάμπυκας ἀγλαοκάρπους ἀλαθέας Ὥρας. The epithet is applied to the Muses *Theog.* 916, Pind. *Isthm.* ii. 1, *Pyth.* iii. 89, to the moon (μήνη) by Maximus περὶ καταρχῶν 81. The ἄμπυξ was the frontlet which formed part of the harness of the chariot-horse (e.g. E 363), and hence the ornament which confined women's front hair (X 469, Eust. *ad loc.*), perhaps a half-circle as distinct from the *stephane* or tiara (below 7, Σ 597), which also probably stood higher.

8. **τρητοῖσι λόβοισι** = Ξ 182.

9. **ἄνθεμ'**: not in Homer, who however has the adj. ἀνθεμόεις

(Ψ 885, γ 440, ω 275) derived by Σ T on Ψ 885 from ἄνθεμα: the word first occurs elsewhere in Pindar *Ol.* ii. 72 (χρυσοῦ).

ὀρειχάλκου: elsewhere first in Hes. *Scut.* 122, then in Stesichorus 88, Ibycus *fr.* 2 (42), Bacchyl. *fr.* 51. The metal, whether copper or a compound, cannot be identified: Plato *Critias* 116 C says it gave out a red gleam (Suid. ὁ διαυγὴς χαλκός, ὁ δόκιμος); cf. Aristotle 92 b 22, 834 b 25, Ap. Rhod. iv. 973. Strabo 610 calls it ψευδάργυρον, an alloy of copper, Pliny *HN.* xxxiv. 2 a natural metal no longer found *iam tempore effeta tellure.* Cf. Philostr. *vit. Apoll.* ii. 7 νομίσματα ὀρειχάλκου τε καὶ χαλκοῦ μέλανος, *ib.* 20 γεγράφαται ὀρειχάλκῳ καὶ ἀργύρῳ καὶ χρυσῷ καὶ χαλκῷ μέλανι ἐλέφαντες ἵπποι κτλ., v. 21 a flute χρυσοῦ τε καὶ ὀρειχάλκου καὶ ἐλάφων κνήμης ξυγκεῖσθαι, *Heroic.* 320 τὸν στύρακα ἐκ τοῦ ἐπὶ θάτερα ὀρειχάλκου ἐμβεβλῆσθαι ἵνα πᾶσα δὴ ἀστράπτουσα ἐμπίπτοι, Libanius xii. 10 οὔτε λιθίνην οὔτε χαλκῆν οὔτε ὀρειχαλκίνην, Julian *or.* iii. 110 D ὀχημάτων . . . χρυσῷ καὶ ἀργύρῳ καὶ ὀρειχάλκῳ μετὰ τῆς ἀρίστης τέχνης εἰργασμένων, P. Lond. 1727. 33 χρυσοις και αργυροις και χαλκοις και οριχαλκοις. See Paul Diergart *Philologus* 1905. 15.

It is a cheap substitute for gold and silver with *stamnum* Suet. *Vitell.* 5; cymbals were made of it *Anth. Pal.* vi. 234. 15, a heart Paus. ii. 37. 3: *EM.* 630. 62 χύμευσις χαλκοῦ τοῦ νυνὶ εὑρισκομένου λευκοῦ χαλκοῦ. The metal intended by Cicero *Off.* iii. 23, Horace *ars poet.* 202 *tibia non ut nunc orichalco vincta tubaeque* | *aemula* and other Latin writers is unknown. The spelling *aurichalcum* is due to false analogy.

12. According to one tradition there were only two Horae (so on the throne of the Amyclaean Apollo Paus. iii. 18. 10 and at Athens *id.* ix. 35. 2, though Pausanias may be mistaken in the latter case, see Robert *de Gratiis Atticis*, P.-R. 478 n. 4). For two Horae in art see Rapp in Roscher i. 2723, 2726. The dual may therefore keep its proper force, and the plural ἴοιεν is a natural irregularity. At the same time the dual in late epos is sometimes equivalent to the plural (see on *h.* iii. 456).

The controversy as to the priority of the division of the year into two seasons or into three is fruitless, as 'will be readily understood by any one who has become familiar with the overlapping and instability of the seasons among primitive peoples', Nilsson

Primitive Time Reckoning 71, 72. All Indo-European-speaking peoples, as early as when we know anything about them, seem to have divided the year both into two seasons, warm and cold (cf. the Egyptian statues of Summer and Winter, Herod. ii. 121), and also into three, spring, summer, and winter. In Homer a fourth season ὀπώρη begins to appear, and for practical purposes was well established by the time of Alcman *fr.* 76. The personifications of the seasons varied mainly between two and three. In art they do not appear as four until Hellenistic times, and rarely in literature (an example in Athen. 198 B).

13. **ἐς χορὸν ἱμερόεντα**: cf. σ 194, and the dance of the Muses and Charites xxvii. 15.

14. Cf. Ξ 187.

16. **ἐδεξιόωντο**: Ap. Rh. ii. 756.

ἠρήσαντο: α 366, θ 336–42.

18. **ἰοστεφάνου**: for this and the variant εὐστ. see on *h.* v. 175.

19. **ἑλικοβλέφαρε**: first in Hes. *Theog.* 16, cf. Pindar *fr.* 123. 5, Orph. *h.* lvii. 4. The meaning is disputed; cf. ἑλικώπιδα κούρην Α 98, ἑλίκωπες Ἀχαιοί 389, ἑλικώπιδος Ἀφροδίτας Pind. *Pyth.* vi. 1, but the sense of ἑλίκωψ itself is uncertain, see Boisacq *in v.* The connexion with ἑλίσσω makes it reasonably certain that the meaning is 'with rolling eyes, ogling, shooting glances'.

γλυκυμείλιχε: only here; *h.* x. 2 μείλιχα δῶρα, *Anth. Pal.* v. 225. 4 Κύπριδι μειλιχίῃ etc.

20. **ἔντυνον**, 'make', i.e. 'inspire' my song. In μ 183 the phrase means 'they began, raised, their song': Max. π. καταρχῶν 454 παιδὶ δαημοσύνην . . . ἐντύνειεν.

VII

Hymn to Dionysus

For references to cult, myths, and other hymns see intr. to *h.* 1, and for a discussion of the different versions Crusius *Philol.* xlviii. 218.

The story of Dionysus and the pirates was a favourite in literature. In Eur. *Cycl.* 11 the Tyrrhenians are inspired by Hera, and the Satyrs man a ship to rescue him. Ovid *Met.* iii. 582–691 and Nonnus xlv. 105–68 give space to the incident, shorter accounts occur in Apollod. iii. 5. 3, Hygin. *fab.* 134, poet. astron. ii. 17[1] (after the *Naxica* of Aglaosthenes), Seneca *Oed.* 449–66, Nonnus xliv. 240–9, *Anth. Pal.* ix. 82 and 524. 20 (= Orph. 284 Abel), Servius on *Aen.* i. 67, Oppian *Hal.* i. 650. Pindar knew the myth according to Philodemus π. εὐσ. p. 48 Π⟨ίνδα⟩ρος δὲ διέρχεται περὶ τῆς λῃ⟨στεία⟩ς Bergk *PLG.* i. 465. It cannot be proved that any of these versions depend on the Homeric hymn. Ovid and Nonnus handle the legend after their characteristic methods; some similarities of expression (noted in the commentary) are due to the subject, which did not admit much variation of treatment.

In art the myth has seldom found a place. The metamorphosis of the pirates does not appear on vases, for the cylix of Execias has no connexion with the Tyrrhenians. On this vase Dionysus sits in a ship from the mast of which a vine loaded with grapes springs. The vacant space round the ship is filled by seven dolphins. The vine indicates the ship which played a part in the cult, the dolphins are a conventional representation of the sea, as often on coins.

The view that the vase refers to a spring festival in which D. was carried in procession through the streets in the model of a ship is confirmed by a b. f. vase from Bologna (Dummler *Rh. Mus.* xliii. 355) and an early b. f. Attic vase from Acragas now in the B. M. reproduced by Farnell (*l. c.* pl. xlii.) together with the Execias cylix; cf. further vase examples in Nilsson *GF.* 270 and the evidence of coins in Usener *Sintflutsagen* 116 n. 2. In literature the festival is attested only for Smyrna and in late authorities (Aristides i. pp. 373, 450 Dind., Philostr. *vit. Soph.* i. 25. 1), but it may have been a pretty general observance, as analogies are abundant. Both in ancient and in modern Europe there has been a widespread practice of carrying an effigy of a ship in procession either at the New Year or at the spring festival (Farnell v. 191, Nilsson *GF.* 268, Dieterich *Kl. Schrift.* 487,

[1] *Astron. vet. script. isagog.* 1589 p. 207, 1681 p. 388.

Mannhardt *BK.* 593, Halliday *Folk-lore Studies* 74). No explanation to cover all the examples has yet been offered. As curious a fact as the procession of Dionysus, who was not a sea God, on a ship is the carrying of the model of a ship by carol-singers in modern Greece at the New Year in honour of St. Basil of inland Caesarea, a saint of no marine functions whatever.

In painting there is a record by Philostratus (*imag.* i. 10) of a picture in which a Tyrrhenian vessel is attacking the ship of Dionysus and his maenads. The metamorphosis has begun, and the God's ship is covered with ivy and vines. The naval battle seems a late invention, to accommodate the myth to other stories of D.'s prowess in war (Crusius, p. 223).

It appears therefore that the choregic monument of Lysicrates (334 B.C.)[1] is the only extant work of art illustrating the myth. In this the story has been much modified. The scene is laid not in a ship, but on the seashore. Dionysus sits on a rock playing with a panther, and the Tyrrhenians are punished by Satyrs. Some of the pirates are being beaten with the thyrsus, others are leaping into the sea half turned into dolphins. Several attempts have been made to give a religious interpretation to the story of D. and the pirates. Crusius, p. 217, thinks that it refers to the victory of D. over fish-like sea Gods, and connects it with theories about the Brauronian festival. Voigt (Roscher i. 1083) detects vestiges of an imaginary Dionysus Delphinius, worshipped by equally hypothetical Thracian thalassocrats who once ruled in Naxos. It will be safe to rule out any explanation (e.g. that of Maas *Hermes* xxiii. 70) which starts from the supposition that D. was once regarded as a marine deity or God of sailors. He was never considered a God of water, fresh or salt, and among his many titles there are three isolated examples which denote a connexion with the sea (*actaeus* in Chios *CIG.* 2214 c, *pelagius* at Pagasae Theopompus ap. Σ Ω 428, *halieus* Philochorus *fr.* 194; to suggest that v. 2 of Hermippus *fr.* 63 on the imports of Athens shows that D. was a sea-God betrays a lack of sense and

[1] It has often been reproduced, e.g. by Müller-Wieseler *Denkmäler* i, plate 37, J. E. Harrison *MMAA* 248, Mitchell *Anc. Sculpt.* 487. A cast in the B.M.

humour alike). These are most probably to be explained as due to the accident of a temple happening to stand on a sea-shore, or of a local legend that the image was picked up out of the sea (Farnell v. 124). The story of Dionysus and the pirates has in fact no religious significance whatever, and throws no light upon cult. The sole *aition* is the explanation of how dolphins came into being. Although metamorphoses provided favourite material for the sophisticated versification of Alexandria, this type of tale, the 'Just-so' story of popular fancy, is common to the folk-lore of all peoples, and has left traces in the early strata of Greek legend. As the interested attention of the landsman was aroused by the song and habits of the spring migrants, nightingale, swallow, and hoopoe, that of the sailor was attracted by the dolphin which accompanied his ship (see on *h.* iii. 400). Stories about the humane and human qualities of these fish were prevalent throughout antiquity, and it was widely believed that their ὁμοψυχία could only be explained on the supposition that they had once been human (see reff. in Wellmann P.-W. iv. 2504). The hymn represents one form in which the Greek genius for creating stories cast this popular belief. The other elements in its composition are easily analysed. From Homer to the end of antiquity capture by pirates is a favourite topic with storytellers. An early example, in which dolphins figure, is the story of Arion (Herod. i. 23); another is the attempted abduction by Tyrrhenian pirates of the statue of the Samian Hera (Menodotus of Samos ap. Athen. 672 A). For the rest we have the miraculous transformations which are commonplaces of Dionysiac cult and legend.[1] Finally, though the Execias and similar vases are not illustrations of the hymn, such representations and the festival to which they refer may have suggested the idea of D. as a passenger by ship, though indeed the unaided flight of imagination, in supposing that a God whose

[1] For epiphanies of D. see on v. 2, for animal shapes on 44, for the miraculous transformation of the tackle cf. the magical vine of Nysa, the design upon the Execias vase, the miracles which attended Bacchic revels (e.g. Pind. *fr.* 104, Eur. *Bacch.* 142, 704, 710, Plato *Ion* 534 A, *Phaedr.* 253A) or the transformation of their weaving utensils into vines, ivy, etc., which did not suffice to convert the Minyades (Ovid *Met.* iv. 1, Ant. Lib. x).

cult was established throughout the Greek islands might sail from place to place, can hardly be denied to the first inventor of the tale.

Date and Place. There is no substantial evidence. The style has been thought to be dithyrambic, but the formula ἀμφί τινα ἀείδειν (see on 1) is not confined to the dithyramb, and sudden transitions (44, 54) are a sign of poor art only. The artistic merit of the hymn is not high; nothing is said about the scene of the event, the description of the bear (46) is clumsy, and no less the indifference shown by the crew after the God has freed himself from his bonds. Ovid, a better artist, makes the pilot infer Dionysus' divinity from his general appearance only. There is, however, nothing in these defects to make the hymn late, and Ludwich's view (*Königsberger Studien*, 1887, 63) that the hymn was a work of the Orphic school of the third or fourth century A.D. is now rejected (P.-W. v. 1039). Ludwich found resemblances in vocabulary between the hymn and the Orphic Argonautica, consisting especially in words denoting haste (τάχα, θοῶς, etc.). These are common to Homeric epic, e.g. to Σ 525–32 (Crusius) or to the hymn to Hermes (see on iv. 70). Still more oddly the position of the hymn in the collection, next to the hymn to Ares, was thought to bear upon its date. This argument has force in the case of the first hymn to Dionysus; but here it would apply at least as well to the ninth hymn. There is equally little reason to make the hymn Alexandrine. No argument can be based on the language, which is normal epic. The double title Διόνυσος ἢ λῃσταί may remind us of Theocritus and Herondas, but it is not given in M and may be an addition of any period. The style, direct and rather rough, is un-Alexandrian; this appears if we compare it with Theocritus xxi, the punishment of Pentheus, a similar subject. The hymn is free from the affected vocabulary (μαλοπάρῃος, ἐθυμάρει) of the idyll. A fifth- or fourth-century date rests entirely on the youthful appearance of Dionysus; this is of no value (see on 3). There is no reason to separate the hymn from the rest of the collection (viii and perhaps one or two others excepted), or to deny it to the sixth or seventh century B.C. Crusius (p. 204) and others on the ground of resemblances to the festival of Dionysus at Brauron have thought the hymn was Attic. Pelasgian pirates carried off Brauronian women (Herod. vi. 138), little girls at the worship were called ἄρκτοι (see on 46), and the only existing representation of the legend is the monument of Lysicrates. The reasoning will not bear reflection. The later accounts (Aglaosthenes, Apollodorus, Ovid) connect the myth with Naxos, the hymn itself may be Naxian.

1. **ἀμφί**: this opening with ἔννεπε, ἀείδειν, ἔσπετε occurs at the beginning of xix, xxii, xxxiii. Together with ἄνακτα it was stereotyped in dithyramb according to Σ Ar. *Nub.* 595, Ꝑ Fiorent. 112 *fr.* E 5. 7, Suid. *in* Ἀμφιανακτίζειν. Cf. Terpander 2, Stesich. 26, Eur. *Troad.* 511.

Σεμέλης . . . υἱόν xxvi. 2.

2. **ἐφάνη**: ἐπιφαίνεσθαι first occurs in Herodotus, ἐπιφάνεια not before the fourth century, but epiphanies are frequent in literature from Homer onwards, cf. xxxiii. 12. See Pfister in *Epiphanie* P.-W. Suppl. iv. 277. They are a feature of Dionysiac mythology, Rohde *Psyche* 305. Ludwich's detection of an Orphic hand on the strength of Orph. *Arg.* 16 (πρῶτος γὰρ ἐφάνθη) is therefore unsound. No locality is indicated. According to Apollodorus D. wishes to cross from Icaria to Naxos, in Ovid *l.c.* 597 he is found in Ceos (*Ciae telluris* Lachmann for *Chiae*), Nonnus localizes the story in the Sicilian sea. In Ovid the God is captured owing to his condition, *mero somnoque gravis.*

3. **ἀκτῇ ἔπι προβλῆτι**: cf. ε 405, κ 89, ν 97, Ap. Rh. ii. 365. The youthful type of Dionysus in art which was once thought to have been created in the age of Praxiteles is now known to go back to Calamis (Roscher i. 1089, 1126). But in any case reference to the date of art-types is irrelevant to the dating of this passage. The transformation is on Homeric analogy, and the God assumes the form of a youth for the occasion. His appearance is not effeminate and voluptuous, but like that of Apollo in *h.* iii. 450 belongs to a young Greek athlete with broad shoulders (5) like Telemachus ο 61.

5. **στιβαροῖς ὤμοις** = ξ 528, ο 61, Orph. *Arg.* 200.

6. For ἀπό cf. xxxiii. 8 οἱ δ' ἀπὸ νηῶν = ναῦται, with no idea of motion. See on *h.* iii. 133.

7. προγίγνεσθαι often implies movement and is followed by ἐς or ἐπί: Σ 525, Hes. *Scut.* 345, Callim. *Dian.* 178 (ἐπί), Theocr. xxv. 134 (ἐς).

8. **Τυρσηνοί**: first in Hes. *Theog.* 1016. In the fifth century B.C. the terms Tyrsenians and Pelasgians were regarded as alternative names for the pre-Hellenic population of the Balkan peninsula (Herod. i. 57, 94, Thuc. iv. 109, Soph. *fr.* 270. 4). To this race the contemporary population of Lemnos was thought to belong. Stories of their exploits, e.g. the rape of the Athenian women at Brauron, or the legend of Hera Lygodesma at Samos (Athen. 672 A) attest their piratical disposition. The Etruscans of tradition were invaders of Italy from the east. Their origin and the date of their arrival in Italy are matters of dispute, but archaeological evidence seems to confirm the tradition that they came from the east by sea, but suggests a date several centuries later than the period of the Trojan war. According to Hellanicus (*fr.* 4 Jac.) the Etruscans were Pelasgians who acquired the name Tyrseni after their settlement in Italy. On the truth of these ethnographical speculations, ancient and modern, there are not yet the means of deciding. Was it Etruscans or Pelasgians that the author of the hymn had in mind? To this question the answer is almost certain. It is true that Etruscans were pirates and harried the Greek colonies of the west, and that late writers on the theme (Philostr. *Imag.* i. 19, Nonnus xv. 104) not unnaturally considered Τυρρηνοί to be Etruscans. But this early poem has no connexion with Sicily or Magna Graecia, and the usual explanation that Tyrsenians = Pelasgians is therefore preferable.

11. **υἱὸν . . . βασιλήων.** He appeared to be a prince from his appearance (cf. *h.* ii. 215) and his purple cloak; this was worn by Telemachus δ 115 and Odysseus τ 225. In Nonnus the God wears jewellery as well.

13. For the miraculous loosing of the bonds cf. Eur. *Bacch.* 447, 498, 616 sq. In Ovid *l.c.* 700 the miracle happens to the pilot Acoetes, when he is imprisoned by Pentheus.

14. **ἐκάθητο**: the usual epic form is καθῆστο. See Veitch p. 347.

22. **αὐτὸν ἀφῶμεν**: *αὐτός* is unemphatic (in the acc. = ἑ) in any position; ζ 277, 308, 329, κ 113, π 370, θ 343, Ι 562, Π 519, Τ 303. Cf. *h.* iii. 155, 181.

24. **ὄρσῃ ἀργαλέους**: ω 110 *ὄρσας ἀργαλέους ἀνέμους*, λ 400 *ὄρσας ἀργαλέων ἀνέμων ἀμέγαρτον ἀυτμήν*. For the hiatus *in thesi* see Monro *HG*. § 38 a.

26. **ἅμα** = *simul*, as you observe the wind.

27. **ἄνδρεσσι**: i.e. men, not cowards.

29. The Hyperboreans, unknown to Homer, occur first in Hesiod *fr.* 209 and the *Epigoni fr.* 3, next in Alcaeus *fr.* 2, Aristeas *frr.* 5, 6, 7, Pindar *Ol.* iii, where they are at the head of the Danube. The historians took account of them, Hecataeus *fr.* 373, Hellanicus *fr.* 96, Herodotus iv. 32, Arethas ap. Σ Pind. *l.c.*, Diodorus ii. 47, Strabo 61, 62, 711 (quoting Ephorus, Onesicritus, Simonides), Pliny *NH.* iv. 89–91, Protarchus, Callimachus, Damastes *ἐν τῷ π. ἐθνῶν* ap. Steph. Byz. *in v.* Herodotus, who quotes Hesiod, neglects this hymn. See Schröder *ARW.* viii. 69, Crusius in Roscher i. 2805, Daelritz in P.-W. ix. 258. The etymology and meaning of the name are still obscure. The Greek derivation from *βορέας* (*οἱ ὑπὲρ τὸν ἄνεμον οἰκοῦσι τὸν βορέαν* Paus. v. 7. 7) is not impossible; cf. *διαβόρειοι* Strabo 86, *καταβόρειος*, -*βορρος* in the lexx., *προσβορέους* Strabo 4, *πρόσβορρος*, *προσβόρειος* Aristotle, *μελαμβόρειον* Strabo 182, *ὑπερβορέου μείζονα φωνεῖς* Aesch. Choeph. 372. Alcaeus and Abaris (ap. Suid. *in* Ἄβαρις) made Apollo go to them. See Farnell *Pindar* i. 19, ii. 64, 217. G. F. Hudson *Europe and China* 1931, 27–52 following Tomaschek identifies them with the Chinese.

ἐς δὲ τελευτήν: cf. Hes. *OD.* 333, Theognis 201, 607, 755, Pindar *Ol.* v. 22.

29. M's *ὀὲ καστέρω* is a survival of *ὅγ' ἑκαστέρω*, cf. υ 245 *ἥδε γε, ἥδέ τε, ἥ δέ ε*.

30. **κτήματα πάντα**, 'their whole income', with a view to ransom.

33. For **ἔμπνευσεν** c. acc. cf. Pind. *Isthm.* ii. 40 *οὖρος ἐμπνεύσαις ὑπέστειλ' ἱστίον*, though the context is ambiguous, Α 481 *ἐν δ' ἄνεμος πρῆσεν μέσον ἱστίον*; *ἐμπίπτειν* c. acc. Nonnus vii. 45.

34. **καττάνυσαν**: Ap. Rh. ii. 933 *κὰδ δ' ἄρα λαῖφος ἐρυσσάμενοι*

τανύοντο | ἐς πόδας ἀμφοτέρους, β 430 δησάμενοι δ' ἄρα ὅπλα, Ovid *l.c.* 663 *vela deducunt.*

37. **πάντας ἰδόντας**: hiatus occurs before ἰδεῖν vv. 8, 42, 48, 52. For the variation cf. φ 112 ὄφρα ἴδωμεν, 122 τάφος δ' ἕλε πάντας ἰδόντας. The last passage defends τάφος here.

38. Cf. Ovid *l.c.* 664 *impediunt hederae remos nexuque recurvo | serpunt et gravidis distinguunt vela corymbis.* In Apollodorus the masts and oars become snakes and the ship is filled with ivy; in Nonnus the mast is changed into a cypress wreathed with ivy, in Oppian *Cyn.* iv. 261 a boat which carried Bacchus across the Euripus was covered with ivy, vines, and smilax. Theophr. *HP.* iv. 4. 1 ἐν Ἰνδοῖς φανῆναι κιττὸν ἐν τῷ ὄρει τῷ μηρῷ καλουμένῳ ὅθεν δὴ καὶ τὸν Διόνυσον εἶναι μυθολογοῦσιν; Lucian *vera hist.* ii. 41.

41. **τηλεθάων**: not in Homer c. dat.

43. **νῆ' ἤδη**: the correction is supported by *h.* iii. 392 ἠμαθόην, corrected by Γ, M m. 2 and Demetrius to νῆα θοήν. Νῆ' ἤδη written in full ΝΗΑΗΔΗ is close to μηδηδη. Cf. Herod. v. 85 μιῇ νιῇ νιή νηι. For ἤδη τότ' ἔπειτα cf. δὴ τότ' ἔπειτα λ 44, Ap. Rh. iv. 718, 1631, Solon 16. 3 εἴην δὴ τότ' ἐγώ. Formerly it was proposed, taking πελάαν intrans., to make a name out of μηδηδη or -δειν, e.g. Μηδείδην, like Φρόντιν Menelaus' pilot γ 282. Cf. Μεγαμηδείδαο *h.* iv. 100. The name should have been mentioned before (e.g. at 15) if at all. In Ovid and Hyginus the pilot is Acoetes.

44. **λέων γένετ'**: a common transformation of Dionysus, Eur. *Bacch.* 1018, Horace *Od.* ii. 19. 23, Nonnus vi. 182, xl. 44. In Ovid and Seneca the God retains his human form, but wild beasts appear at his side (Ovid 668) or occupy the prow and stern (Sen. 457). In Nonnus D. suddenly becomes a giant and animals swarm on the ship's benches. The scene in the hymn resembles the story in Ant. Lib. 10 (Aelian *VH.* iii. 42): in order to frighten the Minyades, who stayed at their homes instead of joining the Bacchanals, Dionysus ἐγένετο ταῦρος καὶ λέων καὶ πάρδαλις, καὶ ἐκ τῶν κελεόντων ἐρρύη νέκταρ αὐτῷ καὶ γάλα.

46. **ἄρκτον ἐποίησεν**: in his contest with Deriades Dionysus takes the form of a bear, among other changes, Nonnus *Dion.* xl. 46. Ovid's *simulacra inania* is in the later spirit.

47. **ἂν δ' ἔστη** must be taken with λέων as well as with ἄρκτος, awkwardly.

52. **πήδησαν**: Prop. iii. 17. 25, 26 *desiluisse*. Of the crew in Oppian iv. 263 κυβίστεον ἀσπαλιῆες.

53. καὶ ἐγένοντο δελφῖνες Apollod. iii. 38. Dolphins according to Lucian *dial. mar.* 8. 1 were once men.

54. **ἔθηκε πανόλβιον**, 'made him wholly blessed': Hesych. πανόλβιος· παμμακάριστος. Theognis 441 οὐδεὶς γὰρ πάντ' ἐστὶ πανόλβιος, epigr. Cougny i. 287. 1 πανόλβιον ἄνδρ' ἀνέθηκε, Philostr. *vit. Apoll.* iii. 43 πανολβίου τινος καὶ ταὐτὸν ἰσχύοντος τῷ Ἀπόλλωνι τῷ Δελφικῷ: a proper name Libanius *ep.* 393. 3 and others in Pape.

55. δῖε κάτωρ: δῖε is natural, but κάτωρ is non-existent. Ἑκάτωρ is conceivably a shortened form of such a name as Ἑκατήνωρ, Ἑκατόδωρος, Ἑκατώνυμος; cf. Ἑκήτορος Diod. v. 50, +κήτορος Parthen. xix, Ἑκατέρω (*sic* gen. Hesiod *fr.* 198 ap. Strab. 471).

59. Cf. i. 19.

VIII

Hymn to Ares

It is evident that this hymn is quite removed from the style and tone of the other hymns in the collection. Ruhnken, Hermann and a large majority of the older critics assigned it a place among the Orphic poems. Coincidences with the hymns of Proclus (see on 5, 6, and 10, and minor verbal coincidences in the vocabulary of 1–3) have been thought to show evidence of his influence. Pfeiffer, on the other hand, draws the contrary conclusion that Proclus wrote with the hymn before him (*Studien zum antiken Sternglauben*, Στοιχεῖα Heft ii. 1916).

Other students of the *Orphica* refuse to put it in the Orphic category (Maass *Orpheus* 198, Abel *Orphica* 102, *Hom. Hymns* 91, who dates it 'in or after the age of Nonnus', Adami 223). The accumulation of epithets, though a marked characteristic of the *Orphica*, is not confined to them (Maass and Adami *l.c.*, Pfeiffer *l.c.* 104; see on *Dem.* 18). The vocabulary is not especially Orphic. The prayer for peace is similar to that in

Orph. *h.* lxv, but that does not prove the Orphic character of the hymn.

The noticeable peculiarity about the hymn as distinct from the others in the collection is its astrological character. It is addressed to the planet Mars rather than to Ares, the God of war. The planet is first mentioned in Plato *Epinomis* 987 C. Upon grounds of subject, therefore, as well as of style, the hymn cannot be earlier than the Alexandrine period, to the earlier part of which Pfeiffer assigns it. The general character of the language and style, however, may be thought to support a much later date. The language resembles that of the hymn to Paean, *IG.* xiv. 1015, or of *IG.* viii. 2, 153, an inscription of the fourth century after Christ.

The cause which led to the inclusion of this hymn among 'Homeric' poems is obscure. If it be due to the inability of the compiler to distinguish the two kinds of poem, the present form of the collection must belong to a very late age (Gemoll); for the Alexandrines, who knew some of the short hymns, would not have been so lacking in critical sense as to include this among them. According to others the presence of the hymn is due to the juxtaposition of Homeric and Orphic poems in a manuscript, which led to the displacement of one hymn, a very slight probability. It is at least as probable that some one at a late period, observing there was no hymn to Ares in the collection, added this one, and put it in the 8th place to come alphabetically before Artemis.

The cult of Ares (Farnell v. 396, Nilsson *GF.* 402, P.-R. 335) was of so little importance that the absence of a genuine Homeric prelude in honour of the God is not surprising. The Orphic hymns lxv, lxxxviii, are addressed to Ares, and *fr. lyr. adesp.* 108 (Bergk) appears to belong to an invocation or hymn to him. This last is also marked by an accumulation of epithets: βρόμιε, δορατοφόρ', ἐνυάλιε, πολεμοκέλαδε, πάτερ Ἄρη.

1–3. Of this string of epithets only ὀβριμόθυμος is definitely a favourite in Orphic literature (of Ares Orph. Εὐχή 10, Orph. *h.* lxv. 1, of Athena *ib.* xxxii. 2, of Hades *ib.* xviii. 1, of Rhea *ib.* xiv. 7, of Hephaestus *ib.* lxvi. 1, of Dionysus *hymn. alph. AP.* ix. 524,

Abel *Orphica* 284), but though not Homeric (in Homer Ares is ὄβριμος E 845, N 444, 521, O 112, Π 613 κτλ.) it is used by Hesiod *Theog.* 140 of the Cyclops Arges, and by Panyasis *fr.* 16. 4 of Ares. In Manetho v. 177 the planet Ares is ὀβριμόεργος. The form ὑπερμενέτης is also not Homeric, but ὑπερμενής is a constant Homeric epithet of Zeus (B 116, 403, H 315, 481, I 23, Λ 727 κτλ.). βρισάρματος of Ares is Hesiodic, *Scut.* 441. χρυσοπήληξ is applied to Ares in Aesch. *Sept.* 106 and Athena in Callim. *h.* v. 43, cf. Proclus *h.* vii. 7. φέρασπις is Aeschylean (*Ag.* 693, *Pers.* 240): it is used of Athena in Proclus *h.* vii. 3 and Christod. *ecphras.* 388. πολισσόος is ἅπαξ λεγόμενον, formed on the analogy of the frequent Homeric epithet λαοσσόος (e.g. N 128, χ 210 of Athena); cf. σαόπτολις, an epithet only used in late writers (Coluth. 140, Nonn. xli. 395, *IG.* viii. 2. 153. 1). χαλκοκορυστής is a good Homeric epithet (e.g. E 699, Z 199, 398); Pfeiffer compares χαλκεομίτρας used of Ares in an astrological poem *Cat. cod. astr.* i. 173. καρτερόχειρ is rare and found only in late authors (e.g. Orph. *h.* lxvi. 3 of Hephaestus, and *AP.* ix. 210 of the emperor Anastasius). ἀμόγητος, as an adjective ἅπαξ λεγ., is formed from the Homeric adverb ἀμογητί. δορυσθένης is found in Aeschylus (*Choeph.* 159) and *AP.* ix. 475; Pfeiffer compares ἐγχεσπάλος of Ares in *Cat. cod. astr.* i. 173, ii. 21 and δορυσσόε of Athena in Proclus *h.* vii. 4. The vocabulary, therefore, does not support the view that this hymn is Orphic.

4. **Νίκης**: in Hes. *Theog.* 384, Apollod. 1, 2, 4 (cf. Bacchyl. *fr.* 72. 1) she is daughter of Styx and Pallas. The relation of Ares here to Nike and Themis is not mythological but symbolical.

5. **ἀντιβίοισι**: as a subst. only here and in Proclus *h.* vii. 50 κάρδος ἐπ' ἀντιβίοισι.

δικαιοτάτων ἀγὲ φωτῶν: possibly there is a verbal reminiscence of N 6, but certainly no allusion to Scythians, as Baumeister supposes. Ares is 'Lord of the Just', the antithesis to which, δίκαιος having an almost technical sense, is represented by κακότης (l. 12), from which he is prayed to grant delivery. It is a remarkable role for Ares (see on 9). Possibly the conception of Ares, Lord of δίκαιοι, may have developed from that of Ares, patron of ἀγαθοί, brave = good as opposed to κακοί, cowards = bad: cf. the conventional epitaphs of young warriors, e.g. *IG.* ii. 3. 2718 on Glauciades, τοὺς ἀγαθοὺς ἔστερξε Ἄρης.

6. **ἠνορέης σκηπτοῦχε**: there is perhaps no parallel for this use in early Greek, but cf. τοξοσύνης σκηπτοῦχε of Apollo Nonn. xxviii. 253, νόθον σκηπτοῦχον Ὀλύμπου of Dionysus Nonn. xlviii. 18, θαλάσσης σκηπτοῦχον of Poseidon *AP.* v. 100. 3, θεῶν σκηπτοῦχε of Aphrodite Orph. *h.* lv. 11. Pfeiffer's explanation (p. 105) that there is a reference to the Egyptian system of astrology in which the planets figure as sceptre-bearers, appears therefore unnecessary. In certain aspects the planet is patron of generals, admirals, members of the body-guard of tyrants, kings and leaders of the people, though these tend at the last to come to a violent end, Manetho, i. 210, 213, ii. 49, 63, i (v) 103, iv. 48.

πυραυγέα κύκλον κτλ., 'wheeling thy red orb among the bodies that move in the sevenfold paths of heaven'. The passage closely resembles Proclus *h.* iv. 17 εἴτε καὶ ἑπτὰ κύκλων ὑπὲρ ἄντυγας αἰθέρα ναίεις, cf. τηλεπόρου δίνης ἑλικαυγέα κύκλον | οὐρανίαις στροφάλιγξι περίδρομον αἰὲν ἑλίσσων of Helios Orph. *fr.* 235 Abel (236 Kern). In Sophocles *OT.* 27 Ares is πυρφόρος θεός (cf. *ib.* 190), and the priests of Ares are called πυρφόροι (Σ Eur. *Phoen.* 1377), but in πυραυγέα here there is an allusion to the distinctive redness of the planet Mars, which was called ὁ πυρόεις Arist. *Mund.* vi. 18. For the terms πυρόεις, πυριλαμπής, and πυρφόρος as applied to the planet in astronomical literature see the references in Brugmann *Epitheta Deorum* p. 42, and upon the name πυρόεις, which possibly was of Mesopotamian origin, Bouché-Leclercq *L'Astrologie Grecque*, p. 60.

7–8. **πῶλοι ζαφλεγέες**: the god Ares is χαλκάρματος πόσις Ἀφροδίτας Pindar *Pyth.* iv. 87; for his car see E 356 sqq., and for its horses Deimos and Phobos O 119. Here, however, the planet is meant, and the horses of its car are fire-breathing like those of Helios (see on xxxi. 14).

8. **τριτάτης ὑπὲρ ἄντυγος** refers to the third planetary zone counting from that farthest from the earth. For this meaning of ἄντυξ see Proclus iv. 17, quoted on 6, τὴν Ἀνάγκην οἱ θεολόγοι τῇ τοῦ παντὸς οὐρανοῦ ἐξωτάτῃ ἄντυγι ἐπέχουσι, Iamblichus *Theol.*

arith. 61, *AP.* viii. 1, Eustath. in *Il.* 483. 12. The order in which the planets were arranged varied in different systems. Saturn, Juppiter, Mars, Mercury, Venus, Sun, Moon is given in Aristotle *de Mund.* 2, the system ascribed to Plato varies only in changing the positions of Venus and Mercury, but some mathematici placed the Sun in the middle (Plut. *plac. phil.* ii. 15 = 889 B). In all systems Mars occupies the third zone, i.e. the fifth away from the earth.

9. **εὐθαλέος** is perhaps due to the influence of *εὐθᾰλής*, but the ᾱ is common in late Greek, e.g. *εὐθαλῆ πλάτανον AP.* ix. 247. 1, *νεοθαλῆ | ἕρπυλον* iv. 1, 53, *τέθαλε ep.* Cougny iv. 30. 12, and cf. *ἀλαθέος* Tryphiodorus 641, *πολυγαθέα AP.* vi. 144. 3, but *νεοθηλέϊ* xxx. 13, *νεοθηλέαν Herm.* 82. No alteration is necessary. *εὐθαλής* and *εὐθαρσής* are post-Homeric. *εὐθαρλέσεος* is a good example of contamination. The general character here perhaps euphemistically attributed to Mars runs counter to astrological doctrine, in which the planet is emphatically *κακοποιός*, see Bouché-Leclercq, *l.c.* 99, 422–5. Mars was, however, connected with manly qualities; Pfeiffer quotes *Cat. cod. astr.* vii. 218 *ὁ Ἄρης ποιήσει θαρσηρούς, ἀλκίμους*, *ib.* 219 *ὁ Ἄρης ποιεῖ εὐμεγέθεις, παχεῖς, θρασεῖς, πολεμιστάς.*

10. **κλῦθι καταστίλβων**: i.e. *κλῦθι καὶ κατάστιλβε*: Matthiae compares Orph. *h.* iv. 9, xxviii. 11, xxxiv. 27.

πρηῢ σέλας: Pfeiffer quotes Babylonian doctrine that if the planet Mars is dull it is auspicious, if it shines brightly it is threatening.

βιότητα: for *βιοτήν, βίοτον* only in late Greek: cf. Manetho iv. 32 *ἐφημερίης βιότητος*, *Proverbs* vi. 23 as quoted in Clem. Alex. *Strom.* i. 29. 181 *ὁδοὺς γὰρ βιότητος ἐλέγχει παιδεία* and two late inscriptions *IG.* xiv. 1449 (= Kaibel 588), 2010. For the general sense of 10 f. Matthiae compares Proclus *h.* iv. 21 *πολύμοχθον ἐμὴν βιότοιο πορείην | ἰθύνοις σέο, πότνα, δικαιοτάτοισι βελέμνοις, | οὐχ ὁσίων παύουσα πόθων κρυόεσσαν ἐρωήν.*

12. **κακότητα**: a word frequently used in Orphic and Neo-Platonic writings for the wickedness and wretchedness of mortal existence, e.g. *κύκλου τ' ἂν λῆξαι καὶ ἀναπνεύσαι κακόκητος* Orph. *fr.* 229 Kern, cf. *frr.* 230, 233.

13. **ψυχῆς ἀπατηλὸν . . . ὁρμήν**: Ares punishes *γόητες* and *φαρμακεῖς* Aelian *HA*. xv. 11.

15. **φυλόπιδος κρυερῆς**: cf. Mimnermus 13. 10 *ἐποίχεσθαι φυλόπιδος κρατερῆς*.

16. Ares is similarly prayed to stay the strife and give peace in Orph. *h*. lxv. 6, cf. *ib*. 9. So Hephaestus as the God of fire is asked to stay the rage of fire, Orph. *h*. lxvi. 12. The principle is that expressed by the proverbial *ὁ τρώσας καὶ ἰάσεται*.

μάκαρ: see on xxii. 7.

17. **βιαίους**: for the termination Baumeister compares Plato *rep*. 399 B, *leg*. 885 A.

IX

Hymn to Artemis

The composer may have been a rhapsodist at Claros, for the marks of locality (the Meles, Smyrna, Claros) are not sufficiently important to be conventional, as for instance the mention of Cyprus and Cythera in connexion with Aphrodite (see *h*. v. introd.). The hymn may have been recited at a common festival of Apollo and Artemis (Baumeister), but there is no proof of such a festival. Colophonian coins of Apollo *Κλάριος* and of Artemis *Κλαρία* have come down from imperial times (Head *HN*. 571), but the two deities are not represented together on the coinage (see also Farnell ii. 532), and the reference to the Clarian Apollo may have a mythological rather than a ritualistic significance (see on 5 and xxvii. 13). Nor do we grasp the meaning of Artemis' drive, nor especially why she starts from the Meles, unless the story is aetiological and explains a procession in which the Goddess was carried between these places.

Wilamowitz imagined that this was a prelude abbreviated from a longer hymn as xviii was from iv, the longer hymn being written in the seventh century B.C. while Smyrna was still a daughter-city of Colophon. This of course rests on no evidence.

On the name Artemis see Kalinka *Klio* 1929, xxii. 255. She is called *Τμωλία θεός* by Diogenes trag., Nauck *TGF*. p. 602 *κλύω δὲ Λυδὰς Βακτρίας τε παρθένους | ποταμῷ παροίκους Ἅλυϊ Τμωλίαν* θεὸν | δαφνόσκιον κατ' ἄλσος Ἄρτεμιν σέβειν. Her hymn was called οὔπιγγος (Pollux i. 38, Athen. 619 B), corrupted in Theodoretus ἑλλ. παθ. θερ. 921 μὴ τῇ Ἀρτέμιδι τὸν ὕποιπον (ᾄσωμεν), and she herself οὖπις (Callim. iii. 204, *EM.* 641. 55).

2. ἰοχέαιρα παρθένος Pind. *Pyth.* ii. 16, παρθ. ἰοχ. Nonnus xx. 70 al., Υ 71 Ἄρτεμις ἰοχέαιρα κασιγνήτη ἑκάτοιο, *h.* iii. 199 Ἀρτ. ἰοχ. ὁμότροφος Ἀπόλλωνι.

3. **ἵππους**: A. is χρυσήνιος Ζ 205 and was εὐρίππα at Pheneos Paus. viii. 14. 5. Cf. Pind. *Ol.* iii. 26 Λατοῦς ἱπποσόα θυγάτηρ, *fr.* 89 ἵππων ἐλάτειραν. She appears with Apollo in a car on coins of Selinus (*HN.* 168, cf. the monolithic statue at Rome Plin. *NH.* xxxvi. 36), and as a driver in Callim. *Dian.* 111. But more often in art she drives stags or deer (e.g. on the frieze of the temple of Apollo at Bassae).

ἄρσασα: for the verb and the construction the edd. quote Euphorion *fr.* 75 οἳ δ' οὔπω Σιμόεντος Ἀχαιίδας ἤρσαμεν ἵππους.

Μέλητος: only in M. The river Meles flowed by Smyrna, and is identified with a stream at Bournoubat, Ramsay *Hist. geog.* 115. Homer was born on its banks (*vit. Herod.* 29 etc., Moschus iii. 70–5) and composed his poems in a grotto hard by (Paus. vii. 5. 12). He was also said to be the son of a nymph by the river-god Meles (*Hom. et Hes. cert.* 9, Suidas *in* Ὅμηρος, etc.). Coins of Amastris in Paphlagonia bear Homer on the obverse and Meles on the reverse (*Cat. Brit. Mus.* Pontus 86 pl. 20. 4); on the coins of Smyrna Meles appears without Homeric associations (*id.* Ionia 265 pl. 27. 16). *Ep. gr.* Kaibel 1030 praises Meles for his help in pestilence, *ep.* Cougny vi. 134 οἳ πάγον οἰκήσουσι πέρην ἱεροῖο Μέλητος. For further reff. see Roscher ii. 2636. A temple of Artemis at Smyrna is mentioned by Quintus xii. 310 Σμύρνης ἐν δαπέδοισι . . . Ἀρτέμιδος περὶ νηὸν ἐλευθερίῳ ἐνὶ κήπῳ.

5. **Κλάρον**: see on *h.* iii. 40. She visits her brother at Claros as she visits Delphi xxvii. 13 (q.v.).

6. **ἑκατηβόλον**: only here of Artemis, but equivalent to ἑκηβόλος Soph. *fr.* 401, Nonnus xv. 187, *ep.* Cougny i. 81, and on a Naxian inscription at Delos *BCH.* iii. 3, and ἑκαέργη (Farnell ii. 465).

7 = xiv. 6, where as here M only preserves the correct θ' for δ'.

X

Hymn to Aphrodite

The hymn, like its parallel, vi, was a prelude recited at a contest (cf. 5). There is no reason to suppose that it was Cyprian in origin. The MSS. offer several singular variants in the few lines of the hymn.

1. **Κυπρογενῆ**: first in Hes. *Theog.* 199 Κυπρογενέα. The variations εὐπρογενῆ etc. are due to the initial being left to the scribe to paint in colour.

Κυθέρειαν: Hes. *Theog.* 196, 198, etc.: in the *Odyssey* (θ 288, σ 193) as a proper name. See Roscher ii. 1769.

2. **μείλιχα δῶρα**: sc. τἀφροδίσια, cf. *h.* ii. 102, Hes. *Theog.* 206, Mimnermus i. 3 κρυπταδίη φιλότης καὶ μείλιχα δῶρα καὶ εὐνή Bacchyl. xv. 10 Κύπριδος [αἰ]νὰ δῶρα, Anacr. *fr.* 90 ἀγλαὰ δῶρ' Ἀφροδίτης, Γ 54 δῶρ' Ἀφροδίτης of Paris, Hes. *Scut.* 47, Theognis 1383, Stesich. 26. 2 ἠπιοδώρου Κύπριδος. Aphrodite Doritis was worshipped at Cnidus (Paus. i. 1. 3). Cf. γλυκυμείλιχε vi. 19.

ἐφ': both prepositions (in 2 and 3) are *in tmesi*; cf. Sappho vii. 9. 4 Lobel ἔρος δ' ἐπ' ἰμέρτῳ κέχυται προσώπῳ. ἐπιμειδάω, ἐπιμειδιάω are common, even more so ἐπιθέω. Cf. also Simonides 128. 2 ἡνίκ' ἀφ' ἱμερτὴν ἔπνεεν ἡλικίην, Anacr. 102. 4 ἀφ' ἱμερτὴν ἔκλυσεν ἡλικίην. For other tmeses cf. iv. 410, Ξ 396.

3. Sappho i. App. 13 σὺ δ' ὦ μάκαιρα | μειδιάσαισ' ἀθανάτῳ προσώπῳ. ἄνθος = bloom, beauty, as *Dem.* 107, *Herm.* 275 and often. θέει is more natural with this than φέρει: cf. trop. ζ 45 λευκὴ δ' ἐπιδέδρομεν αἴγλη, υ 357 κακὴ δ' ἐπιδέδρομεν ἀχλύς, lit. Hippocr. ii. 329. 10 οἱ ἐπιθέει ἐπὶ τὸ στόμα [φλέγμα], Strabo 53 τῷ δὲ κλύδωνι καὶ κῦμα ἐπιτρέχει, Hermippus *fr.* 82. 3 μήλων ἐπιδέδρομεν ὀδμή. φέρει avoids the change of subject, on which see K.-G. ii, § 597. 20.

4. The alternatives are equal in point of sense, but the metre of M's version can hardly be paralleled; cf. *Batr.* 287. For μάκαιρα cf. Sappho above, *Anth. Pal.* xiii. 245 (Callim.), Soph. *Phil.* 400 ἰὼ μάκαιρα (Ge), Eur. *Ion* 457 ὦ μάκαιρα Νίκα, *Alc.* 1004 μάκαιρα δαίμων.

5. **εἰναλίης τε Κύπρου**: cf. Musaeus *H. et L.* 46 εἰναλίης ἀπὸ Κύπρου, *h.* vi. 3. For ῠ cf. Empedocl. 282, 419, Ibycus v. 2, Pind. *Nem.* iv. 46 etc. For the worship of Aphrodite in Cyprus and Cythera see Farnell ii. 740, P.-W. i. 2756.

XI

Hymn to Athena

This and the following hymn have no formula of transition to a rhapsody. Hence it is very doubtful whether the hymn was a prelude at a recitation at Athens or elsewhere. The cult of Athena πολιάς or πολιοῦχος was common to many Greek states (Farnell i. 299).

Other hymns to Athena beside those quoted in the notes will be found in Alcaeus *fr.* 9, Aristophanes *Knights* 581, Proclus *h.* vii, Orpheus *h.* xxxii, *IG.* xiv. ii. 1389. Paus. iv. 17. 2 mentions a hymn in Doric by Gitiadas.

1. **ἐρυσίπτολιν**: the epithet occurs Z 305, *h.* xxviii. 3 of Athena, and is explained in v. 4; cf. also ῥυσίπολις γενοῦ Παλλάς Aesch. *S. c. Th.* 129, ἐρυσίπτολις Ἀθηναίη Tryphiod. 302. Another, perhaps original, form was ῥυσίπτολις as ℨ A *l.c.* This would imply ῥῡ-, and so far agrees with ἐρρύσατο v. 4. The quantity of ῥύομαι varies, see Veitch. The epithet recalls Athena πολιοῦχος (P.-W. 1946); cf. further *scol.* 2 *PLG.* iv. 643 Παλλὰς Τριτογένει' ἄνασσ' Ἀθηνᾶ | ὄρθου τήνδε πόλιν καὶ πολίτας κτλ. The reference to περθόμεναι πόληες (3) does not contradict this character. Athena sacks the enemies' city (Ἀθηναίῃ ληιτίδι K 460 quoted by ℨ Z 305).

2. Athena and Ares are very rarely united in myth or ritual. At Olympia they had a joint altar as patrons of horse-racing (Paus. v. 15. 6); Pindar (*Nem.* x. 84) brackets them as warlike deities; there was a statue of Athena in the temple of Ares at Athens (Paus. i. 8. 4), and occasionally Athena Ἀρεία or Στρατία is mentioned with Ares (Farnell i. 309, 407), but in general the Thracian God and the civilized Goddess had little in common.

3. **περθόμεναί τε πόληες**: cf. Παλλάδα περσέπολιν κλῄζω πολεμαδόκον ἁγνὰν παῖδα Διὸς μεγάλου δαμάσιππον Lamprocles ℨ Ar.

Nub. 967, περσέπτολις Callim. *h.* v. 43, ἑλέπτολις Orph. *Lith.* 679, πτολίπορθος *ep.* Kaibel 768. 7, Tryphiod. 390.

4. **ἰόντά τε νισόμενόν τε**, 'going and coming'. This is one of the cases where νίσ(σ)ομαι has the sense of returning, as νόστος always.

5. With the formula cf. Ion of Chios i. 15 χαῖρε δίδου δ' αἰῶνα, hymns xv and xx, Callim. *Jov.* fin.

XII

Hymn to Hera

This hymn alone in the collection (except viii, which is unique in other respects) has no verse of farewell, or concluding address to the deity. There seems to be no probable explanation of the peculiarity. Possibly the hymn is the opening of a longer poem.

For other hymns see Alcman *fr.* 16, Orph. *h.* xvi.

1. **ἀείδω**: the lengthening of the α in arsi is not Homeric except at ρ 519. See Veitch, and add xviii. 1, *Il. parv.* 1, Theognis 4, etc. ἀείδειν xxxii. 1 is uncertain.

2. **βασίλειαν**: cf. Pindar *Nem.* i. 39, *ep.* Kaibel 268. 3, 822. 7, Nonnus viii. 207. For Basilis and Basilia as cult titles of Hera in Argos, Lebadea, and Pisidia see P.-W. viii. 1. 382.

4. **κυδρήν**: Hes. *Theog.* 328 Διὸς κυδρὴ παράκοιτις. For J's κυδνήν (= κε̆δνήν) cf. the v. ll. ο 26, Ap. Rh. iv. 1333. For Hera's position in Olympian society cf. Δ 58, *h.* v. 41.

XIII

Hymn to Demeter

This cento, as Gemoll calls the hymn, is formed from the longer hymn to Demeter (1 = *h. Dem.* 1, 2 = *h. Dem.* 493) except for the third line, which occurs in Callim. *Dem.* 134 as far as πόλιν. But, although obviously a patchwork, the hymn is not necessarily later than Callimachus. The Alexandrine poet might perhaps have disdained to borrow from such a source; but both he and the hymn-writer may have taken the sufficiently commonplace χαῖρε θεὰ καὶ τήνδε σάου πόλιν from an older hymn. Guttmann's view, that ἄρχε δ' ἀοιδῆς is a mark of late work, is rightly criticized by Gemoll; it is addressed to Demeter herself, who inspires, and so may be said to begin, the recitation; cf. θ 499 ὁ δ' ὁρμηθεὶς θεοῦ ἤρχετο, Alcman *fr.* 45 Μῶσ' ἄγε . . . ἄρχ' ἐρατῶν ἐπέων, Pindar *Nem.* iii. 10.

2. **Περσεφόνειαν**: the Homeric form. The aspirate (*x p* D and Orph. *h.* xli. 5) may be due to the forms Φερσεφόνα(η), Φερσέφασσα, Φερ(ρ)έφαττα. See Förster *Der Raub der Pers.* 276.

3. **σάου**: this form is a variant for σάω ρ 595, Hedylus ap. Ath. 486 B, *Anth. Pal.* vi. 157. 2, the sole form Callim. *Epigr.* 35, Cougny i. 115. 5, *Anth. Pal.* viii. 37, xiii. 2. 4, Quintus xii. 153; on the other hand σάω is given alone in ν 230, Callim. *Cer.* 134, *Aet.* 88, *Anth. Pal.* xxii. 2, *Inscr. gr. metr.* Preger 63. 4. σάου is supported by Nauck *Mélanges* iv. 134, K.-B. ii. 545. σάοζ' in the epigr. Polyb. iv. 33. 3 is presumably the result of σάω (with ωζ' written above), as Σ Callim. iv. 22 σαοῖ· σώζει.

XIV

Hymn to the Mother of the Gods [1]

The goddess commonly identified by the Greeks with Rhea and the Asiatic Cybele and occasionally with Demeter [2] was widely worshipped from early times as simply μήτηρ θεῶν. At Athens her cult in the Μητρῷον was important (see Frazer on Paus. i. 3. 5), she had a festival at Amorgos (*Metroa*, *IG.* xii. 7. 237. 64) and a public offering at Cos (Paton and Hicks, *Inscr. of Cos* 402). In general, however, the Mother of the Gods appears to have been more honoured in private worship than in public cult.[3] The earliest literary mention of her elsewhere is in Herodotus iv. 76.

[1] See P.-R. 638, Nilsson *GF.* 439.

[2] E.g. Suidas *in* βάραθρον, μητραγύρτης; for the quite early identification of Demeter and Cybele see on *h.* ii, p. 115 above.

[3] *IG.* xii. 3. 436 from Thera records the private dedication of land to her, and provision for two sacrifices a year; dedications from Thera *ib.* 437, 438; a *collegium* Ματρὸς θεῶν *IG.* xii. 1. 162. 5. Further references to her

The absence of a personal name (Rhea or Cybele) in the hymn is therefore no indication of lateness. Nor is there any question of Orphic influence; the poem is far removed from the spirit of Orphic compositions and, as Baumeister remarks, is quite 'Homeric'. Two Orphic hymns are dedicated to the Goddess: of these *h.* xiv mentions Ῥέα by name, *h.* xxvii calls her the Mother of the Gods.

1. For Rhea cf. *h.* ii. 60, 442, 459, v. 43. She appears as Mother of the Gods in O 187, Hes. *Theog.* 453, 625, 634; as Mother of Gods and men Orph. *h.* xiv. 9, xxvii. 7. Cybele similarly is μάτηρ θεῶν Pind. *dith.* 79 b, cf. Ar. *Birds* 876 μεγάλῃ μητρὶ θεῶν καὶ ἀνθρώπων.

2. **Μοῦσα λίγεια**: cf. xvii. 1, ω 62, Stesich. *fr.* 44, Alcman *fr.* 1, Terpander *fr.* 6, *fr. lyr. adesp.* 33.

Διὸς θυγάτηρ μεγάλοιο: for the phrase cf. H 24, Antim. *Theb. fr.* 1, *Certamen* 152.

3. **βρόμος αὐλῶν** = *h.* iv. 452; cf. *Anth. Pal.* vi. 165. 5 τυπάνου βρόμον, 217. 5 Κυβέλης ἱερὸν βρόμον, Ap. Rh. i. 1139 ῥόμβῳ καὶ τυπάνῳ Ῥείην Φρύγες ἱλάσκονται. The variant τυμπ- is also found in Apollonius and the Anthology (e.g. Cougny vi. 124. 2), and as a v. l. Strabo 471 and in Aesch. *fr.* 56. 10.

4, 5. Cf. *h.* v. 70 λύκοι χαροποί τε λέοντες, 74 κατὰ σκιόεντας ἐναύλους, hymn *IG. ed. min.* iv. 131 χαροποὶ λέοντες ἢ πολιοὶ λύκοι. The lion is the constant symbol of the Mother in art from the time of Phidias (see Rapp in Roscher ii. 1644).

5. **ὑλήεντες ἔναυλοι** = xxvi. 8.

6 = ix. 7.

XV

Hymn to Heracles

As the compound λεοντόθυμος is not otherwise known in classical literature it has been thought that the title of the hymn is Byzantine. There is not the faintest likelihood that the Byzantines did anything to the Hymns except copy them and

worship will be found in *IG.* iv. 659. 2. 700 (Argos), *ib.* 1034 (Epidaurus), *ib.* vii. 560, 562, 3216, 3315, 3378 (Boeotia).

make a few notes upon them (p. lxxxii). For the compound cf. λεοντόχλαινος *Anth. Plan.* iv. 94, λεοντοδάμαν poet. ap. Lucian. *pro imag.* 19 of Orion's dog, λεοντομάχαν Theocr. *ep.* xxii, and others in the lexx.; for the elements θυμολέοντα E 639, H 228, δ 724, 814, Hes. *Theog.* 1007, Ar. *Ran.* 1041, poet. ap. Lucian. *Philopatr.* 25, Nicander *Ther.* 671, Arist. *Peplos* 18, *Anth. Pal.* ix. 524. 9, *IG. Sic. Ital.* 1003, θυμολέαινα Paul. Silent. *Anth. Pal.* vi. 299. 7, θρασυλέων title of a play by Menander *CAF.* iii. 69 (Θρασυλέων οἶμαι ἦν ὄνομα αὐτῷ ἢ ἄλλο τι τοιοῦτον συμπεπλεγμένον θηρίῳ), cf. Julian *Misop.* 349 c, Ael. *ep.* 9 fin., ἐχθρολέων *ep.* Kaibel 96. 3 = Cougny ii. 172. 3, ἐρεβινθολέων Alciphr. i. 23; apart *Anth. Pal.* vii. 344 b 1 (Callim.) ἀλλ' εἰ μὴ θυμόν γε Λέων ἐμὸν οὔνομά τ' εἶχεν (loqu. leo), Bacchyl. i. 141 λέοντος θυμό[ν ἔχων, *orac.* ap. Plut. *Lucull.* 12 μεγάθυμε λέον, Tyrtaeus *fr.* 10.

The alternative titles of other hymns (xiii, xiv, xxiii, xxv, xxx, xxxiii) may have originated at an early period. The view that the hymn is Attic because Heracles was first worshipped in Attica (Diod. iv. 39) is a mere supposition. As the hymn agrees in sentiment with λ 602 sq. which were condemned as Onomacritean, and with the longer passage in Hesiod's *Catalogi* Ox. pap. 2075 where eight lines are obelized, it has undergone the same influence and is doubtless of the sixth century or later.

In general see Gruppe in P.-W. suppl. iii. 910–1121, Farnell *HC.* 94–174, Robert *Held.* 422–648. Cf. the Orphic hymn xii.

5. The alternatives resemble those in *h.* x. The version of *x p* is unexceptionable (O 639 Εὐρυσθῆος ἄνακτος ἀγγελίης); that of M has no δέ to follow πολλὰ μέν, its ἀεθλεύων κραταιῶς is without construction or metre, and neither κραταιῶς nor the phrase ἔξοχα ἔργα occur elsewhere. Hesiod imperfectly adapted is perhaps the source of these v. ll. Cf. ἀπήμαντος *Theog.* 955 with πημαίνετ', ἔξοχ' ἀεξομένοιο βροτήσια ἔργα πένεσθαι *OD* 773 with ἔξοχα ἔργα.

7. Cf. λ 602 αὐτὸς δὲ μετ' ἀθανάτοισι θεοῖσι | τέρπεται ἐν θαλίῃς καὶ ἔχει καλλίσφυρον Ἥβην, Hes. *Catal.* pap. Ox. 2075 *fr.* 1 *col.* ii. 17 ζωει δ ενθα περ αλλοι ολυμπια δωματ εχον[τες | ἀθανατος και αγηρος εχων καλλ[ισ]φυρον ηβη[ν]. Lucian *dial. deor.* xvi. 1 borrows from λ or Hesiod. For the marriage of Heracles and

Hebe cf. Hes. *Theog.* 950, Sappho *h.* 48 B, Pind. *Nem.* i. 71, x. 18, *Isthm.* iv. 59, and reff. to later literature in P.-W. vii. 2581. In art it was represented on a silver altar by Naucydes in the Argive Heraeum (Paus. ii. 17. 6) and on two surviving reliefs of the fifth century B.C. (see Roscher i. 2241), and was a favourite subject with vase-painters (id. i. 1870, P.-W. vii. 2582). For the cult of Hebe, important in the N. Peloponnese and Attica, see P.-W. vii. 2759. There Hebe was connected with Hera. In cult the association of Hebe and Heracles is rare, and is derived from mythology. It is attested for Cos by Cornutus 31, and ἐν τῇ Εὐρώπῃ by Mnaseas *fr.* 11. Hebe is included with Hercules in a common offering to Helios, Athena, and other deities on an Egyptian inscription (*Österr. Jahresbericht.* 1910 Beibl. 35).

8. **καλλίσφυρον Ἥβήν**: Theocr. xvii. 32 λευκοσφύρου Ἥβας.

9. **δίδου δ᾽ ἀρετήν** κτλ. = xx. 8, Callim. *Iov.* 96. Cf. διδοι δ αρεταν [τε και ολβον inscr. from Ptoeum Buck *Class. Philol.* iv. 76. 437. The phrase is conventional and applicable to any deity, though Heracles was specially the patron of manly virtue (cf. αὐτὸν ἀλεξητῆρα κακῶν, αὐτόν σε δοτῆρα | παντοίης ἀρετῆς κλῄζομεν Ἡράκλεις *IG.* xiv. 1003), both on the battlefield and in the gymnasium (Farnell *HC.* 147), and thence in a general sense, as is shown by his prominence as the prototype of the Stoic 'God's athlete'. Like Hephaestus (xx. 5) Heracles was a bringer of civilization and its arts (P.-W. *suppl.* iii. 1010), and was interested, though this aspect is more certainly attested for the Hellenes of Italy than of Greece, in commerce and therefore in wealth (P.-W. *l.c.* 1015, Farnell, *HC.* 153).

XVI

Hymn to Asclepius[1]

There are no data for determining the place of composition; a certain antiquity may be inferred from the citation of 1–3 in Σ Pindar *Pyth.* iii. 14.

The original nature of Asclepius, heroic or divine, is a matter

[1] See Rose *Handbook* 139, P.-R. 514, Roscher i. 615, P.-W. ii. 1642, Nilsson *GF.* 408, Farnell *HC.* 234 (and on Pindar), where the fullest recent discussion will be found.

of controversy. In Homer he is king of Tricca; his dynasty lasted through Podalirius and Machaon, who appear at Troy, to Alexanor and Sphyrus sons of Machaon (Paus. ii. 11. 5, 23. 4. The names are different, *ib.* 38. 6). In Homer there is no hint that this prince, who like his contemporaries learned medicine in the school of Chiron, was more than mortal or more than exceptionally proficient in a science which was part of heroic education. In Hesiod he has become the son of Apollo and in the end is destroyed by Zeus for bringing the dead to life. Here as in Pindar (*Pyth.* iii. 51), where Asclepius uses soft spells and gentle potions and charms hung round the limbs, he is a magical healer (θελκτῆρ' ὀδυνάων).

The story of the birth to which allusion is here made is that first given by Hesiod *frr.* 122–5. It appears definitely to be a local legend connected with the Lapith house, and belonging to a time earlier than the tribal movements which turned the political map of Thessaly which we find in the Catalogue and *h.* iii. 216 into that of historical times. The story given by Hesiod remained substantially the same throughout antiquity. The only serious rival was the Messenian claim that A. was the son of Arsinoe (Apollod. iii. 10. 3 and further reff. in Frazer's note).[1] In the main the Hesiodic version persisted with minor variations, such as were necessary to support the claims of Epidaurus (Paus. ii. 26. 3) or Tricca (Strabo 647) to be the birthplace of the God.

In the story of Coronis as given by Hesiod has been incorporated a popular story of the *Just-so* type, 'why the crow is black' (cf. the story explaining why the crow's call means rain, Aelian *NA.* i. 47, Eratosth. *Catast.* 41). This characteristically is omitted by Pindar, and by Pausanias also. It formed part of the accepted version and is given by most of our authorities, e.g. Ant. Lib. 20. 7. It told how Apollo loved Coronis daughter of the Lapith King Phlegyas, who lived in the Dotian plain on the Twin Hills (Hesiod), or the town Lacereia (Pindar). Before the birth of her child she was married to (Hesiod) or indulged

[1] For the possibility of an Arcadian version based upon a confusion with Elatus son of Lycaon see on *h.* iii. 210. If true it had no importance, as the obscurity of Cynaethus' version shows.

a passion for (Pindar, Ant. Lib. 20. 7) a mortal, and for this sin was killed either by Artemis or by Apollo himself. Apollo took the child from its mother's body and gave it to Chiron to rear.

The sequel of the story exhibits the servitude of Apollo to Admetus as a consequence of the blasting of Asclepius. This confirms the view that the legend was originally Thessalian.

Other hymns to Asclepius are found *IG. ed. min.* iv. 135 (Isyllus), *IG.* iii. 1. 171, xiv. 967 B, 1015, *ep.* Kaibel 1027, 1035, Orph. *h.* lxvii, Hippol. *Elench.* iv. 23. 3, Origen *c. haeres.* iv. 42. Herondas iv opens with a hymn to Asclepius. Sophocles wrote a paean (Philostr. *vit. Apoll.* iii. 17), a poet in Stobaeus *ecl.* i. 31 A 3 has θείω ἰατῆρος τ' Ἀσκληπιοῦ ὀλβιοδώτα. A title preserved by Hesychius (ἀγλαόπης· ὁ Ἀσκληπιός· Λάκωνες) is unexplained.

1. **ἰητῆρα νόσων Ἀσκληπιόν** = Orph. *fr.* 160. 12 (Abel), 297 a (Kern); cf. ἰητὴρ πάντων Ἀσκληπιέ Orph. *h.* lxvii. 1, ἰητῆρι νόσων φαεσιμβρότῳ Ἀπόλλωνι *ep.* Kaibel 798. 1.

2. **δῖα Κορωνίς**: cf. Ap. Rh. iv. 617. On the story of Coronis see the introduction, for theories of her connexion with the crow (κορώνη) Frazer on Paus. ii. 11. 7. Many personal names in Greek and Latin, in historical as well as legendary times, denote a bird or animal. There is no reason to read into the legendary any more than into the more historical examples an esoteric significance. The meaning of Coronis may have affected the form of the story, it may have caused the scene to be laid at Lacereia (λακέρυζα κορώνη Hesiod *OD.* 745) in many versions, and it is almost certainly the reason of the inclusion in the legend of the story 'how the crow became black'. But in itself Coronis is a real proper name belonging to this district; cf. Coronos the Lapith from the Dotian plain (Soph. *fr.* 386), son of Caeneus and father of Leonteus who represented the Lapith house at Troy B 746.

3. On the Dotian plain or argos, its river Amyros (from which it was also called Ἀμυρικὸν πεδίον), and its town Lacereia see *Catalogue* p. 122, *Origins* 113. The present passage resembles Hesiod *Eoeae fr.* 122

ἢ οἵη διδύμους ἱεροὺς ναίουσα κολωνοὺς
Δωτίῳ ἐν πεδίῳ πολυβότρυος ἄντ' Ἀμύροιο
νίψατο Βοιβιάδος λίμνης πόδα παρθένος ἀδμής, cl. *fr.* 246.

Cf. also a verse in Plut. *qu. conv.* 748 B ἀνὰ Δώτιον ἀνθεμόεν πεδίον, Antim. Λυδή *fr.* 1 γαίης ἔκτοθι Δωτιάδος. The situation is described by Strabo 442 πλησίον τῆς ἄρτι λεχθείσης Περραιβίας καὶ τῆς Ὄσσης καὶ ἔτι τῆς Βοιβηίδος λίμνης ἐν μέσῃ τῇ Θετταλίᾳ, λόφοις δὲ ἰδίοις περικλειόμενον. The δίδυμα ὄρη had been colonized by Delphians *ib.* 647. Cf. also Steph. *in* Δώτιον with many quotations. Dotis was the mother by Ares of Phlegyas father of Coronis and ancestor of the Lapith Kings, Apollod. iii. 5. 5.

4. Cf. *orac.* ap. Hendess 34. 1 ὦ μέγα χάρμα βροτοῖς βλαστὼν Ἀσκλήπιε πᾶσιν | ὃν Φλεγυὴς ἔτικτεν ἐμοὶ φιλότητι μιγεῖσα | ἱμερόεσσα Κορωνὶς ἐνὶ κραναῇ Ἐπιδαύρῳ, *orac.* v. 48 Wolff ὦ μέγα πᾶσιν χάρμα βροτοῖσιν, carm. pop. 47. 18 Bergk = *ep.* Kaibel suppl. 1025 e ὄνειαρ βροτοῖς, Isyllus 52 Diehl τὸν νόσων παύστορα δωτῆρα ὑγιείας, μέγα δώρημα βροτοῖς.

θελκτῆρ' ὀδυνάων: see introd. Cf. θέλγων ἀνθρώπων πολυάλγεα πήματα νούσων Orph. *h.* lxvii. 2, θελγηθρον ανε[ιων *ep.* Kaibel 1032.

5. **λίτομαι**: the form is frequent in the *Orphica*, see Veitch. It is no longer read at xix. 48. Wünsch *Aus einem griech. Zauberpapyrus* 1911 v. 2566 λίτομαι σε ἄνασσα.

XVII

Hymn to the Dioscuri[1]

The lines are no doubt an abbreviation of the longer hymn to the Dioscuri (xxxiii), just as the following hymn is borrowed from iv. Lines 3, 4 are copied with variations from xxxiii. 4, 5. The hymn was apparently not intended for a prelude, as the verse of transition (xxxiii. 19) is here omitted.

1. **ἀείσεο**: the solitary instance of the aor. imper. middle; in xx. 1 ἀείδεο is equally solitary. ἀείσεο was maintained by Buttmann (K.-Z. ii. 103, Veitch *in* Ἀείδω).

5. M's reading had its origin in a graphical corruption of ἐπιβήτορες. Cf. *h.* Apoll. 457 ἐκ μὴ τοῦ δέ for ἐκβῆτ' οὐδέ.

[1] See Introduction to xxxiii.

XVIII

Hymn to Hermes

The shorter hymn to Hermes is merely an abstract from the longer, as is the case with the preceding hymn to the Dioscuri. Neither contains any other indication of the date of its composition, which remains quite uncertain. Nor is the reason for the existence of these abbreviations at all obvious. The original hymn to Hermes (iv) is of course too long to have served as a prelude to an ordinary recitation of epic poetry: it would therefore be natural to suppose that xviii was an abstraction for the use of rhapsodists. But the original hymn to the Dioscuri (xxxiii) hardly exceeds the limits of the usual preludes, and it is not easy to see why it should have been further shortened. Perhaps even a hymn of moderate compass came to be thought excessive by rhapsodists who were anxious to begin the actual recitation. The prelude had become a mere convention, just as a few bars of *God save the King* are now taken to represent the entire national anthem at the conclusion of a play.

2–9 = *h.* Herm. 2–9 with a few variations: 4 *Ἄτλαντος θυγάτηρ* = *νύμφη ἐυπλόκαμος*, 5 *ἀλέεινεν* = *ἠλεύαθ'*, 6 *ἄντρῳ ναιεταόυσα παλισκίῳ* = *ἄντρον ἔσω ναίουσα παλίσκιον*, 8 *εὖτε* = *ὄφρα*, 9 *λάνθανε δ'* = *λήθων*.

10 = *h.* Herm. 579.

12. **χαριδῶτα**: for these words see on i. 2. The *χάρις*, which Hermes has himself received as the special gift of Zeus (iv. 575), he bestows on mortals (*Ἑρμείαο ἕκητι διακτόρου ὅς ῥά τε πάντων | ἀνθρώπων ἔργοισι χάριν καὶ κῦδος ὀπάζει* o 319). A cult of Hermes Charidotes existed at Samos in which a general licence to steal and pick pockets was accorded to the worshippers at the festival (Plut. *qu. gr.* 55). Charidotes or Charitodotes is also recorded as a cult title of Dionysus in association with the epithet Meilichios, and as a cult title of Zeus in association with his aspects as Ktesios and Epikarpios. These analogies and the nature of the ritual suggest that Hermes Charidotes at Samos was a God of

fruitfulness. See further Halliday *The Greek Questions of Plutarch*, p. 206.

δῶτορ ἐάων = xxix. 8, Callim. *Iov.* 91, θ 335, hymn *IG.* iii. 1. 171.

XIX

Hymn to Pan[1]

This hymn, ten lines shorter than that to Dionysus, describes some functions of Pan, as God of sheep, as a hunter, as a piper, a gamboller and tumbler among the nymphs, who accompany him over the hills and sing round the wells about the Olympian Gods and especially Hermes, how he begat Pan and showed him in heaven.

The style is vigorous, abrupt, jerky, and even difficult to follow (14–15); it runs to strings of epithets (2, 5–6, 37, 39). Aspects of nature are described more abundantly and minutely than is usual in epos (4, 8–14, 25–6), in a style resembling drama.

Date of the hymn.

Though the poem cannot be dated with any certainty, scholars are substantially agreed that it is one of the latest in the collection and can hardly have been composed before the age of Pindar at the earliest. This view is supported by mythological considerations. No doubt the wood-spirits who appear in semi-caprine form[2] belong to the oldest creations of Greek folk-lore, but Pan, the shepherd God of Arcadia, has no place among the Gods of Homer and Hesiod, and scarcely won any recognition in literature before the Persian Wars. Until that period his importance seems in fact to have been purely Arcadian and local; hence no doubt the inference of Herodotus (ii. 145) that he was the most recent of Hellenic deities. The earliest reference to him is a

[1] See Farnell v. 431, Nilsson *GF.* 443, P.-R. 738, Roscher iii. 1347, Roscher *die Sagen von der Geburt des Pan* Philologus 1894, Nestle *Archiv f. Religionswissenschaft* 1910, xiii. 467–73. For the etymology of the name, see on 47.

[2] See Mannhardt *AWFK.* ch. iii.

quotation from Epimenides in Σ Theocr. I. 3, Σ Eur. *Rhes.* 36, in which Pan and Arcas are said to be the twin sons of Zeus and Callisto. In Pindar he is a mere attendant of the Great Mother (*Pyth.* iii. 78, *fr.* 6. 1 Ματρὸς μεγάλας ὀπαδέ). It is therefore difficult to believe that a hymn which shows so developed a conception of Pan's nature and Pan-Hellenic importance could have been the product of the seventh or early sixth century, in which all other literature passes over the God in silence, and art (for which see Roscher iii. 1407) ignores him.

On the other hand the hymn does not appear to be Alexandrine. Forms such as πίσῃ (2), τόθι (25), Ἑρμείην (28), ὤν (32), χέρα (40) are foreign to the oldest stage of epic, but there is little or nothing in the language which cannot be paralleled in the really ancient hymns. νύμφη (34) for 'daughter' is un-Homeric, and a number of ἅπαξ λεγόμενα (φιλόκροτος 2, χοροήθης 3, ἀνακέκλομαι, ἀγλαέθειρος 5, αὐχμήεις 6, μηλοσκόπος 11, λιγύμολπος 19, τερατωπός 36) are noticeable, but may belong to an early stage of language. The hymn reads like the product of a good period, perhaps the fifth century.

Place of composition.

The hymn treats of an Arcadian God, and mentions his birth on Cyllene, but as the cult of Pan became the common property of the Greeks from the beginning of the fifth century or a little earlier, there is no internal evidence of locality. For the view of Baumeister and Wilamowitz (*Aus Kydathen* 224) that the hymn is Athenian no reason can be given except that Pan became a favourite at Athens after the battle of Marathon, when his cult, if known before to the Athenians, was first officially organized[1]. The hymn contains no allusion to Pan's services at Marathon, his character is entirely pacific. He is a hunter but no warrior. B.'s further suggestion, that the hymn served as a proem to Homeric recitations at the Panathenaea, is mere guess-work.

Integrity of the hymn.

The unity of the hymn is sufficiently obvious, though the *motif* does not lie in a single episode, as in the hymns to Demeter and

[1] Herod. vi. 105, Simonid. *fr.* 133, Milchöfer *AZ.* 1880, 214.

Aphrodite. There is no question of interpolated lines. The attempt of Groddeck to divide it into two parts, the first (1–27) relating to Pan and the Nymphs, the second (28–47) describing the birth of the God, requires no comment. It may seem singular that the birth of Pan is narrated at the end of the hymn and the chief role given to Hermes, but the order is the same as in xxvii, which ends with a choir directed by Artemis which tells her birth and that of Apollo.

Other poems to Pan: Castorio ap. Clearch. *fr.* 68 (Diehl ii. 261), *scol. anon.* 4, *IG. Sic. Ital.* 1014, Pindar *fr.* 95 (vit. ii West. p. 97), Aratus vit. i. 86, iii. 20 West.

1. **ἀμφί**: see on vii. 1.

Ἑρμείαο φίλον γόνον: the genealogies vary. Roscher (*Philologus* 1894) gives a complete list. For Hermes as the father cf. Herod. ii. 145, Lucian *dial. deor.* 22, *Anth. Plan.* iv. 229, the epithet ἑρμόπαν Choerob. *in Theod. can.* 261. 8.

2. **αἰγιπόδην**: this form is preserved 37, *Anth. Pal.* vi. 57. 3, ix. 330. 2 and is rightly restored here.

Numerous epithets alluded to the goat-footed Pan (αἰγίπαν); e.g. Simon. *fr.* 33 τραγόπουν, Herod. ii. 46 τραγοσκελέα, Ar. *Ran.* 230 κεροβάτας, Theocr. *ep.* xiii. 6, *Anth. Pal.* ix. 433. 6, *IG.* xii. 3. 199 αἰγιβάταν, Orph. *h.* xi. 5 αἰγομέλες, Nonnus xxiii. 151 αἰγείοις πόδεσσι, *Anth. Pal.* vi. 35. 1 αἰγώνυχι.

δικέρωτα: so Thespis *fr.* 4, *Anth. Pal.* ix. 124, Orph. *h.* xxxiv. 25, δικραίρῳ *Anth. Pal.* vi. 32, κερασφόρος Lucian *l.c.*, αἰγοπρόσωπον Herod. *l.c.*, Πᾶνες κερααλκέες Nonnus xiv. 72, ὑψικέρως id. xvi. 187, ἀληθὴς Ζεὺς ὁ κεράστης Orph. *fr.* xi. 12, δισσοκέρας *orac.* v. 91–3 Wolff, Bruchmann p. 186.

3. **ἄμυδις**: not in Homer.

χοροήθεσι: ἅπ. λεγ., like the alteration χορογηθέσι. Cf. χοροπαίγμονες Orph. *h.* xxiv. 2 (Gemoll).

4. **αἰγίλιπος**: on the unknown derivation see Boisacq.

κατ᾽ . . . στείβουσι: a tmesis for καταστείβουσι (καταστείψας πέδον Soph. *OC.* 467). κατὰ by itself would mean 'down', as of waterfalls in the Homeric collocation κατ᾽ αἰγίλιπος πέτρης Ι 15, Π 4. Cf. Max. π. καταρχῶν 522 νομὸν . . . ἐπιστείβοντα πόδεσσιν.

5. **νόμιον**: of Pan *Anth. Pal.* vi. 96. 6, ix. 217. 4, Nonnus xv.

417 al. There was a temple of Pan under this title on the *νόμια ὄρη* near Lycosura Paus. viii. 38. 11.

ἀγλαέθειρον: the adj. is conventional, as in *ἀγλαόκαρπος, ἀγλαόδωρος*, 'fine'.

6. Pan's province was the hills of Arcadia, the chief of which (Lycaeus, Cyllene, Maenalus, Parthenion) were sacred to him. Soph. *Aj.* 695 ὦ Πὰν Πὰν ἁλίπλαγκτε Κυλλανίας χιονοκτύπου | πετραίας ἀπὸ δειράδος φάνηθ', *OT.* 1100 ὀρεσσιβάτα, *Anth. Pal.* ix. 142. 1 κρημνοβάταν, *ib.* 217. 4 ὑλιβάτην, poet. ap. Stob. *Ecl.* i. 387. 31 πετροβάτα, *Anth. Pal.* vi. 32. 3 φιλοσκοπέλῳ, 106. 5 βουνῖτα, 79. 1 λοφιῆτα, ix. 824. 2 ὀρειώτα, *ep.* Cougny vi. 129. 2 βαίνων ὑλήεντα κατ' οὔρεα. Cf. in gen. Eur. *Electra* 699 sq.

νιφόεντα: so Soph. *Aj. l.c.*, Castorio ap. Ath. 455 A σὲ τὸν βολαῖς νιφοκτύποις δυσχείμερον | ναίονθ' ἕδραν θηρονόμε Πὰν χθόν' Ἀρκάδων | κλῄσω, Eur. *Telephus fr.* 697. 2 ὅς τε πέτρον Ἀρκάδων δυσχείμερον | Πὰν ἐμβατεύεις.

7. **κορυφὰς ὀρέων**: ὑψηλῶν ὀρέων κορυφάς M 282, Anacr. 2. 5 (ὑψηλάς).

8. **διὰ ῥωπήια πυκνά** = Ψ 122.

9. **ἐφελκόμενος**, 'drawn', i.e. 'attracted by'. The metaphorical passive is less frequent than the middle, but occurs Thuc. i. 42. 4 μηδὲ . . . τούτῳ ἐφέλκεσθε and often in the *Anthology* (vii. 707. 8, 87. 6, xv. 37. 33 al.). The simple ἕλκεσθαι met. is in Plato *Soph.* 265 E, *rep.* 494 E, Polyb. v. 87 B, xvi. 14. 9, and cf. παρελκομένῃ τῇ συνηθείᾳ Aristaen. i. 19. Matthiae took it literally 'wafted, drifting on', but goats do not take to the water, they drink it, *pascentes a flumine reice capellas Ecl.* iii. 96 (Roscher), cf. the stag κ 159 ποταμὸν δὲ κατήιεν . . . πιόμενος.

11. **μηλοσκόπον**: G.'s correction of the accent is right. From a σκοπία shepherds watched their sheep. Cf. ὑλησκόπῳ Πανί *Anth. Pal.* vi. 107, ὑλοσ[κοπωι] *BCH.* xxvii. 295.

12. **ἀργινόεντα**, 'white', of calcareous rocks. See on iii. 40.

14. **ὀξέα δερκόμενος**: Hesych. Ὑπόσκοπον χέρα· Αἰσχύλος. ὥσπερ οἱ ἀποσκοποῦντες· οὕτω κελεύει σχηματίσαι τὴν χεῖρα ὥσπερ τοὺς Πᾶνας ποιοῦσι, a dance Ath. 629 F ἦν δὲ ὁ σκώψ τῶν ἀποσκοπούντων τι σχῆμα ἄκραν τὴν χεῖρα ὑπὲρ τοῦ μετώπου κεκυρτωκότων. The gesture is described by Lucian *Philopatr.* 19 παπτήνας δὲ ἐς ἅπαντας

καὶ τὴν χεῖρα τοῖς βλεφάροις περικάμψας ἐσκοπίαζον ὀξυδερκέστατα, Sil. Ital. xiii. 340 *obtendensque manum solem infervescere fronti* | *arcet et umbrato perlustrat pascua visu*, Galen iii. 776 ὅσοι διὰ λαμπρᾶς αὐγῆς ἰδεῖν τι βούλονται πόρρωθεν ἤτοι τὰς χεῖρας ὑπὲρ τῶν ὀφθαλμῶν κατ' αὐτὰς τὰς ὀφρῦς παρατείνουσι ἢ τῶν χειρῶν ἄλλο τι μεῖζον καὶ στεγανώτερον. See Roscher *Philol.* 1894, 161, *lex.* 1401.

οἶον = μόνον, 'only at evening'. Cf. Hes. *Theog.* 26 γαστέρες οἶον, Aesch. *Ag.* 136 (gl. μόνον), Pind. *Nem.* iv. 151 (ψιλοῖ Ar.), *orac.* Herod. vii. 140 κοὺ τὸ σὸν οἶον, often later (Theocr. xxv. 199, Ap. Rh. ii. 634, *ep.* Kaibel 1027). It has been so taken in I 355 ἔνθά ποτ' οἶον ἔμιμνε.

15. **ἄγρης**: a certain correction: cf. Theocr. i. 16 ἀπ' ἄγρας | τανίκα κεκμακὼς ἀμπαύεται of Pan, xxv. 87 ἐκ βοτάνης ἀνιόντα of sheep, Ap. Rh. ii. 938 ἄγρηθεν ὅτ' οὐρανὸν εἰσαναβαίνῃ of Artemis, iii. 69 θήρης ἐξανιών of Jason. For Pan as hunter cf. Hesych. Ἀγρεύς· ὁ Πὰν παρὰ Ἀθηναίοις, ὡς Ἀπολλόδωρος, *EM.* 34. 38; ἀγρότας *Anth. Pal.* vi. 13. 2 and 188. 3, ἀγρονόμος *ib.* 154. 1, εὔθηρος *ib.* 185. 4, θηρονόμος Castorio ap. Ath. 454 F, θηρητήρ Orph. *h.* xi. 9. Cf. also Philostr. *imag.* ii. 11, Arrian *cyneg.* 35. 3, Paus. viii. 42. 3, Calpurn. 10. 3. Hunting was the natural occupation of the semi-bestial Pan and the Centaurs. When the chase was unsuccessful images of Pan were beaten by Arcadian boys with squills, Theocr. vii. 107. See further Roscher *Philol.* 1894, 154 *lex.* 1387.

δονάκων ὕπο, 'to the pipes', see on xxi. 1. The pipes are Homeric, Σ 526.

μοῦσαν ἀθύρων, 'playing his tune', cf. Ap. Rh. iii. 949 μολπὴν ἀθύρειν and on iv. 152: συρίζοντος Paus. viii. 36. 8.

17. **ἔαρος πολυανθέος**: apparently gen. of time, but an epithet in this construction is hard to find. Cf. Hes. *Scut.* 153 Σειρίου ἀζαλέοιο (Baumeister). τῶν προτέρων ἐτέων Λ 691 and ἔαρος νέον ἱσταμένοιο τ 519 are hardly parallel, δείλης ὀψίας, ἑῴας are nearer. To take the gen. with ἐν πετάλοισι, 'leaves of spring', is doubtful Greek.

The bird is the nightingale, and the reminiscence Homeric (T 578).

18. **ἀχέει**: the repetition ἐπιπροχέουσα χέει can hardly be toler-

ated. ἀχέει (on its existence see *h.* ii. 479) seems better than ἰαχεῖ (cf. *Anth. Pal.* vii. 201. 2 ἀδεῖν μέλπων ἐκπροχέεις ἰαχάν of a cicala) or ἠχέει (Julian *ep.* 186=420 C Πανὶ μέλος λιγυρὸν ἠχοῦντι).

19. **σφιν**: the use as dat. sing. is not Homeric. It is probable if not certain in Aesch. *Pers.* 759, Soph. *OC.* 1490. Pindar *Pyth.* ix. 205 and *h.* xxx. 9 are uncertain.

For Pan and the nymphs see Roscher iii. 1390 (literature), 1420 (art).

20. **πυκνά**: for the correption cf. Hes. *OD.* 567 ἀκροκνέφαιος, *fr.* 138 ὦ τέκνον, Theocr. xxii. 126 πυκνοὶ δ' ἀράβησαν ὀδόντες, Quintus vii. 15 πυκνὰ μήδεα ᾔδῃ, Emped. 185 τέχνας; Eberhard *Metr.-Beob.* i. 31.

22. **χορῶν**: for the plural cf. xxvii. 18, for the gen. see on *h.* iv. 226, 357. For Pan as a dancer cf. Pind. *fr.* 99 χορευτὴν τελεώτατον θεῶν, Aesch. *Pers.* 451 ὁ φιλόχορος Πάν, Soph. *Aj.* 696 ὦ θεῶν χοροποί' ἄναξ, *scolium* ap. Ath. 694 D ὦ Πὰν Ἀρκαδίας μεδέων κλεέννας | ὀρχηστά, poet. ap. Hephaest. c. 10 Πὰν Πελασγικὸν Ἄργος ἐμβατεύων, Orph. *h.* xi. 9 σύγχορε νυμφῶν, *Anth. Pal.* vi. 32. 2 εὐσκάρθμῳ, Philostr. *Imag.* ii. 11 and 12.

23. **διέπει**: sc. χορούς, as στρατόν B 207.

25. **τόθι**: here first as a relative, v.l. δ 229. The lexx. give for early Greek Mimnermus 11. 5, Pind. *Nem.* iv. 84.

26. For the v.l. cf. Ap. Rh. ii. 843, Moschus ii. 67.

28. **οἷόν θ'**, 'and for example'. Hermes iv. 57 declares the story of his own birth, Artemis xxvii hers and that of Apollo. They announced their pedigree.

30. Cf. *h.* v. 68. For the sheep of Arcadia cf. Bacchyl. xi. 95, Theocr. xxv. 157, *h.* iv. 2.

31. **Κυλληνίου**, 'as of Cyllene'; for the gen. after οἱ cf. ii. 37.

For Hermes Κυλλήνιος see on *h.* iv. 8, and for the same title belonging to Pan Soph. *Aj.* 695, *BCH.* xxvii. 293 υλοσ[κοπωι] κυφαρισσ[ιται] . . . σοι κυφαρισσιτα κυλλανιε, from Crete.

32. **ὧν**: see on iii. 330.

ψαφαρότριχα: the *x* family, as G. observes, offer the Ionic form.

33. **θάλε**, 'waxed, was hot'. The word is frequent of disease in Hippocrates and tragedy; it is used as here of love in verses

quoted by Plutarch *quaest. conv.* 761 B (*PLG.* iii. *fr.* 44) σὺν γὰρ ἀνδρείᾳ καὶ ὁ λυσιμελὴς ἔρως ἐπὶ Χαλκιδέων θάλλει πόλεσιν, Plato *Symp.* 203 E θάλλει καὶ ζῇ (Eros personified), Apostol. *prov.* ix. 3 ἔρως θάλλει μὲν εὐπορῶν, ἀποθνήσκει δὲ ἀπορῶν, sim. Terpander *fr.* 6 ἔνθ' αἰχμά τε νεῶν θάλλει καὶ μοῦσα λίγεια, Critias *fr.* 1. 17 δαίμων ἀφθίτῳ θάλλων βίῳ, Ariphron *PLG.* iii. 597 τέθαλε καὶ λάμπει χαρίτων ὄαρος (?), epigr. Kaibel 1028. 38 τεθαλοτος αρτιον εργου | φεγγος επ αρτιγονον βρεφος αγαγον, Arist. *Probl.* iv. 25 τοῦ μὲν οὖν ἀνδρὸς ἠμαύρωται ἡ δύναμις, τῶν δὲ θάλλει ἐπανισουμένη τῷ ἐναντίῳ, Eur. *fr.* 961 ὁ δ' ἄρτι θάλλων διοπετὴς ὅπως | ἀστὴρ ἀπέσβη, *fr.* 230. 2 ἔτι γὰρ θάλλει πενία | κακὸν ἔχθιστον, φεύγει δ' ὄλβος, of παίδευσις Antiphon Soph. *fr.* 134 ζῇ καὶ θάλλει. Ruhnken's λάθε is usually printed, owing to its air of palaeographical identity, but λαβών for βαλών iv. 256 (and perhaps *ib.* 159 v.l.) and μῦθον for θυμόν *ib.* 457 are the only plausible cases of *anagrammatismus*, and λάθε does not suit Hermes' simple psychology.

34. **νύμφη**: not elsewhere apparently for 'daughter'; the ref. is to Dryope, daughter of Dryops son of Arcas (Ant. Lib. xxii, Virgil *Aen.* x. 551). (Roscher's translation, 'bride', *Philol. l.c.* 368, and the alterations Δρυόπης, Δρυόπῃ are impossible.) An oak-spirit is appropriate as mother of Pan, whom the Arcadians called τὸν τῆς ὕλης κύριον Macrob. *Sat.* i. 22; so Chiron is son of Philyra (Hes. *Theog.* 1001) and Pholus, another centaur, of Melia (Mannhardt *AWF.* 48). Roscher however thinks the genealogy is due to the settlement of the Dryopes in the neighbourhood of Cyllene (see Immerwahr *Kulte und Myth. Ark.* 136), so that the legend may be local and Cyllenian.

36. **ἄφαρ**, 'straightway': δ 85 Λιβύην ὅθι τ' ἄρνες ἄφαρ κεραοὶ τελέθουσιν, Callim. *Apoll.* 103 εὐθύ σε μήτηρ | γείνατ' ἀοσσητῆρα.

38. **τιθήνη** = mother: so Coluthus 84, 87, 99, 174, 372. Cf. τροφός = μήτηρ Soph. *Aj.* 849, τὴν θρέψασαν, 'motherland' Lycurg. *in Leocr.* § 47.

43. The hare is a symbol of Pan on coins of Messane and possibly on those of Rhegium (Head *HN.* 109 and 154). On a coin of the former city Pan is seated on a rock caressing a hare (dated by Head 420–396 B.C.). Pan also has the λαγωβόλον Roscher iii. 1386.

46. **περίαλλα**, un-Homeric: also in Pind. *Pyth.* xi. 5.

On the close connexion of Pan and Dionysus cf. *Anth. Pal.* vi. 154, 315, *scol.* ap. Ath. (quoted on 22), Lucian *dial. deor.* 22. 3, Nonnus xliii. 10, poet. ap. Euseb. *PE.* v. 6 χρυσοκέρως βλοσυροῖο Διωνύσου θεράπων Πάν. The epithet βάγχειος occurs in cult *IG.* iv. 558, vii. 1. 155. On the termination see on *h.* iii. 496.

47. On the Greek etymologies of Pan see Roscher *Philol.* 1894. 368, *lex.* iii. 1405. The true derivation has been supposed to be from the root *pa*, in πάομαι, *pasco*, *Pales*, &c., and the termination Arcadian, as Ἀλκμάν, Ἑρμάν, Ποσοιδάν, but the assumption is highly doubtful. See Gerhard *Wiener Studien* xxxviii. 342.

48. **ἵλαμαι**: so xxi. 5, ἵληθι xx. 8, xxiii. 4. For its use in taking leave of a deity cf. Theocr. xv. 143, Ap. Rh. iv. 1773, Plato *Phaedr.* 95 A. The alternative λίσομαι is taken by Veitch to be a future (τὸ θέμα λίσσω, ὁ μέλλων λίσω *epim.* O[8] *in* Λίσσομαι an. Ox. i. 262): however we have the variants λίτομαι, λισομαι *Anth. Pal.* v. 164. (λίτομαι occurs xvi. 5.)

XX

Hymn to Hephaestus

Hephaestus[1] was possibly in origin an oriental deity of fire, whose worship reached the Greeks from Asia Minor and the adjacent islands and was later spread by Greeks in the volcanic regions of the western Mediterranean. Already in Homer he is a somewhat undignified member of the Greek pantheon, in his Hellenized form as the God of handicraft in general and smith's work in particular. At Athens, where he was associated with Athena, his cult had some importance: in Lemnos, too, his worship was evidently old and prominent. Of his cult in other parts of the Greek world we have sporadic indications, but nowhere else does it appear to have been of great significance, and no festival in his honour is known outside Attica. Only of the Attic cult have we any detailed information. It is especially to be

[1] See Rose *Handbook* 165, P.-R. i. 174, Malten in P.-W. in *Hephaistos*, Farnell v. 374, Nilsson *GF.* 429.

regretted that our knowledge of the facts regarding the Lemnian cult are so meagre.

The fact that Hephaestus and Athena were joined in a common cult at Athens, and (as far as is known) in no other Greek city, gives colour to Baumeister's suggestion that this hymn is Athenian. The two deities were worshipped together as patrons of all arts and crafts; the shops of braziers and ironmongers were near the temple of Hephaestus, in which stood a statue of Athena (Paus. i. 14. 6), and the festival called Chalceia was sacred to both (see Frazer's note *ib.*, P.-R. i. 180, 209). According to Plato (*Critias* 109 C, 112 B), Athena and Hephaestus, φιλοσοφίᾳ φιλοτεχνίᾳ τε ἐπὶ τὰ αὐτὰ ἐλθόντες, became joint patrons of Attica; cf. Solon *fr.* 13 (quoted on 5) and other references in Farnell i. 409. So close was their association that Hephaestia was a cult title of Athena in Athens (*IG.* ii. 1. 114 B, 4, ii. 4, 1659 D). Athena was Ἐργάνη, the Worker; but in a wider sense she was the giver of all civilization; Hephaestus, the Fire-god and the divine smith, gave men the skill (κλυτόμητιν 1, κλυτοτέχνην 5) which differentiated them from wild beasts.[1]

But this aspect of Athena (see on *h. Aphr.* v. 12) and Hephaestus was by no means exclusively Attic. The conjunction of the two deities as patrons of civilization (see esp. also Plato *Laws* 920 D, *Politicus* 274 C, *Protag.* 321 D) appears to have been the common property of Greek religious speculation, and found a place in the Orphic system, though the Orphics attributed the original invention of the arts of civilization, handed on by them to human kind, to the τεκτονόχειρες (πρῶτοι τεκτονόχειρες, οἳ Ἥφαιστον καὶ Ἀθήνην | δαίδαλα πάντ' ἐδίδαξαν ὅσ' οὐρανὸς ἐντὸς ἐέργει, Orph. *fr.* 92, 135 Abel, 178, 179 Kern). In Hesiod, Athena instructs Pandora, the creation of Hephaestus, in weaving (*Op.* 63), and, finally, the conjunction of Athena and Hephaestus as the divine patrons of handicraft is known to Homer. Ἀνὴρ ἴδρις ὃν Ἥφαιστος δέδαεν καὶ Παλλὰς Ἀθήνη is the description of the master jeweller, to the beauty of whose inlay work the looks of Odysseus are com-

[1] Aeschylus indeed attributes these gifts of civilization to Prometheus; but the Titan is purely a culture hero, and as such his importance is almost exclusively mythological.

pared ζ 232. We may therefore fairly look for Epic rather than Athenian influence in the mythology of this hymn.

In general cf. Alcaeus *frr.* 11–12, Orph. *h.* lxvi, *orac.* ap. Ach. Tat. 14. 3 ἔνθ' Ἥφαιστος ἔχων χαίρει γλαυκῶπιν Ἀθήνην.

1. **κλυτόμητιν**: in Homer Hephaestus is κλυτοεργός θ 345 or κλυτοτέχνης Α 571, Σ 143, 391, θ 286 etc.; cf. 5. Athena in *h.* xxviii is πολύμητις, in Orph. *fr.* 279 Abel, 347 Kern πολυεργός.

2. **ἀγλαὰ ἔργα**: here = τέχνας generally; cf. *h.* v. 11 and 15.

3. For ancient poetic accounts of the savage life of primitive man cf. Aesch. *PV.* 463, Eur. *Suppl.* 201, *fr.* 582, *fr. trag.* ap. Nauck 393, Critias *fr.* 1 (*ib.* p. 771), Moschion *fr.* 7, Lucr. v. 933, Juv. xv. 150, Cic. *de invent.* 1. 2.

5. **ἔργα δαέντες**: cf. Solon *fr.* 13. 49 ἄλλος Ἀθηναίης τε καὶ Ἡφαίστου πολυτέχνεω | ἔργα δαείς, Theocr. xvii. 81 βροτῶν ἔργα δαέντων of civilized men.

6. **τελεσφόρον εἰς ἐνιαυτόν**, 'for the full year'. The phrase occurs T 32, *h.* iii. 343 and several times in the *Odyssey.*

8. For the ending cf. xv. 9.

XXI

Hymn to Apollo

1. **ὑπὸ πτερύγων λίγ' ἀείδει**: cf. Ar. *Av.* 771 συμμιγῆ βοὴν ὁμοῦ πτεροῖς κρέκοντες ἴακχον Ἀπόλλω . . . ὄχθῳ ἐφεζόμενοι παρ' Ἕβρον ποταμόν. Aristophanes meant that the note (βοήν) blended with the wings. This is true in nature; we have been favoured with information from ornithological authorities which leaves no doubt on the point: 'the creature has such a very highly developed wind-pipe that one would suppose it associated with the production of loud sound' (Professor Mackinnon); 'the Whooper swan (*cygnus cygnus* or *cygnus musicus*) has a loud deep call described as trumpet-like, unquestionably vocal. But any one who has watched a flock of our ordinary swans flying by will probably have noticed the not unmusical sound made by the passage of air between the flight feathers' (Mr. B. W. Tucker, through Professor

Poulton). In the present passage therefore ὑπό means 'to the accompaniment of', a frequent sense. The ancients however often believed that the sound was produced by the wings only: Σ Ar. *l.c.* διὰ τῆς τῶν πτερῶν κινήσεως ὕμνουν τὸν Ἀπόλλω, Theognis 729 φροντίδες . . . ἔλακον (ἔλαχον codd.) πτερὰ ποικίλ' ἔχουσαι, Pratinas *fr.* 1. 5 οἷά τε κύκνον ἄγοντα ποικιλόπτερον μέλος, Anacreont. 58. 8 ἅτε τις κύκνος Καΰστρῳ | ποικίλον πτεροῖσι μέλπων | ἀνέμῳ συναύλος ἠχῇ, and (with other passages collected by D'Arcy Thompson *Greek Birds* 104 sq.) Philostr. *vit. Apoll.* i. 5 τὰς πτέρυγας . . . ἄραντες ἀθρόον ἤχησαν, *ib.* iii. 49, Himerius *ecl.* xiv. 5 πρὸς ᾠδὴν ἐκδιδόναι μέλλων τὰς πτέρυγας, *ib.* xxi. 1, *or.* xvii. 3 εὐτρεπίζει τὸ πτερὸν πρὸς τοὺς ὕμνους, Dio Prus. xxxiii. 43, Nonnus xxvi. 204; in gen. Hes. *Scut.* 356, Alcman i. 100, Bacchyl. xvi. 6, Eur. *HF.* 692, *Ion* 169, *Electra* 151, *IT.* 1104, *Phaethon fr.* 775. 31, 32. On the other hand the 'swan song' before death (Pratinas i. 5 (*PLG.* iii. p. 558), Aesch. *Ag.* 1145, Plato *Phaedo* 84 E, Polyb. xxx. 4. 7, xxxi. 20. 1, Chrysippus ap. Athen. 616 B, Paus. i. 30. 3) is a fable; 'a low musical sound made in the breeding season' (Tucker), 'probably epigamic, chiefly made by the males' (Poulton). Alexander of Myndos disbelieved in it Ath. 393 D, and so Aelian *VH.* i. 14, Lucian *de Elect.* 4.

3. **Πηνειόν**: the Peneus θοὰς ἐστήσατο δίνας at Apollo's birth, Callim. iv. 149 (G.); other rivers on which swans settle are the Hebrus (Ar. *l.c.*), the Pactolus (Callim. *ib.* 249), the Strymon (Moschus iii. 14), the Cayster (B 461).

4. **πρῶτόν τε καὶ ὕστατον**: cf. I 97 ἐν σοὶ μὲν λήξω σέο δ' ἄρξομαι, Hes. *Theog.* 34, 48, *fr.* 192, Theognis 2, Theocr. xvii. 3, Aratus 14, *h.* i. 18; πρώτῃ πυμάτῃ τε *h.* xxix. 5.

XXII

Hymn to Posidon

The hymn appears to be rather a prayer for safety at sea (7) than an ordinary prelude, although the phrase ἄρχομ' ἀείδειν suggests a rhapsodist. It may be compared with Hom. *ep.* vi (*vit. Herod.* 235), which, however, is more personal in tone and refers to a special occasion, whereas πλωόυσιν ἄρηγε is quite general.

For the cult and mythology of Posidon see Farnell iv. 1, Nilsson *GF.* 64, Roscher iii. 2788.

Other hymns are Orph. *h.* xvii and Arion *fr.* 3; one by Myro Eustathius 327. 11. The hymn mentioned in Xen. *Hell.* iv. 7. 4 (πάντες ὕμνησαν τὸν περὶ τὸν Ποσειδῶ παιᾶνα) was addressed to the earthquake God not to the God of the sea. Simonides wrote a hymn to Posidon Ꙅ Eur. *Med.* 5, and in connexion with the panegyris of Posidon and Amphitrite at Tenos (for which see Strabo 487) the poetess Alimoe is honoured for a hymn to Zeus (?), Posidon, and Amphitrite (*IG.* xii. 5. 812, *s.* iii B.C.), and an unknown poet for a hymn to Posidon and Amphitrite (*ib.* 813).

1. **ἀμφί**: see on vii. 1.

2. **γαίης κινητῆρα κτλ.**: cf. γῆς τε καὶ ἁλμυρᾶς θαλάσσης ἄγριον μοχλευτήν Aristoph. *Nub.* 567, κινητὴρ γᾶς Pind. *Isthm.* iv. 32.

3. **πόντιον**: the epithet, frequent in poetry, was used as a title in cult at Taenarum (Eupolis *fr.* 140 Kock) and Elatea (Ποντίῳ Ἱππομέδοντι Ποσειδῶνι *IG.* iii. 119), cf. *IG.* ix. 1. 130 (Phocis).

Ἑλικῶνα: cf. Υ 404 Ἑλικώνιον ἀμφὶ ἄνακτα. Martin's Ἑλίκην τε is disposed of by Hom. *ep.* vi (*vit. Herod.* 236) εὐρυχόρου μεδέων ἠδὲ ξανθοῦ Ἑλικῶνος. The cult of Posidon Heliconius, which at the Panionium on Mycale formed the religious centre of the Ionian federation, appears to have been common to all states which claimed Ionian descent. The derivation of the title was a puzzle in antiquity. Helice and Aegae upon the Corinthian gulf are mentioned together as sacred to Posidon in Θ 203 (for Helice cf. B 575 and for Aegae cf. N 21, Pindar *Nem.* v. 57: Strabo 386, 405, however, was perhaps rightly of opinion that N 21 referred to the Aegae in northern Euboea, see on *h.* iii. 32). It is perhaps because of this Homeric passage that the derivation of Posidon Heliconius from Helice was widely favoured in antiquity. In Helice Posidon was worshipped as Heliconius (Strabo 384), but the alleged foundation of Priene from Helice (Ꙅ Υ 404) or the participation of the men of Helice in Neleus' expedition to Ionia (Paus. viii. 24. 5) are probably inventions to justify the alleged connexion of the God of the Ionians with Helice. Though this was supported by the authority of Delphi and accepted by the Ionian States who met at the Panionium (see Diod. xv. 49: the date is clearly a little before the destruction of Helice by earthquake in 373 B.C.), it is difficult to believe that a small town in Achaea provided the chief political cult of the Ionians. Further, as Aristarchus (*Et. M.* 547. 16) pointed out, the epithet formed from Helice should be Ἑλικήϊος or Ἑλίκαιος: Heliconius can only derive from Helicon. This Clidemus *an. Bekk.* i. 326) realized when he deduced from the existence of a local cult of Posidon Heliconius at Agrae that the former name of the place was Helicon: similar testimony is borne by the desperate shift adopted by Steph. Byz. (*in* Ἑλίκη) ὁ πολίτης Ἑλίκωνιος ἀπὸ κτίστου Ἑλικῶνος. Against the derivation from Helicon is the fact that no cult of Posidon upon the mountain is known in historical times, though ἵππου κρήνη (Paus. ix. 31. 3) shows association with the God. On the other hand the importance of Boeotia in the Ionian migration, and the prevalence and antiquity there of the worship of Posidon (ἐπεὶ ἡ Βοιωτία ὅλη ἱερὰ Ποσειδῶνος, Aristarchus *l.c.*), make it probable that Heliconius must originally have been derived from Helicon. See further Farnell iv. 30, Nilsson *GF.* 74. The various attempts to evade the difficult choice between Helicon and Helice by means of foolish etymological explanations of the title, e.g. from ἕλιξ as connected with the curling wave (Welcker and Preller), or the shambling kine of Homer (Gruppe), are not worth serious consideration. The Doric form is preserved by Hesychius, Ἀλικανών· ὁ Ποσειδῶν. Σώφρων.

4. The dual character of Posidon, ὅ θ' ἵππιος ποντομέδων ἄναξ (Aesch. *Sept.* 130, cf. the invocation in Aristoph. *Eq.* 551) is as old as Homer (Ψ 307). Hence partly the appropriateness of metaphor of ships as horses of the sea: αἵ θ' ἁλὸς ἵπποι ἀνδράσι γίγνονται, περόωσι δὲ πουλὺν ἐφ' ὑγρήν δ 708, cf. ἵπποισιν ἢ κύμβαισι ναυστολεῖς χθόνα; Soph. *fr.* 127.

5. Cf. Pamphos *ap.* Paus. vii. 21. 9 ἵππων τε δμητῆρα, νεῶν τ' ἰθυκρηδέμνων: Posidon Δαμαῖος was worshipped at Corinth in

association with Athena Chalinitis (Σ Pind. *Ol.* xiii. 90). For Posidon and the origin of the horse see P.-R. 589.

σωτῆρά τε νηῶν: the double function of Posidon resembles that of the Dioscuri (see xxxiii), and the former God is also here called Soter. Almost inevitably the God of the Sea was invoked to help sailors (I 362, cf. Pind. *Isthm.* vii. 52 ἀλλὰ νῦν μοι Γαιάοχος εὐδίαν ὄπασσεν ἐκ χειμῶνος), but the title σωτήρ, frequent in the cult of the Dioscuri, is rare in that of Posidon. It occurs in an inscription of the third century B.C. at Sunium (Ἐφ. Ἀρχ. 1900, 145). But the most famous cult of Posidon Soter, at Artemisium, was commemorative not of safety at sea but of the destruction of the Persian fleet by storm (Herod. vii. 192). Posidon, as the helper of sailors, was more often addressed as Ἀσφάλιος, Ἀσφάλειος, or Ἀσφαλίων, titles originally of the earthquake God which acquired a secondary marine significance (see P.-R. 572 n. 2). Under this title Posidon was often jointly worshipped with Aphrodite Euploia (examples in P.-R. 582 n. 5), and the general practice seems to have been not to attach the title Saviour to Posidon, but to worship Posidon Asphalios in conjunction with a Saviour Deity. The worship of Zeus Soter and Posidon Asphalios at Sparta (Aristides i. 29), and that of Posidon with Athena Soteira at Asea in Arcadia (Paus. viii. 44. 4), may refer to the God of the earthquake, but marine examples are the cult of Zeus Soter and Posidon at Calauria (*Ath. Mitt.* 1895, 288), the naval inscription of the second century B.C. at Delos beginning Διὶ Σωτῆρι Ἀθάναι Σωτείραι Ποσειδᾶνι Ἀσφαλείωι *IG.* xii. 5. 913, and the dedication to Posidon Pontios of statues of ἡμίθεοι σωτῆρες *IG.* ix. 1. 130 (Phocis).

7. Hermann's *Orpheum audire videaris* is rightly refuted by Baumeister; the hymn is 'Homeric' in spirit, although the language of this line suggests Orph. *h.* lxiv. 12 ἀλλά, μάκαρ . . . εὐμενὲς ἦτορ ἔχων (quoted by Gemoll), *h.* viii. 16, and the hymn to Asclepius in Origen *c. haeres.* iv. 32, v. ll.

XXIII

Hymn to Zeus

The appearance of Themis gives the keynote of this hymn. The poet prays for the favour of the God of law and right.

For the Homeric conception of Themis see O 87, Υ 4, β 68. The relationship of Zeus and Themis is determined by the character of the Goddess and that of Zeus as the fount of authority and Θέμιστες. She is variously represented as the wife of Zeus, the second after Metis, Hes. *Theog.* 901, his ἀρχαία ἄλοχος Pindar *fr.* 30. 5. Sometimes in late authors she is an unwedded love of Zeus (Steph. *in* Ἴχναι, Apollod. i. 3. 1, Nonnus v. 620, Claudian *rapt. Pros.* i. 107), but nowhere in antagonism to Hera. Her children by Zeus were the Horae, Eunomia, Dike, and Eirene (Hes. *Theog.* 901), and the Fates, Clotho, Lachesis, and Atropos (*ib.* 904).

Sanctuaries of Zeus Agoraios, Themis and the Fates stood in juxtaposition on the road outside the Neïtan gate of Thebes (Paus. ix. 25. 4). Like Dike (Hes. *OD.* 258, Orph. *h.* lxii. below, cf. Lobeck *Aglaophamus* 396), Themis was Διὸς ξενίου πάρεδρος Pind. *Ol.* viii. 28, cf. Plut. *Alex.* 52, *ad princ. inerud.* 4, Eust. on A 63, Aesch. *Suppl.* 360, Soph. *El.* 1064. In Bacchyl. xi. 51 the title πάρεδρος is applied to Hera as wife of Zeus, and whether Themis is here the wife or merely the adviser must remain uncertain in view of the ambiguous language of v. 3.

Orphic influence has been supposed, from the passage Orph. *h.* lxii. 2 (of Dike) ἣ καὶ Ζηνὸς ἄνακτος ἐπὶ θρόνον ἱερὸν ἵζει. But the connexion of Zeus with Dike or Themis is frequent in poetry, and the hymn is not less 'Homeric' than xx–xxii.

Besides the hymns of Cleanthes and Callimachus, Orph. *h.* xv, xix, xx are addressed to Zeus. Mentions survive of the hymns of Callinus (2) and Terpander (1), and of one by Simonides (Himerius *or.* v. 2).

2. **τελεσφόρον**: the epithet was personified in Telesphorus an attendant or son of Asclepius. It is applied to Μοῖρα Aesch. *PV.* 511, Δίκη Soph. *Aj.* 1390, Γῇ *IG.* ix. 1. 2452, Orph. *h.* xxvi. 2,

or. Sib. iii. 659 in rather different senses. To Zeus it applies in its most general sense, and is the equivalent of τελεσιουργός (a cult title at Miletus, see Cook *Zeus* ii. 1228) or τέλειος, which though sometimes used in a special sense corresponding to that of Hera τελεία and referring to marriage (Plut. *qu. rom.* ii. 264 B, Diod. v. 73, Σ Ar. *Thesm.* 973) referred generally to the 'accomplisher' upon whose will the completion of all things depended: Ζεὺς ἐν θεοῖσι μάντις ἀψευδέστατος καὶ τέλος αὐτὸς ἔχει Aristides ii. 51, Ζεῦ Ζεῦ τέλειε τὰς ἐμὰς εὐχὰς τέλει Aesch. *Ag.* 973, cf. *Eum.* 28, *Suppl.* 524, Pind. *Ol.* xiii. 115. An altar of Zeus Telesphoros from Phrygia is given by Körte *Ath. Mitt.* xxv. 418; for cults of Zeus Teleios at Athens see *IG.* iii. 294, at Tegea Paus. viii. 48. 6.

Θέμιστι: the unmetrical Θέμιτι may be due to the ligature στ, often misread as τ. The Σ Pind. *Ol.* x. 28 expressly read the form at O 87 where there is no trace of it in the MSS. At π 403 it is a v. l.

3. **ἐγκλιδόν**: lit. 'sideways', i.e. bending towards, or leaning on, Zeus. Weniger (Roscher v. 575) quotes the female figures on the east pediment of the Parthenon, and as the converse attitude *h.* iii. 345.

In another sense the word occurs Ap. Rh. i. 790, iii. 1008.

XXIV

Hymn to Hestia

For the cult and mythology of Hestia see Roscher i. 2605, P.-W. viii. 1257, P.-R. 422, Farnell v. 345, Nilsson *GF.* 429.

Hestia is one of the divinities of Greek cult which never became completely personified. She was manifest in the flame of the sacred hearth of home, *prytaneion*, or temple, and was comparatively rarely represented by art in anthropomorphic form (on representations of Hestia see Roussel, 'Hestia à l'omphalos', *Rev. Arch.* xviii. 1911, 86). The hearth of the home, invoked in oaths in Homer (see on 5), was symbolically, as well as actually, the central point of family life. Further, as the well-being of the family depended upon the family hearth, so the well-being of the State depended upon the common hearth. Hence in cult the association of Hestia with such civic deities as Zeus Polieus (see on 5). Above all in importance was the sacred hearth at Delphi, the omphalos or central point of the world (see the many references collected in P.-W. viii. 1288), and from this, new fire was distributed after the Persian War to states whose hearths had been polluted by the Mede (Plutarch, *Aristid.* 20, *Num.* 9).

Whether or not the central hearth was retained in houses of the classical period, the original position of Hestia in relation to the household was never forgotten. Hence Delos is ἱστίη ὦ νήσων εὐέστιε (Callim. *Del.* 325), geographically and religiously the centre of the Cyclades. Philosophic speculation thus came to interpret Hestia as the central principle of the world (e.g. Philolaus *fr.* 7 Diels p. 237 πῦρ ἐν μέσῳ περὶ τὸ κέντρον ὅπερ ἑστίαν τοῦ παντὸς καλεῖ, cf. Orph. *h.* lxxxiv. 2 ἣ μέσον οἶκον ἔχεις πυρὸς ἀενάοιο), and earth was regarded as the common ἑστία of all living things (Arist. *de mundo* 391 b 14).

Hestia is here invoked to make her home, with Zeus, in a building the nature of which cannot be determined. B. thought it was a private house or a palace in which rhapsodists recited epic at a feast. But there is weight in Gemoll's criticism, that Hestia and Zeus would not be invoked into a private house with so much solemnity. The occasion is rather to be sought in the dedication of a temple.

The words Πυθοῖ ἐν ἠγαθέῃ need not imply that the hymn was Delphic: the reference is literary, being due to the fame of Hestia's special connexion with Delphi.

In view of the abrupt style many commentators believe it to be a fragment from a longer hymn; Matthiae marks a lacuna after 3. We need not suppose that the original form of the hymn was widely different from the present tradition.

Other hymns: hymn by Aristonous found at Delphi, *Fouilles de Delphes* iii. 2, no. 192, Pomtow *Phil. Woch.* 1912, 1394, Diehl ii. 301; Simias 5 Diehl ii. 259; Orph. *h.* lxxxiv.

1. Ἑστίη: for the form see on *h.* v. 22.

2. ἠγαθέη is a common epithet of Pytho, θ 80, *Theog.* 499, Pind. *Pyth.* ix. 71, Bacchyl. iii. 62, v. 41, *orac.* Hendess 32. 2:

cf. also *ib.* 45. 1 ὅς ἐμὸν δόμον ἀμφιπολεύει. The hymn of Aristonous to Hestia (Diehl i. 15. 2 a) is similar in sentiment ἃ καὶ Ὀλύμπου καὶ ἐπὶ γαίας μεσόμφαλον ἀεὶ Πυθίαν παρὰ δάφναν κατέχουσα ναὸν ἂν ὑψίπυλον Φοίβου χορεύεις.

3. **σῶν πλοκάμων ἀπολείβεται ὑγρὸν ἔλαιον**: for the phrase cf. η 107. Gods' heads, like those of humans (cf. e.g. Archestratus ap. Ath. 101 C στακτοῖσι μύροις ἀγαθοῖς χαίτην θεράπευε) and horses (Ψ 281), were dressed with oil; Callim. *Apoll.* 38 αἱ δὲ κόμαι θυόεντα πέδῳ λείβουσιν ἔλαια· | οὐ λίπος Ἀπόλλωνος ἀποστάζουσιν ἔθειραι | ἀλλ' αὐτὴν πανάκειαν, *Aetia* i. 4 ἀπ' ὀστλίγγων αἰὲν ἄλειφα ῥέει, Artemid. *onir.* ii. 33 θεῶν ἀγάλματα . . . ἀλείφειν, *IG.* xiv. 978. Hestia had statues (e.g. in the Prytaneum at Athens Paus. i. 18. 3), but in early times her cult was aniconic. Oil was poured on sacred stones (Paus. x. 24. 6, Lucian *Alexandr.* 30, Apul. *Flor.* i. 1, Babrius 48. 6) and on altars (Lucian *deor. conc.* 12, Posidippus ap. Ath. 414 E ἀλλὰ σὺ τούτου | καὶ χρῖε στήλην Ἀττικὲ καὶ στεφάνου). Oil flowed out in front of a temple Paus. ii. 6. 3; it was applied to ivory *ib.* v. 11. 10, and poured on offerings to Demeter at Phigalea *ib.* viii. 43. 11.

4. **ἐπέρχεο θυμὸν ἔχουσα**: θυμὸν ἔχειν occurs in a very doubtful passage in Theognis 444, but seems meaningless here. Hence an epithet has been sought for, as ὁμόφρονα *h.* iv. 391, ii. 434, ἶσον P 720. This does not explain ἐπέρχεο. Tucker's ἕν' ἔρχεο does this, but the phrase ἕνα θυμὸν ἔχειν is always of two people, and here we cannot make σὺν Διὶ μητιόεντι equivalent to a dative after εἷς. ἐπέρχεο marks a heightened emphasis, often met with (Soph. *El.* 850, Eur. *IT.* 984, Ar. *Ran.* 369, *Anth. Pal.* v. 161–3, Orph. *fr.* 192, D. Hal. *ars rhet.* ii. 1), and repetition is common in prayers and magical formulae; see Schmid *ARW.* xix. 277. A lacuna is probable, containing epithets of θυμόν.

5. **σὺν Διὶ μητιόεντι**: cf. *ep.* Kaibel *praef.* 824 a 5 ὦ κραίνουσα Διὸς μεγαλαυχέας οἴκους. The connexion of Hestia and Zeus, which probably originated in the private cult of the home, was extended to public cults where Hestia is specially associated with the God of the State, as e.g. at Cos the offering to Hestia in conjunction with a sacrifice to Zeus Polieus (Nilsson *GF.* 429), and see *IG.* xii. 704 (Camirus), xiv. 7, 8 (Syracuse), Polyb. v.

93. 10 (Aigion), Paus. i. 3. 4 (Athens), *IG.* xii. 1. 701, 704, 707 (Rhodes), P.-W. 1300. In Homer Hestia is not personified, but we find the hearth invoked at the same time as Zeus, e.g. ξ 159, ρ 156, τ 304, υ 231. Hence the development Ζεὺς ἐφέστιος (Soph. *Aj.* 492, Herod. i. 44), and Pindar makes Hestia sister of Zeus *Nem.* xi. 1, where see Farnell.

XXV

Hymn to the Muses and Apollo

The prelude is a cento from Hesiod: 1 is suggested by *Theog.* 1, 2–5 = *Theog.* 94–7, and 6 is modelled on *Theog.* 104. The old view that the lines *Theog.* 94 f. are borrowed from the hymn is no longer entertained. It is rightly pointed out that ἐκ δὲ Διὸς βασιλῆες is motiveless in the hymn, while it is quite suitable to the context of the *Theogony.* But although later than Hesiod, the abstract was doubtless made in ancient times for purposes of epic tradition (cf. 6, 7). Guttmann's arguments for his theory of Byzantine compilation are worthless (see Gemoll, p. 346).

For the joint worship of Apollo and the Muses see on *h.* iii. 189, *h.* iv. 450. Apollo had the titles Musagetes (*IG.* xii. 5. 893 [Tenos], cf. Plato *Laws* 653 D, Strabo 468, Arrian *Cyneg.* 35, Himer. *Or.* 13. 7) and Μουσεῖος (*IG.* vii. 1. 36 [Megara]), cf. τῷ Μουσάρχῳ Λατοῦς υἱεῖ Terp. 3, Μουσάων σκηπτοῦχε *h. mag.* ii. 2. 26 (Abel, p. 288). On the chest of Cypselus πεποίηνται δὲ καὶ ᾄδουσαι Μοῦσαι καὶ Ἀπόλλων ἐξάρχων τῆς ᾠδῆς Paus. v. 18. 3. Apollo, Hermes, and the Muses, who are associated in an inscription from Ozolian Locris (*IG.* ix. 1. 278), possessed a joint temple at Megalopolis *Paus.* viii. 32. 2. Leto, Artemis, Apollo, and the Muses were portrayed together upon one gable at Delphi *Paus.* x. 19. 4. See further P.-W. ii. 38. Apollo was the father of three Muses, Κηφισοῦς, Ἀπολλωνίς, Βορυσθενίς, Eumelus *fr.* 17.

In an inscription from Amorgos *IG.* xii. 7. 273 Aristogenes is described as Ἀπόλλωνος καὶ Μουσῶν μυθογράφον. Terpander 3 is addressed to Apollo and the Muses. Other hymns to the Muses are *IG.* vii. 4240, xii. 7. 95, Jan *Mus. Script. Graec.* suppl. 45, Proclus *h.* iii.

1. For ἄρχομαι cf. μ 163 λίσσωμαι, λίσσομαι.

3. **ἐπὶ χθονί**: ἐπὶ χθόνα in Hesiod *l.c.*, as in *Theog.* 187, *OD.* 11, in Homer ψ 371, *h.* ii. 305, iii. 69; the dative is common, e.g. A 88. The gen. occurs xx. 3.

κιθαρισταί: not Homeric, Hes. *l.c.*, Alcman 20. 2.

4. For the phrasing cf. ὁ δ' ὄλβιος ὅν κε σὺ θυμῷ xxx. 7, Oppian iv. 32, ὁ δ' ἔξοχος ὅν κε φιλήσῃ Theocr. xvii. 74.

6. Hesiod 104, Theocr. xxii. 214.

XXVI

Hymn to Dionysus

The occasion of this hymn was no doubt some festival of Dionysus; the singer hopes to be present for many successive years. It can hardly have been recited at the Brauronia, as Baumeister supposes, for this festival was held every four years, whereas ἐς ὥρας implies an annual rite (see on 12).

1. **κισσοκόμην**: of Dionysus *IG.* xii. 7. 80, Pind. *fr.* 75. 9 κισσοδόταν (sic) θεόν, of a satyr *Anth. Pal.* vi. 56. 1; cf. κισσοχαίτης Ecphant. *fr.* 3, Pratinas *fr.* 1. 42, Delphic paean *BCH.* xix. 147, θεὸν σταφυληκόμον Nonnus ix. 29, κισσοστέφανον *anon. hymn.* Abel p. 284, κισσόβρυον Orph. *h.* xxx. 4. Dionysus Kissos was worshipped at Acharnae Paus. i. 31. 6; at Thebes D. Perikionios, to whom Orph. *h.* xlvii is addressed, was represented by a pillar wreathed with ivy (Σ Eur. *Phoen.* 651, Clem. Alex. *strom.* 413); hence κομῶντα κισσῷ στῦλον θεοῦ (Eur. *fr.* 202); see further Kern in P.-W. v. 1016, *Arch. Jahrb.* xi. 115. For the chewing of ivy by Bacchanals, a vegetable form of σπαραγμός, see Plut. *mor.* 717; Hesych. Βαγχᾶν· ἐστεφανῶσθαι κισσῷ.

Διόνυσον: Διώνυσος in Homer except λ 325. The author of *h.* vii is indifferent (Διώνυσον 1, Διόνυσος ἐρίβρομος 56).

3. For the nurses of Dionysus (τιθῆναι Z 132) see P.-R. i. 663, Roscher i. 1048, ii. 2244, Gruppe *Gr. Myth.* 1435.

8. **φοιτίζεσκε**: also in Ap. Rh. iii. 54, Callim. *fr.* 148.

10. **ἄσπετον ὕλην** = B 455.

11. **πολυστάφυλ'**: not elsewhere of Dionysus. Similar titles,

however, are not only attested in poetry (ἐριστάφυλος Nonnus xii. 251, xlvii. 2, βοτρυηφόρον Orph. *h.* xxx. 5), but also in cult (e.g. Σταφυλίτης Aelian *VH.* iii. 41, Εὐστάφυλος at Lebadeia *IG.* vii. 3098). For other cult titles of Dionysus derived from the vine and other plants see Farnell v. 118.

12. **εἰς ὥρας**: that this expression means 'next year' and not merely 'in the future' appears from Plato *ep.* 346 C μένε . . . τὸν ἐνιαυτὸν τοῦτον, εἰς δὲ ὥρας ἄπιθι (Gemoll), Plut. *Ages.* 22 ἐὰν ἐσπαρμένην τὴν γῆν εἰς ὥρας ἔχωσιν, Theocr. xv. 74 εἰς ὥρας κἤπειτα, *Anth. Pal.* xii. 107 εἰς ὥρας αὖθις ἄγοιτε and no doubt ι 134 μάλα κεν βαθὺ λήιον αἰεὶ | εἰς ὥρας ἀμῷεν, Longinus *ars rhet.* 552 ἑτέραν ὥραν, Babrius 53. 7, Artemid. *onir.* iv. 84, Plut. *Marius* 21; more detailed expressions are εἰς νέωτα πάλιν ὥραις ταῖς αὐταῖς D. Hal. *comp. verb.* 6, εἰς νέωτα ὧραι Philostr. *vit. Apoll.* iii. 37.

An equivalent is εἰς νέωτα (Hesych. Εἰς νέωτα· εἰς τὸ ἐπιόν. Ἐπὶ νέωτα· εἰς ἕτερον ἔτος. Νέωτα· εἰς τὸ ἐπιὸν ἢ νεόν ἔτος) for which see the lexx.

13. **εἰς τοὺς πολλοὺς ἐνιαυτούς**: inscr. Dittenberger *Syll.* 898 εβοησεν ο δημος πολλοις ετεσι τους νεωκορους, *ib.* 110, Julian *ep.* 13 σε ἡ θεία πρόνοια διαφυλάξοι πολλοῖς χρόνοις, id. *ep.* 30, P. Oxy. 123. 23 ερρωσθαι σε ευχομαι πολλοις χρονοις, P. Bour. 25. 16 σε ο κυριος διαφυλαττοι μακροις ειρηνικοις χρονοις: in modern Latin *ad multos annos*, in modern Greek εἰς ἔτη πολλά, 'many happy returns'.

XXVII

Hymn to Artemis

The hymn to Artemis, which gives a pleasant picture of the youthful goddess returning from the chase to take part in the dance at Delphi, seems to belong to a good period. The writer was almost certainly influenced by the hymn to Apollo; Gemoll compares lines 5 f. with the opening scene of that hymn, and 15 f. with *h. Ap.* 189 f. The prelude may have been used at Delphi, where portions of ancient poetry bearing on Delphi and the god were recited (Dittenberger *Sylloge* 703); but it is possible that the scene at that place (13 f.) was introduced for literary effect.

For other hymns to Artemis cf. one quoted by Dicaearchus

ἐν τοῖς περὶ τοῦ τῆς Ἑλλάδος βίου ap. Athen. 636 c (*PLG.* iii. 655), a few lines in Ap. Rh. i. 570, Libanius *or.* 5, Alcman 60–5.

1. **χρυσηλάκατον**: see on *h.* v. 16.

2. **παρθένον**: for this epithet of Artemis see Bruchmann *epith. deor.* 49, παρθένον ἰοχέαιραν ix. 2, παρθένος ἀδμής ζ 109 of Nausicaa after a comparison to Artemis.

ἐλαφηβόλον: not Homeric of Artemis; cf. Anacr. i. 1, Soph. *Trach.* 214, *scolia* 3. 4 Diehl and later, Farnell ii. 433.

4. **ὄρη**: for the form cf. Μουσῶν 15.

For Artemis as inhabiting heights cf. the epithets ὀρειβάτις, ὀρεσίφοιτος, ὀρεστιάς, ὀρειάς in poetry, and cult-epithets such as Acria at Argos, Coryphaea at Mt. Coryphum; the reff. are collected by Pearson Soph. *fr.* 309.

5. **ἄγρῃ τερπομένη**: Φ 470 πότνια θηρῶν | Ἄρτεμις ἀγροτέρη, ζ 104 τερπομένη κάπροισι καὶ ὠκείῃς ἐλάφοισιν, Bacchyl. v. 123: Farnell 562.

8. **κλαγγῆς**: xiv. 4.

10. **ἐπιστρέφεται**: Anacreon ii. 4 ἐπιστρέφεαι δ' | ὑψηλὰς ὀρέων κορυφάς.

11. **θηροσκόπος**: of Artemis Bacchyl. xi. 107.

13–15. The lines do not show that there was a common cult of Apollo and Artemis at Delphi. The Goddess visits her brother to take part in the chorus of Muses and Graces (*h.* ix introd. and note on *ib.* 5). Artemis appears to have no place in the earliest stratum of Delphic legend (see introd. to iii). In historical times she found a place beside her brother and accordingly acquired the cult titles of Δελφινία (Attica, Thessaly) and Πυθίη (Miletus). At Delphi she was always a subordinate figure (Farnell ii. 467). An inscription (379 B.C.) records an amphictyonic oath to Apollo, Leto, and Artemis (*CIG.* 1688), another an oath by the same three deities (*IG. ed. min.* 26. 10). Slaves were sometimes manumitted in the name of Apollo and Artemis (Collitz *Dial. Inschr.* 1810). The eastern pediment of the Delphian temple represented Apollo, Artemis, Leto, and the Muses, but no trace has been discovered.

20. **ἔργμασιν**: post-Homeric, cf. Hes. *OD.* 801, *h.* xxix. 12, xxxii. 19, Bacchyl. xiii. 17.

XXVIII

Hymn to Athena

The style of this hymn is so similar to that of the preceding, that Gemoll confidently attributes both to the same composer. For coincidences of language he points to 3, 10 in this hymn (see notes). It is more to the point to notice that the influence of the hymn to Apollo is probably to be seen here, as in the hymn to Artemis. Gemoll compares 15 with *h. Ap.* 7, and 16 with *h. Ap.* 12.

According to the earliest detailed version of the myth (Hes. *Theog.* 886–900) Zeus swallowed Metis, who was already pregnant with Athena. The Goddess then sprang from the head of Zeus (*ib.* 924–6). Hesiod says nothing of the agency of Hephaestus (or other God who assisted Zeus[1]), nor of an armed Athena. The 𝔖 Ap. Rh. iv. 1310 remarks that Stesichorus (whose poem is lost) first mentioned the panoply of the Goddess at her birth. He passes over the hymn, of the existence of which he was probably unaware, as he could hardly have had enough acumen to place a 'Homeric' hymn later than the time of Stesichorus. The myth next appears in Pindar (*Ol.* vii. 38), who describes the agency of Hephaestus, and the terror of Heaven and Earth at the loud cry of Athena.

For later accounts of the birth see P.-W. ii. 1895, Farnell i. 280, and (from the anthropological standpoint) Lang *Myth, Ritual and Religion* ii. 242. It seems clear that the mention of the panoply, which is elaborated in the hymn (5, 6, and 15), is not part of the primitive myth; but this early became prominent in literature and art (cf. Lucian *dial. deor.* 8, Philostr. *imag.* ii. 27). On archaic vases, down to the time of Phidias, the usual type represents Zeus as sitting in the midst of Gods, while Athena, a small armed figure, issues from his head (see vases in Brit. Mus. B 147, 218, 244, 421, E 15, 410). Phidias probably represented Athena as already born, either standing by the side of Zeus, or moving away from him, as in the well-known relief at Madrid

[1] E.g. Prometheus, *Ion* 455.

(reproduced by Baumeister *Denkm.* fig. 172, and Frazer on Paus. i. 24. 5, where references to the recent literature on the subject are given). See Schneider *Die Geburt der Athena*, Vienna, 1880, Gardner *Handbook Gk. Sculpture* ii. p. 279 f.

Other hymns: Orph. *h.* xxii, hymn at Sparta, s. vi, *BSA.* xxix. 45 π]αλας αθαναια θυ[, Alcaeus 9, one mentioned in Σ Ar. *Clouds* 967.

2. **ἀμείλιχον ἦτορ ἔχουσαν** = I 572 (of Erinnys).

3. **παρθένον αἰδοίην**: of Artemis xxvii. 2.

ἐρυσίπτολιν: see on xi. 1.

4. **Τριτογενῆ**: so τεύχη 15 (but τεύχε' 5); cf. xxvii. 4. The form Τριτογενής is not Homeric.

αὐτός: cf. E 880 ἐπεὶ αὐτὸς ἐγείναο παῖδ' ἀΐδηλον (the only reference in Homer to the birth of Athena); Hes. *Theog.* 924 αὐτὸς δ' ἐκ κεφαλῆς γλαυκώπιδα γείνατ' Ἀθήνην. Cf. *h.* iii. 314, 323.

5. ὅπλοις λαμπομένην χαλκήιον ἄνθος ἰδέσθαι Orph. *fr.* 132 Abel (174 Kern). For the birth in panoply see introduction above.

7. **πρόσθεν**: proleptic; 'she sprang before Zeus, from his immortal head'; Διός is to be taken both with πρόσθεν and καρήνου. The poet may have had in mind representations of the scene after the type of the Madrid relief (see introd.). The actual process of the birth is not described; and this, as Gemoll notes, may account for the omission of Hephaestus with his axe.

9 f. For the terror of all nature at the birth cf. Pind. *Ol.* vii. 38 Οὐρανὸς δ' ἔφριξέ νιν καὶ Γαῖα μάτηρ. The upheaval of Nature is due to this stupendous scene. Later Greek rationalists gave a physical explanation of Athena's birth, in which they are followed by moderns of the school of Roscher; but it is certain that Hesiod, Pindar, and the hymn-writer have no idea of reading a physical interpretation into the myth (see Farnell *l.c.*). Compare the fear inspired by Artemis in the chase, xxvii. 6 f. Adami (p. 231) collects other examples.

10. **ὑπὸ βρίμης**: the manuscript reading ὑπ' ὀβρίμης is scarcely defensible, as ὄβριμος has always ι short. It is true that certain adjectives have a medial lengthening on the analogy of ὀπωρινός ἴφθιμος (Schulze *QE.* p. 473), but there is no authority for extending the list, with Ilgen's obvious correction to hand. βρίμη

does not occur in early epic, but cf. Ap. Rh. iv. 1676 ὑπόειξε δαμῆναι | Μηδείης βρίμῃ πολυφαρμάκου (Σ τῇ ἰσχύϊ); so Βριμώ, βριμώδης, which seem to show that βρίμη is not mere 'strength', but connoted the idea of terror inspired by Athena; Hesych. also explains by ἀπειλή. For δεινὸν ὑπὸ βρίμης Gemoll compares xxvii. 8 δεινὸν ὑπὸ κλαγγῆς. On the derivation of ὄβριμος etc. see Johansson *IF.* iii. 239 n. and Boisacq *in* Βριαρός.

12. ἔσχετο: Baumeister's objection to this word, which he thinks a contradiction of ἐκινήθη, is unfounded; ἔσχετο is defended by στῆσεν . . . ἵππους. Nature was first upheaved by terror at the coming of Athena, and then her regular course was stopped; the sea was 'stayed', and no longer beat on the shore.

13. At the birth of Athena represented on the eastern pediment of the Parthenon, Helios and his horses were sculptured at one end, and Selene in her chariot at the other. This scheme became common, e.g. on the base of the statue of Olympian Zeus depicting the birth of Aphrodite (Paus. v. 11. 8). But the presence of the Sun and Moon gives only a local or temporal frame to these scenes; in the hymn the Sun stops miraculously, from terror. In Σ 239 f. Hera sends the Sun to Ocean before his time; so Athena prolongs the night, ψ 243 f. Cf. also the Sun's threat to disturb the course of nature, μ 383.

In *EM.* 474. 31 *in* Ἱππία the following explanation of the title is given: ἐκλήθη οὕτως ἡ Ἀθηνᾶ, ἐπεὶ ἐκ τῆς κεφαλῆς τοῦ Διὸς μεθ' ἵππων ἀνήλατο, ὡς ὁ ἐπ' αὐτῆς ὕμνος δηλοῖ. This hymn must have been late, if Athena came forth with a chariot and pair. Moreover no old hymn can have existed in the Etymologus' time. It is plain that the lexicographer does not allude to the present hymn, as the horses belong to the Sun.

14. The MS. reading εἰσότε is defended by Fuch *die Temporalsätze mit den Konjunctionem 'bis' und 'so lang als'*, Würzburg, 1902, 41. For the variant see on *h. Apoll.* 501.

XXIX

Hymn to Hestia

Although primarily addressed to Hestia, the hymn is equally in honour of Hermes. If the order of the lines 9 f. is correct Groddeck's inference may be right, that ναίετε δώματα καλά alludes to the cult of the two deities in a common temple. Gemoll further supposes that here, as in xxiv, the hymn was sung at the dedication of a new temple. Baumeister's view that the occasion was a feast in a private house depends on Martin's order of the lines, by which δώματα καλά is joined to ἐπιχθονίων ἀνθρώπων: but see on 9 f. It is difficult to see why Gemoll should call the style of the hymn more lyric than epic; his notion of strophic arrangement (in stanzas of four lines) is also of the slightest, and breaks down if we assume a lacuna after 9.

For the cult and mythology of Hestia see Introduction to xxiv.

The close connexion of Hermes and Hestia (see references in P.-R. 423, Roscher i. 2649), which is attested by their representation as a pair on the basis of the Olympian Zeus of Phidias (Paus. v. 11. 8), has defied satisfactory explanation. For such can hardly be called the suggestion of Preller, that their functions are complementary, Hestia representing family life and Hermes the life of the streets, or that of Campbell (*Religion in Greek Literature*, p. 119) that their functions are akin because Hestia is Goddess of the house and Hermes the God of boundaries.

Whether the view of Baumeister that the hymn refers to a cult in a private house be right or wrong, it may be suggested that the origin of this close association of Hestia and Hermes lay originally in the connexion of both with everyday life in the home. τούτων δὲ λέγεται τὴν μὲν Ἑστίαν τὴν τῶν οἰκιῶν κατασκευὴν εὑρεῖν καὶ διὰ τὴν εὐεργεσίαν ταύτην παρὰ πᾶσι σχεδὸν ἀνθρώποις ἐν πάσαις οἰκίαις καθιδρυθῆναι τιμῶν καὶ θυσιῶν τυγχάνουσαν Diod. v. 68. Nor was Hermes in fact kept outside the door, though even as *propylaeus* he belonged in a real sense to the fortunes of the family before whose door he stood. It is uncertain whether it was Hermes in front of the door or Hermes within doors that the so pious Clearchus crowned and polished at every new moon (Theopompus ap. Porphyr. *de abst.* ii. 16), probably on the fourth of the month (see on *h. Herm.* 19), when the Superstitious Man garnished his Hermaphrodites (Theophrast. *Char.* xvi. 10), but the conjunction with Hecate suggests that his Hermes was inside the house. For as a sender of dreams (*h. Herm.* 14) and a power over ghosts Hermes was a guardian against the terrors of night. His statue stood in the bedroom, and the wise turned their face to it when going to sleep (Apollodorus in Σ ψ 198, cf. Hesychius *ἐπιθαλαμίτης· Ἑρμῆς ἐν Εὐβοίᾳ*). To him men prayed for pleasant dreams: *ἄλλους τε τῶν θεῶν καὶ τὸν Ἑρμῆν ἐπὶ πᾶσιν ἐπικαλούμενος, εὐόνειρον τε ᾔτει τὴν νύκτα* (Heliodorus iii. 5). This aspect of Hermes in the private life of families is clearly old, for the Phaeacians (η 137), like the later Greeks (Plutarch *quaest. conviv.* vii. 9. 6, Athen. 16 B), gave the last libation before going to bed to Hermes, and a 'nightcap' (*οὗ Ἑρμῆς ὑπὲρ ὀνείρων πίνει* Philostr. *Her.* x. 8) was called Ἑρμῆς in Greek (Pollux vi. 16, Hesych. and Phot. *in* Ἑρμῆς, Athen. 473 C, Longus iv. 34. 2). Hestia represented the religious focus of family life at meals, and Hermes was the protector of the sleep of the family. Surely this is the secret of their close association. At bedtime Hermes usurped the prerogative of the last libation, which at other times of the day belonged to Hestia (see on 5).

1–3. Cf. *h.* v. 31, 32. On the form Ἑστίη see on *h.* v. 22, xxiv. 1.

2 = E 442.

3. ἀίδιον: of two terminations, as usually, xxix. 3, Hes. *Scut.* 310; of three Orph. *h.* x. 21, lxxxiv. 6.

πρεσβηίδα, 'venerable', as *h.* v. 32 *θεῶν πρέσβειρα*.

4. τιμήν: neither the repetition of the word in 3, 4 nor the spondee at the pause in 4 is sufficient to shake *τιμήν* in a document of this period.

5. Theognis 1146 *Ἐλπίδι τε πρώτῃ καὶ πυμάτῃ θυέτω.*

At sacrifices Hestia received the first and last libation. Alluding to the myth that Hestia was swallowed first and disgorged the last of the children of Cronos (see on *h.* v. 22), Cornutus (53) says explicitly *μυθεύεται δὲ πρώτη τε καὶ ἐσχάτη γενέσθαι τῷ εἰς* ταύτην ἀναλύεσθαι τὰ ἀπ' αὐτῆς γινόμενα καὶ ἐξ αὐτῆς συνίστασθαι, καθὸ κἀν ταῖς θυσίαις οἱ Ἕλληνες ἀπὸ πρώτης τε αὐτῆς ἤρχοντο καὶ εἰς ἐσχάτην αὐτὴν κατέπαυον. That Hestia received the first libation is not disputed, for it is attested by abundant evidence (e.g. Pindar *Nem.* xi. 6, Soph. *Chrys. fr.* 726, Ar. *Av.* 864, Paus. v. 14. 5 and further reff. in P.-W. viii. 1273). Nor is it disputed that Vesta at Rome had the last libation, but Preuner (*Hestia-Vesta* 3 sq., Roscher i. 2605) considers that the one custom is Greek and the other Roman; and that the divergence is to be explained by an indefiniteness in early 'Aryan' custom. The authority of Cornutus is better than that of Preuner on a question of fact. It is true that the last libation before going to bed was offered to Hermes, and this perhaps explains one bond between the two deities (see Introduction). But the attempt to explain away Cornutus also fails to appreciate the force of the proverb ἀφ' Ἑστίας ἄρχεσθαι which implies total completion, 'lock, stock, and barrel'. This Mair notes on Callim. *Dem.* 108 (ed. Loeb) καὶ τὰν βοῦν ἔφαγεν τὰν Ἑστίᾳ ἔτρεφε μάτηρ: 'the proverb . . . sometimes approaches the sense of τὴν ἀφ' ἱερᾶς κινεῖν, indicating a last desperate move, or something thorough-going'. Cf. the German *von Hause aus*? It is possible that Eur. *Alc.* 162 δέσποιν' ἐγὼ γὰρ ἔρχομαι κατὰ χθονὸς | πανύστατόν σε προσπίτνουσ' αἰτήσομαι κτλ. alludes to the practice of giving the last libation to Hestia.

6. For the omission of τις, which is eased by the presence of the participles, see on iv. 202, K.-G. i, p. 35 g.

9 sq. Martin's arrangement, by which 9 is transferred to follow 11, involves several difficulties: (1) the translation is unmotived graphically, (2) the apodosis, which should include Hestia and Hermes, is thus in the singular (ἐπάρηγε), (3) the clause ἔργματα καλά κτλ. is left with an asyndeton, for θ' after the third word can hardly be a copula to the clause. In the 1896 text an omitted line was assumed after 9, beginning with εἰδότες and perhaps ending with υἱέ (and hence left out) in which Hermes was addressed separately. There is no great difficulty in ναίετε following σύ after an hyperbaton; the construction would be *ad sensum*, Hestia being included in the subject of the verb.

10. **ἵλαος**. Cf. Choerob. *in Theod. can.* 252. 21, who quotes

Parthenius ἵλαος ὦ Ὑμέναιε. Cf. also *IG.* ii. 3. 1336 ἀνθ' ὧν ὦ Διόνυσε ὢν ἵλαος οἶκον ἅμ' αὐτῷ.

12. **εἰδότες ἔργματα καλά**, 'seeing, perceiving, aware of'. Both deities, being domestic, oversee labour. Orph. *h.* xxviii. 9 ἐργασίας ἐπαρωγέ of Hermes (B.). The following word ἕσπεσθε is unique and consequently obscure. Veitch p. 261 quotes the v.l. ἕσπεται = ἔρχεται δ 826, which would make the form a present (Pauw conjectured ἑσπέσθαι for σπέσθαι Pind. *Isthm.* vi. 17). We translate 'ye follow them (ἔργμασι) with mind and vigour'.

13. **χαῖρε Κρόνου θύγατερ** is borrowed by Aristonous in his Delphic hymn to Hestia Diehl ii, p. 301. Cf. also Orph. *h.* lxxxiv. 1 Ἱστίη εὐδυνάτοιο Κρόνου θύγατερ βασίλεια, Simias 5 (Diehl ii, p. 259) Ἱστία ἁγνά.

XXX

To Earth, Mother of All

Groddeck's theory that this hymn is Orphic has rightly met with no support, except from Crusius (*Philolog.* xlvii, 1889, p. 208). It is a genuine prelude in the Homeric style. There are absolutely no indications of date or place; we may, however, infer that it is of no great antiquity, as the writer seems to have borrowed from the hymn to Demeter; Gemoll compares 7, 12, and 18, 19 (see on *h. Dem.* 486, 489, 494–5). The hymn resembles the two following in length, and seems to belong to the same age and perhaps to the same workmanship (Crusius *l.c.*). Orph. *h.* xxvi is addressed to Gaea. Pausanias (x. 12. 10) attributes to the Peleiadae of Dodona the ancient ritual hymn

Ζεὺς ἦν, Ζεὺς ἐστίν, Ζεὺς ἔσσεται· ὦ μεγάλε Ζεῦ.
Γᾶ καρποὺς ἀνίει, διὸ κλῄζετε Ματέρα γαῖαν.

1. **παμμήτειραν.** Cf. μήτειρα a variant for δμήτειρα read by Zen. and Aristoph. Ξ 259; παμμήτωρ τε γῆ Aesch. *PV.* 90. On the epithet see Roscher i. 1570. The Σ Theocr. i. 30 quotes χθὼν παμμήτωρ as Homeric.

ἠυθέμεθλον: only here.

5. For the omission of the subject see on xxix. 6.

εὔπαιδες: in allusion to the title Γῆ κουροτρόφος P.-R. i. 635.

εὔκαρποι: as in the Dodonaean hymn (introd.).

6. **ἀφελέσθαι**: as a chthonian deity.

7. **ὁ δ' ὄλβιος**: see on xxv. 4.

8. **τῷ τ' ἄφθονα κτλ.** = iii. 536 (δ' and *παρέσται*).

9. **σφιν**: probably singular as *h.* xix. 19, q.v.

10. **εὐθηνεῖ**: sc. *ὁ ὄλβιος*.

14. **φερεσανθέσιν**: this correction is already indicated by *x*'s *περεσανθέσιν*: cf. *φερέσβιος* 9, *IG.* xiv. 1015, *φερεσσίπονος ib.*, *φερεσσακέας* Hes. *Scut.* 13, *λιπεσάνορας* Stesich. *fr.* 20. Forms without -*σ*- are *φερανθής* *Anth. Pal.* ix. 363. 2, *φερεαυγέα ib.* 634. 1. For *φ* = *π* cf. *φαρθενε* = *παρθένε* *IG. ed. min.* 555, 650, and *περσεφόνεια φερσ*-.

15. **σκαίρουσι**: a certain correction. The same word gave *σπαίρουσι κ* 412.

17. **θεῶν μήτηρ**: the confusion or identification of Gaea and Rhea as mother of the Gods is early: cf. Soph. *fr.* 290 *Γῆ μήτηρ θεῶν* and reff. in Pearson's note, Solon *fr.* 36 *μήτηρ μεγίστη δαιμόνων Ὀλυμπίων*. In Hesiodean mythology she was mother of the Titans and Cronos.

18. **βίοτον θυμήρε' ὄπαζε**: Orph. *h.* xxviii. 11, lxvii. 8 *βιότου* (-*ῆς*) *τέλος ἐσθλὸν ὀπάζων*.

18, 19 = *h.* ii. 494, 495.

XXXI, XXXII

Hymn to Helios and Hymn to Selene

The resemblances between these hymns are striking. If they are not the work of a single author, as G. and B. (less confidently) suppose, the writer of one hymn took the other as his model. The description of the bright sun is closely parallel to that of the moon, and the language in several places is identical; cf. xxxi. 10, 13 with xxxii. 6, 8 and see further on xxxi. 10. In both hymns we see a search after recondite mythology (Euryphaessa xxxi. 2, Pandia xxxii. 15). The concluding formulae show that they were preludes to recitation. If somewhat florid in style they are in the Homeric manner, and there is not the slightest reason to attribute them to the school of Onomacritus (B.). The hymn to Selene is perhaps recognized by Aristophanes *Birds* 912 οὐκ, ἀλλὰ πάντες ἐσμὲν οἱ διδάσκαλοι | Μουσάων θεράποντες ὀτρηροί | κατὰ τὸν Ὅμηρον. See on xxxii. 20. They have nothing in common with the extant Orphic hymns to the same deities. The place of composition cannot be recovered.

For the mythology and cult of Helios see P.-R. 429, Farnell v. 417, Roscher i. 1993, P.-W. viii. 1. 58, Nilsson *GF.* 427; for Selene P.-R. 443, Roscher *Selene und Verwandtes* 1890 with *Nachträge* 1895, *lex.* ii. 3119, P.-W. ser. 2. ii. 1134. In cult Helios has little and Selene no importance. From Homer onwards Helios was invoked in oaths (see on ii. 62), and throughout the Greek world reverence was paid to him. But only in Rhodes does he figure as a God of real importance in public cult. Survivals in southern Laconia suggest that his worship was once important in the Peloponnese, but elsewhere in Greece Helios played no prominent part in religion until the revival of sun-worship in the age of syncretism.

Selene at no time had importance for cult except in so far as the moon was identified with other Goddesses, Hecate, Artemis, or Persephone.

Other hymns to Helios are Orph. *h.* viii, Proclus *h.* i (Abel, p. 276), *h. mag.* iv (Abel, p. 291), Hepding *Ath. Mitt.* xxxii. 357 (inscr. from Pergamon), C. Jan *Mus. Script. Graec.* suppl. 48. To these may be added the address by Zeus to Helios about Phaethon *IG.* xiv. 2012 A.

Orph. *h.* ix and *h. mag.* v (Abel, p. 292) are addressed to Selene.

XXXI

1. **Ἥλιον**: in Homer only θ 271.

αὖτε, 'now': cf. Terpander *fr.* 2 ἀμφί μοι αὖτε (B.).

2. **Καλλιόπη**: cf. Alcman *fr.* 45 Μῶσ' ἄγε Καλλιόπα θύγατερ Διὸς | ἄρχ' ἐρατῶν ὕμνων, Bacchyl. v. 176 &c. She occurs first, as one of the Nine, Hes. *Theog.* 79. Max. Tyr. i. 2 says δεῖ δέ τινος ἄλλης μούσης ἀνδρικωτέρας ἣν Ὅμηρος μὲν Καλλιόπην ὀνομάζων χαίρει, which if taken literally refers to this place.

Εὐρυφάεσσα: only here. *Theog.* 371 Theia is the mother of the Sun, Moon, and Dawn; cf. Pind. *Isthm.* v. 1. See Roscher ii. 3160.

6. **ῥοδόπηχυν**: Sappho 65. 18 *βροδόπαχυν αὔων.*

7 = Λ 60 *ἠίθεόν τ' ἀκάμαντ' ἐπιείκελον ἀθανάτοισι*, which seemed to Franke to imply the Sun's inferiority compared to the Olympian Gods, but he with Selene and Eos is mentioned with them *Theog.* 9. Probably the writer took the epithet with the line; *ἀκάμας* alone is an epithet of the Sun Σ 239, 484.

8. Cf. γ 2.

9. The conception of the Sun as a driver of a chariot does not appear in Homer, though the Dawn has horses ψ 244; see Rapp in Roscher i. 1998, 2005, Jessen in P.-W. viii. 89. It is however the rule in the *Hymns* (ii. 63, 88, iv. 69, xxviii. 14), appears in Hesiod *fr.* 67, and in later writers *passim.*

10. **χρυσῆς**: xxxii. 6 the MSS. vary between *χρυσοῦ* and *χρυσέου.*

λαμπραὶ δ' ἀκτῖνες: cf. Timotheus 11. 2.

ἀπ' αὐτοῦ: cf. *ἧς ἄπο* xxxii. 3.

11. **παρειαί**, 'cheeks', i.e. cheek-pieces; cf. *παρήιον* of a horse Δ 142 (Hesych. *ὁ παρὰ τὸ γένειον τόπος καὶ κόσμος ἐπὶ μετώπου τῶν ἵππων παρὰ γνάθον*), *χαλκοπάρῃος* of a helmet *passim*; *κρανιδιον . . . παρειας ουκ εχον CIA.* ii. 1. 703, vv. 10, 11, and 676, 701, Pollux i. 89 *τῆς πρώρας τὰ ἑκατέρωθεν παρειὰ καλεῖται καὶ πτερά, ib.* 135 *τὰ δὲ περὶ ταῖς χερσὶ προβλήματα ὁμωνύμως τῷ μέρει χεῖρες καλοῦνται*, Eust. 456. 15 *παρήιον δὲ ἵππων τὸ τοῦ χαλινοῦ παραγναθίδιον· λέγεται δέ ποτε καὶ αὐτὴ ἡ παρειά.* Cf. also *παραγναθίς, παρώπια, πτερύγια, buccula* and in gen. Ach. Tat. i. 14 *ἐκαλλώπιζον τὸ πονηρὸν θηρίον προστερνιδίοις, προμετωπιδίοις, φαλακραῖς ἀργυραῖς*, Xen. *Cyrop.* vi. 4. 1, vii. 1. 2. The sentence is overfull. What it describes is a closed helmet or visor.

14. **πνοιῇ ἀνέμων**, 'in the blast of the winds', the clothing is blown back. Cf. the description of Europa Mosch. ii. 129 *κολπώθη δ' ἀνέμοισι πέπλος βαθὺς Εὐρωπείης | ἱστίον οἷά τε νηός.*

ἄρσενες ἵπποι: the horses, here stallions, of the Sun are swift as birds (*h.* ii. 89, *ὠκύποδες* xxviii. 14); in later literature (e.g. Eur. *El.* 466, *Or.* 1001) and art they are represented as winged. Both in literature and in art the chariot of the sun is drawn sometimes by a pair, sometimes by four horses. For the variations in the names of these fire-breathing steeds see P.-W. viii. 88.

The incomplete statement ὑπὸ δ' ἄρσενες ἵπποι, the absence of a reference to ἔνθ', and the unexplained subjunctive πέμπῃσι require at least another line; and as the omission seems the effect of ἵπποι ἵππους the line followed 14, so Hermann thought. The conditions would be fulfilled by (ὑπὸ) ἀίσσουσ' ὄφρ' ἂν μέσον οὐρανὸν αὐτὸν ἵκωνται (i.e. to the μεσουράνησις) or the like. The sun 'stays his golden chariot and horses' at noon, at the 'peak of heaven' (Shelley), 'when' or 'where he sends them through the sky to the sea': Strabo 173 ἐκκλίναντος δὲ τοῦ ἄστρου πάλιν ἀναχωρεῖν τὸ πέλαγος.

18. **κλῄσω**: the verb is un-Homeric; frequent in the fifth century and later. See Veitch *in v.*, Schulze *qu. ep.* 281 n. 3.

XXXII

1. **ἀείδειν** and **ἕσπετε** seem incompatible, but the parallel line xxxi. 1 ἥλιον ὑμνεῖν . . . ἄρχεο suggests that ἕσπετε may mean 'follow', cf. ἕσπεσθε xxix. 12, ἕπεται διελθεῖν Ar. *Eth. Nic.* iii. 1. 2. Hymn xxxii would then be a 'sequel' to xxxi. The obvious alteration ἔσπετε involves the alteration of ἀείδειν also.

τανυσίπτερον: there appears to be no other example of a winged Selene in literature, and the type is very uncertain in art. Roscher ii. 3140 doubtfully identifies a winged Goddess on a gem (Müller-Wieseler ii. 16, 176 a) as Selene-Nike. The attribution of wings to Selene is due rather to a confusion with Eos than with Nike. Even when she drives a car Eos regularly has wings.

3. **γαῖαν ἑλίσσεται**, 'shoots to the earth', like lightning (?).

4. Cf. πολὺς δ' ὑπὸ κόμπος ὀρώρει θ 380.

6. The epithet 'golden' is at least as common as 'silver' in allusion to the moon; cf. Pind. *Ol.* iii. 19, Eur. *Phoen.* 176 and other reff. in Roscher ii. 3130, 3136. On the στέφανος see *ib.* 3133.

ἀκτῖνες δ': on the metre see *h.* ii. 269 and cf. i. 18.

ἐνδιάονται: this verb is usually active (ἐνδιάασκον Theocr. xvi.

38, -εν xxii. 44, ἐνδιάει Nicander ap. Ael. *NH.* x. 4. 9, ἐνδιάουσα Agath. *Anth. Pal.* v. 291. 6, ἐνδιάων Nonnus xxv. 474, Hesych. ἐνδιά[λ]ῳ· μεσημβρίας ὥρᾳ); the middle occurs in Hesych. ἐνδιῶνται· μεσημβριάζουσιν. The transference from noon to night may be allowed. The word is Alexandrian.

9. **πώλους**: Eos has horses ψ 246, Selene Theocr. ii. 163. On Selene's car see Roscher ii. 3134, 3174.

10. **προτέρωσ'**: un-Homeric, cf. Ap. Rh. i. 306, 1241.

11. **διχόμηνος** = διχόμηνις Pind. *Ol.* iii. 19, Ap. Rh. i. 1231, iv. 167, Aratus 471, Nonnus iv. 281, Io. Gaz. *descript.* i. 203.

ὄγμος, 'orbit', Aratus 749, Nicand. *Ther.* 571.

12. τελέθωσιν of the MSS. is a return to the original construction, which is broken at 11; cf. xxxiii. 9.

13. For **τέκμωρ** or τέκμαρ of the heavenly bodies, cf. Eur. *Hec.* 1273, Ap. Rh. i. 499, iii. 1002 al.

15. **Πανδείην**: here and in Photius (Πάνδια· ἑορτή τις Ἀθήνησι μετὰ τὰ Διονύσια ἀγομένη ἀπὸ Πανδίας τῆς Σελήνης ἢ ἀπὸ Πανδίονος κτλ.) a daughter of the moon, who seems in fact an abstraction of the moon herself. Cf. Ulpian in Dem. *Mid.* 517 οἱ δὲ τὴν Πανδίαν τὴν Σελήνην νομίζουσιν, Orph. *fr.* 11 (Abel) 280 (Kern) πανδῖα Σεληναίη, Max. Phil. 22 al. πανδῖα Σελήνη, 123 al. πανδῖα without substantive. It has been denied by Wilamowitz (*Aus Kydathen* 133) and Robert (P.-R. i. 132) that the Athenian festival Pandia, which they associate with Pandion, had any connexion with the Goddess. But this opinion is not certainly correct. Of the Pandia little is known. Alternative connexions given by the lexicographers are Pandeia, Zeus (so Photius and Pollux i. 37), and Pandion. Except for an account of a deme's expenditure of 650 drs. (*IG.* ii. 1. 570), all we know of the festival is that a sacrifice was offered to all (i.e. the twelve) Gods, and that it came at the end of the Great Dionysia on the 14th Elaphebolion. That however there is some connexion with Pandeia the full moon (see 11) is suggested by the date, which is in fact διχόμηνος (see Mommsen *Feste* 432, 448).

20. For the phrase see Hes. *Theog.* 100–2, Theognis 769, Eur. *El.* 717, Ar. *Av.* 913 (above). The Σ there quote Margites i. 2 Μουσάων θεράπων καὶ ἑκηβόλου Ἀπόλλωνος, but the word ὀτρηροί

does not occur in the line, and the passage in Aristophanes is a parody on a Homeric verse; cf. also Choerilus i. 2, *ep.* Kaibel 101. 3, 415. 3 (θέραψ), Dio Prus. xxxvi. 33, Libanius *ep.* 1461, ἐνυαλίοιο θεράπων Archilochus i. 1, οὐρανίας Bacchyl. v. 14, τοῦ θεοῦ τοῦδε [τοῦ Ἡλίου] θεράποντα Julian *or.* iv. 131 C.

XXXIII

Hymn to the Dioscuri

Although placed all but last in the collection, this hymn is no doubt older than xvii, which seems to be an abstract of it. The poem is a vigorous piece of writing, and upon grounds of style there is no reason to assign it to other than an early date. That it is pre-Alexandrian is certain, for there is little doubt that it was imitated by Theocritus (*Idyll* xxii), whose description of the storm lulled by the Dioscuri is more elaborate than the simple language of the hymn [1]. Further the evidence of the inscription upon a bronze disc said to have been found at Cephallenia (see on 9), almost certainly indicates that the hymn was well known before the sixth century B.C.

The editors do not notice the similarities of language between this hymn and vii (to Dionysus): cf. 1 ἀμφί = vii. 1; 8 ἀπὸ νηῶν = vii. 6 ἀπὸ νηός (a rare use); 12 ἐφάνησαν = vii. 2 ἐφάνη; 14 ἀργαλέων ἀνέμων = vii. 24 ἀργαλέους ἀνέμους; 16 σήματα = vii. 46; 16 οἱ δὲ ἰδόντες = vii. 42; see also on 10. These resemblances, taken singly, are slight; but their number suggests the possibility that this hymn was influenced by that to Dionysus and is therefore later. But if it is older than the Cephallenian inscription, this provides additional confirmation that vii to Dionysus is of early date (see p. 379 above).

The origin and nature of the Dioscuri has been a matter of controversy. One view maintains that they represent the survival in a particular form of Heavenly Twins, deities of the sky, who were worshipped by the ancestors of all the peoples who speak

[1] Of recent editors, Baumeister, Gemoll, and Abel agree on this point; see also Crusius in *Philolog.* xlviii. 202.

an Indo-European language (see Roscher i. 1154). Others have maintained that Castor and Polydeuces were originally separate heroes who were subsequently united and identified with a hitherto nameless pair of twin heroes, who were known as the sons of Tyndareus (see Bethe in P.-W. v. 1087, Robert *Held.* 306). Nilsson has recently connected them, on the other hand, with Minoan religion and the child Zeus of Crete through their function as household deities and the survival in some parts of Greece of the worship of child-gods (Nilsson *MMR.* 469). The view, however, taken here is in the main that more fully set out by Farnell *HC.* 174 (see also Rose *Handbook* 230, Halliday *Plutarch's Greek Questions* 116).

For Homer Castor, tamer of horses (both of them have this function Alcman ii. 1–3), and Polydeuces, the boxer, were the twin sons of a mortal Tyndareus and were buried in Laconia (Γ 236). λ 298 refers to the legend that these heroes 'pass from life to death on alternate days and enjoy equal honours with the Gods' (ἑτερήμεροι λ 303, Julian *or.* iv. 147 A), a curious belief which may have its origin in the combination of a chthonian with a celestial cult (Nilsson *GF.* 417). Hesiod (*fr.* 91) stated that Zeus was the father of the Tyndaridae, but the first literary evidence for the title Διὸς κοῦροι is in this hymn (see on 1). All theories which seek to define the origin and nature of their worship in terms of the title Dioscuri, which thus appears to be a secondary appellation, must necessarily be invalid.

The home of the cult of the Tyndarids was Laconia[1], and from here it seems to have spread at a very early date into Argos and Messenia and eventually into all parts of Greece. In Sparta, as elsewhere, they were the patrons of athletic contests. Perhaps from their prominence in the Argonautic saga they early acquired also the nautical aspect of saviours on the sea, which was to become their most important function. As saviours of sailors in

[1] Throughout antiquity the cult of the twins was prominent in Laconia They were protectors of the household (see Nilsson *MMR.* 470); they were in a special way associated with the two kings of Sparta (Nilsson *l.c.*, Kahrstedt *Griechisches Staatsrecht* i. 126–7) and the Spartan people (Xen. *Hell.* vi. 3. 6).

distress they accompanied Peloponnesian colonization of the West [1] and the eastern expansion of Hellenism round the shores of the Black Sea.[2] This nautical aspect of the Dioscuri, assisted by their common cult title of Anakes and the appellative Soteres (see on 6), led to the frequent identification and confusion of the Dioscuri with the Great Gods of Samothrace, which is prevalent from the third century B.C. onwards.

In Alexandrian and subsequent writers, but with the possible exception of Euripides [3] in no earlier documents, the Dioscuri are placed among the stars, and in the later mythographers they are frequently identified with the constellation Gemini, or with the Morning and Evening Star. Of this stellar theory there is naturally no trace in the hymn. Here the Twin Brethren are identified with the lights (of an electric nature) which appear on the masts or sails of a ship during storms, and consequently have excited in all ages and countries the superstitious attention of sailors.

In the seventeenth century such lights were known to Mediterranean sailors as Corposants (from Corpo Santo), or were believed to be caused by Hobgoblins, Fairies, or Witches, or by spirits of the dead.[4] Even more generally they have been known as St. Elmo's Fire.[5] Their ascription to the Dioscuri is frequent in classical literature: cf. Alcaeus B 5. 3 Lobel, 78. 3 Diehl *προφάνητε Κάστορ | καὶ Πολύδευκες | οἳ κὰτ εὔρηα[ν] χ[θόνα] καὶ θάλασσαν | παῖσαν ἔρχε[σθ᾽] ὠ[κυπό]δων ἐπ᾽ ἴππων | ῥῆα δ᾽ ἀνθρώπ]ο[ις] θα[ν]άτω ῥύεσθε | ζακρυόεντος | εὐσδ[ύγ]ων θρώσκοντ[ες ἐπ᾽]*

[1] Cf. the importance of the cult of the Dioscuri at Tarentum, or the name Tyndaris given to the Messenian colony in Sicily. For coins of Tyndaris on which they bear the title ΣΩΤΗΡΕΣ see Head *HN.* 189.

[2] Here Dioskorias, which bears their name, was founded by Miletus probably before the Ionian Revolt; for coins see Head *HN.* 495.

[3] Euripides *Hel.* 137, 1499, *Electra* 990, 1347, *Or.* 1636 are not unambiguously decisive. They are, however, quite consistent with the view that Euripides identified the Dioscuri, not with stars, but merely with the meteorological phenomenon to which the hymn alludes.

[4] Bent *Early Voyages and Travels in the Levant*, Hakluyt Society 1893, p. 127.

[5] For references see Frazer on Pausanias ii. 1. 9.

ἄκρα νάων | π]ήλοθεν λάμπροι προ[ ] τρ[ ]ντες | ἀργαλέᾳ δ' ἐν νύκτι φ[άος φέ]ροντες | νᾶι μ[ε]λαίνᾳ, poeta ap. Stob. *ecl.* i. 31 a 5 ναυσί τ' ἐπ' ὠκυπόροισι Διοσκούρων ἐπιφαντᾶν (corr. Meineke), id. ap. Plut. *non posse suav.* c. 23 (= *PLG.* iii. 730) ἐπερχόμενόν τε μαλάξοντες βιατάν | πόντον ὠκείας τ' ἀνέμων ῥιπάς, *an seni* 790 D (=Diehl ii. 490. 11) ὅτι Τυνδαριδᾶν ἀδελφῶν ἅλιον ναύταν πόθος | βάλλει, Eur. *Or.* 1636 sq., *Helena* 1495 sq., *Electra* 992, Diod. iv. 43, Sosibius *frr.* 2 and 16, Polemo *fr.* 760, Seneca *QN.* I. I. 13, Pliny *NH.* v. 101, Strabo 48, 232, Plut. *Lysand.* 12, *de def. or.* 30, *de plac. phil.* 889 D, Lucian *dial. deor.* xxvi. 3 *de merc. cond.* 1, *de navig.* 9, *Charid.* 3, Max. Tyr. ix. 7, Horace *Od.* i. 12. 25 sq., Libanius i. 142, lvii. 24, *ep.* 1187; σωτῆρες ἄνακτες Alciphron iii. 68 (in an accident). An explanation is offered by Xenophanes ap. Stob. *ecl.* i. 24. 1=Aetius ii. 13 τοὺς δὲ ἐπὶ τῶν πλοίων φαινομένους οἷον ἀστέρας οὓς καὶ Διοσκούρους καλοῦσι τινες νεφέλια εἶναι κατὰ τὴν ποιὰν κίνησιν παραλάμποντα.[1] In Euripides Helen is associated with her brothers as a saviour, but a later elaboration alleged that two lights were a sign of safety, whereas a single light (identified with Helen = ἑλέναυς) betokened the worst (Pliny *l.c.*, Artemid. *onir.* ii. 9). The twins also saved men driving; Eur. *Heracl.* 854 δισσὼ γὰρ ἀστέρ' ἱππικοῖς ὑπὸ ζυγοῖς, Theocr. xxii. 7.

1. **ἀμφί**: see on vii. 1.

Διὸς κούρους: possibly descriptive rather than a title, and the earliest literary evidence for the appellation (see introduction). By the fifth century B.C. Dioscuri had become an established divine title; cf. Ar. *Pax* 285, *Eccles.* 1069, Thuc. iv. 110 (a Διοσκόρειον at Torone). The earliest epigraphic evidence for the title is an inscription from Thera (*IG.* xii. 3. 359), which may be as old as the seventh century B.C. Festivals called Διοσκόρεια are attested at Sparta, Delphi, and Rhodes (Nilsson *GF.* 420–2). Hesiod *fr.* 91 apparently attributed the parentage of both Tyndarids to Zeus. The story that Zeus was the father of Polydeuces and Tyndareus of Castor first appears in the *Cypria fr.* 6. This

[1] Ovid *Fasti* v. 720, *Amores* II. xi. 29 may refer to St. Elmo's fire, but more probably to the theory that the Dioscuri were the Morning and Evening Star.

view may have been influenced by the theory of their alternate sojourn in the Lower World, to which allusion is made in λ 298; its origin however lies in a belief, prevalent in many parts of the world, that the birth of twins is miraculous, and to be explained by supposing that one of the two is the son of a God or Spirit. Here a Greek parallel is provided in Iphicles son of Amphitryon and Heracles son of Zeus (see Rose *Handbook* 206). The double pair of twins, Pollux and Helen fathered by Zeus, Castor and Clytaemnestra by Tyndareus, is a late invention (Apollod. iii. 10. 7).

2. **Τυνδαρίδας**: according to λ 299 they were sons of Leda and Tyndareus. Here and in xvii they are called sons of Zeus, but also Tyndarids from the putative father; so Castor is Τυνδαρίδης Theocr. xxii. 136, but in the next line both are called Διὸς υἱώ. Tyndaridae, the name by which they were originally known, continued to be used both in literature and in cult throughout classical antiquity. There is no reason to discredit the unanimous view of antiquity that Tyndareus was a human king, or to imagine that the supposed meaning of his name 'hammerer' proves him to have been a Thunder-God (Farnell *HC.* 197). Such a derivation is all but ludicrous.

3. Cf. Γ 237, λ 300, *Cypria* 11. 6.

4. **Ταυγέτου**: so xvii. 3, Τηυγ- ζ 103, *Cypria* 11. 2.

5. That Leda was the mother of the Tyndarids was the unanimous verdict of classical writers. The story that Helen was produced from an egg occurred probably in the *Cypria* 7, certainly in Sappho 56, but in this version the egg was laid by Nemesis and hatched by Leda. The seduction of Leda by Zeus in the form of a swan appears first in Euripides *Hel.* 17. In subsequent versions Leda not Nemesis laid the egg. In the hymn there is neither swan nor egg; the inclusion of the Dioscuri in the story of the miraculous egg seems to be the work of Alexandrian mythography. The motive was no doubt to work in the birth of her brothers with that of Helen, and the revised story may have found support in a misinterpretation of monuments such as those found at Sparta (Farnell *HC.* 194). The story takes various forms. In one Dioscuri and Helen emerge from

the same egg (Serv. *in Aen.* iii. 328), in another from separate eggs (Horace *Sat.* ii. 1. 26, *AP.* 147); in a third two pairs of twins (see on 1) emerge from two eggs. The suggested connexion of the πῖλοι of the Dioscuri with the two halves of the shell is probably Lucian's invention (*dial. deor.* xxvi. 1).

6. **σωτῆρας**: this cult title is applied to other Gods, e.g. Apollo, Hermes, Artemis, Athena, Demeter, Core and Zeus, and among heroes only to those of the highest rank, i.e. who were worshipped also as θεοί, Asclepius, Heracles, and the Dioscuri. To the last the title was applied in connexion with the perils of sailing or fighting. It appears as early as Terpander 4 (ὦ Ζανὸς καὶ Λήδας κάλλιστοι σωτῆρες), and in many authors and inscriptions throughout antiquity, see Roscher xii. 3. 1333, iv. 1254. The hero Menestheus gave them this title and that of ἄνακτες Aelian. *VH.* iv. 5.

8. **ἀπὸ νηῶν**: cf. vii. 6.

9. *IG.* ix. 1. 649, not later than s. vi B.C., reads Εὐσοίδα μ' ἀνέθηκε ΔιϜὸς κώροιν μεγάλοιο | χαλκὸν ᾧ νίκασε Κεφαλλᾶνας μεγαθύμους. Two literary coincidences in a single couplet can hardly be accidental, and it may be concluded that the author borrowed from this line and from B 631. If so, the hymn is older than the inscription.

10. **ἄρνεσσι λευκοῖσιν**: this sacrifice is only appropriate in the cult of the Dioscuri as θεοί (see on 6). The contrast between celestial and chthonian ritual (φαιδρὰ μὲν οὐρανίοις, χθονίοις δ' ἐναλίγκια χροιῇ *orac.* ap. Euseb. *PE.* iv. 9. 2, cf. οὐ θύεται λευκὰ τοῖς τεθνεῶσιν ℬ Ψ 30) is illustrated by Γ 103, where a white lamb is sacrificed to Helios and a black to Earth. See further Farnell *HC.* 183, Stengel *Kultusaltertümer* 151, *id. Die Farbe und das Geschlecht der griech. Opferthiere*, *Neue Jahrbb.* 1886 cxxxiii. 321. Servius' statement (*in Aen.* iii. 18) *tempestati atras pecudes, candidas serenitati immolant* is irrelevant. White lambs are sacrificed to the σωτῆρες in storms.

ἀκρωτήρια: although in Herod. viii. 121 ἀκρωτήρια νηός is a ship's beak, the word means any upper part or 'end', and here is equivalent to ἴκρια, 'deck'. As there were decks fore and aft (Torr *Ancient Ships* 57) πρύμνης is added to limit the word. The sailors crowd to the poop for safety from the waves as in vii. 48 for a different reason.

14. The reading of *p* (ἀέλλαι) shows the same tendency to construe παύω neuter that is observed δ 659, Hes. *Scut.* 449.

16. **πόνου σφίσιν**: one of these words is manifestly corrupt, but the remedy has not yet been found.

18. **ἐπιβήτορες ἵππων**: cf. λεύκιπποι Ibycus 16, λευκόπωλοι Pind. *Pyth.* i. 126. Both in literature and in art the Dioscuri are invariably represented as riding. On the other hand all Greek personifications of light, with the partial exception of Selene, are equally invariably represented as driving a chariot, as are the Indian Aśvins, the Heavenly Twins of Aryan mythology.

Εἰς Ξένους

This poem was included in the Hymn-corpus by *x* (that is by E Π T, L[1] had stopped long before) and by C and D. M also had stopped (at xviii. 4) and we cannot say that its archetype did not contain the poem. It occurs also with the other Homeric 'epigrams' in the Herodotean life of Homer c. 9, vv. 101–5. This document (on which we may refer to *Origins* p. 14 sq.) is of unknown date, but seems referable to the second century after Christ, and to come from Aeolis. Where the compiler found the 'epigrams' is still more obscure. They are obviously older than the Life, and therefore the one here might have come into the Hymn-collection independently of the Life. Some others of the 'epigrams' are found in other places (*vit. Herod.* 135, 417, 425, 479, 515); the hymn to Apollo itself is found alone in S, and hymn xxv alone in the Salamanca MS. (p. xvi).

The poem refers to the neighbourhood of Cyme and the river Hermus, and in its ultimate origin certainly comes from the Aeolic or Chian traditions about Homer, perhaps from the Homeridae. It is perhaps not too much to suppose that the person who made the collection of the Hymns appended it at the end as a sort of *envoi* to the poems in the character of their nominal author.

The distance of the two appearances of the document has produced extraordinary variants:

	Hymns	vit. Herod.
2	πόλιν	πόλου
	νύμφης ἐρατώπιδος ἥρης	κύμην ἐριώπιδα κούρην
3	ἐς ἅδην ἧς πόδα	σαρδήνης πόδα
4	ξανθοῦ	θείου
5	ἕβρου	ἕρμου

The Hymn-version is much the worse. At v. 3 both are at fault, and Stephanus has preserved the real word. Ἕβρου is graphical.

CONIECTURAE VERI MINUS SIMILES

I 12 lacunam hic statuit Matthiae 17 ἴλαθι Ruhnken

II 1 θεὸν Ruhnken 4 χρυσοθρόνου Ruhnken: ὡρηφόρου Bücheler 10 δέ τε Wyttenbach: δ' ὅγε Matthiae 13 κηώδει Ruhnken: κωδείας Mitscherlich: κυδιόωντ' Ignarra: κηώεντ' Ludwich: κύκλῳ ἴει Goodwin 17 Μύσιον Malten: μέσσατον vel νείατον Preller 22 οὔτε θνητῶν Hermann 23 ἀγλαόμορφοι ἑταῖραι Ruhnken: ἀγλαόμορφος Ἀλωάς Schütz, Ἀχαία Voss, Ἀμαῖα vel Ἐλευθώ Mitscherlich: ἐλεῖαι Huschke, Ἕλειαι Ilgen: φωνὴν θεᾶς ἀγλαοκάρπου ἐλεινήν Gemoll 24 οἴη Wackernagel *Rh. Mus.* xliv. 531 29 δέχμενος Cobet 40 χαίτης ἀμβροσίης Hermann 46 οὔτε τις οἰωνῶν οἱ ἐτ. Brunck: οὐδέ οἱ οἰωνῶν τις Hermann 50 ἄσατ' Mitscherlich θάλπετο Mitscherlich: χρό' ἀτάλλετο Ilgen 53 ἀγγέλλουσα Ruhnken: ἄγχι θέουσα Matthiae: ἐγκονέουσα Ludwich 57 γὰρ μὲν Wassenbergh: μὲν γὰρ Voss 58 ὦνα Mitscherlich: αὖ κε vel ὅς κε Voss λέγοι cum lacuna Hermann: λέγειν cum lacuna Ludwich 64 Διὸς ὕπερ Fontein: θεᾶς ὕπερ Voss, θέης Hermann: μ' ἐλέησόν τ' Matthiae 77 οὔ νυ Gemoll 82 χόλον Hermann 85 τιμῇ Schneidewin: τιμῆς Hermann 87 τῶν μέτα ναιετάειν Valckenaer, μεταναιετάειν Puntoni versum post 81 ponit Brunck 111 ἔγνον Cobet 113 χαμαιγενέων Bücheler 117 φιλήσαιντ' Brunck 127 lacunam posuit Hermann 128 δ' ἠρτύνοντο Hermann: δ' ἐντύνοντο Voss: τ' ἐντύνοντο Bücheler 147 ἀχνυμένοις περ ἀνάγκη τετλάμεν ἀνθρώποις Brunck 157 ὀπωπῆς Ignarra 160 δ' ἐθέλεις Hermann 172 ὅσσ' Ruhnken 204 σχέμεν ἦτορ vel ὀργήν Mitscherlich 205 ὀργή Bücheler: εὖαδ' ἑορταῖς Voss 207 γ' οἱ Ruhnken 223 δοίη Matthiae 227 θρέψω τ' vel θρέψασθ' Voss: θρέψαι Hermann: θρέψουσ' Goodwin: θρεψέμεν Agar 229 οὐδοτόμοιο Bergk 232 χείρεσιν Ilgen: χείρεσσ' Cobet 236 θησάμενος ἡ δ' ἦμαρ Matthiae, κατὰ δ' ἦμαρ Voss 236 a ἠματίη μὲν γὰρ καλλιστέφανος Δημήτηρ Voss: ἀλλὰ γὰρ ἤματα μέν μιν ἐυστέφανος Δημήτηρ

Baumeister 240 κρύβδα φίλων Baumeister 241 γὰρ pro δὲ Voss 248 ξείνῃ σ' ἤδ' ἐν πυρὶ πολλῷ Hermann, σε πυρὸς μένει οὔλῳ Schneidewin 253 γ' ἧκε Matthiae: ἔθεν ἧκε Cobet 256 φράδμονες Bücheler 262 γῆρας Huschke 269 ἀθανάτων Stoll ὄνιαρ Voss, ὄναρ Hermann: ὄνειαρ χάρμα τ' ἐτύχθη Ruhnken: κ' ἄρμα τέτυκται Tyrrell: καὶ πολὺ χάρμα Agar 274 ἱλάσκησθε Schäfer 284 ἐλεινήν Ruhnken 289 ἐλοῦοντ' Mitscherlich 300 δαίμονι ἶσος E. White 312 θυέων Hermann 349 ἐρέβεσφι Franke 371 αὐτῇ Voss: ᾄδης Schneidewin ἐπεὶ ἴδε καλὰ πρόσωπα Voss 398 εἰ δ' ἐπάσω Wyttenbach, εἰ δ' ἐπάσω τι πάλιν μὲν Bücheler: εἰ δέ τι πάσσαο πάμπαν Goodwin 403 a λέξον δ' ὅππως ἦλθες ὑπὸ ζόφον ἠερόεντα Hermann 428 ἐμοὶ δόλον vel περίπλοκον Mitscherlich: μοι ἐς δόλον Jacobs: ὑπέρκοτον Bothe: εὔχροον Ilgen: κροκόεντά περ Matthiae: ὥσπερ κόνιν vel αἰπὺν δόλον Hermann: ὑπείροχον vel ὑπερήφανον Voss: ὑπέρτατον Spitzner 441 τὰς Voss μέτ' Hermann 445 νεῖσθαι Voss 448 ἀμέλησε Hermann ἀγγελίῃσι Ranken 451 ἀλλ' ἀπέτηλον Ruhnken 454 ἀνθερίκεσσι Ruhnken 462 ἅς κεν ἕλοιο Ilgen 466 ὥς τοι ὑπέσχετ' ἔσεσθαι Hermann: καὶ ἑοῖ αὐτῷ ἔσεσθαι vel ᾧ ἐνὶ οἴκῳ Bücheler 481 ὁμοίην Fontein 490 ἵλαθ' Hermann

III 4 τιταίνῃ Barnes 5 μεῖνε Schneidewin 6 ὄφρα Bücheler 8 τόξα τ' Schneidewin: τόξα μὲν Stoll 17 κεκλιμένῃ Lenz 20 πεπλήχαται Matthiae: μεμέληται ἀοιδῆς vel μεμέληται ἀοιδοῖς Hermann 32 ἀμφιάλῃ Matthiae 35 'Αντικάνης vel 'Ακροκάνης Ilgen: Αἰγοκάνης Matthiae: ἄντα Κάνης Hermann 40 Αἰγαλέου F. C. Matthiae 42 μερόπων ἀγερώχων Pierson 53 τίσει Ernesti: σ' ὀνήσει Jacobs: ἐσελάσσει Kirchhoff 73 καταστρέψας δ' Franke ᾤσῃ δ' Giphanius 92 αὐτόθι Ilgen: ἐνθάδε Hermann 98 χρυσέοις νεφέεσσι La Roche *HU*. i. 57, 83 104 λίθοισι Peppmüller: χρύσεον ἠλέκτροισιν ἑερμένον Barnes 116 δὴ τότε τὴν Ilgen 125 ἀθανάτοις χείλεσσιν Eble ὀρέξατο Maittaire: ἐπορέξατο Ilgen 138 κῆρ ἔτι Agar *J.Ph.* 1901. 51 139 ἀνθέον ὕλῃ Barnes 142 νηούς Baumeister ἂν ῥία Jacobs: ἄκριας Voss 148 αὐτοὶ Gemoll: αὐτοῖσιν παίδεσσι Hermann 151 φαίης Ruhnken

152 ἀπαντιάσαι Barnes: ὑπαντίασει' Abel: ἐναντιάσει' Ilgen: οἳ τότ' ἐναντία σεῖο γ' Ruhnken 163 αὐτῇ ἑκάστῃ Peppmüller 173 μερόπεσσιν Bothe ἀριστεύσουσιν Barnes 179 hymni in Apollinem Delphicum initium hic statuit Ruhnken 192 ἀμφιδεεῖς Maittaire 207 ἀναμνήσω vel ἐπιμνήσω Gemoll 208 μνηστῦσιν Schulze 209 μωόμενος Lobeck 'Ρηματ. p. 355 211 τριοπηγενεῖ D'Orville (-αγενεῖ Ruhnken): τριόπου γένει Wolf: τριόπεω γόνῳ Hermann: τριόπεω γένος Ilgen 213 τριόπας Ilgen 220 τόθι Ruhnken 231 κῆρ pro περ Ilgen 242 πολύπυρον Barnes 251 ἤπειρον Reiz 281 θείων Hermann 317 ὅν γε μὲν αὐτὴ Ruhnken: ὅν τε καὶ αὐτὴ Creuzer 330 τηλόθι οὖσα Ilgen: τηλόθ' ἐοῦσα Hermann ἀπέσσομαι Groddeck: κοτέσσομαι Gemoll 335 ναιετάουσιν Ilgen 361 θυμὸς Matthiae λεῖβε δὲ φοινὸν | θυμὸν Ruhnken 364 ζώουσα Ilgen 380 προχέειν Barnes 382 ῥόον Gemoll 402 ἐπεφράσατ' οὐδ' ἐνόησε Matthiae: -σαθ' ὥστε νοῆσαι E. White 419 ἑκοῦσα Baumeister 422 Ἀμφιγένειαν ἐραννὴν Ilgen 431 τάχ' ἐφαίνετο Schneidewin 439 ἀμάθοις D'Orville 456 ἕστητε τεθηπότες Matthiae: τίπτε κάθησθ' οὕτω τετιηότες Cobet 475 ἀμφενέμεσθε Cobet 479 τετιμένοι Hermann

IV 6 ἄντρου Baumeister 75 πληνοδίας Schneider, F. D. Allen 79 ἔραψεν Matthiae 82 ὥρης Hermann epist. lvi: νεοθηλέα ἀγκύλῃ ὕλην Ilgen 83 εὐλαβέως Schneidewin: ἀβλαύτοις Pierson 86 δολίην Matthiae 87 νέμων Fick (δέμων Barnes) 103 ἀκμῆτες Ilgen 106 ἀθρό' ἰούσας Barnes 124 ἐπὶ Barnes 152 παλάμης περὶ McDaniel λαίφει ἀθύρων Franke: λαίφεσ' ἀθύρων Ilgen: λαίφεα σύρων Gemoll ἀθύρων et ἐέργων (153) transp. Matthiae 157 δύσμαχ' Radermacher 188 κώκαλον Stahl 259 ἀλιτροῖσι Ilgen: δολίοισι Hermann: ὀλοοῖσι Bothe 272 βουσὶν ἐπ' Schneidewin 280 ἅλιόν τως Radermacher 418 ἄθυρμα Schneidewin 436 πολεύμενε Schneidewin 437 μέμηλε Eberhard, -ώς Ludwich: μέλη· σὰ Lohsee 461 ἔμμεν ἐάσω Stadtmüller, ἔμμεν ὁδεύσω Tucker ἡγεμ. et οὐκ ἀπατήσω (462) transp. Ludwich lacunam postul. Schneidewin

V 23 excl. Heyne 57 ἔκπαγλος Köchly 237 ῥέει Wolf: τρεῖ Hermann ἄσπετον Flach 252 στόματ' ἔσσεται Clarke: στόμα λήσεται vel πείσεται Ilgen, τλήσεται Matthiae: στόμ' ἀχήσεται vel χήσεται Buttmann

X 1 κυπρογενέα Barnes, -νην Fick

XIX 9 ἐφεζόμενος Baumeister

XXII 3 Ἑλίκην τε Martin

XXXI 11 ἔθειραι Pierson, Matthiae

ADDENDA

II. 53. It should have been said that in this construction Polyaenus has the future participle as well as the present, i. 20. 2 αὐτόμολον ἐκπέμπει Σόλων ἀγγελοῦντα, 42. 1, 46, etc., vi. 2. 2 οἱ μὲν Ἀθηναῖοι σπουδῇ ἔθεον . . . ἀγγελοῦντες, and cf. v. 1. 4 ἔπεμψε τοὺς μνησευσομένους ('K', μνηστευομένους 'F') τὴν θυγατέρα, iv. 2. 4 ἀγγελοῦσι, ἀγγέλλουσι. In the present, one lambda is usually wanting.

— 176. Isaiah xlvii. 2 ἀνάσυρε τὰς κνήμας, διάβηθι ποταμούς (to the παρθένος θυγάτηρ βαβυλῶνος).

— 258: Empedocles 129. 2 μήκιστον . . . ἐκτήσατο πλοῦτον.

— 358: Σοφία Σείραχ 2. 15 and 16. 28 ἀπειθεῖν c. gen.

— 386: cf. δάσκιον ὕλην Oppian *Cyn.* iii. 39, iv. 1.

III. 104: Oribasius *coll.* xlvii. 17. 2 [τὸ λίνον] διὰ τοῦ δακτυλιδίου εἴρεται.

— 171: Aretaeus v. 1. 1 ἀμφαιρέουσι ἀφ-, ἀμφαφόωσι ἀφ-.

IV. 43: Oppian *Hal.* v. 660 ὥστε νόημα.

— 48: cf. ἣν διά A 72, Hermesianax 2. 31, ὃν διά Tyrtaeus 4. 2, Simonides 94. 1, Aristotle *Peplos* 13. 1, without variant. In deference to the printer's reader we have retained the conventional accentuation (i.e. not δία), though Blass K.-B. i. 333 observes that it is pedantic. He read ἄνα Bacchylides xii. 75 for ανα of the papyrus. See the passages from the grammarians in Lehrs *qu. ep.* 72.

— 55: ἠύτε κοῦροι | ἡβηταὶ θαλίῃσι παραιβόλα κερτομέουσιν. Ἡβηταί does not mean 'in their youthful prime', but 'in their cups', 'excited': *scolia* 7. 4 Diehl καὶ τὸ τέταρτον [ἄριστον] ἡβᾶν μετὰ τῶν φίλων, 19. 1 σύν μοι πῖνε συνήβα, Theognis 87 ἥβα μοι φίλε θυμέ = 1070 a τέρπεό μοι φίλε θυμέ. An ἡβητής, therefore, is a reveller.

— 77: of the bear Aelian *NA.* vi. 3 ἐσέρχεται οὐ βαδίζουσα ἀλλὰ ὑπτία, ἀφανίζουσα τοῖς θηρευταῖς τὰ ἴχνη.

IV. 83 : for ἀβλαβής ἀβλαβῶς see a note in the *Revue de Philologie* ix. 291, to which add Porphyry *de abst.* i. 5 ἀβλαβῶς act., ii. 12, 43, iii. 1, 26, 27 ἀβλαβές -ής act., Aristotle *Probl.* xxviii. 1. 3 -ῆ act., Paulus Aegin. vi. 88. 4 -ές act., Oribas. *inc.* xxxviii. 38. 7 -ῆ act., LXX Σοφία Σαλ. 18. 3 -ῆ act., Dioscurides i. 116 ult. -εῖς act., iv. 70. 1 -ής act., v. 6. 1 -ῶς act., Julius Africanus *Cest.* 39 (f. 302 b inf.) -ές act, Hippocr. ii. 622 Littré -έα act.

— 108 : Aelian *NA.* xii. 43 πυρεῖα πεύκης τῆς λιπαρωτάτης ; id. *VH.* iii. 7. 9 fire by rubbing stones.

— 119 : Hesychius ἐτέτορεν· ἐτρύπησεν.

— 133 : Galen ii. 898 περαίνει δὲ αὐτὴν εἰς τὸν γυναικεῖον κόλπον, if the text is sound.

— 210 : Oppian *Cyn.* iv. 68 ἐπιστροφάδην δὲ φέβονται, 138 ἐπιστροφάδην δὲ νέονται.

— 231 : Aelian *NA.* xii. 30 καὶ ἐς νῦν ὁ χῶρος (Aborras) εὐωδίαν ἀναπνεῖ.

— 284 : Demetr. π. ἑρμην. 99. 12 (Dionysius) and 243 χαμόθεν οἱ τέττιγες ὑμῖν ᾄσονται.

— 295 : Aristotle *Probl.* 33. 11 ὁ μὲν πταρμὸς μᾶλλον δοκεῖ ἐπισχεῖν τοὺς ἀρχομένους καὶ ἐν τῇ ἀρχῇ, Polyaen. iii. 10. 2 πταρμὸς ἐγένετο· ὁ κυβερνήτης ἐπισχεῖν ἐκέλευσεν, anon. Ox. pap. iii. 413. 3 πορδαί are ἀποτροπαί.

— 486 : Porph. *vit. Pythag.* c. 7 τῇ περὶ τοὺς φόνους φυγῇ καὶ τῶν φονευόντων, *de abst.* i. 8 τῶν μὲν φυγὴν (aversion) παρεσκευάσαι, τῶν δὲ αἵρεσιν, Ar. *Probl.* xxviii. 10 τὸ θερμὸν φεύγει ὅτι ἂν φοβηθῇ. There are similar metaphors in Ar. *de audibil.* 51 and 63, Quintilian ix. 4. 31 (refugit), 87 (fugiat).

— 531 : add Hesych. ἐθέμωσεν· ἠνάγκασεν, ἐποίησεν.

V. 3 : on the power of love, Oppian *Cyn.* ii. 410 sq.

— 90 : for attraction add Longinus τέχν. ῥητ. 564.

— 228 : Herodian i. 7. 5 of Commodus ἴουλοί τε αὐτοῦ κατιόντες ταῖς παρειαῖς ἐπήνθεον, Xen. *Symp.* 4. 23 τούτῳ μὲν παρὰ τὰ ὦτα ἄρτι ἴουλος καθέρπει.

— 260 : Hesych. μακρόβιοι· αἱ νύμφαι Ῥόδιοι.

— 274 : Solon 19. 1 παῖς μὲν ἄνηβος ἐὼν ἔτι νήπιος ἕρκος ὀδόντων |

φύσας ἐκβάλλει πρῶτον ἐν ἑπτ' ἔτεσιν, Quintilian i. 1. 16 Chrysippus . . . quamvis nutricibus triennium dederit . . ., 17 cur hoc . . . usque ad septem annos lucrum fastidiamus?

VII. 53: Oppian *Hal.* i. 650 dolphins once were men Διωνύσοιο δὲ βουλῇ | πόντον ἐπημείψαντο καὶ ἰχθύας ἀμφεβάλοντο.

VIII. 16: On Ares and peace see Eusebius *hist. eccl.* ix. 7. 11.

XIX. 14: see the verb ἐπηλυγάζεσθαι in the lexica.

XXI. 1: for the swan's song see Oppian *Cyn.* ii. 548, *Ixeut.* ii. 19, Ar. *HA.* ix. 124.

XXVI. 12: further evidence for εἰς ὥρας = 'next year' will be found in the *Revue de Philologie* ix. 289.

XXVI. 13: Euseb. *hist. eccl.* x. 5. 20 πολλοῖς ἔτεσι, 21 fin. ἐπὶ πολλοῖς ἔτεσι.

XXXII. 1: Porph. *de ant. nymph.* 21 ἕπεται . . . ζητεῖν τὸ βούλευμα.

XXXIII. intr. (p. 439): Eus. *praep. ev.* xv. 2. 49 also quotes the explanations of Xenophanes (νεφέλια) and Metrodorus (στιλβηδόνες, i.e. flashes from the eyes).

To the note on Ilithyia (iii. 97) may be added a passage in Maximus Tyrius ii. 35 ἡ λεγομένη παρὰ Λυκίοις ἐλευθέρα [sic] of Artemis. Artemis was a goddess of birth, and if Apollo came from Lycia Artemis-Ilithyia-Eleuthera may have done so too.

An unambiguous case of αἰών = μυελὸς νωτιαῖος (iv. 42) is Hippocr. vii. 122 Littré ὁ τὸν αἰῶνα φθινήσας.

INDEXES

I.—INDEX OF GREEK WORDS

This index aims at giving (1) all proper names, (2) the less common epithets of Gods and heroic persons, (3) non-Homeric words, (4) other words for any reason remarkable. The complete vocabulary of the *Hymns* will be found in the *Index Homericus: Appendix Hymnorum vocabula continens, composuit Augustus Gehring*, Lips. 1895, which, in spite of defects in execution (see the review by Eberhard, *N. Phil. Rundschau*, 1895, 289 f., and cf. *CR.* 1895, 415 f.), is indispensable.

Non-Homeric words or forms are marked by a *; a † implies a corruption; conjectures are within square brackets.

II.—ENGLISH INDEX

[The figures refer to pages.]

PRINTED IN
GREAT BRITAIN
AT THE
UNIVERSITY PRESS
OXFORD
BY
JOHN JOHNSON
PRINTER
TO THE
UNIVERSITY